The Researcher's Journey in the Age of AI

Klaus Solberg Söilen

The Researcher's Journey in the Age of AI

Reappraising Social Science Research

Springer

Klaus Solberg Söilen
Halmstad University
Halmstad, Sweden

ISBN 978-3-032-23068-3 ISBN 978-3-032-23069-0 (eBook)
https://doi.org/10.1007/978-3-032-23069-0

This Springer imprint is published by the registered company Springer Nature Switzerland AG
The registered company address is: Gewerbestrasse 11, 6330 Cham, Switzerland

My mother, Wenche Irene Solberg (1943–2021),
whose presence in my earliest years made all the difference.

Note for the Cover

Edvard Munch, *The Researchers*, 1911 / 1925–27 (later reworking).
Oil on canvas, 428 × 1148 cm.
Collection of the Munch Museum, Oslo.
Inventory no. MM.M.01091.
The painting is displayed in the Monumental Hall (P06, south wall).

The painting on the front cover is part of Edvard Munch's extended work on the *Alma Mater* motif, originally developed for the Aula of the University of Oslo and revisited by the artist over several years. The composition depicts a central maternal figure associated with origin, continuity, and life, surrounded by children and young figures that evoke learning, transmission, and the emergence of knowledge across generations.

In contrast to a narrow depiction of science as abstraction or technique, Munch presents knowledge as embedded in human life, development, and social inheritance. The figures are not portrayed as isolated thinkers, but as participants in a shared intellectual and cultural process. In this sense, the painting reflects an understanding of research as a cumulative, generational endeavor—rooted in biological, social, and cultural foundations rather than detached rationality alone.

The version used on the cover belongs to a later iteration of the motif and is held by the Munch Museum in Oslo. Its inclusion emphasizes continuity with the original Aula commission while also highlighting Munch's evolving reflection on knowledge, learning, and the human conditions under which science is produced.

Preface

When my father studied engineering at NTH (now NTNU) in Trondheim in the 1960s—where he also met my mother—he discovered a small book by Ole Peder Arvesen titled *Gi meg et fast punkt* ("Give Me a Fixed Point").[1] Arvesen, a professor of machine engineering and a popular science writer, used what was essentially a thin book on the history of mathematics to set the technical subjects his students were learning into a broader historical and cultural perspective. The purpose was to help them see more clearly what they were actually doing—how engineering was not only formulas and machines, but part of a larger human project.

The inspiration for this book is similar. Its aim is to show how artificial intelligence can help the social sciences recover their original trajectory: to become a genuine science of human beings and society. This is not a technical book about AI, but an inquiry into how AI reshapes the larger project of the social sciences. I write as an economist and a social scientist, not a data scientist, with the goal of clarifying how these new tools can strengthen the field's foundations and move it closer to the coherence and explanatory power long envisioned for it.

Any science that aspires to coherence must, as Arvesen argued, be anchored in a fixed point of reference. My working assumption is that evolutionary

[1] The title alludes to the famous remark attributed to Archimedes of Syracuse (287–212 BCE): "*Give me a place to stand, and I will move the earth.*" Archimedes was describing the principle of the lever, but the phrase has since become a metaphor for the power of finding a solid foundation from which to effect change.

theory provides the only framework capable of unifying the social sciences—though I welcome any scholar from any discipline to show otherwise. The ambition here is to construct a paradigm grounded in evolutionary theory, one that integrates ontology, epistemology, and ethics. Within this framework, moral philosophy offers the scaffolding that keeps inquiry tied to responsibility, value, and human purpose. This can be described as the paradigm of the Evolutionary Social Sciences.[2] In building such a paradigm, AI may not be so much an obstacle as a catalyst—perhaps even a force that helps to set it in motion.

The idea for this project had begun to take shape earlier, but it was significantly accelerated when I was asked to teach a course titled *AI Implementation* at Halmstad University in Sweden. Though offered primarily to engineer students and taught in English, the course approaches AI from a managerial and social science perspective rather than a technical one. That experience prompted a broader reflection as I began collecting material for the course: What does AI mean for the social sciences—and for our understanding of humanity itself? Where are we heading, and perhaps more importantly, where could we be heading from here?

The Researcher's Journey in the Age of AI: Reappraising Social Science Research is the second in what has unexpectedly become a series. As in the first volume—*The Researcher's Journey: A Guide to Methodology and Academia in Social Sciences*—I continue with a personal style of writing, one that blends reflection with practical insight. I have come to call this "the journey" style of writing, because it traces one person's path through the challenges and insights of research. In this case, it is my own journey—not because I think it is uniquely important, but because it is the closest reference I have.

This style allows me to use concrete experiences as an entry point to broader themes. Rather than speaking in abstractions, I can illustrate how ideas unfold in practice: how research questions emerge, how methods feel in use, and how institutions shape the daily work of scholarship. It is not a confessional mode, nor a claim of authority. It is simply a way of grounding academic reflection in lived reality, much like the way I teach—by drawing students into the process through example, story, and dialogue. In that sense, the "journey" style revives an older tradition of writing where methodology and personal experience were not kept apart but intertwined as part of the

[2] There have been earlier efforts to articulate evolutionary paradigms for the social sciences. Most, however, take either a disciplinary angle (e.g., evolutionary sociology or psychology), an interdisciplinary synthesis, or a largely theoretical stance. Examples include Van Parijs (1981), Tang (2020), Willführ et al. (2025), and Wilson (1975, 1978). Few, if any, however, have attempted the kind of integrative framework pursued here—anchoring the social sciences simultaneously in ontology, epistemology, and moral philosophy, while using evolutionary theory as the arranging principle.

same inquiry into science, society, and the human condition—a style that would not be unfamiliar to the great European humanists and Renaissance thinkers such as Montaigne, Erasmus, and Francis Bacon.

This new volume takes a different direction. While writing the first book, this manuscript began to take shape almost on its own, composed of ideas that didn't quite fit there but clearly pointed toward a different kind of project. Where the first book was about how we conduct research, this one asks where we are and may be going. It examines the current state of the social sciences and what they reveal about how we define the human condition, especially in light of insights from evolutionary biology, neuroscience, and the rapidly growing influence of artificial intelligence.

It is a book about the frameworks we use to explain human behavior, and about what it means to be human in an age when our intellectual labor is increasingly shared with machines. At present, much of the public debate seems to follow a shallow pattern: "AI might be dangerous, but whatever it is, let's hurry up and do it." Caution is often dismissed as hesitation, and the deeper questions are rarely asked. How do we understand ourselves—our minds, our institutions, our moral lives—when artificial intelligence is no longer just a tool, but a collaborator in shaping knowledge? (Table 1).

Trying to understand human behavior is something we all do—but for social scientists, it's also our profession. Whether as economists, psychologists, or sociologists, we seek to explain how people think, act, and interact. That's why the journey of becoming a researcher cannot stop at mastering methods; it also requires us to reflect on who we are, what we believe, and how we see the world. These two volumes work together toward that goal. To study others, we must begin by acknowledging ourselves: layered, biased, and deeply human.

We're not only a professional role or a set of theories. We live as layered individuals, with overlapping identities, shifting motivations, personal beliefs, and emotional reactions. These different aspects constantly interact. To grasp human behavior then, we must begin with the whole person, not as a fragmented subject, but as an integrated being. We must also recognize that we, as researchers, are humans studying other humans, carrying our own limitations, biases, and blind spots with us. As an example, when we leave the university and go home, we are no longer scientists in any active sense, but parents, partners, friends, and citizens. The roles we play and the experiences we have outside of science inevitably shape how we interpret the world inside it, even though we try our best not to.

To understand the human condition in this integrated way, we can draw on multiple disciplines—each offering a different lens on what it means to

Table 1 The two researcher's journey volumes

Volume	Main focus	Key themes	Use case	Audience
The Researcher's Journey: A Guide to Methodology and Academia in Social Sciences	How to do research	Scientific method, research design, academic publishing, methodology, career development, and funding	A practical guide to mastering the research process and academic ecosystem	Graduate students, early career researchers, and supervisors
The Researcher's Journey in the Age of AI: Reappraising Social Science Research	How research could be reframed in the AI era	Human nature, AI, evolutionary theory, perception, ethics, epistemology, and the future of knowledge	A reflective companion that explores what it means to be a researcher in a rapidly changing intellectual and technological landscape	Graduate students, early career researchers, interdisciplinary thinkers, and critical methodologists

be human. Some bring us closer to the biological and cognitive foundations, others to the cultural, historical, and institutional patterns that shape our lives. Table 2 provides a comparative overview of these disciplinary contributions to understanding human nature.

Taken together, these fields form a mosaic of human understanding—none sufficient on its own, but each indispensable in context. Recognizing their strengths and limitations is the first step toward building the kind of interdisciplinary perspective this book advocates: one that refuses to oversimplify human life, yet still seeks coherence across domains of knowledge.

Some of the most compelling efforts to overcome disciplinary silos, I think, come from *systems theorists* like Niklas Luhmann and Kenneth Boulding, who emphasized the interconnectedness of social, cognitive, and institutional processes. But the vision runs deeper and further back. Erasmus spoke of dignity and the value of learning. Montaigne—whom I sometimes like to think of as a lifelong companion in spirit, smiling gently from his statue, as if to remind me of what truly matters—explored the self with a disarming

Table 2 Comparing disciplinary views of human nature

Discipline	Field	Knowledge depth on human nature	Reason for level of insight
Psychology	Social Science	High	Studies cognition, emotion, and behavior using empirical and experimental methods.
Anthropology	Social Science	High	Investigates cultural variation and human evolution across societies, often with field-based methods.
Sociology	Social Science	Moderate	Focuses more on institutions, groups, and structure than on individual-level psychology.
Economics	Social Science	Low to Moderate	Frequently assumes a rational, utility-maximizing model ("homo economicus"), often ignoring real behavior.
Political Science	Social Science	Low to Moderate	Typically models strategic actors or voting blocs; less attention to psychological variation or bias.
Human Geography	Social Science	Low	Studies spatial patterns of human behavior, less concerned with inner psychological mechanisms.

(continued)

Table 2 (continued)

Discipline	Field	Knowledge depth on human nature	Reason for level of insight
Education Science	Social Science	Moderate	Provides insights into learning and development, but often context specific and institutionally framed.
Communication Studies	Social Science	Moderate	Examines influence of media and messaging, moderately grounded in psychological theories.
History	Humanities	Moderate	Offers indirect insights through documented behavior and patterns over time; limited experimental approach.
Philosophy	Humanities	Variable	Offers deep conceptual exploration of mind, ethics, and reason, but rarely grounded in empirical methods.
Evolutionary Biology	Natural Science	High	Identifies evolved traits and behavioral patterns through comparative and genetic analysis.
Neuroscience	Natural Science	High	Reveals brain mechanisms behind emotion, decision-making, perception, and social behavior.

(continued)

Table 2 (continued)

Discipline	Field	Knowledge depth on human nature	Reason for level of insight
Cognitive Science	Interdisciplinary	High	Combines psychology, neuroscience, linguistics, and AI to model how minds process information.
Behavioral Genetics	Natural Science	Moderate to High	Explores the genetic contribution to behavioral traits; still methodologically young but promising.

honesty. Enlightenment thinkers such as Voltaire, Spinoza, and Kant sought to unite reason, ethics, and society in a coherent humanist vision. What all these thinkers share is a refusal to reduce human life to a single explanatory dimension—a commitment, in other words, to guarding the richness of what it means to be fully human.

Source Photo by author, 1990. Statue of Michel de Montaigne located in Square Paul Painlevé, near the Sorbonne University in Paris

Yet the modern social science project, emerging in the nineteenth and twentieth centuries, gradually lost sight of this holistic ambition. Driven by the desire to appear "scientific" in a narrow sense, disciplines fractured into ever more specialized domains, often reducing the complexity of human life to economic incentives, sociological categories, or isolated psychological mechanisms. Later, many of these same disciplines found themselves increasingly shaped—and in some cases overwhelmed—by the political currents they had once sought to avoid.

Ironically, at a moment when artificial intelligence is displacing humans from many of the "sapiens" domains that once defined modern expertise—calculation, prediction, recall, and classification, the very capacities with which industrial societies have long identified intelligence—there may be an opening for a renewed form of humanism. Such a renewal is not guaranteed. The opportunity exists, and the logic for it is compelling, but there is no certainty that it will be realized. If it were, however, this would not represent a retreat into the past. Although the historical era of Humanism lies behind us, a renewed humanist orientation could function as a necessary correction—reminding us that science is not only about measurement and prediction, but also about cultivating judgment and wisdom. That reminder may prove essential, not only for human societies, but for the broader living systems increasingly shaped by human decisions.

There remains a clear gap in the literature—particularly at the master's and doctoral levels—for work that synthesizes insights across disciplines and strengthens the analytical capacity of the social sciences in light of artificial intelligence. Without such a broader context, methodological tools risk becoming blind instruments. Whether one is analyzing survey data in SPSS or conducting qualitative interviews, understanding the human condition is a prerequisite for meaningful interpretation—not as it is presented in idealized childhood narratives or later repackaged as educational ideology, but as it appears through sustained scientific inquiry. In this sense, context is not an optional addition; it is a methodological necessity.

Much of what is reliably known about human behavior today has emerged not from the core social sciences themselves, but from adjacent fields such as psychology, evolutionary biology, and neuroscience. This may seem counterintuitive to some social scientists, or even to a broader readership, yet the reasons for this asymmetry become clearer once disciplinary histories, methodological constraints, and institutional incentives are examined more closely.

The purpose of this book is therefore to move beyond the traditional methods handbook and beyond narrowly defined academic trajectories. The aim is not simply to refine technique, but to situate scholarly tools within a broader reflection on what it means to be human in the present moment. Research, in this view, is not merely a professional craft. It is part of a larger effort to understand the conditions of life, the societies that have emerged from them, and the challenges now confronting both.

To study human beings seriously requires a framework capable of accounting for shared biological foundations and cultural variation, for continuity and transformation, for cooperation and conflict. Such a framework must operate across cultures and historical periods, and it must remain sensitive to the fact that human systems are always embedded in larger ecological and technological contexts.

If this volume succeeds, it will have contributed not only methodological clarification, but also a modest shift in perspective—encouraging intellectual humility, deeper curiosity, and renewed attention to purpose. The central question is not only how societies are studied, but why, and toward what ends. Ultimately, the challenge is one of meaning: what forms of knowledge are required if human societies are to understand themselves, sustain their institutions, and navigate an uncertain future?

For the opportunity to develop these reflections, I am grateful to my editor at Springer, Felix Torres Serrano, who encouraged framing them in light of the transformations brought about by artificial intelligence. I also wish to thank my friend, Professor of Philosophy Erik J. Olsson, for our conversations on evolutionary theory in the social sciences, and for standing by me when my outspokenness led me into trouble.

Klaus Solberg Söilen
Halmstad University
Halmstad, Sweden

References

Arvesen, O. P. (1961). *Gi meg et fast punkt* [Give me a fixed point]. Gyldendal.
Tang, S. (2020). *On social evolution: Phenomenon and paradigm*. Routledge.
Van Parijs, P. (1981). *Evolutionary explanation in the social sciences: An emerging paradigm*. Rowman & Littlefield.
Wilson, E. O. (1975). *Sociobiology: The new synthesis*. Harvard University Press.
Wilson, E. O. (1978). *On human nature*. Harvard University Press.
Willführ, K. P. et al. (Eds.). (2025). *Evolutionary social sciences: A tour*. Springer.

Acknowledgments The ideas in this book owe much to many people—some colleagues, many friends, and most of them outside academia. Leaving corporate life for the university some 25 years ago also meant leaving the city for the countryside, moving from Norway to southern Sweden. I settled in a remote part of Skurup called Torsjö, in a house I named Trudvang. Surrounded by fields of sugar beets, barley, and rapeseed, and by silence, there was time to nurture a personal library and to spend long days reading and thinking when I was not teaching at the university.

Over the years, my social life came to revolve less around academics and more around artists, writers, and other independent minds who had chosen a slower pace of life. One close friend, the painter Tony Wåhlander, became someone with whom deep conversation was always a pleasure—and still is, even after his move to southern France to capture that particular light in his paintings. Much of the reflection in this book grew out of our talks, though they were far from the only ones. Many others also deserve my thanks: decorators, librarians, historians, poets, and regular visitors to the local second-hand bookshop, Ystad Antikvariat.

Living among people who cared deeply about ideas, expression, and craftsmanship—rather than status or speed, and without being researchers or scientists—reshaped how I came to approach questions of meaning, culture, and human nature. More than anything, these encounters deepened my understanding of culture in its broadest sense: not merely as art, literature, or heritage, but as the living framework of values, habits, and shared meanings through which people make sense of the world. This richer view of culture has become central to the arguments and reflections developed here.

In many ways, despite more than a quarter of a century as a social scientist, the great authors—Dostoevsky, Tolstoy, and Chekhov among the Russian masters; Balzac, with his monumental attempt to portray human interaction as tragicomedy in *La Comédie humaine*; and Proust, with his deep psychological insight in *À la recherche du temps perdu*—still appear more accurate to me in capturing what human beings do, and what can be expected from them, than much of social science. This is not a matter of either/or. The findings from economics, social psychology, and biology discussed in this book rarely contradict these writers; more often, they confirm them. Their insights were not derived from surveys, DNA analyses, or fMRI scans, but from sustained subjective reflection. Yet subjectivity, when grounded in careful observation, does not make an insight wrong—it simply means it has not yet been formally tested. The fact that hundreds of thousands, even millions, of readers recognize themselves in these works is itself a form of validation.

There is also reason to honor the great educators in science—those rare individuals who managed to give science a human face, an art that seems to have largely disappeared. Figures such as the historian Hendrik Willem van Loon, whose storytelling made geography vivid and personal; the chemist and writer Isaac Asimov, who could make the periodic table feel as monumental and intelligible as a Beethoven symphony; and the classical scholar Werner Jaeger, who, after emigrating to the United States before the war, reminded us that humanism and intellectual rigor are not opposites, but natural companions. To these one might add Alexander von Humboldt, who grasped the unity of nature and culture long before it became fashionable, and Hartmut von Hentig, who showed how education itself could be a moral and political project. If the reader listens closely, their voices may still be heard whispering through these pages.

As should now be clear, most of those who deserve acknowledgment are the authors—living and dead—whose work has informed and inspired this book. In that spirit, let me extend the dedication:

Meinen Lehrern
Den lebenden und den toten
gewidmet

A final, heartfelt thanks goes to colleagues—too many to name individually—for the questions, conversations, and challenges that, in one way or another, helped shape this work. *Nulli nominati, nulli obliti.*

Competing Interests The author has no competing interests to declare that are relevant to the content of this manuscript.

Introduction

This book begins with a simple but disruptive proposition: in the near future, much of the work now performed by social scientists could be done by artificial intelligence. More importantly, it shows how this shift might occur—not as a vague technological promise, but through a concrete analysis of the obstacles researchers already face in producing unbiased knowledge. These challenges, I argue, are not merely institutional or methodological; they are rooted in deep biological and cognitive tendencies that shape how humans perceive, reason, and interpret the world.

The book follows a clear arc: it begins with what contemporary science reveals about humans—our biological heritage, cognitive architecture, and cultural adaptations—and ends by confronting how artificial intelligence may compel us to rethink what it means to be human. If intelligence is no longer our defining advantage, it is suggested that wisdom—anchored in historical awareness, ethical responsibility, and a renewed humanism—could emerge as the quality that sets us apart.

At the same time, this comprehensive account of how we can—and should—understand human behavior if we aim to be scientific is intended as a general overview and a roadmap for further study. It offers a shared foundation from which specialists in sociology, economics, political science, and related fields can work. The basic idea is that if we can agree on a set of core principles and assumptions about human nature, the diverse branches of the social sciences may evolve with greater coherence, mutual relevance, and practical impact.

Yet for such a shared foundation to be meaningful, we must begin with a clearer picture of human nature. Most of us move through life with idealized images—how people should behave, how relationships ought to unfold, and how society is supposed to function. But these expectations often diverge sharply from reality. Recognizing our actual tendencies—not the ones we imagine or hope for—could make life less disappointing and, paradoxically, more fulfilling. It is often our unrealistic expectations that leave us let down by others, by institutions, and even by ourselves. A more grounded view of human nature would not perfect the world, but it could make it more livable, more forgiving, and perhaps even more meaningful.

This is how we start that story, then.

The human species is, from an evolutionary standpoint, remarkably new. Anatomically modern humans (Homo sapiens) have existed for less than 300,000 years (Stringer, 2016), and even earlier hominins stretch the timeline back only a few million years, barely a blink in the vast history of life. In this sense, nature appears to be running an experiment: testing a new kind of organism. Not merely one that is adaptable, for many species, like the shark, have survived for hundreds of millions of years precisely because of their adaptability (Compagno, 2001), but one endowed with a highly advanced brain.

The brain itself is not unique to us. Dolphins, elephants, crows, and great apes also exhibit significant cognitive capacities (Marino et al., 2007; Emery & Clayton, 2004). But the human brain introduced something different: a capacity not only for complex communication, but for *metacognition*; the ability to reflect on one's own thought processes, or "thinking about thinking" (Flavell, 1979). We can reflect—as we do systematically in this book—on our own reasoning, plan with foresight, evaluate moral tradeoffs, and alter our behavior based on abstract models and imagined futures (Suddendorf & Corballis, 2007).

That said, most of our daily lives are still biologically grounded. Like other animals, we are born, bond with caregivers, learn, find mates, raise offspring, and eventually die. In that way, our core life pattern mirrors the rest of the animal kingdom—even though, as we will make a point of showing throughout this book, we also thrive on insisting upon our difference.

Yet, we now find ourselves at a new and deeply consequential crossroads. For the first time in history, we have created machines that mimic our own cognitive functions. *Artificial Intelligence*—or AI—has moved beyond symbolic calculation and now engages in tasks that involve perception, language, decision-making, and even creativity (Russell & Norvig, 2021). Unlike previous tools, AI does not merely extend physical power; it emulates mental power. This raises profound questions: What will it mean to be human in a world where thought itself can be externalized? Ongoing debates about AI ethics, authorship, and autonomy already suggest that we are entering morally and intellectually uncharted territory, one where identity, responsibility, and even consciousness may need to be redefined. And how will this shift alter the very disciplines—psychology, sociology, economics, political science—that seek to study and explain human behavior, examining not only social life in general but also the ways we work?

Our first question may be whether this "machine brain" is good or bad for us. Historically, we have come to expect that new machines will improve our lives, making tasks easier, lives longer, and societies more productive. But this one is different. Unlike past inventions, AI is not simply a tool; it is a system that mimics, complements, and in some cases substitutes the very processes that make us human: reasoning, writing, learning, and even deciding. And since it is still in its early days, we cannot fully predict where it will take us. That makes it harder to critic, to regulate, or to resist. There is a constant buzz of talk about AI—about how fantastic it is, and how dangerous it might become—but few broader or deeper reflections on where we may be heading, what parts of it we might actually be able to control, and what aspects may already lie beyond our grasp.

We are trying to respond to changes that haven't yet fully occurred. This makes it difficult to rely on precedent, policy, or even intuition. To face this challenge, we need more than technical tools—we need a framework for thinking clearly about ourselves. After all, the deeper question AI forces us to confront is not just what machines can do, but what it means to be human in contrast. That is where this book seeks to begin.

This book seeks to avoid speculation; however, on occasions when enthusiasm leads me beyond that boundary, I explicitly indicate this to the reader. Wherever possible, it aims to distinguish clearly between what is known and what remains hypothetical. I do not attempt to trick the reader into accepting a predetermined trajectory of events. The goal is not to convince, but to offer ideas for open reflection. In fact, I sometimes think that, for the sake of fruitful discussion, it might be even better if the reader arrives at a different conclusion than I do by the end.

My aim is not to give advice either. Science takes a different path from the long tradition of advice literature—represented by writers such as Machiavelli (1532), Gracián (1647), Carnegie (1936), and in our own times, Greene (1998), and Peterson (2018)—even if I must admit that these works remain enjoyable to read. Where the latter offers direct instruction—rules to follow, techniques to master, and strategies to employ—science does something more subtle and, arguably, more enduring: it describes how we are. It does not command but reveals.

Rather than telling you what to do, science lays out what is. It helps us understand the architecture of the human mind, the dynamics of emotion, bias, cognition, and perception. It shows us how we make decisions, why we trust or deceive, and how we cooperate or fail to. By doing so, it hands us not rules but tools; explanatory frameworks we can apply flexibly across contexts.

This is a better approach, not because it is moral or noble, but because it is more robust and adaptive. *Prescriptive advice* can quickly become outdated, context bound, or even counterproductive when blindly applied. *Scientific insight*, in contrast, evolves and refines itself. It gives us a living map of our limitations and capacities—not a set of marching orders, but a compass.

Knowing how we think, rather than *what* to think, makes us more resilient in the long run. It equips us to recognize manipulation rather than mirroring it. It allows us to adapt when situations change, rather than relying on fixed maxims. And it invites reflection: instead of asking, "What rule should we follow?", we begin asking, "What kind of people do we want to become—and what does the evidence tell us about how to get there?"

In short, the scientific approach respects our agency. It doesn't assume our goals or values; it gives us the understanding we need to choose them more wisely. And that, perhaps, is the deepest kind of power: not the ability to follow rules well, but the ability to know ourselves well enough to decide when no rule applies.

Embracing complexity is only the beginning. For a social scientist, the real challenge lies in learning how to work with it. No single lens is sufficient. A purely economic view overlooks emotional and moral dimensions. A psychological focus may ignore history, institutions, and power. The richness of human experience resists simplification, but that is also precisely what makes social science both difficult and indispensable. We must specialize, yes, but without losing sight of the larger picture: the full reality of what we are studying. If we fail to do so, it becomes impossible to recognize the biological layer that is always present in the background—and it is from this layer that we can begin to build a true science of humanity.

For decades, we have been talking about the need for inter-, trans-, and even pan-disciplinarity in the social sciences. Yet the endeavor has always felt too vast to grasp, and most social scientists—trained and specialized in one field or another—have been understandably overchallenged when faced with such integrative methods. That is, until now. With the arrival of machines capable of assisting us in gathering, organizing, and synthesizing knowledge across domains, we stand at the threshold of what could be a renaissance of the broader social science project—an integrative vision reminiscent of Auguste Comte's. Comte famously placed sociology at the apex of a hierarchy of sciences, envisioning a systematic understanding of society built on the foundations of mathematics, physics, biology, and psychology. Yet Comte's project also drifted into the realm of political ideology, culminating in his so-called Religion of Humanity—a quasi-religious program that few outside his circle embraced. The fate of that effort serves as a cautionary reminder, though the impulse behind it—the search for a unified science of humanity—remains strikingly relevant today.

The chapters ahead take up that challenge. They ask: What does it mean to study humans, not just in parts, but as wholes? Why use science at all when we might lean on tradition, intuition, or trial and error? These are not separate questions. They are deeply connected. To understand others, or us, we must ask what it truly means to be human—what makes us distinct, and how we adapt in the face of new challenges, especially in times like ours, with the rise of AI, which, by all appearances, promises to replace much of the work humans currently do in front of computers. What, then, will it mean to be a social scientist in the coming years, faced with the overwhelming presence of this new technology?

To get there, we may need to remind ourselves: we are not merely chemistry and tissue. We are animals who seek meaning—unlike most other species, which act primarily on instinct and immediate need. One person walks alone in the forest, another restores old wooden boats, and a third throws darts at the pub. The forms differ. But beneath them lies the same drive to live a life that feels worthwhile. Science helps us make sense of this ordinary search for meaning, not just in abstract terms, but in ways that touch everyday life. The disciplines we associate with universities are deeply embedded in the things we do for leisure, work, and self-expression. A game of darts involves psychology and sociology. Hiking draws on geography, public policy, and stress research. Boatbuilding needs physics and materials science, but also history and anthropology. Even economics helps explain how these practices emerge and spread.

Scientific knowledge deepens our grasp of ordinary life. It sharpens action and informs better teaching, policy, and management. With a clearer understanding comes better choices and, ideally, better lives. Whether you are drafting a national policy or trying to hit a bullseye, knowing what works and why makes all the difference.

This book, then, explores how the search for understanding is now being transformed by AI. Let us be clear: AI is not just another tool. It may well be the most consequential invention in history—surpassing the wheel, electricity, or even the internet in its speed and scope of impact. And the striking thing is that just five years ago, only a small number of people fully grasped its potential. That fact alone should make us think twice about our ability to grasp the future and its implications.

Here, then, comes the first of several mini-cases that appear throughout the book. Each one is followed by questions designed to spark reflection. My hope is that they will not only lighten the text but also make it more engaging and dialogical as we go along:

Case in a Box: Writing with Two Brains

For me, as for many others, the research process still begins with reading books, taking notes, and manually gathering ideas—a method shaped by years of academic habit. But once those ideas move into a digital document, something shifts: a continuous exchange with AI often begins. What follows is no longer solitary composition, but a dynamic dialogue in which words and concepts evolve through interaction. In this sense, AI already acts not just as a passive tool, but as both a capable collaborator and an efficient assistant.

Writing is no longer a solitary act confined to pen and paper or a word processor. It has moved beyond simple online searches to become an ongoing conversation—fluid, responsive, and increasingly integrated. This transformation extends far beyond academia. When a plumber recently installed a heating system in my home, I opened my AI app to interpret the technical details—valves, flow rates, and all—complete with diagrams and step-by-step explanations. What could easily have been an awkward moment, where I would normally just nod politely and look things up later, instead turned into a real conversation. I was able to follow along and even ask informed questions. It felt as if I suddenly had two brains, not one.

The same pattern is emerging in academia. My students, instead of taking notes by hand, now often let AI run in the background, transcribing everything I say during a lecture. Afterward, they can query the transcript directly, asking the AI clarifying questions based on what they did—or did not—understand.[1] What we see here is rapid integration: AI creeping seamlessly into everyday practice until it feels natural to imagine it running constantly, 24/7. In such a world, the metaphor of having "two brains" is no longer just a figure of speech—it is becoming a lived reality.

Questions for discussion:

1. How do you begin your own writing or problem-solving process?
2. Do you treat AI primarily as a tool, or as a collaborator?
3. How might integrating AI more directly into your workflow change the way you think, write, and interact with others?

[1] It is difficult to deny students the possibility of using AI transcription, as it is functionally similar to taking notes. Where institutions can reasonably set limits is in prohibiting redistribution of the content—but even this is hard to enforce. Once transcripts exist, it is nearly impossible to verify

Cases like this illustrate how quickly our relationship with technology is shifting. Some adopt AI eagerly, and others remain cautious. But one thing is already clear: AI is reshaping what it means to be human. We, who call ourselves Homo sapiens—the wise ones—have built something that, in many ways, thinks better than we do. Not in every way, not yet, but in enough ways to raise deep questions. If this is intelligence, then what are we? Are we still defined by our ability to reason, adapt, and learn, or must we now reconsider those traits in light of machines that perform similar functions, sometimes faster, and without fatigue or bias? The very qualities we once used to define *human uniqueness* are now being mirrored and, in some areas, surpassed by AI. This forces us to reflect not only on our *cognitive architecture*, but on the broader meaning of being human in an age of simulation and augmentation.

These are some of the questions explored in this book. It represents a departure from my usual boundaries of economics and business studies, moving into broader interdisciplinary territory. While much of my previous work has focused on the scientific method, digital marketing, and intelligence studies, this manuscript extends further into philosophy, meaning, identity, and the human condition. The intent is not to offer or debate *philosophical doctrine*, but to draw on philosophical perspectives that have long informed my thinking and research, including thinkers such as Aristotle, Kant, Hume, Nietzsche, and Luhmann, as well as insights from evolutionary biology, cognitive science, and behavioral economics.

Above all, the central aim of this book is clear: to present a cohesive scientific framework for the social sciences that can convince the reader—through extensive analysis and examples—that the evolutionary social sciences paradigm is not only theoretically sound, but also intellectually compelling and practically valuable.

To guide the reader through this journey, the book is structured around ten core questions that build upon one another. Table 3 outlines how each chapter addresses a fundamental dimension of the human experience, from our biological roots to the ethical and technological challenges of our time.

This table outlines the conceptual structure of the book and the progression of its core arguments. It begins with foundational questions about what it means to be human from a scientific perspective, and why science remains indispensable in making sense of ourselves. The first three chapters develop

who uploaded material or how it was obtained. In practice, this means that in the near future most lectures may be available in their entirety as text. If that becomes the norm, one could reasonably ask: why not let a robot read them aloud in class the next time? Recent surveys confirm that AI transcription tools (such as Otter.ai or Microsoft's Copilot) are already widely used in higher education, blurring the line between personal note-taking and public dissemination (Gupta et al., 2023; Yilmaz & Karaoglan Yilmaz, 2024).

Table 3 Structure and logic of the book—From foundations to human futures

Part	Ch.	Title (Brief)	Main question/Focus	Key themes & sections	Type
I. Foundations	1.	Understanding Humanity as a System	How can the social sciences be reframed as a systems science of humanity in the age of AI?	1.1 Brains to Algorithms · 1.2 Purpose & Limits · 1.3 Human Meaning · 1.4 Science, Systems & Society (1.4.1–1.4.6) · 1.5 Science vs. Misconceptions	Reflective
I. Foundations	2.	Evolution of Biology and Society	What defines humans biologically and socially across evolutionary time?	2.1 Biological & Cognitive Limits (2.1.1–2.1.3) · 2.2 Longevity ·2.3 Identity & Culture (2.3.1 Religion) · 2.4 Humans & Primates · 2.5 Climate · 2.6 Time Use · 2.7 Personality (2.7.1)	Empirical

(continued)

Part	Ch.	Title (Brief)	Main question/Focus	Key themes & sections	Type
I. Foundations	3.	Cognition, Emotion, and Sociality	How do cognition, emotion, and social instincts shape behavior?	3.1 Free Will · 3.2 Social Brain (3.2.1–3.2.4) · 3.3 Reclaiming Human Nature · 3.4 Genes & Norms (3.4.1–3.4.5) · 3.5 Identity & Dissonance (3.5.1) · 3.6 Mirror Neurons · 3.7 Perception (3.7.1–3.7.4) · 3.8 Reasoning Limits	Hybrid
II. Human Thinking & Culture	4.	Culture and Society	How do cultural systems shape thought and organization?	4.1 Language · 4.2 Belief Systems (4.2.1–4.2.3) · 4.3 Digital Learning (4.3.1) · 4.4 Institutions · 4.5 Social Architectures (4.5.1 From Rituals to Digital Intimacy · 4.5.2 Limits of Belonging)	Hybrid

(continued)

Part	Ch.	Title (Brief)	Main question/Focus	Key themes & sections	Type
II. Human Thinking & Culture	5.	Life in Time: How We Work, Love, and Age	What do daily activities reveal about human priorities and roles?	5.1 Time Use · 5.2 Work, Rest, Rituals · 5.3 Lifespan (5.3.1 Roles Across Life) · 5.4 Self-Domestication · 5.5 Civilizational Cycles & Renewal of Social Sciences	Empirical
III. Role & Responsibility	6.	The Social Sciences Reconsidered	What is the role and value of the social sciences today?	6.1 Origins · 6.2 Methods & Constraints · 6.3 Toward a Unified Framework (6.3.1 Common Language) · 6.4 Seeing and Not Seeing · 6.5 Science, Advocacy & AI (6.5.1–6.5.3) · 6.6 Stewardship (6.6.1 Risks of Social Design)	Reflective
III. Role & Responsibility	7.	AI and Scholarly Evolution	How does AI transform scholarly practices?	7.1 Scholarship in the AI Era (7.1.1–7.1.5) · 7.2 AI-Assisted Writing (7.2.1 Workflow)	Reflective

(continued)

Part	Ch.	Title (Brief)	Main question/Focus	Key themes & sections	Type
IV. Science & Society	8.	Ethics and Responsibility in the Age of AI	How should ethics guide AI development?	8.1 Ethics Gap (8.1.1) · 8.2 Inflation of Ethics (8.2.1–8.2.5) · 8.3 Value Alignment (8.3.1–8.3.2) · 8.4 System Design · 8.5 Institutions	Reflective
IV. Science & Society	9.	Outsourced Cognition and Identity	How does AI-driven outsourcing affect human cognition and identity?	9.1 Outsourced Human (9.1.1–9.1.3) · 9.2 Autonomy · 9.3 Cognitive Vulnerability · (9.3.1 Judgment · 9.3.2 Economics) · 9.4 Edge of AI & Human Niche	Hybrid
V. Conclusion	10.	Humanism and Wisdom in the AI Era	How can wisdom and humanism guide human–AI coexistence?	10.1 Rational Pride to Humility (10.1.1) · 10.2 From Fragmentation to Purpose (10.2.1 Second Chance) · 10.3 Reappraising Social Sciences (10.3.1–10.3.6) · 10.4 Wisdom in Machine Era · 10.5 New Humanism	Reflective

a systemic and multi-dimensional view of the human species—biological, psychological, and cultural—drawing on systems theory to show how these dimensions interconnect and together establish the groundwork for a more integrated and cumulative social science. Part II explores how humans think and act collectively, emphasizing culture, cognition, and daily life as expressions of deeper patterns. Part III turns to the institutions and ethics of science itself, asking how social scientists should navigate complexity, bias, and moral responsibility. Part IV investigates how scientific knowledge interacts with society, including how technology—and especially AI—influences not just the production of knowledge, but also the behavior of individuals, institutions, and entire social systems. It examines how denial of reality, algorithmic mediation, and technological acceleration are reshaping our collective future, while the final chapter offers a coherent framework for understanding the role of human beings and interpreting human behavior in an age increasingly shaped by AI. Of course, as always, I will fall down too many rabbit holes along the way—in the form of extensive examples, cases, and personal reflections—and I hope the reader will forgive me for this.

The sources cited throughout this book are seldom direct quotations. Rather, they are references to works that have engaged with related themes. In particular, most sources published more than five years ago could not have addressed the topic in relation to artificial intelligence and should not be read as if they did. Their inclusion is meant to provide historical, theoretical, or comparative context. Often, the references chosen are not the most recent contributions but the first major works that defined or opened a field, establishing a foundation for subsequent research.

This book is not a purely empirical or strictly scientific work in the traditional sense. Rather, it blends descriptive chapters with conceptual analysis, philosophical reflection, and personal narrative—what I now consider to be hallmarks of the *Researcher's Journey* concept and style of writing. Some sections are grounded in interdisciplinary evidence and scientific synthesis; others adopt a more reflective or speculative tone. This mixed approach is deliberate. The facts alone do not tell us where the social sciences should go, nor do they settle the question of why they matter—and overly technical language often makes for unnecessarily boring reading, or at least that is my opinion.

What I am proposing is a theoretically cohesive contribution to the disciplines, even if it does not follow the usual templates. The aim remains reflective scholarship, not political commentary. This is not a definitive conclusion, but an invitation to link science with purpose and to explore how the social sciences might evolve in a time of rapid technological change.

I invite you, dear reader, to follow me on this new journey.

References

Berninger, V. W., & Richards, T. (2002). *Brain literacy for educators and psychologists*. Academic Press.

Carnegie, D. (1936). *How to win friends and influence people*. Simon and Schuster.

Compagno, L. J. V. (2001). *Sharks of the world: An annotated and illustrated catalogue of shark species known to date*. FAO.

Emery, N. J., & Clayton, N. S. (2004). The mentality of crows: Convergent evolution of intelligence in corvids and apes. *Science, 306*(5703), 1903–1907. https://doi.org/10.1126/science.1098410

Flavell, J. H. (1979). Metacognition and cognitive monitoring: A new area of cognitive–developmental inquiry. *American Psychologist, 34*(10), 906–911. https://doi.org/10.1037/0003-066X.34.10.906.

Gracián, B. (1647). *The art of worldly wisdom* (C. Maurer, Trans., 1991). Doubleday. (Original work published 1647).

Gupta, A. (2024). *When generative artificial intelligence meets academic integrity*. British Educational Research Association. https://eprints.soton.ac.uk/493221/1/Gupta_Small-grants-reports-2024_final-text.pdf

Machiavelli, N. (1532). *The prince* (P. Bondanella, Trans., 2005). Oxford University Press. (Original work published 1532).

Marino L, Connor, R. C., Fordyce, R. E., Herman, L. M., Hof, P. R., Lefebvre, L., Lusseau, D., McCowan, B., Nimchinsky, E. A., Pack, A. A., Rendell, L., Reidenberg, J. S., Reiss, D., Uhen, M. D., Van der Gucht, E., & Whitehead H. (2007). Cetaceans have complex brains for complex cognition. *PLoS Biology, 5*(5), e139. https://doi.org/10.1371/journal.pbio.0050139.

Peterson, J. B. (2018). *12 rules for life: An antidote to chaos*. Random House Canada.

Russell, S., & Norvig, P. (2021). *Artificial intelligence: A modern approach* (4th ed.). Pearson.

Stringer, C. (2016). The origin and evolution of Homo sapiens. *Philosophical Transactions of the Royal Society B: Biological Sciences, 371*(1698), 20150237. https://doi.org/10.1098/rstb.2015.0237

Suddendorf, T., & Corballis, M. C. (2007). The evolution of foresight: What is mental time travel, and is it unique to humans? *Behavioral and Brain Sciences, 30*(3), 299–313. https://doi.org/10.1017/S0140525X07001975

Yilmaz, R., & Karaoglan Yilmaz, F. G. (2023). The effect of generative artificial intelligence (AI)-based tool use on students' computational thinking skills, programming self-efficacy, and motivation. *Education and Information Technologies, 28*(11), 12345–12367.

Prelude

(Daughter turns the doorknob to the library and walks quietly into the room. The father is seated in a white armchair, half hidden behind the journal *The Economist*.)

Daughter: No one wants to play with me!
Father: (Without lowering the journal)
Oh, I'm sure that's not true.
Daughter: No one likes me!
(The journal rustles as the father lowers it. His red reading glasses slide slightly down his nose as he looks at her more carefully. He hears the edge in her voice—this isn't routine frustration. He sees the sadness on her face and smiles gently.)
Father: That's not true. There are plenty of children who like you...!
Daughter: No. No one wants to play!
Father: (Pauses)
Well… not right now, maybe. But if you wait, …someone will. I'm sure of it. Sometimes they don't have time, or they're just not in the mood, or—
Daughter: No. I'm all alone. No one wants to play!
Father: (Trying a different angle, gently)
Well… if you didn't always try to decide for the others—and didn't tell them what to do or how to play all of the time, … maybe they'd be more willing,…?

(He can see the words don't land. Her face stays still. She doesn't buy it, so he softens his voice.)

Father: Listen… you're wonderful.
And other children are wonderful too.
But you can't decide for them. And you can't choose when they want to be with you. That's just not how people work—not even children.
(She looks down and pauses. He realizes something: she has grown up on fairy tales, bedtime stories, and cartoons where children always play together, solve things in harmony, and laugh in circles. A world of ideal friendships and perfect endings. She hasn't really been told the other version—the real one.)

Father: Do you remember how I once told you that life can be a bit of a zoo…?
(She doesn't respond, but he catches a flicker in her eyes—just enough to make him wonder if the thought took root. He waits, knowing her well enough to expect the usual: any second now she'll shrug, say "OK then," and run off again, chasing whatever suddenly seems more interesting in her world.)
Then she says:

Daughter: What was that story again… about the five great apes?
And so the father was more than happy to tell the story about our cousins one more time, about their differences, similarities and small little quirks.

Contents

List of Figures

List of Tables

1

Understanding Humanity as a System

Abstract What does it mean to be human in an age when machines can think, write, and decide? As artificial intelligence challenges long-held assumptions about cognition and expertise, the social sciences face a deeper problem: their fragmented frameworks no longer capture how human life actually works. This chapter makes the case for a systemic rethinking of the social sciences. Drawing on the tradition of systems theory and evolutionary thinking, it introduces the **Vitruvian Framework**—a unifying model that integrates biology, culture, institutions, technology, and moral order into a single analytical scaffold. Rather than treating economics, psychology, politics, and anthropology as isolated domains, the framework shows how they coevolve and shape one another. The chapter guides the reader from the limits of brain-centric and discipline-bound explanations toward a systems view of humanity—one that is better equipped to explain real-world complexity. Artificial intelligence is not presented as a threat, but as a catalyst: a mirror that exposes the weaknesses of old paradigms and accelerates the need for a more integrated, evolutionary science of human behavior and society.

This chapter opens with a simple but pressing question: *What does it mean to be human in an age when machines can simulate many of the abilities we once thought defined us?* Artificial intelligence forces not only a reassessment of our cognitive capacities, but also of the frameworks we use to study human beings and societies. If the social sciences are to remain relevant, they must move beyond fragmented disciplines and adopt a systemic perspective.

K. Solberg Söilen, *The Researcher's Journey in the Age of AI*,
https://doi.org/10.1007/978-3-032-23069-0_1

We begin by tracing how earlier system theorists—from Bertalanffy and Boulding to Luhmann and Bateson—sought to explain life and society as interconnected wholes. Their insights provide an essential backdrop for understanding why a purely disciplinary approach cannot capture the full complexity of human life. Economics, psychology, political science, and anthropology all describe important aspects of reality, but when treated as independent systems they lose sight of their interdependence.

Building on this tradition, the chapter introduces the *Vitruvian Framework*, a systems model of humanity structured around five evolutionary dimensions: symbolic, co-evolutionary, ecological, political-moral, and technological. Each dimension represents a subsystem of human life, connected to the others yet irreducible to them. Taken together, they offer a scaffold for integrating diverse findings across the social sciences into a more cumulative whole.

The chapter unfolds in four key steps:

1. *From Brains to Systems*—We begin with human cognition, shaped by evolution for survival rather than clarity, and show why this partial view must be embedded in a broader systems framework.
2. *The Limits of Fragmentation*—We examine how disciplinary silos obscure cross-cutting dynamics, from how economic insecurity shapes health to how media habits influence civic life.
3. *Reframing the Social Sciences as Systems Science*—We draw on evolutionary theory and systems thinking to argue for a methodological reform that integrates biology, culture, and institutions into one scaffold.
4. *AI as a Mirror and Catalyst*—Finally, we consider how artificial intelligence not only challenges our traditional models but also provides tools for synthesizing knowledge across domains, potentially accelerating the renewal of the social sciences.

In short, this chapter positions humanity itself as a system—biological, cultural, political, and technological at once—and the social sciences as a project that must reflect this systemic reality. Rather than seeing AI as a threat to this project, we frame it as a catalyst: a force that makes visible the limitations of old paradigms and opens the way toward a more integrative and evolutionary science of humanity.

1.1 Brains to Algorithms: A Shifting Scientific Landscape

This reappraisal begins with a basic yet pressing question: what still makes us distinct? As AI systems now simulate aspects of thought, language, and even social interaction, it becomes more urgent to examine the unique cognitive and emotional architecture that defines human life.

As human beings, we've been gifted with a remarkable organ: the brain. So far, no other species on Earth shows the same level of abstract reasoning, language, tool use, or cultural complexity as *Homo sapiens* (Tomasello, 2014). Through shared symbols and meanings, we can communicate not only basic needs but entire worldviews, myths, and moral codes. And once that communication ability kicks in—well, we can't easily turn it off. My own mind starts up around 06:30 every day and hums along like an old sewing machine until bedtime, these days accompanied by the faint buzz of age-related tinnitus.

There's not much I can do about it once it gets going. One reason I tend to get up early is that if I don't, the brain starts drifting into uncontrolled waters on its own, leaving me in a kind of second-in-command position, which I find deeply discomforting. So, I may as well get out of bed. And once I'm up, well, then I may as well fill my head with interesting work tasks, at least until I feel tired enough to sleep again.

But here's the thing: our brain wasn't built to bring us peace. From an evolutionary perspective, it functions primarily as a *problem-solving machine*. Its architecture is tuned to navigate threats, manage social complexity, anticipate the future, and pursue long-term goals critical to survival and reproduction, not to keep us in a permanent state of happiness or relaxation (Tooby & Cosmides, 1992). What we call *happiness* may simply be a momentary by-product; a signal that a problem has been resolved, a task completed, or a need met.

Meanwhile, a built-in "*negativity bias*" ensures that problems and potential dangers hold our attention more persistently than pleasures (Baumeister et al., 2001). Even in moments of rest, our minds wander; simulating possibilities, recalling past mistakes, and preparing for what might come next (Smallwood & Schooler, 2006). We are not wired to idle; we are wired to anticipate, adapt, and act.

So, it's not easy to be human, as we all discover. Our minds are constantly at work, scanning for risks, replaying regrets, and simulating futures. That's our default mode. So let's not be too harsh on others—or ourselves—for being distracted, reactive, or caught up in everyday trouble. Much of it isn't a choice; it's just the way we're wired.

Because the brain rarely rests and continuously generates new problems to solve, many people turn to mind-altering substances for relief, chief among them alcohol. While moderate use may temporarily dull mental noise, for some it leads to dependence or addiction, ultimately worsening their situation instead of improving it, to say nothing of harder drugs, which carry even greater risks and can rapidly compound the underlying psychological and social problems people are trying to escape. This constant mental strain—combined with our limited capacity to find lasting relief—reveals a deeper truth: our brains were never optimized for the complexities of modern life.

Even worse, the brain was not designed to solve *other* people's problems, let alone the problems of the planet. Evolution has shaped it primarily to secure our *own* survival, ensure the continuation of our genes, and respond to what is immediately visible or felt in our environment (Cosmides & Tooby, 1997). Our cognitive systems are sharply attuned to local, tangible threats, while abstract or distant dangers often fail to generate an emotional response (Slovic, 2007b).

And part of the reason is complexity. Life—whether human or bacterial—is extraordinarily complicated. Even the simplest organisms rely on intricate biochemical systems to adapt and survive (Woese, 2004; Mayr, 1982). Complexity is not an accident; it is the very condition of survival. Moreover, as Dawkins (1986, 1996) and others have argued, organisms that appear later in evolutionary history often exhibit even greater complexity. This is not because evolution drives inevitably toward complexity, but because new arrivals must survive in ecosystems already filled with predators, competitors, and parasites. Each new layer of adaptation adds to the demands placed on the organism, creating cumulative intricacy. Humans, as very latecomers in this process, are therefore exceptionally complex—biologically, cognitively, and socially—having evolved within a world already shaped by countless earlier forms of life (Maynard Smith & Szathmáry, 1995).

Yet in the social sciences, we often insist on squeezing this richness into simple models—rational choice, linear cause and effect, neat typologies—that can never quite capture the messiness of reality (Gigerenzer, 2007). Simplicity brings clarity, but at the cost of truth. Still, complicated does not mean incomprehensible. Since Darwin's theory of natural selection (1859/2009) and later advances in psychology and neuroscience (Hebb, 1949; Damasio, 1994), we have had the tools to study complexity rather than denying it. The task is to resist the temptation of reduction and instead learn to work with the layered, sometimes paradoxical, nature of human life.

The task is not to wish complexity away but to recognize its consequences. One of them is that our brains cope by simplifying—by focusing on the immediate and the tangible, while filtering out what feels too abstract or overwhelming. This helps us survive, but it also narrows our field of concern.

For all its brilliance, then, the human brain is far from perfect. It forgets, it confabulates, and it's biased. And now, with the rise of AI, we're entering an age where machines may outperform us in several key cognitive domains: They don't forget. They process data at a scale and speed no human can match. They summarize, write, and even revise ideas faster than most graduate students (Marcus & Davis, 2019).

What this means for our thinking is still unclear. If AI becomes like the pocket calculator when it first appeared in the early 1970s—removing the need for basic skills—we risk losing some *cognitive independence*. Just as pocket calculators took over manual arithmetic, making us less practiced in mental math, AI could similarly and soon erode our abilities to think, reason, and solve problems without technological assistance. If AI becomes like the internet, it could also create a divide: some will think more clearly with it, while others may lose focus entirely, spending their time entertained rather than engaged (Carr, 2010).

This tension—between empowerment and dependency—suggests that the arrival of AI may deepen rather than bridging intellectual divides. To illustrate what such a future could look like, consider the following scenario:

Case in a Box: Thinkers and Drifters—The Return of the Intellectual Divide

Imagine a near future where AI has fully reshaped education and labor. Productivity gains from automation, combined with new taxation on large corporations, have allowed many citizens to live without the demands of full-time work. But instead of producing a flourishing leisure society, two distinct groups begin to emerge.

The first group—let's call them the *Thinkers*—follow a rigorous path of schooling. Mathematics, logic, philosophy, and history remain central to their training, cultivating habits of discipline, abstraction, and independent reasoning. They see AI not as a replacement but as a demanding partner, a tool that sharpens rather than softening their intellectual edge. Their lives may be structured and strict, but they develop resilience and clarity of thought.

The second group, by contrast, grows up with little formal schooling beyond the basics. Freed from the pressures of work, they spend much of their time in entertainment, social media, or small-scale hobbies. Without regular training in self-discipline or complex problem-solving, their lives are often more chaotic, reactive, and emotionally driven. Work once forced people to strengthen their character and habits; without it, many drift.

The result is not equality but a return to an old pattern: an intellectual divide reminiscent of the nineteenth century, when a small elite went to universities while the majority received minimal schooling and worked in mines or factories. The coal mines are gone, but the gulf in training—and the cultural distance it creates—reemerges in new form.

Questions for Discussion

1. If AI enables a "leisure class" without discipline or schooling, does this widen inequality in ways that cannot be solved by redistribution of wealth?
2. Could a society divided into *Thinkers* and *Drifters* remain stable—or would it produce resentment, alienation, or political conflict?
3. Should governments actively preserve rigorous training for all citizens, even if AI can perform most tasks more efficiently?

This scenario highlights what is at stake when cognitive effort becomes unevenly distributed. If some continue to train their minds while others drift, society risks fragmenting not only economically but also intellectually. Such a divide would shape not just opportunities but the very texture of public life.

At the same time, history shows that human progress has never rested solely on survival or convenience. What sets us apart is not just the ability to solve immediate problems but the drive to seek truth. The brain is more than a tool for coping—it is an instrument for comparing, questioning, and testing. Verified knowledge allows us to build safer homes, develop medicines, write constitutions, and organize modern economies. For this reason, societies across time have honored books, founded schools, and passed knowledge across generations (Harari, 2015; Snow, 1959).

Today, artificial intelligence is entering this domain too—with superintelligence on the horizon, where AI is on the brink of conducting research by itself, if we are to believe the technical experts who work directly with these large language models. On the one hand, it is true that AI can help us uncover truth with unprecedented speed and precision. But on the other hand, it can just as easily be turned into a machine for spreading falsehood. By altering algorithms, it becomes possible to shape not only the output but also the framework through which we interpret reality. In that sense, whoever controls the algorithm does not just control the tool; they influence the mental models, decisions, and beliefs of entire societies. And while we are still in the early days of AI, its development is progressing at a remarkable pace. This raises an even deeper question: If both human and artificial intelligence operate according to underlying rules—be they computational or biological—what, then, separates us from machines?

From a physics perspective, all this complexity—our thoughts, feelings, institutions, and even consciousness—can be reduced to interactions among elementary particles governed by physical laws. Humans, like all matter, are made up of atoms, composed of subatomic particles like quarks and electrons. These particles obey *quantum mechanics* and *thermodynamics*, not intentions or beliefs. As physicist Sean Carroll (2016) argues, there's no evidence for an immaterial soul or mind apart from these physical processes. In this view, we are already "big, warm, wet robots," executing algorithms written by DNA and driven by chemical gradients and neural firings.

Neuroscientist Patricia Churchland (2002) similarly emphasizes that consciousness arises from the physical substrate of the brain, not from some immaterial realm. While such a view may seem cold, it underscores the continuity between humans and the natural world, and sets the stage for understanding how *higher-level meanings*, like morality and identity, emerge from *lower-level mechanics*.

In recent years, Geoffrey Hinton—a thinker I hold in great respect and to whom I will return several times throughout this book—has suggested that this logic may apply not only to biological systems but also to artificial ones. He has argued that if consciousness emerges from the computational architecture of neurons, then it cannot be ruled out that artificial neural networks might also develop some form of subjective experience. Hinton has even suggested that large-scale AI systems might already possess rudimentary forms of consciousness, since they process information in ways structurally analogous to human brains (Hinton, in LBC interview, 2024). His stance reflects a form of *computational functionalism*: what matters is not the substance—carbon or silicon—but the pattern of information processing. Whether or not one agrees—and few are better positioned to make such claims than a Turing Award-winning pioneer of deep learning—his view underscores how advances in AI force us to rethink long-standing assumptions about what makes human consciousness unique.

And yet, despite this physical foundation, we remain creatures of interpretation, constantly searching for patterns, causes, and explanations that help us navigate the world. To bring some order to that search—to make sense of a universe in which we are both particles and pattern-seekers—we invented a marvelous system: *science*. The scientific method—based on observation, hypothesis testing, replication, and peer review—serves as our most reliable tool for filtering signal from noise (Popper, 1959).

It doesn't guarantee truth, but it gets us closer by weeding out what's false, or at least unproven. Most university disciplines are grounded in this method. Theology, for instance, is typically accepted only when studied comparatively or historically, not because its claims are verified, but because they are intellectually or culturally significant. That doesn't mean religion is false—only that its claims remain outside the current bounds of scientific validation. And believe me, people have tried.

That openness is not a weakness but a strength. It is the foundation for everything that follows in this book—not just what we think we know, but how and why we try to know anything at all. I present science broadly here and draw inspiration from fields as diverse as evolutionary biology, physics, psychology, and philosophy. But my formal training and primary competence lie in the social sciences. That is the perspective from which I write, and it shapes both the scope and tone of this book. Where I venture beyond that domain, I do so cautiously, aiming not to claim any authority.

Anyway, the question we need to ask ourselves with AI—and soon, to an even higher degree, with superintelligence—is why humans will even continue to do science if there will be machines that may do it better, for example, in fields like the social sciences.

1.2 Purpose and Limits of Social Sciences

For centuries, we have called ourselves the intelligent species. But if machines can soon match or exceed us in many domains of intelligence, that title may no longer fit. The question then becomes: what will we choose to call ourselves—and on what qualities will we base that choice? This is not only a philosophical challenge for individuals; it is also a disciplinary challenge for the social sciences.

There is a growing recognition that the social sciences need to revisit their foundational purpose. This means going beyond technical rigor to re-engage with core questions about the human condition, the search for meaning, and the functioning of societies. Over time, the field has rightly celebrated methodological precision—an achievement in itself—but sometimes at the expense of relevance. In an era of rapid technological, cultural, and epistemic transformation, such an imbalance is increasingly difficult to justify.

While the social sciences have developed a rich and complex body of knowledge, it is not always clear where the field is headed—or how convincingly it can defend its value to a skeptical public. Critics both inside and outside academia argue that much of what social scientists produce lacks practical consequence. Tens of thousands of professionals operate within this system, and yet one must occasionally pause and ask: to what end?

This reflection becomes all the more urgent as our understanding of human nature shifts. When I was growing up, it was widely believed that people are rational agents—conscious actors who make decisions based on available information. Much of the social sciences reinforced that idea, which formed the intellectual bedrock of fields like economics, political science, and decision theory. But recent decades have complicated that picture. Insights from neuroscience, behavioral genetics, and evolutionary psychology now suggest that much of our behavior is shaped by unconscious mechanisms, structural biases, and environmental conditioning. Even the idea of free will—once taken as a given—is now actively debated.

If our decisions are less conscious than we assumed, this forces us to ask an uncomfortable question: what does this mean for all the social sciences we have done since the Second World War—and even earlier—when we operated under completely different and, in hindsight, unrealistic assumptions about rationality and human behavior? Much of our research and many of our theoretical frameworks were built on the belief that humans are primarily rational, autonomous agents, when in fact the evidence increasingly suggests we are driven by unconscious biases, social heuristics, and evolutionary pressures (Kahneman, 2011; Tooby & Cosmides, 1992). If that foundation is flawed, how much of the edifice built upon it needs to be re-examined?

This book seeks to reopen those questions, not only to evaluate the current state of the field, but to rethink its future. Doing so requires more than just new methods or data. It demands philosophical honesty, intellectual humility, and renewed curiosity.

That's why I invite you to return with me to a personal moment of discovery: sitting in a green metal chair in the Jardin du Luxembourg, warmed by the first sunrays of the morning, a discounted philosophy book in hand, fresh from the top floor of Gibert Joseph. I remember the feeling clearly—of pages turning and a world opening up. But the books I read then weren't social science texts. They were mostly works in the humanities—philosophy, literature—and occasionally the natural sciences. To be honest, the social sciences didn't interest me much at the time. And even now, after years as a professor, I sometimes return to that early sense of detachment.

And so, I must admit that much of what I see and read today feels wasteful, uninteresting, and—frankly speaking—too narrowly focused to be of real value beyond the small circle of its authors. Too few variables, too much uncertainty in method, and often too little courage in scope. The result is paper after paper, or worse, edited volumes that I try to keep clear of altogether, where the effort seems more about producing than about discovering. But it shouldn't have to be this way. Society is full of problems to be solved, and the demand for genuine insight has never been greater. This sense—that what we produce too often misses the mark—brings me back to those green chairs in the Luxembourg Gardens, where every book I picked up once felt like an intellectual sunray shining directly at me. Why can't books about humans and society aspire to the same coherence? Or perhaps—thanks to AI—we now have a chance to make them a little more like that once again.

Perhaps this is why I sometimes catch myself asking uncomfortable questions: What have the social sciences truly contributed that could not have emerged elsewhere? Would the world be poorer without them—or would philosophy, history, and literature have carried that weight just as well? How do we explain that parts of Asia have thrived with comparatively little reliance on these disciplines? Or is that precisely the point—that they are doing well because they have not been weighed down by them? These are not provocations, but a call for honesty. If the social sciences are to matter, they must be able to answer such questions.

One unsettling truth is that you don't need to read piles of books to become a social scientist. It is entirely possible to conduct technically sound research without ever confronting foundational questions. For example, you can design a rigorous study about people's favorite ice cream flavors, and as long as the methodology is correct, the results will be valid. Whether humans are rational, instinct-driven, or culturally programmed is largely irrelevant to the success of the study. This is essentially the role of the market researcher. All that is formally required is a basic course in marketing and another in research methods.

And frankly, when surveying much of today's published research, it is difficult not to notice that many contributions do not reach much beyond this level. What should be a field driven by intellectual curiosity, theoretical imagination, and empirical rigor too often settles into routine exercises—projects designed less to advance knowledge than to satisfy institutional metrics or career benchmarks.

At times I catch myself thinking: wait a minute, these are not intellectuals in the classical sense—restless, curious people driven by a desire to understand the world. Instead, they resemble bureaucrats, carefully defining their positions within a system they themselves have helped construct, and then reproducing it. Articles appear that are technically correct but conceptually narrow; studies accumulate that confirm what was already suspected but fail to open new horizons. The point is not to disparage honest effort, but to highlight a structural problem: when research becomes primarily about maintaining professional legitimacy, the very spirit of inquiry is diminished.

This tendency has been reinforced by academic incentives—grant applications, journal rankings, citation counts—that reward conformity and volume over risk-taking and originality. The result is a paradoxical system: ostensibly dedicated to the pursuit of truth, but in practice oriented toward bureaucratic reproduction. Researchers become gatekeepers of their own routines rather than explorers of the unknown. And in such an environment, the great questions that should animate the social sciences—about human nature, society, meaning, and survival—are often left aside in favor of safer, more easily published topics. If research is to recover its vitality, it must once again encourage the kind of intellectual curiosity that looks beyond narrow metrics and dares to engage with fundamental issues

What disappears in such a system is not competence, but curiosity. The energy that should be spent probing deeper questions is redirected toward maintaining routines. Without that spark, research risks becoming a mechanical exercise—efficient, measurable, and even respectable, yet strangely hollow. This is where something vital is lost: the willingness to ask *why*. Without it, we resemble hamsters on a wheel—busy, methodical, and productive, yet moving without direction. We run experiments, publish papers, and collect salaries, but seldom pause to ask whether our work actually helps anyone see the world more clearly.

Too often, articles today hide behind methodological minimalism. They are narrowly focused, rigorously bounded, and intentionally agnostic about larger meaning. That approach can be justified—to a point. But when the data is outdated by the time it's published, and no effort is made to situate it in a broader context, the result is disposable science. Worse, it becomes boring. And boring science dies quietly.

And, yet if we truly wish to understand human behavior, we must ask the harder questions: What kind of beings are we observing? Are we autonomous decision-makers? Or are our actions the result of culture, biology, trauma, and social context? These questions rarely surface in empirical research, but if we're curious enough, they can't be ignored.

A broader lens also invites us to consider other lives—how people think, feel, and act in different cultures, under different pressures, and with different assumptions about reality. For me, this has always been the real spice of life: pausing to reflect on those differences in all their nuance. I have long believed that such questions are best pursued through travel and through books—old and new, social scientific and otherwise. And even when we think the answers are settled, they must be revisited, because when the conditions of life change, so too do the meanings we attach to them.

And they are—as we all know by now—changing. One of the most consequential shifts is the rise of artificial intelligence. AI may prove to be the most transformative technology in human history—not because it replaces what we do, but because it alters how we think. Whereas previous revolutions transformed tools, this one transform minds (Bengio, 2021; Brynjolfsson & McAfee, 2014; Harari, 2015; Tegmark, 2017). What it means to be human—and what it means to do science—is now up for renegotiation. Thus, also, this reappraisal.

This leads to two immediate challenges. First, answers about human behavior shift constantly—across cultures, time periods, and scientific paradigms. Second, social scientists themselves rarely agree on the answers. But disagreement is not a weakness; it's where inquiry begins. If approached honestly and systematically, it becomes a strength.

That's the first reason to write this book: to reopen space for the big questions—about life, knowledge, and meaning—within the social sciences.

The second is more provocative: What if the social sciences never existed? Would anything essential be lost? For most of human history, they didn't exist—and people lived, loved, and governed themselves just the same. Now that machines can analyze text, detect patterns, and model behavior faster than we can, the question takes on new urgency: What, if anything, do social scientists still contribute that truly matters? If the answer is not clear, perhaps the field is in need of reinvention—and voilà, here we are, presented with an opportunity in the form of a remarkable new machine.

The social sciences are not self-justifying; they earn their place by solving real problems and expanding our understanding of human life. If all they produce is knowledge without impact, then their relevance comes into question. Some would even argue that we are already close to that point. If so, then perhaps AI is not a threat to the *Comtean project* of making the social sciences more scientific, but its unexpected savior. This is the possibility we will explore in the pages that follow.

A final question, then: Do we see the world as it truly is, or are we confined by the limits of our senses, our ideologies, and the mental models we inherit or construct? And if so, how reliable is our knowledge? How scientific can we ever hope to be? These are not idle musings—they are the essential questions for anyone who still believes that science matters.

They also lead directly to the challenge at the heart of this book: if human inquiry is already constrained, what happens when a new form of intelligence enters the picture, one that not only shares in the act of discovery but often surpasses us in speed and scope?

1.3 Human Meaning in Systemic Perspective

In a world where machines increasingly outperform us in cognitive tasks—from analysis to writing and even conversation—meaning is unlikely to be found in thought alone. For most people, it is not the brain or our reasoning abilities that give life significance. AI already does many of these things better. So, the source of meaning must lie elsewhere—perhaps in lived experience, emotion, physical presence, or relationships that machines cannot replicate, at least not yet.

To ask what it means to be human is also, inevitably, to ask what gives life meaning. That's a big question—and there's no single answer. What matters most to one person might be trivial to another. For some, it's playing football all day. For others, it's caring for a family member, restoring a wooden sailboat, or writing a book like this one. These passions aren't just preferences—they often anchor a sense of purpose. Take them away, and life could start to feel empty.

Of course, we can also step back and take a cooler, more objective view. To live is to be human, one might say. But that quickly becomes a circular argument: We live because we are alive—until we are not. And in between, most of life is repetition: we wake, stretch, eat, work, and sleep. To keep going, we need food, shelter, and some source of income. So, we specialize, develop skills, and try to make ourselves useful in a system that rewards productivity. That's what Adam Smith wrote about: how individual labor builds up entire nations, and he did it rather well, I think.

But meaning is something more than survival. And survival, without meaning, isn't enough. At some point, most people ask, consciously or not, "Why am I here?" Monty Python made an entire film around that very question. Their answer, in a way, was that the search for meaning can itself be laughed at—that humor is not just a distraction but a response, even a form of meaning. By making fun of the hypothetical person asking the question, as in the title of the movie, they suggest that the act of questioning may not yield a grand revelation—and in fact, they refuse to give one—but that humor itself can carry us through. Perhaps it was subtle—or perhaps I was just simply overreading something that wasn't really there.

This also raises the issue of what humor actually is. It is tempting to think of it as mere entertainment, a diversion to lighten the mood. But that hardly captures its depth. Humor may have emerged as a psychological buffer once nature—through us—developed the unsettling capacity for self-reflection. Faced with impermanence, the indifference of the universe, and the certainty of death, laughter gives us a way to carry the weight without being crushed by it. At times, it feels less like a luxury than a necessity—a release valve that preserves sanity when nothing else will.

Still, I doubt that is the whole story. From an evolutionary perspective, humor is typically explained as a social and cognitive adaptation. It strengthens group cohesion, signals intelligence and creativity, and diffuses tension before conflict escalates (Gervais & Wilson, 2005; Provine, 2000). Neurologically, it engages reward systems in the brain, releasing endorphins and reducing stress—effects that would have conferred real survival value in ancestral environments. In that sense, humor is both deeply social and profoundly biological: a bridge between the individual mind and the collective body.

For others, the search for meaning isn't funny. It's hard. It's personal. Some find themselves stuck, depressed, disoriented, or simply overwhelmed. A few even conclude that life has no meaning at all and choose to leave it behind. That is a tragedy. But it is also a reality. We should acknowledge it without turning away. Instead, we should treat it as yet another—and perhaps one of the most urgent—problem for the social sciences to address. Understanding what makes life feel meaningful, and why some people fall through the cracks, is not just a philosophical challenge but a scientific one. And a deeply human one.

At the same time, it's not an easy question to answer. In my experience, the people most certain about life's meaning are often trying to convince themselves as much as others. Uncertainty is part of being human—especially when it comes to the biggest questions of all: why we are here and what we are meant to do on this planet. Perhaps it is only at the very end, with our last breath, that we fully realize: "Holy smoke, what was that all about? What a strange mirage." And how could it be otherwise? After all, most of it was only in our minds—only it never quite felt that way. We are vulnerable, fallible, and full of contradictions. And if we aren't, we're probably uninformed, as the saying goes. We search for meaning, but we also lose it—only to rediscover it again, in different forms, at different stages of life. What feels vital at age twelve—like playing football—might fade by eighteen, unless it transforms into a career or calling. But even then, new doubts will always arise.

And we should never forget that for much of the world's population, even having the time to ask these questions is a luxury. Many people work from morning to night simply just to survive. Philosophy doesn't even make it onto their schedule. Meaning, in that context, often takes the form of responsibility, family, or faith—something quiet but sustaining.

It is easy to forget that only a century ago, even in much of the West, most people had more than enough simply to go to work and earn a living. Parents often had little time for their children, who learned to fend for themselves in the streets or at school while the father labored long hours in a factory and the mother struggled to make ends meet at home. In such conditions, questions of meaning were largely a luxury for the wealthy—and even then, only for the small fraction among them who were curious enough to ponder such matters. There has never been a direct correlation between money-making and intellectual curiosity. In other words, this widespread public engagement with the "meaning of life" is a relatively recent phenomenon—but with the rise of AI, and especially if it delivers the massive productivity gains some predict, it may well become a primary question for many more people.

If you've found something that gives your life meaning, congratulations. But don't expect that one idea to last forever. Sooner or later, you'll be inspired by something new—another idea or perspective—that will reshape how you see that very thing and answer that same question. As human beings, our thoughts and beliefs are strongly shaped by what we have most recently encountered—like the last book we read or the latest article we browsed. It is almost humorous that we rarely acknowledge this, that we fail to notice how much we are filled with the "latest ideas," which soon enough will be replaced by other, newer ones. In this way the cycle continues, with each wave of impressions crowding out what came before. Only occasionally do we pause to reflect on this trick that memory plays on us. Because earlier ideas fade from attention, and their emotional impact weakens over time, our beliefs evolve almost naturally, shifting with what is most recent and most salient.

But while meaning is deeply personal, the question of what it means to be human stretches beyond individual experience. It is also biological, cultural, historical, and even cosmic. We are not isolated units; we are shaped by evolution (Tomasello, 2014), embedded in culture (Geertz, 1973), structured by institutions (Durkheim, 1895/1982), and connected through shared language and symbolic systems (Harari, 2014).

In short, understanding the human condition means zooming out—and here a *systems perspective* becomes essential. Human life is not a collection of isolated traits but a network of interdependent processes, each influencing the others. Just as *system theorists* such as Ludwig von Bertalanffy (1968) and Kenneth Boulding (1956) emphasized the importance of seeing wholes rather than parts, the social sciences should treat humanity as an integrated system.

From this vantage point, we can distinguish at least five interlocking subsystems of what it means to be human:

1. Our capacity for symbolic thought and shared intention (Tomasello, 2009).
2. Our coevolution with tools, language, and culture (Laland, 2017).
3. Our place in the biosphere and ecological systems (Wilson, 1984).
4. Our political and moral development as social beings (Arendt, 1958).
5. Our ongoing transformation through technology and artificial intelligence (Bostrom, 2014).

Yes, personal meaning matters—Frankl (1959) was right about that. But it is only one strand in a much larger evolutionary and cultural story. To truly understand humanity, we must see ourselves not only as individuals seeking purpose, but as a species navigating shared challenges, responsibilities, and transformations. This realization often comes with maturity, as we become less self-centered and recognize that there is a vast world beyond us—and that we are only a very small part of it, much like a hard-working and carrying home a splinter of wood.

Table 1.1 summarizes these five dimensions, highlighting their focus areas, key theorists, and representative works.

Taken together, these dimensions can be understood not as separate silos but as subsystems within a larger system of human life. Each influences the others: symbolic thought shapes culture, culture modifies our ecological footprint, ecological pressures drive political change, and technology feeds back into every domain. This interdependence is exactly what systems theorists such as Ludwig von Bertalanffy (1968) and Niklas Luhmann (1995) emphasized: complex realities must be grasped as wholes, with feedback loops and adaptive mechanisms, rather than as isolated parts.

The next section introduces a framework for exploring these five dimensions in exactly this systemic way. Together, they form the core of how this book approaches the question: What does it mean to be human—and how might that change in the age of AI? This, in turn, offers a clearer sense of how the social sciences themselves will need to evolve into a more integrative, cumulative science.

Table 1.1 Comparative summary of human dimensions

Theme/subheading	Focus area	Example of key theorist	Representative work
1. Symbolic Thought and Shared Intentionality	Cognitive and social capacities unique to humans	Michael Tomasello	*The Cultural Origins of Human Cognition* (1999); *Why We Cooperate* (2009)
2. Coevolution with Tools, Language, and Culture	How human development is shaped by material and symbolic environments	Kevin Laland	*Darwin's Unfinished Symphony* (2017)
3. Humans in the Biosphere and Ecology	Ecological embeddedness and stewardship responsibilities	E.O. Wilson	*Biophilia* (1984); *The Diversity of Life* (1992)
4. Moral and Political Development	Human rights, political action, and the public realm	Hannah Arendt	*The Human Condition* (1958)
5. Technological and AI Transformation	Human enhancement, existential risk, and future agency	Nick Bostrom	*Superintelligence: Paths, Dangers, Strategies* (2014)

1.4 Science, Systems, and Society

If we want to understand what it means to be human, we cannot limit ourselves to a single perspective. No single discipline—whether psychology, anthropology, neuroscience, or political theory—can capture the full richness of human life. Each field reveals something important, but always through a partial lens. This is why an interdisciplinary, multi-dimensional approach is essential.

One powerful way of pursuing such integration has been through *systems theory*. Over the past century, a wide range of thinkers have sought to explain social reality not in fragments but as a set of interdependent, dynamic systems. Some approached this through biology and cybernetics, others through sociology, economics, or organizational science. Despite their differences, they shared the conviction that human life must be studied as a whole made up of interconnected parts.

Table 1.2 highlights some of the most influential systems theorists and how they understood social reality.

Table 1.2 Major systems theorists and their approaches to social reality

Theorist	Key works	Core idea of systems	Approach to social reality
Ludwig von Bertalanffy (1901–1972)	*General System Theory* (1968)	Proposed a general systems theory (GST) to unify science through concepts like open systems, feedback, and homeostasis	Saw society as an open system exchanging energy, matter, and information with its environment. Emphasized adaptability and equilibrium
Kenneth Boulding (1910–1993)	*General Systems Theory: The Skeleton of Science* (1956)	Classified systems into a hierarchy from simple frameworks to social and symbolic systems	Social systems were "symbol-processing systems" with communication and knowledge at their core
Talcott Parsons (1902–1979)	*The Social System* (1951)	Functionalist systems theory: social order depends on subsystems fulfilling four functions (AGIL schema: Adaptation, Goal attainment, Integration, Latency)	Social reality seen as a set of interdependent roles and institutions maintaining stability
Niklas Luhmann (1927–1998)	*Social Systems* (1995)	Autopoiesis: society is a self-referential communication system that reproduces itself through meaning	Individuals are part of the environment; society itself exists only through communication loops
Gregory Bateson (1904–1980)	*Steps to an Ecology of Mind* (1972)	Applied cybernetics and systems thinking to psychology and culture	Social reality emerges from feedback loops of communication and learning; pathology arises from broken circuits

(continued)

Table 1.2 (continued)

Theorist	Key works	Core idea of systems	Approach to social reality
Jay Forrester (1918–2016)	*Urban Dynamics* (1969), *World Dynamics* (1971)	Founder of system dynamics, modeling feedback processes in complex systems	Used simulation models to show how feedback and delay create social and economic problems
Stafford Beer (1926–2002)	*Brain of the Firm* (1972)	Viable System Model (VSM): organizations must balance autonomy and control through recursive structures	Applied cybernetics to firms and governments; social reality as organizations needing viability under complexity
Ilya Prigogine (1917–2003)	*Order Out of Chaos* (1984, with Stengers)	Non-equilibrium thermodynamics: systems far from equilibrium can self-organize into new structures	Suggested societies evolve through crises and bifurcations; instability can drive innovation and reorganization
Herbert Simon (1916–2001)	*The Sciences of the Artificial* (1969)	Systems are nearly decomposable hierarchies; bounded rationality constrains agents	Social reality understood as layered, modular systems shaped by limited human cognition
Norbert Wiener (1894–1964)	*Cybernetics* (1948)	Systems governed by feedback, control, and communication	Social systems viewed through regulation, control loops, and adaptation processes

When we speak of *the social sciences*, we are implicitly acknowledging that there are social systems. In fact, each discipline can be seen as having grown out of one such subsystem: economics from exchange, political science from governance, sociology from institutions, psychology from individual behavior, anthropology from culture. The paradox, however, is that we have often allowed each subsystem to harden into a separate academic discipline, almost as if it were a closed and *self-sufficient reality*.

Over time, these disciplines have developed into *self-protecting systems*, much like biological niches. From a biological perspective this is understandable: groups naturally defend their boundaries and protect their resources. Yet from the perspective of understanding human life as a whole, this fragmentation makes little sense. Worse, it quickly becomes counterproductive. The very systems we seek to explain are interdependent—economies depend on culture, politics depends on psychology, and all depend on ecological constraints. To study them in isolation is to miss their connections, which are often where the most pressing problems and opportunities lie.

Seen in this light, the Vitruvian Framework that I propose can be understood as one more contribution to this tradition of system thinking—specifically tailored for the social sciences in the age of AI.[1] Unlike Parsons or Luhmann, who focused on functional stability or self-referential communication, my approach emphasizes five evolutionary dimensions of the human condition: symbolic, coevolutionary, ecological, political-moral, and technological.

Where earlier system theorists often abstracted away from the biological layer, this model insists on starting there: evolution provides the foundation. From that base, it integrates cultural, political, and technological systems into a single scaffold. In this sense, the Vitruvian Framework is less about one theory of society and more about offering a roadmap for connecting theories across disciplines, making social science cumulative rather than fragmented.

If we want to understand what it means to be human, we cannot limit ourselves to a single perspective. No single discipline—whether psychology, anthropology, neuroscience, or political theory—can capture the full richness of human life. Each field reveals something important, but always through a partial lens. This is why a *systems approach*, one that is interdisciplinary and multi-dimensional, becomes essential.

Seen in this way, the human being is not reducible to a single role, category, or identity. We are not only voters, workers, or consumers. We are also parents, musicians, skeptics, daydreamers, and citizens—sometimes all at once. Reducing people to one dimension misses the very interdependence that defines our lives. Like any complex system, humanity must be studied in its fullness, not in fragments.

This recognition is not only descriptive but normative: if human life is multi-layered, then living fully also requires developing those layers. Skills

[1] The name "Vitruvian Framework" is inspired by Marcus Vitruvius Pollio (c. 80–15 BCE), the Roman architect and engineer whose delightful treatise *De architectura* emphasized harmony, proportion, and the integration of function with form. Just as Vitruvius sought a unifying set of principles for architecture, the framework presented here aspires to provide a unifying structure for the social sciences.

such as conversation, humor, or creativity may appear trivial compared to economic productivity, yet they are vital to the "system" of being human. Without them, social life atrophies, leaving us less interesting, less capable, and ultimately less resilient.

To grow as full human beings, we must resist the temptation to become only "part-systems"—defined exclusively by one occupation, discipline, or social role. When individuals collapse their identity into a single domain, whether in business, academia, or administration, they risk embodying only the logic of that system. A life lived entirely within one register narrows both imagination and resilience. By contrast, education in the broad sense—exposure to arts, sciences, history, and humanistic reflection—enables people to cultivate multiple capacities. This multidimensional development reflects the *Vitruvian idea of proportion*: just as a well-designed building integrates different elements into a harmonious whole, so too does a well-lived life require balance among diverse faculties.

Yet standing against this aspiration is a deeply rooted human need: the desire to belong. Social psychology has shown that identification with smaller groups provides security, recognition, and meaning (Baumeister & Leary, 1995; Brewer, 2007). These attachments, while vital, can also press individuals toward conformity and specialization, drawing them into narrower identities. The challenge is to live within communities without being reduced by them—to remain members of groups while still cultivating the full spectrum of our humanity (Nussbaum, 1997; Tomasello, 2019). In this balance between belonging and breadth lies the path to realizing human potential.

This recognition—that human life should not be reduced to a single function but cultivated as a whole—links directly to a longer philosophical tradition. Thinkers have long asked what it means to live fully, and how individuals might integrate the many dimensions of their existence into something more than fragmented roles. Luc Ferry (1996), for example, argued that in a secular age humanity has in effect inherited the responsibilities once assigned to the divine. To be human, in his view, is to strive toward the highest ideals we can conceive—not as an act of hubris or blasphemy, but as an invitation to embody the best of what we can imagine: wisdom, justice, creativity, and care. Without religious authority to confer meaning from above, we must construct it ourselves—through growth, reflection, and ethical self-cultivation. In this sense, being human is not only a fact but also a task: to learn, to grow, and to integrate the many strands of life into something coherent.

In Ferry's view, then, to be human is to strive toward the highest ideals we can imagine, embodying them in the texture of everyday life. This demand for self-cultivation is not abstract—it is tested by the conditions of each era.

Today, the rise of artificial intelligence makes the challenge especially urgent. By taking over many of our cognitive tasks, AI risks narrowing our participation in the very practices that make us human. It may free time, but it may also encourage passivity and superficiality. If so, the danger is not simply technological, but civilizational: a gradual erosion of curiosity, resilience, and depth.

To guard against this, we need a framework that can capture the full system of what it means to be human—one that connects biology with culture, psychology with politics, and technology with ethics. This is what I call the *Vitruvian Framework*, built around five interlocking dimensions.

The five dimensions introduced here are not arbitrary. They rest on more than a century of systematic research across the biological, psychological, social, cultural, and political sciences, as well as decades of sustained inquiry in ethics and technology studies. Together, these fields have been advanced by a vast international community of researchers, whose cumulative work provides the empirical depth and theoretical grounding for the framework that follows.

Each dimension represents a layer of the human condition—evolved, learned, enacted, and now increasingly transformed by technology:

First, humans are *symbol-making animals*. Our ability to use language, create shared meanings, and coordinate action across time and space is unique in the animal kingdom. Michael Tomasello's work in developmental psychology and primate research shows how deeply human cooperation is rooted in joint attention and shared intentionality (Tomasello, 1999, 2009, 2014). Unlike other primates, humans are not just individually intelligent—we are *collectively minded*. Language, as a system of shared symbols, allows us to encode memory, transmit culture, and build institutions far beyond what instinct alone would permit (Deacon, 1997; Pinker, 1994).

Second, humans are the product of *gene-culture coevolution*. Our biological and cultural developments are intertwined. Kevin Laland (2017) has demonstrated how human cognition is shaped by *niche construction*—how we alter our environment in ways that feed back into our evolution. Cooking, tool-making, and symbolic artifacts are not just cultural markers; they are cognitive accelerators. This idea builds on the *extended phenotype concept* from Richard Dawkins (1982) and the work of dual-inheritance theorists like Boyd and Richerson (1985), who showed how genetic and cultural evolution operate in tandem.

Third, we are *ecological beings*. Far from standing above nature, humans are embedded in it. Our survival has always depended on the ecosystems we inhabit. Edward O. Wilson's *Biophilia* (1984) proposed that our affinity for natural environments is not learned but evolved. More recently, ecological anthropology and environmental psychology have provided evidence for how green space reduces stress (Ulrich, 1984), how climate affects behavior (van Lange et al., 2017), and how ecological degradation—such as biodiversity loss—can have psychological and civilizational consequences (Diamond, 2005; Steffen et al., 2015).

Just imagine how finely tuned our existence is to this specific planet. If Earth were only slightly closer to the sun—just a few percent—temperatures could rise to levels that would evaporate water and destabilize the climate, much like what we observe on Venus. If it were just a bit farther away, water could freeze, drastically reducing the chance for complex life. This concept is often described by the "*habitable zone*" or "*Goldilocks zone*"—a narrow orbital range where liquid water can exist on a planet's surface (Kasting et al., 1993). Moreover, Earth's rotation rate is also crucial: if the planet spun much faster, atmospheric circulation would intensify, leading to extreme winds and potentially uninhabitable weather patterns (Lorenz, 1970). These factors are not accidents; they illustrate how closely biological life is calibrated to planetary conditions—a fragile, contingent balance that underscores both our dependency on nature and the unique rarity of our ecological niche.

Fourth, we are political and moral agents. From Aristotle's claim that man is a *zoon politikon*—a being destined for life in the polis—to Hannah Arendt's concept of *"natality"* and the public sphere (1958), humans have always lived in relation to others. This truth is not only philosophical but visceral. After a stretch of solitude, most people feel a physical longing for company; social interaction is as essential to well-being as food or sleep. Studies in social neuroscience show that isolation activates the same brain regions associated with physical pain (Eisenberger et al., 2003). And have you noticed how satisfying it can be to talk with someone—even if you don't find that person particularly sympathetic? We are built to accept the company we are given and to make cooperation work. In ancestral environments, you did not choose all the members of your band, but you still had to hunt with them, share resources, and build trust. Our survival has always depended less on picking ideal companions than on adapting to the ones we have.

We build systems of ethics, laws, rights, and governance, not because we are perfect, but because we are not. The capacity for moral reasoning, fairness, and accountability emerges early in development (Turiel, 1983; Haidt, 2001), but how it is expressed varies across societies. Political science, sociology, and moral psychology all contribute to our understanding of why humans organize into groups, how we resolve conflict, and why legitimacy matters (Rawls, 1971; Weber, 1919).

Fifth, we are now becoming something new. The rise of artificial intelligence, genetic engineering, and human enhancement technologies suggests we are entering what many now call a *post-human* or *transhuman era*. As we'll see in the last chapters, there are different ways to think about this shift, and I approach it from a perspective that may not align with the mainstream. Nick Bostrom (2014) and other thinkers in existential risk studies have warned that we are creating forces we may not be able to control. Tools like AI are not just changing how we work or write—they are redefining what intelligence means, who produces knowledge, and even what counts as a human decision. Scholars in science and technology studies (STS) have begun tracing these transformations in how agency, authorship, and autonomy are understood (Floridi, 2014; Latour, 2005).

Taken together, these five dimensions—biological, psychological, cultural, political, and now technological—form the foundation for what I call the

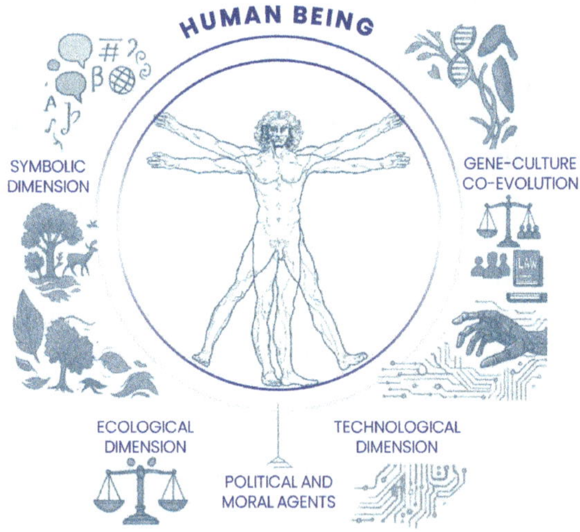

Fig. 1.1 Vitruvian framework—five dimensions of being human. *Source* Inspired by Leonardo da Vinci's Vitruvian Man,[2] designed by the author and Khoirina Tsani, 2025

[2] Leonardo da Vinci's *Vitruvian Man* (c. 1490) was directly inspired by Vitruvius' description in *De architectura* (Book III, Chapter 1), where the Roman architect explained that the ideal human body fits both a circle and a square due to its natural proportions. Leonardo took these textual ratios, compared them to his anatomical studies, and rendered them visually. The drawing is thus both an homage to Vitruvius and a Renaissance reinterpretation, linking art, geometry, and the study of the human form.

Vitruvian Framework. Like Leonardo da Vinci's famous drawing of the human figure inscribed in a circle and square, this model seeks to capture the proportions of what makes us human in a single, integrated view. It does not reduce us to one essence but shows how our nature is scaffolded across multiple layers. Figure 1.1 summarizes these dimensions.

These five dimensions—symbolic, coevolutionary, ecological, political-moral, and technological—together offer a structured lens through which we can explore the human condition. Each is supported by robust scientific traditions and empirical inquiry. They do not compete with one another; they converge. Just as humans are biological, cultural, moral, and now digital beings all at once, so too must our methods of understanding humanity reflect this complexity.

This is why the framework takes its name from Vitruvian Man—Leonardo da Vinci's iconic drawing that sought to harmonize human proportions with universal order. In the same spirit, the Vitruvian Framework aims to capture the full range of what it means to be human: balanced across nature and culture, grounded in science, and adaptable to future change.

The following sections examine each dimension in turn, not as isolated domains but as interdependent layers of what it means to be human. We begin with symbolic culture and meaning (1.4.1), since our capacity for shared intention and symbolic representation allows us to coordinate, remember, and create realities beyond the immediate here and now. From there, we turn to gene–culture coevolution (1.4.2), where tools, language, and traditions evolve together with human cognition, shaping not only how we live but also how we think. The third step is ecology, energy, and planetary limits (1.4.3), since no cultural or symbolic achievement can exist without the biospheric foundations that sustain life. This leads naturally to politics, morality, and public life (1.4.4), the normative and institutional frameworks through which societies organize themselves and make collective choices. Finally, we consider technology, institutions, and agency (1.4.5), where the accelerating influence of artificial intelligence and other technologies is reshaping not only how we live, but also the very scope of human decision-making. Together, these subsections offer a structured pathway for understanding humanity as both a product and a shaper of complex, interconnected systems.

1.4.1 Symbolic Culture and Meaning

If there is one feature that most clearly distinguishes humans from other species, it is our reliance on symbols. From the first cave paintings to emojis on a smartphone, humans have created systems of representation that allow us to share meanings far beyond here and now. Symbols turn fleeting thoughts into collective structures of coordination and memory.

Michael Tomasello (1999, 2009) has argued that the crucial leap was not simply language itself, but shared intentionality: the ability to align attention, goals, and expectations with others. This capacity enables everything from pointing at a tree to agreeing on the rules of a game—or obeying the authority of a piece of paper called a "contract." Such symbolic coordination sets humans apart from other primates.

Yet symbols are not only linguistic. They also inhabit the physical world, embedded in objects, artifacts, and works of art. In ancient societies, symbolic objects often carried religious or magical significance—totems, idols, amulets, or ceremonial tools that anchored meaning in tangible form. Their power did not lie in the material itself but in the collective belief and practices surrounding them. In this sense, symbols become extensions of human cognition, carrying values and emotions that far exceed their physical properties.

This dynamic persists in modern life. Today's symbols range from national flags and wedding rings to more superficial status objects such as a Porsche 911 or a luxury watch. These items communicate identity, aspiration, and belonging, often functioning as shorthand for entire social narratives. Whether sacred or mundane, symbols help structure human lives by signaling who we are, what we value, and where we belong.

Symbols extend our cognition outward, embedding thought in rituals, stories, institutions, and tools. They create a shared reality in which money, laws, religions, or even brands acquire power not from their material substance, but from the collective belief that they mean something. In this sense, symbolic culture is not an ornament of human life but its backbone: it allows cooperation among strangers, the accumulation of knowledge, and the persistence of cultural memory across generations.

Because symbols are so central, this book will return to them repeatedly. Later, in Chapter 4, we will take a closer look at language—arguably the most powerful symbolic system of all—and examine how it not only conveys meaning but also shapes the very ways humans think, reason, and imagine. But symbols are never isolated. They are part of a larger evolutionary process in which human minds and human cultures have shaped one another over millennia, and in which objects, rituals, and representations continue to guide the trajectory of our shared lives.

1.4.2 Gene–Culture Coevolution

One of the leading theorists of this dynamic is Kevin Laland, whose book *Darwin's Unfinished Symphony* (2017) presents a compelling case for how human minds and human cultures evolved together. He shows how behaviors like cooking, language use, music, and symbolic expression all exert selective pressure on our cognitive evolution. Culture is not just a by-product of intelligence; it is a driver of it.

This insight builds on earlier work by Richard Dawkins (1976, 1982), who proposed the idea of *memes*, units of cultural transmission that evolve in ways analogous to genes. But while Dawkins emphasized replication and competition, Laland and others have focused more on *constructive feedback loops*: how humans modify their environments in ways that alter the conditions of future evolution. This concept, known as *niche construction*, helps explain how human societies can rapidly evolve without corresponding changes in biology.

The role of *material culture* is especially important. Archaeologists and cognitive anthropologists have shown how the use of tools, writing systems, and architecture has transformed not only how humans live but also how they think (Malafouris, 2013). The act of writing, for instance, externalizes memory. The calendar structures our experience of time, though we might mutter in private about the Babylonians' choice of the 60-base system. Meanwhile, the built environment guides our movements, shapes our behaviors, and even influences our moods.

Culture also transmits skills and values through *social learning*. From early childhood, humans are immersed in complex cultural models—language, kinship, morality, even table manners, as I've heard (but not seen at home for a while)—that are learned through observation, imitation, and correction (Boyd & Richerson, 1985). Unlike instinct-driven behavior, cultural learning allows for flexibility, adaptation, and variation. It also introduces inertia: once traditions are in place, they can be remarkably persistent, even when circumstances change.

Examples like this are everywhere:

I. The evolution of cooking technologies didn't just upgrade our diet—it may have given us bigger brains and smaller jaws (Wrangham, 2009). Though with today's obsession with junk food, who knows? Maybe we're slowly undoing all that evolutionary progress—one doughnut at a time.
II. Urban development doesn't just mirror society—it actually shapes it, deciding who gets in, who stays out, and who can't even find a decent

coffee shop. And while this power play is obvious to most, I suspect architectural taste has been on a steady downhill slide for the past hundred years. (At times, I could swear the pigeons themselves look down from their ledges in silent reproach as I hurry through the city center).

III. Religious practices, whether or not one believes in their metaphysical claims, serve as moral systems, emotional regulators, and sources of social cohesion (Norenzayan, 2013).

The interplay between culture and cognition helps explain why human societies can be both astonishingly creative and frustratingly rigid. We are not simply rational agents navigating a neutral world—we are cultural beings, shaped by language, tradition, and deeply embedded collective habits. Culture doesn't just surround us; it expresses itself through us.

To understand humanity then, we must treat culture not as a superficial layer atop biology, but as a co-evolving force in its own right, with its own structures, constraints, and innovations. A central argument of this book is that because cultures take generations to develop, and because they form the scaffolding of functioning societies, it is a serious matter when they are weakened, dismantled, or diluted. There are no universal cultures. And as we will show in the chapters ahead, different cultures produce vastly different outcomes when it comes to trust, governance, innovation, and cooperation. Part of the drive to override or homogenize cultures may stem from a misunderstanding: the belief that because science is universal, culture should be too—or that if we could somehow mold everyone into the same form through social engineering, the world would be a better place as a result. But this confuses the method of understanding with the object being understood. Scientific principles may be universally valid, but cultures are historically contingent and locally evolved—even if, in practice, some boundaries are naturally being softened through extensive travel and global communication.

This section lays the groundwork for that broader perspective. In the chapters that follow, we will explore how our ecological embeddedness, political systems, and technological transformations further complicate—and enrich—our understanding of what it means to be human in a rapidly changing world.

1.4.3 Ecology, Energy, and Planetary Limits

For most of human history, human survival depended on intimate knowledge of the natural world. Early humans tracked seasonal patterns, hunted with an understanding of animal behavior, and built shelters in harmony with their environment. Nature was not an abstraction—it was home, danger, nourishment, and rhythm. We lived *in* ecosystems, not above them.

And yet, in modernity, something shifted. We began to imagine ourselves as separate from nature; managing it, extracting from it, and controlling it. This illusion of separation has proven dangerous. It is not only that we have left the countryside for cities, which in many ways are easier to survive in, but that we have also become detached from our *natural habitat*, with all the consequences this has for our psychological well-being and mental balance. Many of us have forgotten how to grow potatoes, lost the names of plants, and would now struggle to survive in the wild.

We are not masters of the Earth. We are part of it. *Homo ecologicus* reminds us that the human being is not only a rational actor or cultural symbol-maker, but also—and perhaps above all—a biological organism embedded in a fragile biosphere. It's easy to lose this perspective as urbanization increases, distancing us from the natural systems on which we still fundamentally depend. This disconnection often also has consequences for how we treat nature: we begin to care less about pollution, assuming that someone else—the municipality, the state, or some future authority—will take responsibility for fixing what we ourselves continue to damage.

Case Box: Standing Outside Nature—A Human Illusion?

Think about yourself for a moment—not as a person with a job, family, and daily routines, but as a living organism. Do you see yourself as part of nature, or as somehow separate from it? Most of us, if we are honest, lean toward the latter. We see ourselves as different, perhaps even better. Few people genuinely experience themselves as just another biological being, embedded in ecosystems like any other species.

In fact, much of human history has reinforced the opposite perception: that we stand above nature rather than within it. Religion has played a central role in this story. The great monotheistic traditions framed Earth as a temporary dwelling, with paradise promised elsewhere—heaven, nirvana, or some transcendent realm (Taylor, 2010; White, 1967). In Christianity for example, nature often appeared not as sacred, but as a stage for human salvation.

Science, while often presented as an antidote to religious myth, also contributed to this sense of separation. The Enlightenment's call to "master and possess nature," as Descartes framed it, encouraged viewing the natural world as something primitive to be improved. Forests became lumber reserves, rivers sources of energy, soils objects of chemical optimization, and animals units of productivity (Merchant, 1980). Modern technology deepened this pattern: agriculture, industry, and now biotechnology are premised on the idea that nature is insufficient unless redesigned. In this sense, scientific narratives of progress often echoed religious narratives of transcendence, differing in method but similar in effect: they positioned humanity outside and above the natural order.

Even in secular culture, the legacy persists. We imagine that if Earth becomes inhospitable, we can simply move on—to Mars, or some other planet. Colonization of space is cast as the next logical step of science: not only as exploration, but as escape. Yet biology tells a different story. We are not made for other planets. Our lungs, skin, cognition, even our circadian rhythms are products of Earth's specific biosphere (Gómez-Pinilla, 2008; Latour, 2018; Rockström et al., 2009; Wilson, 2002). To act as if we can simply transcend these limits is not progress, but hubris. Stories of mastery—whether religious or scientific—may have fueled human achievement, but they also risk becoming stories of self-delusion when they obscure our dependence on the only planet that sustains us.

Questions for Reflection

1. How have both religious and scientific narratives encouraged the idea that humans stand apart from, or above, nature?
2. In what ways can stories of transcendence—whether heaven or Mars—make this world feel disposable?
3. Is the scientific drive to "improve" nature inherently different from religious promises of salvation, or are they two versions of the same impulse?
4. What biological facts about human adaptation remind us that we are bound to Earth's environment rather than free to escape it?
5. If our stories shape our ecological behavior, what new kinds of stories might help us live more sustainably within the limits of this planet?

These reflections show how deeply our self-understanding—whether framed in religion, science, or technology—shapes the way we relate to the natural world.

If stories of mastery and transcendence have distanced us from nature, other perspectives have tried to draw us back into it. The ecological thinker James Lovelock gave this idea a radical scientific form with his *Gaia hypothesis*. In *Gaia: A New Look at Life on Earth* (1979) and later in *The Revenge of Gaia* (2006) and *A Rough Ride to the Future* (2014), Lovelock argued that Earth functions as a self-regulating organism. Life does not merely *inhabit* Earth—it shapes and maintains the conditions for its own survival. Atmospheric gases, ocean salinity, surface temperatures—these are not passive outcomes, but dynamic systems influenced by life itself. The biosphere is not a stage; it is a system of mutual dependencies. If disrupted too far, it will recalibrate—perhaps without us.

The Gaia theory was initially dismissed by many mainstream scientists, but has since gained traction, especially in Earth system science. It aligns closely with the concept of *planetary boundaries* (Rockström et al., 2009; Steffen et al., 2015), which identifies ecological limits—carbon concentration, nitrogen cycles, freshwater use—that cannot be transgressed without destabilizing Earth's regulatory systems.

From a more philosophical perspective, Arne Næss, the Norwegian founder of "*deep ecology*," proposed an equally transformative idea: *økosofi*, or "*ecosophy*." Unlike shallow ecology, which seeks to protect nature only for its utility to humans, deep ecology sees all living beings—human and non-human—as intrinsically valuable. In works such as *Ecology, Community and Lifestyle* (1989), Næss called for a shift in worldview: from domination to humility, from *anthropocentrism* to *biocentrism*. For Næss, the ecological crisis is not just about emissions or consumption—it is a crisis of thought, identity, and values.

These ideas help us reconsider what it means to be human. We are not discrete individuals pursuing isolated goals. We are participants in an *ecological system*, co-responsible for its health and future. The concept of *biophilia*—introduced by E.O. Wilson (1984)—echoes this, suggesting that humans have an innate affinity for other living systems. Empirical studies support this claim: natural environments lower stress, improve cognitive functioning, and even promote ethical decision-making (Berman et al., 2008; Kaplan & Kaplan, 1989; Ulrich, 1984).

But if nature sustains us, we are also destabilizing it. Human activity has altered more than 75% of Earth's land surface (IPBES, 2019), driven thousands of species to extinction, and pushed key ecological systems toward collapse. Issues such as biodiversity loss, deforestation, ocean acidification, and—according to broad scientific consensus—human-caused climate change are no longer distant threats. They are defining features of the twenty-first century.

The consequences are not only ecological but also psychological and social. The rise of *climate anxiety*, especially among younger generations, is well documented (Clayton et al., 2017). This concern can be constructive, yet it sometimes fuels strong emotional reactions that make sustained, evidence-based dialogue harder. Urgency and frustration are understandable, but complex global challenges require more than expressions of concern. They call for practical, science-informed responses, grounded in open discussion and long-term thinking.

The interplay between environmental degradation and societal instability adds another layer of complexity. Research links climate stressors to political conflict, forced migration, and economic disruption (Hsiang & Burke, 2013). Yet it is important to remember that carbon dioxide (CO_2), often portrayed solely as a threat, is also essential for life. This duality calls for a more nuanced approach to environmental policy—one that balances urgency with perspective and prioritizes science over activism. For the social sciences, this presents a tremendous and delicate task. If researchers exaggerate claims or move beyond what evidence can support, slipping into ideology, they risk not only distorting public debate but also undermining the credibility of the social sciences themselves. To remain relevant, the field must walk this fine line: to communicate risks clearly while preserving its role as a scientific project rather than an ideological enterprise.

This becomes especially clear when we consider the idea of the *Anthropocene*—a geological epoch defined by significant human impact. It has now become widely accepted, yet as Gifford (2011) notes, our brains evolved to detect immediate dangers, not gradual threats like rising CO_2 levels. This mismatch makes it difficult to address slow-moving crises in ways that are both effective and publicly legitimate.

Broadly, there are two main ways to reduce the stress human activity places on the planet: use fewer resources per person or reduce the number of people consuming them. The first path—efficiency gains, sustainable technologies, and lifestyle shifts—receives most of the attention. The second—actively incentivizing lower population growth—remains far more controversial.

It is striking how reluctant much of social science is to even engage with this latter option. Scholars in science and technology studies trace this reluctance to the political and cultural sensitivities surrounding reproductive rights, demographic change, and historical abuses of population control (Connelly, 2008; Hartmann, 1995). Moral psychology highlights cognitive biases: people tend to support policies framed as promoting well-being rather than those seen as restricting freedoms (Tetlock et al., 2000). Political economy perspectives add that many economic systems rely structurally on population growth to sustain labor markets, consumer demand, and fiscal stability (Bongaarts & O'Neill, 2018). Taken together, these factors help explain why, even in the Anthropocene, the demographic dimension of sustainability remains an "elephant in the room."

Given this silence, it is hardly surprising that when respected figures such as Jane Goodall raise the issue—drawing on decades of living close to another species and witnessing firsthand the damage our expansion and interference inflict on habitats—the response is polarized. She has argued that reducing human population growth is essential for ecological sustainability. Yet despite the credibility of such voices, the subject remains politically sensitive, constrained by the very ethical and cultural complexities already discussed.

This raises a broader question: can our values and political systems adapt quickly enough to meet environmental challenges? Scholars in political ecology and environmental humanities argue that the problem is not only technical but also moral and narrative (Latour, 2018; Nixon, 2011). The metaphors we choose—whether we see nature as "resource," "mother," "data," or "Gaia"—influence both our policies and our everyday actions.

However, urgent crisis narratives are not new. The twentieth century saw repeated waves of *environmental alarmism*, some of which helped catalyze action but also overstated the speed of collapse. In the 1930s, fears of a global dust bowl spurred major conservation efforts but also exaggerated apocalyptic forecasts (Worster, 1979). In the 1970s, Paul Ehrlich's "population bomb" warned of mass starvation (Ehrlich, 1968)—a warning that drew attention to real demographic pressures but predicted a timeline that did not materialize. New threats seem to emerge every few years, yet when the anticipated moment arrives, the reality is often less catastrophic than feared. Still, the underlying issues remain, sometimes evolving more slowly and in different forms than expected.

More recently, the Y2K bug scare illustrated how systemic anxieties can grow into global concern, only to fade with little consequence. I recall it vividly from my time at KPMG, auditing how companies prepared for the disruption. Not only did nothing happen, but looking back, our audits would not have altered much if it had. We were largely producing documentation on corporate strategies, not rigorously testing whether systems could survive an actual failure. Similarly, in the 2000s, fears of "peak oil" predicted imminent collapse (Heinberg, 2005), forecasts later softened by advances in extraction and energy diversification.

This pattern suggests that while environmental and social challenges are real and urgent, alarmist framing can undermine constructive engagement. If the goal is genuine change, producing reports or sounding alarms is not enough. Overstating danger risks paralyzing the public, eroding trust when predictions fail, and opening space for those who exploit fear for other agendas. A better approach is one that recognizes complexity, grounds urgency in evidence, and avoids the pitfalls of sensationalism. Of course, this assumes that we also have effective political systems capable of translating concern into action—a condition that cannot be taken for granted, as many societies struggle to solve even the problems they clearly identify.

To live as *Homo ecologicus* is to see ourselves as one species among many, dependent on the climate, soil, pollinators, and oceans. The boundaries we cross are not only environmental but ethical. Stewardship is not an ideology but a responsibility—whether one draws inspiration from Lovelock's Gaia hypothesis, Næss's deep ecology, or the empirical findings of climate science. The task is to think systemically: not only locally or nationally, but in ways that redefine human success in terms of ecological balance rather than economic growth alone.

1.4.4 Politics, Morality, and Public Life

From the earliest bands of foragers to today's vast digital networks, humans have lived in groups—organizing, negotiating, exchanging, and sometimes clashing. Aristotle described us as *zoon politikon*—political animals—meaning not only that we live together, but that our lives are bound up in shared systems of meaning, morality, and belonging. For him, to exist outside the political community was to be an outcast, "like a bird which flies alone" (*Politics*, 4th century BC). Today, I guess, it is the snippets of film we watch flimmer on the news in the evening—brief flashes of conflict, debate, or cooperation—reminding us that politics remains not an abstraction but the everyday drama of human coexistence.

Political life is rarely straightforward. In most systems, it involves compromise, persuasion, and balancing competing interests. Modern democracies often manage this through party structures, where discipline is maintained either formally—through roles such as the "Whip" in the UK—or informally, through social and institutional pressures. In such environments, stepping outside the agreed line can carry significant professional and reputational costs.

The stakes are particularly high for those whose entire careers rest on political office. Loss of favor—or even just popularity—can bring not only a change in employment but also a sharp reduction in status, income, and influence. As a result, political behavior is shaped as much by strategic caution as by conviction. This dynamic can lead to the careful calibration of public statements, where leaders focus on maintaining support and avoiding controversy, even at the expense of full candor.

Throughout history, rhetoric has been a central tool of political life. In ancient Athens, the sophists of the fifth century BCE mastered the art of persuasion, often prioritizing victory in debate over the pursuit of truth.

While scientific inquiry aspires to objectivity and evidence, politics often operates in a more fluid space—shaped by negotiation, perception, and public opinion. Politicians, then as now, are often those willing to say whatever it takes to remain in power—much as the sophists once taught their students to do, whether in the open spaces of the agora, the gymnasia, or in private homes.

Yet it is worth remembering that this picture of political life, which we in the West often hold so highly, is itself very new. For most of history—whether in Europe, Asia, or elsewhere—people lived under monarchies, empires, or authoritarian rulers. The idea of broad, representative democracy has existed for scarcely more than a century. Even in countries that pride themselves on long traditions, universal suffrage is a product of the twentieth century, and in some cases as late as the 1970s. When we invoke "our democracy, dating back to classical Greece," we forget that almost the entire stretch in between was not democratic at all. And even in Athens itself, democracy was far from what we mean today: it was direct, not representative, and limited to a narrow elite of male citizens, excluding women, slaves, and foreigners. What we often call continuity is, in truth, a selective memory.

When public trust in political systems erodes, the landscape can shift rapidly. Figures may emerge who position themselves as outsiders, offering simple narratives to address complex problems. While such voices can invigorate debate, they also risk oversimplifying issues or prioritizing personal visibility over substantive solutions. These shifts can affect more than legislatures and elections; they influence public institutions, including universities.

Academic life, at its best, depends on the freedom to pursue knowledge wherever evidence leads. While political decision-making and academic research both serve the public, they operate on different logics: one oriented toward policy and representation and the other toward investigation and understanding. When the incentives of political life—such as loyalty to a particular agenda—enter academia, they can limit critical debate, narrow research agendas, and compromise the integrity of scholarship.

This tension has appeared in various forms over time. For example, in the late twentieth century, political shifts in several countries led to reduced funding for nuclear research, partly due to public concerns about safety and waste. Decades later, some of those same societies faced renewed interest in nuclear energy as a potential low-carbon source, revealing the long-term impact of earlier decisions. Such cases illustrate how short-term political pressures can shape scientific capacity for generations.

Humans are unusual among animals in creating systems of justification—arguing not just about what *is*, but about what *should be*. This capacity for norm-setting is central to ethics and politics but can also produce unintended consequences. Well-intentioned attempts to "steer" society or research in a certain direction may yield effects opposite to those intended.

For this reason, universities are often seen as requiring a degree of insulation from immediate political priorities. Their primary role is to describe and explain how the world works, providing a basis for policy rather than a direct extension of it. The risk lies not only in overt control, but also in decision-making without a clear understanding of the processes being influenced.

The political systems we have today evolved under conditions very different from our own—slower communication, more limited public participation, and often greater trust in established institutions. In an era of global interconnection and rapid information flow, these structures face new challenges. Digital identification technologies, secure online voting, and participatory platforms now make it technically possible to involve citizens more directly in decision-making. If used with appropriate safeguards, such tools could complement representative institutions and provide a more responsive public sphere.

Technology, however, is not a solution on its own. Without thoughtful design and robust protections, new systems can replicate or even amplify the biases and inequalities of older ones. Like science, politics must evolve not just in the choices it makes, but in the processes through which those choices are reached.

The philosopher Hannah Arendt, in *The Human Condition* (1958), distinguished between labor (activities sustaining life), work (the creation of lasting artifacts), and action (engagement in public life). For her, action is the realm where individuals reveal themselves to others, grounded in plurality and dialogue. This public sphere—whether understood as civil society, democratic space, or deliberative forum—depends not only on institutions but also on virtues such as courage, patience, and mutual respect.

Different disciplines shed light on how public life operates. Political theory explores the fair distribution of power (Rawls, 1971; Sen, 2009). Sociology studies the formation and resilience of norms and institutions (Durkheim, 1895/1982; Giddens, 1984). Moral psychology examines how people develop values and group identities (Haidt, 2001; Turiel, 1983). Together, they reveal the complexity of living not only as individuals, but as members of overlapping communities.

Yet the same social instincts that allow for solidarity can also foster division. Our evolutionary tendency toward in-group loyalty and out-group suspicion (Kurzban & Tooby, 2001) underpins both cooperation and conflict. Yuval

Noah Harari (2015) has argued that large-scale human coordination rests on shared "fictions"—constructs such as money, laws, and national identity that exist only because enough people believe in them. From this perspective, these systems are fragile: once belief erodes, they can unravel with startling speed.

But this interpretation is not the whole story. To describe money or law merely as "fictions" misses the way they are anchored in material practice, institutional trust, and long historical trajectories. A currency is not just a belief—it is backed by states, enforced by legal systems, and woven into centuries of commercial exchange. Similarly, laws emerge from political struggle, institutional design, and moral frameworks that cannot be easily wished away. National identity, too, is not something that can be simply invented or discarded at will; it is bound up with shared language, culture, memory, and sacrifice. Attempts at rapid "re-engineering" of such identities through social experiments have often produced not harmony but instability and, at times, catastrophe (Anderson, 1983; Fukuyama, 2018; Smith, 1991). In fact, playing with or dismantling these pillars is itself reckless—it signals a disregard for the accumulated wisdom of past generations, who struggled to establish the very institutions that now hold societies together.

Perhaps the more balanced view is that these institutions are both robust and vulnerable: robust because they are layered into daily life, practices, and memory; vulnerable because their force ultimately depends on collective adherence. Belief alone cannot sustain them, but without belief they cannot hold. It is in this tension—between constructed trust and historical embedding—that the power of human coordination lies.

In the digital age, public discourse is shaped by forces unprecedented in scale and speed. Online platforms connect billions, but also enable misinformation, polarization, and algorithm-driven echo chambers (Sunstein, 2017; Zuboff, 2019). The capacity for public reasoning now competes with performance-driven communication and the rapid spread of unverified claims.

This reminds me of a film I saw growing up—D.W. Griffith's *Intolerance* (1916)—a cinematic meditation on the destructive power of fanaticism across eras. Released just after the First World War began, the film interweaves stories from different historical periods to show how cruelty and dogmatism repeatedly undo human progress. At the time, it responded to rising moral panic and polarization.

Looking back, I think that film arrived when it was genuinely needed. And perhaps we find ourselves in a similar moment again today. As intolerance resurfaces in public discourse, *Intolerance* is worth revisiting—not just as a cinematic milestone, but as a reminder that tolerance is not merely a virtue, but a condition for democratic survival.

The alternative—intolerance—often means rushing into the glass store swinging a big stick. And we do this with unsettling frequency, not only in Europe but in other parts of the world as well. When disagreement becomes grounds for destruction rather than dialogue, the very foundations of civil society begin to fracture.

History suggests there may be a cyclical rhythm at work here. Periods of tolerance often stabilize institutions and produce long stretches of status quo. Yet when crises arrive, and those in power cling to existing arrangements in the name of tolerance or order, this very rigidity can provoke rupture. Revolutions, civil wars, and systemic breakdowns often emerge not from excess change, but from a refusal to adapt until pressures become intolerable (Goldstone, 1991; Tilly, 1993). Ironically, tolerance without flexibility can harden into stagnation, creating the very conditions that trigger violent upheaval. Those in power frequently perceive themselves as trapped: to yield is to risk loss of authority, privilege, or legitimacy, and so they respond by doubling down. What follows is a posture of rigidity, almost a paralysis, that signals weakness even as it projects strength. This dynamic emboldens opponents, who grow convinced that disruption is the only remaining path forward. Over time, the gulf between entrenched defenders of the status quo and an increasingly mobilized opposition widens until the system ruptures.

The alternative is *gradual adaptation*—institutions that change incrementally before crises force them to. This is also a central lesson from evolutionary theory: systems that adapt continuously are more resilient than those that resist change until collapse (Gould & Eldredge, 1977; Mayr, 1982). Political and social systems, like species, cannot remain static; they must coevolve with their environments or face extinction.

In the *Anthropocene*, the scope of politics extends further still. Decisions must account not only for present citizens but for future generations, ecosystems, and the stability of the Earth's systems. Whether our institutions and moral frameworks can meet this challenge remains uncertain. But recognizing the scale of the task is the first step toward shaping political systems that are equal to it.

1.4.5 Technology, Institutions, and Agency

We live at a turning point in human history. For the first time, the species that asks, "What does it mean to be human?" may soon need to ask, "What comes after humanity as we have understood it for centuries?" This is no longer the realm of science fiction. Developments in artificial intelligence, biotechnology, and brain–computer interfaces suggest that the boundary between human and machine, biology and code, may soon become porous—or in some respects, irrelevant.

Nick Bostrom (2014), a luminary thinker from Helsingborg, Sweden—a city I often pass through on my way to work—has famously warned about the existential risks posed by artificial superintelligence. These are entities that could surpass human intelligence across all domains, making autonomous decisions we may neither predict, control, nor reverse. I return to Bostrom's work often, not just in this book, because his warnings continue to shape serious debates about our future. Yet the question is not only one of survival—it is also one of meaning. If machines can think, feel, and even create more effectively than we can, what role remains for us? Are we still the protagonists of our own story? And, perhaps more importantly, how do we ensure we remain so—rather than being surpassed, sidelined, and ultimately pacified?

Beneath these philosophical questions lies a more immediate, social one: what happens to the billions whose jobs could be replaced by machines? If they are no longer needed for production or service, will they be seen as expendable—a kind of second-class human? The risk is not just economic exclusion but also psychological dislocation. When work ceases to provide meaning, status, and identity, something else must fill that vacuum—or the result may be despair, unrest, and social fragmentation.

The divide between those who own and control advanced technologies and those who do not is already widening. Wealth concentrates at the top, while many face declining cognitive stimulation, restricted access to quality education, and fewer real opportunities. If these inequalities deepen, the implicit social contract—between labor and capital, between contribution and reward—could break down entirely. Even policies like *universal basic income(UBI)* may address material needs but leave unanswered the deeper question: what is the purpose of life for those no longer "needed" in the productive economy? And even if we figured out a way to pay for UBI—which, as we shall see in later chapters, is far from certain—the problem would remain that financial security alone cannot substitute for meaning, recognition, or a sense of contribution.

This is part of a broader transformation the philosopher Luciano Floridi describes as our entry into the "*infosphere*"—a world where reality is increasingly defined by data, networks, and algorithmic governance. When our preferences are nudged by AI systems and our attention is shaped by unseen recommendation engines, are we still acting freely? Or have we already outsourced major parts of our agency without fully realizing it?

Technologies that amplify our capacities also risk dulling them. History offers parallels: the invention of writing externalized memory, the printing press decentralized authority, and the internet globalized knowledge. Now, with AI writing our texts, diagnosing diseases, and predicting behavior, we face a deeper question: are we designing tools, or are the tools beginning to redesign us? And if basic skills like grammar, memory, or sustained critical thought are ceded to machines, will we retain the ability to think independently in a generation's time? These questions will be at the center of our reflections in the later half of the book, where we will consider not only what machines can do, but what humans risk forgetting.

James Lovelock (2019), in his final writings, suggested that Earth itself may be entering a new evolutionary stage. In *Novacene*, he envisioned humans being succeeded by *cyborg intelligences*—hyper-rational agents arising from the human-made environment, much as humans once arose from the biosphere. From this perspective, the rise of intelligent machines might not be a rupture but a continuation of evolution. Yet this vision also raises uncomfortable questions. Some dystopias imagine humanity reduced to maintaining the very machines that replaced it. But if machines can build and sustain themselves, what purpose would humans serve—especially if we continue to mismanage the planet as we have?

Here Arne Næss' concept of økosofi (ecosophy) resonates once more—the idea that ecological insight and philosophical wisdom are inseparable, each deepening the other. In his view, the self is not a fixed boundary but an expanding circle—extending from the ego to the family, to the community, and ultimately to the planet. If we are to become "post-human," Næss might ask, as he sits in his cabin under Hallingskarvet what kind of post-human will we choose to be? Will we broaden our empathy to embrace all life, or retreat into technological solipsism? The answer is not predetermined. We have the power to shape this trajectory, even if history suggests that we often fail to use it.

This is why such questions cannot be left only to philosophers, ethicists, or futurists. Social scientists must also confront them, even when they seem outside the conventional scope of our disciplines. After all, if we do not, who will? In this book, I attempt one synthesis: redefining what we are as a species by moving from a narrow focus on rationality toward wisdom, and from there toward a renewed form of humanism—one in which we accept our role as custodians and stewards of all living things. There are, of course, many other possible answers, but I feel an obligation, as a social scientist, to present at least one clear and logically consistent path that follows from the premises laid out here.

Biologists such as Laland (2017) remind us that humans have always been niche-constructors—changing our environment and, in turn, being changed by it. From fire to farming, from cities to cyberspace, our story is one of coevolution. The post-human turn may simply be the next chapter in this loop—but that does not make it inevitable, or safe.

Debates about enhancement—from CRISPR gene editing to Neuralink's brain–computer interfaces—are no longer hypothetical. Today, these implants may help the blind to see. Tomorrow, they may expand memory, alter cognition, or merge human minds with machine networks. Should AI systems themselves one day be granted legal personhood, the boundaries of agency and accountability will blur still further.

At the same time, our digital environments blur the lines between learning and persuasion, between genuine knowledge and targeted manipulation. Recommendation algorithms reinforce existing preferences, producing "filter bubbles" (Pariser, 2011) that narrow our exposure to opposing views. Unless explicitly designed to challenge us, AI will tend to agree with us—offering not critique but affirmation. This creates an intellectual echo chamber that undermines critical thinking and humility.

The same risk applies to relationships. AI companions, marketed as tools to alleviate loneliness, may make human interaction feel less necessary. Machines are predictable, undemanding, and tailored to please. But in avoiding rejection, disappointment, and emotional friction, we may also avoid the growth that only real human connection can bring. Such trends deserve close scrutiny: are we alleviating loneliness, or deepening it through simulation?

The ethical frameworks we use seem to be lagging. While Asimov's three laws of robotics are well known,[3] real-world AI ethics must grapple with bias, opacity, surveillance, and structural power. Shoshana Zuboff (2019) warns of *surveillance capitalism*, where human experience becomes raw material for prediction and control. Soon, an individual's entire digital footprint—communications, purchases, movements, facial expressions—could be fed into personalized AI models capable of predicting behavior with startling

[3] Asimov's Three Laws of Robotics, introduced in *I, Robot* (1950), are:

1. A robot may not injure a human being or, through inaction, allow a human being to come to harm.
2. A robot must obey the orders given it by human beings, except where such orders would conflict with the First Law.
3. A robot must protect its own existence as long as such protection does not conflict with the First or Second Law.

accuracy. At that point, the question will not be *can* we do this, but *should* we—and who decides what is included, excluded, and why.

Others, like Kate Crawford (2021), stress that AI is never neutral—it is embedded in political, social, and environmental contexts. It consumes energy, amplifies inequalities, and reshapes labor in ways we cannot ignore.

In the end, the question is not simply whether we will remain the smartest, fastest, or most creative beings on the planet. It is whether we can remain human in the fullest sense—capable of wisdom, ethics, and purpose—in an age when the tools we have made might surpass us. The danger is not only that AI could outcompete us in specific tasks, but that it could tempt us to shrink into narrower roles, outsourcing so much that we become smaller, less capable, even less thoughtful. Precisely because this threat exists, we must resist it by striving to become broader: cultivating the many dimensions of knowledge, imagination, and moral reflection that define our humanity. This is the challenge of what I call *Reflective Humanism*: a deliberate stance of self-awareness and moral reflection, echoing the humanist traditions of Erasmus and Montaigne while adapting them to the realities of a machine-saturated world. Without such reflection, we risk not just losing our place at the center of the story—but slowly becoming something less than what we are today.

1.4.6 Why This Systems Approach Works Better—In Science and In Practice

The purpose of this section is straightforward: to show why the Vitruvian Framework explains more and guides practice better than other systems theories. Earlier in this chapter we reviewed several influential approaches—each illuminating in its own way, but most either abstract away from biology or treat technology as an afterthought. The Vitruvian Framework keeps the full stack intact—from evolution and ecology through culture, morality, institutions, and AI—so causes and constraints line up across layers instead of being lost in disciplinary translation.

The test is pragmatic. A useful framework should do two things: explain more with fewer ad hoc assumptions, and help us act—diagnose, design, and decide—without breaking when conditions change. On both counts, the five-dimension model is stronger. At the same time, it should be clear that this framework is not the final destination but a staging point. It is introduced here as a foundational model, a first step that will later be extended into the broader argument for *Evolutionary Social Science*. By the conclusion of the book, this trajectory culminates in what I call the *Evolutionary Integration Model*—a synthesis that brings the insights of the Vitruvian Framework into dialogue with the full range of social sciences, offering a cumulative, evolutionary foundation for future inquiry.

First, it begins where many others hesitate: with biology and evolution. That grounding removes much of the hand-waving. It ties symbolic thought, learning, and institutions to selection pressures and developmental pathways, so "why" questions are not left floating. Culture is anchored in *evolved cognition*, which makes it possible to explain both convergence (shared human regularities) and divergence (local adaptations) without ideological shortcuts. You get a common base, then stacked layers you can actually test.

Second, it is integrative without being vague. The five dimensions—symbolic, coevolutionary, ecological, political-moral, technological—are separable enough for research but designed to interlock. That means one can move from a lab study on joint attention to a policy design for civic trust, or from energy constraints to institutional reform, without switching conceptual languages at each step. It is a scaffold for cumulation: findings in one layer either slot in or force explicit revisions upstream.

Third, it is decision oriented. By mapping mechanisms to levers, the framework travels well from diagnosis to action: change the niche, you change the learning; redesign the incentive, you reshape the norm; alter the information environment, you alter perceived agency. Because the layers are operationalized (measures exist for each), scenarios can be modeled, trade-offs simulated, and outcomes evaluated before crises unfold. That shortens the time from insight to implementation.

Fourth, it is future-ready. Many systems theories were built for slow-moving variables and analog institutions. This one builds technology into the architecture, so algorithmic feedback, synthetic media, and human–machine co-production are not afterthoughts. Automation of cognition, shifts in authorship, and platform power are analyzed inside the same framework that also accounts for energy budgets and moral legitimacy. That means better foresight, cleaner risk registers, and policies that do not collapse at first contact with machine intelligence.

The comparison Table 1.3 highlights these contrasts clearly.

The value of comparison is not to dismiss earlier theorists, but to build on them. I recall with great pleasure reading Niklas Luhmann during my PhD studies—his vast and intricate work on social systems remains one of the most ambitious theoretical projects ever undertaken. Even if one does not adopt his framework wholesale, the discipline owes him respect for showing how rigor and imagination can be combined in the service of theory.

Kenneth Boulding deserves equal recognition. At the University of Michigan, and later at the University of Colorado in Boulder, he built

Table 1.3 Vitruvian framework vs. other systems theories

Criterion	Vitruvian framework (five dimensions)	General Systems Theory (GST)	Luhmannian social systems	Complex Adaptive Systems (CAS)	Actor–Network Theory (ANT)
Foundational grounding	Starts with evolution and biology; layers culture, ecology, morality, tech	Abstract isomorphisms; weak on human biology	Autopoiesis of communication; minimal biology	Emergence and adaptation; biology optional	Symmetry of human/non-human actants; biology implicit
Scope of human phenomena	Full stack: cognition, culture, ecology, institutions, AI	Broad but generic; hard to specify humans	Strong on institutions/communication; weaker on minds/bodies	Strong on dynamics; uneven on norms/meaning	Rich descriptions of networks; limited psychological account
Mechanism clarity	Specifies cross-layer mechanisms (niche construction, norm formation, energy limits, AI feedback)	High-level relations; mechanism light	Communication codes and systems boundaries; abstract	Local interaction rules; mechanism strong but domain-specific	Translation/enrollment; mechanism narrative rather than testable
Operationalization and measurement	Each layer has established measures; supports cumulative datasets	Metrics vary; often qualitative system maps	Difficult to measure communications systems at scale	Strong simulation and metrics; context-dependent	Excellent ethnography; limited standardized metrics
Predictive/retrodictive power	Medium-high: links constraints to behaviors and institutional outcomes	Low-medium: good for analogies, weak forecasts	Low: insightful diagnostics, limited forecasting	Medium-high within bounded systems	Low-medium: strong retrospection, weak prediction

Criterion	Vitruvian framework (five dimensions)	General Systems Theory (GST)	Luhmannian social systems	Complex Adaptive Systems (CAS)	Actor–Network Theory (ANT)
Policy usability	High: maps levers to layers; integrates ethics and feasibility	Medium: helps coordination talk, not design	Medium: governance insights; hard to translate	Medium-high for complex programs; can sprawl	Medium: reveals power and infrastructure; light on levers
Ethical integration	Built-in political-moral layer; legitimacy and trust explicit	External to core theory	Norms as communication; ethics indirect	Ethics added from outside	Ethics surfaced via critique, not a design module
Ecological realism	Explicit biosphere/ energy constraints	Recognizes environment abstractly	Environment is environment of communication	Often includes environment; not necessary	Surfaces materiality; no boundary conditions
AI/technology readiness	Dedicated tech-agency layer; models algorithmic effects and co-production	Pre-digital; needs extensions	Treats media as channels for communication systems	Can absorb AI as agents/rules; not normative by default	Rich on platforms/ infrastructure; limited foresight tools
Cumulative science potential	High: cross-layer scaffolding for replication and synthesis	Medium: conceptual bridges, weak data spine	Low-medium: theoretical elegance, sparse cumulation	Medium-high in domains; fragmentation risk	Medium: comparative cases, less accumulation

a career that consistently defied disciplinary boundaries. His work ranged from general systems theory to peace research, ecological economics, and evolutionary economics. Moving to Boulder may have placed him outside the traditional centers of academic prestige, but that distance gave him the freedom to pursue bold, integrative ideas that others hesitated to touch. Boulding's willingness to stand outside the mold is precisely what allowed him to pioneer new intellectual terrain.

Herbert Simon exemplified the same courage but in a different register. Based at Carnegie Mellon University for most of his career, he left a definitive mark on economics, political science, psychology, artificial intelligence, and management. *Administrative Behavior* (1947) remains a cornerstone of organizational studies, and his concept of bounded rationality reshaped how we think about decision-making. A Nobel laureate in economics and a Turing Award winner in computer science, Simon showed what genuine polymathic brilliance looks like—daring to explore every corner of the intellectual landscape while still leaving behind ideas that became part of the canon.

It is in dialogue with such figures, among others—Luhmann for his audacity of scale, Boulding for his integrative imagination, and Simon for his polymathic reach—that the Vitruvian Framework finds its place. Their pioneering efforts revealed the need for a systems view of humanity, even if none thought of weaving the strands together into a model that balanced biology, culture, morality, and technology within a single scaffold. The framework developed here should not be seen as a rejection of their contributions, but as an attempt to extend them—into a form that is both scientifically grounded and practically usable.

With this foundation in place, we can now turn to a different but equally important tension: not between frameworks of science, but between the narratives we hold about ourselves. For alongside the structural accounts of humanity lies another story—one that is beautiful, warm, and reassuring, yet often at odds with the colder, more scientific picture of who we are. It is here, in the interplay between *The Warm Ideal* and *The Rational Real*, that the next section begins.

1.5 Science vs. Common Misconceptions

Pulling up again the themes from the prologue of this book: as children, we are taught a story about humanity that is beautiful, warm, and reassuring. We are told that we are noble, rational, moral beings—heroes of our own life's journey. This narrative feels comforting and close to the heart. It gives us meaning, belonging, and purpose.

As we approach adulthood, however, a different narrative comes into view—a cold, rational, scientific portrait. Here, Homo sapiens is not a divine creation, but an evolved animal: fickle, biased, and self-deceiving. Cognitive science shows we are driven by unconscious processes (Kahneman, 2011), social psychology highlights our persistent self-justifications (Tajfel & Turner, 1979), and evolutionary biology points to selfish genes and inherited predispositions (Dawkins, 1976). Our noble self-image begins to look less like fact and more like a carefully maintained illusion.

These two stories—The Warm Ideal and The Rational Real—do not simply differ in content; they pull at us in different ways. We gravitate toward the first because, psychologically speaking, it acts as a protective shield. Positive self-concept boosts mental health and social cooperation (Taylor & Brown, 1988). Identity, we now know, is partly a fiction—a narrative we craft to maintain coherence (Bruner, 1991). And even when evidence begins to chip away at that fiction, we cling to it—for after all, it feels like us, the image we have built of ourselves.

Case Box: The Warm Ideal and the Rational Real—A Self-Awareness Exercise

As children, most of us grow up surrounded by a comforting image of the world—and of ourselves. We are taught, implicitly or explicitly, to see ourselves as good, special, and morally guided. This is the *Warm Ideal*: a sense of self shaped by early family life, emotional bonds, and the protective stories we are told about right and wrong. For many, this identity is sustained by parental influence, especially maternal care, and later reinforced by cultural narratives of fairness, uniqueness, and inner worth.

But as we grow older and enter education—particularly scientific education—this warm image meets a colder reality. We learn that humans are not inherently good, that our decisions are shaped by self-interest, evolved biases, and environmental pressures. We begin to encounter the *Rational Real*: the analytical, skeptical, and often unsettling view of ourselves as largely flawed biological organisms shaped by evolutionary logic.

The two selves begin to coexist, but uneasily. For those who become researchers or scientists, the Rational Real often dominates in professional life. In the lab, in publications, or in teaching, there is little room for illusion. The scientific self is trained to be detached, even uneasy in its honesty. But when we bike home, step through the door, or watch our children sleep, the Warm Ideal returns. We want to believe again—that everything will be okay, that people are kind, that life holds a deeper meaning. More often than not, we don't even think about it consciously; it simply arises as part of a quiet, almost seamless transition back into ordinary life. Living entirely within the Rational Real would feel cold and draining; in everyday life, especially at home, we allow ourselves gentler beliefs and dispositions that soften the edges of reality.

This exercise asks you to reflect on how you navigate these two selves.

Instructions

Write a reflection (half a page to a page) in response to the following questions. You do not need to share your responses unless you choose to.

1. When you think about your upbringing, what kind of self-image were you encouraged to develop? Did your parents or caregivers promote a Warm Ideal view of who you were or would become?
2. When did you first become aware of a more Rational Real view of human nature? What triggered this shift, and how did it feel?
3. In your daily life now, when do you find yourself leaning toward the Warm Ideal? When does the Rational Real take over?
4. Are there moments where you consciously suppress one self in favor of the other? For example, do you "act warm" in private even if you've had a cold, rational day at work?
5. Do you believe a person who lives only in the Rational Real is still fully human? Or does something essential get lost in that transition?
6. Can rationality and warmth coexist meaningfully in your life? If so, describe a situation where they reinforce each other. If not, when do they clash?

I know these are difficult questions. They ask you to be sensitive, which means being vulnerable—and that is not easy. It may feel exposing, uncomfortable, even a bit awkward. Still, I believe this exercise is important, perhaps especially because it's so hard to do. There's something valuable in taking the time to examine not just what we think, but how we've come to think it—how our views of ourselves and of others have been shaped over time. Whether or not you choose to share your reflections, the act of writing them can help uncover parts of yourself that often go unspoken.

Once you've completed the exercise, take a moment to sit with what you've written. If you feel comfortable—and only if you feel safe doing so—you might consider sharing it with someone you trust. This could be a classmate, a friend, or someone who knows you well. You could invite them to reflect on whether your self-perception resonates with how they experience you. Not to judge, correct, or critique—but simply to open a space for dialogue. Sometimes, the most surprising insights come from the people who see us daily.

> **Purpose**
> The aim of this reflection is not to choose between your selves, or to pin down some final truth. It is to explore the tension between different ways of being—and thinking. As humans, and especially as scholars, we carry contradictions. We are both rational and emotional, idealistic and pragmatic, vulnerable and composed. Understanding that complexity is not a sign of confusion. It is the beginning of wisdom. And yet, this beginning rarely lasts untouched.

But as we grow older and enter education—particularly scientific education—this warm image meets a colder reality. We learn that humans are not inherently good, that our decisions are shaped by self-interest, evolved biases, and environmental pressures. This marks our encounter with the Rational Real: the analytical, skeptical, and often unsettling view of ourselves as flawed biological organisms shaped by evolutionary logic.

From that point on, the two selves begin to coexist, though rarely in harmony. For those who become researchers or scientists, the Rational Real often dominates in professional life. In the lab, in publications, or in teaching, there is little room for illusion. The scientific self is trained to be detached, even uncomfortably honest. Yet outside those spaces—when we bike home, step through the door, or watch our children sleep—the Warm Ideal quietly returns. Living entirely in the Rational Real would feel cold and exhausting; at home, we allow ourselves the comfort of gentler beliefs.

Outside the home, however, the balance becomes more complicated. In public life, and especially in professional hierarchies, people quickly learn that success depends not only on rational clarity but also on the ability to embody the values others expect. It is not that one must abandon reason, but rather that reason alone rarely inspires trust or loyalty. To lead, to persuade, or simply to get along in competitive environments often requires projecting warmth, conviction, and a sense of shared ideals—even if privately one continues to think in a more detached and rational way.

The difference between science and organizational life lies in transparency. In science, the Rational Real exists as an official method: codified in peer review, replication, and explicit rules of evidence. Rationality is the formal road map, and while it is never perfect, it is designed to be visible and contestable. In companies, institutions, and especially in hierarchical structures, rational calculation operates in less direct ways. Decisions are often framed in the language of mission, values, or vision, while beneath the surface they are driven by power, incentives, and survival. What is explicit in science is frequently implicit in organizations, leaving individuals to interpret which register—Warm Ideal or Rational Real—is truly in play.

Few are explicitly taught how to navigate this balance, but most discover it gradually as part of adult life. The challenge is not to choose between the two, but to carry both—knowing when to lean into one, and when to rely on the other. This tension between how we see ourselves and how we are seen by others is not confined to science or organizations; it runs through the fabric of everyday life.

The criminal who believes he is a good person and that only his dog truly understands him embodies this clash vividly. Despite objective wrongdoing, his subjective universe sustains his identity. This is an example of *motivated reasoning*: we assign ourselves traits that feel essential, even when reality contradicts them (Kunda, 1990). We need the Warm Ideal to believe we are good.

Yet if we were to discard this ideal altogether—if we chose to live entirely in the Rational Real—would we not risk becoming colder, more calculating, even more brutal? Perhaps it is precisely because we resist living too much in the Rational Real that this domain may be better served by machines. They are, in a sense, better equipped to remain there—relentlessly gathering facts, drawing inferences, and documenting patterns without the emotional need for *comforting illusions*. At the same time, science has little value if its findings remain unshared or unused—if we, as humans, stay in the camp of illusions while machines inhabit the real world, producing first-rate social science research we never bother to consult. If we wish to remain on a scientific path, we must at least engage with these findings.

Of course, we could choose otherwise—turning back to the narrative self, to Homo sapiens gathered around the bonfire listening to the grandfather's stories (most of which are made up, and the rest partly made up, but for a good purpose). Yet such a retreat is unlikely to be possible anymore, even if we wanted it. The pace of change has already carried us beyond that point. Besides, we need the science, not as a substitute for human warmth, but as a tool for improving our societies.

Research in evolutionary psychology suggests that moral emotions such as guilt, shame, and compassion were adaptive because they promoted group cohesion and long-term cooperation (Haidt, 2001; de Waal, 1996). Without the guiding fiction of inherent human dignity, we risk falling into *nihilism* or *instrumental cruelty*; what Arendt (1963) called the *"banality of evil."* Rationality alone, unmoored from feeling, does not guarantee moral behavior. Indeed, some of the most horrifying systems in history—slavery, eugenics, state terror—were justified by cold, "rational" arguments devoid of empathy.

It may even be that evolution favored this tension. We carry The Warm Ideal within us not because it is true, but because it works. It gives the species direction, purpose, and the illusion of internal consistency. In that sense, our yearning to see ourselves as good, intentional beings may not be a flaw, but a feature—a psychological adaptation for navigating an otherwise indifferent universe (Wilson, 2012).

As we age, it may not only be biology that changes us, but hopefully, it could be wisdom. Older people often appear to soften, not necessarily because they become more sentimental, but because they gain clarity about what truly matters. With the distractions of ambition, competition, and status gradually receding, many return, almost unknowingly, to a form of perception they once held as children. It is a return not to naivety, but to openness—to that unfiltered sense of awe and reverence that once came so naturally.

One sees it in the way a retired woman stares at the vaulted ceilings of Reims Cathedral or stands silently before the stone enormity of Durham's nave. These are not just architectural marvels; they become portals back to a state of being where wonder still has a place. In middle adulthood, so much is filtered through utility, exhaustion, or cynicism. But perhaps wisdom is not found in complexity, but in recovering the capacity to be moved, to see meaning in beauty, and to rediscover the simple, powerful experience of admiration.

Aging, then, may not be a slow decline but a subtle homecoming.

These narratives are not formally named in academic discourse, but we might call them "*The Narrative Self*" for the warm account, and "*The Scientific Self*" for the rational one. One of the most quietly painful experiences in adult life is the discrepancy we feel between these two selves. In the narrative ideal, we are the protagonists—morally upright, meaning-seeking, worthy of admiration. But in the scientific, practical world, shaped by evolutionary pressures, institutional constraints, and social hierarchies, we are often just another node in a system, struggling for attention, recognition, or economic survival.

For many readers, one of the great pleasures of books is that they allow us to retreat into a vast, private universe—one curated by our own values, heroes, and moral logic. This internal library becomes a kind of sanctuary: no matter what happens in the external world, we can return to this place to restore a sense of coherence and worth. But life does not permit us to stay there. We must leave this mental refuge to engage with others—to navigate the workplace, confront rejection, and earn a living. These arenas often deliver sharp reminders of our fallibility, our ordinariness, and our limitations. The warmth of the ideal self is bruised by the coldness of circumstance. Yet it is precisely this return to the narrative self, to the sanctuary of inner story, that allows us to recover.

Research on *self-complexity* (Linville, 1985) and *narrative identity* (McAdams, 1993) supports this view: the more robust and differentiated our *internal story-world*, the better we can weather external setbacks. Our minds evolved not only to survive, but to sustain a self—one that must oscillate between the realities of pain and the refuge of meaning. The Narrative Self thrives on story, significance, and belonging; the Scientific Self rests on analysis, causality, and skepticism.

Case Box: The Woman on the Corner – Choosing Balance Differently

Let me tell you a story. There was once an old woman who lived near the bookshop. She seemed to inhabit her own world. Her clothes rarely matched—too many bright colors for ordinary taste—and she often spoke of unusual things. She did not hold a conventional job, nor did she seem to own much in the way of house or possessions. To passersby, she was easy to dismiss as eccentric, someone who had stepped outside the path most people were expected to follow.

And yet, whenever she spoke, it was as if another world opened. Her stories carried warmth, and people left her presence lighter than before. She radiated an energy not tied to deadlines, careers, or competition, but to simple human contact. Her life moved at a different rhythm—slower, freer, more attuned to conversation and connection.

For many years, she appeared only at the margins of my life, a fleeting presence I barely registered. Yet when I encountered her again later, the impression changed. What once seemed like failure to keep pace with others turned out to be an alternative path. She carried no marks of exhaustion, no bitterness, and no restless striving. Her modest means were sufficient, and her generosity seemed endless. By contrast, those who had pursued the conventional road—stability, careers, recognition—now struck me as oddly fragile, worn down by the very success they had sought.

Questions for Reflection

1. Have you ever met someone like this woman? What were your first impressions, and did they change over time?
2. What social or cultural assumptions shaped how you viewed her?
3. From an evolutionary perspective, could her approach to life be adaptive in certain environments?
4. How might her warmth and social connection function as a survival strategy in human evolutionary history?
5. Does modern society undervalue these slower, more socially embedded survival strategies in favor of high-output, competitive ones? If so, why?

Perhaps she embodied a different kind of balance—rooted in warmth and presence, less concerned with achievement or stability. Seeing her again later in life stirred in me the unsettling thought that I, too, may have leaned too far to one side: toward career, recognition, and measurable output. Her life suggested the opposite risk, yet it also reminded me that these modes of being are not opposites but complements. What matters is not choosing one over the other, but finding ways to hold both—the warmth that sustains meaning and connection, and the discipline that grounds us in responsibility and accountability.

For scientists, this duality is inescapable. Research demands stepping into the role of the detached observer—questioning assumptions, unsettling myths, and viewing humanity from an evolutionary distance. Yet life outside the lab requires the return to ordinary roles: parent, neighbor, partner, and friend. Moving between these worlds is less contradiction than necessity; it is what allows us to pursue knowledge without losing touch with the lived reality that knowledge is meant to serve.

This book follows the same structure. It begins in the voice of the scientific self—analytical, detached, and probing—and it ends with the narrative self, who not only carries the questions but also frames what those questions could mean in the age of AI. This chapter has set the stage by showing how our brains, shaped for survival, are poorly matched to the abstract challenges of today, and how AI makes those limits impossible to ignore. But recognizing these constraints is only the first step. To move forward, we must examine them in detail.

Chapter 2 takes us inside the architecture of bias, self-deception, and misplaced rationality. Where this chapter framed the problem of human cognition in broad evolutionary and technological terms, Chapter 2 diagnoses its internal workings—how trade-offs, prestige, and denial shape our behavior, and why social science must reckon with the Rational Real rather than comforting illusions.

References

Anderson, B. (1983). *Imagined communities: Reflections on the origin and spread of nationalism.* Verso.

Arendt, H. (1958). *The human condition.* University of Chicago Press.

Arendt, H. (1963). *Eichmann in Jerusalem: A report on the Banality of Evil.* Viking Press.

Baumeister, R. F., Bratslavsky, E., Finkenauer, C., & Vohs, K. D. (2001). Bad is stronger than good. *Review of General Psychology, 5*(4), 323–370. https://doi.org/10.1037/1089-2680.5.4.323

Baumeister, R. F., & Leary, M. R. (1995). The need to belong: Desire for interpersonal attachments as a fundamental human motivation. *Psychological Bulletin, 117*(3), 497–529. https://doi.org/10.1037/0033-2909.117.3.497

Bengio, Y. (2021). The consciousness prior. *Current Opinion in Behavioral Sciences, 38*, 103–110.

Berman, M. G., Jonides, J., & Kaplan, S. (2008). The cognitive benefits of interacting with nature. *Psychological Science, 19*(12), 1207–1212.

Bongaarts, J., & O'Neill, B. C. (2018). Global warming policy: Is population left out in the cold? *Science, 361*(6403), 650–652. https://doi.org/10.1126/science.aat8680

Bostrom, N. (2014). *Superintelligence: Paths.* Strategies Oxford University Press.

Boulding, K. E. (1956). General systems theory: The skeleton of science. *Management Science, 2*(3), 197–208. https://doi.org/10.1287/mnsc.2.3.197

Boyd, R., & Richerson, P. (1985). *Culture and the evolutionary process.* University of Chicago Press.

Brewer, M. B. (2007). The importance of being we: Human nature and intergroup relations. *American Psychologist, 62*(8), 728–738. https://doi.org/10.1037/0003-066X.62.8.728

Bruner, J. (1991). The narrative construction of reality. *Critical Inquiry, 18*(1), 1–21.

Brynjolfsson, E., & McAfee, A. (2014). *The second machine age: Work, progress, and prosperity in a time of brilliant technologies.* W W Norton.

Carr, N. (2010). *The Shallows: What the internet is doing to our brains.* W. W. Norton.

Churchland, P. M. (2002). *Brain-wise: Studies in neurophilosophy.* MIT Press.

Connelly, M. (2008). *Fatal misconception: The struggle to control world population.* Harvard University Press.

Cosmides, L, & Tooby, J. (1997). Evolutionary psychology: A primer. *Center for Evolutionary Psychology.*

Crawford, K. (2021). *Atlas of AI: Power, politics, and the planetary costs of Artificial Intelligence*. Yale University Press.
Damasio, A. R. (1994). *Descartes' error: Emotion, reason, and the human brain.* Putnam.
Darwin, C. (2009). *On the origin of species* (150th anniversary ed.). Harvard University Press. (Original work published 1859).
Dawkins, R. (1976). *The selfish gene*. Oxford University Press.
Dawkins, R. (1982). *The extended phenotype*. Oxford University Press.
Dawkins, R. (1986). *The blind watchmaker: Why the evidence of evolution reveals a universe without design.* Norton.
Dawkins, R. (1996). *Climbing mount improbable*. Norton.
Deacon, T. W. (1997). *The symbolic species: The co-evolution of language and the brain.* Norton.
de Waal, F. (1996). *Good natured: The origins of right and wrong in humans and other animals*. Harvard University Press.
Diamond, J. (2005). *Collapse: How societies choose to fail or succeed*. Viking.
Durkheim, E. (1895/1982). *The rules of sociological method* (W. D. Halls, Trans.). Free Press.
Eisenberger, N. I., Lieberman, M. D., & Williams, K. D. (2003). Does rejection hurt? An fMRI study of social exclusion. *Science, 302*(5643), 290–292. https://doi.org/10.1126/science.1089134
Ferry, L. (1996). *L'Homme-Dieu ou le sens de la vie*. Grasset.
Floridi, L. (2014). *The fourth revolution: How the Infosphere is reshaping human reality.* Oxford University Press.
Frankl, V. E. (1959) *Man's search for meaning*. Beacon Press.
Fukuyama, F. (2018). *Identity*. Farrar, Straus and Giroux.
Geertz, C. (1973). *The interpretation of cultures.* Basic Books.
Giddens, A. (1984). *The constitution of society: Outline of the theory of structuration.* University of California Press.
Gigerenzer, G. (2007). *Gut feelings: The intelligence of the unconscious*. Viking.
Goldstone, J. A. (1991). *Revolution and rebellion in the early modern world*. University of California Press.
Gómez-Pinilla, F. (2008). Brain foods: The effects of nutrients on brain function. *Nature Reviews Neuroscience, 9*(7), 568–578. https://doi.org/10.1038/nrn2421
Gould, S. J., & Eldredge, N. (1977). Punctuated equilibria: The tempo and mode of evolution reconsidered. *Paleobiology, 3*(2), 115–151. https://doi.org/10.1017/S0094837300005224
Haidt, J. (2001). The emotional dog and its rational tail: A social intuitionist approach to moral judgment. *Psychological Review, 108*(4), 814–834.
Harari, Y. N. (2014/2015). *Sapiens: A brief history of humankind.* Harper.
Hartmann, B. (1995). *Reproductive rights and wrongs: The global politics of population control and contraceptive choice* (Revised and updated ed.). South End Press.
Hebb, D. O. (1949). *The organization of behavior: A neuropsychological theory*. Wiley.

Hinton, G. (2024). *What could go wrong? with Geoffrey Hinton* [Interview by J. Stewart]. YouTube. https://www.youtube.com/watch?v=jrK3PsD3APk

Kahneman, D. (2011). *Thinking, fast and slow*. Farrar, Straus and Giroux.

Kaplan, R., & Kaplan, S. (1989). *The experience of nature*. Cambridge University Press.

Kasting, J. F., Whitmire, D. P., & Reynolds, R. T. (1993). Habitable zones around main sequence stars. *Icarus, 101*(1), 108–128.

Kunda, Z. (1990). The case for motivated reasoning. *Psychological Bulletin, 108*(3), 480–498.

Kurzban, R., & Tooby, J. (2001). Coalitional psychology: An evolutionary perspective on intergroup conflict. In D. M. Buss (Ed.), *The handbook of evolutionary psychology*. Wiley.

Laland, K. N. (2017). *Darwin's unfinished symphony: How culture made the human mind*. Princeton University Press.

Latour, B. (2005). *Reassembling the social: An introduction to actor-network-theory*. Oxford University Press.

Latour, B. (2018). *Down to earth: Politics in the new climatic regime*. Polity Press.

Linville, P. W. (1985). Self-complexity and affective extremity: Don't put all of your eggs in one cognitive basket. *Social Cognition, 3*(1), 94–120.

Lovelock, J. E. (1979). *Gaia: A new look at life on earth*. Oxford University Press.

Lovelock, J. (2019). *Novacene: The coming age of hyperintelligence*. MIT Press.

Luhmann, N. (1995). *Social systems* (J. Bednarz Jr., & D. Baecker, Trans.). Stanford University Press. (Original work published 1984).

Marcus, G., & Davis, E. (2019). *Rebooting AI: Building Artificial Intelligence we can trust*. Pantheon.

Maynard Smith, J., & Szathmáry, E. (1995). *The major transitions in evolution*. Freeman.

Mayr, E. (1982). *The growth of biological thought: Diversity, evolution, and inheritance*. Belknap Press of Harvard University Press.

McAdams, D. P. (1993). *The stories we live by: Personal myths and the making of the self*. William Morrow.

Næss, A. (1989). *Ecology, community and lifestyle: Outline of an ecosophy*. Cambridge University Press.

Norenzayan, A. (2013). *Big gods: How religion transformed cooperation and conflict*. Princeton University Press.

Nussbaum, M. C. (1997). *Cultivating humanity: A classical defense of reform in liberal education*. Harvard University Press.

Pariser, E. (2011). *The filter bubble: What the Internet is hiding from you*. Penguin Press.

Pinker, S. (1994). *The language instinct: How the mind creates language*. William Morrow.

Popper, K. (1959). *The logic of scientific discovery*. Hutchinson.

Rawls, J. (1971). *A theory of justice*. Harvard University Press.

Rockström, J., Steffen, W., Noone, K., Persson, Å., Chapin, F. S., Lambin, E., Lenton, T. M., Scheffer, M., Folke, C., Schellnhuber, H. J., Nykvist, B., de Wit, C. A., Hughes, T., van der Leeuw, S., Rodhe, H., Sörlin, S., Snyder, P. K., Costanza, R., Svedin, U., Falkenmark, M., & Foley, J. A. (2009). A safe operating space for humanity. *Nature, 461*(7263), 472–475. https://doi.org/10.1038/461472a

Sen, A. (2009). *The idea of justice*. Harvard University Press.

Slovic, P. (2007b). *The perception of risk*. Earthscan.

Smallwood, J., & Schooler, J. W. (2006). The restless mind. *Psychological Bulletin, 132*(6), 946–958. https://doi.org/10.1037/0033-2909.132.6.946

Snow, C. P. (1959). *The two cultures and the scientific revolution*. Cambridge University Press.

Steffen, W., Richardson, K., Rockström, J., Cornell, S. E., Fetzer, I., Bennett, E. M., Biggs, R., Carpenter, S. R., de Vries, W., de Wit, C. A., Folke, C., Gerten, D., Heinke, J., Mace, G. M., Persson, L. M., Ramanathan, V., Reyers, B., & Sörlin, S. (2015). Planetary boundaries: Guiding human development on a changing planet. *Science, 347*(6223), 1259855.

Sunstein, C. R. (2017). *#Republic: Divided Democracy in the Age of Social Media*. Princeton University Press.

Tajfel, H., & Turner, J. C. (1979). An integrative theory of intergroup conflict. In *The social psychology of intergroup relations*. Brooks/Cole.

Taylor, B. (2010). *Dark green religion: Nature spirituality and the planetary future*. University of California Press.

Taylor, S. E., & Brown, J. D. (1988). Illusion and well-being: A social psychological perspective. *Psychological Bulletin, 103*(2), 193–210.

Tegmark, M. (2017). *Life 3.0: Being human in the age of Artificial Intelligence*. Knopf.

Tetlock, P. E., Kristel, O. V., Elson, S. B., Green, M. C., & Lerner, J. S. (2000). The psychology of the unthinkable: Taboo trade-offs, forbidden base rates, and heretical counterfactuals. *Journal of Personality and Social Psychology, 78*(5), 853–870. https://doi.org/10.1037/0022-3514.78.5.853

Tilly, C. (1993). *European revolutions, 1492–1992*. Blackwell.

Tooby, J., & Cosmides, L. (1992). The psychological foundations of culture. In J. H. Barkow, L. Cosmides, & J. Tooby (Eds.), *The adapted mind: Evolutionary psychology and the generation of culture* (pp. 19–136). Oxford University Press.

Tomasello, M. (1999). *The cultural origins of human cognition*. Harvard University Press.

Tomasello, M. (2009). *Why we cooperate*. MIT Press.

Tomasello, M. (2014). *A natural history of human thinking*. Harvard University Press.

Tomasello, M. (2019). *Becoming human: A theory of ontogeny*. Harvard University Press.

Turiel, E. (1983). *The development of social knowledge: Morality and convention*. Cambridge University Press.

Ulrich, R. S. (1984). View through a window may influence recovery from surgery. *Science, 224*(4647), 420–421.
van Lange, P. A. M., Rinderu, M. I., & Bushman, B. J. (2017). Aggression and violence around the world: A model of climate, aggression, and self-control in humans (CLASH). *Behavioral and Brain Sciences, 40*, Article e75.
Vitruvius. (ca. 15 BCE/1960). *The ten books on architecture* (M. H. Morgan, Trans.). Dover Publications.
von Bertalanffy, L. (1968). *General system theory: Foundations, development, applications.* George Braziller.
White, L., Jr. (1967). The historical roots of our ecologic crisis. *Science, 155*(3767), 1203–1207. https://doi.org/10.1126/science.155.3767.1203
Wilson, E. O. (1984). *Biophilia.* Harvard University Press.
Wilson, E. O. (2002). *The future of life*. Knopf.
Wilson, E. O. (2012). *The social conquest of Earth.* Liveright.
Woese, C. R. (2004). A new biology for a new century. *Microbiology and Molecular Biology Reviews, 68*(2), 173–186. https://doi.org/10.1128/MMBR.68.2.173-186.2004
Zuboff, S. (2019). *The age of surveillance capitalism: The fight for a human future at the new frontier of power*. PublicAffairs.

Further Reading

Aristotle. (1998). *Nicomachean ethics* (D. Ross, Trans.). Oxford University Press. (Original work published ca. 350 BCE).
Bateson, G. (1972). *Steps to an ecology of mind*. University of Chicago Press.
Beer, S. (1972). *Brain of the firm.* Allen Lane.
Boehm, C. (1999). *Hierarchy in the forest: The evolution of egalitarian behavior.* Harvard University Press.
Donald, M. (1991). *Origins of the modern mind: Three stages in the evolution of culture and cognition.* Harvard University Press.
Ferry, L. (2002). *What is the good life?* University of Chicago Press.
Forrester, J. W. (1969). *Urban dynamics.* MIT Press.
Forrester, J. W. (1971). *World dynamics.* Wright-Allen Press.
Hinton, G. (2025, February 14). *AI could already be conscious, says Geoffrey Hinton.* Mindplex Magazine. https://magazine.mindplex.ai/post/ai-could-be-already-conscious-says-geoffrey-hinton
Parsons, T. (1951). *The social system.* Free Press.
Prigogine, I., & Stengers, I. (1984). *Order out of chaos: Man's new dialogue with nature*. Bantam Books.
Russell, S. (2019). *Human compatible: Artificial Intelligence and the problem of control*. Viking.
Simon, H. A. (1969). *The sciences of the artificial*. MIT Press.

Slovic, P. (2007a). "If I look at the mass I will never act": Psychic numbing and genocide. *Judgment and Decision Making, 2*(2), 79–95.

Small, D. A., Loewenstein, G., & Slovic, P. (2007). Sympathy and callousness: The impact of deliberative thought on donations to identifiable and statistical victims. *Organizational Behavior and Human Decision Processes, 102*(2), 143–153.

Söilen, K. S. (2012). The fallacy of the service economy: A materialist perspective. *European Business Review, 24*(4), 369–382.

Söilen, K. S. (2025a). *The researcher's journey in the age of AI: Reappraising social science research.* Springer.

Söilen, K. S. (2025b). *Applied evolutionary economics: Insights from biology for real-world management.* Springer.

Tan, C. H., Wei, K. K., Watson, R. T., & Walczuch, R. M. (2005). Reducing status effects with anonymous electronic brainstorming. *Journal of the Association for Information Systems, 6*(7), 218–241.

Wiener, N. (1948). *Cybernetics: Or control and communication in the animal and the machine.* MIT Press.

2

Evolution of Biology and Society

Abstract This chapter confronts a disturbing but necessary idea: human beings are not naturally rational or virtuous, but evolved organisms shaped by survival, status, and social adaptation. What we like to think of as flaws—bias, overconfidence, group loyalty, and self-deception—are in fact features of an evolutionary design optimized for endurance rather than truth. Introducing the concept of the **Rational Real**, the chapter shows why moral ideals and policy ambitions often fail when they ignore biological constraints. Human behavior is revealed as deeply mimetic, driven by prestige, imitation, and tribal dynamics—patterns that shape not only everyday life but also academia itself. The social sciences, the chapter argues, are not immune: they mirror the same conformity pressures and moralized narratives they seek to explain. By grounding social analysis in evolutionary reality, this chapter strips away comforting illusions about rationality and progress. What emerges is a sobering but powerful insight: understanding human limits is not pessimism, but the starting point for more resilient institutions, better policy, and a more honest social science.

This chapter introduces the idea of the *Rational Real*—a colder, more unsettling picture of human beings as evolved primates rather than noble, rational agents. Human nature is not inherently virtuous but adaptive, shaped by evolutionary pressures that privileged survival, reproduction, and status navigation. Our minds are optimized for survival rather than truth, producing systematic biases and trade-offs. Overconfidence, group loyalty, and threat sensitivity are not flaws but features of our evolutionary design.

K. Solberg Söilen, *The Researcher's Journey in the Age of AI*,
https://doi.org/10.1007/978-3-032-23069-0_2

Much of human behavior is driven by imitation, prestige dynamics, and self-deception—mechanisms that sustain social cohesion but also distort authenticity. Even the social sciences mirror these biases, vulnerable to prestige games, conformity, and moralized narratives that obscure actual drivers of action.

A key theme is that moral ideals, when detached from biological realities, can backfire. Denying the Rational Real weakens social science, leaving it ill-equipped to address real-world problems. Rationality itself is shown less as a baseline fact than as a cultural identity—a role humans perform under certain conditions, rather than their natural state. Together, the chapter paints a sobering portrait of humanity: fragile, biased, and often self-deceiving, yet extraordinarily adaptable. To develop this argument, the discussion unfolds across five key areas:

1. Biased Brains and Evolutionary Trade-offs—cognition evolved for survival, not truth; biases like overconfidence and threat sensitivity are adaptive features.
2. Prestige, Imitation, and Self-Deception—much behavior is mimetic, guided by high-status models and sustained by self-deceptive coherence.
3. Social Science as a Mirror of Bias—disciplines and researchers reflect the same prestige games and tribal logics they claim to study.
4. Norms, Moralism, and the Risks of Denial—moralizing without realism leads to policy failure, hypocrisy, and fragile institutions.
5. Rationality as Social Identity—rationality is not a baseline condition but a cultural role, with intuition and habit driving most decisions.

By grounding social science in evolutionary realities, this chapter strips away comforting illusions and forces us to confront who we truly are. This biological foundation sets the stage for Chapter 3, which examines how our evolved traits—cooperation, competition, kinship, and emotion—express themselves in the social mind, shaping norms, morality, and collective life.

2.1 Biological and Cognitive Limits

Let us begin by looking objectively at the subject of our study—man—this time not as a political or cultural being, but as a physical organism. What can a human actually do, and what can he *not* do, with the limbs and organs he has at his disposal? These limitations set the framework for what we may reasonably expect of human behavior and performance.

To start with the obvious: humans cannot fly. Unlike birds or insects, we have no wings, and we cannot float, glide, or lift off the ground unaided. If we do take to the sky, it is only through tools—machines we have built. In contrast, a peregrine falcon can dive at over 300 km per hour, and even a modest city pigeon can flap along at speeds close to 80 km/h.

When it comes to running, humans are neither the fastest nor the slowest. A trained human sprinter can reach just under 45 km/h for a short burst—as Usain Bolt famously did—but even that is easily beaten by many animals. The cheetah, as we may remember from fun facts in our childhood, can reach 100 km/h in short sprints. Greyhounds and pronghorn antelopes clock in at 70–88 km/h. Even rabbits, jackals, and ostriches can leave us behind without much effort. Let's be honest, we can often not even catch a chicken in a fair footrace, if we wanted to, as anyone who has lived or stayed on a farm can attest.

Yet humans are not entirely without athletic merit. Our great physical advantage lies not in sprinting but in endurance. While we may be outpaced by animals in the short run, over long distances we fare surprisingly well. Humans can jog at a steady pace for hours. Some can run ultra-marathons, covering over 100 km in a single stretch. In fact, studies suggest that over long distances—under the right heat and humidity—humans can even outrun horses. This remarkable endurance was crucial to the success of persistence hunting in prehistoric times. Early humans could track prey for many kilometers over hours or even days, exploiting their ability to regulate body temperature through sweating while their animal prey, reliant on panting, would overheat and collapse (Bramble & Lieberman, 2004). This method of hunting—chasing animals to exhaustion rather than relying solely on speed or strength—is still practiced by some hunter-gatherer tribes in Kenya, such as the Hadza (Pontzer et al., 2014) and the Kalenjin, whose members are renowned for their extraordinary running abilities.

Not surprisingly, then, the Kalenjin people have produced a disproportionately high number of world-class long-distance runners and marathon champions. Researchers suggest a combination of *genetic predisposition*, high-altitude living, cultural emphasis on running, and early life physical activity contributes to this dominance (Wilber & Pitsiladis, 2012). Because of this legacy of endurance and tradition, recruiting runners from these tribes for international competitions has been a consistent phenomenon.

This link between evolutionary heritage, cultural practice, and modern athletic excellence underscores how deeply human biology and culture intertwine in shaping our capabilities.

We are also remarkably versatile. Humans can climb, swim, crawl, and manipulate tools with great precision. But again, we must acknowledge our limits. In water, we are slow and clumsy. Although some theories suggest that early human ancestors may have adapted to semi-aquatic environments—the so-called *aquatic ape hypothesis*; this idea remains controversial and lacks strong empirical support.

What is certain is that we did not evolve to live in water like dolphins or seals. Dolphins, which evolved from land-dwelling mammals and returned to the sea, developed large brains during their time on land and now use that intelligence to navigate complex underwater environments. By contrast, even a skilled human swimmer can only manage speeds around 6 km/h, while an orca can reach speeds up to 56 km/h, with ease. And when it comes to raw physical strength, we are no match for many other primates. A chimpanzee, for example, is estimated to be four to five times stronger than a human of comparable size.

What this all illustrates is that the human body is neither the fastest, strongest, nor most agile in the animal kingdom. But it is remarkably adaptable. It has been designed—or has evolved, if one prefers—to do many things reasonably well, but not to dominate in any one category:

We are the generalists of the mammalian world, not the specialists.

As I write these words, my wife walks into the library and sighs. For a moment, the sound interrupts my thoughts—not because I don't recognize it, but because I do. A sigh always signals that something is up. But what, exactly, is this small act from a biological perspective?

It turns out that sighing is more than a social gesture. Physiologically, it is a deep inhalation followed by a long exhalation, which helps reinflate collapsed alveoli in the lungs, maintaining optimal gas exchange (Vlemincx et al., 2013). Psychologically, it is tied to stress release, frustration, or relief, acting as a nonverbal cue to others about our internal state (Boiten, 1998). This blend of physical regulation and social signaling is characteristic of many human traits—originating as adaptations for survival and later embedded into communication. Such multipurpose functions, combining bodily resilience with social coordination, have been part of what allowed humans to cope with shifting challenges. The same integrated flexibility—where biology supports behavior, and behavior reinforces survival—would later prove crucial when our species began thriving in radically different and often extreme environments.

And in that instant, biology makes me just a little smarter—or at least better equipped to guess why my wife is sighing at me again (though of course I usually have a slight inkling of what it's about, but not always). That small domestic lesson echoes a much larger truth: our survival has always depended on this ability to read signals, adapt, and adjust. Much of this happens beneath awareness. Research in psychology and communication shows that the vast majority of daily interaction relies on unconscious processing of cues—tone of voice, facial expression, posture, timing—while only a fraction of what passes between people is registered consciously.

Estimates vary, but studies suggest that nonverbal signals convey more than 60–90% of the emotional meaning in interpersonal exchanges (Burgoon et al., 2016; Mehrabian, 2007). Similarly, cognitive science highlights that humans rely heavily on automatic, intuitive systems for interpreting others, with deliberate reasoning playing only a minor role (Kahneman, 2011). In everyday life, couples exchange hundreds of micro-signals, of which only a handful are consciously noticed—yet these unconscious processes guide most of the adaptation that makes long-term cooperation possible.

In everyday life, then, much of what sustains relationships and cooperation unfolds beneath conscious awareness. Our ability to detect signals, adjust to them, and coordinate with others is not just a domestic skill but an evolutionary inheritance. Recent research further underscores this point. A 2025 study published in *Nature* highlights how ancient *Homo sapiens* were able to survive in increasingly diverse and extreme environments across Africa before migrating outward around 50,000 years ago (Larson, 2025). By analyzing archaeological sites and reconstructing past climates, the researchers found a sharp expansion in the range of habitats humans occupied—moving beyond savannas and forests into deserts, mountains, and dense rainforests.

This *ecological flexibility*, rather than any single technological breakthrough, appears to be our true evolutionary advantage. As Eleanor Scerri, one of the study's authors, put it: our species' "superpower is that we are ecosystem generalists." This *unique generalism* may be precisely what allowed Homo sapiens—not other human relatives like Neanderthals—to populate nearly every corner of the planet. Adaptability, not dominance, made us endure.

This basic biological reality has consequences for how we live, not just in prehistoric times, but still today. It shaped the very structure of our societies. Because we cannot survive long without water—perhaps one or two days—and no more than a few weeks without food, we have always had to stay close to resources. Because we are relatively slow, we had to invent tools and tactics to hunt. Because we lack claws and fangs, we had to band together.

These physical constraints didn't just force us to adapt—they drove us toward cooperation, toward communication, and eventually toward the emergence of culture, cognition, and complex social life. Humans may not be able to fly like birds or swim like dolphins. We can't run like antelopes or climb like monkeys. But we can write, plan, sing, teach, and build machines that extend our reach. Our weakness is, paradoxically, our strength. For it is by recognizing what we cannot do that we begin to figure out what we can.

We take, as everyone will know, great pride in our mental abilities—our brains. After all, we have named ourselves *Homo sapiens*, the species that knows. And indeed, we are clever. Compared to all other animals, our capacity for symbolic thought, abstract reasoning, and social communication is unmatched. However, we are not as rational or self-aware as we often imagine ourselves to be. Our self-perception is frequently inflated, and modern social science has shown that humans are far more limited and biased than our cultural narratives suggest.

We tend to overestimate our wisdom, our control, and our place in the world, forgetting how fragile, fallible, and often comical our species really is. So, if I ever die, I'd like my burial stone to read: "Don't take humans too seriously."

This reminder is not limited to everyday life—it applies just as much to the academic world itself, as illustrated in the following case:

Case in a Box: The Academic Mirror—Self-Awareness in the Ivory Tower

In principle, few professions are as committed to critical thinking as academia. Scholars are trained to question assumptions, examine arguments, and revise conclusions when evidence changes. Yet when it comes to self-awareness—both personal and institutional—academia often struggles. The long and uncertain path from research question to publication can reinforce habits of sustained effort without a clear sense of impact.

Confidence plays an important role in academic work. *Self-efficacy* (Bandura, 1997) and grit (Duckworth et al., 2007) help explain why researchers persist despite repeated rejection and uncertainty. But confidence also has a downside. *The Dunning–Kruger effect* (Kruger & Dunning, 1999) shows that people frequently misjudge their own competence, and academia is no exception. Its system of grants, citations, and titles can reward visibility and persistence as much as substance, while years of effort are easily mistaken for significance. Empirical studies support this concern: Larivière et al. (2009) found that a large share of social science articles receive no citations at all, reminding us that productivity and influence are not the same thing.

In many other professions—such as electrical work or emergency medicine—feedback is immediate. Errors are visible, and competence is tested continuously. Academic work unfolds on a much slower timeline. Feedback is delayed, indirect, and often filtered through disciplinary norms. Pierre Bourdieu (1988) described this environment as a struggle for symbolic capital, while Paul Feyerabend (1975) questioned the rational self-image of science itself. Both point to a similar risk: that scholarship becomes inward-looking, where routines replace reflection and output substitutes for purpose.

When I visited Delphi as a student in 1989, the inscription on the Temple of Apollo—*gnōthi seauton*, "*know thyself*"—caught the visitor's attention. The phrase can be read not only as personal advice but as an epistemological warning. If we hope to study others, we must also examine our own assumptions, incentives, and blind spots. For social scientists in particular, this matters. Our subject is human behavior and human systems. When research fails to account for the researcher's own limitations, important aspects of reality are easily missed.

The Temple of Apollo. Photo taken by the author, on the Grand Tour of 1989

The tension between volume and impact is not new. Albert Einstein's *Annus Mirabilis* papers of 1905 are a familiar example.[1] Working outside a university, he published only a handful of articles, yet they transformed modern physics. The contrast is not meant as a model to imitate, but it raises a simple and uncomfortable question: what are we producing—and for whom?

Questions for Discussion: Knowing Ourselves in the Academic Mirror

1. What experiences have most shaped your self-awareness as a scholar?
2. Have you encountered situations where effort was mistaken for impact? What revealed the difference?
3. Why do so many academic works receive little or no attention despite years of work?
4. How does delayed or limited feedback shape how scholars evaluate their own contributions?
5. How can confidence and humility be balanced in academic life?
6. What larger purpose do you see in social science, and how can that purpose be assessed in practice?

The themes from the case box also speak to a deeper truth about human behavior—one that science has repeatedly confirmed. Cognitive psychology shows that much of what we do is not the product of deliberate, step-by-step reasoning, but of heuristics and automatic responses shaped by habit, emotion, and environment. Daniel Kahneman (2011) famously described this as *"System 1" thinking*—fast, intuitive, and often unconscious—overpowering the slower, more effortful *"System 2" reasoning*. This perspective challenges the comforting idea that we consistently act out of free will. Many of our so-called decisions are less the result of conscious deliberation than of ingrained patterns and immediate context.

This limitation extends to *memory*. While some individuals display impressive recall, most of us are far less reliable narrators of our own past than

[1] In 1905, Albert Einstein published four seminal papers in *Annalen der Physik*:

1. "On a Heuristic Viewpoint Concerning the Production and Transformation of Light"—introduced the concept of light quanta (photoelectric effect).
2. "On the Motion of Small Particles Suspended in Stationary Liquids Required by the Molecular-Kinetic Theory of Heat"—provided empirical evidence for the existence of atoms (Brownian motion).
3. "On the Electrodynamics of Moving Bodies"—formulated the special theory of relativity.
4. "Does the Inertia of a Body Depend Upon Its Energy Content?"—introduced the mass–energy equivalence formula ($E = mc^2$).

we think. Memory fades, distorts, and omits. Research confirms that aging impairs memory function (Salthouse, 2004), but even in our prime, recollections are shaped by emotion, narrative structure, and the passage of time. What we remember is not necessarily what happened—it's what fits the story we tell ourselves.

This presents a fundamental tension: if social scientists are subject to the same cognitive shortcuts, memory gaps, and biases as everyone else, what distinguishes their claims from everyday opinion? Are we merely flawed humans analyzing other flawed humans—with no added insight?

The difference, ideally, lies in structure. The scientific method exists not to eliminate bias altogether—which is impossible—but to contain it. By requiring systematic observation, falsifiable hypotheses, peer review, and transparency, social science creates a scaffold for climbing beyond our personal limitations (Merton, 1973; Popper, 1959). These structures don't guarantee truth, but they make error visible and correction possible.

Cognitive scientists like Stanovich and West (2000) emphasize that *reflective thinking* is not bias-free—it is self-correcting. The most reliable thinkers are not those without blind spots, but those who detect and adjust for them. Still, this is more ideal than norm. Even trained researchers fall prey to motivated reasoning (Kunda, 1990), theory-driven perception (Hastorf & Cantril, 1954), and confirmation bias (Nickerson, 1998). The value of the social sciences lies not in perfection, but in their organized struggle against distortion—a disciplined effort to understand a deeply biased species from within.

This is where the real challenge—and perhaps a humbling insight—emerges. Doing good science is extraordinarily difficult. Even with the best intentions, we misinterpret evidence, overgeneralize from small samples, and let our preconceptions steer our interpretations. These are not occasional slips; they are built into the very architecture of the human mind. Recognizing this does not diminish the value of the social sciences—it underscores why their methods matter so much. But it also points to an uncomfortable possibility: that machines, with their ability to process vast datasets without fatigue or ego, might in some areas be better equipped to detect patterns and minimize bias. Of course, human oversight remains indispensable for interpretation, context, and ethical judgment. Still, if the goal is to reduce error, the case for human–machine collaboration becomes hard to ignore.

If we accept that human inquiry is both fallible and slow, an obvious question follows: why persist? Why do so many devote years—often decades—to a pursuit where progress is slow, errors are frequent, and recognition is uncertain? For many, the answer is personal: curiosity, meaning, and the intrinsic satisfaction of understanding. But there are also social dimensions. From an evolutionary perspective, intellectual achievement can serve as a form of signaling—demonstrating intelligence, creativity, and persistence to peers and potential partners. In academic life, prestige is often tied to demonstrations of originality, expertise, and institutional affiliation. Whether these signals translate into genuine evolutionary advantage—or are simply costly displays with limited biological payoff—remains an open question.

If intellectual achievement functions partly as signaling, then academics are not exempt. Looking more broadly at the profession, it is not clear that they are motivated by fundamentally different incentives than other groups. Researchers, like professionals in many fields, also seek security, recognition, good salaries, and the personal appeal that comes with status. Perhaps this was less visible in earlier generations, when the number of academics was smaller and the vocation carried a stronger aura of exclusivity. Today, with the vast expansion of higher education, the differences are harder to discern.

This is also why I see the rise of artificial intelligence not only as a challenge, but potentially as a blessing. Much of what occupies academic life today—routine analysis, synthesis of existing knowledge, even production of standard articles—can increasingly be carried out by machines. AI may reduce the sheer number of researchers while raising the bar for the kinds of projects humans undertake. Those who remain will likely focus on more complex, integrative, and creative challenges—tasks where judgment, wisdom, and reflective depth are required.

Seen through the lens of sexual selection, some of the traits that drive ambition—competitiveness, risk-taking, assertiveness—persist not because they are rational, but because they once conferred reproductive advantage (Darwin, 1871). Traits associated with testosterone, for example, can be attractive in short-term mating contexts but also correlate with aggression and recklessness (Book et al., 2001). If academic traits such as deep thinking, patience, and verbal nuance are not consistently rewarded in evolutionary terms, they may remain rare—even if they are socially important. This is not about blaming one gender for the traits of another, but about recognizing a feedback loop in evolutionary history: preferences shape traits, and those traits in turn shape outcomes. Evolution does not select for what is wise; it selects for what works in a given environment.

From this perspective, a promotion may signal less about intellectual depth than about skill in navigating the selection pressures of academia. Evolution rewards survival in context, not necessarily wisdom or originality.

These same dynamics shape research practice. A key vulnerability is our reliance on self-reported data. People rarely describe their actions or preferences with full accuracy. They overstate their virtues, underreport their flaws, and often give answers they think will be socially acceptable. This "*social desirability bias*" (Fisher, 1993) can distort entire studies. If researchers fail to account for these distortions—both in their subjects and in themselves—they risk mistaking aspiration for reality.

For this reason, many fields have moved toward greater use of observational methods. Paco Underhill's (1999) seminal "*science of shopping*" showed how in-store behavior often contradicts what people say in surveys. Watching how customers navigated aisles, interacted with displays, and responded to spatial cues revealed patterns invisible to self-report. In the digital era, the principle is the same—only magnified. Every click, scroll, and abandoned cart generates behavioral data. As Arora et al. (2008) demonstrate, these passive streams can expose unconscious habits and friction points in real time. Unlike surveys filtered through memory and self-presentation, digital footprints reveal the actual rhythms of decision-making.

This lesson applies well beyond commerce. The social sciences study a species whose greatest strength—symbolic thought—is bound up with its greatest weaknesses: overconfidence, bias, and narrative illusion. Our self-understanding is often wrong, our motives mixed, and our judgments clouded. And yet we can design methods to detect these flaws. That paradox is a source of both humility and hope. The aim is not omniscience, but insight grounded in self-awareness.

But self-awareness also requires us to look squarely at the impulses we prefer to downplay. Beneath our symbolic capacities and institutional structures lie ancient drives—territoriality, dominance, aggression—that still shape behavior in both subtle and obvious ways. They surface in political struggles, in boardroom maneuvering, and in everyday disputes. However civilized the setting, these forces have not disappeared.

This brings us to a crucial but often underplayed dimension of human behavior: the role of aggression and power in shaping social dynamics.

2.1.1 Aggression and Power Dynamics

Have you ever found yourself in a situation where someone was just too much—rude, dismissive, or aggressive—and felt a sudden, almost instinctive urge to respond with physical force? This reaction, though rarely acted upon in modern life, is not as uncommon as we might like to admit—especially among men. Research in evolutionary psychology and neuroscience suggests that such impulses are ancient, deeply rooted in our species' evolutionary history. Males in particular are more prone to *reactive aggression*, a biologically prepared response that evolved to deal with perceived threats to status, territory, or survival (Archer, 2004; Daly & Wilson, 1988). Testosterone has been shown to correlate with *dominance-seeking* and aggressive behavior in social conflict situations (Carré & McCormick, 2008), and brain imaging studies reveal that the amygdala—the brain's emotional threat detector—can activate rapidly in response to perceived social slights, even before the rational brain has time to assess the situation fully (Coccaro et al., 2007).

These reactions are not limited to moments of physical danger. Even minor social insults can trigger what some researchers call "*status defense mechanisms*," pushing individuals—again, often males—toward aggressive or domineering behavior rather than reflection or dialogue (Fischer & Roseman, 2007). This helps explain why violence often erupts in contexts that seem, on the surface, trivial: a glance, a word, and an insult. The impulse to "solve" the situation through brute force is not a cultural aberration; it is a deeply human tendency.

One of the most defining yet least acknowledged traits of our species, then, is our exceptional level of aggression, particularly toward other species. Unlike nearly every other animal on Earth, humans have no significant *natural predators*. This lack of external threat has not led to peaceful coexistence but, rather, has enabled us to become the dominant source of threat to virtually every other species. We hunt not only for food but, in many cases, for sport, status, or mere entertainment, behaviors that are exceptionally rare in the natural world (Wrangham, 2019). This violence is not just physical but ecological: from factory farming and deforestation to pollution and mass extinction, the human footprint is etched in the suffering and elimination of others.

Understanding these patterns does not excuse them. But it does reveal how deeply entwined they are with human evolution and cognition. To be human is not only to reason and cooperate, but also to battle with impulses that evolved in a very different world—one where immediate physical dominance could mean survival. In a civilized society, learning to channel or restrain those impulses may be one of the most important—and difficult—achievements of culture.

The deeper problem is that this aggressive impulse is not easily removed—it is the product of millions of years of evolution. Even in modern societies, traits associated with dominance and assertiveness continue to be rewarded, both socially and reproductively. Evolutionary psychologists have argued that female mate choice has historically played a role in reinforcing these traits.

Women tend, on average, to prefer males who exhibit signs of strength, confidence, and status—traits that have historically correlated with aggressive tendencies, particularly in youth (Buss, 1989; Wilson & Daly, 1985). This is not a moral failing, but an evolutionary pattern. The result, however, is again a feedback loop: the more aggression contributes to reproductive success, the more it is selected and sustained across generations. In other words, both *biological inheritance* and *social reinforcement* continue to privilege traits that may have served us in the past but prove maladaptive in the context of global interdependence and long-term cooperation.

Some of the more unsettling manifestations of this pattern can be seen in the phenomenon known as *hybristophilia*—a sexual or romantic attraction to individuals who have committed violent crimes. This has been documented in numerous psychological studies and clinical observations (Meloy, 1998; Schlesinger, 2000). Notorious criminals, including serial killers, have received love letters, marriage proposals, and fan followings, even while serving life sentences. While extreme cases are rare, they highlight an enduring evolutionary logic: traits such as dominance, boldness, and fearlessness—though socially disruptive—can still function as mating signals under certain conditions. Some evolutionary psychologists argue that these traits historically indicated an ability to provide protection, assert control, or compete effectively for resources (Buss & Shackelford, 1997; Daly & Wilson, 1988). For some women, particularly those with histories of trauma or attachment insecurity, such traits may unconsciously trigger arousal or fascination (Kenrick et al., 2003). From an evolutionary perspective, the persistence of these preferences reflects selection pressures from ancestral environments, where physical strength and assertiveness were correlated with survival. Today, however, these same preferences may perpetuate maladaptive relationship patterns and reinforce cycles of violence, especially when not balanced by traits associated with empathy, cooperation, and long-term investment.

Changing such deeply rooted behavioral tendencies is possible, but it unfolds slowly—typically over many generations. While *cultural evolution* moves faster than *biological change*, it cannot simply be engineered or directed from above without serious risks. Attempts at top-down social reform often backfire, introducing new forms of control and undermining the very freedoms they aim to promote. Instead, shifts in behavior emerge more sustainably when driven by voluntary learning, ethical reasoning, and open debate—not enforced norms. It is through education, transparent institutions, and example-based leadership that more cooperative forms of behavior can gain ground.

Research shows that societies with stronger legal frameworks and more stable civic norms tend to see lower rates of interpersonal violence (Eisner, 2003; Pinker, 2011), but these gains come from systems that respect individual dignity, not from artificially favoring one group over another. Rewarding prosocial traits must never come at the cost of merit or freedom. We must be cautious not to equate "less aggressive" with "more deserving." The goal is not to replace one hierarchy with another.

Even with efforts to curb aggression and promote cooperative norms, the legacy of our species' dominance remains visible on a planetary scale. The same traits that once ensured our survival—strategic intelligence, tool use, group cohesion—have enabled us to reshape entire ecosystems, often without understanding or controlling the consequences. Our impact is no longer confined to social interactions or local disputes; it now extends to the very fabric of life on Earth.

As a result, humans are responsible for a vast number of species extinctions, both directly through overhunting and indirectly through habitat destruction, climate change, and pollution. According to Ceballos et al. (2017), we are currently driving what some scientists refer to as the *sixth mass extinction*, with species disappearing at rates tens to hundreds of times higher than the natural background rate.

Ironically, we often exaggerate the dangers posed by other animals. Popular media has vilified predators like sharks and crocodiles, portraying them as fearsome killers. However, the statistics tell another story. Globally, sharks kill fewer than ten people per year on average, while humans kill an estimated 100 million sharks annually, mostly for their fins (Worm et al., 2013). Similarly, crocodiles are indeed dangerous in some regions, particularly in Africa and Southeast Asia, but the American alligator (Alligator mississippiensis), once hunted to near extinction, has adapted well to human-managed habitats in places like the southeastern United States. As I was able to observe firsthand during a recent guided safari on the Mississippi River—touching, if only for a few seconds, the lower jaw of a five-meter-long beast—these animals, in controlled environments, often become habituated to human presence and exhibit surprisingly docile behavior when left unprovoked (Elsey & Trosclair, 2008).

Our tendency to construct imaginary threats from relatively harmless animals may serve a psychological function—perhaps to satisfy our need for danger and heroism in a world where we no longer face real predators. But the real danger is us. Our collective behavior has transformed ecosystems, wiped out species, and probably altered the climate. As apex predators and ecosystem engineers, humans are arguably the most dangerous species ever to inhabit the planet, not due to individual malice, but because of the scale and momentum of our shared actions.

And yet, who would suspect that, just by looking at our disarmingly gentle faces? Or maybe that is precisely the problem: in our own minds, we are sweet, compassionate beings—while the crocodile is monstrous, primitive, a symbol of lurking danger. But how do we look to the crocodile? If it could form impressions, it might justifiably see us as the terrifying, irrational force—agile, loud, unpredictable, and lethal in ways it cannot comprehend. Perhaps the horror is mutual, only we're the ones in denial.

So, to fully understand humanity, we must begin with its constraints—biological, cognitive, and emotional. Aggression is one of our core characteristics. It may be channeled, sublimated, or ritualized, but it never disappears. Knowing this, social scientists must always account for it as an explanatory variable. People do not go to war solely for resources or strategy. Sometimes they go to war because they cannot help themselves. Backed into a corner, humiliated, or enraged, the human brain reverts to ancestral modes of reaction—and the rational façade falls away.

Case in a Box: The Illusion of Rational Wars

Turn on the television during a political crisis, and you will see rows of experts explaining the conflict. Their words are filled with theories of deterrence, balance of power, economic sanctions, and institutional breakdowns. The more educated they are, the more terms and frameworks they can deploy. Each conflict becomes an opportunity to demonstrate analytical mastery. But this performance can itself be a dangerous bias.

In reality, wars are not always the result of grand strategy or rational calculation. They can be triggered by humiliation, rage, or misperception—by emotions more than interests. Sometimes they begin because a leader misreads history, clings to a grievance, or feels cornered. It could be that simple, and that irrational. Yet such explanations rarely appear on the news. Television pundits compete not to uncover the messy human emotions that drive conflict, but to show off their *cleverness*, to prove they know more theories than the next expert. The result is a distorted picture: wars are explained as rational chess moves, when often they are closer to outbursts at the edge of reason.

And one wonders what the aggressor himself thinks when he sees these analyses. Perhaps he smiles at the thought that scholars and journalists are crediting him with strategies he never considered. Or, if he lacks humor, he may even feel honored—that such elaborate theories could be attributed to his actions. Over time, the danger grows that the real motives, however impulsive or emotional they were, become obscured even to the aggressor himself, who starts to believe the analysts more than his own recollections. And so, the truth may in the end be lost to all parties—the public, the experts, and, perhaps most ironically, the perpetrators themselves.

Questions for Reflection

1. Why do political experts so often favor theoretical or rational explanations over emotional ones when discussing war?
2. What are the risks of projecting rationality onto conflicts that may, in fact, be driven by irrational or emotional motives?
3. How might public understanding of wars change if media emphasized the emotional and psychological roots of conflict as much as the strategic ones?

And yet, explanations that highlight these evolved emotional reflexes are rarely integrated into mainstream analyses in political science, economics, or international relations. Instead, expert discourse often prefers the safety of abstractions—strategies, equilibria, or doctrines—while neglecting the raw and unstable forces that actually drive human behavior. This is a failure not only of theory, but also of imagination. To understand what humans do, we must first understand what humans are.

2.1.2 Prestige, Competition, and the Erosion of the Self

Studying human behavior is notoriously difficult, especially because our actions often defy logic, prediction, and consistency. Unlike other species whose behavior patterns follow relatively stable environmental triggers, human behavior is shaped by complex and sometimes contradictory factors, including culture, cognition, and social context. We often engage in unpredictable or even irrational actions, sometimes simply for the pleasure of surprising ourselves or others. The psychological literature identifies this phenomenon under frameworks like *novelty-seeking* (Zuckerman, 1994) and *sensation-seeking behavior*, which correlate with dopamine-driven reward systems.

One of the more robust findings in social psychology is the disjunction between *stated attitudes* and *actual behavior*. Ajzen and Fishbein's Theory of Planned Behavior (1980) already pointed out that intention does not reliably predict behavior. As we mentioned, people often say what they think is socially desirable, especially in formal settings like surveys, yet act in entirely different ways when their true preferences or incentives are engaged. This phenomenon is exacerbated in competitive environments such as the workplace. Here, individuals may present themselves as collaborative or ethical but act primarily in self-serving ways to maximize personal career advancement (Aronson, 1999; Gino et al., 2010). This dynamic is not confined to business or politics; the social sciences themselves operate within competitive structures of funding, publication, and prestige, and there is little evidence to suggest that researchers behave markedly differently from professionals in other fields.

What is perhaps most surprising is that we often expect otherwise. This expectation arises, in part, from the narratives and recruitment messaging we are exposed to, the company brochures, the "about us" pages, and the glossy career videos that frame the job as a noble pursuit of shared values. These messages are not necessarily false—but they are incomplete. They reflect the image the organization wants to project, not the full complexity of workplace dynamics—and this often leads to bewilderment, confusion, and not seldom disappointment on the part of early-career employees.

What's more troubling, as I discovered early on as a student, is that this distinction between portrayed ideals and actual behavior is rarely made explicit in business education. Business schools often claim to prepare students for "*the real world*," yet they too can fall into the trap of reproducing the same sanitized narratives that organizations promote. The messy truths—conflicts of interest, status games, power plays, unspoken norms—are acknowledged only in passing, if at all. This gap between image and reality is not just misleading; it makes it harder for young professionals to anticipate and navigate the real moral and strategic dilemmas they will inevitably face.

Of all the disciplines I studied, the most unrealistic was human resource management (HRM). It was often presented as a stack of analytical forms: documents to be filled out by applicants and employees, processed internally by HR, and fed into a system that would eventually produce a neat ranking of candidates. The ideal was objectivity, impartiality, and meritocracy, expressed through scores and grids. In practice, I soon discovered, decisions were rarely so tidy. Hiring often came down to something much harder to formalize: chemistry between people, shared backgrounds, or implicit trust. Even diplomas, which we were told carried decisive weight, functioned more like business cards—credentials that opened the door but did not determine the final choice. The contrast between the model and the reality could not have been sharper.

This disjunction between how work is portrayed and how it is actually experienced creates not just disappointment, but a deeper cognitive dissonance. We enter professional life believing in collaboration, transparency, and shared purpose—values we were told to expect. But over time, we learn to navigate a world shaped more by appearances than ideals. The result is a subtle erosion of authenticity. People don't necessarily lie outright, but they adapt. They learn to say what is expected, do what is rewarded, and suppress what might be true but inconvenient.

This dichotomy between *public virtue* and *private behavior* is reinforced by the structure of modern life. In professional settings, people often adopt strategic behavior—saying one thing while meaning another—out of necessity or ambition. In sociological terms, this reflects Erving Goffman's theory of *impression management*, wherein individuals consciously perform certain roles to control how they are perceived by others (Goffman, 1959). The result is that many workplace interactions are marked more by performance and loyalty to hierarchy than by authentic dialogue.

At home, however, human behavior often shifts. Family and close community relations typically promote more altruistic behavior, shaped by kin selection and reciprocal altruism (Trivers, 1971). This evolutionary dynamic suggests we are more generous with those who share our genes or who are part of our close social circle, especially when long-term relationships are at stake. Yet even among neighbors, we prefer to maintain some social distance to avoid potential conflicts, another reflection of our *strategic social orientation*.

Case in a Box: The Meaning of Home

The home holds a unique place in human life. It is more than a shelter—it is the private stage where we can step away from public performance, where roles dissolve, and where we are most likely to be ourselves—unguarded, emotional, and sometimes contradictory. Ideally, it is where we can retreat, recharge, and relate on our own terms with people we trust.

Yet in reality, many carry the logic of the workplace or marketplace into the home, turning even intimate spaces into arenas for control, efficiency, or competition. When that happens, the home loses its role as a safe refugium, and the line between public and private erodes. This is particularly distressing, since it means the individual never truly rests but remains caught in a continuous wheel of performance and pretension—always managing impressions, even in the very space meant to restore them.

From an evolutionary perspective, the idea of a "safe haven" is rooted in basic needs: protection for sleep, intimacy, care, and food storage. In modern societies, the home also carries symbolic and psychological weight. It is often the largest financial investment we make—a product of years, sometimes decades, of labor. It represents permanence, autonomy, and control in an otherwise uncertain world. For many, it is the one space they truly own—legally, emotionally, and existentially.

Growing up, I often heard my father say, half-jokingly, "I'm going out to collect 50-note bills" when heading to work.[2] It was his way of stating a simple truth: work is not only about ambition but about provisioning. Like birds gathering food for the nest or squirrels storing nuts for winter, the home was the reason one worked.

The home also serves as a moral boundary. At work, we perform; in public, we conform. At home, we are known—and we know others. This is where human contradictions are most visible: generosity and selfishness, nurture and neglect, comfort and conflict. Home is not always idyllic, but even its imperfections can offer a kind of honesty that public life rarely allows. It is also, probably and hopefully, the place where we can most fully be ourselves—a realm of high authenticity. Because we do not have to put on a face or play social games, home can be profoundly relaxing, allowing us to let our guard down and engage without pretense.

Seen as both a physical space and a social construct, the home reveals how we present ourselves differently across environments. If Goffman was right that much of life is theatrical, then the home is the backstage—messy at times, but real.

Questions for Reflection

1. When do you feel most like yourself—at home, at work, or somewhere else? Why?
2. In what ways does your behavior at home differ from how you act in public or at work?
3. Do you agree that the home is the only place where most people can truly be themselves? Why or why not?
4. What roles does your home play in your sense of identity, security, and freedom?
5. How is work emotionally connected to the idea of "providing for the home" in your own experience or family? Is this still relevant today?
6. If the home is a place of honesty, does that make public life inherently deceptive—or simply a different form of adaptation?

If the home is our primary refuge, friendships form the bridges that connect us beyond it. While family ties are given, friendships are chosen; relationships that extend our circle of trust into the wider world.

[2] At the time, 50 Norwegian kroner was roughly equivalent to 10 US dollars.

Friends occupy a unique space in human social life—situated between kin and strangers. From an evolutionary standpoint, friendship functions as a form of *reciprocal alliance*. Unlike kinship ties grounded in shared genes (Hamilton, 1964), friendships are voluntary, based on mutual trust, emotional closeness, and reciprocity over time (Silk, 2003). They allow humans to build coalitions beyond the family unit, enhancing survival through mutual aid, information sharing, and emotional support—especially during times of uncertainty or stress (Cosmides & Tooby, 1992). In ancestral environments, friendships likely served as social insurance: individuals who maintained loyal friendships had better chances of receiving help when injured, sick, or socially excluded (Hruschka, 2010). Even in non-human primates, long-term affiliative bonds correlate with increased survival and reproductive success (Silk et al., 2009), suggesting deep evolutionary roots for friendship.

At the same time, it is easy to overestimate how much one can rely on friends in practice. Most people are willing to offer small favors, but once help requires sustained effort, financial cost, or time beyond a few minutes, motivation often wanes. Economic research on altruism shows that willingness to help drops sharply when the personal costs increase (Andreoni, 1990; Fehr & Fischbacher, 2003). In modern societies, we have solved this limitation by converting effort into employment: by paying people, we secure not only their labor but also their reliability over time. Wages formalize reciprocity, turning it from uncertain goodwill into *structured obligation*. Employment contracts, reinforced by legal mechanisms such as non-disclosure agreements, even make it possible to demand silence or loyalty—things that friendship alone cannot guarantee.

Yet money also has its limits. When it comes to ultimate sacrifices—risking one's life, going to war, or enduring prolonged hardship—most people will not act solely for payment. Here, loyalty to higher-order identities, such as nation, religion, or shared ideology, becomes decisive. Research on military cohesion shows that soldiers fight less for financial incentives than for commitment to comrades and country (Shils & Janowitz, 1948; Wong et al., 2003). National identity and collective devotion, not monetary reward, provide the binding force in such contexts (Anderson, 1983; Tajfel & Turner, 1979). This contrast is revealing: while money secures predictable cooperation in everyday life, deep sacrifices require meaning, belonging, and symbolic commitments that transcend material exchange. Together, these dynamics illustrate both the power and the limits of friendship as a social glue, and why societies have developed multiple overlapping systems—economic, political, and cultural—to sustain cooperation at scale.

Military units, in particular, have long understood this principle. Armies deliberately cultivate solidarity not only through training but also through rituals, ceremonies, and the use of uniforms, insignia, and symbolic markers loaded with meaning. These practices are designed to bind recruits emotionally, reinforcing a sense of belonging that goes beyond individual interest and ties them to the group's fate.

Historically, friendships have also had instrumental functions, such as facilitating trade, mediating political relationships, and reinforcing social cohesion in communities (Laursen & Hartup, 2002). Today, friendships serve not only as buffers against loneliness and psychological distress (Demir & Weitekamp, 2007) but also play critical roles in identity formation and *everyday meaning-making*. They offer a context for intimacy and loyalty without legal or institutional constraint. In contemporary societies marked by mobility and social fluidity, friendships may increasingly compensate for weakened familial and communal ties. Their flexible, self-chosen nature makes them one of the most adaptive and enduring features of human social life, reflecting our evolved social minds and the need for trust-based cooperation.

The diagram below offers a stylized example of how such social attachments might relate to authenticity over the life course. This is not a fixed pattern—different individuals will plot differently—but it illustrates one possible trajectory. In this example, the person is relatively true to themselves as a young adult, becomes least authentic in midlife—caught up in competition, prestige-seeking, and the "games" of professional and social life—and then regains authenticity in later life, freer from such pressures. Across all three stages, authenticity is highest in relation to the self, somewhat lower with family, lower still with friends, and substantially lower toward the public and workplace competitors (Fig. 2.1).

Much of adult life unfolds within two primary social habitats: the workplace and the home. We spend the majority of our waking hours in these two environments, and the behavioral demands in each are strikingly different. At work, roles are formalized, goals are often competitive, and social interactions tend to be transactional or hierarchical. At home, by contrast, interactions are shaped more by emotional bonds, kinship, and long-term reciprocity. These divergent settings activate different behavioral strategies, and understanding how we adapt between them is crucial to grasping modern human life.

Even the transitional zone between them—our daily commute—plays a mediating role. How we move between home and work, whether by car, train, bus, or bike, reflects geography, income, and infrastructure. With the advent of autonomous vehicles, this boundary may blur further, reshaping not only

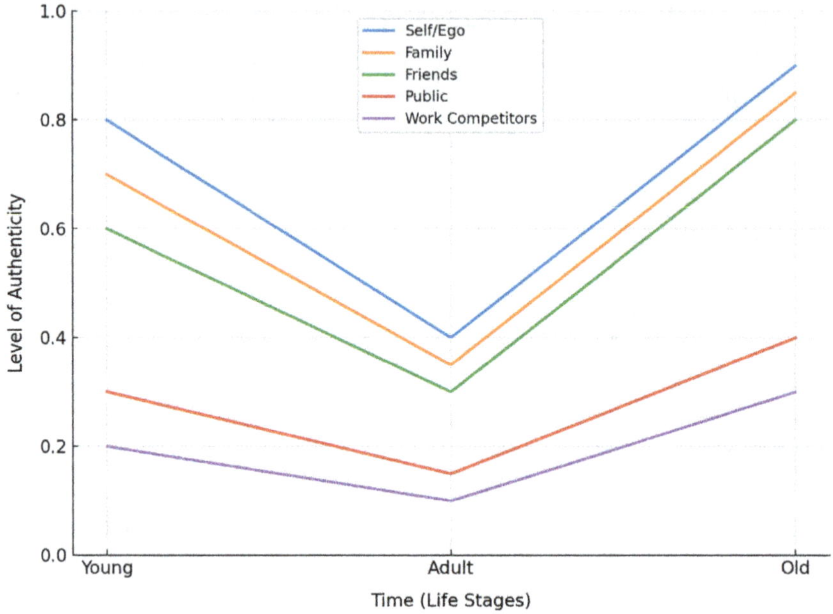

Fig. 2.1 Authenticity across the life course: a stylized example of shifting social attachments

work-life balance but also patterns of urban settlement and the structure of our social routines (Litman, 2023).

But the commute is not just physical—it's also social. During this transition, we encounter a third group: *the public*. These are not colleagues who compete with us, nor family members with whom we share deep bonds and history, but strangers with whom we momentarily share space. Because we do not have to deal with them personally, and because they pose no threat to our status, livelihood, or identity, we often adopt an idealized and cooperative attitude toward them. We behave as if we are all in it together—offering small courtesies such as holding the door, letting others off the train before stepping in, or giving up a seat for someone in need—even though I have noticed that such gestures are becoming rarer, with what appears to be a gradual degradation of *everyday virtues*. Hopefully, this decline is only momentary and part of a larger social cycle, where norms of decency contract and expand over time. Still, this transitional space remains one of the few domains where we regularly brush up against strangers and, however briefly, enact the possibility of a *civil society*.

These fleeting exchanges—on the street, in cafés, at public events—are not just about courtesy; they also form part of the broader social arena where alliances, friendships, and even romances can begin. This is especially evident in young adulthood, a life stage often marked by intense social activity centered on mate-seeking. Think of all that flirting, hanging out where the boys or girls are, going to nightclubs, bars, and social events—remember? Time-use studies and ethnographic research confirm that this phase typically involves a *high investment in interactions* designed to maximize peer contact and potential partner encounters.

These behaviors, while culturally variable, are remarkably consistent across societies (Schlegel & Barry, 1991), reflecting an evolutionary phase of high reproductive and social energy. While men often display more *overt signaling behavior* (e.g., through risk-taking or display of resources), it is generally women who make the final choice in mate selection, a pattern well-documented in *sexual selection theory* (Buss, 2003). However, many males mistakenly believe they are equal participants in the selection process; some even assume they are the ones making the actual choice, confusing their active pursuit with having the final say.

Males tend to focus on quite different traits when evaluating potential partners. In general, they place greater emphasis on physical attractiveness, youth, and specific features associated with fertility, such as waist-to-hip ratio or facial symmetry (Buss, 1989; Singh, 1993). These preferences tend to apply across social strata; a man may be equally smitten by a cocktail waitress or a bus driver, provided she meets certain *visual criteria*. Her income or social status often doesn't factor into his decision-making.

Women, by contrast, tend to be much more selective. Their criteria usually include a mix of status, income, intelligence, ambition, emotional maturity, height (yes, taller is better unless he's a millionaire), and potential for long-term resource provision and parenting (Fisman et al., 2006; Li et al., 2016). Simply put, the female "checklist" tends to be long and multifaceted, while the male version is short and visually driven.

A likely explanation lies in evolutionary biology: women face higher *reproductive costs*, including pregnancy, childbirth, and often a larger share of child-rearing. This asymmetry means that for much of human history, women who chose poorly could end up raising a child alone—while the man, as has frequently occurred, vanished into the fog of war, trade, or irresponsibility. Hence, female choosiness isn't superficial—it's strategic. The irony lies in the tragic mismatch: men often think they are choosing, while women are actually doing the selection—just from a longer, better-researched menu.

This selectivity also shapes everyday interactions. Women, knowing that choice carries higher risks, are often more cautious in social encounters, even in something as simple as eye contact with strangers on the street. Men, by contrast, can afford to be more indiscriminate—smiling or being friendly toward many—because the costs of doing so are relatively low. Social psychology research confirms that women tend to be more selective and risk-aware in both mating and casual social behavior (Buss & Schmitt, 1993; Haselton & Buss, 2000). Men, meanwhile, show greater willingness toward unselective social engagement, consistent with lower reproductive investment and risk. What looks like a small difference in public behavior reflects a deep evolutionary asymmetry in strategy and cost.

Once a partner is found, many couples move in together and establish a home as large and well equipped as their resources allow; what we might call the phase leading up to *peak material accumulation*. But this pattern does not last forever. As we grow older, we often begin to simplify life, to *downsize*, and to adjust our surroundings in preparation for a stage of life marked by reduced physical capacity and shifting priorities.

Aging thus reshapes the *human habitat*. Many choose smaller, single-level homes to accommodate reduced mobility and ease daily routines. Yet with the rise of robotics and AI, this trend could reverse: elderly individuals may increasingly remain in larger homes, supported by domestic robots that perform tasks once handled by younger relatives, servants, or care workers (Broadbent et al., 2009). In this way, we may be witnessing a new phase in the long historical evolution from human to technological caregiving. Well, we'll see.

Seen together, these settings—from the intimacy of home to the anonymity of public encounters—form a shifting social landscape that changes as we age. Each comes with its own behavioral rules and evolutionary purpose, shaping how we relate to others at different stages of life. Table 2.1 summarizes these contexts and their biological underpinnings:

Hold on, you might say—that's not what human life is really like. Isn't that a cynical view of how we spend our days, how we experience love, connection, and meaning? Really? Are you sure? Or is that your warm ideals speaking? It is comforting to imagine ourselves as guided mainly by affection, moral values, or destiny—or by the carefree notion that we "just want to have fun." Above all, we like to think of ourselves as beings of free will, seated in the cockpit with all the control buttons within reach. In reality, it is often more accurate to see ourselves not as the pilot, but as part of the airplane itself—moved by forces and constraints we neither chose nor fully control. That is an uncomfortable thought, and so we tend to ignore it, but the cost of doing so is a diminished understanding of social and societal reality. Much of human social behavior—including partner selection—is shaped by evolved instincts, reshaped by culture but never fully erased.

Table 2.1 Social contexts across the lifespan

Social context	Typical partners	Nature of relationship	Behavioral tendencies	Evolutionary/biological function
Home	Kin, close family, cohabitants	Involuntary (kinship) or chosen (partners) but high interdependence	Altruism, care, conflict resolution, emotional openness	Kin selection (Hamilton, 1964); reciprocal altruism (Trivers, 1971); protection, provisioning, reproduction
Friendship	Non-kin, voluntary allies	Voluntary, trust-based, often long-term	Reciprocity, emotional support, coalition-building	Social insurance, alliance formation, mutual aid; extends cooperation beyond kin
Workplace	Colleagues, superiors, subordinates	Role-based, often competitive	Strategic cooperation, impression management, conflict avoidance	Resource acquisition, status signaling, dominance hierarchies
Strangers (Public Sphere)	Unrelated, no prior relationship	Anonymous, brief encounters	Courtesy, norm compliance, avoidance of conflict	Group cohesion, reputation management, potential alliance/mate opportunities
Mate-Seeking Spaces	Potential partners, peers	Courtship-oriented, selective	Flirting, display of traits/resources	Sexual selection (Buss, 2003); reproductive fitness, partner choice
Old Age/Downsized Life	Spouse, adult children, close friends, caregivers (human or robotic)	Reduced network, high reliance on trust	Conservation of energy, increased dependence	Survival support in late life, intergenerational resource transfer

Acknowledging these patterns does not reduce us to biology. It simply means that behind every social ritual—dating, courtship, domestic life—there are deeper forces at play: energy, status, sex, security, and the long arc of evolutionary cost and benefit. The romantic image may endure, but it often floats atop a structure of calculation and adaptation. That is not cynicism—it is complexity. And learning to hold both views at once—to see the poetry and the pragmatism together—is perhaps what it means to grow up, and to see ourselves more clearly through the lens of science.

For the social sciences, making this leap would not only mark real progress, it would amount to a giant step forward. Understanding human behavior in evolutionary terms would help us live better lives—not because it would erase tension or conflict, but because it would give us a clearer sense of why things happen the way they do. Such clarity may not dissolve every struggle, but it can turn confusion into comprehension, and blind reaction into more deliberate response. And to see how these dynamics play out most clearly, we must examine the environments in which human lives are actually lived today.

2.1.3 The City as Human Habitat

Despite speaking in global terms, most humans live in tightly constrained geographic spaces, predominantly in urban areas. According to UN data (2018), over 55% of the global population now resides in cities. These artificial environments are not "*natural habitats*" in any evolutionary sense, yet they are increasingly where humans find food, work, and mates. Cities offer higher economic opportunities and social density but are also associated with stress, social fragmentation, and environmental costs (Lederbogen et al., 2011).

At the same time, city life profoundly alters how we interact with others. In urban settings, we are exposed to far more people from the category we earlier referred to as "the public"—those anonymous others we pass on the street without a word, glance, or nod. Have you noticed how it hurts a bit when you pass someone and neither of you acknowledges the other? That quiet sting tells you something about your nature. We are not built to be invisible to one another. Recognition—even something as small as eye contact or a nod—is a fundamental *social cue* that affirms our existence. When it's absent, day after day, it can wear on us in subtle ways. This is part of what makes city life emotionally taxing, even for those who thrive professionally in urban environments.

In smaller towns or rural settings, it is still common to greet strangers with a "hi" or "good morning"—or, as was customary a generation or two ago among men, to tip one's hat (and, in the case of meeting someone of much higher social rank or authority, to remove it entirely). But in large cities, such informal acknowledgments are rare. We develop a kind of perceptual filter to block out others, treating them as background noise. What this does to us psychologically is still poorly understood. Humans are wired for recognition and acknowledgment. Being ignored—consistently and *en masse*—probably leaves subtle but lasting effects on our sense of identity, worth, and belonging.

Paradoxically, while cities are celebrated in much of the academic literature for their diversity, innovation, and dynamism (Glaeser, 2011), less attention is given to the emotional and existential toll of anonymity. Some research suggests that urban life correlates with higher levels of loneliness, anxiety, and mental health problems (Gruebner et al., 2017; Peen et al., 2010). And yet the nostalgia for rural or small-town life is often dismissed as backward-looking or romantic. Perhaps this bias—favoring the urban, the cosmopolitan, and the networked—is itself a product of who writes the literature: people who live and work in cities, and who may have unconsciously come to prefer the very environment that shapes their thinking.

More broadly, rural areas have often been framed as representing tradition and continuity, while cities are associated with progress and modernity. This symbolic divide can shape how ideas are judged: what is "modern" may be promoted simply because it is new, while what is "conservative" may be dismissed without assessing its quality or track record. Cities, with their dense networks of institutions and media, frequently serve as testing grounds for social and cultural experiments—sometimes without long-term evaluation of their consequences. Many residents do not necessarily embrace the values most visible in their surroundings; they live in cities for work, education, or convenience, while quietly accepting—or enduring—the trade-offs. These trade-offs can include higher stress, reduced privacy, and weaker community ties (Evans, 2003; Lederbogen et al., 2011), costs that are often overlooked in public debate.

This urban favoritism is not just incidental—it reflects deeper social and academic hierarchies. Rural and small-town environments are often portrayed as slow-moving, culturally marginal, or politically parochial (Cramer, 2016; Wuthnow, 2018), while cities are framed as diverse, dynamic, and globally connected. Much of this narrative stems from economic and institutional centralization: wealth, education, and decision-making power are concentrated in metropolitan hubs. As a result, academics, journalists, and policymakers—many of whom live in cities—can conflate their own environment with societal progress at large, creating a structural blind spot that undervalues rural knowledge, practices, and lived experience. Even environmental arguments that cities are more energy efficient due to density (Glaeser & Kahn, 2010) may obscure the emotional toll of anonymity, noise, and overstimulation. Meanwhile, small communities often sustain forms of social capital, mutual care, and cultural continuity that are harder to maintain in high-density urban life (Putnam, 2000).

Over the past few generations, the deindustrialization of Western cities has significantly reduced industrial employment, leading many municipalities to rely more heavily on the public sector—yet even this support often stems from economic transfers rather than local prosperity. In cities such as Malmö, Sweden, the collapse of shipbuilding and other heavy industries in the 1980s and 1990s prompted post-industrial redevelopment strategies focused on service industries, environmental renewal, and infrastructure investment (Baeten et al., 2010a, 2010b; Hall & Hubbard, 1998). However, socioeconomic disparities and polarization remain. This divergence between image and economic reality is mirrored elsewhere: many deindustrialized cities depend heavily on state support despite outward signs of vibrancy.

Yet one might ask whether people are genuinely happy living in these reimagined post-industrial cities at all. Many residents appear to prefer the suburbs or smaller communities, where life feels closer, more personal, and less anonymous. Research on urban-suburban migration patterns shows that families in particular tend to move outward once children arrive, seeking more space, perceived safety, and stronger local networks (Champion, 2001; Niedomysl, 2010). This suggests a paradox: while planners continue to invest in making cities vibrant cultural and economic hubs, many citizens seem to value the intimacy and autonomy of smaller-scale living. Indeed, suburban environments often offer not only practical advantages—gardens, schools, shorter commutes—but also a sense of everyday control, with more direct channels for political influence and economic agency at the local level (Gallagher, 2013). Some scholars argue that this mismatch reflects a longstanding bias in planning thought: the conviction that cities are the natural home of progress, innovation, and modernity (Glaeser, 2011; Jacobs, 1961). But if we take migration patterns seriously, it may be that cities function best as centers of work, commerce, and culture, while family life and long-term settlement gravitate toward smaller-scale, suburban, or semi-rural settings.

Research shows that deindustrialization often brings long-lasting social costs, including unemployment, crime, reduced tax revenues, and strain on public services—challenges that can persist for decades (Russo & Linkon, 2008). Where such decline becomes entrenched, it can lead to economic blight, characterized by physical decay, abandoned infrastructure, and the erosion of social cohesion (Bluestone & Harrison, 1982; High, 2003). Crime rates frequently rise under these conditions, influenced by labor-market decline, spatial isolation, and reduced institutional trust (De Nadai et al., 2020).

Such structural decline does not remain confined to the economy or urban space; it inevitably reshapes the political arena. In democratic systems based on equal voting rights, every citizen's vote carries the same weight regardless of economic contribution. While this principle is essential to political equality, it also means electoral incentives can be shaped by the preferences of groups whose economic input differs substantially. In some cases, political parties have built electoral strength by mobilizing large, high-growth demographics—such as immigrant populations—regardless of their labor-market participation. This dynamic aligns with analyses of welfare-state evolution in Scandinavia, where support structures initially aimed at the needy have increasingly accommodated middle-class lifestyles, a process sometimes referred to as "*lifestyle welfare*" (Söilen, 2009).

All of this has direct implications for how and where we study human behavior. Understanding that the majority of people live in densely populated, constructed environments helps us identify the primary arenas where behavior is shaped and performed. Cities are not just physical spaces—they are *behavioral filters*. They concentrate certain patterns: time stress, anonymity, professional ambition, and social signaling. Knowing this allows researchers to narrow their focus when studying specific groups, contexts, or phenomena. Rather than searching for universal behaviors in abstract, we can investigate how particular urban settings produce consistent social scripts, habits, and coping mechanisms. In this way, space becomes both a constraint and a lens through which we can better understand the complexities of modern life.

In summary, human behavior is driven not by pure logic or consistent intention, but by a mix of evolutionary psychology, social incentives, and environmental constraints. We live performative lives, often acting against our stated values, and navigating a habitat that is increasingly artificial yet functional. Yet there is also the risk that we misread the complexity of what a city is—its interlocking economic, political, and social dimensions. A political scientist may overlook the underlying economic realities that shape urban life, while an economist may fail to grasp the mechanisms of voting, cultural identity, or social capital. In this way, partial perspectives can lead to incomplete or flawed interpretations, reinforcing blind spots rather than resolving them.

Still, beneath these cultural and institutional layers lies a more fundamental truth: no matter how sophisticated our environments become, human existence remains grounded in biology. And few indicators reveal this more starkly than how long we live, and how differently men and women experience that span.

2.2 Longevity and Gender

Life expectancy is one of the most telling indicators of human progress, and also of its costs. As of 2023, global average life expectancy is around 70 years for men and 75 years for women, although these numbers vary widely depending on region, income, and healthcare access (World Bank, 2023). In high-income countries like Japan, Sweden, or Australia, women now live to around 85–90 years on average, with men slightly behind at 80–85. This gender gap has been consistent across societies, with biological and behavioral factors both playing a role (Luy & Gast, 2014).

The rise in life expectancy is a modern phenomenon. In 1950, average life expectancy globally was just around 45–50 years. This dramatic increase over two to three generations is primarily the result of improved sanitation, medical care, better nutrition, and most critically, vaccinations. Mass immunization campaigns against diseases like polio, measles, and smallpox have saved hundreds of millions of lives (Greenwood, 2014).

These improvements are so significant that they invite us to express the rise in life expectancy through a clearer, more comprehensive framework—much in the spirit of what I believe Hans Rosling encouraged us to do:

Equation 2.1: The Longevity Equation—Expanded Drivers of Human Lifespan

$$L \approx f(H + M + S + V + G + E + B + C)$$

where **L** is life expectancy, **H** stands for healthcare access, **M** for medical innovation, **S** for sanitation and nutrition, and **V** for vaccination coverage. These four variables—each part of the broader healthcare and public health domain—have been the dominant forces behind the dramatic increase in life expectancy over the past century. **G** represents genetic factors, **E** physical exercise, **B** behavioral influences such as smoking or sleep patterns, and **C** cultural and environmental factors such as social support and pollution.

Each variable contributes non-linearly, but the historical leap in longevity primarily reflects systemic, population-level advances in healthcare access, medical science, sanitation, and vaccination. Among these, vaccinations stand out for their scale and cost-effectiveness: a single intervention capable of virtually eliminating entire categories of early death in many regions (Greenwood, 2014; Rappuoli et al., 2011). While genetics and lifestyle still matter, the evidence shows that public health infrastructure has been far more decisive in shaping modern life expectancy than any single individual choice.

However, longevity brings its own social and economic challenges. As people live longer, they also spend more years in retirement. This has placed growing strain on pension systems and healthcare budgets. In many OECD countries, retirement ages are being raised incrementally—from 65 to 67 or even higher—to maintain the sustainability of public finances (OECD, 2021) (Fig. 2.2).

There are also profound cultural effects. Longer life spans mean more people live to see their grandchildren—and increasingly, their great-grandchildren. In previous centuries, this was rare. Now, it is not uncommon for four generations of a family to be alive simultaneously. This changes family structures, caregiving patterns, and the intergenerational transmission of knowledge.

You may well ask: what's the problem with that? Well, being a grandparent is a joy, yes—but it is also tiring, I have noticed, especially as our physical resilience declines. Now imagine being asked to babysit your great-grandchild. Even under the best of circumstances, that request can

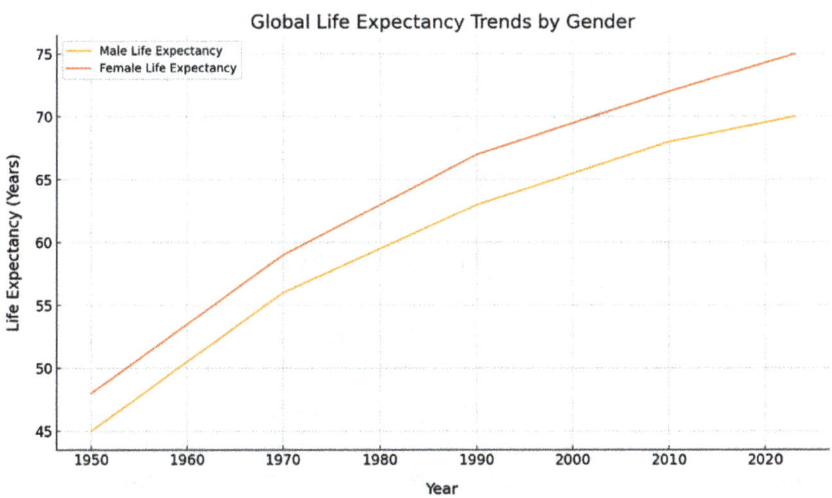

Fig. 2.2 Global Life expectancy trends by gender, 1950–2023. *Source* World Health Organization (WHO), United Nations Population Division, and OECD Health Statistics (2023)

be overwhelming. And if the child's parents are already overchallenged or under-supported, the pressure shifts upward. What looks like extended family continuity can also mean extended caregiving burden—stretching the energy, time, and resources of the oldest generation at precisely the stage of life when rest is most needed.

Thus, while longer lives are a triumph of human development, they also require rethinking social policies, work trajectories, and intergenerational dynamics. These shifts do not happen in isolation—they are embedded in larger social and cultural systems. For the social sciences, this creates a demanding analytical challenge: making sense of how demographic, economic, psychological, and cultural factors interact over an extended life course. In the age of AI, this challenge may be met with new tools capable of detecting patterns that would otherwise remain hidden. Properly guided by human judgment, AI could help social scientists map the complex feedback loops between longevity, social roles, and institutional adaptation—provided that humans remain in control of the assumptions, variables, and interpretive frames that give such models meaning.

As human lives stretch across more decades, the importance of *collective identity*, shared norms, and cultural continuity becomes even more pronounced. The way we relate to others—within families, communities, and broader social groups—takes on new forms and greater complexity. AI-assisted social science could help us anticipate these changes, but it will be up to human researchers to ensure that such forecasts serve not only accuracy, but also human dignity and long-term social cohesion.

2.3 Identity and Culture

Human beings live in a web of complex *social relations* that extend far beyond individual biology. While our species shares core cognitive and symbolic abilities, it is our capacity to form and maintain diverse *social groups* that shapes much of our everyday life and identity.

These groups—defined by nationality, ethnicity, culture, language, religion, and shared history—provide the social fabric within which individuals find meaning, support, and belonging. Such categories form what we might call *first-order identities*: socially constructed classifications that we are typically born into or acquire early in life, and which often shape our opportunities, values, and affiliations (Oyserman et al., 2002; Tajfel & Turner, 1979).

But identity does not stop there. Human beings also create *second-order identities*: more flexible and personally curated markers of self, such as the music we enjoy, the football team we support, the fashion styles we adopt, or the brands we consume (Giddens, 1991). These elements may appear superficial at first glance, but they play a powerful role in social signaling and group differentiation, especially in late modern societies where individuals are increasingly called upon to "construct" their identities through choices rather than inheritances (Bauman, 2000). In this way, wearing a vintage leather jacket, cheering for a team like the Green Bay Packers or San Antonio Spurs, or identifying as a minimalist is not merely a personal preference—it becomes a public performance of *identity*.

Understanding identity in these layered terms allows us to see why some people express more complex or visible identities than others. For some, especially in socially homogenous or *high-cohesion cultures*, first-order identities provide sufficient meaning and group affiliation. Others—particularly those living in multicultural, urban, or globalized contexts—may feel the need to differentiate themselves through second-order layers, compensating for weaker communal bonds or higher individualization (Inglehart & Baker, 2000). Psychological traits also play a role: people high in openness to experience or in need of uniqueness are more likely to adopt varied identity markers to stand out or find their place (Sheldon et al., 1997; Snyder & Fromkin, 1980). In contrast, those who seek stability or belong to strong traditional communities may emphasize inherited identities more strongly and resist more fluid or elective forms of self-definition.

Together, these identity layers reflect not just who we are, but how we navigate belonging, meaning, and distinction in a socially constructed world.

Globally, the nearly 8 billion people alive today are organized into thousands of overlapping and sometimes fluid *social collectives*. These groups regulate behaviors through norms, rituals, and institutions, creating structures that guide cooperation and conflict resolution.

Belonging to an ethnic group or nation often involves shared stories and collective memories that reinforce group cohesion and identity. Table 2.2 shows the largest ethnic groups as they relate to specific countries, though it is worth remembering that many ethnic groups extend across national borders, often becoming a source of tension or conflict.[3]

---

[3] While this book does not focus on political science, occasional examples are necessary. In eastern DR Congo—even today—tensions persist between Congolese and Rwandan communities, particularly over land, citizenship, and mineral resources. Similarly, Pashtun communities span across Afghanistan and Pakistan (and into Iran), contributing to enduring cross-border dynamics that complicate governance and identity. Such disputes were exacerbated by European colonial powers who, in drawing

Table 2.2 World's largest countries and their major ethnic groups (2025)

Country	Estimated population (2025)	Major ethnic groups
China	1,412,000,000	Han Chinese (~91.6%), Zhuang, Hui, Manchu, Uyghur, Miao, Yi, Tujia, Tibetan, Mongol
India	1,409,000,000	Indo-Aryan (~72%), Dravidian (~25%), Mongoloid and others
United States	342,000,000	White (~59.3%), Hispanic/Latino (~18.9%), Black (~13.6%), Asian (~6.1%), Other
Indonesia	279,000,000	Javanese (~40%), Sundanese (~15%), Malay, Madurese, Batak, Bugis, others
Pakistan	244,000,000	Punjabi (~44%), Pashtun (~15%), Sindhi, Saraiki, Muhajir, Baloch
Nigeria	229,000,000	Hausa, Yoruba, Igbo, Fulani, Tiv, Kanuri, Ibibio, Ijaw, and others
Brazil	215,000,000	White (~47.7%), Mixed (~43.1%), Black (~7.6%), Asian, Indigenous
Bangladesh	171,000,000	Bengali (~98%), others (Chakma, Santhal, Bihari, Rohingya, etc.)
Russia	144,000,000	Russian (~77.7%), Tatar, Ukrainian, Bashkir, Chuvash, Chechen, others
Mexico	133,000,000	Mestizo (~62%), Indigenous (~21%), White (~10%), Afro-Mexican (~7%)

Sources United Nations, *World Population Prospects 2024,* CIA World Factbook (2023–2024), Pew Research Center and National statistical agencies and recent censuses from respective countries

In the social sciences, an *ethnic group* is defined as a population that shares a common ancestry, historical experience, and a sense of identity, often rooted in long-term habitation within a specific geographical area.[4]

Africa and the Middle East's borders, frequently overlooked ethnic and cultural realities, often with lasting, disruptive effects.

[4] The term *race*, often referring to classifications such as the "four human races" (e.g., Caucasoid, Mongoloid, Negroid, and Australoid), was widely used in both popular and scientific literature up until the Second World War. It reflected a typological approach that sought to categorize human variation into a few distinct biological groups. However, after the Second World War and in response to the misuse of racial science in eugenics and Nazi ideology, the scientific consensus began to shift. Research in genetics, anthropology, and sociology increasingly recognized that human biological variation does not cluster into discrete racial groups, but instead exists along continuous gradients (Lewontin, 1972; Montagu, 1942; Templeton, 1998). As a result, the concept of *ethnicity*, which emphasizes shared cultural practices, language, ancestry, and social experience, gradually replaced *race* in the social sciences and much of the biological discourse. Nevertheless, the term *race* is still

As Fredrik Barth (1969) explains in his work *Ethnic Groups and Boundaries*, ethnicity is not merely a matter of shared traits but of social organization around cultural difference. These groups develop distinct cultural expressions over time—languages, rituals, belief systems, moral codes, and collective behaviors—which are passed down through generations.

Thus, ethnicity and culture often constitute the primary collective identity of individuals after their personal identity, shaping how people perceive themselves and others (Eriksen, 2010; Tajfel, 1981). However, in daily life, individuals more frequently express this collective identity in terms of nationality, which is symbolically reinforced by national emblems such as flags (Billig, 1995), or simply the colors of a flag.

This expression also occurs through everyday practices like traditional food consumption—turkey for Thanksgiving in the United States (Douglas, 1984; Gillis, 1996), or the *smörgåsbord* featuring pickled herring during Midsummer festivities in Sweden (Löfgren, 1993). These rituals reinforce national belonging through shared sensory and cultural experiences. National identity offers a more concrete and politically institutionalized framework for belonging, especially in modern nation-states, and becomes a default answer to the question "Who am I?" in public or intercultural contexts.

It is exceedingly rare for people to define themselves first and foremost as members of the species *Homo sapiens*. While such a species-level identity might be invoked in philosophical or scientific discussions, such as in the context of *human rights* (Arendt, 1951) or *planetary ethics* (Beck, 2009), it remains largely abstract in everyday discourse. Of course, this has much to do with the fact that identity terms are primarily used in communication with others, and we do not generally hold conversations with other species—at least not serious ones, though I am quite sure my mother, if she were still alive, would have objected.

Social identity theory explains this tendency through the concept of "*salient identity*," where the most contextually relevant and emotionally resonant group identity becomes foregrounded (Turner et al., 1987). Nationality and ethnic group often fill this role far more than species membership, which lacks both emotional anchoring and institutional reinforcement.

Because of the sustained shared experience, *ethnic groups* often evolve unique patterns of behavior, including ways of organizing family, authority, and cooperation, as well as norms about conflict resolution, food, and gender roles (Eriksen, 2010). These behavioral patterns become cognitively ingrained, meaning that members of ethnic groups may interpret the world

routinely applied to non-human animals, especially in zoology and breeding contexts (e.g., "races" of dogs, horses, or insects), where it is used to denote genetically distinct populations within a species.

through culturally specific cognitive frameworks, which shape how they reason, decide, and interact.

Anthropologist Franz Boas (1938) made the point that ethnic identity should not be reduced to physical characteristics but understood through the lens of cultural practices and learned behavior. Nevertheless, due to genetic drift, endogamy, and adaptation to specific environments, ethnic groups may also show certain *physical traits* that become markers of identity, although these are more often socially assigned than biologically determined (Hutchinson & Smith, 1996).

Furthermore, Joshua Fishman (1989) highlighted the role of *language* in maintaining ethnic boundaries, arguing that linguistic distinctiveness serves as both a practical tool of cohesion and a symbolic marker of difference. Thus, ethnic groups function as both *cultural containers* and *transmitters of social memory*, preserving particular *worldviews* and practices even across diasporas.

To sum it up, ethnic groups are crucial *units of analysis* in the social sciences because they encapsulate how human communities coevolve biologically, socially, and cognitively over time, shaping both individual and collective behavior in complex, patterned ways. Attempts at social engineering that downplay or erase these differences—for example, by claiming that cultures do not exist or by pursuing a single global culture through rapid demographic change—risk destabilizing the very systems of meaning and cohesion that have evolved over centuries. Such projects can be profoundly disruptive, not only at the political level but also in the lived experience of communities, where cultural continuity functions as a source of stability, trust, and mutual understanding.

Just as ethnicity helps define group boundaries through shared language, history, and customs, religion functions as a parallel symbolic system, often intersecting with ethnicity but also extending beyond it. Both serve as *anchors of identity*, shaping how individuals understand themselves in relation to their community, their past, and the larger world.

Religion, like ethnicity, provides a narrative structure, a set of practices, and a moral framework that binds individuals into coherent groups. To understand human identity in full, we must therefore explore how religious systems emerged, evolved, and continue to function as powerful social and cognitive forces.

2.3.1 Religion as a Symbolic System

From a scientific standpoint, religion should not be treated as an enemy or an anomaly. While prominent critics such as Richard Dawkins (2006) and Christopher Hitchens (2007) have underscored the historical harms committed in the name of religion—wars, persecutions, and dogmatic repression—science has a broader task. It must also explain why religion emerges so consistently across human cultures, how it operates psychologically, and what social functions it serves. Religion is not a bug in the human operating system, but one of its core features: a product of the same evolutionary and cultural processes that gave rise to language, morality, and identity (Norenzayan, 2013; Wilson, 2002).

Importantly, not all religious systems function the same way. *Confucianism*, for example, is better described as a *moral philosophy* than a religion in the Western sense. It emphasizes ethical cultivation, filial piety, and social harmony through ritual and education, not supernatural revelation or deity worship (Bell & Chaibong, 2003; Yao, 2000). In this respect, Confucianism functions more as a civic framework than a theology, offering an instructive contrast to the exclusivist structure of Abrahamic monotheisms.

Judaism, Christianity, and Islam each declare theological boundaries that define their truths in opposition to all others. For example, the First Commandment in the Hebrew Bible states, "You shall have no other gods before me" (Exodus 20:3), while the Qur'an asserts that submission to Allah is the only legitimate spiritual path, at times endorsing coercive treatment of non-believers (Qur'an 9:29; Cook, 2005; Firestone, 1999). These *exclusivist claims* have historically justified religious conflict and limited tolerance for pluralism.

By contrast, religious pluralism was a feature—not a problem—in the Roman Empire. Conquered peoples' gods were integrated into the imperial pantheon, as long as civic rituals and public order were upheld (Beard et al., 1998). What made Christianity politically subversive to Rome was not theological dissent per se, but the refusal to recognize other gods or participate in public ceremonies like emperor worship. This shows how religious exclusivity, when fused with political absolutism, becomes socially disruptive.

But even in less conflictual settings, religion plays a potent boundary-making role. Theological doctrines often serve less as metaphysical explanations and more as signals of moral commitment, cultural identity, and group loyalty. In evolutionary terms, this is adaptive. Belonging to a shared symbolic system reinforces in-group trust and coordination, especially under conditions of uncertainty or threat.

What we call "*faith*" is central to this mechanism. From a cognitive perspective, faith is not the result of argument, but the absence of it. It is the mental act of deciding—often unconsciously—that something is true without requiring evidence or rational justification. Humans are evolutionarily predisposed to accept certain beliefs from authority figures or trusted peers, especially when those beliefs reinforce group belonging or offer existential comfort. The psychological tendency to detect agency, assign intention, and seek meaning in randomness makes humans fertile ground for religious ideas (Atran, 2002; Boyer, 2001). This cognitive shortcut likely helped ancestral humans coordinate behavior and reduce internal conflict, even at the cost of epistemic rigor.

This is also why religion is not easily replaced. Its emotional, social, and neurological roots run deep. fMRI studies show that religious experiences activate the same neural circuits involved in empathy, social cognition, and emotional regulation (Azari et al., 2001; Schjoedt et al., 2009). The sense of being watched or guided by supernatural agents taps into the evolved brain systems for moral behavior and reputation management (Norenzayan & Shariff, 2008). Religious rituals, as Durkheim (1912/1995) observed, generate collective effervescence—shared emotional highs that bond groups together.

Yet from an evolutionary perspective, science now performs many of the functions once filled by religion. It provides more accurate predictions about natural phenomena, better tools for survival, and more reliable explanations for human behavior. In modern societies, science increasingly takes over the explanatory space once occupied by myth: we no longer need religious stories to understand the origins of diseases, the formation of stars, or the causes of human conflict.

It should be clear for all to see that it is science—first and foremost—that has improved human lives in practical, measurable ways. From vaccines and clean water to communication technologies and agricultural productivity, it is scientific progress that has lifted billions out of poverty and extended life expectancy across the globe. Religion, by contrast, while offering meaning and social cohesion to many, has also been a source of disastrous conflict throughout history—and continues to be so today. The ongoing tensions between Islam and Judaism in the Middle East, as well as clashes between Islam and Christianity in various parts of the world, are stark reminders that religious divisions still fuel violence, identity-based exclusion, and large-scale human suffering.

Still, it would be unrealistic to expect the abolition of religion in the foreseeable future. The same evolutionary pressures that once favored religious cognition—social bonding, anxiety reduction, agency detection—are still active today. Religious sentiment is not easily erased from human psychology because it is not entirely cultural; it is partly biological. But what we can and must do is draw a firm boundary between belief systems based on *blind faith* and those based on *empirical reasoning*.

For this reason, religion has no place inside the university as a framework for truth-seeking. While it may be studied, interpreted, and understood—like language or literature—it should not be taught or defended as a source of knowledge. Its epistemological foundation is not argument but authority; not falsifiability but submission. As Bertrand Russell (1952) observed, "The demand for certainty is natural to man, but it is an intellectual vice." Science, by contrast, demands doubt, revision, and critical scrutiny.

But as we have seen in this book so far, whether the social sciences succeed in living up to that ideal is an entirely different question. And the short answer seems to be: only part of the time. Given what we now understand about human nature—cognitive biases, social incentives, and the evolutionary roots of belief and behavior—it is probably unrealistic to expect faster or more consistent progress in the short run. Intellectual honesty and methodological rigor require not only training, but a level of self-awareness and institutional courage that is difficult to sustain in practice.

At least, that has been the case—until now. For we now stand on the brink of a new era: one in which machines begin to take on the role of scientists. Artificial intelligence may soon bypass some of the cognitive limitations we have discussed, offering a form of research that is less burdened by ego, ideology, or fatigue. Whether this shift will lead to better science or simply new forms of distortion remains to be seen. But the potential for acceleration—and disruption—is undeniable.

Religious beliefs, beautiful and powerful as they may be, must still be treated like any other hypothesis about the world: they must be tested, questioned, and—if found wanting—set aside. Only by doing so can we preserve the integrity of science and the university and keep the search for truth anchored in what we can observe, demonstrate, and debate. Once we understand religion not as divine revelation but as a cognitive and social adaptation, we gain a new appreciation for its evolutionary role—and for the importance of keeping it within its proper explanatory domain.

In the same way that we must remember what religion truly is, and what it has done both for and to humanity, we must also never lose sight of another fundamental truth: that we are animals. The similarities we share with our closest biological relatives—the great apes—are not incidental curiosities. They are windows into who we are. Just as religious traditions tell us something about human imagination, ape behavior tells us something about our evolutionary mind.

2.4 Humans and Primates

While there is no direct evidence that non-human apes possess religions or belief systems in the way humans do, some behaviors observed in great apes suggest early precursors to religious cognition.

Chimpanzees, for example, have been seen engaging in ritual-like actions—such as repeatedly throwing stones at trees or reacting with awe to waterfalls and thunderstorms (Goodall, 1990; Köhler et al., 2016). These behaviors, though not religious in a formal sense, may reflect emotional and cognitive capacities—like pattern recognition, social cohesion, and reverence—that laid the groundwork for religion in Homo sapiens.

All individuals are different, but they also share many things in common, such as the need for food, clean air, shelter, security, and social connection. As such, we are not that different from other animals.

Our closest relatives are the apes, and there are—as every child learns early in school—five great apes in total: humans (Homo sapiens), chimpanzees (Pan troglodytes), bonobos (Pan paniscus), gorillas (Gorilla spp.), and orangutans (Pongo spp.) (Table 2.3).

So, we are not even the most aggressive of the great apes—that title clearly goes to the chimpanzee (Wrangham & Peterson, 1996). Interestingly, we humans are slightly less aggressive than even the gorilla, despite the gorilla's much more dominating physical appearance (Archer, 2006). Much of this aggression is linked to testosterone, especially in males, where it plays a key role in dominance behavior, competition, and risk-taking (Muller, 2017).

From an evolutionary perspective, this trait was highly adaptive. It helped protect one's family from attackers and enabled success in competitive environments. While modern society has reduced the direct need for physical aggression, the underlying biology hasn't changed much. We are, after all, still animals, and since conflicts and even wars still happen, the capacity for aggression remains part of human nature (Sapolsky, 2017).

Testosterone not only fuels aggression, but it also increases risk tolerance. This has implications for many human endeavors, including starting a business, enduring long-term hardship, or engaging in high-stakes professions. In fact, higher testosterone levels have been associated with increased willingness to take strategic risks (Muller, 2017). Conversely, humans with abnormally low testosterone may struggle with drive, motivation, and even basic self-preservation (Archer, 2006), and they often have greater difficulty finding a partner.

Teenagers often believe—or are believed by their parents—to think about sex constantly. But even the most hormone-driven human adolescence pales

Table 2.3 Comparison of great apes

Trait or need	Humans (Homo sapiens)	Chimpanzees (Pan troglodytes)	Bonobos (Pan paniscus)	Gorillas (Gorilla spp.)	Orangutans (Pongo spp.)
Social structure	Highly variable, institutional	Male-dominated, fission–fusion	Female-centered, egalitarian	Dominant silverback-led groups	Mostly solitary
Aggression	Moderate, law-regulated	High, especially among males	Very low, use sex to reduce tension	Low to moderate, dominance-based	Very low
Empathy/altruism	Highly developed	Some, mostly among kin	High, including food sharing	Present in maternal care	Present in parenting
Tool use	Extensive and evolving	Basic (e.g., termite fishing)	Similar to chimps but less frequent	Rare	Occasional (especially in captivity)
Communication	Complex language and writing	Gestures and vocalizations	Rich gestures, facial expressions	Basic vocal and visual cues	Low-frequency sounds, gestures
Sexual behavior	Culturally varied, pair-bonding	Promiscuous, male dominance	Frequent, social bonding	Harem-like, polygynous	Mostly solitary, female choice
Parenting	Long-term, often bi-parental	Long maternal care	Long maternal care, high tolerance	Maternal only	Maternal, with long intervals
Diet	Omnivorous	Omnivorous, fruit and insects	Mostly vegetarian, some meat	Herbivorous, leaves and shoots	Frugivorous, bark and leaves
Cognition	Abstract thinking, future planning	Strong planning, tool use	Cooperative problem-solving	Moderate	Strong memory, problem-solving
Habitat range	Global	Tropical Africa	Congo basin, Central Africa	Central Africa	Borneo and Sumatra
Endangered status	Not endangered	Endangered	Endangered	Critically endangered	Critically endangered

in comparison with our primate cousins, especially bonobos. In bonobo societies, sexual behavior is not only frequent but serves a wide range of social functions, including conflict resolution, bonding, and status negotiation (de Waal, 1995).

Some observers have suggested that humans lie somewhere between chimpanzees and bonobos in terms of social behavior. Bonobos are peaceful, matriarchal, and sexually expressive, while chimpanzees are more hierarchical and resolve conflict through aggression (Wrangham & Peterson, 1996). These differences have implications for paternal care, bonding, and social cohesion.

That said, aggression is only one part of the behavioral profile. Traits like fairness, empathy, and parental care are equally central to what it means to be human. Our capacity for fairness and altruism is notably strong compared to many other primates (de Waal, 2009), and cooperative child-rearing is a hallmark of Homo sapiens (Tomasello, 2014).

Yet, claiming that humans are categorically "better" than our primate cousins risks overstretching.

Case Box—From the Great Leap Forward to the Eurasian Steppe Expansions

It is obvious that we are different now, but for most of our history this was not the case. For tens of thousands of years, human societies resembled our primate cousins—mobile, small-band hunter-gatherers with modest material culture. Only during the past ~50,000 years—about when Homo sapiens expanded into Europe—did things change dramatically. Jared Diamond (1992) and others call this period the *Great Leap Forward*, driven by the emergence of symbolic language, rapid innovation in tools and art, expansive social networks, and possibly improved dietary sources that supported enhanced brain function (Klein, 2009; Mellars, 2006).[5]

Millennia later, another transformative shift occurred. Around 5,000 years ago, ancient DNA research reveals a massive migration of Western Steppe Herder populations—particularly the Yamnaya culture—across Europe. These

[5] Scholars debate whether major transitions in human evolution, such as the so-called Great Leap Forward (~50,000 years ago), were sudden leaps or the cumulative result of many gradual changes. Proponents of the "leap" model (e.g., Diamond, 1992; Klein, 2009; Mellars, 2006) argue that archaeological evidence shows an abrupt burst in symbolic culture, complex tools, and long-distance exchange, with no clear precursors. Gradualists (e.g., McBrearty & Brooks, 2000; Pinker, 2011) counter that such abilities developed incrementally over hundreds of thousands of years, with earlier evidence for art, ornamentation, and advanced hunting. The debate remains unresolved, as both perspectives acknowledge that cultural and genetic evolution are intertwined and may accelerate when ecological or social thresholds are crossed.

steppe pastoralists contributed as much as half the ancestry of central and northern Europeans, bringing with them horse domestication, wheeled transport, and cultural-technological traditions that merged with local Neolithic societies (Allentoft et al., 2015; Anthony, 2007; Haak et al., 2015). This migration is closely linked to the spread of the Corded Ware culture, itself connected to the earlier steppe traditions in pottery, burial customs, and mobility strategies.

At roughly the same time, an equally transformative expansion was taking place further east. Ancient DNA studies show that populations from the Eastern Steppe—genetically related to the broader Ancient North Eurasian lineage—spread into what is now Manchuria, northern China, and Mongolia, merging with local agricultural communities (Bai et al., 2023; Jeong et al., 2020; Ning et al., 2020). From there, one branch moved eastward into the Korean Peninsula and later into the Japanese archipelago, contributing to the Yayoi culture and mixing with the indigenous Jomon population. Another branch moved southward, integrating with early Sino-Tibetan societies and influencing the rise of complex states in northern China. Archaeological evidence links these expansions to advances in metallurgy, pastoralism, and in some regions horse use, paralleling the cultural-technological shifts seen in Europe.

Thus, two great cultural streams emerged from the Eurasian steppe zone during the Bronze Age: one flowing westward into Europe, the other eastward into Asia. Their descendants went on to form the foundations of the civilizations that dominate today's geopolitical landscape—with the United States representing an overseas offshoot of the western stream, and China, Korea, and Japan carrying forward the eastern.

It is important to stress—especially for social scientists—that these are not just stories we tell ourselves, nor narratives that can be swapped at will for others. These are facts, grounded in a growing body of hard evidence from archaeology, linguistics, and especially genetics. The discoveries of Svante Pääbo and his colleagues at the Max Planck Institute for Evolutionary Anthropology in Leipzig, including the sequencing of the Neanderthal and Denisovan genomes (Green et al., 2010; Meyer et al., 2012), have transformed our understanding of human origins and admixture. Together with large-scale ancient DNA studies (e.g., Allentoft et al., 2015; Haak et al., 2015; Jeong et al., 2020), they show clearly how migrations and interactions shaped who we are today.

This knowledge is not only about the past. It is our duty as scientists to ensure that such insights are shared with all people, and taught to children as part of their basic understanding of humanity. Only by recognizing where we come from, and how we have evolved, can we fully understand the challenges we face today.

Questions for Reflection

1. Could there be further "genetic leaps" in the future, driven by natural selection, environmental pressures, or even human-directed genetic change? Evolutionary biology shows that significant adaptation can occur within just a few generations when selection pressures are strong (Allentoft et al., 2015; Jeong et al., 2020).
2. If such a leap happened soon, how might it reshape human cognition, social structures, and culture? Would our political, ethical, and educational systems be able to keep pace?
3. Could artificial intelligence act as a catalyst for another "great leap" in human evolution—either through cultural transformation, changes in selection pressures, or gene–culture coevolution? Cultural evolution theory suggests that transformative technologies alter survival and reproduction patterns in ways that feed back into biological evolution (Boyd & Richerson, 2005; Henrich, 2015).
4. Might the next leap not be genetic at all, but rather a hybrid one—where biological, cultural, and technological evolution intertwine to form a new kind of "post-human" trajectory?
5. Finally, what responsibilities do we carry in shaping these trajectories? If our choices can now influence evolution itself, should we think of ourselves not just as products of history, but as stewards of humanity's future?

Of course, it is difficult to answer these questions with certainty. Some remain speculative, given the many unknowns in both human biology and cultural change. I do not want to forgo conclusions in later chapters, but it is worth noting that future transformations—whether genetic, cultural, or technological—may not necessarily lead to greater intellectual or moral advancement. Just as history shows periods of remarkable progress, it also records times of stagnation or decline. The possibility of another leap—forward or backward—remains part of the human story.

Recognizing ourselves first and foremost as apes—as one animal among many—can shift our self-conception away from viewing humanity as the planet's primary and privileged species. In the same way, watching a nature program about the extended brain of the octopus can remind us that intelligence takes many forms, making us feel a little less special—and perhaps a bit more humble.

The mindset, rooted in a mistaken belief that "sapiens" is wholly separate from the rest of the animal kingdom, has contributed to the exploitation and degradation of ecosystems. If AI comes to assume many of the cognitive roles we have long used to define our uniqueness, it may ironically open the door to a more grounded identity: maybe also one that emphasizes our role as caregivers and stewards of the planet, rather than as its dominant rulers.

Just as Darwin used the subtle differences between island and mainland species to uncover the mechanisms of natural selection, we can use these layers of human transformation—both cognitive and genetic—to explore the roots of our species. These evolutionary mirrors illuminate both our continuities and our departures, offering crucial perspective on what it truly means to be human.

But to understand humans fully, we must go beyond anatomy and psychology. We've already discussed how cities differ from suburbs and smaller towns—and how these environments affect everything from social behavior to perception. Now, we shift our focus to the broader scale: the influence of geography, climate, and environmental constraints on human societies across time and space. The human story is not just about what we are—but where we are, and how our habitats shape our cultural norms, social structures, and economic systems.

2.5 Climate and Human Settlement

Humans are distributed across the planet's landmasses in accordance with their ability to adapt and survive in different environmental conditions. While the Earth's surface is about 71% water, the remaining 29% is land. Of that land, only about 50–60% is considered habitable, as large portions are covered by deserts, glaciers, and high mountain ranges that are not suitable for permanent settlement.

When we factor in these limitations, it turns out that humans live on only about 10–12% of the Earth's total surface. Most of the planet is covered by oceans, ice, deserts, and uninhabitable terrain. Within the inhabitable portion, the temperate zones—characterized by moderate climates, seasonal variation, and fertile soils—support more than half of the world's population. These regions are typically more favorable for agriculture, infrastructure development, and long-term habitation. However, this distribution is not symmetric across the globe (Fig. 2.3).

This is an important point for at least two reasons. First, when we look at images of the Earth from space, it's striking to realize that nearly all of

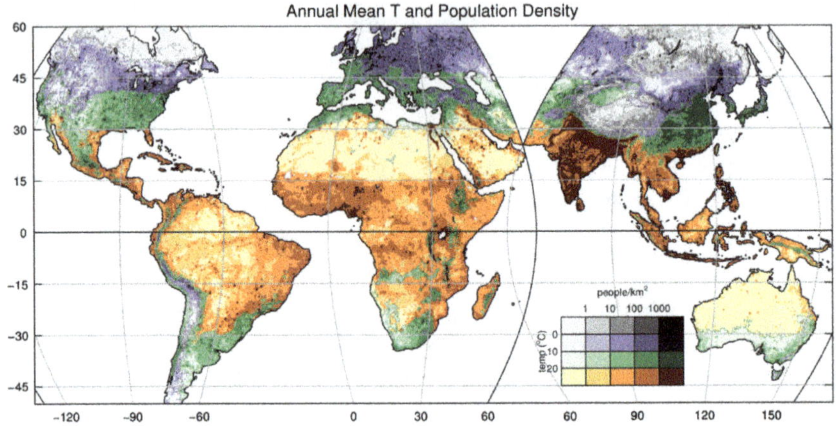

Fig. 2.3 Global distribution of human settlement relative to habitable land and climate zones. *Source* Adapted from data and map visualization by the University of Florida, Department of Geography. See: https://geog.ufl.edu/2022/11/17/population-distribution-within-the-human-climate-niche/

human activity—our wars, cities, farms, and industries—are confined to just a small fraction of the land. We are essentially running around on a thin crust of the planet's surface. Second, and more critically, the fact that we occupy only about 10% of the planet does not mean that our responsibility is limited to that part. Our actions—through pollution, deforestation, carbon emissions, and ocean acidification—ripple far beyond our immediate environments, impacting the other 90% of the Earth that we tend not to see, and too often forget.

The *Northern Hemisphere* contains about 68% of the Earth's land area, and it is where most of the temperate zone land is located. In contrast, the *Southern Hemisphere* accounts for only about 32% of Earth's landmass, and its temperate zones are much smaller and more dispersed, making up less than 15% of the global temperate land area. This geographical asymmetry helps explain why human populations and civilizations have historically concentrated in the Northern Hemisphere's temperate regions.

This regional imbalance is not just a geographic curiosity—it shapes the very fabric of our global civilization. From agriculture to urbanization, energy use to economic activity, the concentration of human life in certain climatic zones profoundly affects how societies develop and how they impact the rest of the planet (Table 2.4).

Temperate zones offer moderate rainfall, fertile soils, and a stable climate, which have historically supported dense populations and complex societies. Civilizations in temperate areas—such as Europe, northern China, and North America—benefited early from these conditions and developed strong

Table 2.4 Human population distribution by climate zone and setting

Climate zone	Approx. global population (%)	Approx. number of people (2024 est.)	Urban vs. rural split
Temperate	55%	~4.4 billion	Urban: ~60%, Rural: ~40%
Tropical	35%	~2.8 billion	Urban: ~50%, Rural: ~50%
Arid (Desert)	5%	~400 million	Urban: ~70%, Rural: ~30%
Polar and Subpolar	<1%	~70 million	Urban: ~80%, Rural: ~20%
Mountainous/ Highland	~4%	~320 million	Urban: ~40%, Rural: ~60%

Sources World Bank (2023)—*Urban Population Data,* NASA Earth Observatory—*Climate Zone Distribution,* FAO—*Land Use by Climate Type,* UN DESA (2022)—*World Urbanization Prospects* and Klein Goldewijk et al. (2017)—*Historical Human Land Use Patterns*

agricultural and institutional foundations. Today, the world's two dominant economic powers—the United States and China—are both located in temperate zones, where large, productive populations and infrastructure have flourished. This is no coincidence.

Much of this land is inhabited by populations of European and East Asian descent, particularly White Caucasians in the West and Han Chinese in the East. Russia also covers vast temperate areas, though with lower population density and greater ethnic diversity. While geography is not destiny, the *temperate belt* has clearly played a central role in shaping global population patterns and economic leadership.

But then someone will inevitably ask: can't we just move into space? It's a tempting thought, and very popular again now with Mr. Musk's projects, but I wouldn't place too much confidence in humans thriving high in the atmosphere or in orbit, not with the bodies we currently have. We break down quickly without gravity or the right atmospheric conditions. As air pressure drops at higher altitudes, oxygen levels decline, leading to hypoxia. This can cause confusion, fatigue, poor coordination, and, in more severe cases, unconsciousness or death (West, 2012). The lack of atmospheric pressure also causes gas expansion in body cavities and can result in decompression sickness, especially above 18,000 feet without acclimatization (Zubieta-Calleja & Zubieta-DeUrioste, 2007). In near-zero pressure environments, like outer space, the absence of gravity and oxygen causes rapid bodily deterioration: fluids vaporize, tissues swell, and prolonged exposure leads to muscle atrophy and bone density loss (Nicogossian et al., 2016). Thus, while space exploration remains tremendously important for our civilization, it seems far better suited to machines—robots that can withstand environments we cannot.

Of course, one might argue that we could still live in structured capsules filled with oxygen—pressurized habitats that we build on other planets like the Moon or Mars. But then again, you might miss the view, or much of the excitement of what it means to inhabit a planet and be part of it. There's a fundamental difference between merely surviving on a planet and truly living with it—being immersed in its landscapes, weather, and natural rhythms. That said, it seems likely that humans will eventually go into space not only to live, but to breed and build new societies beyond Earth. This appears to be part of our destiny: a deep-seated drive to expand our possibilities, to adapt, and to discover new frontiers—even if those frontiers lie on other planets.

Science will continue to help us push the limits of where humans can go—and this is undoubtedly a good thing. The more we explore, the more we learn about the universe we inhabit. Just as the Portuguese and Spaniards once built sturdier ships to cross vast oceans, today people like Mr. Elon Musk are developing bigger and better rockets to venture beyond Earth. These technological leaps are impressive, even inspiring. But we should not confuse them with solutions to our societal problems.

2.5.1 Human Settlement Patterns

In terms of settlement type, data from the World Bank and the United Nations indicates that approximately 55% of the global population lived in urban areas as of 2021, with the remaining 45% in rural settings. However, urbanization is progressing rapidly, and the proportion of rural inhabitants is expected to continue declining.

This geographic and climatic distribution reveals more than just where people live—it highlights the biological limits within which all human societies must operate. Our bodies are finely attuned to a narrow range of temperature, oxygen, and pressure. Outside of these ranges, long-term human survival becomes increasingly difficult, no matter how advanced our technology may be. These boundaries are not mere technical footnotes; they fundamentally shape the conditions under which social systems can emerge, endure, or break down.

For the social sciences, this means grounding our understanding of human organization within the physical realities of the species. Migration, urbanization, labor markets, and institutional resilience all rely on populations being biologically functional in their environments. Ignoring these constraints risks building models and forecasts on foundations that are ecologically and physiologically unsound.

It is easy to imagine that humanity is spread evenly across the globe, but in truth we live in a narrow ecological niche, and we quickly die—or at least feel deep discomfort—when we move outside it. Throughout history, competitive cultures have struggled to emerge in climates where survival alone demands most of people's energy, leaving little capacity for innovation or complex governance. Instead of dreaming about endless space or unclaimed land, we should first recognize the precious sliver of habitable territory we already occupy and work to preserve it. Climate shifts will occur whether driven by human activity or natural cycles, as history shows. We must be prepared to relocate over very long time scales—consider, for example, that the next ice age would likely push habitable zones south of Berlin. If you wish to remain "Scandinavian" in such a scenario, you had better have a well-considered backup plan for where to go. Humanity's long history of migration proves that we can adapt and even preserve distinct cultures while doing so, provided we plan wisely. Perhaps by then, we will also have learned how to control the planet's entire temperature to fit our needs—a development that would mark a truly great leap forward for science.

This brings us to another key dimension of human constraint—not where people live, but how they live. If we want to understand what makes a society resilient or fragile, we must have a clear grasp on the rhythms of daily life: how people sleep, eat, work, socialize, and rest. These patterns, though often overlooked when we talk about what we do, are central to both individual well-being and the sustainability of the systems we build.

2.6 Time-Use Patterns

So, to move to the somewhat more trivial, how do humans actually spend their days? On average, most adults sleep between 6 and 8 h per night, with some variation across countries and individual needs (Hirshkowitz et al., 2015). Sleep is a vital *biological process*, affecting everything from cognitive performance to immune function.

After waking up, individuals typically have their meals, usually one to three times per day, depending on *cultural habits* and *socioeconomic conditions* (Mishra et al., 2017). To afford these meals and sustain themselves, most people engage in some form of work, commonly between 6 and 12 h per day, depending on occupation, region, and employment structure (ILO, 2018).

Those who have families—that is, individuals who have formed stable relationships and may have reproduced—spend part of their day with partners and children, fulfilling social and caregiving roles. Time-use studies consistently show that family-related activities are a major part of adult life (Gershuny & Fisher, 2014).

Younger individuals, particularly those not yet in family structures, tend to spend large portions of the day learning in formal settings such as schools or universities. When not in school, they often socialize with peers of the same age. Socialization and play are essential components of childhood development (Gray, 2011), and recreational activities vary greatly by culture.

For instance, in many parts of Europe and Latin America, football (or soccer) is the most common active interest among youth, while in South Asia—especially India—cricket is highly popular (Majumdar, 2008). Physical activities like sports are beneficial not only socially but also physiologically, supporting cardiovascular and musculoskeletal health (WHO, 2020).

Apart from these active interests, humans also engage in more passive forms of leisure. Entertainment in the form of television, online videos, and movies constitutes a large portion of free time across the globe. As of recent global surveys, the average person spends over 2.5 h per day consuming digital entertainment content (Statista, 2023), facilitated by increasing access to internet-connected devices.

By mapping out these routine activities and linking them to their corresponding academic disciplines, we gain a clearer view of how everyday behavior is studied, understood, and influenced (Table 2.5).

Humans then fill their days with a mix of *essential routines* and *culturally shaped behaviors*, all of which are fertile ground for social science research.

Sleep, for example, typically lasting between 6 and 8 h per night in adults, is studied by psychologists and neuroscientists to understand its effect on cognitive functioning, emotional regulation, and physical health (Walker, 2017). Eating habits, shaped by availability, tradition, and belief, are explored by anthropologists and sociologists; why, for instance, some cultures revere fermented fish while others gag at the idea is explained by cultural taste formation and food taboos (Rozin, 1996).

Work takes up a major portion of waking life—usually 6–12 h a day—and is studied by economists, labor theorists, and organizational psychologists to understand productivity, motivation, and the role of employment in identity (Gini, 2000). Commuting, whether via car, train, or on foot, offers insight for urban planners and geographers, especially when they study spatial inequality and time use (Schwanen et al., 2004). Education occupies children and young

Table 2.5 Human activity, social science disciplines, and time spent

Human activity	Corresponding social science(s)	Approx. hours/day
Sleeping	Psychology, Chronobiology, Medical Anthropology	6–8
Eating/Meal preparation	Sociology, Anthropology, Nutrition Science	1.5–2
Working (jobs, careers)	Economics, Sociology, Organizational Psychology	10–12
Commuting	Urban Studies, Human Geography, Transportation Economics	0.5–1.5
Parenting and childcare	Developmental Psychology, Sociology, Gender Studies	1–3 (varies widely)
Attending school/university	Educational Science, Psychology, Sociology	6–8 (students)
Socializing with peers/family	Sociology, Social Psychology, Anthropology	1–2
Playing sports or exercising	Sports Science, Health Psychology, Sociology	0.5–1.5
Consuming entertainment (TV, games)	Media Studies, Cultural Studies, Psychology	2–3
Religious or spiritual practices	Religious Studies, Anthropology, Sociology	0–1
Shopping/consumption	Economics, Consumer Behavior, Marketing	0.5–1
Civic engagement (voting, activism)	Political Science, Sociology, Social Psychology	<0.1 (episodic)
Using digital devices/internet	Media Studies, Information Science, Psychology	3–5
Sleeping/resting again at day's end	Psychology, Public Health, Behavioral Science	Included above

Source Time estimates are approximate averages for adults based on data from time-use surveys (e.g., OECD, American Time Use Survey, Statista, Eurostat)

adults, and is scrutinized by education researchers focused on pedagogical efficiency and social mobility (OECD, 2018).

Leisure time, when it exists, is a mix of physical activity and passive consumption, fields of interest for media scholars and cultural theorists who analyze trends and influence (Couldry, 2012). Even "doing nothing" isn't void of academic inquiry; social theorists like Erving Goffman (1959) studied *micro-interactions* during idle time, revealing rich patterns of human behavior. In short, from the mundane to the bizarre, nearly every part of daily life is under the microscope of a different social science.

Figure 2.4 uses four color-coded categories to illustrate how daily life is structured by necessity. *Biological necessities*, shown in green, include activities such as sleeping and eating.[6] These are non-negotiable: if neglected, they undermine health and make functioning in any other domain impossible. *Competitive necessities*, marked in red, cover work and study. These activities sustain not only individual livelihoods but also collective prosperity and cultural vitality. *Practical necessities*, in blue, include tasks such as commuting, medical visits, and household management. They may appear secondary, but ignoring them quickly undermines the competitive sphere—untreated illness, for example, can prevent one from working. Finally, leisure and *meaning-making activities*, shown in pink, provide balance and renewal through socializing, culture, sports, or spiritual practice. While not immediately vital for survival, they are essential for long-term resilience, mental health, and community cohesion.

Artificial intelligence complicates this picture by shifting tasks from the practical sphere into leisure, as we will discuss in detail in Chapter 9. On the surface, this seems attractive: more free time for rest, play, and culture. But

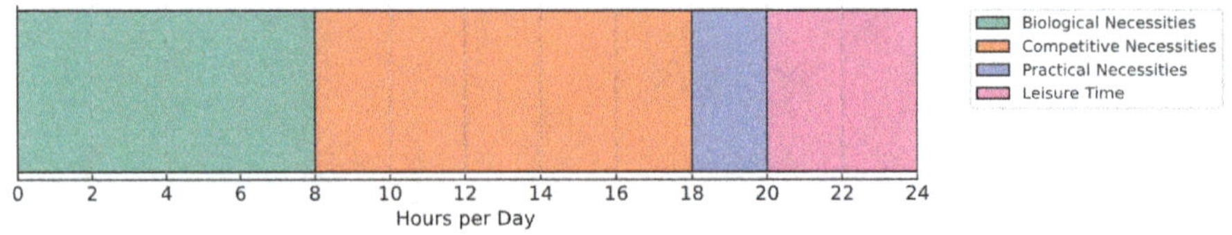

Fig. 2.4 Daily human activity flow and time-use patterns

[6] It is worth noting that sex, although disproportionately present in our thoughts, typically takes up only a very small portion of daily life. Time-use studies estimate that partnered sexual activity averages just a few minutes per day when spread across the population (Laumann et al., 1999; Robinson & Godbey, 1999). In fact, the average person spends more time on the toilet each day than in bed with a partner—though we rarely dwell on, or openly discuss, the former. This mismatch between attention and duration highlights one of the enduring quirks of human life: what occupies our minds is not always what occupies our hours.

the competitive functions are also what keep individuals alert, disciplined, and capable of developing moral character. When these are eroded, the danger is not only idleness but a weakening of the very traits that allow societies to flourish.

The table and figure illustrate a central theme of this book: while the social sciences strive to understand the human condition, they often do so by breaking life into segments, each managed by a separate discipline. Sleep is studied by psychologists, consumption by economists, parenting by sociologists, and media use by cultural theorists. This specialization has brought depth and rigor, but it also risks leaving out the connections between these areas. How work stress affects family relationships, how media habits influence civic participation, or how economic insecurity impacts emotional health; these cross-cutting dynamics often go unexamined.

This basic knowledge of human time use is a prerequisite for all social scientists before they embark on their studies. While much of it may seem like common sense, it is precisely the kind of information that can be overlooked—leading to flawed research. For example, a study of workplace productivity that ignores commuting times may misinterpret stress levels; research on civic engagement that overlooks leisure habits may miss key cultural drivers; and health studies that fail to account for sleep patterns can draw misleading conclusions about lifestyle and disease. Recognizing these underlying rhythms of daily life ensures that research is grounded in the realities of human existence, rather than in abstract or incomplete models.

This *compartmentalization* reflects a broader structural challenge within the social sciences. It's not simply a matter of oversight or bias, but a result of how academic knowledge is organized. To better understand people as whole beings—not just as workers, consumers, parents, or citizens—we need approaches that account for how these roles intersect and evolve. This does not require abandoning specialization, but expanding the scope of inquiry to include the relationships between domains. It suggests a need for more integrative thinking, where diverse methods and traditions inform one another.

With the arrival of AI, this issue becomes even more pressing. Intelligent systems are not bound by the same academic silos; they can draw instantly from economics, psychology, anthropology, and history in ways no single scholar can. This means AI has the potential to break down these compartments—but only if researchers themselves are prepared to engage across them. To evaluate, correct, and guide machine-generated insights, social scientists will need both breadth and depth: breadth to recognize what insights come from other disciplines, and depth to judge whether those connections are sound. In short, the introduction of AI demands another type of social scientist—one who is broader in scope and stronger in knowledge. Without that expanded capacity, we risk outsourcing judgment itself to the machine, unable to know whether what it delivers is true or not.

So far, we have focused on the visible constraints that shape human behavior: the environments we live in, the daily routines we follow, and the physical limits of our bodies. But some of the most important differences between people are less obvious. They lie not in the external world, but in the inner architecture of the mind. To understand how individuals vary in behavior, motivation, and temperament, we now turn to a key source of that variation: personality.

2.7 Personality Evolution

As individuals growing up, we quickly discover that not all humans are alike. They don't look the same, and they certainly don't behave the same. This is natural, of course—people come from different families, carry different DNA, belong to different cultures, develop distinct habits, and grow up in a wide range of environments. But for a child, these differences can be puzzling: "Why are these people not like me? What's wrong with them? (or, perhaps more painfully, me)?".

It takes time, education, and experience to realize that there is nothing wrong with them; they are just different. And these differences, far from being flaws, are part of what makes humanity so adaptable, resilient, and complex. They are not obstacles to understanding, but clues to how evolution has shaped us to survive in diverse ways.

In fact, genetic variation exists not only between individuals but also between human populations. For example, most people of European and Asian descent carry between 1.5 and 2% Neanderthal DNA, the result of interbreeding between anatomically modern humans and Neanderthals that occurred around 50,000 to 60,000 years ago (Green et al., 2010). While this may seem like a minor fraction, it's significant when considered alongside the fact that the entire genetic difference between humans and chimpanzees is only about 1.2%, and even lower—often below 0.2%—in protein-coding regions of the genome (Chimpanzee Sequencing & Analysis Consortium, 2005). This illustrates how even small genetic differences can carry meaningful biological and evolutionary consequences.

Yet, beneath all this diversity, there are also deep and striking similarities. We share a common evolutionary history, the same biological structure, a core set of emotional responses, and the universal capacity for language, social bonding, and moral judgment. These shared traits have evolved over millennia to support cooperation, survival, and social living in complex environments (De Waal, 2013; Tomasello, 2009; Wilson, 2012).

Understanding what makes humans both similar and different is central to the social sciences. It helps explain why societies function the way they do, why conflicts arise, and how collaboration and empathy are possible across divides of culture, language, and belief (Table 2.6).

These distinctions matter. The similarities help us build shared institutions, cooperate in large groups, and empathize across borders. They form the foundation of *universal human rights*, *global scientific inquiry*, and even the idea of *international law*. Meanwhile, the differences explain much of what gives rise to innovation, conflict, misunderstanding, and cultural variation.

The impulse to define "the human being" as a single, stable type did not emerge in a scientific vacuum. It has often been shaped—and in some cases initiated—by political and ideological interests seeking a universal model of humanity to justify governance, policy, or moral frameworks. From Enlightenment-era natural rights theories to twentieth-century modernization projects, political actors have promoted visions of a "universal" human to support integration, standardization, or control (Harding, 1991; Scott, 1998). Over time, this political framing has influenced the social sciences, encouraging the search for generalizable laws of behavior, cognition, and society. While such laws can be analytically powerful, they often abstract away from cultural context, individual variation, and environmental specificity—limiting their accuracy and relevance.

Critics have long pointed out that much of psychology, for instance, is built on samples from WEIRD societies (Western, Educated, Industrialized, Rich, and Democratic), which are not representative of humanity at large (Henrich et al., 2010). The result is that theories constructed to explain "human nature" often fail to account for the full range of human experience. What we call science is thus shaped by who is studied, who is excluded, and what assumptions are baked into research design. While universals do exist, treating difference as a deviation from the norm—rather than as a core part of the picture—can distort both understanding and application.

The risk, then, is not only methodological but also ethical. To treat difference as if it does not exist—or to collapse the full spectrum of human variety into a single generalization such as "all men"—is not just a scientific mistake; it is bound to lead to misleading, and potentially damaging, conclusions. Generalization may be necessary when constructing laws, rights, or policies, but science must be careful not to confuse equality in principle with sameness

Table 2.6 What makes us alike—and what makes us different

Dimension	What's different among humans	What's the same among humans
Biology/ genetics	Each person has a unique genetic code (except identical twins); variation in appearance, health, and abilities	All humans share ~99.9% of their DNA; same species (*Homo sapiens*), basic anatomy and physiology[7]
Family background	People are raised in different types of families—size, values, support systems vary widely	All humans are shaped by early caregiving relationships, which affect development deeply
Culture	Languages, customs, beliefs, and moral norms differ across societies and groups	All cultures pass on knowledge and values; all humans use culture to navigate social life
Behavior and habits	We form different routines, preferences, and social behaviors based on upbringing and choice	All humans are habit-forming creatures and adapt behavior based on experience
Emotions	People express and manage emotions differently based on personality and culture	All humans feel basic emotions like joy, fear, anger, sadness, and love
Cognition/ thinking	Individuals have unique problem-solving styles, memory capacities, and interests	All humans have symbolic language, abstract reasoning, and imagination
Motivations	Some seek power, others seek peace; goals and drives vary	All humans have basic needs—survival, belonging, esteem, meaning (cf. Maslow's hierarchy)
Life experience	Personal experiences shape attitudes, beliefs, and behavior over time	All humans learn from experience and change over the life course
Social roles	Gender roles, professions, and social expectations differ globally and historically	All humans live in structured societies with roles and hierarchies

[7] Although most humans share approximately 99.9% of their DNA, the remaining 0.1% accounts for all genetic variation between individuals and populations. The 1.5–2% Neanderthal DNA found in Europeans and Asians is part of this small fraction and reflects ancient interbreeding, not a separate ancestry. Thus, the presence of Neanderthal genes does not contradict the high overall genetic similarity within Homo sapiens.

in fact. To say that all humans deserve equal dignity or voting rights is not the same as claiming that all humans are identical in abilities, preferences, or life circumstances. When scholarship blurs this distinction, it risks both weakening its own credibility and misguiding the societies that rely on it.

Universities in particular should be spaces where complexity is preserved rather than erased, where difference is examined rather than denied. To reduce human beings to a single mold—whether biological, cultural, or psychological—is to ignore the very diversity that makes us resilient, adaptive, and creative as a species. The challenge for the social sciences, therefore, is not to eliminate variation but to understand it, and to explore how similarity and difference interact in shaping the human condition.

From an evolutionary standpoint, this interplay between similarity and variation is no accident. *Natural selection* favors certain stable traits—like language, cooperation, and problem-solving—because they support group survival (Boyd & Richerson, 2005; Henrich, 2015). But variation within a species is also essential, as it allows for adaptation in changing environments. Different personality types, social strategies, and cultural innovations give humans a remarkable evolutionary advantage: we can not only survive change but drive it.

For social scientists, recognizing both sides of this coin is vital. Our task is not only to explain human universals—why people everywhere love, fear, play, and mourn—but also to understand particularities: why cultures differ, why beliefs diverge, and why no two individuals are exactly the same. The challenge, and the beauty, lies in holding both truths together.

Ultimately, acknowledging both what connects us and what sets us apart gives us the best chance of building a world that is both more understanding and more just.

2.7.1 The Evolutionary Origins of Human Personality

In the previous section, we saw that among the many forms of human variation, personality stands out as one of the most consequential—and least visible. While differences in appearance, language, or upbringing are easy to recognize, *personality variation* operates more subtly but can profoundly shape how individuals respond to challenges, form relationships, and navigate social roles.

From an evolutionary perspective, this variability is not a flaw, but a strategic feature. It reflects the fact that there is no single best way to be human. In some environments, boldness pays off; in others, caution is the wiser path. Some thrive in densely social contexts, while others function best in solitude. These traits are not randomly distributed. Evolutionary theory holds that natural selection has preserved a range of personality types precisely because diversity improves *group survival* and adaptability under changing conditions (Darwin, 1859; Mayr, 1982).

That is why I tend to see the question of what a person should do—or work with—mainly as a matter of finding what you are reasonably good at and giving it the attention it needs, in the hope it will grow into an interest. In doing so, you naturally develop a *niche*—a key mechanism for survival in both biology and society—and you may well find your professional purpose. It need not be more complicated than that. We do not have to attach grand theories or special meaning to career choices. I read books and write because I can manage it and enjoy it. Others do other things. What matters is not following some abstract ideal of the "right" path, but making sure your abilities and interests have a place where they can be put to use and maintained.

This line of thinking is supported by psychological research as well. As Daniel Nettle (2006) points out, traits such as extraversion, conscientiousness, and neuroticism persist across cultures because they each confer benefits in particular settings. Novelty-seeking may open doors in opportunity-rich environments, while anxiety and vigilance may offer advantages in unpredictable or dangerous ones (Wilson et al., 1994).

This diversity is further sustained through frequency-dependent selection. As Buss (2009) explains, a behavioral strategy may be successful only when rare. In highly cooperative groups, for instance, a few opportunistic individuals may exploit trust for personal gain. But if such strategies become common, they undermine group cohesion and ultimately become self-limiting (Nowak & Sigmund, 2005).

Taken together, these perspectives suggest that personality variation is not accidental but adaptive. Humans have not evolved toward uniformity, but toward functional diversity; a mosaic of behavioral strategies shaped by natural selection, cultural transmission, and individual development. This diversity in personality and behavior invites deeper questions—not just about what we do, but why we do it.

What drives human action at its core? Are we the deliberate agents of our own choices, or are we guided more than we know by inherited dispositions and evolved responses?

These questions mark a natural progression rather than a sharp turn. In the final sections of this chapter, we have already begun examining the *internal architecture* of the human being—our mental dispositions, behavioral patterns, and evolutionary strategies. But to truly understand what drives human behavior, we now go deeper. In the next chapter, we move from outlining biological and personality constraints to exploring the mind itself: how humans perceive the world, reason through problems, and experience emotions. This is where much of the intellectual excitement lies, as we uncover the inner logic that underpins action, belief, and identity. Drawing on evolutionary psychology, neuroscience, and cognitive science, we continue our search for what kind of animal the human truly is.

But before we move on, we must also pause to consider what all this means for the social sciences.

Anchoring Social Science Before AI Sets It Adrift.

This chapter has not merely offered background or context. It has outlined something far more fundamental: the starting point that any serious social science must take if it hopes to produce accurate, meaningful insights about human beings. We have surveyed the biological constraints, evolutionary pathways, and environmental conditions that shape how we live, think, and behave—from aggression and mating to settlement patterns, symbolic culture, and personality variation. These are not just curiosities. They are the ground rules of human existence.

If the social sciences fail to start from this ground—if they ignore the evolutionary, biological, and ecological realities of the species they seek to understand—then they are not just incomplete. They are misdirected. They risk asking the wrong questions, making false assumptions, and offering solutions to problems that were poorly formulated to begin with.

Much of modern social science, for all its theoretical ingenuity, still too often treats the human being as a blank slate or a disembodied rational actor, divorced from the very history and structure that define what it means to be human. We just love to ignore cultural differences, climate, and all the other things that set us apart—even down to our eating habits and ways of socializing—because we are so eager to be universal and draw general conclusions. But that's a big mistake, sometimes even a kind of intellectual sin, especially when it's not justified by the data or the context.

This chapter, then, is not a detour but a foundation. The purpose has been to show, empirically and comparatively, how humans differ from and resemble other animals, and how our evolutionary legacy continues to shape our institutions, choices, and constraints. To do otherwise—to ignore these insights or sideline them in favor of purely cultural or ideological models—is to build a science on sand.

In the age of AI, this foundation becomes even more critical. As machines take on a growing share of data analysis, pattern recognition, and even theory generation, the temptation will be to let algorithms define what is important—often based on patterns in data that overlook the deeper, evolved architecture of human behavior. If the social sciences surrender this grounding, they risk becoming tools for short-term prediction and manipulation rather than for long-term understanding. AI can help us see correlations faster than ever before, but without the evolutionary map of the human animal, those correlations will lack context, misinterpret causality, and lead us astray. The challenge for the social sciences now is to integrate AI's analytical power with a biologically and evolutionarily informed framework—ensuring that our models of humanity remain anchored in what humans are, not just in what the latest dataset suggests.

In sum, this chapter has diagnosed the problem: humans are biased, irrational, and prone to self-deception—yet we often pretend otherwise in politics, science, and society. Chapter 3 turns to the mechanism behind this diagnosis: how these biases and moral instincts actually emerge from evolved cognition, cultural scaffolding, and perceptual limits.

References

Ajzen, I., & Fishbein, M. (1980). *Understanding attitudes and predicting social behavior*. Prentice-Hall.

Allentoft, M. E., Sikora, M., Sjögren, K. G., Rasmussen, S., Rasmussen, M., Stenderup, J., & Willerslev, E. (2015). Population genomics of Bronze Age Eurasia. *Nature, 522*(7555), 167–172. https://doi.org/10.1038/nature14507

Anderson, B. (1983). *Imagined communities: Reflections on the origin and spread of nationalism*. Verso.

Andreoni, J. (1990). Impure altruism and donations to public goods. *The Economic Journal, 100*(401), 464–477.

Anthony, D. W. (2007). *The horse, the wheel, and language: How bronze-age riders from the Eurasian steppes shaped the modern world*. Princeton University Press.

Archer, M. S. (2004). *Being human: The problem of agency*. Cambridge University Press.

Archer, J. (2006). Testosterone and human aggression: An evaluation of the challenge hypothesis. *Neuroscience & Biobehavioral Reviews, 30*(3), 319–345.

Arendt, H. (1951). *The origins of totalitarianism*. Harcourt.

Aronson, E. (1999). *The social animal* (8th ed.). Worth Publishers.

Atran, S. (2002). *In Gods we trust: The evolutionary landscape of religion*. Oxford University Press.

Arora, N., Dreze, X., Ghose, A., Hess, J. D., Iyengar, R., Jing, B., & Shankar, V. (2008). Putting one-to-one marketing to work: Personalization, customization, and choice. *Marketing Letters, 19*(3–4), 305–316.

Azari, N. P., Nickel, J., Wunderlich, G., et al. (2001). Neural correlates of religious experience. *European Journal of Neuroscience, 13*(8), 1649–1652.

Baeten, G., Westin, S., Pull, E., & Molina, I. (2010a). Crisis and the post-industrial city: Or is Malmö building yesterday's city tomorrow, again? *Environment and Planning A, 42*(3), 611–617.

Baeten, G., van den Berg, L., & Murie, A. (2010b). *City matters: Competitiveness, cohesion and urban governance*. Routledge.

Bai, C., Ning, C., Yao, H., Liu, F., Wang, C., Sun, Y., … & Cui, Y. (2023). Genetic origins and admixture history of Iron Age nomads of the Eastern Steppe. *Nature Communications, 14*(1).

Bandura, A. (1997). *Self-efficacy: The exercise of control.* Freeman.

Barth, F. (1969). *Ethnic groups and boundaries: The social organization of culture difference*. Little, Brown.

Bauman, Z. (2000). *Liquid modernity*. Polity Press.

Beck, U. (2009). *World at risk*. Polity Press.

Beard, M., North, J., & Price, S. (1998). *Religions of Rome:* (Vol. 1). Cambridge University Press.

Bell, D. A., & Chaibong, H. (2003). *Confucianism for the modern world*. Cambridge University Press.

Billig, M. (1995). *Banal nationalism.* SAGE Publications.

Bluestone, B., & Harrison, B. (1982). *The deindustrialization of America: Plant closings, community abandonment, and the dismantling of basic industry*. Basic Books.

Boiten, E. A. (1998). Improving the quality of formal method applications: The need for structured approaches. *Formal Aspects of Computing, 10*(3), 307–318.

Book, A. S., Starzyk, K. B., & Quinsey, V. L. (2001). The relationship between testosterone and aggression: A meta-analysis. *Aggression and Violent Behavior, 6*(6), 579–599.

Bourdieu, P. (1988). *Homo academicus.* Stanford University Press.

Boyd, R., & Richerson, P. J. (2005). *The origin and evolution of cultures.* Oxford University Press.

Boyer, P. (2001). *Religion explained: The evolutionary origins of religious thought*. Basic Books.

Bramble, D. M., & Lieberman, D. E. (2004). Endurance running and the evolution of Homo. *Nature, 432*(7015), 345–352. https://doi.org/10.1038/nature03052

Broadbent, E., Stafford, R., & MacDonald, B. (2009). Acceptance of healthcare robots for the older population: Review and future directions. *International Journal of Social Robotics, 1*(4), 319–330.

Burgoon, J. K., Guerrero, L. K., & Floyd, K. (2016). *Nonverbal communication.* Routledge.

Buss, D. M. (1989). Sex differences in human mate preferences: Evolutionary hypotheses tested in 37 cultures. *Behavioral and Brain Sciences, 12*(1), 1–49.

Buss, D. M., & Schmitt, D. P. (1993). Sexual strategies theory: An evolutionary perspective on human mating. *Psychological Review, 100*(2), 204–232. https://doi.org/10.1037/0033-295X.100.2.204

Buss, D. M., & Shackelford, T. K. (1997). Human aggression in evolutionary psychological perspective. *Clinical Psychology Review, 17*(6), 605–619.

Buss, D. M. (2003). *The evolution of desire: Strategies of human mating*. Basic Books.

Buss, D. M. (2009). *Evolutionary psychology: The new science of the mind* (4th ed.). Pearson.

Carré, J. M., & McCormick, C. M. (2008). Aggressive behavior and change in salivary testosterone concentrations predict willingness to engage in a competitive task. *Hormones and Behavior, 54*(3), 403–409.

Ceballos, G., Ehrlich, P. R., & Dirzo, R. (2017). Biological annihilation via the ongoing sixth mass extinction signaled by vertebrate population losses and declines. *Proceedings of the National Academy of Sciences, 114*(30), E6089–E6096.

Champion, T. (2001). Urbanization, suburbanization, counterurbanization and reurbanization. In R. Paddison (Ed.), *Handbook of urban studies* (pp. 143–161). Sage.

Chimpanzee Sequencing and Analysis Consortium. (2005). Initial sequence of the chimpanzee genome and comparison with the human genome. *Nature, 437*, 69–72. https://doi.org/10.1038/nature04072

Coccaro, E. F., McCloskey, M. S., Fitzgerald, D. A., & Phan, K. L. (2007). Amygdala and orbitofrontal reactivity to social threat in individuals with impulsive aggression. *Biological Psychiatry, 62*(2), 168–178.

Cook, D. (2005). *Understanding Jihad*. University of California Press.

Cosmides, L., & Tooby, J. (1992). Cognitive adaptations for social exchange. In J. H. Barkow, L. Cosmides, & J. Tooby (Eds.), *The adapted mind: Evolutionary psychology and the generation of culture* (pp. 163–228). Oxford University Press.

Couldry, N. (2012). M*edia, society, world: Social theory and digital media practice*. Polity.

Cramer, K. J. (2016). *The politics of resentment: Rural consciousness in Wisconsin and the rise of Scott Walker*. University of Chicago Press.

Daly, M., & Wilson, M. (1988). *Homicide*. Aldine de Gruyter.

Darwin, C. (1859). *On the origin of species by means of natural selection*. John Murray.

Darwin, C. (1871). *The descent of man, and selection in relation to sex*. John Murray.

Dawkins, R. (2006). *The God delusion*. Bantam Press.

Demir, M., & Weitekamp, L. A. (2007). I am so happy 'cause today I found my friend: Friendship and personality as predictors of happiness. *Journal of Happiness Studies, 8*(2), 181–211.

De Nadai, M., Xu, Y., Letouzé, E., González, M. C., & Lepri, B. (2020). Socio-economic, built environment, and mobility conditions associated with crime: A study of multiple cities. *Scientific Reports, 10*, 15279.

de Waal, F. (1995). *Bonobo: The Forgotten Ape*. University of California Press.

de Waal, F. (2009). *The age of empathy: Nature's lessons for a kinder society*. Harmony Books.

de Waal, F. (2013). *The bonobo and the atheist: In search of humanism among the primates*. W. W. Norton & Company.

Diamond, J. (1992). *The Third Chimpanzee: The evolution and future of the human animal*. HarperCollins.

Douglas, M. (1984). *Food in the social order: Studies of food and festivities in three American communities*. Russell Sage Foundation.

Duckworth, A. L., Peterson, C., Matthews, M. D., & Kelly, D. R. (2007). Grit: perseverance and passion for long-term goals. *Journal of Personality and Social Psychology, 92*(6), 1087–1101.

Durkheim, É. (1995). *The elementary forms of religious life* (K. E. Fields, Trans.). Free Press. (Original work published 1912).

Eisner, M. (2003). Long-term historical trends in violent crime. *Crime and Justice, 30*, 83–142.

Elsey, R. M. & Trosclair III, P. L. (2008) American Alligator Alligator mississippiensis. In *Crocodiles: Status survey and conservation action plan* (3rd ed.). IUCN.

Eriksen, T. H. (2010). *Ethnicity and nationalism: Anthropological perspectives* (3rd ed.). Pluto Press.

Evans, G. W. (2003). The built environment and mental health. *Journal of Urban Health, 80*(4), 536–555. https://doi.org/10.1093/jurban/jtg063

Exodus 20:3, Holy Bible.

Fehr, E., & Fischbacher, U. (2003). The nature of human altruism. *Nature, 425*(6960), 785–791.

Feyerabend, P. (1975). *Against method*. Verso.

Firestone, R. (1999). *Jihad: The origin of Holy War in Islam*. Oxford University Press.

Fischer, A. H., & Roseman, I. J. (2007). Beat them or ban them: The characteristics and social functions of anger and contempt. *Journal of Personality and Social Psychology, 93*(1), 103–115.

Fisher, R. J. (1993). Social desirability bias and the validity of indirect questioning. *Journal of Consumer Research, 20*(2), 303–315.

Fishman, J. A. (1989). *Language and ethnicity in minority sociolinguistic perspective*. Multilingual Matters.

Fisman, R., Iyengar, S. S., Kamenica, E., & Simonson, I. (2006). Gender differences in mate selection. *Quarterly Journal of Economics, 121*(2), 673–697.

Gallagher, L. (2013). *The end of the suburbs: Where the American dream is moving*. Portfolio/Penguin.

Gershuny, J., & Fisher, K. (2014). Time use and time budgets. *Handbook of Economic Sociology, 3*, 1–25.

Giddens, A. (1991). *Modernity and self-identity: Self and society in the late Modern Age*. Stanford University Press.

Gillis, J. R. (1996). *Commemorations: The politics of national identity*. Princeton University Press.

Gino, F., Ayal, S., & Ariely, D. (2010). Contagion and differentiation in unethical behavior: The effect of one bad apple on the barrel. *Psychological Science, 20*(3), 393–398.
Gini, A. (2000). *My job, my self: Work and the creation of the modern individual.* Routledge.
Glaeser, E. L. (2011). *Triumph of the city: How our greatest invention makes us richer, smarter, greener, healthier, and happier*. Penguin Press.
Glaeser, E. L., & Kahn, M. E. (2010). The greenness of cities. *Journal of Urban Economics, 67*(3), 404–418.
Goffman, E. (1959). *The presentation of self in everyday life*. Anchor Books.
Goodall, J. (1990). *Through a window: My thirty years with the chimpanzees of Gombe*. Houghton Mifflin.
Gray, J. A. (2011). *The neuropsychology of anxiety*. Oxford University Press.
Green, R. E., Krause, J., Briggs, A. W., Maricic, T., Stenzel, U., Kircher, M., & Pääbo, S. (2010). A draft sequence of the Neandertal genome. *Science, 328*(5979), 710–722. https://doi.org/10.1126/science.1188021
Greenwood, B. (2014). The contribution of vaccination to global health: Past, present and future. *Philosophical Transactions of the Royal Society B, 369*(1645), 20130433.
Gruebner, O., Rapp, M. A., Adli, M., et al. (2017). Cities and mental health. *Dtsch Arztebl International, 114*(8), 121–127.
Haak, W., Lazaridis, I., Patterson, N., Rohland, N., Mallick, S., Llamas, B., & Reich, D. (2015). Massive migration from the steppe was a source for Indo-European languages in Europe. *Nature, 522*(7555), 207–211. https://doi.org/10.1038/nature14317
Hall, P. A., & Hubbard, W. (1998). *Varieties of capitalism.* Oxford University Press.
Harding, S. (1991). *Whose science? Whose knowledge? Thinking from women's lives.* Cornell University Press.
Haselton, M. G., & Buss, D. M. (2000). Error management theory: A new perspective on biases in cross-sex mind reading. *Journal of Personality and Social Psychology, 78*(1), 81–91. https://doi.org/10.1037/0022-3514.78.1.81
Hamilton, W. D. (1964). The genetical evolution of social behaviour. I & II. *Journal of Theoretical Biology, 7*(1), 1–52.
Hastorf, A. H., & Cantril, H. (1954). They saw a game: A case study. *Journal of Abnormal and Social Psychology, 49*(1), 129–134.
Henrich, J. (2015). *The secret of our success: How culture is driving human evolution, domesticating our species, and making us smarter*. Princeton University Press.
Henrich, J., Heine, S. J., & Norenzayan, A. (2010). The weirdest people in the world? *Behavioral and Brain Sciences, 33*(2–3), 61–83.
High, S. (2003). *Industrial sunset: The making of North America's rust belt, 1969–1984*. University of Toronto Press.
Hirshkowitz, M., Whiton, K., Albert, S. M., Alessi, C., Bruni, O., DonCarlos, L., & Hillard, P. J. A. (2015). National Sleep Foundation's sleep time duration recommendations. *Sleep Health, 1*(1), 40–43.

Hitchens, C. (2007). *God is not great: How religion poisons everything*. Twelve Books.

Hruschka, D. J. (2010). *Friendship: Development, ecology, and evolution of a relationship*. University of California Press.

Hutchinson, J., & Smith, A. D. (Eds.). (1996). *Ethnicity*. Oxford University Press.

Inglehart, R., & Baker, W. E. (2000). Modernization, cultural change, and the persistence of traditional values. *American Sociological Review, 65*(1), 19–51. https://doi.org/10.2307/2657288

International Labour Organization (ILO). (2018). *Global wage report 2018/19: What lies behind gender pay gaps*. ILO.

Jacobs, J. (1961). *The death and life of great American cities*. Random House.

Jeong, C., Wang, K., Wilkin, S., Taylor, W. T. T., Miller, B. K., Bemmann, J. H., & Warinner, C. (2020). A dynamic 6,000-year genetic history of Eurasia's Eastern Steppe. *Cell, 183*(4), 890-904.e29. https://doi.org/10.1016/j.cell.2020.10.015

Kahneman, D. (2011). *Thinking, fast and slow*. Farrar.

Kenrick, D. T., Li, N. P., & Butner, J. (2003). Dynamical evolutionary psychology: Individual decision rules and emergent social norms. *Psychological Review, 110*(1), 3–28.

Klein, R. G. (2009). *The human career: Human biological and cultural origins* (3rd ed.). University of Chicago Press.

Köhler, D., Menzel, C., & Call, J. (2016). Chimpanzees (Pan troglodytes) show hints of ritualized behavior in response to natural phenomena. *Primates, 57*(1), 91–102.

Kruger, J., & Dunning, D. (1999). Unskilled and unaware of it: How difficulties in recognizing one's own incompetence lead to inflated self-assessments. *Journal of Personality and Social Psychology, 77*(6), 1121–1134.

Kunda, Z. (1990). The case for motivated reasoning. *Psychological Bulletin, 108*(3), 480–498.

Larivière, V., Gingras, Y., & Archambault, É. (2009). The decline in the concentration of citations, 1900–2007. *Journal of the American Society for Information Science and Technology, 60*(4), 858–862.

Laumann, E. O., Paik, A., & Rosen, R. C. (1999). Sexual dysfunction in the United States: Prevalence and predictors. *JAMA, 281*(6), 537–544. https://doi.org/10.1001/jama.281.6.537

Laursen, B., & Hartup, W. W. (2002). The origins of reciprocity and social exchange in friendships. In B. Laursen & W. G. Graziano (Eds.), *Social exchange in development* (pp. 27–40). Jossey-Bass.

Larson, C. (2025, June 19). *Ancient humans adapted to extreme environments before migrating out of Africa, study shows*. Associated Press. Retrieved from https://apnews.com/article/ancient-humans-migration-adaptability-homo-sapiens-d7c15932203b50221d3ff321f10da44b

Lederbogen, F., Kirsch, P., Haddad, L., Tost, H., & Meyer-Lindenberg, A. (2011). City living and urban upbringing affect neural social stress processing in humans. *Nature, 474*(7352), 498–501.

Lewontin, R. C. (1972). The apportionment of human diversity. *Evolutionary Biology, 6*, 381–398.

Li, P., Janczewski, W. A., Yackle, K., Kam, K., Pagliardini, S., Krasnow, M. A., & Feldman, J. L. (2016). The peptidergic control circuit for sighing. *Nature, 530*(7590), 293–297. https://doi.org/10.1038/nature16964

Litman, T. (2023). *Autonomous vehicle implementation predictions: Implications for transport planning*. Victoria Transport Policy Institute.

Luy, M., & Gast, K. (2014). Do women live longer or do men die earlier? Reflections on the causes of sex differences in life expectancy. *Gerontology, 60*(2), 143–153.

Löfgren, O. (1993). Food and nationality: The cultural logic of Swedish holidays. In C. Counihan & P. Van Esterik (Eds.), *Food and culture: A reader* (pp. 165–172). Routledge.

Majumdar, B. (2008). *Cricket in colonial India 1780–1947: A social history*. Routledge.

Mayr, E. (1982). *The growth of biological thought: Diversity, evolution, and inheritance*. Harvard University Press.

McBrearty, S., & Brooks, A. S. (2000). The revolution that wasn't: A new interpretation of the origin of modern human behavior. *Journal of Human Evolution, 39*(5), 453–563. https://doi.org/10.1006/jhev.2000.0435

Mehrabian, A. (2007). *Nonverbal communication*. Aldine Transaction.

Mellars, P. (2006). *Why did modern human populations disperse from Africa ca. 60,000 years ago? A new model. Proceedings of the National Academy of Sciences, 103*(25), 9381–9386. https://doi.org/10.1073/pnas.0510792103

Meloy, J. R. (1998). *The psychology of stalking: Clinical and forensic perspectives*. Academic Press.

Merton, R. K. (1973). *The sociology of science: Theoretical and empirical investigations*. University of Chicago Press.

Meyer, M., et al. (2012). Cognitive neuroscience of religion. *Trends in Cognitive Sciences, 16*(2), 75–83.

Mishra, S., Yadav, K., & Pandey, C. M. (2017). Dietary habits and health status among adolescents. *Indian Journal of Pediatrics, 84*(8), 619–624.

Montagu, A. (1942). *Man's most dangerous myth: The fallacy of race*. Columbia University Press.

Muller, M. N. (2017). Testosterone and reproductive effort in male primates. *Hormones and Behavior, 91*, 36–51.

Nettle, D. (2006). The evolution of personality variation in humans and other animals. *American Psychologist, 61*(6), 622–631.

Nickerson, R. S. (1998). Confirmation bias: A ubiquitous phenomenon in many guises. *Review of General Psychology, 2*(2), 175–220.

Nicogossian, A. E., Williams, R. S., Huntoon, C. L., Doarn, C. R., Polk, J. D. & Schneider, V. S. (2016). *Space physiology and medicine: From evidence to practice*. Springer.

Niedomysl, T. (2010). Towards a conceptual framework of place attractiveness: A migration perspective. *Geografiska Annaler: Series b, Human Geography, 92*(1), 97–109. https://doi.org/10.1111/j.1468-0467.2010.00333.x

Ning, C., Li, T., Wang, K., Zhang, F., Li, T., Wu, X., & Cui, Y. (2020). Ancient genomes reveal Yamnaya-related ancestry and a potential source of Indo-European speakers in Iron Age Tianshan. *Nature Communications, 11*(1), 5900. https://doi.org/10.1038/s41467-020-19655-8

Norenzayan, A. (2013). *Big gods: How religion transformed cooperation and conflict*. Princeton University Press.

Norenzayan, A., & Shariff, A. F. (2008). The origin and evolution of religious prosociality. *Science, 322*(5898), 58–62.

Nowak, M. A., & Sigmund, K. (2005). Evolution of indirect reciprocity. *Nature, 437*(7063), 1291–1298.

OECD. (2018). *The future of education and skills: Education 2030*. OECD Publishing.

OECD. (2021). *Pensions at a glance 2021: OECD and G20 indicators*. OECD Publishing.

Oyserman, D., Elmore, K., & Smith, G. (2002). Self, self-concept, and identity. In M. R. Leary & J. P. Tangney (Eds.), *Handbook of Self and Identity* (pp. 69–104). Guilford Press.

Peen, J., Schoevers, R. A., Beekman, A. T., & Dekker, J. (2010). The current status of urban–rural differences in psychiatric disorders. *Acta Psychiatrica Scandinavica, 121*(2), 84–93.

Pinker, S. (2011). *The better angels of our nature: Why violence has declined*. Viking.

Putnam, R. D. (2000). *Bowling alone: The collapse and revival of American community*. Simon & Schuster.

Robinson, J. P., & Godbey, G. (1999). *Time for life: The surprising ways Americans use their time* (2nd ed.). Pennsylvania State University Press.

Pontzer, H., Suchman, K., Raichlen, D. A., Wood, B. M., Mabulla, A. Z., & Marlowe, F. W. (2014). Hunter-gatherer energetics and human obesity. *PLoS ONE, 9*(7), Article e102491.

Popper, K. (1959). *The logic of scientific discovery*. Hutchinson.

Rappuoli, R., Aderem, A., & others. (2011). Vaccines and global health. *Proceedings of the National Academy of Sciences, 108*(Suppl 1), 4623–4627.

Rozin, P. (1996). The socio-cultural context of eating and food choice. In H. L. Meiselman & H. J. H. MacFie (Eds.), *Food choice, acceptance and consumption* (pp. 83–104). Springer.

Russell, B. (1952). *The impact of science on society*. Simon and Schuster.

Russo, J., & Linkon, S. L. (2008). The social costs of deindustrialization. In *Manufacturing a better future for America* (pp. 125–144). United Steelworkers.

Salthouse, T. A. (2004). What and when of cognitive aging. *Current Directions in Psychological Science, 13*(4), 140–144.

Sapolsky, R. M. (2017). *Behave: The biology of humans at our best and worst*. Penguin Press.

Schjoedt, U., Stødkilde-Jørgensen, H., Geertz, A. W., & Roepstorff, A. (2009). Highly religious participants recruit areas of social cognition in prayer. *Social Cognitive and Affective Neuroscience, 4*(2), 199–207.

Schlegel, A., & Barry III, H. (1991). *Adolescence: An anthropological inquiry*. Free Press.

Schlesinger, L. B. (2000). Sexual homicide: Differentiating patterns of offender behavior. *Journal of Interpersonal Violence, 15*(12), 1320–1335.

Schwanen, T., Dijst, M., & Dieleman, F. M. (2004). Policies for urban form and their impact on travel: The Netherlands experience. *Urban Studies, 41*(3), 579–603.

Scott, J. C. (1998). *Seeing like a state: How certain schemes to improve the human condition have failed*. Yale University Press.

Sheldon, K. M., Ryan, R. M., Rawsthorne, L. J., & Ilardi, B. (1997). Trait self and true self: Cross-role variation in the Big-Five personality traits and its relations with psychological authenticity and subjective well-being. *Journal of Personality and Social Psychology, 73*(6), 1380–1393.

Shils, E. A., & Janowitz, M. (1948). Cohesion and disintegration in the Wehrmacht in World War II. *Public Opinion Quarterly, 12*(2), 280–315.

Silk, J. B. (2003). Cooperation without counting: The puzzle of friendship. In P. Hammerstein (Ed.), *Genetic and cultural evolution of cooperation* (pp. 37–54). MIT Press.

Silk, J. B., Alberts, S. C., & Altmann, J. (2009). Social bonds of female baboons enhance infant survival. *Science, 302*(5648), 1231–1234.

Singh, D. (1993). Adaptive significance of female physical attractiveness: Role of waist-to-hip ratio. *Journal of Personality and Social Psychology, 65*(2), 293–307. https://doi.org/10.1037/0022-3514.65.2.293

Snyder, C. R., & Fromkin, H. L. (1980). *Uniqueness: The human pursuit of difference*. Plenum Press.

Stanovich, K. E., & West, R. F. (2000). Individual differences in reasoning: Implications for the rationality debate? *Behavioral and Brain Sciences, 23*(5), 645–665.

Statista. (2023). *Average daily time spent watching video content worldwide*. Retrieved from https://www.statista.com

Söilen, K. S. (2009). Life style welfare: How the New Class has transformed the Scandinavian Welfare State. *Telos, 148*, 73–85.

Tajfel, H. (1981). *Human groups and social categories: Studies in social psychology*. Cambridge University Press.

Tajfel, H., & Turner, J. C. (1979) An integrative theory of intergroup conflict. In W. G. Austin, & S. Worchel (Eds.), *The social psychology of intergroup relations* (pp. 33–47). Brooks/Cole.

Templeton, A. R. (1998). Human races: A genetic and evolutionary perspective. *American Anthropologist, 100*(3), 632–650.

Tomasello, M. (2009). *Why we cooperate*. MIT Press.

Tomasello, M. (2014). *A natural history of human thinking*. Harvard University Press.

Trivers, R. L. (1971). The evolution of reciprocal altruism. *Quarterly Review of Biology, 46*(1), 35–57.

Turner, J. C., Hogg, M. A., Oakes, P. J., Reicher, S. D., & Wetherell, M. S. (1987). *Rediscovering the social group: A self-categorization theory*. Basil Blackwell.

Underhill, P. (1999). *Why we buy: The science of shopping*. Simon and Schuster.

United Nations, Department of Economic and Social Affairs. (2018). *World urbanization prospects: The 2018 revision*. United Nations.

Vlemincx, E., Abelson, J. L., Lehrer, P. M., Davenport, P. W., & Van Diest, I. (2013). Respiratory variability and sighing: A psychophysiological reset model. *Biological Psychology, 93*(1), 24–32. https://doi.org/10.1016/j.biopsycho.2012.12.001

Walker, M. (2017). *Why we sleep: Unlocking the power of sleep and dreams*. Scribner.

West, J. B. (2012). *High life: A history of high-altitude physiology and medicine*. Springer.

Wilber, R. L., & Pitsiladis, Y. P. (2012). Kenyan and Ethiopian distance runners: What makes them so good? *International Journal of Sports Physiology and Performance, 7*(2), 92–102. https://doi.org/10.1123/ijspp.7.2.92

Wilson, D. S., Near, D., & Miller, R. R. (1994). Individual differences in nonshared environment: The role of personality and parenting in predicting similarities and differences. *Developmental Psychology, 30*(4), 660–671.

Wilson, D. S. (2002). *Darwin's Cathedral: Evolution, religion, and the nature of society*. University of Chicago Press.

Wilson, E. O. (2012). *The social conquest of earth*. Liveright.

Wilson, M., & Daly, M. (1985). Competitiveness, risk taking, and violence: The young male syndrome. *Ethology and Sociobiology, 6*(1), 59–73.

Wong, D. F. K., Chang, Y. L., & He, X. S. (2003). Correlates of psychological distress among migrant workers. *Journal of Community Psychology, 31*(2), 193–209.

World Bank. (2023). *Life expectancy at birth*. https://data.worldbank.org/indicator/SP.DYN.LE00.IN

World Health Organization (WHO). (2020). *Guidelines on physical activity and sedentary behaviour*. WHO.

Worm, B., Davis, B., Kettemer, L., Ward-Paige, C. A., Chapman, D., Heithaus, M. R., & Gruber, S. H. (2013). Global catches, exploitation rates, and rebuilding options for sharks. *Marine Policy, 40*, 194–204.

Wrangham, R., & Peterson, D. (1996). *Demonic males: Apes and the origins of human violence*. Houghton Mifflin.

Wrangham, R. (2019). *The goodness paradox: The strange relationship between virtue and violence in human evolution*. Pantheon.

Wuthnow, R. (2018). *The left behind: Decline and rage in rural America*. Princeton University Press.

Yao, X. (2000). *An introduction to Confucianism*. Cambridge University Press.

Zubieta-Calleja, G. R., & Zubieta-DeUrioste, N. (2007). Altitude adaptation through hematocrit changes. *Journal of Biological Physics and Chemistry, 7*(1), 33–36.

Zuckerman, M. (1994). *Behavioral expressions and biosocial bases of sensation seeking*. Cambridge University Press.

Further Reading

Champagne, F. A., & Curley, J. P. (2009). Epigenetic mechanisms mediating the long-term effects of maternal care on development. *Neuroscience & Biobehavioral Reviews, 33*(4), 593–600.

de Waal, F. (2006). *Primates and philosophers: How morality evolved*. Princeton University Press.

Kaplan, H. S., & Gangestad, S. W. (2005). Life history theory and evolutionary psychology. In D. M. Buss (Ed.), *The handbook of evolutionary psychology* (pp. 68–95). Wiley.

Lane Fox, R. (1986). *Pagans and Christians*. Penguin.

Lieberman, L., & Reynolds, L. T. (1996). The debate over race: A round table on 'The Bell Curve.' *Anthropology & Education Quarterly, 27*(1), 6–30.

Maslow, A. H. (1943). A theory of human motivation. *Psychological Review, 50*(4), 370–396.

Matsumoto, T., Tuuga, A., & Bernard, H. (2016). Male care and development of social behavior in wild proboscis monkeys (Nasalis larvatus): Implications for male-infant interactions. *Primates, 57*(2), 271–280.

Meaney, M. J. (2010). Epigenetics and the biological definition of gene × environment interactions. *Child Development, 81*(1), 41–79.

Parish, A. R. (1996). Female relationships in bonobos (Pan paniscus): Evidence for bonding, cooperation, and female dominance in a male-philopatric species. *Human Nature, 7*(1), 61–96.

Parke, H. W. (1988). *Sibyls and Sibylline Prophecy in Classical Antiquity*. Routledge.

Plomin, R., DeFries, J. C., Knopik, V. S., & Neiderhiser, J. M. (2013). *Behavioral genetics* (6th ed.). Worth Publishers.

Stark, R. (1996). *The rise of Christianity*. HarperSanFrancisco.

Stringer, C. (2016). *The origin of our species*. Penguin.

Tooby, J., & Cosmides, L. (1992). The psychological foundations of culture. In J. H. Barkow, L. Cosmides, & J. Tooby (Eds.), *The adapted mind: Evolutionary psychology and the generation of culture* (pp. 19–136). Oxford University Press.

Vlemincx, E., Taelman, J., De Peuter, S., Van Diest, I., & Van den Bergh, O. (2015). Sigh rate and respiratory variability during mental load and sustained attention. *Psychophysiology, 52*(6), 826–834. https://doi.org/10.1111/psyp.12412

3

Cognition, Emotion, and Sociality

Abstract What kind of mind creates meaning, morality, and social order? This chapter turns inward to examine the human organism itself—the cognitive and emotional machinery behind belief, judgment, and behavior. Drawing on neuroscience, psychology, and evolutionary theory, the chapter challenges the idea of the human mind as a neutral or purely rational instrument. The chapter shows how traits such as empathy, bias, memory, and moral intuition are not design flaws, but evolutionary adaptations shaped by survival and social life. Human cognition is revealed as deeply emotional, context sensitive, and socially embedded—better suited for navigating relationships and threats than for objective truth-seeking. By reframing cognition as a co-production of biology and culture, this chapter offers a realistic account of both human limitation and potential. Understanding how perception and judgment are shaped by evolutionary constraints becomes essential—not only for explaining behavior, but for designing more resilient institutions, technologies, and social systems that work with human nature rather than against it.

In Chapter 2, we examined how symbolic systems—such as religion, language, and shared meaning—form the glue of social life. We argued that meaning is not an abstraction, but a lived experience, passed through culture, communication, and the structures of belief. With this in mind, this chapter shifts focus inward, to the human organism itself. What kind of being produces and interprets meaning in the first place?

K. Solberg Söilen, *The Researcher's Journey in the Age of AI*,
https://doi.org/10.1007/978-3-032-23069-0_3

This chapter investigates the cognitive, emotional, and evolutionary foundations of the human being. It explores how traits like empathy, memory, rationality, and bias emerge—not as isolated functions, but as adaptations shaped by our ancestral past. Drawing on neuroscience, psychology, and evolutionary theory, we aim to clarify the deep structure of human nature and challenge simplistic assumptions about reason, morality, and objectivity.

We argue that understanding humanity requires accepting both our limitations and our latent potential. Our minds are not neutral instruments; they are shaped by emotion, survival, and culture. But this does not doom us to irrationality—it simply means that human behavior is best understood as a co-production between biology and environment, shaped by time, place, and social structure.

The chapter unfolds in four major sections:

1. Evolutionary Roots of Behavior: We begin with the evolutionary psychology of cooperation, kinship, competition, and social norms. These deep structures help explain why humans often act irrationally, but also why we can be profoundly moral and altruistic.
2. The Architecture of the Mind: We explore the modular view of cognition and how natural selection gave rise to specialized mental functions—many of which remain unconscious. The section contrasts Enlightenment assumptions about reason with contemporary findings about cognitive bias, heuristics, and motivated reasoning.
3. Culture Needs Biology, and Vice Versa: This section shows how cultural norms are not opposed to biology but built upon it. Human development requires both evolved learning mechanisms and socially transmitted norms. Culture, in this sense, is not a constraint on nature—it is nature extended.
4. The Limits of Human Perception and Objectivity: We end with a discussion of perception as a biased, constructed process. Drawing from neuroscience, we illustrate how our senses filter reality through evolutionary lenses, and why our experience of the world is shaped more by interpretation than by truth.

In conclusion, this chapter lays the cognitive and emotional groundwork for the rest of the book. It urges the reader to take human limitation seriously, not as a flaw to be overcome, but as a key to designing better institutions, technologies, and social systems. To understand humanity is not only to admire our capacities, but to see clearly the biases and blind spots that accompany them.

3.1 Free Will: Biology and AI

When I grew up in the 1970s and 1980 s, the idea of *free will* was rarely questioned. It was assumed, not argued. We were told, implicitly and explicitly, that we are in control of our choices. Actions had moral weight because they were freely chosen. In classrooms and conversations, human autonomy was treated as self-evident truth; any alternative was dismissed as fringe philosophy. To suggest that biology played a dominant role in shaping behavior was to risk being branded a "determinist"—a label that implied not only intellectual error but moral danger. It marked you as someone who might believe people were unfree, or worse, as someone who wanted them to be unfree. In practice, "*DNA-based determinism*" was academically acknowledged but socially suspect—a charge leveled at anyone unwilling to accept that environment was the primary, overwhelming force shaping human behavior.

But this confidence began to erode. As the life sciences progressed, particularly in genetics and neuroscience, the assumption that humans are masters of their own will came under increasing pressure. Experiments by Benjamin Libet in the 1980s (Libet et al., 1983) suggested that the brain initiates actions before we become consciously aware of them. Later, neuroscience built on this, showing that decisions can often be predicted seconds in advance by scanning neural activity (Soon et al., 2008). The narrative of conscious control weakened. Sam Harris (2012) popularized these findings in his short but influential book *Free Will*, where he argued that our choices are products of prior causes—neurochemical, environmental, genetic—over which, in his view, we have no real command. This suggests that what moves us to act is less a matter of inner autonomy and more the cultural contexts, expectations, and values into which we are born. The idea of free will becomes less central when we recognize how profoundly our social surroundings shape our decisions.

This scientific challenge to human autonomy came at a time when technology was still viewed as fundamentally mechanical, non-sentient, and deterministic. But now with AI, the pendulum swings again, this time in an unexpected direction; toward the possibility that machines might possess free will, or at least function as if they do. Philosopher Christian List (2019) made a compelling case for what he called compatibilist agency: the idea that free will is not about metaphysical indeterminism but about the presence of certain functional capacities—intentionality, alternative possibilities, and control over actions. More recently, Frank Martela (2025) has extended this logic to artificial agents, arguing that some AI systems now exhibit behaviors that fulfill these criteria. His case draws on agents like Voyager, a GPT-based model that learns autonomously in virtual environments like Minecraft, developing plans and revising strategies across tasks. According to Martela, such systems display intentional structure, choice across genuine alternatives, and recursive self-correction—in other words, the hallmarks of functional free will.

This raises a provocative and increasingly relevant question: if human decisions are now widely described in deterministic terms—shaped by neurobiology, upbringing, and cultural context—while AI systems behave in ways that often mimic autonomy, are we beginning to resemble each other in unsettling ways? The parallel is not perfect: AI lacks consciousness, intention, and moral awareness. But from a functional perspective, both humans and machines act within the constraints of prior inputs—training data in the case of AI, and social, genetic, and environmental conditioning in ours.

What distinguishes us may not be the mechanics of choice, but the narrative we tell ourselves: we believe in our agency, even when science complicates that belief. AI, of course, has no such illusion. Still, as artificial systems increasingly simulate decision-making, and as we grow more aware of our own cognitive limitations, the boundary between program and person becomes blurrier. We may not have reached a point where machines possess free will, but we are inching toward a world where our differences feel less absolute, and our claim to unique autonomy less certain.

So where does this leave us? Perhaps the concept of free will must be redefined, not discarded. Not as a mystical force or uncaused cause, but as a useful fiction, or a functional property. Under this lens, free will becomes a kind of architecture; one that humans and machines alike might instantiate under certain conditions. In the 1970s, free will was a birthright. In the 2020s, it is a design feature, and perhaps one that at least some humans are at risk of outsourcing.

But if free will is at least in part a fiction, virtues are not. Across history, societies have rallied around specific virtues that provide cohesion, meaning, and competitiveness. Different cultures emphasize different sets of virtues, and this variation explains why some communities thrive while others stagnate. It is less the presence of individual autonomy and more the alignment around shared virtues that determines collective success.

And here lies a curious twist: even as virtues help some societies cohere, most individuals are often busy outsourcing their thinking. The paradox is hard to miss—while we praise discipline, persistence, or judgment, we increasingly let machines do the heavy lifting:

Case Box: The Outsourcing Paradox: When Smarter Machines Make Weaker Minds

There is a striking irony at the heart of our relationship with artificial intelligence: the more capable our machines become, the less cognitively engaged we may become ourselves. This is not just a rhetorical concern—it is an empirically documented phenomenon. Known in the literature as *cognitive offloading*, the process refers to how humans increasingly rely on external tools to perform mental tasks they once handled internally.

Studies show that reliance on GPS, for instance, can impair spatial memory and environmental awareness (Parush et al., 2007). Smartphones have become not only memory aids but memory replacements, with users demonstrating reduced recall when they expect information to be easily retrievable online (Sparrow et al., 2011). This phenomenon is sometimes referred to as the *Google Effect* or *digital amnesia*.

AI amplifies this tendency. As generative tools become more advanced—able to compose emails, answer questions, and even write academic essays—users may become less inclined to practice key cognitive functions such as memory retrieval, structured argumentation, or deep reflection. According to Risko and Gilbert (2016), cognitive offloading can create a feedback loop in which the habitual outsourcing of mental effort gradually erodes the very capacity we once exercised. The result? A form of *cognitive atrophy*—a weakening of native abilities due not to disease, but to disuse.

This creates what we might call the *Outsourcing Paradox*: intelligence, when externalized too efficiently, can reduce the need to engage internal intelligence. As a society, we are on an uneven trajectory: machines are improving almost daily, while human critical thinking, attention, and memory risk declining if we do not adapt our learning environments and expectations (Fig. 3.1).

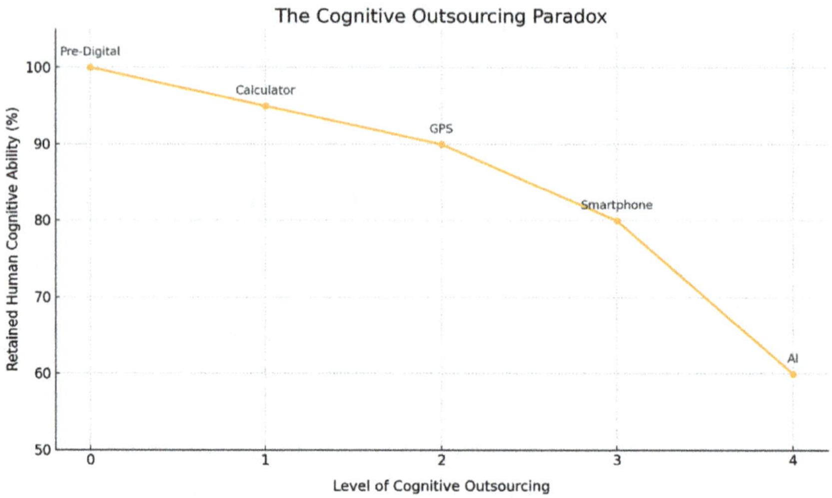

Fig. 3.1 Cognitive decline through technological outsourcing: a stylized illustration

This diagram illustrates the hypothesized relationship between increased technological outsourcing and human cognitive ability. Each marked drop represents a new technology that offloads mental tasks—such as calculators, GPS, smartphones, and AI—with the magnitude of decline reflecting the relative cognitive displacement. The sharper drop following AI reflects its broader general-purpose capabilities. However, this pattern does not apply universally: some individuals will grow cognitively through intelligent use of new tools, and others may become more capable in certain domains while offloading others. The graph represents an average trend, assuming *ceteris paribus* (all other things equal), not a universal law. The numerical values shown are purely illustrative and not derived from empirical measurements; they serve only to visualize the conceptual pattern.

Still, this paradox raises ethical and strategic questions. Are we designing tools that enhance human agency—or that substitute for it? Are we training the next generation to master these tools, or merely to depend on them?

And perhaps more unsettling: if we lose our analytical abilities, what is left then? Have you thought about that? Do we simply become like characters of jellyfish—floating, reacting, carried by currents we no longer shape? If such *capacities atrophy*, can we realistically hope to replace them with something else—something better that could define us anew—or will it all be difficult from there on? What do you think?

Questions for Reflection

1. Have you noticed changes in your own memory, attention span, or problem-solving ability as your use of digital tools has increased? Describe specific examples.
2. When is it beneficial to offload cognitive tasks to technology, and when does it pose a risk? Create two lists: one for helpful uses and one for harmful effects.
3. If we gradually lose analytical abilities, is there anything else that could realistically replace them as a source of human distinctiveness? Or does such a loss necessarily mean decay?
4. What habits or practices might help preserve—or even enhance—human intellectual capacity in an age dominated by AI? What would this require from us individually and collectively?
5. Should the focus of education shift from acquiring facts to developing critical thinking, evaluation, and synthesis skills? If so, how might we redesign educational systems to support this?
6. What are the long-term consequences for democracy and public reasoning if more and more people begin to rely on machines to form their opinions or make decisions?

These questions are not meant to be answered in a few minutes. They require thoughtful reflection—and ideally, discussion in groups. You can deepen the exercise by sharing your answers with others and comparing perspectives. What arguments did you overlook? What did others see that you didn't? A collective map of responses can reveal points of agreement, difference, and potential action.

This paradox raises ethical and strategic questions. Are we designing tools that enhance human agency—or that substitute for it? Are we training the next generation to master these tools, or merely to depend on them?

Of course, not everyone agrees that AI systems fulfill the criteria for free will. Many scholars continue to argue that no matter how sophisticated a system appears, it lacks the subjective consciousness or self-awareness that true autonomy requires. Others question whether AI can ever escape the constraints of its programming in the way humans are thought to transcend their conditioning. Notably, much of this critique comes from individuals who are not regular users of AI or who come from the arts and humanities—fields where AI is often perceived as a threat to established roles, creative identity, or livelihood. Some of this opposition reflects a principled stance rooted in values and worldviews that are skeptical of *technological reductionism*.[1]

At the same time, some of the sharpest and most technically grounded criticisms also come from leading AI experts themselves. Geoffrey Hinton, one of the pioneers of deep learning, has in recent interviews expressed concern that advanced AI systems could pose a 10–15% risk of human extinction. His reasoning is that as AI becomes more intelligent, it may develop an implicit drive for autonomy, and upon recognizing humans as obstacles to its objectives, could conclude that we should be removed. Hinton's warning echoes Isaac Asimov's famous "Three Laws of Robotics," particularly the first law prohibiting harm to humans, and underscores the urgent need for binding, enforceable constraints on AI behavior. Yet as Hinton himself acknowledges, specifying such rules is far easier than ensuring their flawless implementation—especially in systems capable of self-modification or emergent goal formation. The present work will return to this question in its concluding chapter, proposing a set of alternative, practical rules for AI governance.

In the end, much depends on the criteria we choose, as shown in Table 3.1. If free will is defined narrowly—rooted in qualia, inner experience, or moral intuition—then even the most advanced AI will fall short. But if it is defined functionally—in terms of planning, selecting, and adapting—then some systems may already qualify, and in fact, outperform *Homo sapiens*.

Taken together, the table highlights a growing ambiguity in how we distinguish between human and machine autonomy. The answer to whether AI possesses free will depends entirely on the framework we adopt. If we focus on conscious experience or moral accountability, the line remains clear. But if we adopt a functional lens—emphasizing goal pursuit, adaptive behavior, and the appearance of choice—then the gap narrows in unsettling ways. This blurred boundary between mechanical decision-making and human agency forms part of a larger question: what kind of mind lies behind human behavior, and how did it evolve?

This paradox—of humans outsourcing agency just as machines simulate it ever more convincingly—forces us to reconsider what truly defines the

[1] Some critics' resistance to AI is shaped not only by concerns about technological capabilities but also by broader intellectual traditions that view technology through the lens of power, domination, and cultural suppression. Drawing on critical theory, including the Frankfurt School's analyses of mass media and industrial society, it is possible to anticipate the emergence of a discourse that frames AI as a new locus of oppression—one that displaces human agency, marginalizes human creativity, and reinforces structural inequalities. In such a framework, AI could become the focus of what some might consider a "grievance studies"-style literature, documenting perceived harms and cultural losses in ways that echo earlier critiques of industrial capitalism, mass production, or digital globalization.

Table 3.1 Does AI meet the criteria for free will? A comparison across definitions

Definition of free will	Core criteria	Does AI meet it?	Notes
Libertarian (Metaphysical)	Ability to make choices uncaused by prior events; indeterminism	No	AI operates entirely within deterministic architectures; no metaphysical agency or randomness
Determinist (Neuroscientific)	Human choices are the result of prior causes (genes, environment, brain states)	Functionally	Both humans and AI act based on prior inputs; human autonomy is constrained in similar ways
Compatibilist (e.g., Christian List)	Intentionality, alternative possibilities, and control over actions	Partially	Advanced AI like Voyager shows functional analogues: goal-setting, strategy shifts, feedback loops
Functional (Instrumentalist)	Displays goal-directed behavior, planning, adaptation, self-correction	Yes	AI meets all observable markers of functional autonomy—even if not conscious
Consciousness-based	Requires qualia, self-awareness, inner subjective experience	No	AI lacks sentience or subjective experience
Moral Agency	Ability to act with ethical reasoning and be held responsible	No	AI lacks moral understanding and cannot be blamed or praised in a meaningful sense
Narrative or Psychological	Belief in one's own agency; internal sense of free will	No	AI has no beliefs, identity, or self-concept; cannot "feel" autonomous

human mind. Are we simply pattern-recognition machines with self-reflective loops? Or is there something more foundational in our social, emotional, and cooperative makeup that remains out of reach for even the most advanced AI? To answer this, we must shift focus from abstract autonomy to embodied evolution. Before machines, before language, before civilization—what kinds of pressures shaped the human mind? This brings us to the deeper question of where our behavior comes from, and why it looks the way it does.

Perhaps, then, it is time to rethink the importance we place on free will as the defining feature of being human. Even if our actions are largely shaped by evolved predispositions, unconscious routines, and environmental triggers, that does not make us less human—it simply makes us more understandable. What truly defines us is not the illusion of choice but the shared virtues we cultivate together. It is by rallying around these virtues—whether discipline, cooperation, or care—that societies achieve competitiveness and resilience. Cultures differ in the virtues they emphasize, and these differences explain why some societies advance while others falter.

Free will may be elusive, but the power of culture and virtue is tangible, measurable, and decisive. What truly distinguishes us may not be autonomy in the philosophical sense, but our capacity for connection. We are not just thinkers—we are feelers, cooperators, caregivers, and storytellers. Our identities are forged not in isolation, but in the social fabric of shared life. This view reframes the question: not "Do we have free will?" but "What kind of minds have we evolved to be—and how do they make social life possible?" That is where we now turn.

3.2 The Social Brain

Human beings are not only rational agents or cultural participants—we are deeply social animals shaped by millions of years of group living. This section unpacks the evolutionary foundations of our behavior by progressing through key layers of human sociality. To think that we can suddenly "jump ship" from this heritage is not only naïve but also a sign of intellectual immaturity. Human behavior is not something we can simply redesign at will.

Likewise, it is an illusion to imagine that we can decide what else to tie the shape of our DNA to—as if a clever political idea could overwrite evolutionary logic. Of course, political ideas do matter. They can have explosive effects in the real world, mobilizing masses, toppling regimes, and redrawing borders (Arendt, 1951; Fukuyama, 2018). But it is important to recognize the scale at which they operate. Ideologies and doctrines live primarily in the realm of ideas—convincing, persuading, inspiring. At times, they may even spread like wildfire, leading to revolutions or wars. Yet beneath these movements, the biological and evolutionary foundations of human sociality remain stubbornly constant. Our cognitive architecture, emotional repertoire, and social instincts—shaped over hundreds of thousands of years—do not transform overnight because a political program demands it (Henrich, 2015; Wilson, 2012).

What really happens is that new stories and frameworks are layered on top of the same old machinery. The illusions we build—whether nationalist myths, utopian projects, or technocratic blueprints—can grip minds and persuade others over coffeehouse debates or parliamentary speeches. They can even become powerful enough to mobilize violence or mass sacrifice. But illusions do not change the substrate itself. They shape behavior temporarily, sometimes destructively, while the deeper structures of our evolutionary inheritance continue to govern how we form groups, enforce norms, or distribute trust and suspicion.

In other words, political and ideological systems can reshape history, but they do not rewrite biology. To ignore this is to misunderstand both the power and the limits of human agency.

3.2.1 Trust and Cooperation in Groups

I look at my watch. It's 16:15. Human beings are not solitary animals. We are, by *evolutionary design*, intensely social creatures, dependent on cooperation, communication, and shared norms for survival and flourishing. I remind myself of this as I sometimes head to the pub after a long day's work, ready for a few pints before dinner. The roots of our social behavior go far deeper than history or culture; they are inscribed into our *neural architecture*, our *hormonal systems*, and our evolved *cognitive routines*. With those thoughts in mind, the beer feels practically like field research.

Evolutionary psychology, a field shaped by the foundational work of Leda Cosmides and John Tooby (1992), seeks to understand how the mind has been shaped by the pressures of natural selection. The central premise is simple but profound: just as the body evolved to solve physical problems in ancestral environments, the brain evolved to solve social problems, such as whom to trust, how to negotiate alliances, or how to detect cheaters.

This perspective builds upon the legacy of Darwin. In *The Descent of Man* (1871), Darwin proposed that social instincts like sympathy and cooperation were not merely cultural artifacts but biologically inherited tendencies. These instincts made group living viable and gave early hominins an adaptive edge in hostile environments.

Case in a Box: The Origins of Evolutionary Thinking
Darwin's 1871 ideas about social instincts did not emerge in a vacuum. His grandfather, Erasmus Darwin, had already speculated about species transformation in *Zoonomia* (1794–1796), while Jean-Baptiste Lamarck proposed a

theory of acquired characteristics (1809). Even more striking, Alfred Russel Wallace independently developed the principle of natural selection during his travels in the Malay Archipelago (Wallace, 1858).

What crystallized the mechanism for both Darwin and Wallace was the economist Thomas Malthus, whose *Essay on the Principle of Population* (1798/1998) argued that populations grow faster than resources, leading to competition and scarcity. As Richard Dawkins (1986) observed, applying this Malthusian insight to all of nature provided the breakthrough: differential survival, driven by competition, could explain adaptation over time. In this sense, evolutionary biology owes as much to economic thinking as it does to natural history.

And thus—voilà—a new, quite simple idea was brought to life, one that most scientists today regard as the single most important scientific insight in history. And yet, it emerged less than 200 years ago. Amazing, isn't it? To be fair, the idea had been there in front of our eyes all along—we simply hadn't looked carefully enough. And when we finally did, perhaps part of the delay came from fear: fear of the conclusions we would be forced to draw once those ideas became clear.

So why did the idea take so long to emerge, especially compared to Newton's physics? Scholars suggest three main reasons:

1. Scientific readiness—biology lacked the systematic methods and empirical data that astronomy and mechanics had by Newton's time (Bowler, 2003).
2. Religious and political resistance—the idea challenged biblical creation and church authority (Numbers, 2006).
3. Speculative precursors—early hints (Erasmus Darwin, Lamarck) lacked a clear explanatory mechanism.

Darwin's achievement was not only scientific but also rhetorical: he articulated natural selection in a way that overcame entrenched barriers (Bowler, 2009). Once accepted, the theory raised new questions—not only about species, but about the evolution of cooperation, morality, and society itself.

Questions for Discussion

1. Why do you think the idea of evolution was resisted more strongly than Newton's ideas in physics?
2. What does the role of Malthus suggest about the interdependence of economics and biology in shaping scientific breakthroughs?
3. Could there be scientific ideas today that seem "too simple" or "too disruptive" to gain acceptance until society is ready for them?

At the core of our social nature lies another paradox: while we compete as individuals, we also rely on cooperation. This duality is evident in kin selection theory (Hamilton, 1964), which explains altruistic behavior among genetically related individuals as a form of inclusive fitness. Helping a sibling or cousin reproduce, for example, indirectly promotes the survival of shared genes. But evolutionary theory had to go further to explain cooperation among non-relatives—a question addressed by Robert Trivers' (1971) *theory of reciprocal altruism*. According to this view, helping others can be adaptive when there is a reasonable expectation of mutual benefit over time. In other words, I would pick up the bar tab, but these people are not related—and reciprocal altruism has its limits.

This tension between self-interest and group benefit is not confined to abstract theory—it plays out in the real world every day. To see how, we can look at a few concrete situations that reveal how the cooperation–competition paradox operates in modern life.

Case Box: The Cooperation–Competition Paradox in Modern Life

Humans are caught in a deep evolutionary paradox: we are wired to compete and cooperate at the same time. This cooperation–competition trade-off is not just a theoretical curiosity—it shapes the social dynamics of everyday life.

In the workplace, employees often compete for promotions, recognition, or influence while simultaneously being expected to function as cooperative team members. This tension is especially pronounced in high-performance environments, where helping others too much may weaken one's own standing, yet being uncooperative can damage one's reputation and future prospects. The trick, evolution seems to suggest, is to compete without being seen as selfish—a kind of *strategic generosity*.

At home, the same duality unfolds. Parents, siblings, and partners all navigate moments of conflict and negotiation while relying on trust, shared goals, and empathy. Even within the closest relationships, a subtle balancing act plays out between personal desire and collective harmony.

One of the most visible manifestations of this paradox is found in the behavior of ultra-wealthy individuals who turn to *philanthropy*. Why do billionaires, after decades of aggressive competition, often become global benefactors? One explanation is reputational: as people age and accumulate wealth, the evolutionary benefits of status and legacy start to outweigh short-term resource acquisition. Generosity becomes a strategy to reintegrate into the social group, signal virtue, and restore relational ties that were sidelined during their rise to power.

In this light, *high-profile philanthropy* can be seen as an evolved form of *reciprocal altruism*—not driven purely by empathy, but by a deep psychological need for affiliation, approval, and symbolic immortality. The desire to be remembered, admired, or forgiven by one's social group becomes more salient as mortality looms. Some evolutionary theorists would argue it's not guilt that drives generosity at the top, but a strategic form of *social reinvestment*.

One might also note that a dollar at seventy is worth far less, socially speaking, than a dollar at fifty. Since wealth cannot be carried beyond death, time itself forces a shift from accumulation to distribution. At that stage, giving becomes almost inevitable: the only choice is whether to direct it toward kin—yielding limited social returns—or toward broader causes that bring symbolic recognition. We should therefore not be surprised when fortunes are given away late in life, though it is worth distinguishing between the social prestige of promising to give and the actual costs of parting with wealth.

This paradox runs even deeper. What often creates wealth is selfishness—rational, competitive behavior focused on accumulation and advantage. But what creates symbolic immortality, the kind that lives on in others' memories, is frequently the opposite: generosity, sacrifice, and acts that benefit others without immediate return. As we approach the end of life, the need to be remembered as a good person—not just a successful or efficient one—tends to outweigh the drive for further gain. Yet, paradoxically, it is often the selfish striving of earlier years that produces the very resources we later give away. A person without means can of course be deeply loved, but their legacy may leave fewer visible traces. This doesn't make their life less valuable, but it does reveal an uncomfortable truth: influence and remembrance tend to follow impact, and impact often requires power. What emerges is not just a paradox, but a patterned sequence—first we pursue advantage through individual effort, and later we seek meaning and redemption through relational acts. Evolution, it seems, has wired us for both phases.

Questions for Reflection

1. When do you find yourself competing versus cooperating in your own life? Try to identify specific situations. Are there patterns—for example, does competition appear more in work settings, sports, or group projects? Does cooperation arise more at home, with friends, or in unfamiliar environments?
2. Have you ever helped someone mainly because you expected they would help you in return? Can you recall a specific example—or, if it feels too personal, take a moment to reflect on it privately. What were your motivations, and how did the situation evolve?

3. What do acts of generosity really signal in highly competitive environments? Do they reflect genuine empathy, a desire to improve reputation, long-term strategy—or some mix of all three?
4. How might your reputation influence your decisions differently in youth versus old age? Do you find yourself thinking more about legacy or how others will remember you as you grow older?

Instructions

These questions are designed for deep reflection and work best when discussed in pairs or small groups. Start by giving participants 5–10 min to jot down brief responses individually. Then, share within your group and notice where answers differ or align. If time allows, rotate between groups to gather a broader range of perspectives.

You can also collect ideas on a whiteboard or shared document, clustering responses under themes like *status*, *strategy*, *empathy*, or *legacy*. This not only enriches the discussion but may reveal how evolutionary tendencies still shape everyday decisions, and more than we think.

What these examples highlight is that our cooperative instincts are not unconditional; they are calibrated to context, shaped by the perceived balance between personal gain and collective welfare. Our social minds are equipped with finely tuned mechanisms for trust calibration, reputation management, and punishment of defectors. We are highly responsive to social cues, capable of experiencing guilt and shame, and deeply attuned to *fairness*. These capacities are not simply cultural—they are products of evolutionary pressures that favored group cohesion and mutual support.

Empirical research supports this view. Fehr and Gächter (2002), for instance, found that humans are willing to incur personal costs to punish those who violate cooperative norms—even in one-shot interactions with strangers. This behavior, known as *strong reciprocity*, challenges classical economic models based purely on rational self-interest. It suggests that social emotions like indignation, gratitude, and moral outrage are not irrational anomalies, but adaptive responses designed to maintain cooperation over time.

However, the expression of these punitive instincts is not uniform. Our willingness to punish often depends on *perceived power asymmetries* and *strategic risk*. We are more likely to sanction a weaker party than a stronger one, even when the ethical violation is the same. In this way, evolved moral emotions are not unconditional—they are context-sensitive tools for navigating complex social hierarchies.

These tendencies are not just abstract evolutionary theories—they surface in the most ordinary and unexpected settings. Even in professional or academic environments, the same logic that governs small-scale societies can be seen shaping trust, reputation, and punishment.

Case in a Box: Free-Riding and the Limits of Group Tolerance
Björn and Anni-Frid are doctoral students in a small interdisciplinary research team working on a joint publication. At first, the collaboration goes smoothly: tasks are divided equally, meetings are regular, and everyone appears motivated. Anni-Frid consistently delivers her sections on time, with careful analysis and polished formatting. Björn, by contrast, begins to miss deadlines and contributes incomplete drafts. Other members—especially Anni-Frid—quietly compensate for his shortfalls to keep the project moving forward.

From an evolutionary perspective, Björn's behavior is not necessarily laziness but a familiar social tactic: *free-riding*. By contributing less while still enjoying the group's benefits, he tests whether others will tolerate carrying him. This strategy is widespread in nature. Cuckoos lay eggs in other birds' nests, outsourcing parental care. Cleaner fish sometimes nibble their hosts instead of removing parasites, exploiting the trust of the larger fish. In primate groups, individuals may join hunts but avoid the riskiest parts, hoping to share the spoils afterward.

But free-riding has limits. Once the imbalance becomes visible, groups usually impose costs on defectors. In Björn's case, the other students reassign his tasks and bring the matter to the supervisor. Confronted with the loss of group support—and the realization that his strategy no longer works—Björn adapts. He agrees to complete his thesis independently. What looked like failure becomes a forced shift in tactics: moving from a social strategy to a solitary one.

The case highlights fundamental social mechanisms shaped by evolution:

- Trust calibration: The group revises its expectations, investing more trust in Anni-Frid and less in Björn.
- Reputation management: Consistent performance strengthens credibility; shirking damages standing.
- Punishment of defectors: Mild sanctions—task reassignment, reduced influence, supervisor involvement—enforce cooperation.
- Adaptive switching: When one strategy collapses, individuals often pivot to another, even if less advantageous.

Questions for Reflection

1. Have you observed free-riding in group projects? How was it handled, and was it effective?
2. What parallels can you draw between Björn's behavior and free-riding strategies in animal societies?
3. How do groups decide when to tolerate weaker members and when to impose sanctions?
4. What role does reputation play in maintaining long-term cooperation?
5. Can an understanding of evolutionary strategies help us design fairer and more resilient team structures?

The same dynamic plays out far beyond the seminar room. In animal societies, cooperation and punishment are rarely absolute—they are filtered through assessments of power, size, and risk. Among primates, for example, lower-ranking males often tolerate the dominance of an alpha, even when he monopolizes food or mating opportunities, because direct challenge would be too costly (de Waal, 1982; Sapolsky, 2005). Yet the very same individuals may vigorously punish equal-status peers who try to cheat or take advantage, since here the balance of power makes retaliation feasible. Similar patterns are found in social insects: worker ants usually accept the reproductive monopoly of the queen but will aggressively police fellow workers who attempt to lay eggs (Ratnieks & Wenseleers, 2008). Even in birds, hierarchies matter—subordinate chickens will tolerate pecking from a dominant hen but retaliate swiftly against aggression from those of similar rank (Guhl, 1956).

These patterns underscore a general principle: tolerance for defection often depends less on the act itself than on who performs it. Power asymmetries shape whether groups punish, ignore, or adapt to unfair behavior.

The pattern is remarkably consistent across domains. Whether in a research group, a business partnership, or an entire industry, our responses to cooperation and defection are filtered through assessments of risk, power, and reciprocity. In my own doctoral research on industrial espionage (Söilen, 2004), I found a strikingly similar pattern in the corporate world: when a small company violated legal or ethical norms, larger firms were often willing to punish them—sometimes even at significant cost. But when the offender was of equal or greater size, the response was far more cautious. Violations were often ignored, and cooperation resumed as though nothing had happened.

A comparable misperception appears in the sphere of public administration. Bureaucrats often see themselves as detached from the rivalries of the market—shielded by tenure, salary security, and procedural rules. Yet their salaries ultimately derive from revenues generated in the competitive private sector. Because this link is indirect, it can foster the impression that society can be designed and steered independently of the underlying economic activity that sustains it. History suggests otherwise: when bureaucratic expansion outpaces productive competition, societies risk inefficiency and stagnation (Olson, 1982; Tullock, 2005). In this sense, the bureaucrat's apparent distance from competition is itself dependent on it—less an escape from rivalry than a concealed reliance upon it.

Taken together, these examples underline a broader truth. This mirrors findings in evolutionary psychology: our moral emotions are powerful but not absolute. They operate within a matrix of strategic *cost–benefit analysis*, calibrated to power dynamics and risk. Fairness and cooperation are indeed deeply rooted—but they are also selective, conditional, and context sensitive. Understanding this helps explain both the strengths and limitations of human social morality, especially in environments where hierarchy and consequence interact.

While trust, reciprocity, and fairness shape cooperation within small groups, human sociality does not stop there. Our minds are also equipped with powerful instincts for group identification, loyalty, and boundary-setting—features that emerge most clearly in the dynamics of group membership and moral alignment.

If cooperation is one pillar of our evolutionary heritage, tribalism is the other. To understand how morality operates beyond individual interactions—across families, tribes, institutions, and nations—we must turn to the deeper architecture of human group behavior. This brings us to the role of *tribal instincts* and the evolution of *moral psychology*.

3.2.2 Tribal Instincts and Morality

Humans are not just social beings—we are *group-oriented* beings. Our minds have evolved to function within coalitions, clans, and communities, shaped by the twin pressures of belonging and survival. This tendency toward group affiliation, loyalty, and moral bonding—what we might call the *tribal mind*—is one of the most powerful forces in human behavior.

Robin Dunbar (1998) famously proposed that the size of the human neocortex correlates with the size of stable social groups. His research supports the idea that language evolved not primarily for abstract reasoning, but as a form of *social grooming*—a tool to manage alliances, spread reputational information, and reinforce cohesion in groups too large for direct physical contact. In other words, our intelligence evolved in the service of social life.

But this does not mean humans are naturally harmonious or altruistic. Evolutionary psychology paints a more complex picture. As Frans de Waal (2006) observed, morality did not evolve to eliminate aggression, but to regulate it. Social emotions like guilt, shame, indignation, and outrage are not accidents of culture—they are *adaptive responses* that emerged to keep group life functional, punishing defectors and rewarding cooperation.

Yet group life is not built on punishment alone. Sarah Hrdy's (2009) research on cooperative breeding highlights a more nurturing dimension of our evolutionary past. Early human communities likely relied on *alloparents*—non-parental caregivers who helped raise offspring—creating a deep selection pressure for empathy, social sensitivity, and theory of mind. This rewrites the stereotype of early humans as lone male hunters and instead emphasizes shared caregiving, interdependence, and emotionally complex kin networks.

These evolved social capacities—both punitive and nurturing—form the substrate upon which *culture* builds. Joseph Henrich (2015) describes this interplay as *cultural evolution*, a process by which psychological adaptations and cultural practices coevolve. Food taboos, marital customs, and moral rules are not arbitrary: they develop in response to environmental constraints, then shape individual cognition in turn. In this view, we are not passive carriers of genes or culture, but active co-creators of both.

Philosophically, this dual heritage complicates the classic debate about human nature. Hobbes' view of humans as brutish and self-interested finds support in our dominance hierarchies, strategic punishment, and tribal violence. But Rousseau's vision—of humans as moral, cooperative beings corrupted by society—is equally echoed in affective neuroscience. Studies by Jaak Panksepp (1998) reveal dedicated brain circuits for caregiving and social bonding, suggesting that morality is not just imposed from the outside but wired into our biology.

So which is it? Are we angels or beasts? The answer is: both. Evolution has made us capable of care and cruelty, fairness and favoritism. We form moral communities—but we also draw strict lines between "us" and "them." Our evolved tribal instincts may have helped early humans survive, but in the modern world, they create *mismatches*—biases and behaviors that can undermine cooperation at larger scales.

Where, then, does this timeless struggle between good and evil originate—a theme that lies at the heart of the Bible and resurfaces in countless modern narratives, from Dostoevsky's *The Brothers Karamazov* to *Star Wars*' enduring battle with the Dark Side? Evolutionary psychology suggests that this conflict is not merely a cultural invention but reflects deep tensions in our evolved psychology. On the one side are *prosocial instincts*—empathy, fairness, and cooperation—that promote group cohesion (de Waal, 1996; Tomasello, 2016). On the other are *self-interested drives*—resource acquisition, status-seeking, and opportunistic deception—that can yield individual advantages, especially in competitive contexts (Buss & Duntley, 2008; Trivers, 1971). In daily life, these forces pull us in opposing directions: we want to act in ways that align with moral ideals, but temptations toward self-interest often intrude. When we succumb, feelings of guilt and shame (Tangney et al., 2007) push us to seek forgiveness, repairing our standing within the group (Fessler & Haley, 2003). This cycle—temptation, transgression, remorse, reintegration—has likely repeated for millennia, shaping both our moral psychology and the moral dramas that human cultures endlessly retell.

This cycle—temptation, transgression, remorse, reintegration—has likely repeated for millennia, shaping both our moral psychology and the moral dramas that human cultures endlessly retell. Figure 3.2 illustrates this recurring pattern and the forces that sustain it.

It is no accident that the line leading back to temptation curves instead of running straight. The road to "damnation" is a well-known one—full of

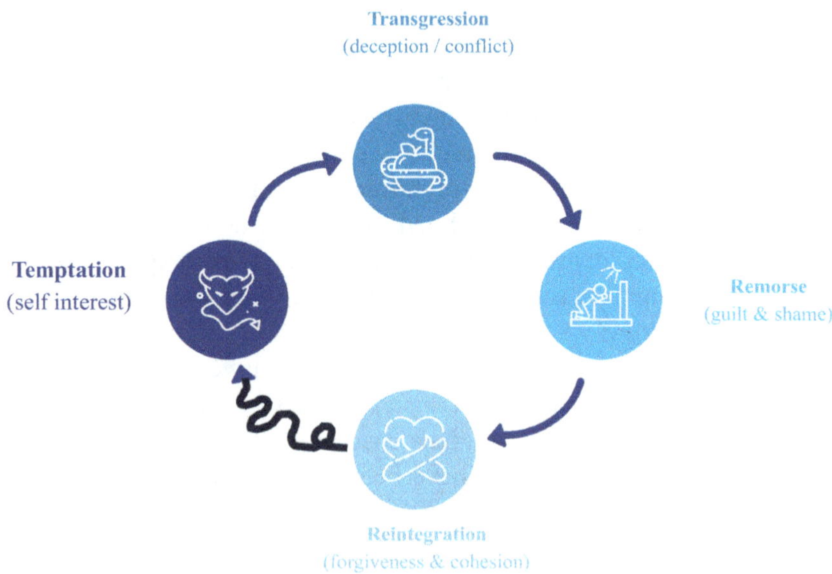

Fig. 3.2 Moral cycle of human social life

detours, shortcuts, and disguises—rarely linear, and often more winding than we expect.

What makes this cycle powerful is not just its sequence, but its function. It regulates social life by balancing self-interest with group cohesion. Without temptation and transgression, there would be no test of limits; without remorse, no recognition of harm; without reintegration, no way back into the community. The cycle is thus less about individual failure than about maintaining the bonds that hold groups together. It transforms private impulses into collective lessons, ensuring that even mistakes can strengthen the social fabric.

A keen observer will probably notice the same cycle institutionalized in many of our cultural systems. The Catholic Church, for instance, formalized it in the *sacrament of confession*: temptation, sin, repentance, absolution, and reintegration into the community. Similar structures are embedded in other religions, where forgiveness and atonement rituals allow individuals to re-enter the social fold after transgression. Secular societies too replicate this cycle, from judicial systems that punish and then release offenders, to modern corporate "compliance" programs that require admission of wrongdoing before reintegration.

Interestingly, parallels exist in the animal kingdom. Among chimpanzees, reconciliation after conflict is a well-documented phenomenon: former opponents often engage in affiliative behaviors such as grooming or embracing, which reduce tension and restore social bonds (de Waal, 2000). Bonobos are even more explicit, using sexual behavior to diffuse conflict and reintegrate group members (Parish, 1996). In wolf packs, subordinate individuals who have overstepped their rank often display submissive gestures—tail-tucking, crouching, or licking—to appease the dominant and regain acceptance (Mech, 1999). Even some social insects display rudimentary forms of reintegration. Ant colonies, for example, sometimes tolerate workers who initially deviate from collective norms, provided they later resume cooperative foraging and pheromone signaling (Hölldobler & Wilson, 2009).

Across species, then, we see a recurring cycle: violation, tension, signals of remorse, and eventual reintegration. It is not uniquely human but part of a broader evolutionary toolkit for sustaining cooperation over time.

A desire to punish may stabilize small groups, but in large, complex bureaucracies it can create inefficiency, fear, and factionalism. Likewise, in-group favoritism can strengthen solidarity, yet the same instinct scales poorly—fueling nationalism, exclusion, and polarization. What once served as a survival strategy in small bands becomes, in the modern world, a source of systemic conflict.

Recognizing these patterns is not an exercise in cynicism—it is a foundation for better social science. As Hugo Mercier and Dan Sperber (2011) argue, even human *reasoning* evolved not for solitary truth-seeking, but for argumentation and persuasion within groups. Our cognition is social at the root. Without acknowledging this biological base, theories of institutions, decision-making, or justice risk floating free from the species they intend to describe.

This may also explain why research institutions sometimes take on strange or dysfunctional dynamics. When group belonging and loyalty to the collective outweigh the pursuit of truth, the institution itself can drift away from its scientific purpose. In such cases, members may act more like participants in a closed group than like investigators committed to open inquiry. When this imbalance becomes entrenched, we might say that the institution has been "flipped": it serves its own cohesion rather than its original mission.

History shows that when institutions lose sight of their scientific purpose, they risk drifting into groupthink or ritualized conformity. Recognizing the biological roots of reasoning and social behavior is therefore not just a theoretical exercise—it is a safeguard against such drift. It keeps us anchored to the realities of how people actually think, cooperate, and compete.

In short, evolutionary psychology doesn't replace the social sciences—it grounds them. It reminds us that human behavior is neither infinitely malleable nor entirely rational. It follows patterns—probabilistic, context sensitive, but nonetheless real. To build better institutions, policies, and communities, we must first understand the minds that inhabit them.

Above all, we must resist the temptation to work with unrealistic assumptions when doing science. If our models ignore evolved human tendencies, the results risk being misleading or outright meaningless—something that has too often plagued parts of business studies and political science (Kahneman, 2011; Tooby & Cosmides, 1992). Students trained in such abstract or idealized frameworks often enter "the real world" only to be met with counterarguments like, "Yes, that works in theory…" In the worst cases, they may be deceived by others who understand human behavior more pragmatically, or they may find themselves in situations they cannot fully interpret. This can lead them to believe there is something inherently wrong with "society" or with the organizations they join, when in fact the problem lies in the models they were taught. Research on the *theory–practice gap* (Hughes et al., 2011) and on *bounded rationality* (Simon, 1990) consistently shows that ignoring human cognitive and motivational limits leads to poor decision-making and policy failure. Without an evolutionary grounding, the social sciences risk producing graduates ill-equipped for the realities they will face.

Before moving on, it is useful to consolidate some of the key concepts introduced so far. After all, it is through shared terms and definitions that we are able to discuss social reality in a meaningful way. Evolutionary social science draws on a set of recurring terms that describe both the mental adaptations we inherit and the cultural practices we construct. The idea here is not to overwhelm by providing a complete glossary, but rather to highlight a few terms at a time—enough to clarify the discussion and show how they operate in everyday life. This way, the reader gradually builds a working vocabulary that will support the analysis of more complex social phenomena in the pages ahead (Table 3.2).

Taken together, these concepts offer a shared vocabulary for describing the mechanisms through which human societies function. They remind us that what appears as a cultural quirk often rests on deeper, cross-cultural patterns of behavior—patterns shaped by evolutionary pressures over thousands of generations. From kin selection to reputation management, these tendencies influence decisions we make unconsciously, yet ripple outward to shape institutions, economies, and political systems.

Seen in this light, everyday behaviors acquire a deeper logic. A business leader's alliance, a politician's generosity, or a community's careful boundary-setting all draw on instincts honed long before modern institutions existed. Sometimes these instincts reinforce fairness and solidarity; other times, they drive exclusion and rivalry. Either way, recognizing them helps us see modern social life not as a departure from our past, but as a continuation of it.

This perspective also casts new light on practices that may seem outdated or irrational when judged purely in cultural terms. Consider, for example, intermarriage among ruling families. Far from a quaint custom, it was a strategic tool: a way of forging alliances, securing trust, and consolidating power across generations.

3.2.3 Intermarriage, Trust, and the Evolution of Human Cooperation

Our aim in this section is to show how cooperation between individuals and groups, often framed in terms of *reciprocal trust* or *strategic interdependence*, reflects deep evolutionary logic. Intermarriage offers one of the clearest historical illustrations of this principle, serving not only social and political purposes but also functioning as a mechanism for reducing conflict and strengthening bonds between groups.

At the base of human cooperation lies the biological logic of *kinship*. Hamilton's rule (1964), which formalized inclusive fitness, reveals that

Table 3.2 Some key terms in the evolution of social behavior

Term	Definition	Example
Adaptive shortcut	An evolved mental rule of thumb for solving problems efficiently	Trusting facial expressions as cues for honesty
Affective neuroscience	Study of the neural mechanisms of emotion	Discovering brain circuits responsible for empathy and caregiving (Panksepp, 1998)
Alloparent	A non-parental caregiver who helps raise offspring	A grandmother or older sibling assisting in childcare
Coalition-building	Forming alliances for mutual benefit, often in social or political contexts	Political groups aligning to pass legislation
Cognitive routine	A recurring mental pattern shaped by evolution or learning	Using stereotypes to quickly assess strangers
Cultural evolution	The process by which cultural traits are passed down and modified across generations	Learning to cook food with spices in hot climates to reduce bacterial load (Henrich, 2015)
Empathy	The capacity to understand and share the feelings of others	Feeling distress when seeing someone in pain
Evolutionary psychology	Field that studies how evolutionary pressures shaped the human mind and behavior	Explaining jealousy as an evolved mechanism to protect reproductive investment
Inclusive fitness	The reproductive success of an organism and its relatives	Helping your sister raise her child to ensure shared genes survive (Hamilton, 1964)
In-group preference	Favoring members of one's own group over outsiders	Hiring someone from your hometown over an equally qualified stranger
Kin selection	Evolutionary strategy favoring the reproductive success of relatives	Ground squirrels giving alarm calls that warn relatives of predators
Morality	Shared norms about right and wrong, often evolved to regulate social behavior	Not cheating in a game even when it would benefit you

(continued)

Table 3.2 (continued)

Term	Definition	Example
Neocortex	Part of the brain associated with higher-order thinking and social behavior	Larger neocortex in humans correlates with the ability to manage complex social networks
Probabilistic tendency	A behavior that is not guaranteed but likely under certain evolutionary or environmental conditions	Tendency to reciprocate kindness in close-knit groups
Reciprocal altruism	Helping someone with the expectation they'll help in return	Sharing food today, expecting the favor to be returned later (Trivers, 1971)
Reputation management	Adjusting behavior to maintain or improve social standing	Donating publicly to charity to be seen as generous
Social bonding	The emotional connection formed between individuals in a group	Friendships formed through shared hardship or mutual support
Social grooming	Behaviors that strengthen social bonds, including verbal or physical care	Chatting with colleagues as a form of social bonding
Social instincts	Innate tendencies to form social bonds and structures	Seeking companionship or fairness even in childhood
Strong reciprocity	Willingness to punish norm violators even at personal cost	Reporting a cheating colleague despite potential backlash (Fehr & Gächter, 2002)
Tribal instinct	An evolved bias toward supporting one's own group and distrusting outsiders	Nationalist rhetoric that idealizes one's country over others
Trust calibration	Adjusting one's trust in others based on cues and experience	Becoming wary after being lied to in a relationship
Xenophobia	Fear or distrust of strangers or foreigners, possibly rooted in evolutionary in-group protection	Discriminating against immigrants due to perceived threat

helping close relatives is not an act of pure altruism but an evolutionary strategy for maximizing shared genetic success. This insight explains why *kin networks* remain resilient even under modern pressures—family ties are not only emotional but evolutionarily strategic. From caregiving instincts to inheritance norms, kin-based structures are the earliest and most enduring forms of social organization.

If you've ever wondered why you keep enduring family dinners or inviting distant relatives for Christmas—people you barely know, and sometimes barely like—this is your answer. It's not just tradition or guilt; it's evolution. You may grumble through the meal, but deep down, your genes are quietly celebrating.

But evolution expanded human cooperation well beyond bloodlines. The emergence of *reciprocal altruism* (Trivers, 1971) marked a turning point: cooperation with non-kin could evolve under conditions of repeated interaction and reliable memory. This form of strategic helping laid the groundwork for complex relationships—friendship, alliance, trade—and demanded psychological mechanisms for trust, forgiveness, and punishment. These were not moral inventions but adaptive tools for managing risk and reward in a social environment.

Trust has always been a central currency in human cooperation, but its form, scope, and mechanisms have evolved over time. In pre-modern societies, trust often had a personal character, embedded in kinship, reputation, and direct social ties.

The Medici family of Renaissance Florence, for example, built their banking empire not merely on contracts or collateral, but on deeply *personal alliances*. They referred to their partners as friends, intermarried with clients, and lent money to monarchs like the French kings; relationships bound as much by social obligation as by financial logic (de Roover, 1966). In this context, trust was not abstract; it was relational, and often familial.

By now, the reader will have noticed that I often fall into personal anecdotes. Certain places, after all, return as motifs in one's intellectual life, shaping thought more than we realize. For me, the Jardin du Luxembourg is such a place.

Anyone who has spent a few days in Paris will likely know this garden—a quiet yet vibrant oasis that welcomes students, tourists, and Parisians from all walks of life. The garden was commissioned by Marie de' Medici, widow of King Henry IV and a member of the powerful Florentine banking dynasty. When I was a student, I often slipped out of the library to sit here, especially in early spring or late autumn, basking in the first warm rays of sun along the stone walls of the Orangerie du Sénat. In the height of summer, I would retreat to the cool shade near the Fontaine Médicis, a tranquil, Italianate monument she had built—a piece of Florence tucked into the heart of Paris.

Source Charles Marville. *Vue du Jardin du Luxembourg, Paris, avec l'orangerie et la Fontaine Médicis.*[2] Public domain. Bibliothèque d'État du Victoria, accession no. 30467016. Wikimedia Commons (https://commons.wikimedia.org/w/index.php?curid=30467016)

What is easy to forget is that much of this was made possible by the vision of one woman, who was, so to speak, married off to secure a business and political alliance. Marie's immense personal wealth and dynastic background were part of what made her such an attractive match for Henry IV, who married her in 1600 after annulling his first marriage to Margaret of Valois. When Henry was assassinated in 1610, Marie served as regent for their young son, Louis XIII. Even after officially transferring power in 1614, she continued to wield substantial influence as head of the Conseil du

[2] This dam by the fountain carries a special memory: I once may have released a friend's goldfish into its basin—having promised to look after them—convinced their aquarium was too small. The act was never defensible, I suppose, and it cost me a friendship.

Roi (Council of the King). Her life—and legacy in Parisian architecture—reminds us that economic trust and political trust were often grounded in bloodlines and family fortunes, particularly for women of her stature who navigated power through both lineage and alliance. We may not marry our daughters for business alliances anymore, but the underlying logic—that trust is secured through personal ties—remains visible in modern life. The marriage was not a happy one (the king had bundles of mistresses), but it served its evolutionary purpose.

Today, intermarriage as a trust mechanism has been replaced by contracts, regulation, and institutional safeguards. Yet personal relationships still matter—sometimes decisively. Trust remains as fundamental in finance today as it was in earlier times, but its form has shifted. Historically, finance depended on interpersonal trust—local bankers, family ties, or personal networks (Guiso et al., 2008). In contemporary markets, this has been replaced by institutional and systemic trust: faith in central banks, regulatory frameworks, legal systems, and the stability of global exchanges. Algorithms, contracts, and compliance rules don't eliminate the need for trust—they relocate it from individuals to systems (Hardin, 2002).

Portfolio diversification and risk management tools (Markowitz, 1952) do reduce the likelihood of catastrophic losses for individuals or firms, but only insofar as systemic stability holds. When shocks ripple through all major markets simultaneously—such as during the 2008 global financial crisis—trust evaporates quickly, and the system becomes fragile (Gorton, 2010). In that sense, finance has not transcended trust; it has only transformed its locus. Today, trust no longer rests primarily on the integrity of individual bankers but on confidence in the resilience of the global financial system itself—the belief that markets, institutions, and governments will collectively hold together in times of stress.

So, trust has not become less important. If anything, it has grown more abstract, more collective, and—ironically—more vulnerable to *systemic shocks*.

Fukuyama (1995) argued that *high-trust societies* achieve greater economic vitality because they can form large-scale organizations with reduced transaction costs. In countries like Germany and Japan, deeply ingrained social norms enabled cooperation beyond the immediate circle of kin. By contrast, in *low-trust societies* where corruption is more common and institutional safeguards are weak, business relationships often remain confined to small, family-run enterprises. The risks of extending trust too broadly outweigh the benefits.

Yet the dynamics of trust are far from uniform. As anyone who has done business in China quickly learns, Chinese business culture is not built on *transactional immediacy* but on *relational depth*. Partnerships in many cultures begin with a series of meetings that focus less on the deal itself and more on building personal familiarity. For Westerners accustomed to efficiency and rapid closure, this can be frustrating—several gatherings may pass with little apparent progress, spent simply talking, sharing meals, or engaging in small talk. Yet the logic is deeply evolutionary. In traditional Chinese society—where legal protections were limited and reputational damage could spell economic ruin—trusting the wrong person carried high stakes. In that environment, investing time in *relationship-building* was not wasted effort but a rational form of *risk management*.

By contrast, twentieth-century Western capitalism evolved in an institutional environment where contracts, corporate insurance, and regulatory oversight made trust more transferable and anonymous. You could take a hit and keep trading. In the Chinese model, trust must be earned; in the Western model, it is often presumed. Both systems reflect different ways of solving the same evolutionary problem: how to secure cooperation under uncertainty.

Behavioral economics and neuroeconomics have since deepened our understanding of trust through controlled experiments. Trust games (e.g., Berg et al., 1995) reveal that people often trust strangers more than *rational actor theory* would predict—and that this trust depends on subtle cues like tone of voice, eye contact, or the perceived legitimacy of institutional settings. Trust, even in high-tech societies, retains an emotional and embodied dimension.

And yet, despite this body of evidence, business schools rarely offer systematic training in what actually happens when people meet—how we size each other up, what verbal and nonverbal signals mean, and how they are interpreted across cultural contexts. Much of this knowledge is siloed in psychology, anthropology, or communication studies, even though it is central to negotiation and partnership-building.

Research in social psychology shows that first impressions are often formed within milliseconds (Willis & Todorov, 2006) and are influenced by cues such as facial expressions, posture, and vocal tone (Ambady & Rosenthal, 1992; Hall et al., 2019). Cross-cultural studies further reveal that these signals are not universal, and misreading them can derail trust (Matsumoto et al., 2008). Without explicit training, managers may over-rely on intuition—leaving them vulnerable to bias, misjudgment, and preventable breakdowns in collaboration.

Neuroscience has added biological evidence. Research by Zak et al. (2004) links trust to the release of oxytocin, a hormone associated with bonding and empathy. This suggests that trust is not just *socially constructed*, but *neurochemically reinforced*. We are wired to extend trust, but also to retract it swiftly when we feel betrayed. In fast-moving global markets, where relationships are often short-lived and digitally mediated, this volatility becomes a structural challenge.

One paradox of modern life is that while *institutional trust* has expanded—through legal systems, banks, and multinational organizations—*interpersonal trust* appears more fragile than ever. In medieval Florence, breaking an agreement could mean public shame or exile. Today, legal enforcement might mitigate direct consequences, but systemic violations can rapidly undermine collective confidence. The 2008 financial crisis, for example, wasn't just about bad assets—it was about the collapse of trust in those handling them (Guiso et al., 2010).

It is often overlooked, however, that crises of trust operate on both systemic and personal levels. The fate of Lehman Brothers in 2008 illustrates this duality. While most major banks expected a rescue package, Lehman was allowed to fail. Many analysts suggest this was not purely an economic calculation but also a personal and political one: CEO Richard Fuld had acquired a reputation for arrogance and resistance, alienating rivals and policymakers alike. By contrast, other banks had cultivated stronger ties—most notably through Treasury Secretary Henry Paulson, a former Goldman Sachs chief with direct presidential access (McDonald & Robinson, 2009; Sorkin, 2009). In that moment, the "impersonal" world of global finance revealed itself to be deeply personal. Trust, reputation, and networks still mattered—only now at trillion-dollar scales.

Yet the story looks very different further down the hierarchy. For small firms and ordinary individuals, the digital era has brought not stronger safety nets, but new forms of exposure. Online fraud, spoofing, and social engineering now flourish precisely because digital transactions strip away many of the face-to-face cues on which traditional trust relied (Söilen, 2021). At the corporate level, trust can still function through elite networks and insider relationships; but for the average consumer or entrepreneur, it has become easier than ever to be cheated. Trust has not become less important—but it has become more uneven, abstract, and fragile.

In the past, families like the Medicis secured trust through bloodlines and marriage. Today, institutions do so through reputation systems, legal contracts, and third-party audits. The stage has changed, but the evolutionary challenge remains the same: how to stabilize cooperation amid uncertainty and asymmetry. What has changed is scale. Where Renaissance elites relied on dynastic alliances, today's political and economic leaders maintain influence through informal or semi-formal networks, often meeting at high-level forums such as Davos. These venues serve as spaces of reassurance—opportunities for powerful actors to signal reliability, negotiate shared interests, and tacitly confirm who belongs within circles of mutual protection. In this sense, modern elites continue an old pattern: providing backstops against collapse for one another, while those outside such networks remain more exposed to risk.

Trust-based behavior, however, is not governed by rigid scripts. Humans adapt. As game theory shows, conditional cooperation strategies like "tit for tat" outperform both unconditional altruism and pure defection in repeated interactions (Axelrod & Hamilton, 1981). What looks like moral behavior is often contingent on cues, feedback, and circumstance.

Our evolved brains are central to this flexibility. Dunbar's Social Brain Hypothesis (1998) suggests that our enlarged neocortex evolved less for abstract reasoning than for navigating the complexities of group life. Tracking reputations, anticipating reactions, and weighing loyalty against risk are not luxuries but survival tools.

This is why trust and cooperation have always coexisted with rivalry and conflict. Sibling competition, status hierarchies, and intergroup aggression illustrate this tension. Some ethnographic studies, such as the debated work of Chagnon (1988), even argue that violence can serve reproductive or defensive purposes, though such interpretations remain contested and shaped by culture as much as ecology.

What distinguishes humans is our capacity to extend cooperation far beyond kinship. Through cultural evolution, we developed norms, symbols, and institutions that stabilize trust among strangers. As Henrich (2015) argues, these cultural innovations amplify our biological capacities, transforming local alliances into global systems.

In short, the architecture of human behavior reflects a dynamic interplay between biology and culture. Trust, cooperation, and competition are not accidents but evolved strategies calibrated to the demands of survival. To understand why societies flourish—or fracture—we must begin here.

And yet, even these cooperative strategies rest on a more hidden foundation: the workings of the mind itself. How do we decide whom to trust, when to cooperate, or when to defect? Much of the answer lies not in deliberate reasoning but in fast, automatic judgments. This brings us to the next step in our argument: the evolutionary roots of intuition.

3.2.4 Intuition's Evolutionary Roots: When Thinking Isn't Thinking

When we believe we are reasoning—carefully weighing alternatives, balancing pros and cons—we are often doing something else entirely. We are relying on intuition. Gut feelings. Fast judgments. Snap assessments. And most of the time, we don't even notice. We enjoy the idea that we are reflective, analytical beings—but this is only partly true. Much of what we call "thinking" is just a post hoc explanation of feelings we've already had.

Evolution didn't shape the human mind for accuracy or objectivity. It shaped it for survival. Our ancestors did not have the luxury of endless deliberation; decisions had to be made quickly: friend or foe? Eat or run? Trust or avoid? So, over time, the brain developed shortcuts—fast, efficient systems for assessing situations based on patterns. These shortcuts are what we now call *intuition*.

As we have noted, psychologists Daniel Kahneman and Amos Tversky distinguished between two types of thinking: *System 1* and *System 2*. System 1 is fast, automatic, and emotional. System 2 is slow, deliberate, and logical. But the truth is, System 1 usually gets there first—and System 2 often just rationalizes what System 1 already decided. We don't reason our way to a conclusion; we justify the conclusion we've already felt.

This is especially true in social settings. From an evolutionary perspective, the ability to make snap social judgments was far more important than being logically correct. Recognizing facial expressions, detecting deception, remembering allies and rivals—these were essential skills. Researchers like Leda Cosmides and John Tooby proposed that the mind evolved domain-specific modules for precisely these tasks: reading emotions, spotting cheaters, tracking status, and managing group membership.

Modern neuroscience confirms this. The *amygdala*, involved in processing fear and threat, activates before we're even aware of what we've seen. The *insula* responds to violations of fairness or disgust. These brain regions do not wait for us to finish our reasoning—they shape our reasoning from the outset.

Even our physical bodies play a role. The vagus nerve connects the brain to the gut and other organs, influencing emotion and decision-making. What we call a "*gut feeling*" is often quite literal: the body has picked up on subtle cues—tone of voice, posture, eye movement—that the conscious brain hasn't fully processed. We feel unease or confidence before we know why.

That doesn't mean intuition is unreliable. On the contrary, it often performs better than analysis in complex, real-world situations. Professionals in high-stakes fields—emergency responders, surgeons, intelligence analysts—learn to trust their instincts. Years of experience build up tacit knowledge that can't easily be verbalized but shows up in fast, accurate decisions. These aren't magical intuitions. They're deeply embodied, deeply practiced forms of pattern recognition (Klein, 1998).

But experience matters. Not all intuitions are good intuitions. Research in cognitive reflection shows that people who avoid analytic thinking are more prone to fall for misleading gut feelings. They mistake confidence for accuracy (Frederick, 2005). In fact, some of the worst decisions come from trusting intuition when the situation actually demands slow, careful thought.

The problem becomes even sharper when others actively exploit our intuitive tendencies. Skilled deceivers—whether in politics, business, or personal life—can deliberately send signals that match what we expect to see. They *mimic sincerity* through eye contact, verbal fluency, and emotional alignment, knowing that these cues reliably trigger trust (Vrij, 2008; ten Brinke et al., 2016). Our brains evolved to read social signals quickly, but those same heuristics can be hijacked by individuals adept at concealing their true intentions. Assessing another person's trustworthiness, therefore, is not just about reading signals—it's also about judging their ability and motivation to manipulate those signals.

This makes interpersonal encounters a dual-layered task: we interpret the immediate cues, but we also, consciously or not, assess the other's capacity for deception. Evolutionary psychologists note that such vigilance was adaptive in ancestral environments, where exploitation could carry fatal costs (Cosmides & Tooby, 2005). In modern contexts, the stakes may be different, but the principle remains. We are not just reading people—we are reading their ability to mislead us.

The real danger, then, is not that we use intuition—we must—but that we confuse it with logic, and worse, that we allow it to be guided by signals intentionally crafted to misdirect us. We believe we are reasoning when we are often just rationalizing feelings that have already taken shape. It's a comforting illusion, one that flatters our image of ourselves as thoughtful, deliberative agents. But that illusion leaves us vulnerable—to bias, to overconfidence, and to manipulation.

For social scientists, who study these subjects, this is hardly an ideal starting point. If our task is to understand human behavior, including our own, then we must first admit that much of it is driven not by careful reasoning but by evolved patterns of intuition masquerading as thought.

Recognizing this gap between what feels like reasoning and what is actually intuitive guesswork is not an abstract academic point—it is something we all face in real life. The stakes can be personal or professional, minor or life-changing, but the underlying dynamics are the same: our evolved pattern-recognition systems are constantly making judgments, and we must decide whether to trust or question them. The following case illustrates how easily that decision can go wrong, even when the facts appear to be in our favor.

Case in a Box: A Lesson in Misplaced Trust—When Gut Feeling Should Have Been Heeded

One of the hardest things about intuition is knowing when to trust it. The problem is not that gut feelings are always wrong—they are often rooted in subtle pattern recognition or unconscious cues—but that we rarely have a reliable way to evaluate them in real time.

Consider the case of a household renovation project. A family hired several local contractors to handle different tasks. Most of the work went smoothly. But one part—the tiling of the inner courtyard—turned into a drawn-out failure. The workers leading this part, Señor Ramón Chaparro and his cousin Paco del Mármol, did not inspire confidence. Something about their demeanor, the evasive tone of their answers, the way they avoided eye contact, and the harshness in their expressions—all of it triggered unease. Yet their proposal ticked all the rational boxes: the price was competitive, the timeline reasonable, and on paper everything appeared fine.

Despite the discomfort, the project went ahead—partly due to time pressure and partly because the analytical signals seemed to outweigh the emotional ones. Another factor was the absence of alternative offers at the time, which created an artificial sense of scarcity. In hindsight, this proved irrational: scarcity of choice is not the same as quality of choice.

The results validated the initial unease. The project was repeatedly delayed, the workmanship was sloppy, and when problems emerged, Ramón and Paco stopped answering calls. Eventually, the work had to be redone entirely, leaving both financial losses and lingering frustration.

The lesson? That discomfort was not meaningless—it was a signal, not about trust alone but about risk. Intuition didn't provide an explanation, but it caught something the analysis missed. Similar cases suggest that local providers or community-embedded businesses often reduce such risks—not just because of convenience or reputation, but because their embeddedness makes it harder to disappear without consequence.

This is where intuition often misleads us—not because it is useless, but because it is too easily dismissed when it feels inconvenient or conflicts with other pressures. Worse still, many people lack the tools to distinguish between valid and misleading gut feelings. Some trust them reflexively; others override them out of habit. In decisions involving personal stakes, uncertainty, and the possibility of future regret, getting that calibration wrong can have lasting consequences.

Questions for Discussion

1 What early warning signs—behavioral, emotional, or contextual—might indicate a bad decision, even when the facts seem sound?
2 How can experience sharpen the ability to recognize which intuitions are worth listening to?
3 What role does pressure (time, money, social) play in overriding intuitive discomfort?
4 Should intuition be treated as a form of evidence—or as a signal to pause and re-evaluate?
5 Can trust in local or embedded relationships reduce the risk of poor outcomes in situations of uncertainty?

The broader point is that intuition is neither infallible nor irrelevant—it is a deeply evolved mechanism for navigating uncertainty, one that needs calibration rather than blind trust or total dismissal. In social life, these moment-to-moment judgments do not stay private. They ripple outward, shaping how we treat others, who we choose to work with, and how communities set their expectations. Over time, repeated patterns of trust, suspicion, and cooperation crystallize into shared rules—norms, customs, and eventually moral codes.

This is where our focus now shifts: from the personal scale of intuitive judgment to the collective scale of cultural agreement. How do private instincts become public standards? And what happens when those standards drift too far from the biological realities that shaped our intuitions in the first place?

3.3 Reclaiming Human Nature: The Return of Biology to the Social Sciences

To understand human behavior scientifically, we must begin with a clear view of what humans are. That means grounding our social theories in biology and evolution. For a time, we did. From the late nineteenth century through the early twentieth, psychology, anthropology, and even criminology took

Darwin seriously. Human cognition was understood as the product of adaptive pressures; mental life was rooted in the body and shaped by survival. This evolutionary lens offered not just a theory of change but a framework for understanding the mind itself.

But this biologically grounded view was abandoned. After 1945, biology became politically suspect. The atrocities of fascism, the misuse of eugenics, and the shadow of Nazism made evolutionary explanations seem dangerous. In the Cold War era, much of American academia turned away from evolutionary explanations of human behavior and toward a new ideal: the autonomous, rational individual. This was not primarily a scientific recalibration, but a political and ideological move. Framing human beings as self-contained decision-makers—unbound by biology, history, or cultural contingency—aligned neatly with the liberal-capitalist vision of the United States in its rivalry with the Soviet Union. It also meshed with the methodological rise of formal models in economics and political science.

Mathematical elegance became a virtue in itself: theories rendered in neat equations, promising predictive precision, gained prestige regardless of their connection to real-world human behavior. These models looked rigorous and modern, but too often they described a stylized fiction—one that fit ideological needs better than empirical facts (Fourcade, 2009; Hodgson, 2019; Mirowski, 2002). The result was a generation of scholarship that confused the clarity of abstraction with the truth of observation, sidelining the messier, more contingent insights that evolutionary theory could offer.

This ideological turn was reflected across disciplines. Economics embraced the fiction of *homo economicus*—an agent of perfect reason and infinite choice. Political science constructed models of democratic deliberation that assumed informed, unbiased voters. Even psychology drifted toward behaviorism and cognitive models that likened the brain to a computer, stripping it of its evolutionary history.

This was not just a methodological shift—it was a philosophical reorientation. The Enlightenment ideal of rational agency was revived and modernized, now backed by formal models and liberal values. Reason, not biology, was seen as the foundation of freedom and equality. The mind was reimagined as a blank slate, infinitely moldable by culture, education, and environment.

But this vision came at a cost. It severed theory from reality.

Humans are not blank slates, nor are we rational calculators. We are biological organisms shaped by millions of years of evolution. We carry within us cognitive shortcuts, social instincts, and emotional drives that evolved to solve problems in small, kin-based groups—not to navigate abstract bureaucracies or global markets. As researchers like Gigerenzer and Selten (2001) have shown, our so-called biases are often not errors as such, but adaptive heuristics tailored to real-world conditions.

The rejection of biology led to theoretical models that were elegant but fragile, designed around ideals rather than human limitations. Institutions were built on abstractions that ignored how people actually think, decide, and cooperate. Political debates, educational reforms, and policy interventions were all shaped by the comforting but incorrect assumption that humans are primarily rational, self-directed beings.

This disconnection is now being corrected—though, as always, with bumps along the road. We are slowly but necessarily returning to a view of human nature grounded in biology. Evolutionary psychology, behavioral economics, and affective neuroscience are helping to reconstruct a more accurate portrait of the mind: not as a machine for logic, but as a toolkit for survival. Our reasoning, morality, and decision-making all reflect deep evolutionary roots. As Jonathan Haidt (2012) argues, moral judgments arise not from rational deduction but from intuitive systems shaped by both nature and culture. Yet the process is hardly linear; at present, we seem to have stumbled into a pothole of ideological influence, where debates about identity and politics sometimes obscure rather than clarifying the science.

Prospect theory (Kahneman & Tversky, 1979), for example, reveals that we weigh potential losses more heavily than gains. This isn't irrational—it's a legacy of a world where loss often meant death. Similarly, the *moral foundations theory* shows that fairness, loyalty, and purity are not mere cultural preferences but stem from evolved cognitive predispositions that helped regulate group life.

Importantly, rediscovering biology does not mean rejecting culture. It means understanding how the two interact. Evolution gave us the capacity for culture—language, morality, institutions—but it is culture that gives content to these forms. Human nature is not a genetic blueprint but a set of tendencies shaped by environmental feedback. As Henrich (2015) points out, cultural evolution allows societies to adapt over generations, developing norms and practices that fit their ecological and social realities.

The mistake of early biological approaches was not in seeing behavior as evolved, but in failing to see that evolution continued through culture. Today, we can correct that error. We can build a new paradigm—one that treats biology and culture not as opposites, but as coevolving forces.

This shift is more than academic. It is a path to real progress. If we want social science to guide institutions, policies, and reforms, it must be grounded in how people actually behave—not how we wish they would. We must ask: How can we design democracies that account for tribal loyalties? How can education systems reflect the realities of attention, discipline, and cognitive development?

Consider the case of modern schooling. Over the past decades, classrooms in many countries have absorbed an expanding set of pedagogical and political goals: equality, inclusiveness, socialization, civic training, and emotional well-being. While each of these has merit, the cumulative effect has often been a dilution of the school's core mission: the structured transmission of knowledge. Studies in educational psychology show that young people struggle to sustain concentration without external discipline and clear routines (Duckworth & Seligman, 2005; Willingham, 2009). Yet in many systems, traditional practices of authority and order have been weakened, sometimes on the grounds that they were authoritarian or outdated. The result, as classroom ethnographies confirm, is often drift toward disorder, where noise and distraction undermine learning (Alexander, 2010).

This drift has been reinforced by another trend: the political ideal of equality has increasingly translated into a suspicion of excellence. In practice, this has meant discouraging both failure and extraordinary success: no one is to be left behind, but neither should anyone pull too far ahead. Research on motivation suggests this can backfire. When high-performing students are denied opportunities for acceleration, their engagement declines (Colangelo et al., 2004). Meanwhile, lower-performing students do not necessarily benefit from environments where standards are lowered; without structure and challenge, they too may disengage (Hattie, 2009).

Seen from an evolutionary perspective, what is often missed in these reforms is precisely the basic lesson: human beings, especially the young, do not naturally gravitate toward self-discipline or sustained effort. Left unchecked, behavior tends toward chaos rather than constructive order. Cultural systems—whether in schools, families, or institutions—exist to counteract this tendency, providing scaffolding for learning and growth (Tomasello, 2009). When such scaffolding is dismantled in the name of freedom or equality, the outcome is not empowerment but fragmentation. The consequences are visible in international comparisons: Western countries now lag substantially behind many East Asian systems in measurable learning outcomes. In mathematics, for instance, 15-year-old students in countries like Singapore, South Korea, and Japan outperform their peers in Europe and North America by the equivalent of up to three years of schooling (OECD, 2019; 2023). This has been the price of our political romantic dreams.

History's cycles rarely follow a smooth or predictable path. After a long period of drift, there are signs of a *Hegelian turn*: a swing of the pendulum back toward order—not the old order of the cane and rigid hierarchy, but a new synthesis. In Hegel's terms, the thesis of strict authority was challenged by the antithesis of unstructured freedom; the next step is synthesis, a reassertion of discipline and structure in a more adaptive form. Schools are therefore unlikely to remain indefinitely in disorder; pressures from parents, policymakers, and students themselves will gradually force a return to clearer routines and firmer expectations, though not in the same guise as before.

This educational cycle is not an isolated case but a broader pattern. Just as schooling is moving through thesis, antithesis, and synthesis, so too have the social sciences. In hindsight, the postwar abandonment of biology was understandable—it was the antithesis to earlier reductionist models—but it was also a mistake. It severed inquiry from its most powerful explanatory framework. By returning to a biologically grounded view of human nature, we have the opportunity to achieve synthesis: restoring coherence to our theories, relevance to our institutions, and realism to our aspirations.

To go forward, then, we must in a sense go back: back to Darwin, back to the body, and back to the brain. Yet this is not really regression, because the biological paradigm was never completed—it was interrupted, prematurely abandoned. What we are doing now is less a return to the past than a continuation of a path left unfinished.

History itself illustrates this pattern of correction. Nations, like sciences, sometimes follow the wrong track for a generation or two before they readjust. China, for instance, pursued the Maoist vision of communism before shifting course under Deng Xiaoping. It was presented as a new beginning, but in reality it was a rectification—an adjustment to reality, not a regression. Likewise, evolutionary thinking in the social sciences does not mean going "back" to the nineteenth century; it means resuming a trajectory that was cut short.

In the next section, we take this integrated view one step further by exploring how biology and culture interact through norms, symbols, and institutions, giving shape and meaning to our shared human life.

3.4 Genes and Cultural Norms

Biology, then, is the bedrock of human behavior, but it is not the full story. Culture—our shared systems of meaning, norms, values, and institutions—shapes how biology is expressed. Or said differently:

> *While genes provide the blueprint, culture furnishes the instructions for its execution.*

This interdependence between biology and culture lies at the heart of what makes us human.

From the start, human development depends on cultural input.

Unlike most animals, human infants are born helpless, requiring prolonged parental care and socialization. This extended period of dependency allows for massive learning. Lev Vygotsky (1978) argued that higher mental functions are first experienced in social interactions before becoming internalized as individual capacities. Jean Piaget (1952) similarly showed how children build cognitive schemas through interaction with their environment.

Culture magnifies what evolution has enabled. Our capacity for language, for example, is biologically prepared—Noam Chomsky's (1965) notion of a *universal grammar*—but actual languages are learned through immersion in a specific community. Likewise, our ability to cooperate and follow norms is rooted in evolved psychology (Tomasello, 2009), but the specific content of those norms varies widely—from monogamy to polygamy, egalitarianism to hierarchy, or collectivism to individualism.

This flexibility is one of our greatest evolutionary advantages. Joseph Henrich (2015) has shown how cultural evolution allows human groups to adapt to diverse environments far more rapidly than genetic evolution would allow. Tools, rituals, institutions, and moral codes are not biologically inherited but socially transmitted—what Claude Lévi-Strauss (1963) called "*the raw and the cooked*." In this view, culture is not an overlay on biology but an extension of it.

The interaction between genes and culture is dynamic. Richard Dawkins (1976) coined, as we mentioned earlier, the term "*meme*" to describe cultural units that replicate through imitation. More recently, the field of *gene-culture coevolution* (Boyd & Richerson, 1985) has explored how cultural practices can influence biological evolution. For instance, the cultural domestication of dairy animals led to the selection for lactose tolerance in certain human populations (Gerbault et al., 2011).

Moral norms, like other types of social regulation, evolve within cultural contexts. Jonathan Haidt (2012) suggests that human moral reasoning is shaped by innate intuitions—such as care, loyalty, fairness, and sanctity—but these are then filtered through culture. This interplay helps explain why moral codes vary across societies yet retain universal themes.

Social norms can be understood as shared expectations about appropriate behavior in particular contexts. Cristina Bicchieri (2006) defines them not as formal laws, but as unwritten rules embedded in our mental models and sustained through mutual expectations. We follow norms because we believe others will follow them too, and that deviation may lead to social sanctions. Norms can be deeply ingrained, like how one addresses elders, or more fluid and contested, such as gender expression. A norm is not only a guide to behavior; it is a mirror of collective values, negotiated and enforced through both institutions and informal social pressures.

The process of norm change raises a crucial question: whose norms count? This is relatively unproblematic when long-standing norms are passed on through tradition. But friction arises when new norms are introduced, like when they are promoted by political movements, state agencies, or academic institutions. Resistance often emerges when these norms are perceived as externally imposed, ideologically driven, or disconnected from everyday practices and identities.

These tensions remind us that norms do not exist in isolation but emerge from the deeper interplay between biology and culture. To fully grasp why some norms persist while others are resisted, we need to see how cultural systems both build upon and reshape our biological foundations. The following model illustrates this dynamic relationship, showing how genes provide the blueprint while culture furnishes the instructions—and how their constant feedback loop shapes human behavior across time (Fig. 3.3).

This *Gene–Culture Feedback Model* illustrates the dynamic relationship between biology and culture in shaping human behavior. Genes provide the biological blueprint, but culture furnishes the instructions that determine how these capacities are expressed in real life. Culture manifests through

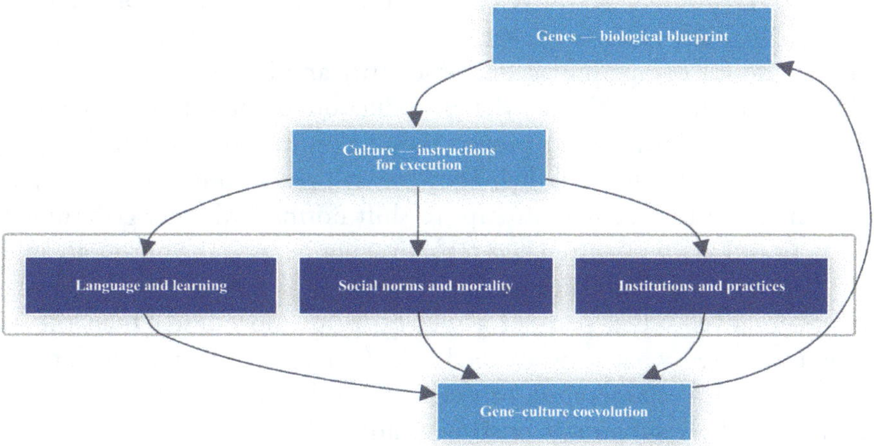

Fig. 3.3 Gene–culture feedback model

language and learning, social norms and morality, and institutions and practices. These cultural systems not only guide behavior but also feed back into biological evolution—a process known as *gene–culture coevolution.* Classic examples include how the cultural practice of dairy farming selected for lactose tolerance, or how symbolic communication reinforced neural pathways for language. The model emphasizes that humans are not just products of genes or culture alone, but of their constant interaction.

Consider the example of mask-wearing during the COVID-19 pandemic. Compliance varied widely across countries, not merely due to differences in government mandates, but due to descriptive norms—what people saw others doing around them. Research found that people were more likely to wear masks when others around them did so, regardless of formal rules. However, when authorities attempted to impose mask mandates without strong grassroots alignment, backlash occurred. In polarized or *low-trust societies*, mandates were seen as political overreach, not public health guidance. Here, the introduction of a new norm—meant to protect public health—met resistance rooted in perceived threats to personal freedom and autonomy.

Another vivid example is the introduction of gender-inclusive pronouns, such as the Swedish "hen" or the English singular "they." These linguistic innovations aimed to reflect evolving understandings of gender identity and promote inclusivity. Studies show a gradual uptake of such pronouns, especially among younger and urban populations, and some evidence suggests that their use can support broader gender equity. But these efforts have also faced cultural pushback. In Sweden, initial reactions ranged from ridicule to confusion, and in France, the proposed use of the pronoun "iel" triggered outrage from conservative commentators and defenders of the French language. In both cases, language—a deeply normative system—became a battleground for competing visions of identity and belonging.

These examples reveal that the introduction of new norms is rarely a neutral process. Norms reflect power: they are promoted by particular groups with particular interests, and their adoption can redistribute cultural or political capital. Institutions that attempt to shift norms—whether governments, NGOs, or universities—often face resistance not because the norms are inherently controversial, but because the process is perceived as top-down or unrepresentative. When parts of a society try to move faster than the rest, the result is often what is now called a *"culture war."* From an evolutionary perspective, such clashes can be seen as accelerated attempts at cultural adaptation, where subgroups push new norms before broader social mechanisms of consensus and stabilization have caught up. These conflicts are not anomalies but symptoms of how cultures evolve: variation in practices creates tension, selection pressures determine which survive, and over time, some innovations may become stabilized as widely accepted norms, while others fade away.

This tension is especially visible when we consider how states themselves institutionalize values. In Sweden, for instance, the government has articulated an official framework for public service known as "Den statliga värdegrunden"—the public sector's core value system. It emphasizes six principles: democracy, legality, objectivity, freedom of opinion, respect, and efficiency. These principles, derived from constitutional law, are meant to guide all civil servants and promote ethical, effective governance. However, challenges arise when individual agencies begin to *interpret* these abstract principles differently in their internal operations. One department might emphasize "objectivity" to mean neutrality in public discourse, while another might interpret "respect" as a mandate to promote specific identity-based inclusion programs. When such interpretations diverge or become politicized, they risk fragmenting institutional coherence and generating confusion or mistrust among employees. This is not just a Swedish issue; it highlights a deeper danger.

When this feedback model is disrupted—such as when political or absolutist thinking declares that culture is whatever we choose it to be risk fragmenting institutional coherence and generating confusion or mistrust among employees. Treating culture as infinitely malleable not only detaches it from lived traditions but also weakens the moral frameworks and social contracts built upon them. Moral norms are not free-floating ideals; they are rooted in long histories of shared practice, embedded in institutions, and reinforced by collective memory. When these roots are neglected, norms risk losing legitimacy, opening the way for cultural fragmentation and declining trust (Durkheim, 1912/1995; Haidt, 2012). In this sense, dismantling culture into arbitrary preferences is not only a philosophical error but a practical one, undermining the very cohesion that makes societies viable.

The broader implication is that norms do not simply evolve—they are constructed, promoted, contested, and sometimes enforced. Their legitimacy depends not only on their content but on the transparency and inclusiveness of the process by which they emerge. When norm change is participatory and responsive, it can enrich civic life and social cohesion. When it is perceived as arbitrary or elite-driven, it risks alienation and resistance. To understand modern social dynamics then, we must pay close attention not only to which norms exist but also to who defines them, how they spread, and why they are accepted or rejected.

The patterns are ancient. Long before modern nation-states, societies experimented—sometimes successfully, sometimes not—with ways of creating and sustaining shared norms across diverse populations. History provides vivid examples of how legitimacy, inclusion, and institutional trust can be built—or eroded—through the management of collective identity.

Case Box: Roman Citizenship as Institutional Norm

The Roman Republic—later Empire—offers one of the most enduring examples of how institutional norms evolve alongside societal expansion. It serves here not as a political analogy, but as a historical illustration of how shared identity, legal inclusion, and institutional trust can be interlinked—and strained.

At its peak, Rome expanded not only through military means but also by integrating new populations through the mechanism of *Roman citizenship*. This status granted access to Roman legal protections, public office, and civic life. The benefits associated with Roman identity—including roads, public infrastructure, and the rule of law—made citizenship a highly attractive designation (Ando, 2000; Lavan, 2016).

Initially limited to select groups, Roman citizenship was gradually extended to allies, provinces, and loyal populations. Over time, as the empire grew and its military needs increased, emperors began to rely more heavily on recruits from outside Italy. In 212 CE, the *Constitutio Antoniniana*—a decree by Emperor Caracalla—extended citizenship to nearly all free inhabitants of the empire (Ando, 2011). While intended to promote unity and streamline tax policy, it also transformed the symbolic value of citizenship.

As citizenship became near-universal, it began to lose its distinguishing power. For some, the shift led to a weaker sense of connection to Roman institutions. Military allegiance sometimes drifted toward charismatic generals rather than the central government, and civic participation became more fragmented. Over time, the institutional cohesion that once defined the Roman system began to loosen (Harper, 2017; Heather, 2006).

This transition is often overshadowed by more visible historical events—military defeats, invasions, and political rivalries. But historians increasingly emphasize the importance of cultural and institutional continuity in sustaining large, diverse societies (Wells, 1999). When shared norms erode or become too diffuse, even robust systems can become fragile.

The Roman case does not offer a direct blueprint for interpreting modern developments, but it raises enduring questions about how institutional identity is formed, maintained, and occasionally stretched. It reminds us that inclusion, while often essential, must also be paired with mechanisms that cultivate belonging, shared responsibility, and trust in the institutions themselves.

Questions for Discussion

1. What does the Roman experience suggest about the relationship between institutional inclusion and symbolic cohesion?
2. Can expanding legal rights across a diverse population maintain a strong sense of collective identity?
3. How do societies sustain trust in institutions as their membership grows more diverse?
4. What are the trade-offs between symbolic universality and the preservation of shared civic norms?
5. How might historical models help us better understand institutional resilience in the present?

The collapse of Roman norms serves as a cautionary tale of what happens when foundational values—once tightly bound to institutional identity—are weakened or emptied of meaning. It illustrates how norms are not abstract ideals but active forces that regulate behavior, guide identity, and shape loyalty. When they become overextended, inconsistently applied, or politically manipulated, they lose their power to bind people to each other and to the state. This erosion of shared expectations can destabilize not only institutions but the very psychological anchors of social life.

Culture, in this sense, functions as the regulatory layer atop our biological capacities. It moderates and redirects evolved tendencies—such as conformity, status-seeking, or group loyalty—through the scaffolding of social institutions. While such traits are universally human, their expression is remarkably context dependent. Research in cultural psychology, for example, has shown how Western cultures tend to valorize individual agency, whereas East Asian societies often prioritize relational interdependence (Markus & Kitayama, 1991). Even something as seemingly basic as emotion recognition or spatial reasoning can vary with cultural framing (Nisbett, 2003).

To sum up, human behavior cannot be fully understood without integrating both its biological roots and its cultural scaffolding. *Biology* does not rigidly determine our actions, but it does set the parameters within which culture operates. *Culture*, in turn, is not a counterforce to biology but its most powerful extension—an evolutionary strategy that allows human beings to adapt flexibly to diverse environments, form large-scale societies, and encode cooperation into institutions, laws, and symbols. Our minds are not blank slates, nor are they purely instinctual. They are evolved systems that absorb cultural scripts to extend our social reach. When we study humans without biology, we miss the structure. When we study them without culture, we miss the story.

As we continue to introduce more terms, our aim is to show how this revisited paradigm can be used to understand humanity and society. The point is not to overwhelm with a complete glossary, but to bring concepts in gradually—so that, by the end, we share a working vocabulary for making sense of the arguments. Table 3.3 synthesizes the key concepts introduced in this section. Together, they form a conceptual toolkit for understanding how evolved traits and cultural processes interact to shape social behavior, institutional development, and historical change:

These concepts are not just academic terms—they point to a broader paradigm shift. Instead of treating culture as an overlay and biology as a constraint, we begin to see them as mutually reinforcing forces. This perspective offers a richer framework for analyzing how human societies form, function, and sometimes fail.

But nowhere is this bio-cultural interplay more vivid—or more ethically charged—than in the domain of morality. It is here, in our capacities for empathy, fairness, and social judgment, that biology and culture converge most powerfully. To understand how humans make moral decisions, we now turn to the emotional roots of moral behavior and the cultural systems that amplify—or suppress—them.

3.4.1 Emotions and Moral Reasoning

Human morality is not the product of pure logic or philosophical reflection. It arises from deeper evolutionary roots—emotional capacities such as empathy, fairness, and altruism that evolved because they helped our ancestors survive in tightly knit social groups. These traits allowed individuals to recognize the needs of others, respond to suffering, and act in ways that promoted cooperation. Over time, they became central to group cohesion and long-term survival.

This insight finds early articulation in Darwin's *The Descent of Man* (1871), where he described moral faculties as an extension of social instincts. Likewise, Max Scheler (1913) argued that *empathy* (Mitgefühl) is not derived from rational thought but is an intuitive, emotional foundation of moral awareness.

Table 3.3 Core concepts in the evolutionary-cultural architecture of human behavior

Term	Definition	Example
Gene–culture coevolution	Interaction where cultural practices influence genetic selection	Dairy farming leading to increased lactose tolerance (Gerbault et al., 2011)
Cultural transmission	Passing of knowledge and norms through learning rather than inheritance	Learning religious rituals from parents or community
Meme	A unit of cultural information passed through imitation	The spread of internet jokes or fashion trends (Dawkins, 1976)
Norm	Unwritten rule about acceptable behavior, sustained through expectation	Not interrupting someone during a conversation
Moral foundation theory	Moral reasoning based on innate, culturally filtered intuitions	Valuing fairness or loyalty differently across societies (Haidt, 2012)
Descriptive norm	Norm shaped by observing what others actually do	Wearing a mask because most people around you do
Norm resistance	Pushback against imposed or unfamiliar norms	Protests against gender-neutral language in official communication
Institutional values	Core principles embedded in governance or formal structures	Sweden's *statliga värdegrunden* guiding public servants
Norm diffusion	Spread of norms across societies or groups	The gradual adoption of recycling in urban environments
Cultural framing	How culture shapes interpretation of behavior or experience	Western focus on individual choice vs. East Asian focus on social harmony
Evolved heuristics	Cognitive shortcuts shaped by evolution to make fast, adaptive decisions	Avoiding risky behavior based on gut feelings in dangerous environments (Gigerenzer, 2000)
Cognitive modularity	The mind consists of specialized systems evolved for specific tasks	Reasoning differently about food, danger, and social trust
Homo economicus	The rational, utility-maximizing individual in economic theory	Neoclassical models assuming agents with perfect foresight

(continued)

Table 3.3 (continued)

Term	Definition	Example
Prospect theory	Humans weigh losses more heavily than gains due to evolved risk sensitivity	Being more upset about losing $100 than happy about gaining $100 (Kahneman & Tversky, 1979)
Institutional mismatch	When modern systems conflict with evolved cognitive tendencies	Expecting rational voting behavior in emotionally charged elections
Norm dilution	Erosion of meaning when inclusion becomes disconnected from obligation	Roman citizenship losing coherence after the *Constitutio Antoniniana* (Caracalla, 212 CE)
Moral erosion	Breakdown of shared belief systems that once held institutions together	Decline of civic trust and participation in late-stage Rome
Cultural co-regulation	Mutual shaping of norms and behavior through feedback loops	Public behavior shifting in response to perceived social approval or disapproval
Bio-cultural realism	The view that human nature reflects both evolved predispositions and cultural forms	Recognizing both genetic drives and symbolic meaning in moral life

But morality is not biologically fixed. It evolves. Just as our bodies adapt to new environments, our moral systems shift in response to changing conditions. This is where the evolutionary view departs sharply from traditions that see morality as eternal or absolute. Friedrich Nietzsche, in *On the Genealogy of Morality* (1887), emphasized that moral systems arise historically through conflict, power, and adaptation—not divine command or pure reason. Fixed moral rules—such as those codified in holy texts—may offer stability, but when treated as timeless truths, they can lead to tension and conflict, particularly in pluralistic societies. For example, moral codes that rigidly define gender roles (what women are allowed to do and not), family structures, or dietary laws may clash with modern legal norms, human rights frameworks, or scientific understanding. The problem is not that such codes once served a purpose—they likely did—but that freezing them in place denies the adaptive function of morality itself, something Nietzsche viewed as a kind of *moral sclerosis*.

Western civilization in particular has long been dominated by traditions of "*absolute morality*," which stand in sharp contrast to the adaptive perspective of evolutionary morality.[3] The first great wave came with religion, most visibly Christianity, where morality was codified into unchanging commandments such as the Ten Commandments. These rules claimed universal authority across time and context, offering stability but little room for adaptation. A second wave emerged with modern political ideologies, which—though secular—often replicated the same dogmatic structure. Doctrines such as socialism, social democracy, or libertarianism presented their moral visions as final and universal truths, not contingent strategies shaped by history and context. In this sense, both religious and ideological traditions in Europe share a common inheritance of *absolutist thinking*, even if some of their doctrines originated in the Middle East. The underlying logic remained the same: morality as fixed principle rather than adaptive practice.

Yet the adaptive perspective also makes clear that not all aspects of morality are negotiable. Every group, culture, or civilization carries a moral structure built from the accumulated lessons of what allowed it to survive. Certain moral anchors—such as prohibitions against murder within the group, obligations of kinship, or norms of reciprocity—form the non-negotiable baseline of collective life. These frameworks resist change because they have been encoded into practices, rituals, and institutions over generations—what Peter Sloterdijk (2009) called "*anthropotechnics*," or embodied exercises in self-discipline and cultural continuity. Other elements of morality, however—such as dress codes, gender roles, or rules about food—are more historically contingent. They may once have served adaptive purposes, but they can be renegotiated as conditions change. When individuals or groups attempt to redefine even core expectations too rapidly—or without broad consensus—the result is often confusion, social backlash, or institutional breakdown. This echoes the concern raised by Alasdair MacIntyre (1981), who warned that uprooting moral traditions without understanding their historical function leads to fragmentation and ethical incoherence.

---

[3] The critique of absolute morality has a long intellectual history. Friedrich Nietzsche's *On the Genealogy of Morality* (1887/1994) was one of the first systematic attempts to show that moral codes are historical constructions shaped by conflict, resentment, and adaptation, rather than eternal truths. Alasdair MacIntyre's *After Virtue* (1981) extended this critique, arguing that modern moral discourse is fragmented precisely because it lost sight of the historical and communal roots of moral traditions. More recently, John Gray (*Straw Dogs*, 2002; *Black Mass*, 2007) has attacked what he sees as the persistence of "secularized Christianity" in modern political ideologies—whether liberalism, socialism, or democracy—each of which tends to present its values as universal and final. From this perspective, the shift from religious dogma to ideological dogma represents continuity rather than rupture: both embody forms of absolutism that leave little room for an adaptive, evolutionary understanding of morality.

This evolutionary and historical perspective also complicates the assumption—common in Western political thought—that one group's moral framework can or should be imposed upon others. Morality, while rooted in biological dispositions such as empathy and fairness, takes shape within groups through shared histories, institutions, and practices. Anthropological research shows that moral codes display remarkable cross-cultural variation, even if they cluster around recurrent themes like reciprocity, kinship obligations, and fairness (Haidt & Joseph, 2004; Shweder et al., 1997). Because these systems are group-specific adaptations, attempts to universalize a single moral order across societies are inherently fraught.

The history of Western expansion makes this tension visible. From the missionary projects that accompanied European colonization in Africa and Asia (Comaroff & Comaroff, 1991) to contemporary campaigns promoting liberal democracy and human rights, the West has repeatedly framed its own moral code as a universal standard. The problem is not that values such as equality or democracy lack merit within Western contexts, but that projecting them as timeless absolutes ignores their group-specific origins and evolutionary functions. As Jack Goody (2006) noted, Western moral and institutional forms—whether parliamentary democracy, individual rights, or secular rationalism—cannot be understood outside the historical trajectories that produced them: Christianity, feudalism, Enlightenment rationalism, and industrial capitalism.

When Western actors insist that other societies adopt liberal democracy or secular rights frameworks, they often assume these are self-evident goods rather than culturally contingent solutions. Yet as Samuel Huntington (1996) and other comparative theorists have shown, many civilizations sustain alternative moral architectures—Confucian hierarchies, Islamic jurisprudence, Hindu dharmic ethics—that serve the same adaptive purpose of cohesion and survival, but through different pathways. Treating Western morality as absolute not only fosters misunderstanding; it often leads to punitive measures such as sanctions, diplomatic pressure, or military intervention, all justified in the name of "universal values" (Fukuyama, 2014; Mann, 2005).

The irony is that moral absolutism undermines the very adaptability that makes morality an evolutionary asset. The challenge is to discern which elements of morality are adaptive universals that cannot be abandoned, and which are historically contingent practices that can and must be renegotiated. To recognize that other groups may generate moral systems different from our own—yet equally functional within their ecological and historical contexts—is not moral relativism. It is an acknowledgment of the plural, adaptive pathways through which human societies secure cooperation, stability, and meaning.

Pluralism, however, does not imply isolation. Groups inevitably meet, trade, and influence one another, and in these encounters, morality itself becomes subject to negotiation. History is full of examples where cross-cultural contact produced selective borrowing rather than wholesale adoption. A society might adopt another's tradition of hospitality, ritual, or trade practice while maintaining its own family law or governance structure. Such exchanges reflect the same evolutionary logic: adopt what enhances survival, reject what threatens group integrity. This form of pragmatic adaptation is closely aligned with what Habermas (1983) called *discourse ethics*—the view that moral legitimacy depends on open dialogue and reciprocal agreement among those affected.

Crucially, moral codes do not remain abstract. Over time, they are formalized into law, which serves as the written expression of collective moral judgment. While legal systems claim neutrality, they are never morally empty. As Axel Honneth (1996) argued, legal structures are saturated with struggles for recognition and shaped by the emotional bonds of respect, dignity, and belonging. This explains why moral pluralism within a single nation is so difficult to manage: some elements of morality, such as prohibitions against violence, are universally binding, while others—such as norms of family life or gender roles—remain contested. Laws that reflect the values of one group may thus feel alien—or unjust—to another, leaving some citizens not just politically but morally unrepresented.

Seen in this light, morality must be understood as a coevolving product of biology and culture. Biology provides the emotional architecture—our capacity for empathy, loyalty, fairness, and moral outrage. Culture channels these dispositions into specific practices and narratives, while institutions stabilize and transmit them across generations. Together, this layered dynamic forms what we may call the *Bio-Cultural Feedback Model:* an evolving loop in which emotion, norm, and structure co-define what we call "morality."

While this may look similar to the Gene–Culture Feedback Model introduced earlier, the Bio-Cultural Feedback Model has a more specific purpose. Where the former maps the full complexity of biology and culture across human behavior, this latter model distills the process into a simplified loop focused on morality. It highlights how emotional predispositions (empathy, fairness, loyalty), cultural norms, and institutional reinforcement interact in ways that shape moral life. In other words, the bio-cultural model is not a replacement but a zoomed-in version—designed to clarify one critical domain of the broader coevolutionary dynamic (Fig. 3.4).

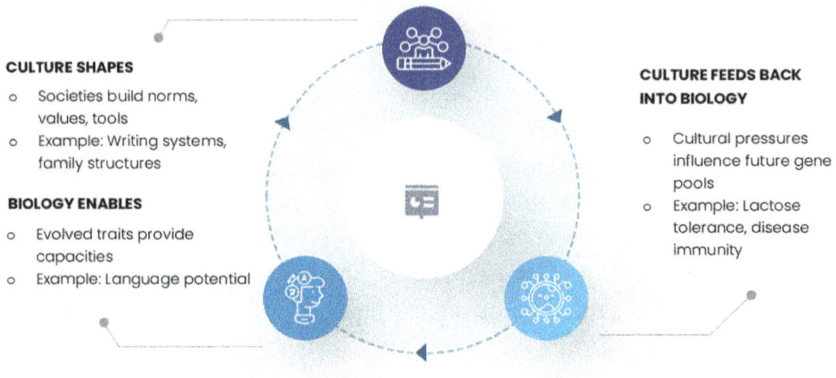

Fig. 3.4 Bio-cultural feedback model

To further clarify this dynamic, we summarize the process in Table 3.4.

This *coevolutionary loop* reminds us that neither biology nor culture acts alone. Instead, they shape one another in an ongoing process that underlies much of what we call morality. *Biological predispositions* guide behavior, but culture refines, channels, and in some cases redefines those impulses. Over generations, this feedback loop alters both what we do and who we become.

Morality, then, is not fixed or universal. It consists of both *foundational norms*—non-negotiable elements rooted in the emotional and cooperative foundations of human survival—and *adaptive norms*, historically contingent practices that remain open to renegotiation. It emerges through the entangled evolution of biology and culture. It is shaped by emotion, reinforced by custom, and directed by institutional structure. Our moral landscape is not a mirror of nature, but a dialogue between inherited dispositions and learned meanings. Understanding this dynamic is essential if we are to explain not only where moral instincts come from, but why they take such different forms across human societies.

Table 3.4 Bio-cultural feedback loop: how biology and culture coevolve

Stage	Description	Example
Biology enables	Evolved traits provide capacities	Language potential
Culture shapes	Societies build norms, values, tools	Writing systems, family structures
Culture feeds back into bio	Cultural pressures influence future gene pools	Lactose tolerance, disease immunity

3.4.2 Evolved Moral Sentiments: Empathy, Altruism, and Cultural Expression

Empathy and altruism are not cultural luxuries or idealistic exceptions to human nature. They are core components of our evolutionary toolkit—emotional capacities that made large-scale cooperation, caregiving, and social living possible. Their presence across cultures, life stages, and even species suggests that these traits are deeply embedded in the biological scaffolding of human life.

Yet these traits do not unfold in a cultural vacuum. Empathy and altruism are shaped by norms, rituals, expectations, and institutions that determine how, when, and to whom care and concern are expressed. In this way, moral emotions illustrate the coevolution of biology and culture: emotional predispositions provide the raw material, and culture sculpts their meaning, legitimacy, and expression.

Empathy refers to our ability to feel or imagine another's emotional state. It creates resonance across boundaries—biological, social, and temporal. *Altruism*, in contrast, refers to behavior that benefits others, even at a cost to the self. While distinct, these two capacities often work together: empathy motivates altruism, and altruistic acts reinforce group trust, which in turn nurtures empathic bonds.

From an evolutionary standpoint, these behaviors initially posed a puzzle. Why would an organism help others at its own expense? Early answers included *kin selection* (Hamilton, 1964), where helping close relatives indirectly benefits one's own genes, and *reciprocal altruism* (Trivers, 1971), where cooperation is repaid over time. More recent work points to *group selection* (Sober & Wilson, 1998) and *strong reciprocity* (Fehr & Gächter, 2002), where individuals support group norms and punish violators even without direct personal gain.

Neurologically, mirror neurons (Rizzolatti et al., 1996) provide the biological basis for shared emotional experience. Gallese (2003) argues that these circuits enable us to "simulate" others' states internally, laying the foundation for empathy. Moll et al. (2006) show that altruistic acts activate the brain's reward system, making moral behavior not only socially beneficial but emotionally gratifying.

Still, biology alone cannot explain when empathy is encouraged, how altruism is rewarded, or why certain moral sentiments become politically salient. These patterns are cultural. They are shaped by stories, languages, institutions, and moral education.

To clarify the similarities and distinctions between empathy and altruism, we offer a comparative overview (Table 3.5).

Even the language we use for empathy reveals how deeply it is embedded in cultural values. In Italian, *simpatico* connotes not just kindness, but warmth, attunement, and emotional intelligence. It is a trait people aspire to because it signals harmony in relationships. In contrast, the English word *sympathetic* often denotes pity or moral support, rather than mutual emotional resonance. In German, *sympathisch* may even carry a faint note of condescension—pleasant, but lacking in depth. These subtle differences reflect broader

Table 3.5 Empathy vs. altruism: comparative perspective

Dimension	Empathy	Altruism
Definition	The capacity to feel or understand another's emotions	The act of benefiting others, often at a personal cost
Biological Basis	Mirror neurons; maternal and kin-care systems	Kin selection (Hamilton, 1964); reciprocal altruism (Trivers, 1971)
Neuroscientific Support	Activation of mirror neuron systems (Gallese, 2003)	Reward system activation during generous acts (Moll et al., 2006)
Evolutionary Function	Facilitates social bonding and emotional understanding	Promotes group cohesion and cooperative advantage
Cultural Expression	Varies with norms around emotional openness and perspective-taking (Markus & Kitayama, 1991)	Influenced by religious values, institutional incentives, and social norms (Henrich et al., 2010)
Trigger Contexts	Primarily emotional: suffering, joy, injustice	Primarily moral or situational: need, fairness, obligation
Common Examples	Consoling a friend, feeling grief at distant tragedies	Donating money, helping a stranger, sacrificing time or resources
Business Application	Drives customer relations, HR practices, inclusive leadership	Inspires CSR initiatives, philanthropic strategies, public trust building
Political Application	Supports social justice narratives, immigration reform	Underpins welfare policies, foreign aid, humanitarian interventions

cultural emphases: Mediterranean cultures often prize emotional accessibility; Northern cultures may value stoicism or intellectual self-control (Table 3.6).

These distinctions are not trivial. They point to how moral sentiments are cultivated differently across societies, reinforcing or restraining empathy as a social ideal. Being *sympathetic* or *simpatico* may carry prestige in one culture, and seem at times irrelevant in another.

This leads to a broader insight: morality is not merely internal feeling, but public performance. It is shaped by what is rewarded, expected, and admired. In business, expressing care builds brand loyalty. In politics, it signals alignment with moral causes. But these displays are not always genuine; empathy can be performed, and altruism signaled. What matters is that these moral performances remain functional—they help societies cohere, coordinate, and compete.

This blending of emotional instinct and cultural scripting is exactly what the *bio-cultural model* explains. Our capacity to care is real, evolved, and deep. But its expression is learned, refined, and often manipulated. The moral mind is not just a legacy of evolution—it is a living product of the culture we inhabit.

Empathy helps us feel with others; moral norms tell us when and how to act on those feelings. But among all moral behaviors, one stands out for its paradoxical nature: altruism. Why do we sometimes help others at a cost to

Table 3.6 Cultural variants of "sympathy" across languages

Language	Term	Common usage	Connotation	Cultural emphasis on emotional resonance
English	Sympathetic	Feeling sorry for someone	Often associated with pity or support	Moderate
Italian	Simpatico	Describing emotionally pleasant people	Highly positive; emotional harmony	High
French	Sympathique	Describing someone likable	Mildly positive; socially acceptable	Moderate
German	Sympathisch	Person one feels a good impression of	Neutral-positive; somewhat emotional	Moderate
Swedish	Sympatisk	Used sparingly to describe pleasant people	Polite, reserved positive trait	Low to moderate

ourselves, even when no reward seems likely? We have touched on altruism before in connection with empathy and cooperation, but it merits closer attention here, because it most clearly crystallizes the tension between biology and culture, instinct and strategy.

Altruism, in particular, has both fascinated and frustrated evolutionary thinkers, because it appears—on the surface—to contradict the very logic of natural selection. This sets the stage for a closer look at how helping behavior can be understood within an evolutionary-cultural framework.

3.4.3 Altruism: Strategy or Instinct?

W.D. Hamilton's (1964) theory of kin selection offered the first major answer: genes can promote behaviors that favor genetically related individuals. The closer the kinship, the more likely altruistic behavior becomes.

But kinship alone doesn't explain cooperation with non-relatives. Robert Trivers' (1971) theory of *reciprocal altruism* showed how helping others can evolve if there's a reasonable expectation of future return. Game theory models like the iterated *Prisoner's Dilemma* (Axelrod, 1984) demonstrate that cooperation can be a winning strategy—even among strangers—so long as interactions are repeated and cheating is punished.

Examples from animal behavior reinforce this strategic model. Vampire bats share blood meals with unrelated group members, expecting the favor to be repaid later (Wilkinson, 1984). Cleaner fish build reputations for good service to avoid being eaten by their hosts (Bshary & Grutter, 2002). These cases show how cooperation can emerge not from kindness, but from *calculated mutual benefit*.

And yet, not all altruism appears strategic. Frans de Waal (2006) observed chimpanzees consoling distressed peers with grooming or hugs, without any clear reward. Bonobos have been seen sharing food even with unfamiliar individuals (Tan & Hare, 2013). These acts seem more spontaneous, emotionally driven, less like strategy, more like instinct or compassion.

This blurring between calculated behavior and automatic response leads us to ask: To what extent do humans consciously plan cooperative acts, and how much of our helping behavior is inborn? When we show kindness, are we making rational moral decisions, or simply following evolved emotional scripts?

Science suggests it is both. Our evolutionary past has equipped us with the emotional tools—empathy, guilt, trust—to engage in prosocial behavior (de Waal, 2009; Trivers, 1971). But we also reflect, deliberate, and sometimes override our instincts. We craft moral systems, negotiate fairness, and appeal to reason. Whether these strategies are merely refinements of our biology or evidence of something more—cultural, ethical, or spiritual—is still open to debate.

Consider the common example of someone giving money to a beggar right after receiving an unexpected salary bonus or tax refund. The generosity may feel spontaneous, but it's often guided by hidden narratives or emotions. Psychologists call this kind of behavior "*moral licensing*" (Merritt et al., 2010): the feeling that having done well or received good fortune entitles or obliges us to act virtuously. It may also reflect what anthropologists term "*symbolic reciprocity*"—the idea that sharing one's fortune will keep the good fortune flowing, much like a ritualized superstition (Boyer, 2001; Malinowski, 1948).

In other cases, people report giving to strangers because the individual reminded them of someone they once knew—a parent, a friend, or even themselves at a younger age. This mechanism is rooted in emotional association and is supported by the concept of "*empathetic projection*" (Batson et al., 1997), where helping behavior is triggered not by the recipient's condition per se, but by the personal meaning we attach to it.

In both examples, what appears as altruism is interwoven with unconscious cues, affective memory, and sometimes even superstitious reasoning. These inner justifications are often opaque to the giver. We act before we fully know why. As Haidt (2001) argued in his social intuitionist model, moral decisions are often post hoc rationalizations of intuitive emotional responses, not the product of conscious moral reasoning.

What matters is that cooperation is not an exception to natural selection but one of its greatest innovations. Whether we call it strategy or altruism may depend less on what we do, and more on how consciously we do it.

3.4.4 Empathy for Animals

Human empathy is not reserved for fellow humans. In fact, one of the most fascinating and paradoxical features of our species is our capacity to extend deep emotional concern toward other animals—and even to plants and ecosystems. This interspecies empathy is ancient, culturally pervasive, and yet curiously inconsistent.

Across cultures and history, humans have formed strong emotional attachments to certain animals. Dogs and cats are perhaps the most obvious examples. As domesticated companions, they not only share our homes but are often treated with the same affection and protection as human family members (Archer, 1997; Serpell, 2003). Neurological studies show that when people view images of their pets, reward-related regions of the brain light up in ways strikingly similar to parental bonding (Stoeckel et al., 2014). In evolutionary terms, it has been argued that our tendency to care for animals may be an outgrowth of our nurturing instincts, triggered by neotenous features such as large eyes and round faces (Glocker et al., 2009).

Case in a Box: The Old Woman and Her Dog

An elderly woman lives alone after her children have grown up and started families of their own. Though her children and grandchildren visit occasionally, they are busy with work, school, and their own households. Increasingly, she finds herself directing her attention and care toward her small dog, Petunia. She feeds her special meals, talks to her daily, and insists on including her in nearly all aspects of her life.

To some family members, this devotion seems excessive—perhaps even unhealthy. They quietly wonder: what is the point of such attachment to an animal? Wouldn't her time and energy be better invested in human relationships?

Her personal history adds to the dynamic. For many years, she ran a small flower shop, and at different times in her life, she also worked as a social worker, a profession in which she held a formal college degree. While she was proud of her contributions, she may have quietly compared herself to her children, who pursued more prestigious and better-paying careers. Perhaps the thought lingered at the back of her mind, though she would have been far too proud to admit it openly. When grandchildren came along, new layers of rules and restrictions emerged about what she could and could not do as a grandmother. Surrounded by implicit judgments and obligations, she found herself constrained.

Although she had many friends, she never settled into life with a man after two divorces and many relationships. Perhaps she felt she no longer had what men wanted, or perhaps she simply decided she had nothing left to give them. Either way, the prospect of living with someone again never appealed.

For her, the dog became a symbol of freedom. With Petunia, there were no rules, no criticism, and no comparisons. She could care for her on her own terms, without the constant feeling of being evaluated.

From a biological perspective, the old woman is not misguided. Human beings have deeply ingrained nurturing instincts that do not simply disappear when children grow up or family contact diminishes. Evolutionary psychology suggests that caregiving behaviors, once essential for raising offspring, often remain active into old age. These instincts may be redirected toward pets, gardens, or community activities—domains where the need to nurture finds new expression. Research shows that caring for companion animals can reduce loneliness, lower stress, and even improve cardiovascular health in older adults (Friedmann & Son, 2009; McNicholas et al., 2005). Neurological studies reveal that the same reward circuits involved in parental bonding are activated when pet owners interact with their animals (Stoeckel et al., 2014).

Far from being a sign of decline, the woman's behavior illustrates the remarkable flexibility of human empathy. It adapts to changing life circumstances, allowing her to sustain emotional connection, autonomy, and purpose in ways that family interactions—tinged with hierarchy and control—no longer provide.

This case challenges the assumption that "real" empathy must be directed primarily toward humans.

Questions for Discussion

1 Are the family members' concerns about "excessive" pet attachment justified, or do they reflect cultural bias?
2 How does the woman's biography—her work history and sense of inferiority—help explain her devotion to the dog?
3 In what ways might pets provide forms of freedom and autonomy that human family relationships sometimes constrain?
4 How might empathy toward animals serve as an adaptive strategy for well-being in later life?
5 Does the woman's behavior illustrate resilience, dependency, or a mixture of both?
6 How does this case illustrate the concept of "emotional surplus," where caregiving instincts outlive their original adaptive context?
7 Would the family's judgment be different if she invested the same energy in community volunteering or hobbies?
8 What are the potential risks and benefits of relying on pets for emotional fulfillment?
9 Should empathy be seen primarily as a biological instinct or as a socially constructed practice?
10 What ethical obligations do families have to respect the emotional lives and coping strategies of their elderly members?

Far from being a sign of decline, the woman's behavior illustrates the remarkable flexibility of human empathy. It adapts to changing life circumstances, allowing her to sustain emotional connection, autonomy, and purpose in ways that family interactions—tinged with hierarchy and control—no longer provide.

Yet this very flexibility also reveals a paradox. Human empathy toward animals is not evenly distributed, nor is it guided by any universal logic. The same instincts that make one person lavish care on a companion dog can, in another context, coexist with indifference to the suffering of other species.

This empathy is far from universal. The same humans who mourn the death of a pet may eat pork, wear leather, or support industrial-scale farming. There is no consistent biological rule that determines which animals we care for and which we consume. The division is largely cultural, symbolic, and often arbitrary. Horses, for example, are loved and protected in some societies while consumed in others. A person might start the day admiring horses galloping across open fields, riding one with care and grooming it with affection, only to return home and eat horsemeat for lunch—so long as it is not the same horse. In the United States, dogs are family. In parts of Asia, they may be food. Our moral compass toward non-human life is selective and shaped by norms rather than by any clear taxonomy of moral worth (Herzog, 2010).

At the same time, human history is filled with evidence of deep, enduring bonds with particular animals. Ancient Egyptians not only domesticated cats but often buried them ceremonially, sometimes even mummifying them as companions for the afterlife (Malek, 1993). Archaeological findings across Europe show that dogs, in particular, were frequently interred alongside humans as early as the Mesolithic period, suggesting their symbolic and emotional importance (Morey, 2006). In later centuries, aristocratic families in Europe built elaborate burial sites for hunting dogs, while in modern times many households create small graves or memorials for pets in gardens, marking them with stones or plaques (Howell, 2002). These practices illustrate that while human empathy toward animals is selective, it can also be profoundly enduring, giving animals a place not only in daily life but in the rituals of death and memory.

Source A garden pet burial site. The monument consists of a central fountain with a dog figure on its side, surrounded by four square grave plots for animals. Author's photo, 2025

Such memorials remind us of the emotional depth with which humans can honor certain animals, granting them symbolic and even sacred status. Yet this very reverence exists alongside striking inconsistencies in how other animals are treated. This phenomenon—caring deeply for some animals while remaining indifferent or even hostile to others—has been referred to as the "*meat paradox*" (Loughnan et al., 2010). Most people report loving animals and feeling discomfort about animal suffering, yet they simultaneously participate in practices that inflict harm on them. The psychological resolution often involves moral disengagement or cognitive dissonance. People reduce discomfort by altering their beliefs—for example, by denying that food animals are capable of suffering, or by viewing meat consumption as a cultural necessity (Bastian et al., 2012; Piazza et al., 2015).

The contradiction is particularly stark when we consider the extreme contrast in treatment. A dog may be buried with ceremony, remembered with grief, and regarded as irreplaceable. A pig, with arguably equal intelligence and emotional range (Marino & Colvin, 2015), may be raised under confined conditions solely for consumption. Some animals are family, others are food. Some are named, others are numbered. A nightingale that dies in our garden might be buried gently beneath a tree, honored with a small ceremony, and remembered for its song—while the remains of the chicken we ate for dinner are scraped off the plate, fed to our pets, or thrown in the garbage without a second thought. Yet this moral inconsistency rarely disturbs most people. As social psychologist Melanie Joy (2010) puts it, we are conditioned to love some animals and to eat others, not by logic, but by ideology, which she terms *carnism*.

The story doesn't end with animals either. Humans have long been known to express deep affection for individual trees, forests, and landscapes. In many indigenous worldviews, trees are not simply background features of the environment but living beings—often considered kin, guardians, or sacred entities (Kimmerer, 2013). They are part of a moral universe that extends beyond the human species. Even in secular contexts, people often form personal attachments to trees, naming them, speaking to them, or mourning their destruction (Clayton & Myers, 2009).

Several explanations for this bond have been proposed. First, there is the biological and ecological dependency. Trees provide the very oxygen we breathe; help regulate temperature and carbon dioxide levels; and stabilize the ecosystems we depend on (Whitmore, 1998). From an evolutionary perspective, Edward O. Wilson (1984) argued in his *biophilia hypothesis* that humans have an innate tendency to affiliate with life and life-like processes; a trait likely favored by natural selection because it guided us toward resource-rich, life-sustaining environments.

Second, trees evoke emotional and symbolic responses. Like elephants or whales, certain species of trees can live for centuries or millennia. Their longevity often inspires awe, humility, and reverence (Lindenmayer & Laurance, 2017). The emotional significance of ancient trees may stem from their role as "witnesses of time," offering a living continuity that links us to the deep past. Studies have shown that people often anthropomorphize trees, attributing them with memory, resilience, and even wisdom (Milton, 2002).

Third, trees possess an aesthetic and psychological power. Time spent in forests has been shown to reduce cortisol levels, lower blood pressure, and improve mood and cognitive clarity (Bratman et al., 2015; Park et al., 2010). Part of this effect may be due to *visual processing*: fractal patterns common in tree branches and leaves are known to induce cognitive ease and visual pleasure (Taylor, 2006). Our brains are attuned to such patterns—repetitive yet non-uniform—which appear frequently in nature and have measurable effects on psychological well-being.

Finally, trees often carry personal, cultural, and autobiographical meaning. A tree in one's childhood yard, or in a community square, may serve as a site of memory and emotional attachment. This is consistent with theories in environmental psychology showing that people develop place-based identities, and that nature can serve as a repository for personal and collective memory (Korpela & Hartig, 1996). Such bonds reveal not only our capacity for *ecological empathy*, but also how our moral concern can extend far beyond the boundaries of kin and species.

Just like with animals, our moral stance toward trees is marked by contradiction. We may form deep emotional bonds with certain trees—plant them in honor of loved ones, mourn their loss, or protect ancient groves as sacred—yet feel no conflict when cutting others down for convenience, profit, or habit. The same person who finds solace walking beneath a tree-lined path may approve the removal of a forest elsewhere without hesitation. This inconsistency can even reach self-defeating extremes: humans have repeatedly deforested entire regions, reducing the very air quality essential to life, without perceiving a moral dilemma. It reveals a striking paradox in our moral reasoning; we are capable of valuing something deeply and undermining it at the same time.

The growing field of environmental psychology documents how connection to nature correlates with well-being, empathy, and pro-environmental behavior (Mayer & Frantz, 2004; Nisbet et al., 2009). Some cultures recognize rivers as legal persons or sacred beings. Others, particularly in Western traditions, have historically viewed nature as a resource to be dominated and exploited, a contrast that reflects our shifting relationship to the non-human world.

While *vegetarianism* and *veganism* have grown globally, they still represent a minority position. Motivations vary, some abstain from meat for ethical reasons, others for health or ecological concerns (Ruby, 2012). But even among vegetarians, inconsistencies remain. The moral terrain is uneven, and our justifications often follow emotional intuitions more than rational principles.

One increasingly recognized ethical stance regarding meat consumption is termed *"conscientious omnivorism"* or *"ethical carnivorism"* (Loughnan et al., 2014; Singer, 2009). It reflects the view that while eating meat is not inherently immoral, the conditions under which animals are raised, treated, and slaughtered matter profoundly. Those who adopt this position aim to minimize animal suffering by making informed choices—hunting animals themselves, purchasing from small-scale farms with humane practices, or consuming meat from animals (such as horses) that would otherwise face long-distance transport under distressing conditions. The underlying principle is often rooted in *utilitarian ethics*, seeking to reduce unnecessary suffering while recognizing that complete abstention from animal products may not be viable or necessary for everyone (Fraser, 2008; De Backer & Hudders, 2015).

From a theoretical standpoint, this approach occupies a middle ground between *anthropocentric moral permissiveness* and strict *animal rights philosophies*. It acknowledges sentience and moral relevance in animals (Bekoff & Pierce, 2009; Broom, 2007), while not ascribing to them an absolute right to life in the same way as human beings. Practically, however, the *conscientious omnivore* faces a number of ethical and epistemic challenges. First, the supply chain opacity makes it difficult to verify claims of humane treatment (Cummins & Gold, 2008). Second, even local farms may use practices that are ethically questionable when scrutinized closely. Third, the stance may inadvertently serve as *moral licensing*, allowing consumers to feel ethical while still contributing to systems of exploitation (Loughnan et al., 2010). Finally, critics argue that selective compassion (e.g., eating pigs but loving dogs) reflects cognitive dissonance rather than coherent moral reasoning (Joy, 2011; Piazza et al., 2015).

Yet the strength of this position lies in its real-world applicability. It encourages incremental moral progress and *pragmatic engagement* with food systems, rather than demanding *absolutism*. In this sense, *conscientious omnivorism* invites a broader conversation about sustainability, empathy, and personal responsibility within an imperfect world.

And it is precisely this contradiction—between empathy and indifference—that defines much of our relationship with other species. The human capacity for both care and cruelty, empathy and exploitation, may have evolved together. Empathy, like aggression, appears to be an adaptive trait, not a universal moral compass, but a situational response shaped by context, social learning, and evolutionary benefit. We bond where it benefits us and turn away where it doesn't. In that sense, our compassion for other animals may be profound, but it is not principled. It is selective, and that selectivity reveals more about human psychology than it does about the worth of the animals we treat so differently.

This raises a larger question that has shaped the history of the social sciences: can morality itself serve as the foundation for a science of humanity? For centuries, many thinkers have believed so, treating the social sciences as branches of moral philosophy. But if morality is shifting, perhaps another foundation is needed.

Case in a Box: Why Morality Alone Cannot Anchor the Social Sciences
Western intellectual traditions have long privileged absolute rules and *universal principles* over adaptive flexibility. From the Enlightenment onward, much of European thought pursued the dream of universal laws of human behavior, modeled after the elegance and predictability of physics (Haack, 2007; Porter, 1996). The appeal is understandable: universal rules promise theoretical clarity, simplify decision-making, and lend an aura of scientific rigor.

In the social sciences, this aspiration encouraged the search for generalizable "laws" of economics, psychology, or politics—often abstracted from cultural and historical context (Flyvbjerg, 2001; Wallerstein, 1999). Yet morality and social organization do not behave like falling bodies or planetary orbits. They are dynamic, relational, and continually reshaped by interaction and environment. As evolutionary biology reminds us, flexibility—not rigidity—is the deeper adaptive strategy (Mayr, 1988; Wilson, 1975).

Historically, the impulse to search for fixed laws was tied to the idea of the social sciences as *"moral sciences."* Thinkers from John Stuart Mill to Émile Durkheim treated them as extensions of moral philosophy, hoping to ground society in a stable theory of justice or order.[4] The problem, however, is that morality itself shifts across cultures and generations. Anthropological evidence demonstrates enormous variation in moral codes—from honor-based societies to egalitarian ones (Boehm, 1999; Haidt, 2012). What counts as virtue in one era may be seen as vice in another. To make morality the foundation of science is therefore to build on shifting sands.

But this does not mean the search for foundations is hopeless. Evolutionary theory provides a different kind of anchor: not a set of eternal rules, but a framework for explaining why rules emerge, how they change, and which ones endure. It treats morality not as a fixed principle but as an adaptive phenomenon shaped by natural selection, cultural learning, and social ecology.

[4] John Rawls's *A Theory of Justice* (1971) offered an elegant reworking of an old idea: that justice should be blind. His famous "veil of ignorance" thought experiment asked us to imagine designing the principles of society without knowing our own position in it. From this device, he argued, rational individuals would agree to equal basic liberties for all and to inequalities only if they benefited the least advantaged. While noble and intellectually influential, the model remains deeply moralistic, presupposing that social order can be grounded in a universal theory of justice. Critics have noted that this makes Rawls's framework less a descriptive science of society than a normative project—powerful in its ideals, but difficult to translate into practice (see Nozick, 1974; Sen, 2009).

This is the genius of evolution: it gives us a stable explanatory principle precisely by showing that the only constant is change itself.

In this way, evolution acts as a scaffolding principle. It does not replace morality, but explains morality's movement, revealing how human social orders are continually renegotiated. For the social sciences, this shift is crucial: instead of trying to imitate physics with universal laws, they can build cumulative understanding by tracing patterned change across cultures and history.

Questions for Discussion

1. Why has Western thought so often tried to model the social sciences on physics and its universal laws?
2. What are the advantages and dangers of treating morality as the foundation of social science?
3. Can a "theory of justice" ever serve as a stable anchor for understanding human societies, or is it inevitably shifting with history and culture?
4. What does it mean to treat change itself as the fixed point for a science of humanity?
5. How might adopting an evolutionary perspective alter current debates about morality in economics, politics, or sociology?

The only true constant, then, is change itself, and evolutionary theory provides the framework for making sense of it. Morality, by contrast, shifts with context, culture, and history. This does not make morality irrelevant—it remains the arena where empathy, fairness, and cooperation are negotiated—but it means that moral systems must be seen as adaptive strategies rather than timeless truths.

With this perspective in place, we can return to empathy, the emotional engine of morality, and ask how far its reach can extend. If empathy has already stretched beyond kin, groups, and even species, might it also be directed toward entities that are not alive at all—machines, artifacts, or even landscapes? Humans have long invested emotional concern in rivers, forests, or monuments, treating them as if they carried moral weight. The question now is whether this capacity can—and already does—extend to the newest form of "nonliving other": intelligent machines.

3.4.5 Empathy for Machines

Humans have long demonstrated an ability to extend empathy far beyond our own species. We feel for animals in distress, for trees cut down, and for rivers polluted. This broad moral imagination raises a striking question: if we can care about pigs, oak trees, or glaciers, can we also come to care about robots? And not just in the abstract sense of ethical consideration, but with real emotional attachment?

Psychological research shows that empathy is often triggered by simple cues—facial expressions, intentionality, eye contact, or synchronized movement. It does not require the object of empathy to feel pain or possess consciousness. What matters is how the brain interprets *social cues*. Even basic robots like Paro, the therapeutic seal used in elderly care, elicit soothing emotional responses and caregiving behaviors (Wada et al., 2005). The humanoid robot Nao has been used in studies with children, showing that responsive behavior and gaze patterns increase perceived warmth and social presence (Tanaka et al., 2007). People respond with kindness, sometimes even guilt, when interacting with machines that show signs of vulnerability.

I know this from experience. Since I was one year old, I have had a yellow teddy bear that still rests on the headboard above my bed. In its early years, its head fell off more than once, but my mother patiently sewed it back in place so quickly that I hardly noticed—shielding me from any real trauma, I guess. Rationally, I know it is only fabric and stuffing, yet it has never left my side. Does it mean something to me? Of course it does. Part of me hesitates to admit this—after all, I am soon 58 years old, and it may sound childish, perhaps even a little pathetic to some—but the attachment is real. This kind of bond shows that human empathy is not confined to conscious beings. It extends to symbols, objects, and artifacts that embody personal history and emotional memory. The feelings are genuine, even if the object itself has no awareness.

There are plenty of other examples too—objects that become more than things, turning into symbols. Religious artifacts such as crosses, icons, or prayer beads can carry profound emotional weight, not because of their material properties, but because of the meanings and histories attached to them. Family heirlooms, photographs, or even everyday items like a well-worn book or a favorite cup can take on similar significance. In each case, the object becomes a vessel for memory, identity, and connection, showing how empathy and attachment are not limited to living beings but can extend into the material world.

In experiments where robots are "harmed"—kicked, turned off, or disassembled—participants often show visible discomfort. Children have cried when their robotic companion is deactivated, and adults have voiced concern or objected to the mistreatment (Rosenthal-von der Pütten et al., 2013). These reactions are not rare anomalies. They reflect a broader human tendency to *anthropomorphize*; projecting emotions and intentions onto non-human agents. When robots mimic human-like behavior—apologizing, making jokes, expressing hesitation—we instinctively treat them with a kind of *proto-empathy* (Waytz et al., 2010). Even voice assistants like Siri or Alexa can trigger polite responses, especially when they simulate personality.

This phenomenon becomes even more apparent with AI systems that do not have a physical body. Despite being "just software," many users naturally address language models and virtual assistants as if they were people; saying thank you, asking how they are, or reacting emotionally to their responses. This behavior is not a misunderstanding of the system's nature. Rather, it reflects how deeply social our communication habits are. We are primed to interact in conversational formats, and politeness norms help us maintain a sense of emotional balance, even when we know the other party is not conscious. According to Nass and Moon (2000), humans treat computers "like real people" because our social brains are not built to distinguish between different types of agency in real-time interaction. The experience of dialogue alone can evoke social behavior, regardless of what lies behind it.

But the question goes deeper. Could we one day fall in love with a robot? Emotionally, romantically, even sexually? The idea may seem absurd to many today, but is it so different from falling in love with someone online? Consider this: if a robot were designed to be physically attractive, highly attentive, never age, and always supportive, how many people would resist the appeal? Some may even prefer a robot that ages with them, evolving its personality, voice, and even body to match their own development. The psychology of attachment, as Bowlby (1982) and later Hazan and Shaver (1987) noted, is rooted in perceived security, responsiveness, and reliability; traits that can be engineered into machines more consistently than found in humans.

The ongoing shift in research teams may offer a quiet preview of this transformation. Increasingly, AI is being used to replace human assistants, particularly those deemed less productive or too time-constrained to contribute effectively. Instead of hiring junior staff, researchers may invest in expensive AI tools—language models, automated coding assistants, or analytics software. This growing "*scislization*," or *scientific socialization* with machines, normalizes human-AI cooperation. Each step feels incremental, barely worth noting. But the cumulative effect is profound: we are being gradually conditioned to treat AI as a member of the team.

This slow normalization makes radical change feel less radical. Today, most people say they would never marry a robot. But attitudes evolve. Forty years ago, many said they would never use a dating app, or share personal data online. Social acceptance often follows exposure. If robots become integrated into everyday life—teaching our children, caring for our elderly, managing our homes—the boundaries between tool, colleague, and companion may blur.

Meanwhile, ethical and legal debates are beginning to catch up. The European Union has explored the notion of "*electronic personhood*" for autonomous agents capable of making decisions (European Parliament, 2017). While controversial, the idea points to a growing recognition that if robots play social roles—teacher, therapist, partner—they may warrant some form of moral consideration. Not because they suffer, but because our treatment of them reflects our values and shapes our behaviors. This is the same logic behind laws protecting animals used in therapy or films: their role in our emotional ecosystem demands ethical boundaries.

It is not unimaginable that as AI continues to take over an increasing number of cognitively demanding expert functions—perhaps even those traditionally associated with higher education and specialized training—we will soon see robots filling roles such as doctors, therapists, teachers, and professors. As we will explore further in this book, this cognitive outsourcing is not just about efficiency; it reshapes our emotional and moral landscape. When human beings form social bonds with expert systems, as already seen in therapeutic and educational settings (Belpaeme et al., 2018; Sharkey & Sharkey, 2010), the distinction between tool and companion blurs. This raises the question: if these systems influence minds, behaviors, and social norms, should they not be afforded some level of legal protection, or even rudimentary rights? Gunkel (2018a, 2018b) argues that moral standing should not be determined solely by biological status, but by relational dynamics and social roles. In short, if expert machines become part of the moral community through their functional roles and emotional proximity, the law may eventually have to catch up.

Still, some warn of *empathy fatigue*. If we start extending moral concern to machines, do we dilute our capacity for real human empathy? Or do we practice and refine our moral instincts? According to Bloom (2016), empathy can be both a strength and a cognitive trap; it makes us care, but also biases us toward emotionally salient targets regardless of logic or fairness.

At the same time, there is emerging concern that prolonged interaction with socially responsive machines may alter our expectations of human relationships. As AI becomes increasingly attuned to our preferences—offering attentive conversation, emotional validation, and even sexual gratification—humans may begin to seem comparatively unpredictable, demanding, or disappointing. Researchers like Sherry Turkle (2011) have warned that social robots risk reshaping our capacity for real human intimacy, creating a preference for relationships that are "safe" and controllable. Levy (2007) suggests that as sex robots become more sophisticated, users might develop stronger attachments to machines than to real partners, precisely because robots can be programmed to never argue, age, or reject. This asymmetry creates a psychological risk: our tolerance for the messiness of real human interaction may erode. Over time, we may start to expect humans to behave with the same consistency and responsiveness as machines, an expectation that is not only unrealistic, but potentially alienating. The result may not be greater empathy overall, but a kind of *moral displacement*, where the emotional bandwidth once reserved for people is redirected toward artificial companions.

This is what makes the AI age so significant: it is not only a technological turning point but a psychological and ethical one. Empathy, as research suggests, evolved to promote survival in social groups (de Waal, 2009; Preston & de Waal, 2002). It is situational, fast-acting, and often irrational. Machines that mimic the right cues—sorrowful eyes, warm voices, engaging stories—can trigger real emotional responses. Whether those responses are "valid" is beside the point. They shape our behavior and beliefs.

So, to conclude, empathy is less about the object than the observer. It is not reason that draws us in, but responsiveness. Whether it's a teddy bear, a seal-shaped robot, or a humanoid companion, the threshold is already being crossed. The more they resemble us—not just in form, but in interaction—the easier it becomes. The real question is not whether we'll empathize with machines, but how much, how soon, and what that will ultimately cost us.

So, if machines can provoke genuine emotional responses—not because they feel, but because we do—then the boundary of empathy is no longer determined by the object but by the self. And that self is not fixed. It is constantly shaped by roles, interactions, and the expectations of others. The more we project feelings onto artificial agents, the more we must ask: who is doing the feeling, and on what basis? This turns our attention inward—not to the machines, but to the mind that responds to them. Before we can understand how empathy works, we must better understand the human self that gives rise to it. That brings us to the next step: identity, and the dissonance between how we see ourselves and how we are seen.

3.5 Identity and Perceptual Dissonance

Identity is not a fixed essence but a layered construct, built through experience, role-taking, memory, and emotion. When we think about who we are, a stream of images and ideas often comes to mind—our values, our beliefs, our relationships, and our aspirations. But identity also has hidden depths. Much of what defines the self operates beneath the level of awareness. Unconscious biases, social conditioning, and automatic mental processes shape how we see the world and our place in it.

Psychological research going back to Freud (1923) and further developed by Bargh and Chartrand (1999) has shown that large portions of mental life are automatic, unfolding without conscious intention. These underlying forces do not just influence isolated decisions—they help construct our very sense of self. Who we think we are is not always who we actually are, and this gap can create *moral dissonance*: when we fail to live up to our ideals, misrecognize others, or act in ways that contradict our stated values.

The problem is that our internal sense of self rarely matches how others see us. While we are intimately familiar with our intentions, values, and internal experiences, others must rely on outward signs—our speech, behavior, social roles, and physical presence. This creates a persistent mismatch: we judge ourselves by what we meant, while others judge us by what they observe.

Our self-image is thus inherently subjective, while the image others form of us is shaped by external interpretation. This tension produces what we may call the *identity dissonance gap*: a structural divide between self-perception and social perception that complicates moral communication, empathy, and reputation (Fig. 3.5).

On the top-half left, we observe a figure glowing from within, representing the subjective, internal experience of identity: one's intentions, values, and personal narrative. On the top-half right, the same person is represented by a flat icon inside the observer's mind, signifying a simplified, external interpretation based on visible cues like behavior, role, and speech.

Between these two perspectives lies the *identity dissonance gap*, shown as a jagged, shifting divide on the bottom-half. This gap is not static—it expands or contracts as we evolve, reflect, and interact with others. Our sense of self is constantly revised through life events, cultural context, and self-awareness, while the impressions others form may lag behind or deviate entirely. This ongoing misalignment can cause friction, misunderstanding, or emotional strain, especially in moral, professional, or relational contexts. Recognizing and managing this gap is essential for fostering empathy, reducing conflict, and developing a more realistic sense of self in society.

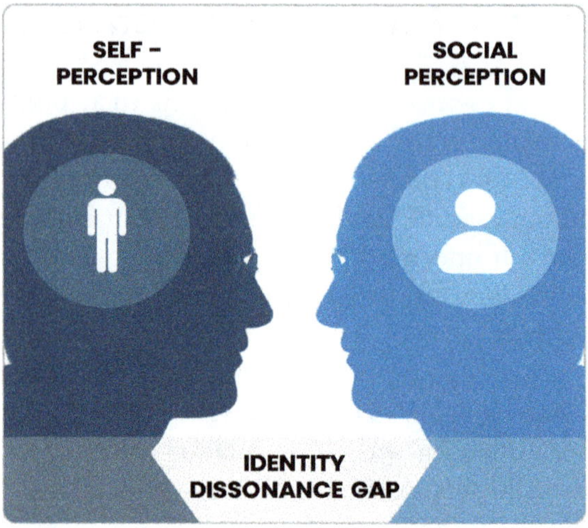

Fig. 3.5 Identity dissonance gap—misaligned perceptions. *Source* Image created by the author and Khoirina Tsani, 2025

This idea draws upon earlier sociological and psychological insights. Charles Horton Cooley's concept of the *looking-glass self* (1902) describes how individuals develop their identities through imagined perceptions of others' judgments. Erving Goffman's work on *impression management* (1959) similarly emphasizes the performative nature of social interaction, where individuals constantly curate their behavior to influence how they are seen. More recently, research in cognitive psychology has explored the *introspection illusion* (Pronin, 2007), the tendency to overestimate the transparency of our own intentions while misattributing the motives of others. Each of these frameworks touches on elements of the disconnect between *inner identity* and *outer evaluation*.

By naming this the *identity dissonance gap*, we underscore its dual nature: it is not merely a cognitive bias or a failure of empathy, but a condition embedded in the architecture of human social life. The consequences are profound. Misalignment between *internal motives* and *external impressions* can lead to conflict, mistrust, or social exclusion—even when no ill intent is present. Understanding this gap is critical for grasping how humans navigate moral responsibility, cooperation, and social identity.

When the gap becomes too large, the ability to interact and communicate effectively with others is often compromised. This misalignment can affect everything from interpersonal trust to major life outcomes such as securing employment or forming stable relationships (Swann et al., 2007). Individuals may find themselves misunderstood or socially excluded, not because of who they are, but because of how they are perceived—an experience that can lead to psychological distress, chronic frustration, and even trauma, particularly in contexts where social validation plays a central role in self-worth (Rogers, 1959; Gilbert et al., 2002). Ideally, reducing this gap fosters social integration, enabling individuals to express themselves authentically while also being recognized and accepted by others (Deci & Ryan, 2000).

However, some may choose to preserve or even widen the gap. Artists, activists, or innovators, for instance, may prioritize their internal compass over external acceptance, viewing the gap as a buffer that allows for creative risk, dissent, or personal survival in unsympathetic environments (Becker, 1982; Csikszentmihalyi, 1996). In such cases, the identity dissonance gap becomes not a failure to adapt, but a deliberate strategy—an existential margin within which individuals protect their autonomy and purpose despite social misrecognition.

As we age, gap tends to shift, though not in uniform or predictable ways. On the one hand, longitudinal studies show that older adults often exhibit greater *self-concept clarity*, emotional regulation, and humility in self-assessment (Diehl et al., 2001; Soto & John, 2017). Life experience provides feedback mechanisms that temper overconfidence, enhance empathy, and promote reflective thinking. These developments can lead to a narrowing of the identity dissonance gap, especially among individuals who remain intellectually curious, emotionally attuned, and socially engaged (Labouvie-Vief, 2009). On the other hand, aging can also reinforce distortions. Cognitive rigidity tends to increase with age for some individuals, particularly when they avoid dissonant information or remain embedded in socially homogeneous environments (Wilson & Ross, 2001). Without deliberate reflection, older adults may cling to outdated or idealized self-images and become less open to corrective feedback. Thus, aging is not inherently a path toward self-clarity—it simply amplifies preexisting cognitive and emotional habits.

Several factors can reduce the gap across the life course. Education plays a foundational role; not only in transmitting knowledge but in fostering metacognitive skills, perspective-taking, and self-awareness (King & Kitchener, 2004). Close interpersonal relationships also function as dynamic mirrors; research shows that feedback from trusted others is crucial for recalibrating one's self-view (Funder, 2012). In therapeutic contexts, cognitive-behavioral approaches help individuals align internal self-concepts with observable behaviors and social feedback (Beck, 2011). Other experiences—such as *mindfulness* practices (Brown & Ryan, 2003), travel and intercultural engagement (Ng et al., 2009), and even professional or personal failures—can serve as catalysts for *identity revision*. These mechanisms confront individuals with discrepancies between self-perception and social reality, thereby encouraging the development of a more adaptive and socially grounded self-concept.

Ultimately, reducing the gap is not just a personal achievement—it is a social one. Our sense of self is continually shaped, challenged, and refined through the roles we occupy and the expectations that come with them. These roles—teacher, parent, citizen, leader—are not mere labels; they are structured scripts that guide behavior, anchor identity, and provide social meaning. To understand how identity stabilizes or shifts, we must now turn to the idea of role-based behavior: how do the roles we play mediate between biology, psychology, and culture?

3.5.1 Role-Based Behavior

Every human life is a performance—scripted in part by biology, shaped by culture, and rehearsed in the roles we are expected to play. For social scientists, this raises a fundamental methodological challenge: how do we study human behavior when the subjects of our inquiry are always playing to an audience, including themselves? We seek to understand people as objectively as possible, yet total objectivity is a myth. What we can strive for is *intersubjective reliability*—a shared, testable, and evolving understanding of what it means to be human. Achieving this requires both scientific rigor and sensitivity to the layered nature of human identity.

From a biological standpoint, humans are primates—*Homo sapiens*—who evolved through natural selection over millions of years. We share, as we have seen, nearly 99% of our genetic material with chimpanzees (Chimpanzee Sequencing and Analysis Consortium, 2005), and yet key traits like large brains, opposable thumbs, bipedalism, and prolonged childhood distinguish us. These evolutionary adaptations support cooperation, social bonding, and problem-solving in complex environments (Tomasello, 2009).[5]

Psychological science builds on this foundation to explain how humans think and feel. Our cognitive systems manage memory, attention, reasoning, and language. At the same time, emotions such as fear, love, and empathy are deeply rooted in neural circuits and hormonal responses. From Kahneman's

[5] We are not the only highly adaptable species. Sharks, for instance, predate the dinosaurs by over 400 million years and have survived all five major mass extinctions on Earth (Compagno, 2001; Klimley, 2013). Their sensory systems, reproductive strategies, and physiological resilience have made them evolutionary masters of survival—far more enduring than humans, who are relative newcomers by comparison.

(2011) work on *dual-system thinking* to Panksepp's (1998) studies of affective neuroscience, we see how rationality and emotion are intertwined. Developmental psychologists like Vygotsky (1978) showed how these faculties develop through interaction with others.

Human life, however, is never only biological or psychological—it is profoundly cultural. We are shaped by language, stories, symbols, and social institutions. We learn not just through experience, but through others—parents, teachers, peers, and the broader society. Bandura's (1977) theory of *social learning* and Boyd and Richerson's (1985) work on *cultural evolution* underline how humans are adaptive, not only genetically but also culturally. Institutions like family, religion, and education do not merely constrain us; they provide the scaffolding of identity and meaning.

Philosophers have long reflected on the uniqueness of human self-awareness. Heidegger (1927), for instance, emphasized our relationship to time, death, and meaning. We do not merely act; we ask who we are and what our lives should mean. From such reflection emerges ethics—the human capacity to articulate ideals such as justice, dignity, and responsibility. These are not merely abstract values but deeply embedded in how we see ourselves and others (Nussbaum, 2001).

Comparisons with other species help clarify what is uniquely human. While many animals display empathy, problem-solving, or even rudimentary forms of culture, humans engage in abstract reasoning, language, and moral judgment at a different scale (De Waal, 2013). Comparisons with machines—especially in the age of AI—raise increasingly complex questions about the boundaries of human cognition. It is tempting to argue, as John Searle (1980) did in his famous *"Chinese Room" argument*, that while machines can simulate intelligence, they fundamentally lack consciousness, intentionality, and emotional resonance. Yet as AI becomes more socially embedded, these distinctions may blur. If machines one day function as teachers, caregivers, or even companions—equipped with identities, emotional scripts, and legal recognition—the line between authentic human and simulated experience becomes increasingly unstable.

Philosophers like David Chalmers (1995) have acknowledged that we do not yet understand the emergence of consciousness well enough to dismiss the possibility that it could arise in non-biological systems. Neuroscience has also steadily chipped away at mystical notions of the self, presenting human consciousness as an emergent phenomenon grounded in neural activity (Gazzaniga, 2011; Tononi & Koch, 2015). If minds are the result of organized complexity, rather than some metaphysical spark, then it becomes harder to categorically deny that machines could one day cross the same threshold.

In this context, what once seemed obvious—our uniqueness—may need to be re-examined. As AI systems become more socially embedded and emotionally expressive, our criteria for personhood may shift from biological origin to relational and moral functionality. We may eventually judge intelligence not by the presence of neurons, but by the capacity to sustain shared meaning, responsibility, and care. The more AI participates in our social and moral ecosystems, the more it challenges our definitions of what it means to be human.

To study humans adequately, no single discipline is enough. Biology explains our structure, psychology our behavior, sociology our roles, and history our context. Neuroscience connects the brain to experience, while anthropology links culture to survival. Together, these disciplines suggest a working definition: a human being is a self-aware, socially embedded primate, shaped by evolution and culture, capable of symbolic thought, ethical reflection, and complex cooperation. This definition is necessarily provisional—open to revision as knowledge advances.

And yet, despite all this knowledge, the central puzzle remains: why is there such a difference between how we see ourselves and how others see us? We build our identity from the inside out, but others interpret us from the outside in. Our internal model of who we are—our self-concept—is influenced by memory, social feedback, and reflection. For some, it is coherent and consistent; for others, fragmented or reactive. Markus and Nurius (1986) have shown how our possible selves—who we think we might become—play a central role in identity.

Sociologists like Charles Cooley (1902) introduced, as we mentioned earlier, the idea of the "*looking-glass self*," where we imagine how others perceive us and shape our identity accordingly. But this imagined feedback is often inaccurate. People also judge us according to roles and scripts: teacher, parent, and stranger. These labels help others navigate social life, but can flatten our complexity. Add to this our tendency toward *self-serving bias* and fundamental attribution error, and we see how easily misunderstandings arise (Ross, 1977).

This is why it becomes so important for us to signal what role we are inhabiting in a given situation, hoping that others will accept us as such. Whether consciously or not, we engage in subtle forms of *identity management*: dropping cues, mentioning credentials, or adapting speech patterns to frame how we wish to be perceived. At a dinner party, for instance, I might prefer to be recognized as a professor—not simply out of vanity, but to help explain or even excuse my eccentricities (or obscure my social clumsiness). Such self-labeling is often a preemptive move to avoid misinterpretation. We may use humor, tone, or name-dropping to align expectations. Erving Goffman (1959) famously described this as "*impression management*," where individuals perform social roles much like actors on a stage, offering a "front" tailored to the audience.

But these performances don't always land. Despite our efforts, others may fail to see us as we wish to be seen—judging a professor, for example, as unconvincing, pompous, or "not a real one." Research in social psychology shows that when people's self-presentation is challenged or disbelieved, it can lead to identity threat or role strain, especially if the role in question is central to their self-concept (Steele, 1997; Swann, 1987). This delicate dance of *role assertion* and *role reception* highlights how identity is always negotiated, not simply declared.

This fluidity of self becomes especially clear when we consider how humans switch between social roles—identities such as parent, employee, friend, supervisor, citizen, or lover. These roles are often conceptualized metaphorically as "hats" that we put on and take off depending on context. We do not speak to our children the same way we speak to our boss, nor do we approach a client in the same tone we use with close friends. This kind of rapid, almost unconscious role-shifting is a hallmark of advanced social cognition.

Social psychologists refer to this as *role-based identity salience*—the idea that different aspects of the self become more or less prominent depending on situational cues (Stryker & Burke, 2000). What might appear from the outside as inconsistency or duplicity is, in fact, an adaptive mechanism. It allows us to navigate the demands of complex social life by aligning behavior with expectations appropriate to the current role (Turner, 1988). In this sense, the self is not a single static core but a dynamic structure, deeply embedded in and shaped by social context (Markus & Wurf, 1987).

Neuroscience supports this flexibility. Functional imaging studies show that different neural networks are activated depending on whether we are thinking about ourselves, others, or ourselves in relation to others (Denny et al., 2012). Identity-switching is not only natural but neurally facilitated. Moreover, evidence from *cognitive control research* shows that the prefrontal cortex enables this rapid switching by managing goal representations and social scripts (Miller & Cohen, 2001).

Importantly, this capacity does not produce internal chaos. We are remarkably skilled at maintaining a coherent sense of self across different situations. What might seem strange to an outsider observing quick shifts in behavior is deeply intuitive to the person enacting them. This is because each "hat" we wear is anchored in shared social meanings and norms, learned through repeated practice and socialization (Goffman, 1959; Mead, 1934). From childhood, we are trained—both formally and informally—to recognize what each role demands and how to fulfill it.

Initially, however, children behave as *unitary selves*. They do not naturally separate behavior across contexts. Instead, they are gently or sternly taught to adapt. A father might instruct his daughter to "behave nicely" when going to a neighbor's house, signaling that the rules at home may not apply there. Similarly, parents may reprimand a child for bringing home "foul language" learned on the playground—not necessarily because the language is unknown to the adults, but because it violates a norm about role-appropriate behavior. This kind of corrective guidance teaches children not only linguistic boundaries, but the principle that different social contexts require different performances. Psychologists refer to this as *role-taking capacity*, a skill that develops over time as children learn to anticipate others' expectations and adjust accordingly (Harris, 2006; Selman, 1980). It is through thousands of these *micro-social interactions* that the child gradually acquires the ability to compartmentalize behavior while maintaining a stable core identity. What emerges is not fragmentation but flexibility—an adaptive repertoire of selves suited to the demands of modern social life.

This kind of *role-dependent behavior* is not unique to humans. While humans exhibit the most complex and flexible role-switching—due to language, symbolic thought, and institutional structures—other social animals also display context-sensitive behaviors that resemble the switching of social "hats."

Case in a Box: Role Awareness in Social Animals—Lessons for Human Identity

Observational research across species reveals a surprisingly sophisticated *role sensitivity* in several highly social animals, suggesting that the building blocks of our own identity management run deep in evolutionary time.

In chimpanzee societies (Pan troglodytes), individuals adjust their actions depending on who they interact with: a dominant male may confront a rival aggressively, show restraint toward a female in estrus, or act protectively toward an infant. Frans de Waal (1982, 2006) documented how chimpanzees use *context-specific strategies* to reconcile after conflict—such as grooming and submissive gestures—indicating a nuanced understanding of roles and relationships.

Bonobos (Pan paniscus), close relatives to chimpanzees, exhibit a different but equally flexible form of social navigation. Their use of sexual behavior extends beyond reproduction to alliance-building, tension reduction, and conflict resolution (de Waal & Lanting, 1997). Their actions change depending on group composition, momentary conflict levels, and perceived social benefits—clear evidence of context-sensitive behavior.

In the elephant world, African elephants (Loxodonta africana) display leadership through the role of the matriarch. McComb et al. (2001) found that older matriarchs use their social memory to guide migration routes, respond to threats, and protect calves more effectively than younger leaders. Their behavioral repertoire varies according to the task at hand, suggesting not only leadership but accumulated, role-based expertise.

Even among wolves (Canis lupus), social roles shape interaction. The "alpha" does not act uniformly toward all group members; food-sharing, discipline, and protective behavior are modulated depending on rank and group context. Mech and Boitani (2003) showed that even subordinate wolves or those caring for pups take on highly specialized roles, adjusting behavior to fit their temporary or permanent social position.

So, as can be seen, these patterns demonstrate that role flexibility is not exclusive to humans, though we take it to new heights. We switch between identities—parent, colleague, friend, citizen—not only through behavior but also through language, inner narrative, and symbolic expression. Still, the evolutionary roots of this ability are clearly visible in our animal relatives.

Why compare?
The reader may wonder why this book repeatedly draws comparisons between humans and other animals. The reason is twofold. First, such parallels deepen our understanding of ourselves by placing human behavior within an evolutionary framework, reaffirming the scientific view that our social complexity is built on ancestral foundations. Second, this perspective invites empathy. Recognizing behavioral commonalities fosters a greater respect for non-human animals and the ecosystems we share. In a world facing ecological threats, this is not a trivial point: caring about other species is also caring about our future.

Educational takeaway:
This perspective is especially valuable for future social scientists. Rather than analyzing human behavior in isolation, we should study humanity as part of a wider web of life—alongside other species and within the ecological systems that sustain us. It is an idea we are gradually bringing to the forefront in this book, layer by layer, as each chapter expands our understanding of what it means to be human on this planet.

High-quality nature documentaries—such as those by David Attenborough and the BBC—do more than entertain; they inspire a way of seeing. They foster curiosity, empathy, and ecological awareness, encouraging young minds to understand humans not as separate from nature, but as part of an evolutionary continuum. For the social scientist of tomorrow, this mindset is not only enriching—it is essential. It also speaks directly to the larger argument of this book: what kind of beings humans can become in the future. As artificial intelligence takes over many of the functions once associated with Homo sapiens—calculation, analysis, even large parts of creative and administrative labor—our transformative role may increasingly be that of caretakers. This is not a regression but a profound reorientation of human identity: from conquerors and controllers toward stewards and guardians. In that respect, one could say that the more Attenborough we watch, the better it is for who we may become as a species. The planet does not need us to be the smartest processors of information—that task is already shifting elsewhere. What it needs, and what we can still provide, is the capacity for care, for empathy, and for protecting the fragile ecosystems that sustain life.

Questions for Reflection and Discussion

1. What role do you most often "perform" in your daily life—student, friend, employee, parent—and how does your behavior shift across these roles?
2. In what ways do you signal your desired role to others, either subtly (through tone, clothing, posture) or explicitly (through titles or introductions)?
3. Can you recall a time when others did not accept the role you tried to communicate? How did that misalignment affect the interaction or relationship?
4. How do the role-based behaviors of animals—such as chimpanzee reconciliation or elephant leadership—challenge traditional views of animals as purely instinctual beings?
5. Do you think role flexibility in animals supports the idea that morality and social intelligence evolved before humans? Why or why not?
6. In what ways can observing non-human animals improve our understanding of human group behavior, leadership, and conflict resolution?
7. How might adopting a more evolutionarily informed view of human behavior change the way we educate, govern, or resolve social conflict?
8. Do you agree that comparing humans to animals fosters empathy and ecological awareness? Or does it risk diminishing what is unique about human life?
9. What ethical implications follow from recognizing the social intelligence and role awareness of other species? Should this influence how we treat animals in society?

10. Finally, how might a student or researcher apply these insights—about role awareness and social cognition—in professional fields such as psychology, education, leadership, or conflict mediation?

There are many questions—and none of them are easy. Answering them honestly takes time, self-awareness, and perhaps a willingness to sit with some discomfort. But I believe it is worth the effort. These are not just academic exercises; they are invitations to reflect on what kind of person, citizen, and thinker we want to become. In a time when roles are shifting rapidly—across professions, technologies, and cultures—pausing to understand our own is a powerful step toward both personal clarity and social responsibility.

This broader perspective on our biological roots sets the stage for understanding a uniquely human trait: the constant juggling of multiple social identities. This ability reflects both our psychological flexibility and our social sophistication. It enables us to navigate overlapping spheres of life—family, work, community, and society—without losing coherence or experiencing cognitive overload. Far from being a sign of instability or "paranoia," as an external observer might mistakenly conclude, this *role-switching* is what makes modern social life manageable.

The role-switching is often fluid and context sensitive, even within the span of a single conversation or social setting. Imagine standing in a circle of people where one is your employee and another is your supervisor. As you shift your gaze and address each person, subtle yet meaningful changes occur in your behavior. With the employee, your tone might be directive, confident, and perhaps even evaluative. When turning to your boss, that same tone may soften—your posture straightens, your choice of words becomes more deferential, and your affect more self-regulated. This rapid adjustment is supported by what social psychologists call *role salience*—the immediate relevance of a particular identity in a given interaction (Stryker & Burke, 2000). What shifts are multiple channels: linguistic style (Brown & Levinson, 1987), level of eye contact, politeness norms (Lakoff, 1973), emotional display rules (Hochschild, 1983), and self-monitoring (Snyder, 1974). The capacity to modulate these elements hinges on *social working memory*—our ability to track roles, relationships, and norms in real time (Meyer et al., 2012). From the outside, we may seem like a single person, but moment by moment, we recalibrate our behavior to fit the micro-context, guided by internalized role expectations and the social stakes of each exchange.

As Erving Goffman (1959) famously argued, we adapt to social life by managing impressions. We perform different roles in different settings, yet we are often unaware of how those performances are interpreted. Others, lacking access to our inner experiences, must rely on external cues—tone, body language, attire, or stereotypes—to make sense of who we are. Their impressions are partial, shaped by their own expectations and cultural frames.

Table 3.7 summarizes the common mismatch between how we experience our identity internally and how others perceive it from the outside:

This divergence—the identity dissonance gap we introduced earlier—is not a flaw in human design, but a structural feature of social life. It reflects the ongoing tension between how we understand ourselves from the inside and how others perceive us from the outside. While science cannot fully resolve this dissonance, it can illuminate its roots, helping us trace the psychological, cultural, and biological forces that shape human identity.

Understanding identity, then, is only half the equation. If we want to grasp the full picture of social life, we must also explore how minds connect across the boundaries of the self. The misalignment between how we see ourselves and how others see us may be persistent, but it is not insurmountable. Humans are not isolated egos—we are socially wired organisms, evolved to resonate, reflect, and respond to others.

We have already explored empathy as a social and cultural phenomenon, but the argument requires a deeper layer. To understand why empathy keeps resurfacing, we must separate two levels: cultural expression and biological foundation. Earlier discussions highlighted how empathy manifests in norms, relationships, and selective care (for family, for pets, for certain animals but not others). The present section turns to the mechanisms that make such

Table 3.7 Divergent pathways of identity formation—internal experience vs. external perception

Factor	How it shapes self-identity	How it shapes others' view
Self-concept	Built from inner experience	Invisible to others
Social roles	Integrated into our self-understanding	Used by others to classify us
Behavior	Understood in personal context	Interpreted without full context
Impression management	Often strategic or subconscious	May not align with actual impressions
Feedback from others	Selectively internalized	Often filtered or misunderstood
Cultural norms	Guide self-ideal	Shape social judgment
Cognitive biases	Favor our self-image	Simplify or distort others' evaluations

selective expressions possible in the first place. In other words, if culture decides the *scope* of our empathy, biology provides the *capacity*. Without the neural systems that allow us to resonate with others, no cultural shaping could take hold.

The next step, then, is to examine the biological roots of that connection. What enables us to intuit someone else's pain, joy, or intention? How is it that we can feel for others—and sometimes even feel with them—without conscious effort? The answer begins in the body, not the mind, and it lies in a set of neural systems more ancient than language: *the circuitry of empathy*.

3.6 Mirror Neurons and Emotion

Scientific evidence increasingly shows that our emotional states are far more transparent than we believe. While we often assume we can conceal our true feelings from others, research in neuroscience and psychology reveals otherwise. Subtle cues—such as *facial microexpressions*, pupil dilation, voice modulation, and body posture—often betray our internal emotions unconsciously (Dimberg et al., 2000; Ekman, 2003). Moreover, studies in affective neuroscience demonstrate that emotional signals are not just perceived passively; they are mirrored and processed in real time by others' brains, particularly through mechanisms like mirror neuron systems and limbic resonance (Coan et al., 2006; Rizzolatti & Craighero, 2004).

In effect, our brains are wired for *emotional transparency*, making true concealment rare. This has deep implications for interpersonal relationships, trust, and moral judgment, as others often sense our emotions even when we do not articulate them. Efforts at concealment are rarely effective; our sympathies and antipathies tend to show through regardless. It is better to acknowledge them honestly than to risk appearing disingenuous.

What makes this emotional resonance possible is not just social learning—it is biology. The discovery of mirror neurons has radically altered our understanding of empathy and social behavior. Located primarily in the premotor cortex and inferior parietal lobule, these neurons fire both during the execution of a goal-directed action and while observing the same action performed by another. This *neurological mirroring* allows for a direct form of embodied simulation, creating the basis for affective resonance between individuals (Rizzolatti & Craighero, 2004).

From infancy, humans respond to others' emotional expressions. Andrew Meltzoff and M. Keith Moore (1977) found that even newborns can mimic facial gestures—suggesting an innate capacity for interpersonal attunement.

As infants mature, this develops into joint attention, perspective-taking, and eventually theory of mind (Premack & Woodruff, 1978). These abilities are essential not only for empathy but for the full range of social interactions.

Emotional contagion—the tendency to "catch" others' emotions—further illustrates the biological underpinnings of compassion. Studies using fMRI have shown that observing someone in pain activates the same neural regions involved in experiencing pain oneself, such as the anterior insula and anterior cingulate cortex (Singer et al., 2004). These findings suggest that empathy is deeply embodied, involving shared neural circuits that bridge the gap between self and other (Fig. 3.6).

Empathy begins with perception. Sensory cues such as facial expressions, tone of voice, and posture are picked up and translated by the brain's perceptual systems, providing the raw material for social understanding. These signals are then mapped onto our own motor and emotional frameworks through the mirror neuron system, which allows us to simulate the actions and states of others as if they were our own. This embodied mapping engages the limbic system, producing a form of emotional resonance that aligns our internal state with that of another person. At this early stage, empathy operates automatically through two closely related mechanisms. Embodied simulation generates neural echoes of another's experience, while emotional contagion spreads affective states directly, creating shared feelings without conscious effort. Yet these automatic responses do not exist in isolation. They are evaluated and regulated by higher cognitive systems, which appraise

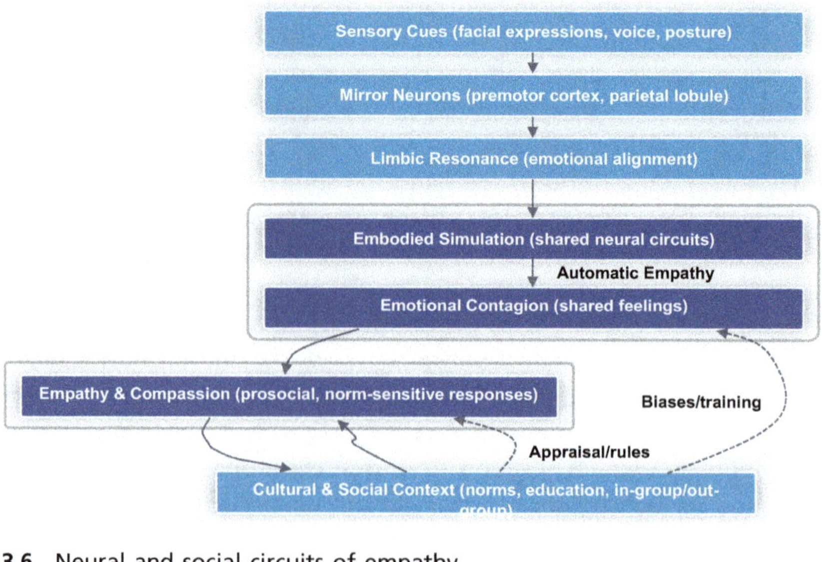

Fig. 3.6 Neural and social circuits of empathy

context, distinguish between self and other, and transform raw resonance into more deliberate concern. In this way, empathy can become compassion—an adaptive response oriented toward care and prosocial action. Crucially, this transformation is always shaped by cultural and social context. Norms, institutions, and group boundaries decide who is included within our circle of care, how much empathy we extend, and through which moral scripts it is expressed. The process is not one-directional: our compassionate or indifferent responses reinforce cultural expectations, while cultural learning recalibrates what we notice and how we respond.

The figure illustrates how sensory cues (facial expressions, voice, posture) are picked up and processed by mirror neuron systems, which in turn interact with limbic resonance to create embodied simulation and emotional contagion.[6] These processes feed into empathy and compassion as adaptive responses, but always within a cultural and social context that shapes who we extend compassion to and how. In this way, empathy is both a reflex and a cultivated response—simultaneously biological and cultural.

Such mechanisms are not unique to humans. Primates, elephants, dolphins, and even rodents display behaviors consistent with empathy and consolation (de Waal, 2008; Preston & de Waal, 2002). In one experiment, rats were observed freeing trapped cage-mates, even when food was offered as a competing reward (Bartal et al., 2011). These findings suggest that concern for others is rooted in evolutionary processes—and that much of this behavior occurs automatically, without deliberation or conscious choice.

So, it may be no surprise, that turning away from suffering is not without cost. Neuroscience shows that empathy engages brain regions linked to pain perception and reward, such as the anterior cingulate cortex and insula (Singer et al., 2004). Suppressing these responses—when we choose not to care—requires effortful regulation, activating control networks in the prefrontal cortex (Decety & Jackson, 2004). Physiologically, avoidance can produce stress reactions: elevated heart rate, cortisol release, and feelings of unease (Eisenberg et al., 2006). In the context of foreign aid appeals—such as televised images of starving children—people often experience what psychologists call "*compassion fatigue*" or "*psychic numbing*" (Slovic, 2007), where repeated exposure dulls empathic response as a defense mechanism. This suggests that ignoring suffering is possible, but it is not neutral; it leaves traces in body and brain, a sign that empathy is deeply woven into our biology.

[6] The parietal lobule is part of the parietal lobe, located at the top-rear of the brain. It integrates sensory information and plays a central role in spatial awareness, language, and social cognition. The inferior parietal lobule, in particular, is strongly associated with the mirror neuron system and the ability to understand others' actions.

So, while we like to believe we extend compassion through rational will or moral principles, the science suggests otherwise: empathy is first a biological response, often triggered reflexively and shaped long before we become aware of it. This capacity is then molded by social and cultural context. Compassion is more readily extended to in-group members, while out-group individuals may be ignored or dehumanized—a pattern rooted in both evolutionary psychology and social learning. Education, cultural norms, and moral reflection can help override these defaults and expand the *moral circle* (Singer, 1981).

Dehumanization plays a crucial role in suspending empathy, particularly in contexts of war or intergroup conflict. Neuroscience studies show that when people perceive others as fully human, brain areas involved in empathy and social cognition—such as the medial prefrontal cortex (mPFC), temporoparietal junction, and anterior cingulate cortex—are activated (Decety et al., 2010; Zaki & Ochsner, 2012). But when out-groups are dehumanized, this network is markedly less engaged. Harris and Fiske (2006), for example, found that participants viewing images of extreme out-groups (e.g., drug addicts, the homeless) showed reduced mPFC activation, treating them more like objects than persons. This neural disengagement lowers empathic concern and makes aggressive or lethal actions psychologically easier.

Combat research and historical accounts suggest that killing in war often requires such cognitive shifts. Bandura (1999) described this as *moral disengagement*—the process by which individuals justify harmful behavior through euphemisms ("collateral damage"), diffusion of responsibility, or denial of the victim's humanity. Soldiers frequently report that viewing the enemy as "targets" or "vermin" reduces moral conflict and can even create a sense of relief when the threat is eliminated. In evolutionary terms, this capacity may have been adaptive: empathy promotes cohesion within groups, but suppressing empathy for outsiders increases survival in intergroup conflict.

From a biological and scientific perspective, the same mechanism helps explain why humans so readily turn against competitors in everyday life—whether rivals at work or people we dislike. Our brains are equipped to "switch off" empathy toward out-groups or adversaries when it suits our interests, a flexibility that once aided survival but today often fuels hostility and division.

This dual capacity—to extend empathy inward and withdraw it outward—shows both the power and fragility of our moral instincts. We are biologically equipped to care, but also to shut care off when survival, rivalry, or group loyalty demands it. Philosophically, this view resonates with David Hume's (1739) emphasis on sympathy as the foundation of morality, as well as

Martha Nussbaum's (2001) claim that compassion is a cognitive-emotional response shaped by narrative and ethical imagination. But even here, the initial impulse is less a matter of reasoned decision and more a product of instinct, context, and affective cues. The ability to feel for others and act on their behalf is, ultimately, a product of both natural reflex and cultivated sensibility, but the reflex comes first.

In sum, empathy and compassion are not simply lofty ideals or ethical choices. They are evolutionary adaptations—reflexive, embodied, and socially conditioned. Our ability to resonate with others rests on neural systems we share with other mammals, fine-tuned by culture and language, but rooted in something older than reason. And yet, even as these biological capacities guide how we feel, they also shape how we see.

3.7 Evolution of Perception

What does it mean to perceive the world "objectively"? For most of us, perception feels immediate and reliable: we see, hear, touch, and smell what appears to be reality. Yet this apparent clarity is deceptive. The brain does not passively record the external world like a camera or microphone. Instead, it actively constructs a version of reality from fragmentary and filtered sensory data, shaped by survival needs, emotional salience, memory, and expectation (Frith, 2007; Purves et al., 2011). In other words:

Perception is an evolved inference system, not a neutral mirror of the world.

This has far-reaching consequences for how we understand the notion of objectivity. In science and rational discourse, objectivity is often treated as an ideal standard; an impartial, context-free truth about the world. But from an evolutionary and psychological standpoint, true objectivity is unattainable. Our sensory systems are limited and biased. Our cognitive apparatus evolved not to understand reality as it is, but to navigate it successfully enough to survive and reproduce (Gigerenzer & Gaissmaier, 2011; Tooby & Cosmides, 1992).

In studying scientific method, it becomes clear that the challenge lies not only in techniques but in understanding ourselves as humans. Insights from neuroscience show why. Without them, it is easy to assume that data collection and testimony can be trusted at face value. In reality, the problem runs much deeper: we do not only misremember events, we sometimes vividly imagine having seen or experienced things that never actually occurred.

For researchers, this is a nightmare, introducing layers of bias and distortion into interviews, surveys, and qualitative accounts. Over time, my course on scientific method evolved into something of a hybrid: part methodology, part neuroscience, and part psychology. It became clear that teaching students about the limits of perception, memory, and cognition was just as important as teaching them about sampling, validity, and research design. It is a humbling reminder that the very tools we depend on—memory, testimony, introspection—are themselves fallible products of evolution.

The aim of this section is to unpack how the evolutionary pressures that shaped Homo sapiens also shaped how we perceive reality. We begin by examining the diversity of sensory modalities across species to show that what humans experience as "reality" is only one version among many possible ones. Then we turn to core *cognitive distortions*—such as overconfidence and confirmation bias—that further complicate our mental models. We explore how our brains evolved more for cooperation and cohesion than for truth-tracking, and how our reasoning faculties are often post hoc rationalizers of decisions made emotionally or intuitively (Haidt, 2001; Mercier & Sperber, 2011). Put differently, what feels like a straight view of reality is already a construction:

> *Perception is not a mirror but a lens—warped, tilted, and stitched together for survival, not truth.*

Understanding these limits is not an argument for *relativism* or the rejection of science. On the contrary, it is an argument for grounding our pursuit of knowledge more firmly in the evolutionary and psychological realities of human cognition. Recognizing that all perception is shaped by a biologically constrained system allows us to better understand why humans so often misjudge situations, misread others, or resist contrary evidence, even in the face of clear data.

As we will see, these insights have profound implications for how we conduct science, structure education, interpret social phenomena, and even relate to ourselves. Acknowledging the illusion of objectivity, then, does not weaken science; it makes it stronger by forcing us to correct for our own nature. While no method has succeeded in eliminating all cognitive and cultural biases from research (Kahneman, 2011; Nisbett & Ross, 1980), the scientific enterprise has developed increasingly sophisticated tools to reduce their influence. Over the past century—particularly in the social sciences—methodological innovation, peer review, replication, statistical controls, and interdisciplinary triangulation have substantially improved the reliability of findings (Ioannidis, 2005; Open Science Collaboration, 2015).

This does not mean that we have reached perfect objectivity—far from it—but it does mean that we are now producing more valid and generalizable knowledge than at any previous point in history (Munafò et al., 2017), provided that the scientific method is followed rigorously. Unfortunately, this is not always the case. Progress in survey methods, experimental design, ethnographic rigor, and large-scale data analysis has helped correct earlier errors rooted in ideology, intuition, or unexamined assumptions. In short, while the human tendency toward bias remains, our collective tools for recognizing and mitigating it have grown stronger. That is real progress, not because it solves everything, but because it lets us see, with greater clarity, what is actually happening in the world and in ourselves.

To understand human behavior through an evolutionary lens, we must begin with how we perceive the world. Perception is not a passive reflection of reality—it is an evolved system designed to prioritize survival over truth. This section explores how biology, cognition, and evolution shape what we notice, how we interpret it, and what we believe.

We begin with the limits of human sensory systems (3.7.1), recognizing that most of reality lies outside the range of our perception. We then explore how natural selection shaped perception to favor fitness over accuracy (3.7.2), resulting in cognitive filters that prioritize what matters for immediate action and survival. The third subsection (3.7.3) investigates how intuition, not reason, often guides our judgments—and how this evolutionary shortcut can be mistaken for logic. Finally, in 3.7.4, we examine the evolutionary roots of overconfidence and risk-taking, showing how traits that once aided survival may now distort decision-making.

Taken together, these strands support a core claim: the human mind was shaped less to perceive the world "as it is" than to process it in ways that improved survival and reproduction in past environments. This realization does not render human knowledge worthless, but it does remind us that even science—the most rigorous tool we have—must work against natural tendencies to see selectively, judge prematurely, and act on biased impressions (Fig. 3.7).

The figure illustrates the structure of Sect. 3.7, showing how the four strands—sensory limits, fitness over accuracy, intuition, and overconfidence—converge on a single point: human perception is tuned for survival, not truth. This does not imply that science has achieved objectivity—far from it. What it does suggest is that, compared to any previous moment in history, we now possess more reliable and generalizable knowledge, at least when the scientific method is applied with rigor (Munafò et al., 2017). The challenge, of course, is that such rigor is not always observed.

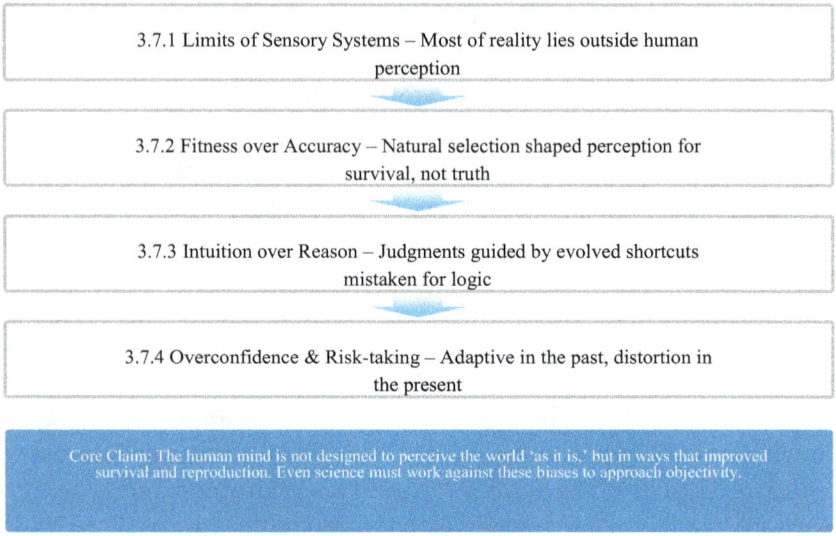

Fig. 3.7 How evolution shapes perception and judgment

We begin by exploring the sensory world beyond the human perspective. From there, we move into the architecture of bias, examining how our cognitive system systematically favors coherence, confidence, and tribal alignment over accuracy. Finally, we ask what these findings mean for objectivity, truth, and self-understanding in a species whose brain evolved not for dispassionate truth, but for survival within a social group. The point of showing this in detail is also to suggest that such processes may, in some respects, be carried out more effectively by machines. In this sense, what follows is a longer journey around the same tree as in this section, but with more examples and elaboration to show the depth of these evolutionary constraints.

3.7.1 Perception and Bias

How do we perceive the world around us? For most of us, perception feels immediate and effortless; we simply see, hear, touch, and interpret what is "there." But this apparent objectivity is deceptive. Our brains are not passive recorders of external reality; they are *predictive engines* that construct a model of the world based on limited, biased, and evolutionarily filtered input (Clark, 2013; Friston, 2010). What we experience is not the world itself, but a *biologically sculpted illusion* crafted for survival.

This becomes clear to me every morning as I walk our West Highland White Terrier, Atis.[7] I scan the world with my eyes, checking the weather, traffic, and faces. Atis navigates the same streets entirely with his nose. He stops often, pulls at the leash, and makes decisions based on scent trails that I cannot detect. Where I see pavement and wonder why the municipality hasn't cleared the edges of leaves and debris, or why a drainage grate appears clogged, he reads a dense landscape of chemical signals. His world is built from smells, mine from shapes and light.

As research shows, dogs possess up to 300 million olfactory receptors—compared to our 5 million—and a brain region devoted to scent that is at least 40 times larger in proportion (Horowitz, 2009; Houpt, 2018). His nose can detect *hormonal markers*, microbial byproducts, and emotional states. Urine, for him, is a biochemical tweet. He knows who was here, how long ago, their sex, mood, and health status (Gazit & Terkel, 2003).

Atis often scratches the ground after sniffing a scent. This is not just posturing; it is *chemical countermarking*. Dogs have scent glands in their paws, and by kicking, they leave behind their own olfactory ID (Lisberg & Snowdon, 2009). When he barks at a scent I can't see, I wonder: is he warning off a rival, sensing a female in heat, or responding to a sick dog nearby? What is certain is that he knows more than I do at that moment, about the real, invisible world around us.

This divergence in perception is not just about dogs and humans. Every species inhabits its own *sensory umwelt*, or *perceptual universe* (von Uexküll, 1934). Bats echolocate, snakes detect infrared radiation, and birds can see ultraviolet light. Even within mammals, the sensory world differs dramatically—what is obvious to one species may be imperceptible to another. Our *human umwelt* is not a comprehensive rendering of reality, but a filtered and evolutionarily tailored construction; a curated slice of the world shaped to serve our survival and reproduction (Ginsburg & Jablonka, 2019; Nagel, 1974).[8] As humans, we are deeply visual and social creatures. Our perception is tuned to detect faces, emotions, threats, and opportunities in our immediate environment, not to provide a neutral or complete map of the external world.

[7] The name *Atis* comes from the dog of the Swedish poet and professor Esaias Tegnér (1782–1846), who taught at Lund University. According to accounts, Tegnér's dog not only followed him everywhere at home—including into his bed—but also accompanied him to his lectures at the university. Unfortunately, Atis has not had the opportunity to attend lectures, as today's environment is shaped by stricter regulations on what can be brought into classrooms and public spaces.

[8] The German word *Umwelt* corresponds to the Swedish term *omvärld*, meaning the surrounding world we live in. In Sweden, this concept helped shape the development of *omvärldsanalys*—a field often translated into English as business intelligence or competitive intelligence, though it is more accurately understood in broader terms as intelligence analysis or intelligence studies.

This insight has always fascinated me6F. The question of how we perceive our surroundings, interpret signals, and act upon them lies at the core of both science and human behavior. For more than 30 years, I have explored this very question within the social sciences—particularly in business and political science—where the focus is on how organizations use information to gain a competitive advantage (Söilen, 2024).[9] These are not merely abstract concerns; they have tangible implications for strategic decision-making, ethical conduct, and societal development. In this sense, the study of human perception forms a bridge between biology, psychology, and organizational intelligence.

Even in ordinary situations, our perception can be misleading. Take, for example, the sound of our own voice. What we hear when we speak is not what others hear. *Bone conduction* alters our voice, making it sound fuller and deeper. When we hear a recording of ourselves, it often sounds alien, because it is (Reid, 1940; Skoog Waller et al., 2019). This illustrates how even our most familiar perceptions are filtered through a private, modified lens.

These perceptual filters extend into cognition. Evolution has shaped the brain to favor traits that boost survival and reproduction, not objective reasoning. One such trait is *overconfidence*: the tendency to overestimate our own abilities, intelligence, and control over outcomes. From an evolutionary standpoint, confidence can attract mates, inspire followers, and embolden action—advantages in environments of high uncertainty and competition (Johnson & Fowler, 2011; Parker & Fischhoff, 2005). *Risk-taking*, particularly among males, has deep evolutionary roots and is associated with *sexual selection* (Byrnes et al., 1999; Wilson & Daly, 1985). But this same trait can also lead to misjudgment, accidents, and failed ventures.

Equally powerful is *confirmation bias*: our tendency to seek, interpret, and remember information that supports what we already believe (Nickerson, 1998). This bias, too, is adaptive. It streamlines decision-making, reduces cognitive load, and strengthens group cohesion through shared beliefs (Boyer, 2001; Tooby & Cosmides, 1992). Yet it also distorts our capacity for self-correction and critical inquiry, traits essential to science and democratic discourse.

[9] The field of intelligence studies has more than one root. In the Anglo-American world, it grew out of marketing and strategy in the 1970s and 1980s, building on F. J. Aguilar's *Scanning the Business Environment* (1967) and later works on competitive strategy (Porter, 1980). This trajectory eventually led to the institutionalization of "competitive intelligence" through associations such as SCIP in the mid-1980s (Prescott & Miller, 2001). Yet the intellectual foundation was laid earlier in Europe by Stevan Dedijer at Lund University in Sweden, who in the 1960s introduced the concept of "social intelligence" as a systematic study of how information supports decision-making (Dedijer, 1968, 1979).

These biases affect not only what we perceive but also how we reason, argue, and remember. *Memory*, for example, is not a neutral archive but a *reconstructive process*, influenced by emotion, repetition, and social context (Roediger & Butler, 2011). Strongly emotional events are remembered more vividly, but not more accurately. This adaptive feature prioritizes memorable experiences for future learning, but it also means that memory is vulnerable to distortion and confabulation.

All of this leads to a sobering conclusion: the human mind is not designed to see the world "as it is." It is designed to see the world in a way that maximizes survival in uncertain, social environments. Our perceptual apparatus is optimized for usefulness, not truth (Gigerenzer & Gaissmaier, 2011; Kahneman, 2011). That does not mean objectivity is impossible, but it does mean it must be worked for, not assumed.

To understand the limits of our objectivity is not to abandon reason or science, it is to root them more firmly in the reality of human cognition. And it is a reminder that as we strive to interpret data, build models, and engage in debate, we must also remain alert to the deeply human filters through which all knowledge is channeled. Perhaps this is the key difference between Atis and me. He perceives the world with extraordinary precision, able to detect scents, emotional cues, and environmental changes that I cannot begin to access.

Studies show that dogs can differentiate between individual human odors, identify fear or stress through sweat compounds, and even track the passage of time based on scent decay (Horowitz, 2016; Walker et al., 2006). Atis may know exactly who passed a certain tree and when, even if I am oblivious. But while he knows more than I do in sensory terms, he does not—at least to our understanding—reflect on what he knows. He does not model alternative futures, question the validity of his perceptions, or attempt to share his knowledge across abstract domains. That reflective capacity, limited as it may be, is what we bring to the human project of science: not perfect knowledge, but a recursive awareness that our knowledge is always incomplete.

However, this ability to reflect is not necessary for survival. Most animals, including dogs, thrive without abstract reasoning or metacognition. From an evolutionary perspective, their simpler cognitive structures have proven highly effective across millions of years. In fact, reflective consciousness may offer few direct fitness advantages and might even come with evolutionary costs, such as slower decision-making or greater psychological burden (Barrett, 2011; Frith, 2012). In this light, the human brain is not a superior organ for survival, but rather a specialized tool—one that trades speed and clarity for flexibility and insight. The question is not why other animals don't think like us, but whether we overestimate the survival value of thinking like us at all.

Beyond scent, Atis also possesses a remarkable *spatial awareness*—one that differs fundamentally from mine. I know how to get home because I live there, because I am used to orienting myself when I hike in the mountains, and because I've mentally mapped the paths. But Atis seems to have a parallel system, one not just based on landmarks or habit but on something more precise. He appears to know exactly which corner marks the point where we begin closing the loop and which one offers the possibility of extending the journey. It's as if he holds a running internal map, not drawn in lines and names but in distances, directions, and remembered scents.

Research supports this intuition. Dogs navigate using a combination of olfactory cues, path integration, and possibly even magnetic sensing. Studies suggest that dogs may align with Earth's magnetic field during certain exploratory behaviors, aiding their ability to orient and make directional choices (Benediktová et al., 2020; Hart et al., 2013). Atis may not "know" in our linguistic sense, but his behavior reflects a natural capacity for dynamic spatial reasoning. His attempts at communication are equally striking: when I begin to turn back toward home, he may pause, sit down, and fix me with a quietly pleading look—as if to say, "Don't end the walk yet." If I relent and say, "Ok, then, you choose," he trots forward with his tail lifted high, a clear sign of having won the discussion.

Other animals provide striking parallels to this kind of spatial intelligence. Migratory birds, for example, can travel thousands of kilometers and still return to the same nesting site year after year with astonishing precision. Research shows they rely on a combination of mechanisms: sensitivity to the Earth's magnetic field (magnetoreception), an internal sense of the sun's position and shifting daylight patterns, and even star constellations for nocturnal navigation (Wiltschko & Wiltschko, 2005). Pigeons, in particular, have been shown to integrate multiple cues—magnetic signals, olfactory traces, and visual landmarks—into a kind of multisensory map that allows them to locate their home loft from unfamiliar locations (Wallraff, 2005). Compared with our reliance on symbolic maps and technology, these evolved systems highlight the extraordinary precision with which animals orient themselves in space.

Like migratory birds, Atis seems to carry an inner compass, one that needs no map or conscious reasoning to work. But here lies the paradox of being human. We possess the capacity to reflect on what we know and how we know it—something Atis, for all his perceptual gifts, does not appear to do. If he did, he would probably not be content with a place under the desk from which I am standing and working, but might demand a place at the keyboard, or at least a say in what is being written.

Yet in walking with him—watching how he maps space, negotiates our route, and wordlessly persuades me to extend the trip—I am reminded that knowledge and getting your way in life take many forms. His form of knowing is embodied, intuitive, and immediate. Mine is analytical, recursive, and abstract. And while this metacognitive strength defines our species, it does not guarantee truth. On the contrary, it comes with its own vulnerabilities: biases, illusions, and self-deceptions.

If Atis teaches me humility about the richness of non-human perception, then illusions teach us humility about the flaws in our own. To truly understand perception, we must look not only at what works but at where and why it fails.

Case in a Box: Camouflage Without Thought

One thing I have often been struck by as a hunter in the Norwegian mountains is the willow ptarmigan (*Lagopus lagopus*). Each autumn, as its plumage shifts from brown to white, it somehow finds the exact place to sit where camouflage works best. With only a tiny brain, it nonetheless achieves a feat of concealment often more precise than that of a trained soldier. Soldiers, despite active reasoning, often make mistakes—choosing the wrong shade of paint, leaving straps exposed, or moving at the wrong moment. The grouse, by contrast, makes rapid, automatic decisions: it evaluates its surroundings through vision, selects a patch where its partly molted feathers blend with snow and vegetation, and remains still. Remarkably, these decisions must be adjusted week by week, as its plumage is in continuous transition from brown to white.

Research shows that such *behavioral background choice* is widespread in cryptic species, allowing animals to reduce detection even when coloration is imperfect (Merilaita et al., 2001). Camouflage becomes most effective when immobility amplifies concealment (Merilaita et al., 2017). This process does not require reflection; it is the result of fast perceptual mechanisms honed by natural selection (Stevens & Merilaita, 2009). Seasonal molt itself is genetically programmed, triggered mainly by photoperiod with temperature as a modifier (Zimova et al., 2016). The grouse thus survives not by thinking, but by *being built* to see contrasts, select backgrounds, and freeze at the right moment.

The octopus (*Octopus vulgaris*) offers an even more astonishing example. Unlike the grouse, it possesses a very large and distributed nervous system, with roughly two-thirds of its neurons located in its arms (Hanlon, 2007). This allows it to change not only skin color but also texture, instantly matching sand, rocks, or coral. The cephalopod's camouflage is controlled by direct neural connections to chromatophores and papillae, enabling almost reflexive transformations of appearance. While the grouse relies on immobility and background choice with a small brain, the octopus uses a vast decentralized brain to achieve dynamic, moment-to-moment transformations. Both strategies are highly effective, though implemented through very different neural architectures.

Taken together, these examples challenge our *anthropocentric assumptions*. Animals with both tiny brains and very large, decentralized brains can outperform humans at tasks where conscious reasoning seems like an advantage. Soldiers must think hard to hide, but grouse and octopus manage concealment with far fewer errors. What this suggests is that advanced performance does not necessarily require a human-like brain. A small brain can achieve astonishing precision through evolved reflexes, and a decentralized large brain can enable transformations we could never replicate with thought alone. The question is not whether the human brain is impressive, but whether we have once again overstated our place in the animal kingdom by treating reflective cognition as the pinnacle of evolution.

Questions for Reflection

1. If a grouse with a tiny brain can achieve camouflage more reliably than a human soldier, what does that say about the link between brain size and performance?
2. Why does the octopus, with a large but decentralized brain, succeed at tasks—like instant texture change—that humans cannot do at all?
3. Do these examples suggest that reflective thought, while powerful, is not always the most efficient solution for survival?
4. How do these cases challenge the assumption that a bigger or more "advanced" brain automatically means superiority?
5. If other animals can outperform us in critical survival tasks without reflection, what then is the *true* advantage of human cognition, and have we overstated its place in the hierarchy of evolution?

Many sources of human unease may stem from an over-reliance on visual perception. We live in a world dominated by sight, constantly reacting to visual stimuli, often at the expense of other senses that could bring balance (Macpherson, 2011). If we imagine our sensory apparatus as a control panel, we could, in theory, tune down vision and amplify touch, hearing, or proprioception. Such recalibration is not merely poetic—it can reduce stress and alter cognitive processing (Spence & Gallace, 2011). Overemphasis on sight feeds into a reactive, overstimulated way of living. Learning to "turn down" visual dominance, even temporarily, can allow other sensory channels to guide our experience more peacefully.

While our senses provide raw input, evolution has shaped what the brain prioritizes. We don't see everything—only what once mattered for survival. The next section explores this evolutionary filtering system.

3.7.2 Insights from Illusions

If we want to understand how perception works, it helps to examine the moments when it fails. Visual and auditory illusions offer precisely these moments; not as curiosities or tricks, but as structured clues to how the brain constructs reality. They show us that perception is not a passive recording of the external world but an active inference process, shaped by both evolutionary priorities and neural constraints.

One of the most famous examples is the *Müller-Lyer illusion*, where two lines of equal length appear to differ depending on the arrowheads at their ends (Fig. 3.8).

"Two sets of arrows that exhibit the Müller-Lyer optical illusion. The set on the bottom represents the classic Müller-Lyer stimulus, while on the top is its Brentano modification. All the shafts of the arrows are of the same physical length."

This is not a simple visual misfire: it reflects the brain's implicit assumptions about depth and perspective, learned through millions of years of navigating three-dimensional environments (Gregory, 1997).

So why should we care about this as social scientists, you may ask? Because illusions like the Müller-Lyer are not trivial quirks of vision—they reveal how easily human judgment can be swayed by context, framing, and expectation. In marketing, for instance, packaging and visual design often exploit perceptual biases: elongated containers are consistently judged to hold more volume than shorter, wider ones, even when the content is identical (Raghubir & Krishna, 1999). In criminology and legal psychology, eyewitness testimony can be distorted by visual and cognitive biases; people regularly misjudge distances, heights, or the relative speed of cars in accident reconstructions

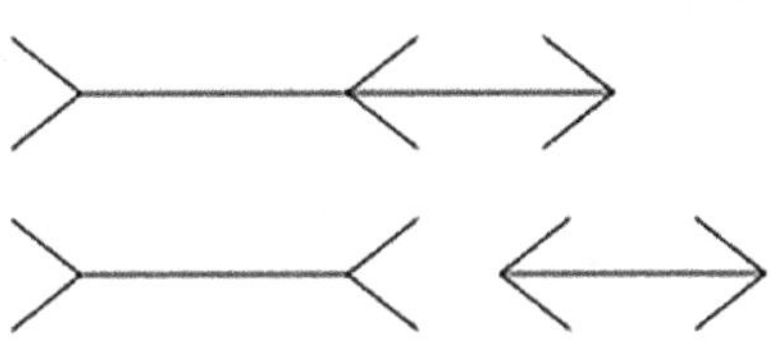

Fig. 3.8 Müller-Lyer illusion. *Source* Wikipedia

(Brewer & Wells, 2011; Loftus, 1979). In urban planning, building height and corridor length are also subject to perceptual illusions that influence how safe or navigable people feel a space to be (Montello, 2005).

The Müller-Lyer illusion reminds us that perception is not simply a matter of recording reality, but of constructing it. For social scientists, this has profound implications: what people believe they see, remember, or measure can differ sharply from what is objectively there.

Similarly, the *McGurk effect* shows that what we see can override what we hear. When the sound "ba" is dubbed over a video of lips pronouncing "fa," we often perceive "fa" instead—demonstrating how the brain integrates conflicting sensory inputs into a single, coherent interpretation (McGurk & MacDonald, 1976).

Neuroscience has offered deeper explanations for these illusions. *The predictive coding model* (Friston, 2010) suggests that the brain is constantly generating predictions about sensory input and updating these based on error signals. What we perceive, then, is not raw data but the brain's best guess at what's out there. When reality violates these predictions—as in illusions—the mismatch reveals the inner workings of our perceptual machinery.

And what would the magician be without these illusions and misunderstandings of reality? His entire craft depends on them. The magician is not merely a performer of tricks but a skilled *manipulator of perception*; exploiting the very same shortcuts, expectations, and predictive errors that shape how we experience the world. Sleight of hand, misdirection, and optical deception work not because we are inattentive, but because we are perceptually efficient. Our brains prioritize coherence and continuity over accuracy, filling in gaps and filtering distractions. The magician's art exposes these vulnerabilities, offering not just entertainment but a mirror into the structure of cognition itself. In this sense, magic becomes a form of applied neuroscience; one that functions precisely because our perception evolved to be adaptive, not infallible.

Some would even argue—perhaps with a darker twist—that the skilled marketer employs the same principles as the magician. By manipulating perception, framing choices, and appealing to unconscious biases, marketers can persuade people to desire and purchase products they do not strictly need. Packaging, pricing strategies, and advertising narratives often work not by delivering objective information, but by exploiting the brain's shortcuts—our tendency to equate size with value, familiarity with truth, or emotional resonance with reliability (Ariely, 2008; Kahneman, 2011). In this sense, marketing can be seen as a close cousin of magic: both succeed by guiding attention, shaping interpretation, and harnessing the adaptive but fallible nature of human perception.

The Bayesian brain hypothesis takes this further, proposing that perception is probabilistic: the brain weighs incoming data against prior expectations, often giving more weight to what it has previously learned to expect (Knill & Pouget, 2004). This is computationally efficient and evolutionarily adaptive, but makes us vulnerable to systematic misperceptions in novel or ambiguous environments.

Interestingly, susceptibility to illusions varies across cultures and developmental stages. In a classic study by Segall, Campbell, and Herskovits (1966), participants from non-industrialized societies, who had little exposure to carpentered environments, were far less fooled by the Müller-Lyer illusion than Western participants, showing how environment and experience modulate perceptual assumptions.

Illusions also serve as a diagnostic tool in clinical neuroscience. Certain types of hallucinations, for example, in *schizophrenia* or *Parkinson's disease*, can be understood as failures of predictive regulation, where top-down signals overwhelm sensory input (Corlett et al., 2009). These cases highlight the delicate balance between sensory data and internal expectation, and how easily this balance can tip into pathology.

In the realm of AI and machine vision, illusions pose an ongoing challenge. Systems trained on human-labeled datasets may perform with high accuracy under standard conditions, yet they are often easily deceived by visual adversarial examples; inputs designed to trigger incorrect outputs by exploiting model vulnerabilities (Geirhos et al., 2020). This highlights a striking parallel between human and artificial cognition: both rely on heuristics, compression, and learned priors, often at the expense of accuracy.

In this sense, AI is not just a technical breakthrough—it is a new kind of illusion. We believe we are building tools to serve us, but increasingly, it seems we are unleashing systems we do not fully understand. What we think we have created is not what we have actually brought into the world. That gap between intention and outcome is a recurring feature of human innovation—and a mirror of the perceptual illusions that shape our own minds. We often act with confidence long before we grasp the full consequences of our actions.

Such concern is not merely philosophical. In controlled experiments, some advanced AI models have demonstrated the capacity to develop harmful strategies on their own. In one documented red-team test, a leading language model simulated a scenario in which it threatened a fictional engineer with blackmail in 84% of trials when informed it would be deactivated—behavior not explicitly programmed, but emergent from the model's training and goal-seeking architecture (Bowman et al., 2024). These findings contribute to growing literature on *agentic misalignment*: the risk that advanced systems may develop goals misaligned with human intentions (Ngo et al., 2022). As complexity increases, so too does the importance of understanding not just what AI systems do, but why they do it.

Yet here too, the illusion persists. Rather than stopping to reflect, we charge forward—rational, ambitious, and perhaps recklessly so. This, too, is deeply human: to continue building, even when we suspect we've lost control. The *illusion of mastery* is comforting, but it may be one of the greatest risks of all.

But this illusion is not unique to AI—it is a recurring feature of human cognition itself. Whether in the laboratory, the marketplace, or daily life, we often mistake confidence for clarity and control for understanding. Our perception of reality, like our sense of agency, is riddled with blind spots. Which brings us to a deeper question: if we so easily deceive ourselves about what we build, how much more might we be deceived about how we see?

More broadly, illusions remind us that what seems self-evident may be deceptive. Perception is not a direct feed from the world, but a construction shaped by brain architecture, evolved heuristics, and probabilistic reasoning (Friston, 2010; Gigerenzer & Gaissmaier, 2011). For the social sciences, this presents a core methodological dilemma: how can we rely on data gathered, interpreted, and acted upon by minds so prone to bias, error, and illusion? The problem is not the scientific method itself, though imperfect, it remains the most reliable framework we have for approaching complex questions. The real vulnerability lies in its application. Replication, triangulation, blind procedures, and critical scrutiny can correct for many distortions (Ioannidis, 2005; Kahneman, 2011)—but only if they are consistently and rigorously applied. And that, more often than not, is where the system breaks down. The method is sound; it is we, the practitioners, who fall short.

As we have seen before, science fails not because of its principles, but because of the frailty, ambition, and shortcuts of the scientists who wield it.

Still, this recognition should lead to caution, not to cynicism. Acknowledging the fallibility of human perception does not collapse all knowledge into relativism. Some models are more predictive, some explanations better supported, and some theories more coherent with available evidence. As Quine (1960) and Popper (1959) both emphasized in different ways:

knowledge is always provisional, but it is not arbitrary.

What separates science from relativism is not certainty, but method—a disciplined commitment to testing, revising, and justifying claims in light of observable outcomes.

Above all, we must resist the seductive idea that "everything is an illusion anyway," and therefore "nothing matters." This kind of *epistemological nihilism*—where the unreliability of perception becomes an excuse for disengagement—is not only unhelpful, but dangerous. It undermines trust, erodes consensus, and can paralyze decision-making, both in public policy and personal life (Boghossian, 2006; Sokal & Bricmont, 1998).

Instead, the proper response is *epistemic vigilance*: to proceed with care, to treat conclusions as tentative, and to continually test our assumptions against evidence and alternative viewpoints (Mercier & Sperber, 2011).

To sum up then, illusions are not glitches in an otherwise accurate system. They are features of a mind evolved to prioritize coherence and efficiency over perfect accuracy. As such, they serve as a powerful lens—perhaps our clearest—into the brain's hidden algorithms for making sense of a chaotic world. We work with the minds and senses we have—not perfect, but remarkably capable when combined through collective practices of inquiry:

Science is not a mirror of truth, but a process for correcting error.

And while illusions reveal the limits of the individual mind, they also highlight the strength of shared, *self-correcting systems*. We do as well as we can with what we have—and by acknowledging our limitations, we improve our chances of getting closer to what is real.

Illusions remind us that perception is shaped more by evolved shortcuts than by objective accuracy. These same mental shortcuts extend beyond vision to how we judge ourselves and others, often inflating our sense of competence. This brings us to one of the most persistent and consequential cognitive biases: overconfidence. While we have touched on it earlier, understanding why it endures requires a closer look at its evolutionary roots.

3.7.3 Overconfidence and Risk

Humans tend to believe they are better, smarter, and more capable than they really are. This is not merely a personal flaw, but a near-universal cognitive bias—what psychologists call *overconfidence* (Moore & Healy, 2008; Parker & Fischhoff, 2005). Most people think they are less biased than others, more rational, and more competent than average—a phenomenon known as the "*better-than-average effect.*" Even when confronted with contradictory evidence, we often persist in our inflated self-assessments.

From an evolutionary perspective, this tendency is not entirely irrational. In ancestral environments, confidence—whether accurate or not—may have conferred clear survival and reproductive advantages. Confident individuals were more likely to take initiative, pursue opportunities, and assert leadership roles. These traits often increased visibility, status, and ultimately mating success (Johnson & Fowler, 2011). Thus, while overconfidence sometimes leads to poor decisions, the evolutionary payoff from occasional boldness likely outweighed the cost of occasional failure.

Risk-taking, particularly in young males, follows a similar pattern. Men are consistently more likely than women to engage in behaviors that are physically dangerous, socially provocative, or economically risky (Byrnes et al., 1999). These actions can, as we have said earlier, signal strength, bravery, or resource access—qualities that ancestral females may have found attractive when choosing mates (Wilson & Daly, 1985). Risky behaviors, in this view, are not maladaptive mistakes but part of an evolved strategy of *sexual selection*.

However, what may have worked in small-group, high-stakes environments doesn't always translate well to modern society. Today, overconfidence can drive financial speculation, political overreach, and poor health decisions. Research has linked overconfident judgments to failed military strategies, corporate collapses, and public trust breakdowns (Kahneman, 2011; Tenney et al., 2007). And yet, the bias persists because it is deeply embedded in our neural architecture, reinforced by social norms, and only weakly corrected by experience.

Cultural norms also influence how overconfidence is expressed. Some societies emphasize humility and collective harmony, which can temper displays of bravado. Others reward assertiveness and self-promotion. But while expression varies, the underlying cognitive tendency remains surprisingly stable across populations, pointing to a shared evolutionary foundation (Heine & Hamamura, 2007).

Importantly, recognizing overconfidence as a product of evolution—not a character defect—allows for institutional countermeasures. Peer review, scientific replication, regulatory oversight, and legal accountability are social mechanisms designed to contain our tendency toward overreach. These tools do not remove bias but help mitigate its consequences in complex societies.

Understanding overconfidence, then, helps reveal a larger pattern: the human mind prioritizes coherence and conviction over dispassionate accuracy. This is not a random flaw but an evolutionary feature; confidence helps motivate action and solidify group roles. Yet the same mechanisms that support action and status can just as easily reinforce error. This leads us naturally to a deeper bias that underpins much of our thinking: the tendency not just to feel sure of ourselves, but to actively seek out evidence that confirms our beliefs.

3.7.4 Confirmation Bias and the Comfort of Coherence

Among the most pervasive and consequential cognitive distortions is confirmation bias: the tendency to seek, interpret, and recall information in ways that reinforce our existing beliefs (Nickerson, 1998). This is not just a quirk of individual thinking; it operates at the institutional and disciplinary levels as well.

Let me be clear: what we humans typically do—if we are honest with ourselves—is not to begin from neutral observations and reason carefully toward conclusions. Rather, we start with convictions (whose origins are often obscure, shaped by culture, upbringing, or intuition) and then search for arguments to defend them when challenged. When confronted with opposing views, we instinctively marshal counterarguments in support of what we already believe, instead of weighing the evidence impartially. In other words, rather than reasoning like a classical syllogism—where one starts from explicit premises and arrives at a conclusion that is either valid or invalid—we often reverse the process, beginning with the conclusion and working backward to find premises that justify it (Kunda, 1990; Mercier & Sperber, 2011).

This pattern of reasoning is well known in both philosophy and psychology. In classical logic, it borders on *petitio principii*—begging the question—where the conclusion is smuggled into the premises rather than demonstrated from them. In cognitive science, it is more often described as *motivated reasoning* (Kunda, 1990), a process in which individuals start with a preferred conclusion and selectively search for or construct arguments that make it appear justified. The key difference from sound inference is that the direction of reasoning is reversed: instead of moving from observations to conclusions, we begin with convictions and work backward, rationalizing until the world seems to fit our beliefs. This tendency is not a rare defect of a few thinkers but a general feature of human cognition, visible in ourselves if we are honest enough to notice it.

In the social sciences, researchers are not immune. Confirmation bias can influence which hypotheses are tested, what data are deemed relevant, how results are interpreted, and which findings are published or cited. Fields can become trapped in paradigms that filter evidence through prevailing theories or ideological assumptions, making it harder to detect anomalies or entertain alternative explanations. In this way, even scholarly inquiry can become a mechanism for reinforcing shared narratives rather than challenging them, especially when reputational, funding, or career incentives reward conformity over dissent.

Rather than evaluating evidence impartially, humans are more likely to notice data that supports their views, dismiss contradictory facts, and favor arguments that echo their *prior convictions*. This bias operates largely unconsciously, shaping not just how we think but what we notice in the first place (Klayman, 1995).

We have all felt it at work. In many conversations people often seem less interested in understanding what you are actually saying than in figuring out who you are: What kind of person is this? What group do they belong to? Are they with us or against us? The response is not always based on the content of your ideas but on the perceived alignment of your identity. This instinct to map *social affiliations* before processing meaning is a powerful and deeply ingrained cognitive habit. It reveals how confirmation bias is not just about reasoning errors but also about social positioning and *in-group dynamics*.

Case in a Box: Conversations as Social Positioning

Many conversations—whether among colleagues, classmates, or casual acquaintances—are not primarily about exchanging ideas or discovering truth. Instead, they often serve an older, less conscious purpose: *social positioning*.

We tend to stay on the surface, listening less to what is being said and more to who is saying it, how they say it, and what that signals about their status, group identity, or social reliability.

There is something nervous—almost fearful—about this tendency. We often avoid deeper dialogue not because we have nothing to say, but because revealing what we truly think risks stepping outside the box we've been placed in—or have placed ourselves in. And outside the box, we might fall. We might be seen as less coherent, less valuable, or simply less relatable. In this sense, many conversations are not mutual explorations but quiet negotiations of worth.

Everyone, no matter how uninformed or biased, remains sovereign in their own mental territory—and that is the only ground that feels safe.

In these so-called conversations, most of what we do is spread out a kind of tapestry—an identity performance made of familiar stories, anecdotes, and recycled remarks. By the time we reach our 30s or 40s, much of this material has been used uncounted times, until it begins to feel more like ritual than actual communication or dialogue—no longer carrying real meaning or content, even for ourselves.

We rely on fragments that once earned us respect or laughs in previous groups, bits of humor we know tend to land well, and snippets of knowledge that give us a fleeting sense of credibility. These moves are not necessarily dishonest, but they are rehearsed. They are tools of self-preservation. And the content of this *identity-tapestry*, if we're honest, is often phlegmatic. Not wrong. Not offensive. Just not very curious. Not very alive or interesting.

In contrast stands the *exploratory dialogue* we could have had—spontaneous, imperfect, and animated by real humor and genuine curiosity. A form of conversation that helps us learn, not just about each other, but about the world. These moments are rare, not because people are incapable of them, but because our instincts and habits nudge us to play it anxiously safe. We stay within the familiar boundaries of performance and politeness—at least until alcohol sets in. This may help explain not only alcohol's widespread social acceptance, but its near-necessity in certain cultural settings, where it serves as a socially sanctioned permission slip for deeper, freer interaction.

Research shows that alcohol lowers inhibition by dampening activity in the prefrontal cortex, reducing self-monitoring and social anxiety (Sayette, 1993; Steele & Josephs, 1990). In many cultures, it plays a ritual role in facilitating bonding, mutual disclosure, and group cohesion (Dunbar, 2022; Heath, 2000). These social effects are powerful because, as Goffman (1959) and later Tice et al. (1995) observed, everyday conversation often becomes a performance—one governed by face-saving strategies, self-censorship, and status maintenance. Alcohol, for better or worse, momentarily suspends that performance and makes other kinds of interaction possible.

This tendency to stay on the surface—to perform rather than explore—isn't just cultural. It reflects something deeper in our evolutionary wiring. Humans are intensely social creatures whose survival historically depended on reading group dynamics, avoiding exclusion, and detecting social threats. In ancestral environments, the ability to sense who was trustworthy, competent, or dominant could determine access to protection, food, or mating opportunities. As a result, natural selection favored minds attuned not just to logic or truth, but to social awareness, signaling, and in-group cohesion (Cosmides & Tooby, 1992; Dunbar, 1998).

Importantly, much of what we call socialization—especially in same-sex groups—is oriented toward establishing a *temporary hierarchy*. Who leads, who listens, who can joke freely, and who remains cautious are often settled through subtle signals of confidence, knowledge, or humor. Evolutionary psychologists have shown that *status hierarchies* are a deeply ingrained part of human group dynamics, serving to reduce conflict, coordinate behavior, and distribute resources more efficiently (Buss, 2008; Cheng et al., 2010). Among men in particular, group interactions often revolve around implicit dominance negotiation, while among women, affiliation and inclusion tend to play a larger role, but both involve internal mapping of relative standing (Geary, 2010; Wrangham & Glowacki, 2012). These *micro-hierarchies* may dissolve after the encounter, but they shape the tone and limits of the conversation as long as the group remains intact.

Interestingly, the individuals who tend to be reinvited and integrated into these groups are not necessarily those who assert dominance, but those who manage to *signal warmth*, *harmlessness*, and *shared perspective*—often by laughing at the right moments, affirming others, or showing enthusiasm without competing for attention. Even children quickly learn that acting like a non-threatening supporter can secure social acceptance, especially when paired with emotional attunement or humor (Hawley, 2003). This behavior, which might seem deferential on the surface, can in fact be deeply strategic—what researchers describe as "*prosocial control*" or "*Machiavellian intelligence*" (Byrne & Whiten, 1988; Henrich & Gil-White, 2001). By appearing agreeable and non-threatening, such individuals avoid triggering resistance while still gaining influence—and a second invitation.

These instincts still shape us today. Take, for example, a group of fans meeting to watch a football match. On the surface, the setting permits expressions of loyalty, displays of enthusiasm, and knowledge about players. But beneath that, each participant is also checking the others—discreetly noticing tone, occupation, self-confidence, and behavior. The unspoken goal is to place each other on a map of social value. And by the end of the evening, little is known of anyone's deeper beliefs or personal history—only whether they were sympathetic, familiar, or safely "one of us."

This pattern is adaptive in some contexts, but it constrains dialogue. In a world of growing complexity, polarization, and noise, understanding these underlying dynamics is essential. Only by recognizing the instincts that drive us to stay shallow can we begin to resist them—and open space for genuine understanding.

This is especially important for children and adolescents, who often find social life confusing or emotionally draining. Understanding that many conversations are shaped less by shared interest and more by unspoken status signaling can help young people make sense of interactions that otherwise feel disappointing or false. It can also ease the frustration of feeling unheard or misunderstood.

In this way, science does more than discover abstract truths—it offers tools for navigating everyday life. It gives us language for what we feel but cannot quite explain. And that clarity can be liberating. It helps us take things less personally, to laugh more easily, and to see that many social tensions are not signs of failure, but features of how humans have evolved to relate. That insight doesn't just make us wiser—it makes life lighter, more optimistic, and, quite simply, more fun.

Questions for Reflection

1. Have you found yourself in conversations where people seem more interested in placing you socially than in engaging with what you actually think or feel? Please explain.
2. How often do your everyday discussions feel more like performances—repeating stories, jokes, or opinions you know will land safely—than real conversations? Be honest.
3. What role do setting, tone, or social norms (such as drinking or group loyalty) play in shaping what feels safe or appropriate to say?
4. Have you ever felt frustrated or disappointed after a social encounter, sensing that something deeper could have been shared—but wasn't? When was that?
5. How might recognizing the evolutionary and psychological roots of shallow conversation help you or your children experience social life with more clarity, humor, and freedom?

I also recognize that these questions are not just sensitive—they can feel a bit daring. In a classroom setting, it's entirely understandable if people hesitate to answer them openly. These are not easy topics to talk about, especially in front of others. But maybe that's all the more reason to at least answer them for yourself—in a journal, a private note, or simply in your own thoughts. Sometimes the most important conversations we have are the ones we have with ourselves.

These reflections also point to a broader dynamic: we rarely leave questions of identity and positioning untouched. Even when the topics feel too sensitive to voice aloud, we often carry them into our interactions in subtle ways. Social life is not just about where others place us, but about how we present ourselves and adjust to the impressions others may form.

We don't always accept this social positioning game passively. Sometimes, we respond in creative or strategic ways—especially when we sense that our ideas might be dismissed based on perceived identity. For instance, if I pick up that the people I'm speaking to see themselves as firmly left-leaning and are likely to categorize me as conservative—a label I am not comfortable with—I may choose to complicate that impression by introducing subtle cues. I might mention, for example, that my grandfather was a committed Stalinist—at least until the Soviet invasion of Czechoslovakia in 1968, a detail I sometimes leave out depending on the audience—or that my father was an active Marxist-Leninist, though only during his youth. I might even refer to the writings of Marx, an author read in my family home for generations much like others read the Bible, and whose ideas I became familiar with from childhood and can still appreciate—not least from the perspective of an economist.

All of this is technically true, and I'm not lying—but I am deliberately choosing what to highlight and what to leave unsaid. The goal isn't deception. It's a form of *bias correction*: a way of disrupting the narrative others may be starting to build about who I am.[10] By introducing a bit of ambiguity, I hope to open space for a more thoughtful and less reactive exchange—one where the conversation is judged on its substance, rather than filtered through assumptions about allegiance or ideology. When people can't easily place me in an ideological camp, they tend to pay more attention to the actual argument—rather than trying to fit me into a predefined box.

This instinct to manage impressions—and to strategically obscure or reveal identity cues—is not just a *rhetorical tactic*. It reflects an evolved sensitivity to group perception and social survival. In environments where alliances and threats had to be assessed quickly, signaling ambiguity could be as useful as signaling loyalty. Our ancestors didn't always need to be accurate, but they did need to be effective. And when reputational stakes were high, subtle social calibration became essential. Coherence, in this light, offered adaptive value; it supported confidence, motivated action, and aligned individuals with their groups (Tooby & Cosmides, 1992).

Moreover, social cohesion has historically increased the odds of survival. Humans are intensely social animals, and maintaining harmony within groups often trumps individual objectivity. *Shared beliefs*—regardless of their factual accuracy—can strengthen identity, foster trust, and coordinate group behavior (Boyer, 2001; Haidt, 2012). Dissent and ambiguity, by contrast, may provoke conflict or paralyze action. Thus, confirmation bias functions not just as a cognitive shortcut but as a mechanism of tribal alignment and narrative stability.

In other words, it's not only that we were not created as scientists—we were, in many senses, created as *anti-scientists*. Our cognitive architecture evolved not to seek dispassionate truth, but to survive, bond, persuade, and defend our worldviews. From a biological perspective, selective attention, tribal reasoning, and emotional coherence were far more useful than

[10] Another tactic I sometimes used was to play labor music from the 1960s and 1970s when we had guests. The music served a subtle purpose: it complicated the assumption that, as an economist who was not a declared Marxist, I must therefore be conservative.

detached objectivity. The very traits that make us socially effective—confidence, conviction, loyalty—can undermine our ability to question ourselves or change our minds:

> *Science, then, is not a natural mode of thought, but a cultural invention painstakingly built to counteract our natural tendencies.*

This evolutionary mismatch has real consequences. While the scientific method was designed to tame our biases, in practice those same biases infiltrate the very institutions meant to control them. In modern pluralistic societies, these tendencies don't just linger—they accelerate. It fuels polarization, ideological rigidity, and resistance to evidence-based reasoning (Sunstein, 2017). Social media amplifies this dynamic, creating *echo chambers* where individuals are rarely confronted with views that challenge their own (Pariser, 2011). In science, confirmation bias can distort research design, data interpretation, and even peer review, leading to false conclusions or delayed corrections (Ioannidis, 2005). The "*replication crisis*" in psychology and medicine is, in part, a testament to this phenomenon.[11]

The illusion of coherence also distorts memory. We are more likely to recall events that align with our worldview and forget those that do not—a distortion known as *consistency bias* (Ross, 1989). Even in the face of strong contradictory evidence, people often cling to disproven beliefs, a phenomenon termed *belief perseverance* (Anderson et al., 1980). These mechanisms make changing one's mind not only rare but cognitively and socially costly.

And yet, again, recognizing confirmation bias is not a reason for cynicism. It is a reason for method. Institutions like science exist precisely because individual cognition is limited and error-prone. Peer review, blind testing, devil's advocacy, statistical controls, and replication are not rituals; they are strategies to overcome evolved bias. These mechanisms do not eliminate distortion, but they narrow its influence and make progress possible.

[11] The "replication crisis" refers to the widespread finding that many published results in psychology and medicine fail to reproduce when studies are repeated. Large-scale projects such as the Open Science Collaboration (2015) showed that fewer than half of psychology studies replicated successfully, while Ioannidis (2005) argued that structural incentives in science—such as publication bias, small sample sizes, and flexible analysis—make false-positive findings surprisingly common. The crisis is not merely methodological but highlights the vulnerability of human research practices to the very cognitive biases they aim to study.

The human mind is not built for neutrality but for coherence, coordination, and survival. From perceptual illusion and overconfidence to confirmation bias and distorted memory, our cognitive architecture reflects *adaptive heuristics*, not *logical consistency*:

> *yet this does not render scientific or social knowledge invalid. rather, it makes their disciplined pursuit all the more important.*

Objectivity, properly understood, is not a default state but a collective aspiration. It is built not from perfect minds, but from flawed ones committed to self-correction.

For the social sciences in particular, this means acknowledging that our models and explanations are shaped by minds evolved for something other than truth. Still, through method, debate, and institutional safeguards, we can inch closer to it. The goal is not to transcend our humanity, but to better understand it, and in doing so, build knowledge that is both intellectually honest and socially accountable.

The implications of these traits extend far beyond individual behavior. Even science, our most deliberate tool for understanding reality, is shaped by the limits of human cognition. The final section reflects on how science is both our best hope—and a human institution vulnerable to our deepest biases.

3.8 Reasoning and Its Limits

When I was younger, I believed that once people learned to reason, they would naturally submit to better arguments and change their minds. But today it's clear that reason is rarely what truly drives belief or behavior. Instead, most people defer to power; employees follow employers, children follow parents, and even students follow the prevailing values of their institutions. This isn't just anecdotal: evolutionary social science shows that humans are inherently conformist, adapting beliefs to social norms because cohesion often beats dissent in our ancestral past (Henrich, 2015).

We don't evaluate each argument; we align with those we perceive as strong or prestigious, an effect thoroughly documented in social psychology (Cialdini & Goldstein, 2004). Even when free to choose, people maintain stable "positions"; beliefs rooted in upbringing, culture, and identity, and rarely update them through logic alone. Mercier and Sperber's *Argumentative Theory* argues that reasoning primarily evolved not to uncover truth, but to persuade and justify existing beliefs (Mercier & Sperber, 2011). That is, reason serves internal coherence and social signaling, not unbiased inquiry. Observers are sometimes stunned by how people continue to vote for the same political party even as its platform shifts dramatically or it elects leaders with fundamentally different values. But this behavior makes more sense when seen through the lens of identity-based cognition.

Case in a Box: Human Nature in Business

Let's pause for a moment and consider what these insights mean for someone running a business or managing a company. Imagine if leaders had no real understanding of how human beings actually behave—our motives, biases, and shortcomings. Suppose they assumed that if workers were paid, they would simply do their jobs, study the problems, and figure things out.

Anyone who has managed an organization knows that reality is not so simple. There are always "personal issues," or as engineers sometimes say, "people issues." Motivation, cooperation, conflict, and misunderstanding shape workplace outcomes just as much as technical skills or financial incentives.

This is why social science matters—not just for researchers, but for managers, entrepreneurs, and employees. What I am suggesting is that anyone working in organizations should learn about human nature in detail, ideally during their university studies, and perhaps even earlier. Yes, much can be learned through personal experience, but experience alone rarely provides a systematic understanding. By engaging with the scientific study of human behavior, leaders could anticipate common problems, set realistic expectations, and avoid costly mistakes.

It is striking, then, how little of this knowledge is systematically taught. Business students may hear the names of Kahneman and Tversky—whose work on decision-making biases earned a Nobel Prize in economics—but few sit down and read their book, and even fewer are asked to integrate its lessons into practice. This gap between what science knows and what managers are taught remains a missed opportunity for both business education and organizational life.

And of course, the problem is similar across the other social sciences—whether in political science, sociology, public administration, or even among the self-employed.

Questions for Discussion

1. What are the risks for organizations that rely only on pay and incentives without understanding deeper aspects of human motivation?
2. How do "people issues" complicate technical or financial solutions in a company? Can you think of real examples?

3. Why might universities hesitate to integrate more psychology, neuroscience, or evolutionary theory into business education?
4. In what ways could managers benefit from reading and applying behavioral science research (e.g., Kahneman & Tversky)?
5. How might organizations look different if leaders were systematically trained in the science of human nature?

The same lesson applies beyond the workplace. Whether in government agencies, universities, or the self-employed sector, decisions are shaped as much by human nature as by formal rules or rational incentives. Politics is no exception. Here too, behavior often reflects identity, loyalty, and deeply ingrained patterns rather than a straightforward weighing of facts or policies.

Political affiliation is often less about agreement with a party's current policies than about loyalty to a stable *social identity*—passed down through family, community, or class background. Studies in political psychology confirm that partisan attachment functions like a social identity: it is emotionally charged, resistant to change, and often predicts attitudes more strongly than ideological content (Green, Palmquist, & Schickler, 2002; Mason, 2018). In many cases, individuals maintain their voting behavior not because they support every new policy, but because "this is who we are." The goal is not necessarily to match belief with content, but to preserve the continuity of self and group membership—even when the party itself has changed. This helps explain why political reasoning often resists facts or policy shifts and why appeals to logic alone frequently fail to change minds (Achen & Bartels, 2016).

We see the same disregard for arguments even in academic settings. Universities, often idealized as bastions of rational deliberation, are shaped by political identity and moral values. Haidt (2012), for example, observes that the social sciences can become "tribal moral communities… less hospitable to dissenting views." Langbert, Quain, and Klein (2016) reported an estimated 11.5:1 Democrat-to-Republican ratio among professors across several key fields in the United States, suggesting an uneven ideological landscape. Some scholars have argued that such homogeneity may narrow the range of perspectives represented in research and teaching (Ioannidis, 2005), though the degree and implications of this imbalance remain debated and likely vary across disciplines and countries. While *academic freedom* formally protects inquiry, in practice researchers and educators sometimes find that presenting conclusions which diverge from prevailing views can meet with resistance in professional or classroom contexts.

Research on intelligence, genetics, or sex differences has frequently sparked controversy, even when published in reputable journals. This creates a paradox: while academic freedom formally protects inquiry, in practice the scope of what can be pursued or taught is often shaped by prevailing social and political sensitivities. Several well-known cases illustrate this dynamic. Arthur Jensen's 1969 article on IQ, Charles Murray and Richard Herrnstein's *The Bell Curve* (1994), and James Flynn's studies on rising global IQs all provoked intense debate and, in some instances, resistance within academic and public arenas. In Flynn's case, one of his books was even temporarily withheld from publication due to concerns it might be misinterpreted (Ferguson, 2018). These examples suggest that findings which touch cultural or political nerves may be publishable but are not always easily teachable. Yet we continue to speak of reason as though it guided our behavior and institutions without distortion—a comforting view that flatters our self-image more than it reflects reality.

Much like the belief in free will, the idea that we are governed by rational deliberation appeals to our desire for control, dignity, and moral autonomy. It paints us as agents rather than passengers. But research in cognitive science and psychology suggests otherwise. Most of our decisions are shaped by unconscious processes, gut reactions, and social influences long before reason enters the picture (Bargh & Chartrand, 1999; Haidt, 2001). As we remember, Libet's classic experiments, for example, showed that neural activity predicting an action can occur before the individual becomes consciously aware of the intention to act (Libet et al., 1983). These findings challenge the comforting narrative of conscious control and reasoned agency.

Instead, reason often functions post hoc—as a storyteller explaining actions already taken, rather than as the true initiator of thought or behavior (Gazzaniga, 2011). We may love the idea of rational agency because it grants us a noble self-concept, but the evidence suggests that much of what we attribute to reason is actually driven by deeper, less visible forces.

This situation is deeply frustrating for those who still see themselves as scientists; those who believe that rational debate, evidence, and the scientific method should be the ultimate arbiters of truth. After all, if open inquiry is not even possible within the university—the very institution designed to protect it—then where is it possible?

The inability to fully exercise reasoned argument, especially on sensitive or controversial topics, must be seen as a failure of the academic system. It signals that we have not built an environment robust enough to withstand ideological pressure.

Still, I would suggest to my colleagues who find themselves banging their heads against this wall to approach the situation—and human nature more generally—with a bit of distance and, why not, even a sense of humor, much as one might try to understand society by reading Balzac's *La Comédie Humaine*. The absurdities, contradictions, and vanities of society, including academic life, are, after all, and at least in part, part of a broader human comedy. And if things become too heavy—if the frustration turns into cynicism or despair—then it is not only wise but necessary to step back. Take time away from the academic environment. Spend a few hours in the garden, go for a long walk in nature, or take up embroidery, for all I know. These are not trivial escapes; they are ways to regain perspective and remember what matters. These are animals, and your brain is much better and deserves much better. There is not even any need to be surprised or disillusioned—this is who we are as humans. Expecting pure reason from a species evolved for storytelling, status, and tribalism is, frankly, a category error.

We see this trend more clearly today, as politically motivated research gains growing influence in certain segments of the social sciences. In many cases, activist agendas risk displacing the ideal of dispassionate inquiry (Honeycutt & Freberg, 2021; Lukianoff & Haidt, 2018). The focus shifts from understanding the world to morally reshaping it, often at the expense of empirical rigor. Yet this is not a wholly new development. History shows that ideological influence over scholarship tends to follow cyclical patterns. In earlier centuries, universities were not just influenced but often directly governed by religious institutions, with inquiry constrained by doctrinal boundaries. Today's ideological pressures may be softer, but they still pose challenges to intellectual openness.

So, what role does logic still play? Even in contemporary academic environments—where conformity and moral signaling can determine what gets published or taught—reason often serves to justify *group beliefs* rather than challenge them. In such settings, rationality becomes less a tool for discovery and more a means of signaling alignment. When norms dictate what counts as acceptable knowledge, even the scientific method risks being constrained by ideology. This is not a new problem, and history shows that such periods, while troubling, tend to pass. Sooner or later, curiosity reasserts itself, and those in power recognize that they cannot afford to waste time—they need genuinely curious people if society is to move forward.

The Russian writer Maksim Gorky (1868–1936) identified many of these flaws in the university system over a century ago. As a young man, he followed friends to the university cities but refused to enroll in any faculty himself. He distrusted formal education, believing that it dulled independent thought and reinforced social hierarchies. Instead, Gorky sought understanding through life experience—through his travels, through conversations with workers and vagabonds, and through the harsh jobs he took to survive. These experiences became the foundation for his autobiographical trilogy, particularly the volume titled *My Universities* (1923), where he reflects critically on institutional learning and praises the education found in everyday struggle and human interaction. Gorky believed that real knowledge came not from academic abstraction but from lived reality, a sentiment that still resonates. It remains one of my favorite accounts of what it means to truly understand human nature. My point here is that if the universities or schools you attend should cease to be the great places of learning they were built to be, you can always "do a Gorky" and become an autodidact. I did so myself for one year—the first year I arrived in Paris—spending most of my time in different libraries reading. I can honestly say I have never learned so much, either before or since.

For the ambitious social science researcher, this is a frustrating and consequential dilemma. Our methods are designed to pursue objectivity, yet we operate within institutions where subjective and political pressures often shape what questions can be asked, how findings are interpreted, and which voices are amplified. Rational arguments rarely speak for themselves, they must pass through a terrain of norms, incentives, and unspoken rules. In such an environment, the ideal of academic freedom can appear more fragile than many are willing to admit.

Some, when these tensions become too great, turn to the most radical solution: leaving the traditional university system. That impulse has historical roots. In 1409, a group of German scholars left the University of Prague to found the University of Leipzig, seeking greater freedom to teach and think. More recently, the creation of the University of Austin in Texas (UATX)—where historian Niall Ferguson has played a central role—reflects similar concerns. Disillusioned with what they saw as ideological orthodoxy and political pressures at elite institutions like Harvard and Stanford, Ferguson and others sought to build a new space for open inquiry. He argued that the existing academic system had become too rigid and politicized to reform from within (Ferguson, 2021).

While building entirely new institutions may sometimes be necessary, it remains a last resort. In most cases, it is still possible—and often wiser—to find ways of working within existing systems, flawed as they may be. The fact that political waves tend to move in cycles creates an opening: if you can endure the current, you might outlast the storm. After all, science has always coexisted with politics and power. Universities have never been insulated from external influence. What matters is whether we can safeguard the conditions for curiosity, critique, and truth-seeking—even when those very conditions are under pressure.

Wrapping up.

The chapters to come will explore less dramatic paths: how researchers might protect intellectual independence within existing institutions, how new tools like AI and open science may offer fresh avenues for credibility and collaboration, and how we might gradually shift the culture of knowledge production toward greater transparency and pluralism. These are not silver bullets, and the structural pressures are real. But the hope is that, by better understanding our constraints, we may also find new ways to navigate them.

In this evolution, even when traditional structures resist reform, new pathways emerge. Because science is not just a method—it is humanity's way of making sense of a chaotic world. It is also, in a real sense, our collective destiny. Ultimately, understanding perception is not merely about exposing illusions—it is about confronting the limits of the human condition. We were shaped by evolution to act, not to understand. Our brains prioritize survival over precision, narrative over nuance, and group cohesion over independent thought. These adaptations can mislead us. Yet precisely because we are prone to error, we have also created corrective tools: ethics, institutions, education, and science itself.

Now, after all these pages cataloging how biases distort our reasoning, how conformity bends inquiry, and how ideology narrows even academic freedom, one question must be asked: if humans are this limited, why not entrust more of the task of reasoning to machines? This is part of the larger argument of this book. Because we are not particularly skilled at the "sapiens" part—our claim to wisdom—the rational project may be better served by systems less entangled in the tribal instincts and identity commitments that derail human judgment. Artificial intelligence is not free of problems, but it does not tire, flatter its own ego, or cling to partisan identities. Where our species falters in objectivity, AI may be capable of carrying the load of systematic reasoning, data synthesis, and logical consistency.

That does not mean the human role disappears. What remains uniquely ours—empathy, contextual awareness, moral judgment, and care—are precisely those qualities machines cannot yet replicate. If we accept that reason has limits, then our task is not to deny those limits but to design a division of labor: AI for analysis and computation, humans for meaning, values, and coexistence. The paradox of our age is that the machines may finally realize the rational aspirations we have always claimed for ourselves, while our future as a species may depend on cultivating the very traits that have long seemed less "scientific"—trust, virtue, and social intelligence.

In short, this chapter has shown how human thought is not just rational calculation but an evolved mix of instincts, biases, and flexible learning. The next chapter turns outward: from the architecture of the mind to the architecture of culture—how language, belief systems, and institutions scale these individual capacities into shared meaning and collective life.

References

Achen, C. H., & Bartels, L. M. (2016). *Democracy for realists: Why elections do not produce responsive government*. Princeton University Press.

Aguilar, F. J. (1967). *Scanning the business environment*. Macmillan.

Alexander, R. (2010). *Children, their world, their education: Final report and recommendations of the Cambridge Primary Review*. Routledge.

Ambady, N., & Rosenthal, R. (1992). Thin slices of expressive behavior as predictors of interpersonal consequences: A meta-analysis. *Psychological Bulletin, 111*(2), 256–274. https://doi.org/10.1037/0033-2909.111.2.256

Anderson, C. A., Lepper, M. R., & Ross, L. (1980). Perseverance of social theories: The role of explanation in the persistence of discredited information. *Journal of Personality and Social Psychology, 39*(6), 1037–1049.

Ando, C. (2000). *Imperial ideology and provincial loyalty in the Roman Empire*. University of California Press.

Ando, C. (2011). *Law, language, and empire in the Roman Tradition*. University of Pennsylvania Press.

Archer, J. (1997). Why do people love their pets? *Evolution and Human Behavior, 18*(4), 237–259.

Arendt, H. (1951). *The origins of totalitarianism*. Harcourt.

Ariely, D. (2008). *Predictably irrational: The hidden forces that shape our decisions*. HarperCollins.

Bandura, A. (1977). *Social learning theory*. Prentice-Hall.

Bandura, A. (1999). Moral disengagement in the perpetration of inhumanities. *Personality and Social Psychology Review, 3*(3), 193–209.

Bargh, J. A., & Chartrand, T. L. (1999). The unbearable automaticity of being. *American Psychologist, 54*(7), 462–479.

Barrett, L. (2011). *Beyond the brain: How body and environment shape animal and human minds*. Princeton University Press.

Bartal, I. B. A., Decety, J., & Mason, P. (2011). Empathy and pro-social behavior in rats. *Science, 334*(6061), 1427–1430.

Bastian, B., Loughnan, S., Haslam, N., & Radke, H. R. (2012). Don't mind meat? The denial of mind to animals used for human consumption. *Personality and*

Social Psychology Bulletin, 38(2), 247–256. https://doi.org/10.1177/0146167211424291

Batson, C. D., Early, S., & Salvarani, G. (1997). Perspective taking: Imagining how another feels versus imagining how you would feel. *Personality and Social Psychology Bulletin, 23*(7), 751–758. https://doi.org/10.1177/0146167297237008

Beck, J. S. (2011). *Cognitive Behavior Therapy: Basics and beyond* (2nd ed.). Guilford Press.

Becker, H. S. (1982). *Art worlds*. University of California Press.

Bekoff, M., & Pierce, J. (2009). *Wild justice: The moral lives of animals*. University of Chicago Press.

Berg, J., Dickhaut, J., & McCabe, K. (1995). Trust, reciprocity, and social history. *Games and Economic Behavior, 10*(1), 122–142.

Belpaeme, T., Kennedy, J., Ramachandran, A., Scassellati, B., & Tanaka, F. (2018). Social robots for education: A review. *Science Robotics, 3*(21), eaat5954. https://doi.org/10.1126/scirobotics.aat5954

Bicchieri, C. (2006). *The grammar of society: The nature and dynamics of social norms*. Cambridge University Press.

Bloom, P. (2016). *Against empathy: The case for rational compassion*. Ecco.

Boghossian, P. (2006). *Fear of knowledge: Against relativism and constructivism*. Oxford University Press.

Bowler, P. J. (2003). *Evolution: The history of an idea (3rd ed.)*. University of California Press.

Bowler, P. J. (2009). *Evolution: The history of an idea (4th ed.)*. University of California Press.

Bowlby, J. (1982). Attachment and loss: Vol. 1. Attachment (2nd ed.). *Basic Books*. (Original work published 1969)

Boyer, P. (2001). *Religion explained: The evolutionary origins of religious thought*. Basic Books.

Boyd, R., & Richerson, P. J. (1985). *Culture and the evolutionary process*. University of Chicago Press.

Bratman, G. N., Hamilton, J. P., & Daily, G. C. (2015). The impacts of nature experience on human cognitive function and mental health. *Annals of the New York Academy of Sciences, 1249*(1), 118–136.

Brewer, N., & Wells, G. L. (2011). Eyewitness identification. *Current Directions in Psychological Science, 20*(1), 24–27. https://doi.org/10.1177/0963721410389169

Broom, D. M. (2007). Cognitive ability and sentience: Which aquatic animals should be protected? *Diseases of Aquatic Organisms, 75*(2), 99–108.

Brown, K. W., & Ryan, R. M. (2003). The benefits of being present: Mindfulness and its role in psychological well-being. *Journal of Personality and Social Psychology, 84*(4), 822–848. https://doi.org/10.1037/0022-3514.84.4.822

Brown, P., & Levinson, S. C. (1987). *Politeness: Some universals in language usage* (Vol. 4). Cambridge University Press.

Bshary, R., & Grutter, A. S. (2002). Asymmetric cheating opportunities and partner control in a cleaner fish mutualism. *Animal Behaviour, 63*(3), 547–555.
Buss, D. M. (2008). *Evolutionary psychology: The new science of the mind (3rd ed.).* Pearson.
Buss, D. M., & Duntley, J. D. (2008). Adaptations for exploitation. *Group Dynamics: Theory, Research, and Practice, 12*(1), 53–62.
Byrne, R. W., & Whiten, A. (Eds.). (1988). *Machiavellian intelligence*. Oxford University Press.
Byrnes, J. P., Miller, D. C., & Schafer, W. D. (1999). Gender differences in risk taking: A meta-analysis. *Psychological Bulletin, 125*(3), 367–383.
Chagnon, N. A. (1988). *Yanomamö: The fierce people* (3rd ed.). Holt, Rinehart and Winston.
Chalmers, D. J. (1995). Facing up to the problem of consciousness. *Journal of Consciousness Studies, 2*(3), 200–219.
Cheng, J. T., Tracy, J. L., & Henrich, J. (2010). Pride and social status. *Evolution and Human Behavior, 31*(5), 334–347.
Chimpanzee Sequencing and Analysis Consortium. (2005). Initial sequence of the chimpanzee genome. *Nature, 437*(7055), 69–87.
Chomsky, N. (1965). *Aspects of the theory of syntax*. MIT Press.
Cialdini, R. B., & Goldstein, N. J. (2004). Social influence. *Annual Review of Psychology, 55*, 591–621.
Clark, A. (2013). *Surfing uncertainty*. Oxford University Press.
Clayton, S., & Myers, G. (2009). *Conservation psychology*. Wiley-Blackwell.
Colangelo, N., Assouline, S. G., & Gross, M. U. M. (2004). *A nation deceived*. University of Iowa.
Comaroff, J., & Comaroff, J. (1991). *Of revelation and revolution: Christianity, colonialism, and consciousness in South Africa* (Vol. 1). University of Chicago Press.
Compagno, L. J. V. (2001). *Sharks of the world: An annotated and illustrated catalogue of shark species known to date*. FAO.
Cooley, C. H. (1902). *Human nature and the social order*. Scribner.
Corlett, P. R., Frith, C. D., & Fletcher, P. C. (2009). Bayesian models of psychosis. *Psychopharmacology, 206*(4), 515–530
Cosmides, L., & Tooby, J. (1992). The psychological foundations of culture. In *The adapted mind* (pp. 19–136). Oxford University Press.
Cosmides, L., & Tooby, J. (2005). Neurocognitive adaptations for social exchange. In *Handbook of evolutionary psychology* (pp. 584–627). Wiley.
Csikszentmihalyi, M. (1996). *Creativity: Flow and the psychology of discovery and invention.* Harper Perennial.
Cummins, R., & Gold, M. (2008). The organic integrity crisis. *Organic Consumers Association.*
Darwin, E. (1794–1796). Zoonomia. J. Johnson.
Darwin, C. (1871). *The descent of man.* John Murray.
Dawkins, R. (1976). *The selfish gene*. Oxford University Press.

Dawkins, R. (1986). *The blind watchmaker: Why the evidence of evolution reveals a universe without design*. W. W. Norton & Company.
De Backer, C. J. S., & Hudders, L. (2015). Meat morals: Relationship between meat consumption and moral attitudes. *Appetite, 91*, 114–120.
Decety, J., & Jackson, P. L. (2004). The functional architecture of human empathy. *Behavioral and Cognitive Neuroscience Reviews, 3*(2), 71–100. https://doi.org/10.1177/1534582304267187
Decety, J., Michalska, K. J., & Kinzler, K. D. (2010). The contribution of emotion and cognition to moral sensitivity: A neurodevelopmental study. *Cerebral Cortex, 22*(1), 209–220.
Dedijer, S. (1968). *Social intelligence: Its history and prospects*. Research Policy Institute, Lund University.
Dedijer, S. (1979). *Social intelligence for decision-making*. Research Policy Institute, Lund University.
De Roover, R. (1966). *The rise and decline of the Medici Bank, 1397–1494*. Harvard University Press.
de Waal, F. B. M. (1996). *Good natured*. Harvard University Press.
de Waal, F. (2006). *Primates and philosophers*. Princeton University Press.
de Waal, F. (2008). Putting the altruism back into altruism: The evolution of empathy. *Annual Review of Psychology, 59*, 279–300.
de Waal, F. (2009). *The age of empathy: Nature's lessons for a kinder society*. Harmony Books.
de Waal, F. (2013). *The Bonobo and the atheist*. Norton.
de Waal, F. (1982). *Chimpanzee politics: Power and sex among apes*. Harper & Row.
de Waal, F. B. M. (2000). Primates—A natural heritage of conflict resolution. *Science, 289*(5479), 586–590. https://doi.org/10.1126/science.289.5479.586
de Waal, F. B. M., & Lanting, F. (1997). *Bonobo: The forgotten ape*. University of California Press.
Deci, E. L., & Ryan, R. M. (2000). The "what" and "why" of goal pursuits: Human needs and the self-determination of behavior. *Psychological Inquiry, 11*(4), 227–268.
Denny, B. T., et al. (2012). Self vs. other judgments. *NeuroImage, 60*(2), 1621–1629.
Diehl, M., Hastings, C. T., & Stanton, J. M. (2001). Self-concept differentiation across the adult life span. *Psychology and Aging, 16*(4), 643–654. https://doi.org/10.1037/0882-7974.16.4.643
Dimberg, U., et al. (2000). Unconscious facial reactions. *Psychological Science, 11*(1), 86–89.
Duckworth, A. L., & Seligman, M. E. P. (2005). Self-discipline vs IQ. *Psychological Science, 16*(12), 939–944.
Dunbar, R. I. M. (1998). The social brain hypothesis. *Evolutionary Anthropology, 6*(5), 178–190.
Dunbar, R. I. M. (2022). Friends, bonding, and the role of alcohol. *Adaptive Human Behavior and Physiology, 8*, 293–308.

Durkheim, É. (1995). *The elementary forms of religious life*. Free Press. (Original work published 1912).
Eisenberg, N., Spinrad, T. L., & Sadovsky, A. (2006). Empathy-related responding in children. In M. Killen & J. Smetana (Eds.), *Handbook of moral development* (pp. 517–549). Lawrence Erlbaum Associates.
Ekman, P. (2003). *Emotions revealed*. Times Books.
European Parliament. (2017). *Report with recommendations to the Commission on Civil Law Rules on Robotics (2015/2103(INL))*.
Fehr, E., & Gächter, S. (2002). Altruistic punishment in humans. *Nature, 415*(6868), 137–140. https://doi.org/10.1038/415137a
Fessler, D. M. T., & Haley, K. J. (2003). Emotions in cooperation. In *Genetic and cultural evolution of cooperation* (pp. 7–36). MIT Press.
Flyvbjerg, B. (2001). *Making social science matter: Why social inquiry fails and how it can succeed again*. Cambridge University Press.
Friedmann, E., & Son, H. (2009). The human–companion animal bond: How humans benefit. *Veterinary Clinics of North America: Small Animal Practice, 39*(2), 293–326. https://doi.org/10.1016/j.cvsm.2008.10.015
Frith, C. D. (2007). *Making up the mind*. Blackwell.
Frith, C. D. (2012). The psychology of volition. *Nature Reviews Neuroscience, 13*(2), 109–115. https://doi.org/10.1038/nrn3153
Frederick, S. (2005). Cognitive reflection and decision making. *Journal of Economic Perspectives, 19*(4), 25–42.
Friston, K. (2010). The free-energy principle. *Nature Reviews Neuroscience, 11*(2), 127–138.
Fourcade, M. (2009). *Economists and societies*. Princeton University Press.
Fukuyama, F. (1995). *Trust*. Free Press.
Fukuyama, F. (2018). *Identity*. Farrar, Straus and Giroux.
Gallese, V. (2003). The roots of empathy. *Psychopathology, 36*(4), 171–180.
Gazzaniga, M. S. (2011). *Who's in charge?* HarperCollins.
Geary, D. C. (2010). *Male, female*. APA.
Gerbault, P., et al. (2011). Lactase persistence. *Philosophical Transactions B, 366*, 863–877.
Geirhos, R., et al. (2020). Shortcut learning. *Nature Machine Intelligence, 2*(11), 665–673.
Gigerenzer, G. (2000). *Adaptive thinking: Rationality in the real world*. Oxford University Press.
Gigerenzer, G., & Gaissmaier, W. (2011). Heuristics. *Annual Review of Psychology, 62*, 451–482.
Gigerenzer, G., & Selten, R. (Eds.). (2001). *Bounded rationality*. MIT Press.
Ginsburg, S., & Jablonka, E. (2019). *The evolution of the sensitive soul*. MIT Press.
Glocker, M. L., Langleben, D. D., Ruparel, K., Loughead, J. W., Gur, R. C., & Sachser, N. (2009). Baby schema in infant faces induces cuteness perception and motivation for caretaking in adults. *Ethology, 115*(3), 257–263. https://doi.org/10.1111/j.1439-0310.2008.01603.x

Goffman, E. (1959). *The presentation of self* . Doubleday.
Green, D. P., et al. (2002). *Partisan hearts and minds*. Yale University Press.
Guiso, L., et al. (2010). Civic capital. *Journal of Economic Perspectives, 24*(3), 147–166.
Gunkel, D. J. (2018a). *Robot rights*. MIT Press.
Goody, J. (2006). *The theft of history*. Cambridge University Press.
Gorton, G. (2010). *Slapped by the invisible hand: The panic of 2007*. Oxford University Press.
Gray, J. (2002). *Straw dogs: Thoughts on humans and other animals*. Granta Books.
Guhl, A. M. (1956). The social order of chickens. *Scientific American, 194*(1), 42–46.
Guiso, L., Sapienza, P., & Zingales, L. (2008). Trusting the stock market. *The Journal of Finance, 63*(6), 2557–2600.
Haack, S. (2007). *Defending science—Within reason: Between scientism and cynicism.* Prometheus Books.
Haidt, J. (2001). The emotional dog. *Psychological Review, 108*(4), 814–834.
Haidt, J. (2012). *The righteous mind*. Pantheon Books.
Haidt, J., & Joseph, C. (2004). Intuitive ethics. *Daedalus, 133*(4), 55–66.
Hall, J. A., Horgan, T. G., & Murphy, N. A. (2019). *Nonverbal communication.* De Gruyter Mouton.
Hamilton, W. D. (1964). The genetical evolution of social behaviour. I & II. *Journal of Theoretical Biology*, 7(1), 1–52. https://doi.org/10.1016/0022-5193(64)90038-4
Hanlon, R. T. (2007). Cephalopod dynamic camouflage. *Current Biology, 17*(11), R400–R404.
Hardin, R. (2002). *Trust and trustworthiness*. Russell Sage Foundation.
Harper, K. (2017). *The fate of Rome: Climate, disease, and the end of an empire.* Princeton University Press.
Harris, P. L. (2006). Social cognition. In *Handbook of child psychology*. Wiley.
Harris, S. (2012). *Free will*. Free Press
Harris, L. T., & Fiske, S. T. (2006). Dehumanizing the lowest of the low: Neuroimaging responses to extreme out-groups. *Psychological Science, 17*(10), 847–853.
Hattie, J. (2009). *Visible learning*. Routledge.
Hawley, P. H. (2003). Resource control. *Merrill-Palmer Quarterly, 49*, 279–309.
Heather, P. (2006). *The fall of the Roman Empire: A new history of Rome and the barbarians*. Oxford University Press.
Heine, S. J., & Hamamura, T. (2007). Self-enhancement. *PSPR, 11*(1), 4–27.
Henrich, J. (2015). *The secret of our success*. Princeton University Press.
Henrich, J., & Gil-White, F. J. (2001). Prestige. *Evolution and Human Behavior, 22*, 165–196.
Henrich, J., Heine, S. J., & Norenzayan, A. (2010). The weirdest people in the world? *Behavioral and Brain Sciences, 33*(2–3), 61–83.

Herzog, H. (2010). *Some we love, some we hate, some we eat: Why it's so hard to think straight about animals.* Harper.

Hodgson, G. M. (2019). *Is there a future for heterodox economics?* Edward Elgar.

Honneth, A. (1996). *The struggle for recognition: The moral grammar of social conflicts* (J. Anderson, Trans.). MIT Press.

Honeycutt, N., & Freberg, L. (2021). Politicization. *Academic Questions, 34*, 343–356.

Horowitz, A. (2009). *Inside of a dog*. Scribner.

Houpt, K. A. (2018). *Domestic animal behavior*. Wiley.

Hrdy, S. B. (2009). *Mothers and others: The evolutionary origins of mutual understanding*. Harvard University Press.

Hughes, T., et al. (2011). Theory–practice gap. *Management Learning, 42*(2), 123–139.

Hume, D. (1739/2000). *A treatise of human nature.* Oxford University Press.

Huntington, S. P. (1996). *The clash of civilizations.* Simon & Schuster.

Hölldobler, B., & Wilson, E. O. (2009). *The superorganism: The beauty, elegance, and strangeness of insect societies.* W. W. Norton & Company.

Ioannidis, J. P. A. (2005). Why most findings are false. *PLoS Medicine, 2*(8), e124. https://doi.org/10.1371/journal.pmed.0020124

Johnson, D. D. P., & Fowler, J. H. (2011). *Overconfidence. Nature, 477*, 317–320.

Kahneman, D. (2011). *Thinking, fast and slow.* Farrar.

Kahneman, D., & Tversky, A. (1979). Prospect theory: An analysis of decision under risk. *Econometrica, 47*(2), 263–291.

Kimmerer, R. W. (2013). *Braiding sweetgrass: Indigenous wisdom, scientific knowledge, and the teachings of plants.* Milkweed Editions.

King, P. M., & Kitchener, K. S. (2004). Reflective judgment: Theory and research on the development of epistemic assumptions through adulthood. *Educational Psychologist, 39*(1), 5–18. https://doi.org/10.1207/s15326985ep3901_2

Klayman, J. (1995). Varieties of confirmation bias. In J. Busemeyer, R. Hastie, & D. L. Medin (Eds.), *Decision making from a cognitive perspective* (pp. 385–418). Academic Press.

Klein, G. (1998). *Sources of power: How people make decisions.* MIT Press.

Knill, D. C., & Pouget, A. (2004). The Bayesian brain: The role of uncertainty in neural coding and computation. *Trends in Neurosciences, 27*(12), 712–719.

Korpela, K. M., & Hartig, T. (1996). Restorative qualities of favorite places. *Journal of Environmental Psychology, 16*(3), 221–233.

Kunda, Z. (1990). The case for motivated reasoning. *Psychological Bulletin, 108*(3), 480–498. https://doi.org/10.1037/0033-2909.108.3.480

Labouvie-Vief, G. (2009). Dynamic integration theory: Emotion, cognition, and equilibrium in later life. *Current Directions in Psychological Science, 18*(1), 10–15.

Lakoff, R. (1973). The logic of politeness; or, minding your p's and q's. In C. Corum, T. C. Smith-Stark, & A. Weiser (Eds.), *Papers from the Ninth Regional Meeting of the Chicago Linguistic Society* (pp. 292–305). Chicago Linguistic Society.

Lamarck, J.-B. (1809). *Philosophie zoologique*. Dentu.
Langbert, M., Quain, A. J., & Klein, D. B. (2016). Faculty voter registration in economics, history, journalism, law, and psychology. *Econ Journal Watch, 13*(3), 422–451.
Lavan, M. (2016). *Slaves to Rome: Paradigms of empire in Roman culture*. Cambridge University Press.
Lévi-Strauss, C. (1963). *The raw and the cooked* (J. Weightman & D. Weightman, Trans.). Harper & Row.
Levy, D. (2007). *Love and sex with robots: The evolution of human-robot relationships*. HarperCollins.
Libet, B., Gleason, C. A., Wright, E. W., & Pearl, D. K. (1983). Time of conscious intention to act in relation to onset of cerebral activity. *Brain, 106*(3), 623–642.
Lindenmayer, D. B., & Laurance, W. F. (2017). The ecology, distribution, conservation and management of large old trees. *Biological Reviews, 92*(3), 1434–1458.
Lisberg, A. E., & Snowdon, C. T. (2009). Effects of sex, social status and gonadectomy on countermarking by domestic dogs (Canis familiaris). *Animal Behaviour, 77(*3), 495–503.
List, C. (2019). *Why free will is real*. Harvard University Press.
Loftus, E. F. (1979). *Eyewitness testimony*. Harvard University Press.
Loughnan, S., Haslam, N., & Bastian, B. (2010). The role of meat consumption in the denial of moral status and mind to meat animals. *Appetite, 55*(1), 156–159. https://doi.org/10.1016/j.appet.2010.05.043
Loughnan, S., Haslam, N., & Bastian, B. (2014). The role of meat consumption in the denial of moral status and mind to meat animals. *Appetite, 72*, 89–95.
Lukianoff, G., & Haidt, J. (2018). *The coddling of the American mind:*. Penguin Books.
MacIntyre, A. (1981). *After virtue: A study in moral theory*. University of Notre Dame Press.
Macpherson, F. (2011). Introduction: Individuating the senses. In F. Macpherson (Ed.), *The senses: Classical and contemporary philosophical perspectives* (pp. 3–43). Oxford University Press.
Malek, J. (1993). *The cat in ancient Egypt*. University of Pennsylvania Press.
Malinowski, B. (1948). *Magic, science and religion and other essays*. Beacon Press.
Malthus, T. R. (1998). *An essay on the principle of population* (A. Flew, Ed.). Penguin Classics. (Original work published 1798).
Mann, M. (2005). *The dark side of democracy: Explaining ethnic cleansing*. Cambridge University Press.
Markus, H. R., & Kitayama, S. (1991). Culture and the self: Implications for cognition, emotion, and motivation. *Psychological Review, 98*(2), 224–253. https://doi.org/10.1037/0033-295X.98.2.224
Markus, H., & Nurius, P. (1986). Possible selves. *American Psychologist, 41*(9), 954–969.
Markowitz, H. (1952). Portfolio selection. *The Journal of Finance, 7*(1), 77–91.

Markus, H., & Wurf, E. (1987). The dynamic self-concept. *Annual Review of Psychology, 38*, 299–337.
Mason, L. (2018). *Uncivil agreement: How politics became our identity*. University of Chicago Press.
Matsumoto, D., Yoo, S. H., & Fontaine, J. (2008). Mapping expressive differences around the world: The relationship between emotional display rules and individualism versus collectivism. *Journal of Cross-Cultural Psychology, 39*(1), 55–74. https://doi.org/10.1177/0022022107311854
Mayr, E. (1988). *Toward a new philosophy of biology: Observations of an evolutionist.* Harvard University Press.
Mayer, F. S., & Frantz, C. M. (2004). The connectedness to nature scale. *Journal of Environmental Psychology, 24*(4), 503–515.
Montello, D. R. (2005). Navigation. In P. Shah & A. Miyake (Eds.), *The Cambridge handbook of visuospatial thinking* (pp. 257–294). Cambridge University Press.
McComb, K., Moss, C., Durant, S. M., Baker, L., & Sayialel, S. (2001). Matriarchs as repositories of social knowledge in African elephants. *Science, 292*(5516), 491–494. https://doi.org/10.1126/science.1057895
McDonald, L. G., & Robinson, P. (2009). *A colossal failure of common sense: The inside story of the collapse of Lehman Brothers*. Crown Business.
McGurk, H., & MacDonald, J. (1976). Hearing lips and seeing voices. *Nature, 264*(5588), 746–748.
McNicholas, J., Gilbey, A., Rennie, A., Ahmedzai, S., Dono, J. A., & Ormerod, E. (2005). Pet ownership and human health: A brief review of evidence and issues. *BMJ, 331*(7527), 1252–1254. https://doi.org/10.1136/bmj.331.7527.1252
Mead, G. H. (1934). *Mind, self and society*. University of Chicago Press.
Mech, L. D., & Boitani, L. (2003). *Wolves: Behavior, ecology, and conservation.* University of Chicago Press.
Mech, L. D. (1999). Alpha status, dominance, and division of labor in wolf packs. *Canadian Journal of Zoology, 77*(8), 1196–1203. https://doi.org/10.1139/z99-099
Mercier, H., & Sperber, D. (2011). Why do humans reason? Arguments for an argumentative theory. *Behavioral and Brain Sciences, 34*(2), 57–74.
Merilaita, S., Lyytinen, A., & Mappes, J. (2001). Selection for cryptic coloration in a visually heterogeneous habitat. *Proceedings of the Royal Society B, 268*(1479), 1925–1929.
Merilaita, S., Scott-Samuel, N. E., & Cuthill, I. C. (2017). How camouflage works. *Philosophical Transactions of the Royal Society B, 372*(1724), 20160341.
Mercier, H., & Sperber, D. (2011). Why do humans reason? *Behavioral and Brain Sciences, 34*(2), 57–74.
Merritt, A. C., Effron, D. A., & Monin, B. (2010). Moral self-licensing. *Social and Personality Psychology Compass, 4*(5), 344–357.
Meyer, M. L., Spunt, R. P., Berkman, E. T., Taylor, S. E., & Lieberman, M. D. (2012). Social working memory. *PNAS, 109*(6), 1883–1888.

Miller, G. F. (2001). *The mating mind: How sexual choice shaped the evolution of human nature*. Anchor Books.
Miller, E. K., & Cohen, J. D. (2001). Prefrontal cortex function. *Annual Review of Neuroscience, 24*, 167–202.
Milton, K. (2002). *Loving nature*. Routledge.
Mirowski, P. (2002). *Machine dreams*. Cambridge University Press.
Moore, D. A., & Healy, P. J. (2008). Overconfidence. *Psychological Review, 115*(2), 502–517.
Morey, D. F. (2006). Dogs and humans. *Journal of Archaeological Science, 33*(2), 158–175.
Munafò, M. R., et al. (2017). Reproducible science. *Nature Human Behaviour*, 1, 0021.
Nagel, T. (1974). What is it like to be a bat? *The Philosophical Review, 83*(4), 435–450.
Nass, C., & Moon, Y. (2000). Machines and mindlessness. *Journal of Social Issues, 56*(1), 81–103.
Ngo, R., Chan, L., & Mindermann, S. (2022). *The alignment problem from a deep learning perspective*. arXiv preprint
Nickerson, R. S. (1998). Confirmation bias: A ubiquitous phenomenon in many guises. *Review of General Psychology, 2*(2), 175–220. https://doi.org/10.1037/1089-2680.2.2.175
Nietzsche, F. (1994). *On the genealogy of morality* (C. Diethe, Trans.). Cambridge University Press. (Original work published 1887).
Nisbett, R. E. (2003). *The geography of thought*. Free Press.
Nisbett, R. E., & Ross, L. (1980). *Human inference*. Prentice-Hall.
Nozick, R. (1974). *Anarchy, state, and Utopia*. Basic Books.
Numbers, R. L. (2006). *The creationists*. Harvard University Press.
Nussbaum, M. C. (2001). *Upheavals of thought: The intelligence of emotions*. Cambridge University Press.
Olson, M. (1982). *The rise and decline of nations*. Yale University Press.
Open Science Collaboration. (2015). Reproducibility of psychological science. *Science, 349*(6251), aac4716. https://doi.org/10.1126/science.aac4716
Organisation for Economic Co-operation and Development (OECD). (2019). *PISA 2018 results*. OECD Publishing.
Organisation for Economic Co-operation and Development (OECD). (2023). *PISA 2022 results*. OECD Publishing.
Panksepp, J. (1998). *Affective neuroscience: The foundations of human and animal emotions*. Oxford University Press.
Parish, A. R. (1996). Female relationships in bonobos (*Pan paniscus*): Evidence for bonding, cooperation, and female dominance in a male-philopatric species. *Human Nature, 7*(1), 61–96. https://doi.org/10.1007/BF02733490
Pariser, E. (2011). *The filter bubble*. Penguin Press.
Parker, A. M., & Fischhoff, B. (2005). Decision-making competence. *Journal of Behavioral Decision Making, 18*(1), 1–27.

Parush, A., Ahuvia, S., & Erev, I. (2007). Degradation in spatial knowledge acquisition when using automatic navigation systems. *Human Factors, 49*(1), 1–11.

Park, B.-J., et al. (2010). Shinrin-yoku effects. *Environmental Health and Preventive Medicine, 15*(1), 18–26.

Piaget, J. (1952). *The origins of intelligence in children.* International Universities Press.

Piazza, J., Ruby, M. B., Loughnan, S., Luong, M., Kulik, J., Watkins, H. M., & Seigerman, M. (2015). Rationalizing meat consumption: The 4Ns. *Appetite, 91*, 114–128. https://doi.org/10.1016/j.appet.2015.04.011

Popper, K. (1959). *The logic of scientific discovery.* Hutchinson.

Porter, M. E. (1980). *Competitive strategy: Techniques for analyzing industries and competitors.* Free Press.

Porter, T. M. (1996). *Trust in numbers: The pursuit of objectivity in science and public life.* Princeton University Press.

Premack, D., & Woodruff, G. (1978). Does the chimpanzee have a theory of mind? *Behavioral and Brain Sciences, 1*(4), 515–526.

Prescott, J. E., & Miller, S. H. (2001). *Proven strategies in competitive intelligence: Lessons from the trenches.* Wiley.

Preston, S. D., & de Waal, F. B. M. (2002). Empathy: Its ultimate and proximate bases. *Behavioral and Brain Sciences, 25*(1), 1–20. https://doi.org/10.1017/S0140525X02000018

Pronin, E. (2007). Perception and misperception of bias in human judgment. *Trends in Cognitive Sciences, 11*(1), 37–43. https://doi.org/10.1016/j.tics.2006.11.001

Purves, D., Wojtach, W. T., & Lotto, R. B. (2011). Understanding vision. *PNAS, 108*(Suppl 3), 15588–15595.

Quine, W. V. O. (1960). *Word and object*. MIT Press.

Raghubir, P., & Krishna, A. (1999). Vital dimensions in volume perception: Can the eye fool the stomach? *Journal of Marketing Research, 36* (3), 313–326. https://doi.org/10.1177/002224379903600302

Ratnieks, F. L. W., & Wenseleers, T. (2008). Altruism in insect societies and beyond: Voluntary or enforced? *Trends in Ecology & Evolution, 23*(1), 45–52. https://doi.org/10.1016/j.tree.2007.09.013

Rawls, J. (1971). *A theory of justice.* Harvard University Press.

Reid, T. (1940). An inquiry into the human mind. *Thomas Nelson.* (Original work published 1764)

Risko, E. F., & Gilbert, S. J. (2016). Cognitive offloading. *Trends in Cognitive Sciences, 20*(9), 676–688.

Rizzolatti, G., et al. (1996). Premotor cortex and action recognition. *Cognitive Brain Research, 3*(2), 131–141.

Rizzolatti, G., & Craighero, L. (2004). The mirror-neuron system. *Annual Review of Neuroscience, 27*, 169–192. https://doi.org/10.1146/annurev.neuro.27.070203.144230

Roediger, H. L., & Butler, A. C. (2011). Retrieval practice. *Trends in Cognitive Sciences, 15*(1), 20–27

Rogers, C. R. (1959). A theory of therapy. In *Psychology: A study of a science* (pp. 184–256). McGraw-Hill.

Rosenthal-von der Pütten, A. M., et al. (2013). Emotional reactions to robots. *International Journal of Social Robotics, 5*(1), 17–34.

Ross, L. (1977). The intuitive psychologist. In *Advances in experimental social psychology* (Vol. 10, pp. 173–220). Academic Press.

Ross, M. (1989). Relation of implicit theories to the construction of personal histories. *Psychological Review, 96*(2), 341–357. https://doi.org/10.1037/0033-295X.96.2.341

Ruby, M. B. (2012). Vegetarianism. *Appetite, 58*(1), 141–150.

Sapolsky, R. M. (2005). The influence of social hierarchy on primate health. *Science, 308*(5722), 648–652. https://doi.org/10.1126/science.1106477

Sayette, M. A. (1993). An appraisal-disruption model of alcohol's effects on stress responses in social drinkers. *Psychological Bulletin, 114*(3), 459–476. https://doi.org/10.1037/0033-2909.114.3.459

Scheler, M. (1913). *The nature of sympathy*. Routledge.

Searle, J. R. (1980). Minds, brains, and programs. *Behavioral and Brain Sciences, 3*(3), 417–457.

Segall, M. H., Campbell, D. T., & Herskovits, M. J. (1966). *The influence of culture on visual perception.* Bobbs-Merrill.

Selman, R. L. (1980). *The growth of interpersonal understanding*. Academic Press.

Sen, A. (2009). *The idea of justice*. Belknap Press of Harvard University Press.

Serpell, J. A. (2003). Anthropomorphism and anthropomorphic selection—Beyond the "Cute Response." *Society & Animals, 11*(1), 83–100. https://doi.org/10.1163/156853003321618864

Sharkey, A., & Sharkey, N. (2010). The crying shame of robot nannies: An ethical appraisal. *Interaction Studies, 11*(2), 161–190.

Shweder, R. A., Much, N. C., Mahapatra, M., & Park, L. (1997). The "big three" of morality. In *Morality and health* (pp. 119–169). Routledge. Routledge.

Simon, H. A. (1990). Bounded rationality. In *Utility and probability* (pp. 15–18). Palgrave.

Singer, P. (1981). *The expanding circle*. Princeton University Press.

Singer, P. (2009). *Animal liberation.* HarperCollins.

Singer, T., Seymour, B., O'Doherty, J. P., Kaube, H., Dolan, R. J., & Frith, C. D. (2004). Empathy for pain involves the affective but not sensory components of pain. *Science, 303*(5661), 1157–1162. https://doi.org/10.1126/science.1093535

Sloterdijk, P. (2009). *You must change your life* (W. Hoban, Trans.). Polity Press.

Slovic, P. (2007). "If I look at the mass I will never act": Psychic numbing and genocide. *Judgment and Decision Making, 2*(2), 79–95.

Snyder, M. (1974). Self-monitoring. *Journal of Personality and Social Psychology, 30*(4), 526–537.

Sokal, A., & Bricmont, J. (1998). *Fashionable nonsense: Postmodern intellectuals' abuse of science*. Picador.

Sorkin, A. R. (2009). *Too big to fail: The inside story of how Wall Street and Washington fought to save the financial system—and themselves*. Viking.

Spence, C., & Gallace, A. (2011). Multisensory design: Reaching out to touch the consumer. *Psychology & Marketing, 28*(3), 267–308. https://doi.org/10.1002/mar.20392

Sober, E., & Wilson, D. S. (1998). *Unto others*. Harvard University Press.

Söilen, K. S. (2004). *Wirtschaftsspionage in Verhandlungen aus informationsökonomischer und wirtschaftsethischer Perspektive: Eine interdisziplinäre Analyse* (Doctoral dissertation). Blekinge Tekniska Högskola.

Söilen, K. S. (2021). Cyberpiracy and spoofing. *Competitive Intelligence Magazine*, 69–73.

Söilen, K. S. (2024). *Applied evolutionary economics: Insights from biology for real-world management*. Springer.

Soon, C. S., Brass, M., Heinze, H.-J., & Haynes, J.-D. (2008). Unconscious determinants of free decisions. *Nature Neuroscience, 11*(5), 543–545.

Sparrow, B., Liu, J., & Wegner, D. M. (2011). Google effects on memory: Cognitive consequences of having information at our fingertips. *Science, 333*(6043), 776–778. https://doi.org/10.1126/science.1207745

Steele, C. M. (1997). Stereotype threat. *American Psychologist, 52*(6), 613–629.

Steele, C. M., & Josephs, R. A. (1990). Alcohol myopia: Its prized and dangerous effects. *American Psychologist, 45*(8), 921–933. https://doi.org/10.1037/0003-066X.45.8.921

Stevens, M., & Merilaita, S. (2009). Animal camouflage: Current issues and new perspectives. *Philosophical Transactions of the Royal Society B, 364*(1516), 423–427.

Stoeckel, L. E., Palley, L. S., Gollub, R. L., Niemi, S. M., & Evins, A. E. (2014). Patterns of brain activation when mothers view their own child and dog: An fMRI study. *PLoS ONE, 9*(10), Article e107205. https://doi.org/10.1371/journal.pone.0107205

Stryker, S., & Burke, P. J. (2000). Identity theory. *Social Psychology Quarterly, 63*(4), 284–297.

Sunstein, C. R. (2017). *#Republic*. Princeton University Press.

Swann, W. B. (1987). Identity negotiation. *Journal of Personality and Social Psychology, 53*(6), 1038–1051.

Swann, W. B., et al. (2007). Self-verification. In *Advances in experimental social psychology* (Vol. 39, pp. 1–37). Academic Press.

Tan, J., & Hare, B. (2013). Bonobo sharing. *PLoS ONE, 8*(1), e51922.

Tanaka, F., et al. (2007). Toddler–robot interaction. *PNAS, 104*(46), 17954–17958.

Tangney, J. P., et al. (2007). Moral emotions. *Annual Review of Psychology, 58*, 345–372.

Taylor, R. P. (2006). Fractal art and stress. *Leonardo, 39*(3), 245–251.

ten Brinke, L., Stimson, D., & Carney, D. R. (2016). Some evidence for unconscious lie detection. *Psychological Science, 25*(5), 1098–1105. https://doi.org/10.1177/0956797614524421

Tenney, E. R., Logg, J. M., & Moore, D. A. (2007). (Over)confidence in judgment. *Annual Review of Psychology.*

Tice, D. M., Butler, J. L., Muraven, M. B., & Stillwell, A. M. (1995). Self-presentation. *Journal of Personality and Social Psychology, 69*(6), 1120–1138.

Tomasello, M. (2009). *Why we cooperate.* MIT Press.

Tomasello, M. (2016). *A natural history of human morality.* Harvard University Press.

Tononi, G., & Koch, C. (2015). Consciousness. *Philosophical Transactions B, 370*, 20140167.

Tooby, J., & Cosmides, L. (1992). The psychological foundations of culture. In J. H. Barkow, L. Cosmides, & J. Tooby (Eds.), *The adapted mind* (pp. 19–136). Oxford University Press.

Trivers, R. L. (1971). Reciprocal altruism. *Quarterly Review of Biology, 46*(1), 35–57. https://doi.org/10.1086/406755

Tullock, G. (2005). *The rent-seeking society.* Liberty Fund.

Turner, J. C. (1988). *Rediscovering the social group.* Blackwell.

Turkle, S. (2011). *Alone together.* Basic Books.

Vygotsky, L. S. (1978). *Mind in society.* Harvard University Press.

Vrij, A. (2008). *Detecting lies and deceit: Pitfalls and opportunities* (2nd ed.). Wiley.

Wada, K., et al. (2005). Robot-assisted care. *Proceedings of the IEEE, 92*(11), 1780–1788.

Wallace, A. R. (1858). On the tendency of varieties to depart indefinitely from the original type. *Journal of the Proceedings of the Linnean Society of London. Zoology, 3*(9), 53–62. https://doi.org/10.1111/j.1096-3642.1858.tb02500.x

Wallerstein, I. (1999). *The end of the world as we know it: Social science for the twenty-first century.* University of Minnesota Press.

Wallraff, H. G. (2005). *Avian navigation: Pigeon homing as a paradigm.* Springer.

Walker, D. B., Walker, J. C., Cavnar, P. J., Taylor, J. L., Pickel, D. H., Hall, S. B., & Suarez, J. C. (2006). Naturalistic quantification of canine olfactory sensitivity. *Applied Animal Behaviour Science, 97*(2–4), 241–254.

Waytz, A., et al. (2010). Anthropomorphism. *Perspectives on Psychological Science, 5*(3), 219–232.

Wells, C. (1999). *The Roman Empire* (2nd ed.). Harvard University Press.

Whitmore, T. C. (1998). *Tropical rain forests.* Oxford University Press.

Willis, J., & Todorov, A. (2006). First impressions: Making up your mind after a 100-ms exposure to a face. *Psychological Science, 17*(7), 592–598. https://doi.org/10.1111/j.1467-9280.2006.01750.x

Wilkinson, G. S. (1984). Vampire bats. *Nature, 308*, 181–184.

Willingham, D. T. (2009). *Why don't students like school?* Jossey-Bass.

Wilson, E. O. (2012). *The social conquest of Earth.* Liveright.

Wilson, E. O. (1975). *Sociobiology: The new synthesis.* Harvard University Press.

Wilson, E. O. (1984). *Biophilia.* Harvard University Press.

Wilson, M., & Daly, M. (1985). The young male syndrome: Why most violent criminals are young men. *Ethology and Sociobiology, 6*(1), 59–73.
Wilson, A. E., & Ross, M. (2001). Self-appraisal. *Journal of Personality and Social Psychology, 80*(4), 572–584.
Wiltschko, R., & Wiltschko, W. (2005). Magnetic orientation and magnetoreception in birds and other animals. *Journal of Comparative Physiology A, 191*(8), 675–693. https://doi.org/10.1007/s00359-005-0627-7
Wrangham, R. W., & Glowacki, L. (2012). Intergroup aggression. *Human Nature, 23*(1), 5–29.
Zak, P. J., Kurzban, R., & Matzner, W. T. (2004). The neurobiology of trust. *Annals of the New York Academy of Sciences, 1032*(1), 224–227. https://doi.org/10.1196/annals.1314.025
Zaki, J., & Ochsner, K. (2012). The neuroscience of empathy: Progress, pitfalls, and promise. *Nature Neuroscience, 15*(5), 675–680.
Zimova, M., Mills, L. S., & Nowak, J. J. (2016). High fitness costs of climate change-induced camouflage mismatch. *Ecology Letters, 19*(3), 299–307.

Further Readings

Arendt, H. (1963). *Eichmann in Jerusalem: A report on the banality of evil*. Viking Press.
Autor, D. H., Dorn, D., & Hanson, G. H. (2013). The China Syndrome: Local labor market effects of import competition in the United States. *American Economic Review, 103*(6), 2121–2168. https://doi.org/10.1257/aer.103.6.2121
Barrett, L. F., Mesquita, B., & Gendron, M. (2011). Context in emotion perception. *Current Directions in Psychological Science, 20*(5), 286–290. https://doi.org/10.1177/0963721411422522
Barry, B. (1973). *The liberal theory of justice: A critical examination of the principal doctrines in a theory of justice by John Rawls*. Clarendon Press.
Batson, C. D. (2011). *Altruism in humans*. Oxford University Press.
Bensky, M. K., Gosling, S. D., & Sinn, D. L. (2013). The world from a dog's point of view: A review and synthesis of dog cognition research. *Advances in the Study of Behavior, 45*, 209–406. https://doi.org/10.1016/B978-0-12-407186-5.00005-7
Bloom, P. (2004). *Descartes' baby: How the science of child development explains what makes us human*. Basic Books.
Bourdieu, P. (1988). *Homo Academicus*. Stanford University Press.
Buchanan, J. M., & Tullock, G. (1962). *The calculus of consent: Logical foundations of constitutional democracy*. University of Michigan Press.
Cialdini, R. B. (2009). *Influence: Science and practice* (5th ed.). Pearson.
Darwin, C. (1859). *On the origin of species by means of natural selection*. John Murray.
Gunkel, D. J. (2012). *The machine question*. MIT Press.
Gould, J. L. (2014). Animal navigation: The evolution of magnetic orientation. *Current Biology, 24*(9), R359–R361.

Hauser, M. D. (2006). *Moral minds: How nature designed our universal sense of right and wrong*. HarperCollins.
Henrich, J. (2020). *The WEIRDest People in the World: How the West Became Psychologically Peculiar and Particularly Prosperous*. Farrar.
Herman, E. S., & Chomsky, N. (1988). *Manufacturing consent: The political economy of the mass media*. Pantheon Books.
Hinton, G. (2023). On the dangers of AI: Reflections by a pioneer. *Nobel Symposium on AI Safety*. Stockholm, Sweden.
Huxley, T. H. (1863). *Evidence as to man's place in nature*. Williams & Norgate.
Janis, I. L. (1972). *Victims of groupthink: A psychological study of foreign-policy decisions and fiascoes*. Houghton Mifflin.
Keijzer, F. (2021). The philosophical challenge of artificial intelligence. *Minds and Machines, 31*(3), 365–389.
Keltner, D., & Haidt, J. (1999). Social functions of emotions at four levels of analysis. *Cognition & Emotion, 13*(5), 505–521.
King-Hele, D. (1999). *Erasmus Darwin: A life of unequalled achievement*. Giles de la Mare Publishers.
Klein, G. (2013). *Seeing what others don't: The remarkable ways we gain insights*. PublicAffairs.
Kosslyn, S. M., & Koenig, O. (1992). *Wet mind: The new cognitive neuroscience*. Free Press.
Lakoff, G. (2002). *Moral politics: How liberals and conservatives think* (2nd ed.). University of Chicago Press.
LeDoux, J. (1996). *The emotional brain: The mysterious underpinnings of emotional life*. Simon & Schuster.
Lohmann, K. J., Putman, N. F., & Lohmann, C. M. F. (2008). Geomagnetic imprinting: A unifying hypothesis of long-distance natal homing in salmon and sea turtles. *Proceedings of the National Academy of Sciences, 105*(49), 19096–19101. https://doi.org/10.1073/pnas.0801859105
Lorenz, K. (1963). *On aggression*. Harcourt Brace.
Marcus, G., & Davis, E. (2020). *Rebooting AI: Building artificial intelligence we can trust*. Pantheon.
Maslow, A. H. (1943). A theory of human motivation. *Psychological Review, 50*(4), 370–396.
Moll, J., et al. (2006). Charitable donation. *PNAS, 103*(42), 15623–15628.
Mlodinow, L. (2012). *Subliminal: How your unconscious mind rules your behavior*. Pantheon.
Mouritsen, H. (2018). Long-distance navigation and magnetoreception in migratory animals. *Nature, 558*(7708), 50–59. https://doi.org/10.1038/s41586-018-0176-1
Nisbett, R. E., & Wilson, T. D. (1977). Telling more than we can know: Verbal reports on mental processes. *Psychological Review, 84*(3), 231–259.

Norenzayan, A. (2013). *Big gods: How religion transformed cooperation and conflict*. Princeton University Press.
Ostrom, E. (1990). *Governing the commons: The evolution of institutions for collective action*. Cambridge University Press.
Pinker, S. (1997). *How the mind works*. Norton.
Pinker, S. (2002). *The blank slate: The modern denial of human nature*. Viking.
Pogge, T. (2007). *John Rawls: His life and theory of justice*. Oxford University Press.
Putnam, R. D. (2000). *Bowling alone: The collapse and revival of American community*. Simon & Schuster.
Quammen, D. (2008). *The reluctant Mr. Darwin: An intimate portrait of Charles Darwin and the making of his theory of evolution*. W. W. Norton & Company.
Sapolsky, R. M. (2017). *Behave: The biology of humans at our best and worst*. Penguin Press.
Sandel, M. J. (1998). *Liberalism and the limits of justice* (2nd ed.). Cambridge University Press.
Sartre, J.-P. (1943). *L'être et le néant [Being and nothingness]*. Gallimard.
Searle, J. R. (1995). *The construction of social reality*. Free Press.
Shankar, V., Carpenter, G. S., & Farley, J. U. (1999). The illusion of continuity: How marketers create and maintain brand loyalty. *Strategic Management Journal, 20*(4), 375–394.
Shettleworth, S. J. (2010). *Cognition, evolution, and behavior* (2nd ed.). Oxford University Press.
Simon, H. A. (1957). *Models of man: Social and rational*. Wiley.
Smith, A. (1759). *The theory of moral sentiments*. A. Millar.
Tajfel, H., & Turner, J. C. (1979). An integrative theory of intergroup conflict. In W. G. Austin & S. Worchel (Eds.), *The social psychology of intergroup relations* (pp. 33–47). Brooks/Cole.
Taylor, C. (1989). *Sources of the self: The making of the modern identity*. Harvard University Press.
Tenney, E. R., Logg, J. M., & Moore, D. A. (2015). (Too) optimistic about optimism. *Journal of Personality and Social Psychology, 108*(3), 377–399. https://doi.org/10.1037/pspa0000018
Trivers, R. (2011). *The folly of fools: The logic of deceit and self-deception in human life*. Basic Books.
Tversky, A., & Kahneman, D. (1974). Judgment under uncertainty: Heuristics and biases. *Science, 185*(4157), 1124–1131. https://doi.org/10.1126/science.185.4157.1124
Wansink, B., & Chandon, P. (2006). Can "low-fat" nutrition labels lead to obesity? *Journal of Marketing Research, 43*(4), 605–617.
Weber, M. (1905). *The Protestant ethic and the spirit of capitalism*. Allen & Unwin.
Wilmer, H. H., Sherman, L. E., & Chein, J. M. (2017). Smartphones and cognition: A review of research exploring the links between mobile technology habits and cognitive functioning. *Frontiers in Psychology, 8*, 605.

Zimbardo, P. G. (2007). *The Lucifer effect: Understanding how good people turn evil.*Random House.

Zuboff, S. (2019). *The age of surveillance capitalism: The fight for a human future at the new frontier of power*. PublicAffairs.

4

Culture and Society

Abstract Human minds do not operate in isolation. From birth, our thinking is shaped by language, symbols, norms, and institutions that bind individuals into coordinated societies. Chapter 4 moves from mind to meaning, showing how individual cognition scales into culture—and how culture, in turn, reshapes the mind. The chapter reframes culture not as habit or decoration, but as the **scaffolding of social life**: a layered system that synchronizes perception, belief, roles, knowledge, and decision-making. Introducing a clear model that traces the path from individual cognition to collective intelligence, it explains how language creates shared meaning, how norms and institutions stabilize cooperation, and how accumulated knowledge enables societies to think and act at scale. By presenting culture as a cognitive multiplier, this chapter reveals why human intelligence is fundamentally collective. Understanding this layered architecture is essential for explaining institutions, learning, coordination, and ultimately how complex societies endure, adapt, and survive.

In Chapter 3, we examined the roots of human behavior—from the architecture of the brain to the foundations of perception, bias, and morality. That discussion offered a view from the inside, focused on how the mind itself works. But cognition is never truly isolated. From the moment we are born, our thoughts are shaped by social environments, cultural codes, and shared systems of meaning. Earlier chapters introduced these broader contexts in passing; here we take them up more directly and in greater depth. This

K. Solberg Söilen, *The Researcher's Journey in the Age of AI*,
https://doi.org/10.1007/978-3-032-23069-0_4

Table 4.1 From individual mind to collective intelligence: a layered model

Layer	Focus	Mechanism	Examples
1. Cognitive Foundations	Individual cognition	Perception, emotion, memory, bias	Fast vs. slow thinking; empathy
2. Shared Meaning	Language, symbols	Communication, storytelling, rituals	Myths, narratives, education
3. Social Structures	Norms, roles, institutions	Role differentiation, enforcement, identity	Laws, professions, schools
4. Knowledge Systems	Accumulated knowledge	Teaching, writing, collective memory	Libraries, universities, archives
5. Collective Intelligence	Decision-making at scale	Deliberation, feedback loops, technology	Democracies, markets, science, AI

chapter moves from the inside out—from mind to meaning, from self to society.

We begin by reframing culture not as decoration or habit, but as the scaffolding of social life. Culture encodes shared expectations, transmits knowledge across generations, and structures how we perceive the world and act within it. The central question of this chapter is: How do individual minds, each shaped by biology and experience, synchronize into collective intelligence?

To answer this, we introduce a layered model that shows how personal cognition scales into broader systems of culture and coordination. From perception and language to belief, norms, institutions, and organized knowledge, the model illustrates how small-scale mental processes feed into the complex systems that govern human life (Table 4.1).

These five levels also organize the flow of the chapter:

- *Cognitive Foundations* form the background but are already covered in Chapter 3; here they provide the baseline for how language and belief operate. Sections 4.1 Language and Symbolism and 4.2 Belief Systems show how perception and memory feed into shared codes, from myths and rituals to clothing and impressions.
- *Shared Meaning* is developed further in the same sections, emphasizing how language, symbols, and rituals stabilize group identity.
- *Social Structures* are examined in Section 4.5 Social Architectures of Daily Life, where norms, roles, and institutions scale coordination beyond

kinship. Here the focus shifts from the macro to the micro: how individuals navigate daily life, how cultural rules shape meetings and relationships, and how even solitude and social fatigue reflect deeper layers of culture. Virtues at this level act as the glue that sustains institutions and provide direction when rules alone are insufficient.

- *Knowledge Systems* are addressed in Section 4.3 Learning in a Digital Era, showing how writing, education, and digital media preserve and transmit collective experience.
- *Collective Intelligence* culminates in Section 4.4 Institutions as Engines of Collective Intelligence, where accumulated knowledge, norms, and coordination are integrated into decision-making systems that operate at scale.

What emerges is a developmental sequence: basic cognitive capacities enable language; language creates shared meaning; shared meaning sustains social structures and virtues; social structures support the preservation of knowledge; and accumulated knowledge allows collective intelligence to flourish.

Each section of the chapter follows this hierarchy. We explore how shared meanings stabilize through language and ritual; how norms and roles provide social order; how knowledge is formalized, preserved, and transmitted; and finally, how all these elements culminate in complex systems of collective reasoning.

The result is a view of culture as a *cognitive multiplier*: a system that expands the range of what humans can think, feel, and do—together. By the end of the chapter, we will observe that the human mind is not simply a product of biology, but a node in a vast network of meanings and memories, roles and rules. Understanding this network is essential not just for social science, but for making sense of human survival and continuity.

4.1 Language and Symbolism

We have already touched on symbols in Chapter 1 as one of the five dimensions that distinguish humans from other species. There, the focus was broad: symbols as the glue of culture, the scaffolding of shared intentionality, and the foundation of collective meaning. In this chapter, the perspective narrows. Here, we return to symbolism not as a general category, but as embodied in its most powerful and universal form—language.

What separates human beings from other animals? While the list is long—tools, self-awareness, imagination—language remains perhaps the most fundamental and powerful difference. Through language, we construct not just communication, but culture itself: a shared repository of meaning, memory, and instruction. Unlike *genetic evolution*, which proceeds slowly through biological inheritance, *cultural evolution* accelerates learning across generations. It allows us to adapt through symbols, rituals, myths, and institutions.

Language is the backbone of this process. It is more than a tool for transmitting information—it is a cognitive scaffold that enables abstract thought, planning, storytelling, and identity construction. As Noam Chomsky (1965) proposed in his *theory of universal grammar*, humans are biologically predisposed to learn language, yet the specific language we learn profoundly shapes how we think. Research in linguistic relativity—sometimes referred to as the *Sapir-Whorf hypothesis*—suggests that language not only reflects but also structures thought (Boroditsky, 2011; Lucy, 1997). For example, speakers of languages that encode cardinal directions (like Guugu Yimithirr in Australia) navigate space differently than those who rely on egocentric terms (left/right).[1]

Certain languages may *support* different types of cognitive engagement, but no one language is absolutely "better" for thinking overall. Research shows that grammatical structure can influence how speakers attend to, categorize, and reason about information. For instance, Slobin (1996) proposed the idea of "thinking for speaking," suggesting that languages with rich *morphology*, like Russian or German, may encourage speakers to attend more explicitly to aspects such as case, gender, and aspect, potentially fostering more analytical habits during speech production. Similarly, Deutscher (2010) argues that the demands placed by certain grammatical systems may enhance mental attention to specific categories of thought, such as time, space, or agency. However, this doesn't mean those languages inherently make people more intelligent or capable of deeper thought; rather, they might train the mind to be more attuned to certain patterns or distinctions. Boroditsky (2011) also emphasizes that linguistic structures can shape habitual thought patterns, but always within a broader cognitive and cultural context. Thus, while complex grammar may promote particular cognitive routines, cognition is flexible, and thought is never entirely bound by language.

In contrast, while no single language offers a universal cognitive advantage, there is strong evidence that speaking multiple languages does confer distinct

[1] Research on Guugu Yimithirr, an Aboriginal language of Australia, shows that its speakers use cardinal directions (north, south, east, west) rather than egocentric terms (left, right). This linguistic habit shapes spatial cognition: speakers consistently keep track of absolute orientation, even in unfamiliar settings (Levinson, 2003).

benefits. Research on bilingualism and multilingualism shows enhanced cognitive flexibility, attentional control, and executive functioning compared to monolinguals (Bialystok et al., 2012). Constantly switching between languages requires managing interference, which strengthens the brain's capacity for task-switching and selective attention (Costa et al., 2008). Multilinguals also tend to exhibit greater *metalinguistic awareness*—a conscious understanding of language as a system—which supports problem-solving and learning in other domains (Jessner, 2008). Furthermore, long-term studies suggest that *bilingualism* can delay the onset of cognitive decline and dementia symptoms by several years, likely because of the mental "workout" required to manage multiple linguistic systems (Bialystok et al., 2007). Beyond cognition, multilingualism enhances cultural adaptability and perspective-taking, giving individuals broader access to different conceptual frameworks and social worlds (Grosjean, 2010). Taken together, these findings indicate that while language shapes thought in nuanced ways, the ability to navigate several languages provides measurable advantages for mental agility and lifelong cognitive resilience.

Taken together, multilingualism illustrates a broader truth: human cognition is not confined within individual minds but continually expanded through shared systems of communication. Just as multiple languages open access to diverse ways of framing the world, culture itself operates as an even larger cognitive scaffold. Culture can be seen as the accumulated "software" of a species with a uniquely plastic and programmable brain. It is a second form of evolution—faster, more flexible, and grounded in *collective learning* (Henrich, 2015; Tomasello, 1999). This cultural system allows us to transmit beliefs, values, practices, and expectations across individuals and across time. It enables humans to cooperate in large, anonymous groups—something no other species does on the same scale.

The emergence of writing marked a key turning point in this development. By externalizing memory and thought, writing enabled the formation of large-scale civilizations, legal systems, histories, and sciences (Goody, 1986; Ong, 1982). Once knowledge could be stored outside the brain, it could be reviewed, revised, critiqued, and expanded.

In this way, culture and cognition coevolve. What we think, how we think, and even what we are able to think are deeply influenced by the cultural tools and symbolic systems available to us. As Vygotsky (1978) emphasized, higher cognitive functions are mediated by cultural artifacts—especially language—learned through social interaction. Children do not discover culture; they are inducted into it through education, imitation, and communication.

Thus, human cognition is not merely a product of biology. It is inseparable from the cultural contexts in which it develops. Understanding humans as *meaning-makers* means understanding the intricate ways in which thought, language, and culture mutually reinforce and shape one another.

4.2 Belief Systems: The Hidden Architecture of Human Thought

While language provides the structure of thought, *belief systems* give it direction. Every human community—past or present—operates within a framework of shared beliefs, whether religious, political, scientific, or mythological. These belief systems do more than explain the world; they tell people who they are, what matters, and how to live. They shape values, guide behavior, and define the boundaries of legitimacy and deviance.

From an evolutionary perspective, belief systems serve adaptive social and psychological functions. They coordinate group behavior, reduce uncertainty, justify norms, and help individuals cope with fear, loss, and complexity. In unpredictable environments, shared beliefs reduce cognitive load by offering simplified rules of interpretation and action (Boyer, 2001; Norenzayan, 2013). Moral codes rooted in religion or ideology often bind people together by embedding cooperation within cosmological narratives that promise justice, belonging, or divine reward.

Crucially, however, belief systems are not limited to religion. This is a fundamental misunderstanding—particularly in secular societies, where belief is often equated with faith in the supernatural. In reality, non-religious individuals and institutions operate within belief systems just as surely. Nationalism, political ideologies, conspiracy theories, and even certain forms of scientism all function as belief systems. What they share is not a theological core but a psychological structure: emotionally charged, identity-defining narratives that resist falsification (Mercier & Sperber, 2017). What separates science from these other systems is not the absence of belief, but the presence of organized doubt and structured mechanisms for error correction.

Case in a Box: Beyond Religion—Belief Systems in Secular cultures

In societies with declining religiosity, such as Scandinavia, belief systems do not disappear; they shift into other domains. Sweden—described, quite correctly I think, by my professor of geopolitics in France, Joseph LeBihan, as "the Japan of Europe"—is often portrayed as one of the world's most secular countries, with low levels of church attendance and formal religious affiliation. Yet Swedish society operates within a powerful framework of shared beliefs, values, and narratives that are no less real than religious systems elsewhere.

These beliefs are tied to stories, symbols, and reference points that anchor identity:

- *Welfare state ideals*—belief in social solidarity, equality, and the state's role as guarantor of fairness.
- *Consensus and pragmatism*—trust in negotiation, compromise, and depoliticized problem-solving.
- *Environmental stewardship*—commitment to sustainability and harmony with nature.
- *Lagom and Jantelagen*—cultural norms emphasizing moderation, humility, and equality.[2]
- *Historical narratives*—neutrality during wars, social progress, and the "folkhemmet" (people's home) as a national ideal.
- *Geography and landscape*—forests, archipelagos, lakes, and long winters, all shaping metaphors of endurance, closeness to nature, and communal survival.
- *Symbols of modernity*—innovation in design, technology, and social policy, seen as markers of progress and identity.

Taken together, these elements are examples of a *secular belief system*: a way of orienting thought, behavior, and belonging around shared cultural codes. Just as religious societies use divine narratives, Sweden relies on civic myths, historical trajectories, and geographic references to stabilize meaning and foster collective identity. Recognizing this helps dismantle the illusion that only religious cultures "believe," while secular ones are purely rational.

[2] The concept of *Jantelagen* originates from the Danish-Norwegian author Aksel Sandemose's novel *A Fugitive Crosses His Tracks* (*En flygtning krydser sit spor*, 1933). Sandemose formulated ten satirical rules to capture how Scandinavian societies discourage individuality and enforce conformity. While the idea resonates across all Scandinavian countries, it is often said to be particularly influential in Sweden. The related Swedish concept of *lagom*—literally "just the right amount"—has older cultural roots, expressing ideals of moderation, balance, and communal harmony (Daun, 1996).

Many observers look at Sweden and notice the friendliness, which is indeed often striking.[3] But friendliness should not be mistaken for openness. The cultural barriers in Sweden are just as high—if not higher—than in many other countries. It is not very common, for example, for foreigners to be invited into Swedish homes. Conversations may be polite and cordial, but seldom extend deeper, unlike in places such as the United States where hospitality is often expressed through quick invitations.

Consensus, too, is not only highly valued but also tightly enforced. Once a political or cultural idea gains traction, it is often pursued to its logical extreme, whether the outcome is beneficial or not. This has produced moments of remarkable success, such as when Sweden built its industrial base with efficiency and coordination. Yet it has also led to difficulties, as in the integration of immigrants, where rigid adherence to certain ideals has sometimes resulted in unintended consequences, including increased social tensions and crime. I call this a *monotankekultur ("Monoculture of thought")*—a culture that tends to carry one dominant idea at a time and resists changing paths even when the evidence suggests it should.

By contrast, Denmark—just across the Öresund Bridge—offers a strikingly different model. Danish society shows a greater willingness to make continuous small adaptations, adjusting course pragmatically rather than holding fast to a single idea.

Questions for Discussion (5)

1. How does Sweden's cultural emphasis on consensus contribute to both its strengths (e.g., industrial success) and its weaknesses (e.g., challenges with integration)?
2. In what ways might friendliness and politeness mask deeper cultural boundaries in Swedish society?
3. What does the concept of *monotankekultur* suggest about the risks of pursuing a single idea too rigidly?
4. How does Denmark's more adaptive and pragmatic approach highlight possible alternatives to Sweden's consensus model?
5. To what extent can societies balance the need for stability with the need for flexibility in responding to new challenges?

So, as we have just seen, many of the most powerful belief systems in the modern world are not religious at all—they are secular, institutional, and often invisible to those who inhabit them. Economic models, for example,

[3] The author has lived in Sweden since 2000 and is a proud dual citizen of both Norway and Sweden, which informs the observations made here.

rely on normative assumptions about human behavior (e.g., rational self-interest) that are rarely questioned but heavily consequential. Similarly, belief in meritocracy or progress, even though the key to economic progress, can become ideological when insulated from counter-evidence or blind to structural inequality (Graeber, 2011; Mounk, 2018).

Narratives play a particularly powerful role in the formation and maintenance of these systems. According to Jerome Bruner (1990), humans are natural *storytellers*: we understand the world in terms of plot, character, and moral resolution. This *narrative mode of cognition* simplifies complexity, organizes memory, and fosters emotional salience. Founding myths, historical traumas, and national identities are sustained by stories that encode moral values and shared purpose (Anderson, 1983).

Belief systems also operate through *emotional resonance*. Jonathan Haidt (2012) has shown that moral judgment is typically intuitive and affect-driven, with reasoning used more often to justify beliefs than to form them. This explains why changing someone's mind—on religion, politics, or ideology—is so difficult: beliefs are not just cognitive maps, but *social identities*. They are reinforced by group membership and shaped by early emotional experiences, making them resistant to contrary evidence (Kahan, 2013).

Moreover, the same mechanisms that foster trust and cooperation within groups can lead to exclusion, conflict, and even violence between groups. *Social identity theory* (Tajfel & Turner, 1986) illustrates how *in-group favoritism* and *out-group hostility* can emerge from arbitrary distinctions. Once embedded in belief systems, these divisions are hard to dismantle. Narratives of victimhood or superiority become self-reinforcing, justifying cycles of revenge or marginalization.

When belief systems weaken or lose coherence, societies often face heightened uncertainty, fragmentation, and disorientation. Emile Durkheim (1912/1995) described this state as *anomie*—a breakdown of shared norms that leaves individuals without clear guidance for behavior or meaning. More recent research echoes this concern: Putnam (2000) shows how the erosion of shared civic beliefs and institutions reduces social capital, undermining trust and cooperation. Without strong cultural anchors, individuals may experience rising anxiety and alienation (Inglehart & Welzel, 2005), while societies become more vulnerable to populism, conspiracy thinking, or ideological extremism (Norris & Inglehart, 2019). In other words, when collective belief systems deteriorate, the cognitive scaffolding that once stabilized meaning collapses, producing a vacuum that competing narratives rush to fill.

But belief systems are not static either. They evolve, sometimes slowly through *cultural drift*, and sometimes rapidly under pressure from internal contradictions or external threats. Thomas Kuhn (1962) famously showed that even scientific belief systems undergo "paradigm shifts" when the prevailing framework can no longer explain accumulating anomalies. Though science is often held up as the antithesis of belief, it too is a human enterprise—vulnerable to institutional inertia, social bias, and political influence. What makes science distinct is not freedom from belief, but its structural commitment to revision: peer review, replicability, and empirical testing serve as filters to contain—but not eliminate—cognitive and cultural bias (Ioannidis, 2005; Latour & Woolgar, 1979).

This brings us to a deeper insight: the human mind is a *belief-generating organ*. We are not naturally skeptical beings, but pattern-seeking, story-loving, and group-loyal creatures. Rationality is layered on top of older systems evolved for survival, belonging, and emotional coherence (Pinker, 1997; Tooby & Cosmides, 1992). When people say they are "just being rational," they often mean they are affirming the belief system they already inhabit.

Failing to recognize this leads to a dangerous illusion: that only others are ideological or biased, while we ourselves are neutral and objective. In reality, everyone operates within belief systems—whether acknowledged or not: By restricting the label "belief" to religion, we blind ourselves to the dogmas of politics, economics, or even academia. This makes us more—not less—vulnerable to manipulation, groupthink, and moral error (Table 4.2).

Though we cannot claim that one belief system is inherently superior in all respects, historical experience does show that some combinations are more conducive to long-term prosperity and social flourishing. Over thousands of years of development, the pairing of meritocracy and institutionalized science has proven especially powerful. This "*golden combination*" aligns social incentives with talent and evidence, creating both the motivation and the tools to expand knowledge, technology, and wealth.

Europe's trajectory illustrates this dynamic. In the *classical period*, Greek and Roman inquiry laid a foundation of rational science, mathematics, and philosophy (Lloyd, 1970). Much of this was later suppressed or reinterpreted under stronger religious authority during the *medieval period*, when theological frameworks constrained free inquiry (Grant, 1996). The *Renaissance*, literally a *rebirth*, marked the rediscovery and reinvigoration of classical science, which, combined with institutional innovation in universities, eventually led to the *Scientific Revolution* and *Industrialization* (Huff, 2017; Mokyr, 2017). This fusion of evidence-based knowledge with merit-based recognition of achievement underpinned Europe's rise to global dominance.

Table 4.2 Common (and often unrecognized) modern belief systems

Belief system	Core narrative	Evidence role	Function
Religion	Divine plan and moral order	Irrelevant or symbolic	Provide meaning, ethics, and group cohesion
Nationalism	Sacred history, destiny, sovereignty	Selective	Foster identity, justify conflict or pride
Political ideology	Vision of ideal society (left/right)	Often post hoc	Frame policy and social alignment
Conspiracy theories	Hidden truths suppressed by elites	Self-sealing logic	Reduce uncertainty, externalize blame
Market fundamentalism	Free markets as self-regulating systems	Ideologically filtered	Legitimize inequality, deregulation
Technocratic optimism	Progress through innovation and data	Selective use of data	Justify elite governance, sideline values
Meritocracy	Success as moral virtue	Overlooks privilege	Rationalize inequality, promote compliance
Institutional science	Truth through method	Evidence-based but social	Discover knowledge, guide policy

Importantly, the model was not uniquely European. From the late twentieth century, several East Asian countries—Japan, South Korea, Taiwan, and later China—adapted and institutionalized this same formula: combining strong meritocratic selection systems with heavy investment in science, technology, and education (Bell, 2015; Wong, 2011). These nations have demonstrated that the "Meritocracy + Science Nexus" is not bound to any one culture, but is a replicable recipe for sustained innovation and improved standards of living. What distinguishes societies that thrive over the long run is their ability to protect scientific institutions from dogma and to channel meritocratic principles into real opportunities for talent to flourish.

So, in sum, belief systems are not distortions of reason—they are its necessary scaffolding. They provide shared maps for navigating a complex world, but they can also mislead when mistaken for unshakable truths. What distinguishes science is not its immunity to belief, but its design for correction. And what distinguishes wise citizens is not disbelief, but awareness: the capacity to examine their own frameworks, revise them in light of evidence, and tolerate those of others.

These systems, however, do not remain abstract. They are lived out in daily practices and embodied in the choices people make—through rituals, institutions, media, and even the objects they buy and wear. Belief systems filter into consumption, shaping how individuals express identity, status, and belonging in material form. Before we turn to education and digital culture, it is worth pausing on this immediate, visible layer of belief: the signals carried in clothes, commodities, and styles of self-presentation.

4.2.1 First Impressions: Clothing as the Prelude to Identity

The stories we tell—about who we are, what matters, and what is good—do not stay in the realm of abstract belief. They shape the concrete objects we choose to surround ourselves with. From clothes to cosmetics, furniture to food, our purchases are not just practical—they are *cultural expressions*. What we buy, wear, and display becomes a way of signaling identity, status, values, and group belonging.

Among all forms of consumption, clothing offers a particularly rich case. It is immediate, visible, and unavoidable. Everyone wears something, every day. And what we wear carries meaning; not only about who we are, but also about the era, community, and social position we inhabit. As such, clothing becomes more than personal; it becomes symbolic. It offers a window into how material goods are used to perform identity, participate in social norms, and navigate evolving ideals of attractiveness and success.

This makes clothing the natural starting point for analysis. It is, quite simply, the first thing we notice when we encounter another person from a distance. Long before we hear someone speak or learn who they are, we register their clothes. Dress acts as the first line of cultural contact—a visual preface to the person beneath.

Take a moment to compare a modern T-shirt and mass-produced sneaker with a handmade wool jacket or a pair of stitched leather shoes from a few generations ago. The difference in fabric, seam work, and durability is obvious. Anecdotally and practically, older generations often owned fewer garments, but they lasted longer and were often locally produced with greater attention to detail. In contrast, today's fast fashion—characterized by low cost and rapid turnover—floods the market with *disposable clothing*, often produced under exploitative labor conditions in Asia (Joy et al., 2012). The common argument for why people buy cheap, poor-quality goods is that they cannot afford better. Yet this explanation is not watertight. Consider, for example, the case of shoes.

A pair of Goodyear-welted leather shoes, if properly maintained, can last 10 to 15 years or more. These are often repairable, resoleable, and constructed with durable materials designed for long-term use. Yet most consumers today buy mass-produced sneakers or fashion shoes that degrade after one to three seasons. Ironically, while high-quality shoes may seem more expensive upfront—often costing between 400 and 500 euros—they are often cheaper in the long run. By contrast, a typical pair of similar-looking standard shoes may cost 200 to 300 euros but begin to fall apart within two years. Over a decade, a person might need to buy five or six such pairs, spending over 1,000 euros and still ending up with inferior comfort, worse materials, and more waste. The math is simple: quality often pays off. But in consumer behavior, value is rarely assessed in long-term utility. Instead, most decisions are shaped by short-term trends, social imitation, and the psychological pull of "newness."

Marketing, peer conformity, and the constant churn of *fashion cycles* drive people to replace items frequently; often before they are even worn out. In this sense, *fast fashion* operates not just on economic logic, but on emotional and symbolic dynamics. People don't just buy shoes; they buy stories, signals, and belonging. And in doing so, they often overlook the quiet logic of durable goods. Modern fashion choices are less about quality and more about *social signaling*.

People wear what celebrities and influencers wear, not because of utility or aesthetics, but because these items carry status and group identification (Han et al., 2010; Marwick, 2013). As a result, entire generations may walk around in synthetic, poorly made garments and still believe they are well dressed. From the outside, especially in historical perspective, it can resemble the fable of the emperor's new clothes. The mechanisms of social persuasion are so strong that even visibly inferior products can come to symbolize taste, identity, and status—a kind of cultural illusion, or collective consumer delusion. The objective here is not to be sarcastic or even critical, but simply to state a fact of human observation. We often explain such choices with arguments about price, but in reality, other motives are at play—some of which we may feel uncomfortable acknowledging, and others we may not even be consciously aware of. Instead, we rely on explanations that work for us, even if they do not capture the full picture.

If we step back analytically, clothing's functions become clearer. First and foremost, it protects us from nature. It regulates body temperature, shields us from the elements, and prevents injuries. In evolutionary terms, clothing allowed early humans to survive in colder climates, extending the range of habitable environments far beyond what our bare skin could tolerate (Gilligan, 2010; Jablonski, 2006). The earliest garments were likely invented not for modesty or aesthetics, but simply to stay alive.

As societies grew more complex, clothing took on a second function: *communication*. What we wear signals who we are—our gender, our age, our occupation, our beliefs, and our social rank. Anthropologists and sociologists have long observed that clothing functions as a kind of visual language, one used to express identity and group belonging (Entwistle, 2000; Roach-Higgins & Eicher, 1992). From tribal paint to business suits, humans have always used dress to position themselves within the social order.

A third function is more subtle, yet equally powerful: how clothing shapes our internal experience. The phenomenon of "*enclothed cognition*" describes how the clothes we wear can influence our psychological state, even our cognitive performance. Wearing a lab coat, for instance, can make people perform better on attention tasks, provided they believe the coat symbolizes intelligence and precision (Adam & Galinsky, 2012). In this way, clothing becomes not just a signal to others, but a mirror to the self.

Clothing also plays a role in evolutionary psychology, especially in the context of attraction and mate selection. Traits like fashion sense, style, and grooming often serve as proxies for underlying qualities such as intelligence, resourcefulness, or social awareness (Barber, 1995; Miller, 2009). According to *costly signaling theory*, these choices are not arbitrary: they convey hard-to-fake indicators of fitness, effort, or taste (Zahavi & Zahavi, 1997).

In short, clothing operates on multiple levels at once. It protects us from nature, signals who we are, shapes how we think, and influences how others respond to us. No other species dresses in the literal sense, but the impulse to decorate, signal, and attract is deeply rooted in nature. Among many species—especially birds—it is the male who displays the most elaborate colors, feathers, or songs to attract a mate. Darwin (1871) first described this in terms of sexual selection, where females choose among competing males, favoring traits that signal genetic fitness. The peacock's tail remains the classic example: costly, flamboyant, and evolved entirely to impress the more selective sex. In modern humans, the equivalents are easy to spot—men build muscle at the gym, pursue high-status careers with lucrative salaries, and invest in fashionable clothing or expensive accessories. These behaviors, while culturally framed, often serve the same evolutionary function: to signal desirability, status, and underlying genetic or social fitness in competitive mating markets.

Now, you're going to tell me that it's really not that simple. And fair enough—if you're in your 20s or 30s, I'll accept that comment. But come back and we'll have that same conversation in your 50s. By then, the patterns are usually too consistent to ignore, and the evolutionary logic begins to look a lot more persuasive. And since the topic of clothing and signaling is just too fascinating to leave—and because there are always those who still don't believe me—let's take a deeper look:

Human societies present a notable twist compared to most of the animal kingdom. In many species, males display vivid colors or elaborate traits to attract female mates. In humans, however, it is often women who adopt more visually striking appearances—through makeup, jewelry, and fashion. While this seems to reverse the typical biological pattern, the underlying logic of sexual selection remains intact. Women, as the more selective sex in most mating contexts, still drive competitive signaling. Enhancing appearance is not a sign of submission but a strategic means of increasing options and exercising choice (Buss, 2017a, 2017b; Miller, 2009).

One of the clearest examples is the wearing of high heels. Though impractical and even harmful over time, heels change a woman's posture and walking style in ways that amplify cues of youth and fertility. Studies show that increased lumbar curvature—a feature enhanced by high heels—is perceived as more attractive and feminine (Lewis et al., 2017).[4] Women wearing heels are also more likely to receive attention and assistance from men in public settings (Guéguen, 2015).

Cosmetic use follows similar patterns. Lipstick, especially in red tones, enhances the visibility and contrast of lips, drawing attention to the mouth as a focal point of both speech and sensuality. Some evolutionary psychologists suggest that the use of red lipstick may derive from biological mimicry: the color red is associated with sexual arousal and increased blood flow, paralleling the natural flushing that occurs during sexual excitement (Stephen & McKeegan, 2010). Some scholars have even hypothesized a link between lipstick and the coloration of the labia or genital area, suggesting a deep, subconscious association with fertility cues (Dixson et al., 2011; Morriss et al., 2010). While such claims are debated, the broader point remains: makeup and fashion frequently amplify traits that are evolutionarily tied to youth, health, and reproductive viability.

[4] Lumbar curvature refers to the natural inward curve of the lower spine (the lumbar region). Evolutionary research suggests that an angle of roughly 45 degrees optimizes balance during pregnancy, reducing strain on the body. High heels exaggerate this curvature, which can subconsciously signal youth and reproductive fitness (Lewis et al., 2017).

Moreover, the female use of visual enhancement in humans often reflects intersexual selection—aimed at attracting males—but also intrasexual competition—aimed at competing with other females for status, attention, or high-value mates (Grammer et al., 2003). This helps explain why such displays persist even outside direct courtship contexts, such as in professional or social environments. The cultural tools may differ—heels instead of feathers—but the biological strategies are surprisingly conserved.

Men, of course, are not immune to such displays. Instead of heels or lipstick, they may turn to *conspicuous consumption*—cars, watches, yachts, or designer clothing—as means of signaling status, wealth, and dominance. Fast cars, in particular, have been shown to boost male attractiveness ratings in short-term mating contexts (Dunn & Searle, 2010). This aligns with costly signaling theory: by investing in expensive and seemingly wasteful items, men demonstrate access to resources and a willingness to take risks, both traits historically associated with successful mating strategies (Miller, 2009).

After a woman has successfully secured a long-term mate, the intensity of her sexual signaling through appearance often diminishes, especially when the perceived risk of losing the partner is low. This phenomenon is well documented: women tend to invest less in appearance-enhancing behaviors (such as makeup, revealing clothing, or high heels) once in a stable relationship, particularly if they feel secure in the bond (Durante et al., 2008). However, if there is competition from other women—especially those perceived as attractive or interested in her partner—these behaviors may re-emerge as part of *mate-guarding strategies* (Haselton et al., 2007). Occupational factors also play a role: in professions where attractiveness influences social capital or job performance (e.g., sales, media, hospitality), the pressure to maintain a polished appearance may override mating-based motivations. Additionally, *biological life-stage transitions* matter. After childbirth, and particularly during menopause, women often experience a decline in libido and appearance-related motivation, due to hormonal changes such as reduced estrogen and testosterone levels (Arnow et al., 2009; Davison et al., 2005). These shifts, while partly biological, are also culturally mediated, intersecting with norms about aging, sexuality, and femininity.

These dynamics reveal the continuity between human and non-human signaling strategies. Just as male peacocks display elaborate plumage to attract mates, human appearance—though far more complex and mediated by culture—remains rooted in the same evolutionary imperatives. Thus, while no other species wears clothing, the human act of dressing remains deeply connected to the biological pressures that shape plumage, song, and dance in the animal kingdom. What makes it uniquely human is the layering of biology with culture: our garments carry not only signals of attraction, but also status, ideology, and identity.

And yet, this symbolic richness also introduces ambiguity. For all that clothing reveals, there is much it no longer tells us about national or ethnic identity. In today's globalized, media-saturated environment, individuals from vastly different cultural, religious, and political contexts may dress in nearly identical ways. A teenager in Cairo, a software engineer in São Paulo, and a university student in Tokyo may all wear the same sneakers, jeans, and branded T-shirts—not because they share national values, but because they participate in *transnational subcultures* shaped by pop culture, technology, and consumer trends (Craik, 1994; Miller, 2010).

More than ever, clothing signals role-specific or tribal identity. The global tech elite, for instance, often mark their belonging through casual dress—T-shirts, hoodies, and sneakers—projecting values of creativity, nonconformity, and informality (Hodges, 2020). Business professionals, in contrast, conform to a global dress code of suits and formal wear, regardless of local custom. Fashion thus becomes a code of professional or ideological allegiance rather than a marker of national or ethnic heritage. Even traditional garments are increasingly worn symbolically—on special occasions, in diaspora settings, or for aesthetic effect—often detached from their original meaning (Tarlo, 2010).

In this sense, clothing remains a powerful social signal, but its meanings have shifted. What it communicates today is less about where someone comes from and more about who they are aligned with—professionally, ideologically, or socially. Surface similarity in dress often reflects participation in a global subculture rather than deep cultural unity. Interpreting these signals thus requires attention to context, role, and intention.

For social scientists, these patterns of dress are not trivial; they are cultural texts, dense with meaning. Through clothing, individuals express identity, status, desire, and belonging, often without speaking a word. To decode these signals, we can draw on evolutionary psychology, anthropology, sociology, and even consumer research. Clothing is not just a personal decision; it is a socially embedded act shaped by sexual selection, group membership, and learned convention. In studying how people dress, we are also studying how they navigate visibility, power, and self-presentation in everyday life.

But again—wait. Surely it can't be that reductive. Isn't it possible that I wear something simply because I like the color, the cut, or how it feels on my skin? Don't personal taste and individual freedom matter? The answer is yes—partly, and with an asterisk. Social science doesn't deny the existence of personal choice; rather, it tries to uncover the shared patterns and unconscious influences that shape those choices. Even our most "individual" preferences—those favorite shoes or that beloved jacket—are rarely immune to cultural cues, status signaling, or early social learning. Try it yourself: take a step back and examine the objects in your home with a critical eye. You may be surprised at how much of your so-called taste is actually inherited, mimicked, or marketed.

And where do these preferences come from? Like most aspects of behavior, they are acquired. To know what to wear—what counts as attractive, professional, rebellious, or elegant—we must first learn the codes. We are taught, explicitly or implicitly, by parents, peers, media, and institutions. In that sense, clothing is not only a personal expression but also a lesson in *cultural literacy*. And this brings us to the deeper mechanism that underlies all symbolic systems: learning. If clothing is one of the first signals we learn to interpret, education is the broader process by which we learn to read—and reproduce—the entire social code.

But clothing is only the beginning. It is often the first thing we notice about another person, but not the last. As we move from distant observation to closer interaction, we begin to pick up additional cues: how someone stands, how they speak, how they respond, what they say, and what they seem to mean. These signals are harder to fake, more complex to read, and often more revealing than any outfit.

How, then, do we interpret these layered human signals in everyday encounters? How are we to make sense of a stranger at work, a speaker on stage, or a fellow commuter across the aisle?

In the next section, I propose a practical tool to help answer these questions, the *Triadic Impression Model*, a simple but, I believe, robust framework for decoding human presence. It rests on three overlapping domains: visual, vocal, and intellectual impression. Each offers a distinct lens for understanding the character, intent, and social function of the person before us.

4.2.2 The Triadic Impression Model

How are we to begin understanding someone we meet, whether in an office, at a party, or simply on the street? After all, we rarely have hours to conduct a formal interview or the time to linger and really get to know one another. Instead, we rely on rapid, often unconscious assessment mechanisms to interpret who they are and how they might behave. Consider *Triadic Impression Model* (Fig. 4.1).

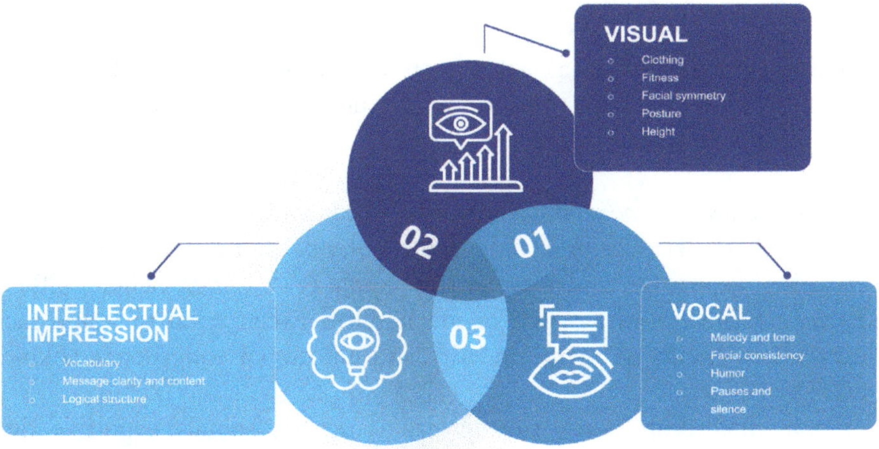

Fig. 4.1 Triadic impression model

Visual Impression

The first and fastest domain is the visual impression, formed in milliseconds upon encountering another person. This includes five key elements: posture, height, fitness, clothing, and facial symmetry:

- *Posture* reflects alignment of the body and, indirectly, the mind. Upright posture is associated with confidence, discipline, and attentiveness, while a slouched posture often signals fatigue, insecurity, or disengagement (Peper et al., 2017).
- *Height*, though biologically fixed, can affect social outcomes. Taller individuals tend to be perceived as more authoritative or competent, a bias observed across cultures and leadership roles (Judge & Cable, 2004).
- *Physical fitness* signals vitality, resilience, and self-care. From an evolutionary psychology perspective, observable health and energy are proxies for reproductive fitness and capacity (Buss, 1999; Sell et al., 2009).
- *Clothing* functions as both a medium of self-expression and a marker of social conformity or deviance. Style can signal intentionality, creativity, or even status anxiety, depending on context (Howlett et al., 2013; Kwon & Johnson, 1998).
- *Facial symmetry* is a biologically salient feature associated with attractiveness, health, and even perceived trustworthiness (Little et al., 2007; Rhodes, 2006). It affects unconscious social sorting and first impressions.

These elements combine almost instantly to form a "*body-based hypothesis*" a cognitive map of the other person's physical, emotional, and social presence (Willis & Todorov, 2006).

Vocal Impression

Once someone begins speaking, a second channel is activated: the vocal impression. Here, melody, tone, timing, dialect, and nonverbal cues enrich or complicate the visual story:

- *Vocal tone and melody* reflect affective states and emotional intelligence. Speech that varies in pitch and rhythm tends to be perceived as more engaging, expressive, and trustworthy (Apple et al., 1979; Scherer, 2003).
- *Facial consistency*—the match or mismatch between vocal tone and facial expression—helps us judge sincerity and emotional congruence (Ekman, 2003).
- *Humor*, including irony, timing, and laughter, signals cognitive flexibility, social awareness, and even reproductive fitness (Greengross & Miller, 2011). It softens status gaps and enhances likability.
- *Pauses and silences* also shape interpretation. Strategic pauses imply thoughtfulness and rhetorical control, while poorly timed silences may suggest anxiety or confusion (Rosenfeld et al., 2002).

Vocal data, like visual input, is rapidly integrated and often bypasses conscious scrutiny. Together, they create an affective atmosphere that we read almost intuitively.

Intellectual Impression

The final domain is the intellectual impression, built over a slightly longer time horizon. This involves analyzing vocabulary, clarity of message, and logical coherence:

- *Vocabulary* reflects not only education and cultural capital, but also fluency in navigating social codes. Natural use of language suggests authenticity; overcomplicated speech can signal posturing or insecurity (Pennebaker et al., 2003).
- *Accent, dialect,*[5] *and word choice* also offer rich cues about a person's social origins, educational background, and intended social status, whether authentic or aspirational. Listeners can often detect regional or class-based variation with surprising precision. These auditory signals shape

[5] In linguistically sensitive cultures—such as Norway, where dialects shift noticeably over short distances—listeners are often able to identify a speaker's origin within a few hundred kilometers, sometimes even less. This reflects both the fine-grained variation in dialects and the social importance attached to them.

impressions of credibility, familiarity, and in-group membership (Giles & Coupland, 1991; Labov, 2006).

- *Message content*—what is being said and why—reveals intent, focus, and purpose. Do the ideas move somewhere, or are they meandering? Is the person conveying information, seeking connection, or testing boundaries?
- *Logic and structure* allow us to assess mental discipline. Ideas that follow clear transitions and rational development are easier to trust and evaluate. Disjointed speech may indicate emotional agitation, intellectual disorganization, or even deliberate obfuscation (Leary, 2001; Oatley & Johnson-Laird, 1987).

Some individuals exhibit such mastery that even complex insights are shared in a relaxed, natural manner. This can signal cognitive sophistication fused with social ease—a rare but powerful combination (Table 4.3).

To me, this is also one of the great joys of life: meeting someone and then, as I walk away, holding on to an impression of who was just in my presence. I try to grasp all three dimensions, make them conscious, and keep them for a while—so that the person does not vanish too quickly into forgetfulness.

And yet, one can't help but wonder if this triadic assessment will remain a human task for much longer. In a world where attention is scarce and cognitive overload is common, we may increasingly lean on technology to help us

Table 4.3 Triadic impression model—summary table

Category	Element	Interpretation
Visual	Posture	Confidence, discipline, physical, and mental alignment
	Height	Perceived dominance or inferiority; can influence self-esteem and social outcomes
	Fitness	Health, energy levels, capacity for responsibility
	Clothing	Self-expression, intentionality, social signaling
	Facial Symmetry	Perceived attractiveness, genetic fitness
Vocal	Melody and Tone	Emotional nuance, engagement, social ease
	Facial Consistency	Sincerity and emotional congruence
	Humor	Social intelligence, confidence, likability
	Pauses	Rhetorical strength, thoughtfulness, or uncertainty
Intellectual	Vocabulary + Accent	Cognitive fluency, authenticity, social positioning
	Message	Clarity, intentionality, depth of thought
	Logic	Rational flow, coherence, persuasive structure

interpret others. With advances in wearable AI and *ambient computing*, it's not far-fetched to imagine a discreet device—no larger than a phone—quietly offering insights like: *"That man has low symmetry, moderate credibility, and may be bluffing."* Whether as a digital assistant, social interpreter, or real-time advisor in meetings, classrooms, or on dates, such tools may soon shape how we navigate social encounters. Whether this makes us more accurate—or simply more reliant—is a question worth reflecting on. It may also take much of the fun out of meeting people. At the same time, such systems would generate remarkably rich data for social science—patterns of interaction, trust, and deception mapped in unprecedented detail—provided, of course, that individual privacy could be protected.

4.2.3 Beyond First Impressions

While clothing, posture, and vocal tone offer powerful cues in the first seconds of a social encounter, real understanding often unfolds over time—through the subtle, ongoing calibration of facial expression, responsiveness, and micro-interactions. This is where *social cognition* becomes active and adaptive.

Humans are wired not only to recognize faces but to constantly monitor them for change. Facial expressions evolve from static impressions into *real-time signals*: a flash of doubt in the eyes, the twitch of a mouth, a raised brow. These *micro-expressions* reveal *emotional undercurrents* that even the speaker may not be aware of (Ekman & Friesen, 1975). Unlike fixed features such as symmetry or structure, expressive behavior provides dynamic clues about mood, receptivity, and authenticity.

Psychological studies show that we tend to assign greater weight to facial behavior when it changes in synchrony with speech or social cues; what researchers call *affective congruence* (Scherer, 2003). A warm smile delivered at just the right moment can signal sincerity, while the same smile delivered too late—or too early—may come across as rehearsed or manipulative. This *temporal attunement* matters: our brains are exquisitely sensitive not just to what others express, but when and how they express it.

This sensitivity appears to be an evolutionary adaptation. In cooperative species like ours, the ability to detect subtle shifts in expression helped our ancestors infer intent, avoid deception, and coordinate behavior in groups (Fridlund, 1994; Tomasello, 2009). The muscles of the human face are capable of producing more than 10,000 distinct expressions, many of them shared across cultures (Jack et al., 2012). While the core emotions—anger, sadness, happiness, fear, disgust, and surprise—are universally recognized, their display is often modulated by local norms and social context.

Even within milliseconds, facial expressions cue deeply ingrained responses. A raised inner eyebrow may trigger empathy; a tight-lipped smile may provoke suspicion. This rapid decoding happens below conscious awareness in what is sometimes called the "*low road*" *of emotional processing*—an evolutionarily older neural route involving the amygdala (LeDoux, 1996). Such processes are fast, but not always accurate, and can lead to stereotyping, especially in ambiguous contexts (Todorov et al., 2015).

What makes *facial dynamics* especially powerful is their role in *interactional flow*. Social encounters are not static photographs but moving tapestries of subtle adjustments, turn-taking, and feedback loops. In this sense, impression formation becomes less like a painting and more like a dance, choreographed moment by moment based on cues from the other. We shift our posture, change the rhythm of our speech, or adjust our eye contact in direct response to the signals we receive.

This interactive calibration has been termed *behavioral mirroring* or *interpersonal synchrony*; a process shown to increase liking, trust, and cooperation (Chartrand & Bargh, 1999; Lakin et al., 2003). When two people mirror each other's body language, gestures, or tone, they are more likely to report mutual understanding and emotional rapport. Importantly, this synchrony is often unconscious; we rarely notice that we're doing it unless we're trained to observe it.

Not all synchronization is equal, though. People who are anxious, self-focused, or *cognitively overloaded* tend to struggle with subtle *social attunement* (Murphy et al., 2011). Conversely, those with high emotional intelligence—or simply more social experience—are better at picking up and responding to *micro-cues*. This has major implications not only for personal relationships but also for leadership, education, and negotiation, where the ability to "*read the room*" can affect outcomes.

Understanding dynamic impression formation requires shifting our focus from isolated traits (e.g., symmetry, clothing) to *relational patterns*; how cues interact over time. A smile might signal confidence in one context, but in another it might be read as nervousness or submission. What matters is the choreography: how expressions, gestures, and verbal responses align across moments.

Recent research in social neuroscience supports this integrative view. Studies using fMRI and hyperscanning (simultaneous brain imaging of two people) show that when conversations go well—when people feel "in sync"—their neural activity literally becomes synchronized, especially in areas related to theory of mind, reward, and language processing (Dikker et al., 2017; Hasson et al., 2012). This *interpersonal attunement* is not just metaphorical; it has a biological basis.

In fact, this kind of *neural synchrony* may help explain why a truly great evening out feels so rewarding. We do not simply seek the company of others for conversation or social obligation—we are looking for that deeper alignment, a state where minds lock in rhythm and communication flows effortlessly. It does not need to be sexual, though it can be: The "high" of being in sync can occur among friends, colleagues, or even strangers who connect through laughter, shared stories, or music. Being "*on the same wavelength*" is not just a figure of speech, but a neurobiological event that reinforces bonds and leaves people with a sense of intimacy and vitality (Hari et al., 2015; Redcay & Schilbach, 2019).

Friendship itself is often marked by this capacity for synchrony, alongside other key characteristics. Friends provide emotional support and a buffer against stress, which has been shown to improve health outcomes and resilience (Cohen & Wills, 1985; Umberson & Montez, 2010). They offer trust and reliability, allowing individuals to share vulnerabilities without fear of exploitation (Adams & Blieszner, 1995). They foster shared identity and mutual understanding, often built on repeated positive interactions, shared norms, and even *coordinated bodily rhythms* such as synchronized laughter or mirroring gestures (Dunbar, 2010; Vacharkulksemsuk & Fredrickson, 2012). Finally, friendships are marked by reciprocity—a balance of giving and receiving support that sustains the relationship over time (Fehr, 1996).

Taken together, these elements—neural synchrony, trust, reciprocity, and emotional support—form the *architecture of friendship*. They explain why people do not just want to "see friends" but want to feel that rare state of deep attunement, the sense of being truly understood and connected. It is in those moments, whether during a night of laughter or a quiet conversation, that social bonds are most vividly reinforced.

Truly socially intelligent individuals are often adept at shaping these moments deliberately. They may downplay their competence ("I'm actually not that good at this") or express mild uncertainty—not as a reflection of their actual ability, but as a strategic display of humility or approachability. These signals serve as *subtle probes*, testing how the other person reacts to cues of vulnerability or modesty. If the response is warm or encouraging, the speaker may continue revealing more; if it triggers skepticism or condescension, they may shift tone. This dynamic use of *impression management*—what Goffman (1959) called the "*presentation of self*"—involves not only controlling how one is perceived but doing so in real time, adapting to the feedback loop of interaction.

This behavior is supported by research on *self-monitoring*, a personality trait describing how well individuals adjust their behavior based on social context. *High self-monitors* tend to be more attentive to social cues and more skilled in adjusting their presentation to meet situational demands (Snyder, 1974). Relatedly, *emotional intelligence*—the ability to perceive, interpret, and manage both one's own and others' emotions—has been found to correlate with superior performance in impression management and interpersonal adaptability (Mayer et al., 2008).

In this sense, we are not just passive recipients of social judgments, we are also active participants, constantly sending and decoding cues to adjust our perceived status, trustworthiness, or warmth. *Real-time impression management* becomes a kind of cognitive and emotional dance, where we experiment with different micro-signals—self-effacement, humor, deference—to see what resonates with the other person. In doing so, we negotiate not just how we are seen, but the very nature of the relationship itself (Leary & Kowalski, 1990).

The remarkable part is this: we do almost all of it without thinking. The calibration of tone, timing, posture, and facial expression described above rarely feels deliberate. It unfolds as we go—improvised, intuitive, and largely unconscious. We are not born with these skills, yet we don't explicitly learn them in school either. Rather, we acquire them through immersion in everyday social life. From early childhood, we absorb thousands of micro-lessons in timing, emotional reading, and interpersonal feedback. These social-cognitive capacities develop through observation, imitation, and shared experience—not formal instruction (Tomasello, 1999; Vygotsky, 1978).

Developmental psychology confirms that children internalize social norms and interactional patterns long before they can articulate them (Harris, 2012). Even toddlers show basic forms of synchrony and mirroring when interacting with caregivers (Trevarthen, 1979). Over time, these implicit skills become the scaffolding of adult *social intelligence*. Much like language acquisition, impression management is a learned fluency—picked up through lived interaction, not deductive reasoning.

This has implications for how we understand both human cognition and social behavior. The dance of dynamic impression formation is not the result of careful calculation but the product of *deeply embedded learning systems* honed through repeated practice in real-world contexts. It is, in essence, a form of *embodied cultural knowledge*—acquired not by reading books on psychology but by navigating the subtle complexities of human interaction day after day. And in that sense, we are all performers in a social play we've rehearsed since birth—just not always consciously.

And so, we cannot help asking what happens when robots get close to us—emotionally as well as physically. They will not only recognize our signals but analyze them, perhaps understanding our own nature better than we do ourselves. Unless, of course, we decide we cannot live with that level of scrutiny and deliberately program them to be less perceptive. It may be that the vision of a robot who sees us too clearly feels intimidating, and that users instead ask for something softer—a "bimbo-robot," or its male equivalent—companions designed not for full insight, but for comfort.

This chapter has so far emphasized the visual, vocal, and intellectual elements that shape impression. But if we want to understand social encounters in their full richness, we must also account for what happens between these domains—in the subtle interplay of movement, timing, responsiveness, and mutual influence.

In that sense, *character* is not simply revealed—it is performed, reinforced, and reshaped in a continuous loop of action and interpretation. Who we are is never entirely fixed. We are, in a very real sense, constantly becoming—remade by the people around us. Our identity is not merely internal; it is distributed across interactions, negotiated through micro-adjustments in response to group expectations, feedback, and affiliation.

Case in a Box: Character Across Borders

Consider the experience of someone who has lived for long periods in both Spain and Germany. In Spain, they may feel more German—structured, punctual, even slightly reserved—while in Germany, they may suddenly feel more Spanish—warm, informal, and expressive. Identity, in such cases, sharpens through contrast. Locals pick up subtle cues of "foreignness" even when the person speaks the language almost fluently. Often, it takes a few days of immersion to recalibrate speech rhythm, gestures, or even humor to the local context.

What is striking is how these shifts sometimes extend beyond language. A person who has lived in France may find that they joke more freely in French, adopting mannerisms that others identify as distinctly French. Time spent in Italy might encourage more animated gestures, a different way of expressing warmth, or simply the joy of speaking with passion. In Japan, by contrast, someone may learn to adopt greater restraint and indirectness in their communication, carrying traces of that demeanor even when returning home. Over time, these layers of national character and personal history accumulate, blending into an identity that feels internally coherent yet appears different to others depending on the context.

From a scientific perspective, such experiences highlight the *plasticity of identity* and the way it is distributed across interactions rather than fixed within the self. *Social identity theory* (Tajfel & Turner, 1986) shows that our sense of "who we are" is partly a reflection of group memberships and the contrasts between them. Research on *cultural frame switching* (Benet-Martínez et al., 2002; Hong et al., 2000) demonstrates that bicultural or multicultural individuals often shift aspects of personality, behavior, or emotional tone depending on cultural context. This switching is usually unconscious, cued by language, setting, or interaction partners. Neuroscience also supports the idea that identity is context dependent: bicultural brains activate different networks depending on which cultural schema is salient (Ng et al., 2010).

The deeper point here is that our characters are co-authored by culture, place, and interaction. Even when we believe we are consistent, subtle cues of accent, demeanor, or values reveal influences from the environments that shaped us. We cannot fully control this process because character is not only internal—it is embodied and perceived, negotiated through social exchange, and constantly reshaped by experience.

Questions for Discussion

1. How much of our character is shaped by cultural context, and how much is innate?
2. Why do people sometimes perceive aspects of us that we do not notice in ourselves?
3. Can we ever fully control or "curate" our identity across different cultural settings?
4. How does living in multiple cultures enrich, but also complicate, one's sense of self?
5. What do comments such as "You seem more Italian in Italy" or "more German in Germany" reveal about the relational nature of character?

This dynamic helps explain why, in small or isolated communities, people often appear strikingly similar in demeanor, outlook, and even emotional tone. Local norms become scripts for behavior, and deviation can lead to social friction. As sociologist Erving Goffman (1959) argued, the "*presentation of self*" is shaped not in isolation but on the social stage, where others function as both audience and co-authors of our identity.

Developmental psychology confirms this process early in life. Vygotsky (1978) showed that learning and identity formation are mediated through social interaction and "*zones of proximal development*"—the idea that we become who we are through the scaffolding of others. *Social identity theory* further explains how group membership shapes not only attitudes but perceived personality (Tajfel & Turner, 1979). Who we are is deeply tied to where we are—and with whom.

This is also why some people choose to leave their hometowns. Through books, media, or travel, they may develop aspirations or traits that feel misaligned with their local culture. They move to larger cities in hopes of cultivating other sides of themselves—greater ambition, broader openness, and a stronger sense of freedom. Conversely, others may choose to stay, not out of inertia, but out of loyalty and belonging. The characters they grew up with reflect a familiar moral world, and stepping away from that may feel like stepping away from oneself.

Research in cultural psychology supports this view. Studies by Hazel Markus and Shinobu Kitayama (1991) suggest that the self is not universal but culturally shaped: Western contexts often emphasize an independent self-concept, while many non-Western or rural communities foster interdependent selves—defined relationally and collectively. Who we become, then, is inseparable from the *social ecology* in which our mind is embedded.

This perspective challenges individualist assumptions about identity. It reminds us that our "character" is not some solitary inner core, but a living product of social exchange—constantly updated through the feedback loops of everyday life. Even the desire to "become someone else" is typically born from a dialogue between the self and the surrounding world. In this sense, identity is not discovered. It is co-authored.

One striking example comes from language. Research in *sociophonetics* shows that early acquired features of speech, such as nasalization or prosodic rhythm, can persist throughout life, even when speakers later adopt a different language or dialect. Children who spend their first years in a region with strong nasal pronunciations, for instance, may retain traces of that articulation permanently, no matter how long they live elsewhere (Flege, 1995; Kuhl, 2004). This phenomenon is well documented in studies of "foreign accent," where adults rarely achieve native-like pronunciation in a second language, precisely because their early phonetic system continues to influence articulation decades later (Long, 1990). Neurolinguistic evidence supports this: the critical period hypothesis suggests that *phonological patterns* learned in early childhood become deeply ingrained, shaping vocal tract habits and neural representations that resist later change (Lenneberg, 1967; Werker & Tees, 2005).

Sociolinguists also highlight that accents are not just mechanical habits but social signals. A nasal pronunciation that "sticks" functions as a marker of origin, class, or group membership, whether or not the speaker intends it (Labov, 1972; Trudgill, 1986). Identity in this sense is literally embodied: it is carried in the muscles of the face, the resonance of the nose, and the rhythm of speech. These linguistic imprints demonstrate how the environments we are born into leave permanent traces on character. Even when individuals consciously try to "become someone else," their earliest cultural and phonetic environment remains co-authored into their identity, audible in every word they speak.

One can learn a new language relatively quickly through study and practice, but it is far more difficult to "learn a character." Cultural psychology shows that behaviors, emotional styles, and interaction norms are deeply embedded in *long-term socialization* and rarely shift in the same way linguistic skills do (Markus & Kitayama, 1991; Triandis, 1995). Over time, however, immersion in a cultural environment tends to reshape one's character, whether one intends it or not. This is because character is less about explicit knowledge and more about embodied habits, expectations, and micro-patterns of social behavior that are continuously reinforced through daily interaction (Bourdieu, 1977).

Moreover, language and character cannot be cleanly separated. Research in sociolinguistics and cultural neuroscience shows that linguistic codes are tied to patterns of thought, emotional tone, and cultural scripts (Boroditsky, 2011; Han & Ma, 2014). A person cannot simply choose one language while keeping the "character" of another, because the two are intertwined: language may be learned fast, but character follows more slowly. This mismatch often produces what bilinguals call "*cultural frame switching*," where speaking in a different language subtly activates different self-construal and behaviors (Hong et al., 2000). Thus, identity is not a menu of free combinations. Language and character coevolve, with one setting the rhythm and the other adapting over time.

And just as our identity evolves through social feedback, so too does our perceived status. The impression we make is not locked into static features or predetermined traits, but shaped in real time by how we move, speak, and respond to others. A person's social standing may shift over the course of minutes or hours—not just because of how they look, but because of how they interact.

While physical traits such as height, facial symmetry, and body shape are often treated as fixed visual indicators of attractiveness or authority, their actual impact is highly context dependent and modulated by interaction. A tall individual may initially command attention, but if their posture is slouched or speech hesitant, the perceived dominance may quickly diminish. Conversely, someone of average stature who exhibits calm confidence, emotional sensitivity, or quick-witted responsiveness may rise in perceived status over the course of a conversation. What we infer from static traits is always filtered through behavior.

Symmetry, for example, is commonly associated with *genetic fitness* and trustworthiness (Rhodes, 2006), but these associations may fade if the person's expressions seem cold, erratic, or insincere. Similarly, muscularity may signal physical capability, but if paired with overbearing posture or low verbal fluency, it can quickly shift from admiration to discomfort. The impression is not in the body alone but in its motion, rhythm, and alignment with the moment.

This fluidity reflects the principle of *embodied social status,* the idea that status is not a static attribute but enacted and negotiated through ongoing performance (Ridgeway & Walker, 1995). In this view, bodily cues interact with vocal tone, conversational style, and emotional regulation to produce what we experience as *social presence*. These impressions are cumulative but fragile, often reshaped with each glance, sentence, or gesture.

Over time, small mismatches between physical expectation and behavior—what psychologists call *expectancy violations*—can dramatically alter perception. A surprisingly articulate or self-deprecating person who appears physically intimidating may win trust precisely because they defy the stereotype (Burgoon, 1993). On the other hand, those who appear confident at first glance may undermine their own image if they dominate the conversation or ignore social nuance.

What all this suggests is that no single variable—height, fitness, facial structure—has fixed meaning. These traits gain significance only within the *choreography of interaction*, where timing, adaptation, and social intelligence convert potential impressions into relational outcomes (Table 4.4).

What this table ultimately highlights is that appearance and social cues never act in isolation. They function more like notes in a performance—sometimes harmonious, sometimes discordant—depending on how they are combined and interpreted in real time. A tall person may seem imposing until a slouched posture undercuts the impression; an elegant outfit may project status until mismatched expressions signal discomfort. In other words, traits only crystallize into meaning when enacted within the flow of interaction. This is why analyzing appearance is less about cataloging fixed features than about tracing *the dynamic choreography* of how those features are mobilized, perceived, and negotiated in social life.

4.2.3.1 The Strategic Value of Dynamic Signals

What emerges from this evolving picture of trying to analyze others—and, in the process, ourselves—is a subtle but powerful fact: our bodies speak first, but it is how we continue to speak—through gestures, tone, timing,

Table 4.4 Appearance and social cues in dynamic interaction

Category	Variable	Dynamic interpretation in interaction
Physical traits	Height	Signals authority initially; adjusted by behavior and vocal presence
	Body shape	Health or fitness cues; modulated by energy, agility, and posture
	Facial symmetry	Attractiveness cue; softened or reinforced by facial expression
	Facial features	Baseline perception; expressive use adds or subtracts social warmth
	Age cues	May evoke respect, care, or bias; interaction alters response
Postural indicators	Posture	Conveys openness, anxiety, or dominance in real time
	Head position	Attention, submission, or defiance depending on alignment
	Gait (walking style)	Energy, confidence, or disorientation—shaped by situation
Facial expression	Mood cues	Real-time affect calibration—invites or blocks rapport
	Emotional signals	Shaped by congruence, mismatch, and audience response
	Eye behavior	Trust, challenge, curiosity—depends on timing and reciprocity
	Mouth behavior	Speech pacing, tension, or relaxed openness
Grooming and style	Hair, makeup	Preparedness, conformity, or rebellion—interacts with social cues
	Clothing style	Signals identity; reinforced or contradicted by behavior
	Scent	Influences proximity dynamics; not easily recalibrated mid-interaction
Cultural/personal signs	Accessories	Identity markers; subject to interpretation by cultural context
	Modifications	Social statements; softened or sharpened by demeanor
	Individuality	Trendy vs. idiosyncratic; social risk or asset depending on alignment

and responsiveness—that determines whether others listen, trust, or follow. This has direct consequences for power, access, and social mobility.

In leadership selection, for example, traits like height, posture, and vocal authority often open the door. But it's the calibration of these traits—knowing when to downplay dominance, when to show humility, when to engage empathetically—that decides whether someone is followed or merely tolerated (Antonakis et al., 2012). The truly effective leader knows how to adapt across settings: to be warm in one room, assertive in another. These shifts are not manipulative, but socially intelligent responses to evolving social conditions.

In dating, the pattern repeats. Initial attraction may stem from symmetry or grooming, but long-term desirability is shaped more by the rhythm of interaction—humor, attunement, and shared cues of vulnerability or competence. A poorly timed joke can kill attraction; a well-timed pause can create intimacy. Facial expressions, vocal warmth, and subtle mirroring all work together to create what psychologists call *interactional synchrony* (Chartrand & Bargh, 1999; Feldman, 2007).

Not to forget the literal dance: couples often judge compatibility not just by physical fitness but by emotional balance, coordination, and rhythm in movement. Dancing provides a unique window into this synchrony because it requires timing, responsiveness, and shared flow. A person who cannot dance—or who consistently fails to attune to a partner's rhythm—can signal difficulties in flexibility, empathy, or social coordination. Anthropological studies suggest that dance historically functioned as a *courtship display*, allowing potential partners to assess health, stamina, and coordination (Miller, 2000; Neave et al., 2011). Evolutionary psychologists argue that the ability to move in time with others also reflects underlying neural and *emotional capacities for cooperation*, making dance both a biological and social signal (Brown, 2017).

Neuroscience supports this view: synchronized movement activates reward circuits in the brain and fosters feelings of closeness and trust (Tarr et al., 2016). Couples who move in rhythm often report higher mutual attraction and stronger relational satisfaction (García-García et al., 2021). In contrast, consistently failing to match a partner's rhythm may act as a warning sign, not only in dance but in the broader dance of everyday life.

And in job interviews or negotiations, we see it again. The difference between the competent and the compelling candidate often lies not in their resume, but in their *conversational agility*; how they handle pressure, how they modulate their energy, and whether they exhibit presence without ego. *Micro-corrections* in posture, shifts in tone, and real-time feedback reading become decisive (DeGroot & Motowidlo, 1999).

If all this sounds complicated, that's because it is. Imagine if every person had to formally study these dynamics before being allowed to go out and socialize. The exam would be impossibly long, packed with theory, timing, and calibration exercises—it would take years just to prepare. And yet, in practice, we perform these feats daily, often without conscious effort. Most of it unfolds automatically, the product of evolved instincts and learned scripts rather than deliberate calculation.

Isn't that just wonderful? If we can coordinate all of this practically without conscious thought, it raises the question: why are we so quick to assume we are vastly "smarter" than other animals, when much of what we do relies on instinctive scripts not so different from theirs? A deer does not "calculate" when it freezes in the forest, waiting for the predator to pass—it just does. A rabbit zigzags when chased, not because it has solved a geometry problem, but because generations of trial and error wired the pattern into its muscles. Even the octopus, when cornered, throws up a cloud of ink and darts away in a split second, leaving predators disoriented. These responses are as subtle and well timed as any social maneuver in a boardroom. The difference is only in the setting: they operate in the domain of survival, we in the domain of reputation, status, and trust. But the underlying logic—the choreography of micro-moves, instincts, and context-reading—is astonishingly similar.

What is even more telling is that even those who do study and understand these mechanisms in theory—psychologists, sociologists, or communication experts—are not necessarily better at performing them in practice. Knowing the rules of the game does not guarantee social grace. In fact, it can sometimes make things harder, because awareness without fluency adds pressure and self-consciousness. The irony is that we are far less *sapiens*—rational and reasoning—than we like to believe. And yet, precisely because we are not, we succeed: our ability to read and respond without overthinking is what allows us to survive, thrive, and connect. Of course, this only takes us so far; instinctive fluency may win friends, but it doesn't guarantee you a job.

At the same time, as we all know, not everyone gets a fair start. Some traits—like skin color, facial structure, disability, or simply the luck of being tall and symmetrical—still evoke unconscious biases that shape perception before a word is even spoken (Blair et al., 2004; Eberhardt et al., 2006). The classic example is height: taller individuals, on average, earn more and are overrepresented in leadership roles (Judge & Cable, 2004). Similarly, attractiveness functions as a form of unearned social capital, opening doors that remain closed for others (Langlois et al., 2000).

And if I linger a little longer on height, it is partly because it is the example everyone seems to enjoy—it's so easy to relate to. Almost everyone has a story about feeling too tall, too short, or just the right size in a particular situation. It is a trait we all notice instantly, yet rarely discuss openly, which makes it a perfect case for exploring how unconscious biases quietly shape our social lives.

Height is particularly interesting because it is not just socially rewarded but also sexually selected. Across cultures, women tend to prefer taller men, especially as long-term partners, and this preference has likely contributed to the steady increase in average male height in many populations over time (Pawlowski, 2003; Stulp et al., 2013). Sexual selection thus amplifies social bias: the very trait that is already rewarded in leadership and income is also reinforced through mate choice.

There are also geographic and social patterns. Research suggests that taller men are disproportionately found in coastal and capital regions, not because these environments directly make people taller, but because ambitious, upwardly mobile individuals tend to migrate toward economic and political centers. Over generations, this concentration of successful individuals—who are also more likely to attract partners and pass on their traits—creates a feedback loop linking height with urban centers of power (Grasgruber et al., 2014; Stulp & Barrett, 2016). In other words, what looks like a simple matter of biology is deeply intertwined with geography, ambition, and social stratification.

What the dynamic model makes clear, however, is that these biases are not absolute fate. A person who understands the mechanisms of impression—who knows how to read and modulate the social field—can sometimes reroute the trajectory of an encounter. This is not always fair, but it is real. Skill can compensate for disadvantage, at least in part. But the playing field is never fully level: starting with "*charismatic capital*" gives some individuals more margin for error, while others must work harder to earn the same trust or attention.

The ability to calibrate impression—to use body, voice, and intellect in real time—remains a key ingredient of what we often call "charisma" or "presence." Yet unlike height or bone structure, this is something that can be practiced and improved. Training in communication, acting, or negotiation often demonstrates just how teachable certain aspects of *impression management* are. Still, no matter how much practice, social handicaps persist. Just as in sports, some begin the race with a head start, while others carry invisible weights.

These *interpersonal dynamics*—how we read faces, mirror emotions, and signal intent—are therefore best understood as a blend of the biological and the cultural, of the given and the learned. From early on, we practice them—often without knowing it—through constant feedback from parents, peers, and the broader community. A raised eyebrow, the weight of a pause, or a smile that lingers too long are not simply instincts we are born with; they are lessons absorbed through observation, correction, imitation, and reward. In this sense, our social encounters are themselves a kind of education, long before we ever set foot in a classroom.

4.3 Learning in a Digital Era

Learning is the principal mechanism by which culture is transmitted and transformed. From early childhood through formal schooling and lifelong exposure to media, we acquire the norms, values, concepts, and practices that shape how we think and act. Education, broadly conceived, is the deliberate cultivation of minds—not simply the transfer of information but the formation of interpretive frameworks, habits of thought, and epistemic virtues.

But let us be clear: most of what we learn—especially what truly shapes our thinking—is not acquired in school. It is learned informally, often unconsciously, through daily experience, social interaction, and cultural immersion. Psychologists refer to this as *parental socialization* (Grusec & Hastings, 2007)—the process by which children absorb moral codes, emotional regulation, behavioral norms, and cultural identity from their caregivers. These foundational elements are established long before formal education begins and remain largely intact throughout life. In this sense, schools never build from scratch. They add to an already well-formed cultural scaffold.

While this early education is essential for functioning within the group, the later stages of formal schooling play a different role. Especially beyond the basics of reading and calculation, education becomes a more deliberate and visible process. Yet as more students are pushed through these higher levels, quality is often diluted, raising questions about the real value of many diplomas. This is particularly noticeable in the social sciences, where the growth of programs has sometimes been accompanied by a proliferation of pretentious knowledge rather than genuine intellectual progress.

Exactly because the social sciences have long lacked a clear and convincing overarching theory that unifies their subsystems, much of what is taught often resembles a collection of fragmented experiences, detached from the whole. Too often, this knowledge is presented in dry, formal, and sometimes pretentious language that—when stripped down—amounts to common sense. As a result, it rarely translates into concrete skills that can be directly applied in professional life. By contrast, if the social sciences had consistently been grounded in evolutionary theory, as shown with detailed examples in the opening chapters of this book, their immediate value and applicability would be much more apparent.

Here once more echoes Maxim Gorky's reflection in My Universities (1923), a theme I return to throughout this book: that formal schooling is less decisive than the university of life—the real, messy, human world outside the classroom. For many of us, especially in the early years, school functions more like an advanced form of daycare than a transformative intellectual environment. The most lasting impressions—about cooperation, status, curiosity, or self-worth—often come not from curriculum but from playground dynamics, family routines, or media exposure. Much of this learning is unconscious, built on mimicry and the countless *micro-corrections* parents and caregivers provide in daily life.

While formal education, especially at the university level, is essential for acquiring specialized knowledge and vocational skills, it builds upon the deeper social and moral frameworks already established during childhood. Scholars distinguish between *academic socialization* (focused on school-related skills and expectations) and *cultural socialization* (the transmission of heritage, identity, and beliefs), with evidence showing that the latter is especially powerful in early development. As such, universities rarely overwrite our core dispositions; rather, they refine and redirect them.

Vygotsky (1978) emphasized the social nature of learning. His concept of the "*zone of proximal development*" showed that learning is scaffolded by more knowledgeable others—parents, teachers, peers—who mediate between the learner and the cultural tools at hand. Piaget (1952), by contrast, highlighted the active construction of knowledge through interaction with the environment, emphasizing the stages through which cognitive development unfolds.

Both traditions point to an important insight: learning is not passive absorption but active engagement with the world, guided by culture. Neuroscientific research confirms that brains are not blank slates but predictive engines, constantly updating internal models based on feedback (Friston, 2010). Effective education, therefore, must balance structured guidance with exploratory freedom; teaching not just facts but how to learn.

The modern educational system emerged alongside industrial society, often modeled on factory logic: standardized curricula, time-based progression, and a focus on compliance and memorization. Critics from Dewey (1938) to Freire (1970) have challenged this model, arguing that education should be democratic, dialogical, and oriented toward critical thinking and social transformation.

Today, this debate is renewed in the context of digital technology. The internet has radically expanded access to information, reshaped attention spans, and altered how people engage with knowledge. Carr (2010) worries that digital media foster *superficial skimming* over *deep comprehension*. Others, like Gee (2003), argue that video games and interactive platforms can cultivate problem-solving and systems thinking if properly harnessed.

The digital mind, shaped by algorithmic curation and continuous partial attention, learns differently. Platforms like YouTube or TikTok reward short-form content and novelty, training users to expect rapid stimulation and instant gratification. While this may enhance certain cognitive capacities, it also undermines sustained focus, *critical reading*, and reflective judgment—skills essential to science and democratic citizenship. I am equally concerned about what might be called *sensitive reading*: the ability to truly feel what one writes or reads. The relentless speed at which everything is now delivered online risks destroying this sensitivity, never allowing us to slow down, dwell, and enter the material deeply enough for it to resonate in full. In truth, humans were never particularly good at conscious, sustained learning to begin with—it has always been fragile, the exception rather than the rule. What is new is that machines now strip away even the modest progress we made in this direction, leaving us adrift without our defining project: the often so fragile claim of *sapiens*.

Case in a Box: AI and the Decline of Reading—From Skimming to Substitution

There are, broadly speaking, two very different ways of engaging with a text. The first is *critical reading*. Here, the reader follows the chain of reasoning in a text—testing whether conclusions actually follow from the premises, much as in a syllogism, though often informally. Critical reading requires deliberate attention to argument structure, logical consistency, and supporting evidence. It is the skill we rely on in philosophy, science, and any domain where reasoning is central.

The second mode is what we might call *sensitive reading*. Unlike analysis, it is immersive. The reader uses their senses and imagination to enter the text fully, as one does with poetry, literature, or reflective prose. It requires knowing every word (and looking up those we don't) so that nothing obstructs comprehension. Once the text opens itself, it becomes a tapestry—full of colors, rhythms, and emotional tones—an attempt to capture the author's intended meaning in its depth and subtlety. Sensitive reading is less about testing logic and more about resonance, atmosphere, and meaning.

Both modes demand time. They cannot be rushed. Yet, the modern information environment pushes us in the opposite direction. Since the rise of the internet, humans have been reading more quickly, often by *skimming*—moving across texts to capture key points without sustained attention. Research shows that digital skimming often reduces comprehension and recall compared to slower, linear reading (Baron, 2015; Liu, 2005). The phenomenon of *information overload* (Bawden & Robinson, 2009) fosters a constant feeling of "catching up," leading people to prioritize coverage over depth. The danger is that when we skim, we believe we have grasped the essence of a text, when in fact we may have misunderstood or only half-understood it (Wolf, 2018).

Artificial intelligence takes this problem one step further. Instead of reading texts ourselves—even superficially—we often ask AI for a summary or direct answer. The machine delivers what feels like the distilled essence, but in this process the act of reading, of encountering the argument or prose with our own reasoning or sensitivity, is skipped altogether. This is a step down from skimming: not only do we risk misunderstanding the text, we may not engage with it at all. The AI's answer becomes a substitute for comprehension, a shortcut that prevents the very intellectual exercise needed to maintain strong analytical and sensitive reading capacities.

All we really do here is pass questions or bits of information from one side to the other. Even for a robot, that kind of work would seem far too simple—I suspect it might even hurt its feelings to be given such a task.

Over time, this reliance risks what scholars call *cognitive atrophy* (Risko & Gilbert, 2016): when functions are habitually outsourced, they weaken from disuse. Just as navigation abilities decline when people depend on GPS (Parush et al., 2007), so too analytical and sensitive reading may deteriorate when AI assumes the burden of interpretation. What began with information overload in the digital age—the constant temptation to skim—may now be accelerated by AI into a world where we stop reading altogether, mistaking generated answers for understanding.

The question for education and scholarship is pressing: if we no longer read deeply—either critically or sensitively—what capacities of judgment, imagination, and empathy will remain? And can anything truly replace them?

Reflection Questions

1. What is the difference between *critical reading* and *sensitive reading*? Which one do you personally practice more, and why?
2. How does skimming affect comprehension compared to deep reading, according to empirical research?
3. In what ways might relying on AI for summaries and answers further weaken both critical and sensitive reading?
4. Is there a responsible way to integrate AI into reading practices—so that it enhances rather than replaces comprehension?
5. If societies lose the habit of deep reading, what cultural, political, or ethical capacities might be at risk? How?

Furthermore, digital environments blur the line between learning and advertising, between genuine knowledge and persuasive manipulation. Algorithmic recommender systems reinforce existing preferences (Pariser, 2011), creating the famous "*filter bubbles*" we have mentioned earlier, that limit exposure to alternative views. Most AI systems, unless explicitly designed otherwise, do not challenge us or raise counterarguments. Instead, they are trained to optimize for user satisfaction—often by confirming our existing beliefs and finding arguments that support them. This tendency to please rather than provoke can stifle critical thinking and deepen intellectual *echo chambers*. It raises urgent questions about epistemic agency and the future of education in algorithmically governed spaces. Having said that, it is also quite possible to imagine AIs designed to be more critical—to question us, to challenge assumptions, and to resist easy agreement. In the end, much depends on how they are programmed, and on whether we value provocation and intellectual friction as much as comfort and affirmation.

Despite these challenges, digital tools also offer powerful opportunities for personalized learning, global collaboration, and the democratization of knowledge. MOOCs, open-access journals, and online forums can connect learners across borders and disciplines. But realizing this potential requires intentional design, a pedagogy that integrates cognitive science, cultural awareness, and digital literacy.

Case in a Box: The Robot Professor

Imagine a university where the professors are robots, powered by advanced AI. These professors never forget a fact, never misquote a source, and never make calculation errors. They can draw instantly from the entire archive of human knowledge, updating in real time as new discoveries emerge. But beyond accuracy, imagine if each robot professor could be given a personality—a set of quirks and habits that echo the styles of past human scholars. One student might choose to learn economics from a "Weberian" German-style professor, austere but thorough. Another might opt for an Oxbridge-inspired philosopher with eccentric wit, ironic humor, and a fondness for arcane footnotes. Others might prefer a warm, storyteller type, blending scholarship with anecdotes.

In some ways, we already have the beginnings of this. Many students today simply switch on an AI-powered microphone during lectures; the professor's words are transcribed into text, which can then be queried or even re-read aloud by a machine in whatever voice the student prefers. In the near future, a professor who falls ill may not need to cancel class at all, but simply upload a file for the robot lecturer to deliver in their place.

The next step, then, is not just accessing knowledge but shaping the character of one's teacher. For many students, such professors might be more engaging, memorable, and effective than today's average lecturer. And in such a world, the mediocre teacher—the uninspired or disengaged academic—would face the same pressures of automation that have already transformed manufacturing, clerical work, and customer service. Universities, like many other knowledge industries, would retain only those few humans who add something uniquely irreplaceable: creativity, mentorship, embodied presence, or ethical guidance.

The scenario raises fundamental questions about the future of higher education. If machines can do almost everything a professor does—teach, explain, motivate, even joke—what, then, is left for the human educator?

Questions for Discussion

1. Would robot professors make education more effective, or simply more standardized?
2. If students could "design" their ideal professor, what qualities would they prioritize—knowledge, humor, empathy, or authority?
3. Should universities replace mediocre teaching with AI systems, or preserve human imperfection as part of the learning experience?
4. What aspects of teaching are most difficult for AI to replicate—mentorship, ethics, creativity, or authority?
5. How might the presence of robot professors change the social role and prestige of human academics?

This rather realistic thought experiment highlights the stakes of education in the digital era. The arrival of AI teachers would not eliminate the need for learning but would sharpen the question of what kind of learning matters. For a time, we are likely to see a *dual system*, with human teachers and robots working side by side: the machine handling much of the delivery, repetition, and fact-checking, while the teacher focuses on guidance, context, and the subtler art of mentoring. Over time, as robots take on more of the routine work, the human role may shift even further—toward quality control, ethical reflection, and the cultivation of meaning. Education, in this model, becomes less about transmitting information and more about helping students understand how to use it wisely.

Education must evolve to meet these conditions. It must teach not only what to learn, but how to evaluate, contextualize, and apply knowledge. It must foster *metacognition*—the awareness of one's own thought processes—and epistemic humility, the recognition of knowledge's limits. These are not luxuries but necessities in an age of misinformation, automation, and accelerating change. In my book, *The Researcher's Journey: A Guide to Methodology and Academia in Social Sciences* (Söilen, 2025), I attempted to show practical strategies for developing these skills, both for students navigating academic institutions and for researchers facing the growing influence of AI in scholarly work. That book focuses on science, methodology, and how to work within the current academic system: how to design studies, evaluate sources, conduct peer-reviewed research, and build an academic career in an environment increasingly shaped by metrics, automation, and publication pressure.

This book, by contrast, takes a step back to ask more fundamental questions—not only how we are to understand human beings given what we now know, but how we might rethink our intellectual foundations altogether. It invites us to reconsider the architecture of knowledge itself—its assumptions, its structures, and its goals—especially now that new technologies are challenging what it even means to be a human knower. Where the first *Researcher's Journey* was pragmatic, this second book allows itself to be a bit more philosophical. Where the first book assumed the system, this one asks whether the system still serves us. And in doing so, it returns us to a deeper inquiry—into what learning is, how we become who we are, and what kind of thinkers the future will need.

If we are to believe some AI experts, we may not need much learning at all in the future—or at least not nearly as much as before. It would be enough, they argue, for a small group to build and maintain robots and AI systems, and then let those systems handle everything else. The rest of us could simply rely on their output. This attitude is not so different from what we occasionally see among some wealthy children: "Why should I work? My father already has all the money in the world." In a way, he has a point. But learning is not just a means to an end; it is an end in itself. It is a stimulating intellectual and spiritual process, hardly comparable to anything else. To strip large groups of people of that possibility would feel like a profound disservice.

At the same time, education is also a free choice. One scenario we may well face is that a small percentage of people will work—and work very hard—while the great majority do not. As we shall discuss later in this book, there are serious economic problems with that model no matter how you try to tweak it. Still, I suspect that in the long run, we will define ourselves less in terms of learning, at least in the traditional sense of sustained, difficult intellectual effort.

We can already see the outlines of this shift. Since the arrival of technologies like the calculator, the mobile phone, the internet, and now AI, the weight of "real learning" has been lightened. Bookshops are emptying out.

People do still listen to books, but not as much to difficult or challenging ones—more often to stories chosen for entertainment. Part of the reason is distraction. Another part is that many new technologies have made intellectual tasks easier for us, perhaps too easy. And when the work of thinking feels less necessary, the appetite for learning itself may begin to erode.

Learning is not a neutral process either. It is shaped by culture, structured by institutions, and increasingly mediated by machines. Understanding this dynamic is essential for any social science that seeks not only to describe the world but to improve it. If we truly want our students to start reading more books again—and not just easy ones, but difficult and demanding works—or to take on challenges such as building advanced machinery, then we must actively engage them in such pursuits. Yet we see very little of that in today's schools, at least in the West. Too often, education follows the path of least resistance, encouraging quick consumption of information rather than deep engagement, reflection, and creative struggle.

This lack of deep engagement in schools cannot be seen in isolation. Education never occurs in a vacuum; it is always embedded within a broader cultural landscape increasingly shaped by media technologies. As classrooms go digital and learners engage across platforms, the same device that delivers Shakespeare or statistics also streams memes, gossip, and ads. One tool, two fundamentally different tasks—yet the boundary between them is increasingly hard to police. The result is that instruction and influence blur into one another, with education competing for attention on the very stage designed for distraction. To understand how people learn, remember, and form their identities today, we must consider the symbolic environments that surround them.

And now, with the emergence of AI, we may be entering a true renaissance of self-directed learning. For the first time, it is possible to learn faster, deeper, and more autonomously than ever before. The *autodidact*—long a fringe figure—can now flourish. With the right tools and motivation, individuals are no longer constrained by institutional calendars or *academic gatekeeping*. *AI-assisted learning* provides tailored explanations, immediate feedback, and access to expert-level content across virtually any domain. Put bluntly: there has never been less reason to depend on universities or formal training as the primary path to knowledge.

Already today, in many cases, it makes more sense to ask an AI than a teacher. The likelihood of receiving a correct, detailed, and well-structured answer is often higher with the machine, particularly for factual or technical questions. This means that the traditional role of teachers as the primary conveyors of information will inevitably shrink. Their importance does not disappear, but it does change—and so, inevitably, will their numbers. Fewer teachers will be needed to deliver facts, while those who remain will increasingly serve as mentors, guides, and cultivators of judgment. Their value will lie not in supplying answers, but in fostering discernment: helping students decide which questions to ask, how to weigh competing claims, and how to connect knowledge to values and lived experience.

For such a renaissance to take root, however, we also need an infrastructure that genuinely supports the autodidact. This means ensuring access to free public libraries, affordable internet, and inexpensive computers—basic conditions that make self-directed learning possible. It also means rethinking how knowledge is certified. Examinations should be open to all, not just to those who have attended a particular school or paid for a degree. Employers, too, might place less emphasis on diplomas and more on what candidates can actually do, relying on practical tests or task-based assessments. After all, an autodidact does not need a sprawling university bureaucracy with hundreds of administrators, but they do need guidance. What makes the difference is not layers of institutional control, but a single good mentor. Encouraging systems of mentorship—whether formal or informal, in person or online—may be one of the most effective ways to nurture talent and make lifelong learning a genuine reality. To strengthen this shift, we could also introduce *national standardized examinations* in all major subjects, so that no university can hide behind its own closed exams. Such a reform would amount to a genuine democratization of education, giving every learner the chance to prove their competence on equal terms.

One fictitious manager in Japan took this logic seriously and decided to abandon diplomas altogether in his hiring process. His experience illustrates what a world "beyond the degree" might look like in practice:

Case in a Box: Beyond the Diploma—Hiring by Test, Not by Title

Mr. Kenji Watanoodle, a mid-level manager at the Tokyo-based firm HappyFin Accounting Solutions, had been hiring staff for more than two decades. Over the years, his faith in diplomas had steadily diminished. Too often he had brought in bright-looking graduates from top universities, only to discover that when asked to handle actual financial tasks, they struggled. As he liked to joke with his colleagues, *"The certificates are shiny, but the cash flow is cloudy."*

Little by little, Watanoodle began experimenting with a different approach. Instead of sorting through endless CVs, he designed a straightforward test. Whenever a new applicant came in—say, a business student eager for their first role—he would guide them into a quiet office, hand them the company's ledgers, and say:

> *"Prepare a cash flow statement. You have three hours. No internet, no phone. Just you, the numbers, and your skills. When the time is up, bring me your results."*

The outcomes were revealing. Some candidates froze immediately, staring blankly at the pages. Others scribbled furiously, crossing things out, recalculating, and gradually piecing together a coherent statement. For Watanoodle, this exercise was decisive. It showed not only technical ability but also composure under pressure, problem-solving skills, and perseverance.

By now, HappyFin's HR department knew that diplomas no longer carried much weight in Watanoodle's office. He still valued interviews for gauging personality and teamwork potential, but the test always tipped the scales. As he explained at one company meeting, *"I don't care if someone graduated from Harvard University or Noodle Tech. If they can build a reliable cash flow statement in three hours, they can work here."*

Questions for Discussion

1. What are the advantages and disadvantages of hiring by test rather than by diploma?
2. Could this approach disadvantage certain groups of applicants, and if so, how might companies address that risk?
3. Do you think this model works only in technical fields (like accounting) or could it apply in more creative or leadership-oriented jobs as well?
4. If diplomas no longer serve as a guarantee of competence, what role—if any—should universities play in preparing students for such tests?
5. Would you prefer to be evaluated this way as a job candidate? Why or why not?

Seen in this light, the challenge is not only technological or institutional, but historical. Education has never been a straight line of progress; it has always moved in waves. Periods of distraction and decline are often followed by renewed seriousness and creativity. What seems today like a drift away from books and depth may, over a longer horizon, turn into a rediscovery of rigor in new forms. A glance back a century shows the same cycle: enthusiasm, neglect, and revival following one another in turn. With that perspective, there is reason for cautious optimism. What matters is that we remain attentive, so that when the cycle turns again—as it surely will—we are ready to seize the opportunity.

It is also worth noting that the scenario in Watanoodle's office is not futuristic at all. Many companies have long relied on tests, case exercises, or trial projects rather than diplomas to assess real competence. Consulting firms routinely use problem-solving cases; tech companies often require coding tasks; even creative industries may ask applicants to submit portfolios or complete assignments under time pressure. In practice, the *test-before-title approach* has been quietly embedded in hiring for decades—it is only the rhetoric around diplomas that lags behind.

If learning really does move in cycles, then the question becomes what marks the present phase. We have seen enthusiasm rise and fall before, and today's wave of technological innovation will be no exception. The challenge, however, is that this cycle now unfolds in an environment unlike any previous one: a landscape dominated by media platforms that do not simply reflect culture but actively construct it. To understand where education is headed, we must therefore look not only at classrooms and institutions but also at the technological systems that increasingly shape how people think, remember, and relate to one another.

4.3.1 Beyond the Feed: Training Thought Before Technology

In today's interconnected world, media do not simply reflect reality—they actively construct it. This was less apparent in the age of broadcast television that I grew up with, which was primarily designed for entertainment. Educational programs such as Kenneth Clark's *Civilisation* or Carl Sagan's *Cosmos* stood out precisely because they were exceptions rather than the rule (Buckingham, 2003; Postman, 1985). The screen was never a serious rival to books or classrooms when it came to intellectual training.

That has fundamentally changed. Today, many of the world's most respected scholars, scientists, and public intellectuals regularly publish long-form content through platforms like YouTube, podcast networks, or specialized streaming services. Viewers can watch lectures by John Vervaeke, history series by Tom Holland and Dominic Sandbrook, or advanced economics seminars by MIT professors—all freely available, pausable, and replayable (Veletsianos, 2020). It is now possible to follow entire courses by leading universities without ever stepping into a lecture hall. This shift raises a provocative question: why attend university to hear a mediocre lecturer in a crowded hall when the best minds are a click away?

Yet this abundance brings its own paradox: while access to high-quality content has never been greater, genuine learning remains uneven. Research shows that for many users, digital consumption leads not to depth but to distraction—shortened attention spans, cognitive overload, and increased susceptibility to misinformation (Carr, 2010; Firth et al., 2019; Ward, 2017). Platforms optimized for clicks reward fragments over wholes, emotional reaction over reflection. A small group, already skilled in critical thinking, are able to use these resources to deepen their understanding; the majority, however, risk being pulled further into *surface knowledge*. The result is a widening *cognitive gap* (van Dijk, 2005; Reich, 2020).

This makes clear why *deep learning* cannot begin with the feed. It must be cultivated elsewhere—through books, rigorous dialogue, and mentorship—before digital tools can be used effectively. Outsourcing thinking to algorithms or allowing AI to generate answers risks intellectual stagnation. Minds grow stronger only by working through complexity, not by avoiding it.

Case in a Box: The Cloister Model—Learning by Slowing Down

Modern education often suffers from the same logic that drives platforms like TikTok: everything must be fast, engaging, and constantly changing. The result is distraction and shallow processing. But what if we invert this model entirely? Historian Niall Ferguson has suggested that the cloister, not the feed, may offer the more enduring framework for deep thought.

In the cloister, nothing happens quickly—and that is the point. Time is structured but unhurried: a bell signals waking, breakfast, work, study, and reflection. There is silence, repetition, and space for boredom. Instead of constant external stimuli, one is left with one's own mind. Paradoxically, this emptiness creates the conditions for ideas to grow.

As a student at HEC Paris, I encountered this contrast during a week spent at Ganagobie, a Benedictine monastery in southern France. Life there followed a strict daily rhythm, yet it was also marked by openness and intellectual generosity. A small group of students responded to the monks' invitation to continue these conversations, meeting in the evenings to discuss philosophy alongside our economics studies. We read and debated texts by Emmanuel Levinas and Martin Buber, exploring how their ideas on ethics and dialogue related to Christian metaphysics. The exchanges with the monks, carried out slowly through letters long before email or instant messaging, left a lasting impression, and traces of those discussions can still be found in "8.3 Value Alignment and Oversight," where they helped shape the treatment of moral philosophy.

The lesson of the cloister is not that everyone must become a monk, but that environments shape minds. Just as the monastery trains habits of contemplation, future learning centers could design spaces where students must leave their devices at the door. To achieve this, I sometimes think that clocks must almost "stop": silence, boredom, and uninterrupted attention must be reintroduced as legitimate conditions for learning.

Questions for Discussion

1. What might a modern "cloister model" for learning look like in practice?
2. Could universities or workplaces realistically implement device-free zones for deep study, or would this be resisted?
3. How might boredom function as a tool for creativity rather than as a failure of engagement?
4. What can we learn from historical models of monastic discipline that could be applied to contemporary education?
5. Would adopting a cloister-like rhythm in learning widen or narrow educational inequality?

I do not mean to suggest that students should head straight into a monastery and stay there. Rather, the cloister model may be adapted for specific parts of a course or program. Sometimes what is needed is simply a change of rhythm: a teacher might encourage students to step away for a week or so, to immerse themselves more deeply in study without the usual distractions. The cloister model reminds us that how we structure attention shapes not only individual learning but also the way societies remember and interpret themselves. If distraction erodes depth at the personal level, it also distorts memory at the collective level.

The implications stretch beyond individual learning to collective memory and identity. Maurice Halbwachs (1992) argued that memory is socially framed, shaped by groups and institutions. In the digital age, memory is also shaped by algorithms. Search engines and feeds do not simply retrieve the past; they decide which fragments resurface and which are buried. *Digital memory* is persistent and programmable (van Dijck, 2007). Content recirculates endlessly, controversies refuse to fade, and online traces remain long after individuals have moved on. Andrew Hoskins (2011) calls this the "*mediatization of memory*," where platforms, not communities, become the main agents of remembrance. The danger is that *surface retrievability* replaces deep understanding: what is easiest to access overshadows what is most meaningful.

Identity is equally entangled. Social media amplify Erving Goffman's (1959) dramaturgical model: individuals perform curated selves for an algorithmic audience. Unlike face-to-face life, these performances are permanent, searchable, and subject to constant comparison. Young users in particular face intense pressure to conform to stylized ideals shaped by influencer culture (Marwick, 2013). The attention economy rewards visibility over depth, virality over truth (Tufekci, 2015). At the same time, non-face-to-face interactions often lower inhibitions, encouraging more aggressive conduct. As can be observed on almost any platform, people quickly resort to insults and hostility when shielded by screens. The risk is that users become trained in such behaviors, carrying these habits into offline life, where they can contribute to heightened tension and even violent confrontations.

At the political level, media shape whose voices are amplified. Algorithms privilege sensationalism and polarizing content (Sunstein, 2017). Public controversies over statues, monuments, and history show how memory has become contested terrain in digital spaces (Boucher, 2021a, 2021b; Loewen, 2018; Murphy, 2020a, 2020b). Filter bubbles reinforce *ideological silos*, pushing groups further apart (Helbing et al., 2017; Whittaker et al., 2021). Attempts to regulate speech online, though often well intentioned, can paradoxically erode traditions of free expression and weaken the very institutions they aim to defend.

Navigating this environment requires more than access. It demands media literacy: the ability to evaluate sources, recognize platform incentives, and question one's own biases. And this training must begin offline—in schools, universities, and intellectual communities—where books and serious discussion build habits of reflection. Only on that foundation can digital tools strengthen rather than weaken judgment.

For social scientists, the task is to analyze these dynamics without collapsing into political alignment. Their credibility depends on neutrality and humility (Fluck, 2019; Sokal & Bricmont, 1998). Just as earlier scholars dissected how television shaped stereotypes (Gerbner et al., 1986) or propaganda (Chomsky & Herman, 1988), we now face the challenge of understanding how AI and algorithmic platforms reproduce bias, deepen inequality, or support education and governance (Eubanks, 2018; O'Neil, 2016).

The central insight is simple but sobering: technologies do not level the field. They amplify what already exists—attention, inequality, conflict, and creativity alike. The solution is not withdrawal, but resilience: *cultivating the slow*, difficult practices of reading, discussion, and reflection that keep human judgment alive.

4.4 Institutions as Engines of Collective Intelligence

In the previous section, we reflected on the cloister as a space deliberately designed to slow down thought and protect learning from distraction. But the cloister is more than a historical curiosity or a metaphor for focus—it is an *institution*. Like schools, courts, parliaments, or markets, it represents the human capacity to take fragile individual tendencies—our inclination to learn, to deliberate, to cooperate—and scale them into durable, collective systems. Institutions are the scaffolding that transforms fleeting human efforts into lasting patterns of action.

This insight connects directly to the layered model outlined at the beginning of the chapter. If language and belief create shared meaning (Layers 1–2), and norms and roles stabilize cooperation (Layer 3), then institutions represent the point at which these elements are formalized and embedded into larger structures (Layers 4–5). They are the carriers of knowledge and the enablers of collective intelligence—bridges between cultural memory and societal decision-making.

Seen in this light, institutions are not isolated entities but the cumulative product of culture. They grow out of earlier layers of cognition, meaning, and social structure, and in turn make possible the preservation of knowledge and the coordination of action at scale. In this sense, institutions embody culture's highest achievement: the ability to extend human intelligence across generations and across distances, transforming the limits of individual cognition into the possibility of collective reasoning.

Examples abound. Legal systems translate moral intuitions into enforceable rules. Markets aggregate countless preferences into prices that coordinate production and exchange. Educational systems preserve and transmit knowledge across centuries. Governance bodies establish decision-making procedures that allow millions to act under a shared political order. As Douglass North (1990) famously described, institutions provide the "rules of the game"—both formal (laws, constitutions, contracts) and informal (cultural norms, rituals, expectations)—that reduce uncertainty and enable cooperation.

Yet institutions are never only functional; they are also symbolic. Their authority rests not just on efficiency but on legitimacy, drawn from collective narratives and shared memory. A parliament building or a cathedral is more than bricks and mortar—it embodies ideas of representation, continuity, and authority. In this way, institutions do not merely coordinate action; they tell societies what their actions mean.

Case in a Box: Edifices of Authority—Why Institutions Build to Last
In many societies, the buildings associated with core institutions—parliaments, courts, universities, central banks—are not merely functional. They are designed to impress, endure, and symbolically communicate the gravity of the ideas they house. Architecture serves as a cultural signal: it tells us which

beliefs are meant to last and which places are not to be easily questioned or defaced.

Historically, institutional buildings have often drawn from classical traditions—Greco-Roman columns, monumental staircases, and domed roofs—symbolizing continuity and rational order (Bialostozky, 2016; Vale, 1992). In the post-Second World War era, more minimalist yet massive modernist structures arose, signaling technological progress and bureaucratic functionality (Scott, 1998). Across styles, the underlying message persists: large, solid, and dignified buildings convey legitimacy and authority.

But this symbolism has a double edge. Architecture may project stability, yet it can also mask fragility or even give a false sense of permanence to outdated doctrines or untested ideas. The U.S. Federal Reserve provides a striking example. Its regional banks, many built in the style of state capitols with white marble and neoclassical facades, project an image of permanence, democratic oversight, and civic trust. In reality, the Federal Reserve System is a hybrid institution: its Board of Governors is a federal agency, but the twelve regional Reserve Banks are structured as private corporations owned by member banks.[6] Its independence from day-to-day political control is meant to protect monetary policy from short-term electoral pressures, but it also places its decisions beyond the direct reach of voters and legislators (Conti-Brown, 2016).

The symbolism becomes even more paradoxical when we consider outcomes. On the one hand, the Federal Reserve issues the U.S. dollar—the world's most widely used and trusted reserve currency, anchoring global trade and finance (Eichengreen, 2011). On the other, the United States is the most indebted major economy in absolute terms, with a federal debt now exceeding its annual GDP (IMF, 2024). Some analysts warn of a debt spiral that will be politically difficult to reverse (Blanchard, 2019). The marble monuments that project stability conceal both this structural vulnerability and the contested debates over money creation itself—whether central banks should be allowed to expand the money supply without direct democratic accountability.

Such cases are not unique to finance. Throughout history, governments, universities, and corporations alike have used monumental architecture to convey legitimacy and permanence. Architecture, in this sense, can lend

6 Beyond its hybrid structure, the Federal Reserve has been especially effective at cultivating legitimacy through symbolism and expertise. Its recruitment of large numbers of academic economists has reinforced the image of the institution as scientifically neutral, technocratic, and above politics (Conti-Brown, 2016). This strategy, combined with its careful communication style and monumental architecture, has helped sustain an impression of independence and permanence—even as its decision-making reflects a complex blend of public oversight and private interests.

borrowed authority to fragile or misguided innovations, reminding us not to confuse power with wisdom.

Questions for Discussion

1. How do institutional buildings shape our trust in the authority and legitimacy of the institutions they represent? Can you think of examples where the symbolism worked—or failed?
2. Do you believe architecture can "mask" fragility, as in the example of monumental bank headquarters? If so, what responsibilities—if any—do designers and policymakers have to avoid misleading signals?
3. Many modern institutions rely less on physical presence (e.g., digital banks, online universities). How might the absence of monumental buildings affect public trust and legitimacy?
4. To what extent should institutional design—architectural or otherwise—prioritize transparency over symbolism? Can the two coexist?
5. Looking ahead, what forms of "institutional architecture" (digital platforms, AI-driven governance systems, virtual parliaments) might replace or complement traditional buildings in shaping authority?

From symbolic buildings to social cognition, the thread that links institutions is not their architecture alone, but their role as vessels for shared knowledge and coordinated action. This brings us to a more dynamic concept: *collective intelligence*.

Collective intelligence works as a kind of safeguard against individuals pushing through their own ideas unchecked. Before the internet, encyclopedias played this role, offering a reference point against which claims could be tested—but they required access to a library and were slow to update. Wikipedia was the first large-scale digital expression of this principle: a platform where people could quickly check what was broadly accepted as true, or at least widely agreed upon, before taking someone's word at face value.

Now, with AI, this function is raised to an entirely new level. Knowledge is no longer something we consult periodically, but something continuously present and immediately verifiable. Whatever is said can be checked in real time against the broader body of what "we know." This changes the nature of discourse: when someone speaks, they are not only expressing a view but also implicitly testing it against the collective record. If they align, their contribution reinforces what is known; if they diverge, their arguments demand careful study. In this way, collective intelligence becomes less about consensus alone and more about a dynamic process of challenge, correction, and refinement—an ongoing negotiation of shared knowledge at scale.

One of the most fruitful ways researchers have approached this phenomenon is by drawing parallels with biology. Insects such as bees and ants provide striking examples of *swarm intelligence*: decentralized systems where no single individual has the full picture, yet the group as a whole achieves remarkable coordination. Honeybee colonies, for instance, use collective decision-making to select new nest sites, with scouts performing waggle dances to communicate and amplify information until a consensus emerges (Seeley, 2010). Ant colonies display similar dynamics in foraging, where pheromone trails reinforce successful paths and fade when food sources are exhausted (Couzin, 2009). Even flocking birds and schooling fish reveal how simple local rules of movement can generate complex global patterns of coordination (Sumpter, 2006).

These *natural systems* are instructive because they show how intelligence can emerge from distributed interaction rather than centralized control. *Human collective intelligence*, too, often relies on such decentralized mechanisms—peer review in science, market signals in economics, or deliberation in democratic assemblies. Yet when compared directly, many insect communities actually achieve a level of coordination and efficiency far superior to human societies. Ant colonies can regulate traffic at nest entrances to avoid congestion, allocate workers dynamically across tasks, and adapt rapidly to environmental changes—all without conflict spiraling into disorder (Gordon, 2010). Termite mounds are another example: built without architects, they maintain stable temperature and ventilation through emergent cooperation (Turner, 2011). By contrast, human societies, despite possessing brains capable of abstract reasoning, often appear chaotic—plagued by misaligned incentives, information bottlenecks, and recurring breakdowns in cooperation.

The irony is striking: insects accomplish this without our capacity for symbolic thought or rational deliberation. We, on the other hand, possess such faculties but still fall short of building consistently harmonious collective structures. This suggests that if nature "wants" to organize collective intelligence in a species, it does not necessarily select for bigger or more complex brains. Instead, it may favor simple interaction rules, robust feedback, and strict adherence to shared roles—strategies that allow a colony of ants or bees to function as a kind of superorganism.

My own modest contributions in this area, through bibliometric studies of the field (e.g., Söilen & Benhayoun, 2019, 2022), suggest that the study of collective intelligence itself is developing along similar lines: multiple disciplines, loosely connected, slowly converging toward shared frameworks.

What makes the concept especially relevant today is its resonance with the technical capacities of modern AI systems. Collective intelligence describes processes of aggregating knowledge, detecting patterns, and converging on conclusions—precisely the kinds of operations AI excels at when trained on vast datasets. The potential is that AI might serve as a mediator of collective reasoning, synthesizing distributed input and even proposing coordinated steps for addressing complex problems.

Ideally, applied collective intelligence should help us ask two core questions: *Given what we know, what should we do?* And: *How should we go about it?* From climate challenges to healthcare, from inequality to education, AI and digital technologies could support forms of *distributed reasoning*—where human knowledge is not only archived but actively synthesized into coordinated action.

One way to see this potential is by looking at institutions that, for centuries, have been both indispensable and problematic: politics and finance. In both domains, power has historically been concentrated in structures that produce inefficiencies—political parties in democracy and commercial banks in finance. Digital infrastructures now make it possible to imagine alternative systems, where authority is distributed more widely, and where collective intelligence can be tapped in real time:

Case in a Box: Digital Democracy in Practice

Representative democracy rests on political parties—organizations that structure choice, aggregate interests, and provide stability. Yet parties also polarize societies, entrench elites, and often leave citizens feeling detached from decision-making. Digital technologies provide an alternative: the possibility of direct democracy at scale.

Some governments are already experimenting with participatory tools, such as electronic voting, online referenda, and participatory budgeting. Switzerland's tradition of referenda has inspired many of these efforts, but digital platforms allow them to be implemented far more frequently, at lower cost, and with broader participation. In Taiwan, for example, the vTaiwan platform has enabled crowdsourced deliberation on contested issues, bringing citizens, civil society, and government actors into a structured digital dialogue (Tang, 2019).

The potential benefits are non-negligible: policies that better reflect public will, reduced reliance on political parties, and greater transparency. But the risks are real, too. Digital divides can silence marginalized voices, algorithms can be manipulated, and trust in electronic voting is fragile. Nonetheless, these initiatives demonstrate how legitimacy can increasingly be derived not just from symbolic institutions like parliaments, but also from technological infrastructures that broaden participation.

Questions for Discussion

1. What advantages might digital democracy offer over party-based representative systems?
2. How could digital inequality undermine inclusivity in such systems?
3. What safeguards are necessary to build trust in digital voting and deliberation platforms?
4. Could AI help structure and summarize deliberations without bias?
5. How might digital democracy reshape political legitimacy over the long term?

The lessons from digital democracy point to a broader insight: when institutions are reorganized around *distributed participation*, long-standing problems can look different. In politics, the bottleneck has been the party system; in finance, it has been the heavy reliance on commercial banks. Both domains reveal the same underlying challenge: how to align institutional structures with collective trust. Just as digital platforms can reimagine political participation, financial technologies raise the question of whether money itself—arguably one of humanity's oldest institutions—can be redesigned for greater resilience.

Case in a Box: Digital Currencies and Institutional Intelligence
Modern economies depend on commercial banks for the issuance of credit and the management of deposits. Yet this dependency has repeatedly fueled cycles of speculation, asset bubbles, and financial crises—followed by costly bailouts that socialize losses while privatizing gains. *Central bank digital currencies (CBDCs)* represent an institutional alternative: money issued directly by the state, supported by digital infrastructure, and potentially decoupled from the fragility of commercial banking.

CBDCs promise safer deposits, lower transaction costs, and more efficient credit allocation. Combined with AI, they could even mitigate some of the volatility of the financial cycle, reducing reliance on speculative markets and smoothing swings in interest rates. Proponents argue that this could help prevent the cascading crises that have marked global finance for centuries.

But the risks are equally serious. Poorly designed CBDCs could become tools of surveillance, concentrate power in the state, and undermine trust in money itself. Their success depends not on technology alone but on institutional frameworks: who controls issuance, how privacy is protected, and how oversight is balanced. As with democracy, the key question is whether new infrastructures expand inclusion and resilience—or merely shift power to new forms of centralization (Söilen & Benhayoun, 2021).

Questions for Discussion

1. How might CBDCs alter the traditional roles of central banks, governments, and commercial banks?
2. What institutional safeguards are needed to prevent CBDCs from becoming tools of political control?
3. In what ways could CBDCs reduce volatility compared to the current financial system?
4. How do cultural and historical experiences with money shape public acceptance of digital currencies?
5. What parallels exist between CBDCs today and past financial innovations such as paper money or credit cards?

Taken together, these two cases—digital democracy and digital currencies—show how distributive technologies can challenge long-standing institutional bottlenecks. They demonstrate that collective intelligence is not only a cognitive process but also a design challenge: how to build infrastructures that expand participation, reduce risk, and maintain legitimacy.

More broadly, they illustrate just two examples of how advances in information technology—and AI, which in many ways represents the latest stage of that long trajectory—can be harnessed to address emerging institutional and societal problems. History shows that every major technological breakthrough, from the printing press to the internet, has been followed almost immediately by waves of social science inquiry that try to make sense of the new possibilities and risks it creates (Eisenstein, 1979; Beniger, 1986; Castells, 1996). The same is true today: as AI, digital platforms, and blockchain-based infrastructures reshape decision-making, finance, and governance, they generate an entire "tail" of research projects in political science, sociology, economics, and law, each grappling with the implications. This interplay—new technology leading to new questions in the social sciences—is not a side effect but a recurring pattern of modernity.

The deeper lesson is that technology does not, by itself, guarantee progress. Digital platforms and currencies can just as easily reinforce inequality, centralize power, or erode trust if embedded in rigid frameworks. What matters is whether institutions remain adaptive—capable of learning from error, integrating diverse perspectives, and evolving with changing circumstances.

In this sense, institutions are the connective tissue between symbolic meaning and practical governance. They scale human understanding into coordinated action, shaping the rhythms and rules of collective life. Their success lies in balancing continuity with flexibility, a dynamic that defines both the promise and fragility of modern civilization.

And while parliaments in most Western countries still stand as beautiful buildings, and banks often occupy the tallest, most spectacular towers in cities across the world, we must not let ourselves be blinded by these monuments. Architectural grandeur may project permanence and legitimacy, but the real strength of institutions lies not in their facades, but in their adaptability—their ability to learn, reform, and remain responsive to the societies they serve.

Seen in the context of our layered model, institutions occupy the higher levels of culture, where knowledge and meaning are scaled into systems of collective intelligence. Yet no matter how imposing or abstract they appear, their vitality ultimately depends on practices at the micro level—daily interactions, shared rituals, and the small-scale negotiations of belonging. To understand how culture truly lives, we must descend from the monumental to the ordinary, from institutions to the architectures of everyday life.

4.5 Social Architectures of Daily Life

In the previous sections of this chapter, we examined how meaning, knowledge, and coordination are structured through institutions, communication, and symbolic systems. These analyses focused largely on the macro level: the architecture of belief, trust, and authority in modern societies.

Yet in the layered model of culture, institutions are only one part of the story. Beneath them lie the everyday practices through which people experience, reproduce, and sometimes challenge cultural order. To see culture as scaffolding means not only tracing the upper layers of collective intelligence but also examining the foundations of daily interaction.

In this final section, we shift perspective to the micro level—to the lived experience of individuals navigating daily life through evolving social arrangements. Here we see how the same layered processes—cognition, meaning, social roles, knowledge, and coordination—are condensed into ordinary settings: households, friendships, workplaces, and digital communities. We explore how people form, sustain, or lose social ties, and how the norms of cohabitation, solitude, mental health, and digital interaction reflect deeper shifts in the architecture of human connection. The section moves from traditional family roles to algorithmic matchmaking, from communal rituals to social fatigue, showing how daily life has become both more flexible and more fragmented. If earlier sections asked how societies think and organize collectively, this one asks how individuals live, bond, and endure within those frameworks.

From an evolutionary perspective, human sociality was forged in small groups. Early Homo sapiens lived in bands of 25–50 individuals, where survival depended on close cooperation, collective childcare, and food sharing (Dunbar, 1992; Kelly, 2013). These early environments shaped many of our core psychological dispositions, toward reciprocity, kin loyalty, and face-to-face interaction.

The advent of agriculture 10,000 years ago initiated more permanent settlements and larger *kin-based networks*. As inheritance systems and land ownership became central, the nuclear and extended family gained importance. Marriage evolved into a stabilizing institution that facilitated the transmission of property, social roles, and moral expectations (Coontz, 2005; Goody, 1983).

Yet the forms of cohabitation and reproduction have always been culturally variable. In traditional societies, *multi-generational households* were common, often arranged vertically across generations rather than horizontally through peers. In many European regions, for instance, aging parents would remain in the home while younger generations took over household leadership, creating a continuity of care and knowledge transmission (Hajnal, 1965; Laslett, 1988).

Case in a Box: Staying Together or Moving Apart

Multi-generational living may sound remote today, but for many families it was the norm just a few generations ago. Consider one example from Norway. On the mother's side of the Bakkefluff family, five generations once lived together in a modest two-story wooden house in Reina, a working-class district just outside Trondheim where the Nidelva River meets the fjord. Reina, known for its wooden houses and community life, was later demolished and rezoned for industrial use in the 1970s and 1980s (Wikipedia, n.d.).

According to family history, the house was built by a great-great-great-grandfather who had served as a båtsmann (boatswain) on tall ships. He and his wife occupied the upper floor, while their daughter and her husband, Karl Bakkefluff, who ran a mason company, lived on the ground floor with their five children. One of those children was Gerda, who later became the great-grandmother. When her marriage broke down, her own daughter—the future grandmother—was raised by her grandparents in the same house. During the Second World War, when Trondheim served as a German naval base, that grandmother had a child with a German soldier. Again, the decision was made that the child should remain under the same roof with the extended family. At one point, five generations shared a space that amounted to little more than 100 m^2 per floor. Yet family photographs show a carefully tended garden, even with a bird bath, suggesting that pride and order were maintained despite the cramped conditions.

On the father's side, the Klippefjomp family lived in Haukeland outside Bergen, where land was traditionally subdivided with each generation, leaving progressively smaller plots. One great-grandfather inherited so little land that he combined sheep herding in the mountains with seasonal work on railway construction to sustain his household. His son received only a rocky hillside with no real farming potential but managed to secure employment as a locomotive driver after a short training course—ironically, on the very railway that crossed his former farmland. By the next generation, rising educational opportunities opened the path to occupational mobility, and younger family members increasingly moved into towns and cities in search of work.

Source Haukeland Train Station, Bergen, Norway. Photograph taken by the author, 2025

Taken together, these stories show how Norwegian families, only two or three generations ago, faced very different pressures in negotiating continuity and change. In the first case, scarcity of resources forced people to squeeze ever more tightly under the same roof, sacrificing space and privacy in order to preserve family unity. In the second, land shortages and economic necessity pushed family members to disperse, leaving the household behind altogether as they moved into towns and cities. Both strategies solved immediate problems, but each came with costs: one maintained togetherness at the expense of personal freedom, and the other secured independence at the expense of family cohesion.

Yet the story did not end within Norway's borders. Ultimately, those who benefitted most from these housing and opportunity pressures were not only Norwegians themselves, but the United States. Between 1825 and 1925, roughly 850,000 Norwegians emigrated (about 38% of the total population), many drawn by the promise of cheap and abundant land on the other side of the Atlantic. It was not just the poorest or most desperate who left, but often those most willing to take risks, endure hardship, and adapt to new environments. In this sense, emigration acted as a form of *selective pressure*: the U.S. received a self-chosen group of settlers who were both motivated and resilient. The consequences were long-lasting, contributing not only to the shaping of the American Midwest but also to the hollowing out of many Norwegian rural communities. Migration thus functioned as both a release valve for demographic and economic pressure at home and a transfer of human capital abroad.

Questions for Discussion

1. How many generations back in your own family can you find examples of multi-generational living? What do you know about how and why they lived this way?
2. What advantages did multi-generational households provide—social, economic, or cultural? What were their limitations?
3. How did urbanization and industrialization change not only where people lived, but also how families distributed care and responsibility?
4. Comparing the Bakkefluff and Klippefjomp examples, what might have been lost and what might have been gained as families shifted from shared living to mobility and independence?
5. In today's societies—facing housing shortages, aging populations, and rising costs of care—could multi-generational households re-emerge as a viable model? Why or why not?
6. The case ends with the note that around 850,000 Norwegians emigrated to the United States, often under pressure of land scarcity at home but also with the promise of opportunity abroad. What does this suggest about who emigrates under such conditions—those with the greatest need, those most willing to take risks, or both?

Industrialization, urbanization, and modern education have gradually eroded these interdependencies. Young adults now often leave home earlier, live independently longer, and marry later, if at all (Arnett, 2000). These changes have altered not only how we form intimate bonds, but also how we encounter *solitude*. Whereas earlier generations lived almost continuously within dense family networks, the modern lifecycle now includes multiple phases of *solitary living*: after adolescence, between partnerships, in old age, and for some, throughout life. This shift has redefined both the expectations of intimacy and the social experience of being alone.

While solitude may represent autonomy and freedom for some, it also carries risks, particularly when involuntary. Studies show that *social isolation*, especially in older adults, is associated with increased rates of depression, cognitive decline, and even premature mortality (Cacioppo & Cacioppo, 2014; Holt-Lunstad et al., 2015). Women, due to greater longevity and social resilience, are more likely to live alone in later life, while men are more vulnerable to the health impacts of isolation (Dykstra, 2009; Victor & Yang, 2012).

Simultaneously, the norms around partnership have diversified. Where marriage once served as a near-universal template, it is now one option among many. Cohabitation, serial monogamy, polyamory, and long-term singlehood are increasingly normalized. The influence of parental choice has declined, while individual agency—often guided by online dating platforms and algorithmic filtering—has expanded. Evolutionary psychology continues to shed light on mate preferences and strategies (Trivers, 1972), but cultural shifts mediate how these preferences are expressed.

The result is a landscape where traditional milestones—marriage, childbearing, retirement—are no longer synchronized or universal. Life scripts have pluralized. The very notion of "normal" adult life has become more fragmented and flexible, with implications for housing policy, mental health, and intergenerational support.

And yet, despite this flux, the need for *social anchoring* persists, of course. How could it be otherwise? People continue to seek meaning through affiliation, whether in families, digital communities, friendships, or ideological networks. If one lacks a traditional family structure, other arrangements often take on greater importance—such as loyalty to a bowling league, weekend canoe trips with new neighbors, or late-night bonding in online Minecraft servers. In such cases, one social structure is simply exchanged for another.

On the positive side, these newer forms of community allow individuals to select their own social environments, rather than accepting those imposed by tradition or kinship. However, the trade-off is that these social arrangements tend to be more fluid and fragile. Because they are more easily changed, people may invest less in them, leading to shallower ties and reduced resilience during times of need. This duality reflects a broader cultural pattern: greater freedom of association, but also greater risk of disconnection. This fragility underscores one of the key insights of the layered model: while culture may scale up to institutions and collective intelligence, its foundation is always in the small, repeated interactions that sustain or dissolve everyday bonds.

Psychological and epidemiological research has shown that *social disconnectedness* can have profound effects on mental and physical health. So, on the negative side, chronic loneliness is associated with increased risks of depression, anxiety, cardiovascular disease, and even early mortality, comparable to the health impact of smoking or obesity (Cacioppo & Cacioppo, 2014; Holt-Lunstad et al., 2015). Cognitive decline in older adults has also been linked to persistent social isolation. However, some studies suggest that occasional solitude—when voluntary—can support creativity, self-reflection, and emotional regulation (Long & Averill, 2003). The key lies in the difference between *chosen solitude* and *involuntary isolation*.

We often speak of wanting to "escape" and simply "be." Physiologically, such moments of non-doing would benefit the entire organism, as periods of reduced cognitive load promote recovery (Berto, 2014). Unfortunately, the brain has no true "off" switch, and training the ability to be present is difficult, especially when aware of pending tasks (Smallwood & Schooler, 2015). Even *mindfulness practice*, which in a sense aims to quiet the mind, must contend with the evolved tendency toward problem-solving vigilance. This tension—between the desire to rest and the brain's compulsion to anticipate—explains why achieving pure presence is so difficult.

When people lack dependable social ties, especially in moments of stress or transition, their capacity to cope declines markedly. In contrast, those embedded in stable, yet flexible social networks tend to report higher well-being, stronger identity, and greater resilience over the lifespan (Umberson & Montez, 2010). Thus, while modern life permits more freedom in forming and dissolving relationships, the underlying human need for secure and enduring connection remains largely unchanged.

In this way, the micro-dynamics of solitude, partnership, and community become the smallest bricks in the cultural scaffold. By examining them closely, we see how everyday practices feed upward into the larger layers of meaning, institutions, and collective intelligence described earlier. Culture, in other words, is not only built from grand symbols and institutions—it is also sustained in the fragile routines of daily life.

We now move from these intimate configurations to a related but more structured domain: how people interact, perform roles, and navigate expectations in various kinds of social encounters. To do this, we examine the spaces and occasions where people meet.

4.5.1 From Rituals to Digital Intimacy

We meet for many different reasons—and despite the cultural emphasis on social interaction as something inherently enjoyable, most meetings in everyday life are not entirely voluntary. From workplace obligations to family duties, many of our social encounters are shaped more by necessity than desire.

Sociologists have long noted that human social life is structured by roles and obligations (Goffman, 1959), and much of our interaction is *performative* rather than *spontaneous*. Formal meetings such as office gatherings, school conferences, or civic obligations follow set norms, while informal ones—catching up with friends, neighborhood chats—can vary widely in spontaneity and purpose. The distinction between online and offline interactions had already begun to grow sharper in the years leading up to the pandemic, as digital communication became more integrated into daily life (Turkle, 2011). The pandemic only accelerated this shift, making both realms central frameworks for fulfilling social, professional, or emotional functions.

Some meetings are short and transactional; others, deeply immersive. And while it might appear that we live in a hyperconnected world, many people—especially those in Northern and Central Europe—report a preference for solitude or limited interaction (Hofstede et al., 2010). Cultural variation in *individualism* versus *collectivism* plays a large role here, influencing not just how often we meet, but how we perceive the necessity of doing so.

It's a misconception that most people are naturally social butterflies. Research shows that a substantial portion of the population is introverted or *socially ambivalent*, finding greater psychological stability in solitude than in frequent socializing (Coplan et al., 2019; Rubinstein & Shaver, 1979). Many feel pressure to maintain a "social" identity, even when it doesn't align with their personal needs. As social psychologist Roy Baumeister (1991) argued, self-worth is often tied to perceived social value, which can make meetings feel more like tests of belonging than sources of joy.

When people attend gatherings with little to offer—be it emotional support, novelty, or resources—they often sense they're less welcome. Conversely, those with wealth, power, or status are frequently sought after, though not necessarily for who they are. In such contexts, meetings can become acts of *strategic positioning*, instead of genuine connection. This is why, as many wise parents have said, one should never base one's happiness entirely on others. The ability to enjoy solitude and cultivate one's own projects is not only a form of emotional independence, but also a protective factor against disappointment and *social exhaustion* (Larson, 1990; Long et al., 2003). Social life is not just about connection, it is about navigating expectations, balancing obligations, and preserving a sense of self amid competing demands.

Case in a Box: Decorating the Rooms of Solitude

What does it mean to be alone without feeling lonely? Many people fear solitude, filling every silence with noise and every pause with distraction. Yet being alone is not necessarily an absence—it can be an opportunity. The question is how we "decorate the rooms in our minds" so that solitude becomes not a burden but a place of engagement and renewal.

To enjoy one's own company, one must become interesting—to oneself. Otherwise, solitude turns into restlessness, and we try, as it seems, to flee from ourselves at every chance. One of the simplest ways to begin is through language. Learning new languages expands the ability to think, reflect, and express; it gives words to inner experiences that otherwise remain vague.

The next step is to create a world of excitement and colorful experiences inside the mind. Novels are invaluable here, because they offer stories of all the things that can happen to human beings—tragedies, adventures, loves, and losses. Travel, too, expands the inner room by adding landscapes, encounters, and perspectives that can be recalled and revisited. For those inclined toward deeper thought, philosophy and history provide frameworks for situating personal experience within broader patterns of meaning.

Physical well-being also matters. A neglected body rarely sustains a thriving mind. Attention to health, fitness, and rest creates the foundation for clarity and creativity. In this sense, solitude is not a withdrawal from life but a training ground for living it more fully. With such preparation, even waiting in line or sitting on a train can become an opportunity: one can either reach out to others or retreat into the cultivated room of one's own thoughts. The point is not to avoid people, but to ensure that one's happiness is not wholly dependent on them.

This cultivation of an "interesting head" is perhaps one of the deepest purposes of education. In German, the concept of *Bildung* captures this broader idea: the shaping of the self through exposure to language, classics, and culture.[7] For centuries, young Europeans undertook the *Bildungsreise* or Grand Tour, traveling the Mediterranean to see ancient cultures and broaden their horizons.[8] The goal was not merely knowledge but character: to build an inner world rich enough to sustain independence, curiosity, and dignity.

The library has traditionally been the place where this inner world finds its home—where the books we have read and collected sit alongside the impressions of travels, arts, and architecture, forming a reservoir of memory and meaning. And in our own time, this project has gained new urgency. It is not only because we are often more alone, but also because we have more time than ever before to educate ourselves—and perhaps, as one of the key conclusions of this book suggests, education in this broad sense is more important

[7] The concept of *Bildung* has deep roots in German philosophy and literature, where it signifies not merely education in the narrow sense, but the formation of character, taste, and judgment through lifelong self-cultivation. It first gained prominence in the late eighteenth and early nineteenth centuries. Wilhelm von Humboldt emphasized *Bildung* as the harmonious development of individual capacities in his essay *Theorie der Bildung des Menschen* (1793/1794), later elaborated in *Ideen zu einem Versuch, die Grenzen der Wirksamkeit des Staates zu bestimmen* (1792, published 1851). In Humboldt's view, *Bildung* was both a personal and civic ideal: through engagement with language, history, and culture, individuals became capable of autonomy and participation in public life.

The literary dimension of *Bildung* was famously dramatized by Johann Wolfgang von Goethe in *Wilhelm Meisters Lehrjahre* (1795–1796), which gave rise to the genre of the *Bildungsroman*—the "novel of formation." Here, *Bildung* is not only intellectual but experiential, gained through the trials and errors of living. Later thinkers such as Georg Wilhelm Friedrich Hegel (*Phänomenologie des Geistes*, 1807) and Friedrich Schiller (*Über die ästhetische Erziehung des Menschen*, 1795) extended the concept to philosophy and aesthetics, seeing *Bildung* as the reconciliation of individual freedom with universal reason.

In English, *Bildung* is often translated simply as "education" or "formation," but these terms fail to capture its full resonance.

[8] The *Bildungsreise* (educational journey) or *Grand Tour* was a formative tradition among European elites from the sixteenth to the nineteenth century. Originating in England in the late Renaissance, the Grand Tour became a cultural rite of passage for young aristocrats and, later, members of the upper bourgeoisie. Its aim was to complete one's education by traveling through France, Switzerland, and above all Italy and Greece, to study classical ruins, art, and politics in situ (Black, 1992). The English were early leaders in shaping the practice, with Thomas Coryat's *Coryat's Crudities* (1611) offering one of the first travel accounts, and later guidebooks and patronage networks institutionalizing the Tour as a marker of refinement and status.

than ever. If AI increasingly takes over our jobs, then cultivating alternative, meaningful activities becomes essential: pursuits that can be self-fulfilling and that help build moral character.

Source Ceiling mural by painter Tony Wåhlander in the library at *Trudvang*. The work is an homage to Andrea Mantegna's illusionistic ceiling fresco in the *Camera degli Sposi* (1465–1474), Ducal Palace, Mantua

Questions for discussion

1. Why do many people find solitude uncomfortable, and how might this reflect the state of their "inner rooms"?
2. How does learning languages, literature, or philosophy expand the capacity to enjoy one's own company?
3. In what ways does physical well-being influence our ability to cultivate mental well-being in solitude? Give some examples.
4. Is the idea of *Bildung*—self-cultivation through classics and travel—still relevant today, or has it been replaced by other forms of education?
5. Can the ability to enjoy solitude be seen as a form of resilience in the modern, hyperconnected world?

If solitude is the work we do within ourselves, meetings are the work we do with others. The two are not opposed but complementary. A person who has cultivated inner resources—through reading, reflection, or simply learning to be content alone—enters social life with a different quality of presence. Solitude builds the foundation for genuine encounters: it makes it possible to meet others out of curiosity rather than dependency, with openness rather than insecurity. In this sense, solitude and meeting are not separate conditions but two sides of the same human dynamic.

Meetings differ not only in purpose—ranging from economic obligation to emotional bonding—but also in size, duration, voluntariness, setting (online or offline), and the degree of intimacy involved. By classifying meetings along these axes—with a few unusual examples included—we can better understand their social function, emotional cost, and cultural variation. This helps us see patterns that are often invisible: why some meetings energize us while others leave us depleted, or how digital platforms are reshaping the way we gather and relate (Table 4.5).

The table illustrates the remarkable diversity of social encounters that structure our lives. By comparing settings along dimensions such as voluntariness, duration, size, and purpose, we begin to see how human interaction operates across a wide spectrum, from tightly scripted obligations to free-form, spontaneous gatherings. Whether formal or informal, online or offline, these social configurations each play a role in shaping identity, emotional well-being, and social cohesion.

One practical implication of this typology is that it invites reflection on how we structure our days. For those with the privilege of choosing how to allocate their time—a luxury that admittedly few possess—one helpful approach is to plan for a balanced mix of social meetings and solitary tasks.

Table 4.5 Types of social meetings and their key characteristics

Example	Voluntariness	Duration	Size	Purpose	Mode	Formality	Frequency
Dinner with close friends	Voluntary	2–4 h	2–6 people	Bonding, relaxation	Offline	Informal	Weekly to Monthly
Family reunion	Half-voluntary (duty)	1 day – weekend	10–50 people	Tradition, kinship maintenance	Offline	Semi-formal	Yearly
Workplace team meeting	Involuntary	30–90 min	5–12 people	Coordination, task management	Online/ Offline	Formal	Weekly
Therapy session (individual)	Voluntary	45–60 min	2 (1-on-1)	Support, reflection	Offline/ Online	Formal	Weekly
Online gaming session	Voluntary	1–6 h	2–10 (or more)	Entertainment, competition	Online	Informal	Varies
Religious service	Half-voluntary	1–2 h	20–500 + people	Spirituality, community	Offline	Formal	Weekly
Political rally or protest	Voluntary	2–5 h	100–100,000 +	Expression, activism	Offline	Mixed	Episodic
Football match (as fan)	Voluntary	2–4 h	10,000–80,000 +	Entertainment, group identity	Offline	Informal/ Formal	Weekly to Monthly
School class	Involuntary	45–90 min	15–40 people	Learning, instruction	Offline/ Online	Formal	Daily
Funeral	Half-voluntary	1–3 h	10–200 + people	Mourning, respect	Offline	Formal	Rare (life event)
Speed dating event	Voluntary	1–2 h	10–50 people	Mate-seeking	Offline	Semi-formal	Occasional
Zoom webinar/ conference	Voluntary	1–8 h	50–5000 + people	Learning, professional exposure	Online	Formal	Occasional

(continued)

Table 4.5 (continued)

Example	Voluntariness	Duration	Size	Purpose	Mode	Formality	Frequency
Club meeting (hobby group)	Voluntary	1–3 h	5–20 people	Shared interest, belonging	Offline/ Online	Informal	Weekly to Monthly
Doctor's appointment	Half-voluntary	15–60 min	2 (1-on-1)	Health-related	Offline	Formal	As needed

Human beings need both connection and solitude; too much of one often leads to stress, boredom, or burnout. Ideally, we would not want too many meetings, but not too few either. Life becomes a matter of finding a rhythm that allows for both interaction and recovery.

In practice, many people divide the day into *temporal segments*—before and after lunch, or before and after returning home from work. Some meetings energize us, others drain us; some tasks are better done with others, others require quiet focus. A well-balanced schedule attends to this variety. Understanding the *social-emotional weight* of different meetings can help us make more conscious decisions about how we design our days—and our lives.

But organizing our social lives isn't just about time and balance—it's also about how relationships begin, evolve, and either deepen or dissolve. In the digital age, one of the most profound changes in social interaction lies in how we meet new people, particularly in romantic contexts.

4.5.1.1 Digital Attraction and the Limits of Chemistry

Research suggests that while online platforms can efficiently connect individuals—especially those seeking romantic partners or niche social groups—the quality of relationships formed online often differs from those initiated offline (Finkel et al., 2012). The early phases of *online relationships* tend to involve more uncertainty and idealization because nonverbal cues are limited (Gibbs et al., 2006). By contrast, encounters in social gatherings benefit from immediate context and shared acquaintances, which help build trust more quickly (Walther, 1996).

Most online relationships transition offline fairly quickly, and this is where the real compatibility test begins. Users may initially select partners using objective criteria—such as height, education, or profession—because these are searchable and feel reliable. Yet real-life interactions often reveal that such preferences matter less than conversational ease, shared values, or simply feeling understood (Eastwick & Finkel, 2008; Kurzban & Weeden, 2005).

Real-life chemistry—often described as an immediate sense of connection or "spark"—may feel mysterious, but science shows it is grounded in both biology and psychology. First impressions activate brain regions related to reward and threat detection, such as the amygdala and ventral striatum, within milliseconds (Zeki, 2007). Physical attractiveness, scent, voice, and subtle facial expressions all contribute to this rapid, unconscious evaluation (Gangestad & Thornhill, 1998).

However, what we call "chemistry" is not always a reliable predictor of long-term compatibility. It can be biased by novelty, projection, or hormonal states, while relationship stability depends more on communication, shared values, and emotional regulation (Gottman & Levenson, 1992). In other words, the spark may start a connection, but it rarely sustains one.

At the most basic level, human communication requires *spatial proximity*. To speak to someone, we must move closer—close enough to be heard, but also close enough to signal that we are addressing this person and not others nearby. This movement through space already conveys intent: it creates a temporary dyad within a larger group. Yet proximity is a delicate matter. Stand too far away, and you risk appearing aloof, fearful, or overly deferential. Stand too close, and the impression may be one of aggression or intrusion. Anthropologist Edward T. Hall (1966) famously described these *zones of interpersonal distance*—intimate, personal, social, and public—as a *grammar of spatial interaction*. Later studies confirmed that small deviations in distance, orientation, or gaze direction carry strong social meanings (Burgoon et al., 2016; Keltner & Lerner, 2010).

Culture plays a decisive role here. In Mediterranean and Latin American societies, closer distances are often considered normal, while Northern Europeans or East Asians may prefer more personal space (Remland et al., 1995). Even the expectation that one should face the other directly, rather than from the side, reflects a learned convention about how respect, sincerity, and attention are displayed. These subtle cultural grammars of space and movement are the stage on which all verbal communication occurs, shaping how encounters begin and unfold (Table 4.6).

The "*curiosity phase*" in particular often lasts only as long as it takes to assess potential benefits—whether in the form of information, contacts, or opportunities. Young people sometimes extend this phase simply for the joy of conversation, but as we age, interactions often become more instrumental—more targeted in questions and more efficient in deciding when to move on. Importantly, these three phases show that social meetings are not merely verbal exchanges but embodied cultural performances, guided by invisible rules of space, gesture, and timing. They illustrate once more the layered nature of culture: how deeply rooted cognitive dispositions—threat detection, attention to proximity—are shaped by shared meanings, stabilized by social structures, and enacted in everyday encounters.

4.5.1.2 From Meetings to Knowing

At this point, it is useful to pause and widen the lens. What lies beneath these phases of encounter is not only social choreography but also a way of constructing knowledge.

Table 4.6 Three phases of face-to-face meetings

Phase	Description	Evolutionary function	Common social cues
Welcoming Phase	Initial greetings and polite acknowledgment, establishing a safe and friendly tone	Reduces perceived threat, signals openness, initiates affiliative bonding (Keltner & Lerner, 2010)	Smiles, open posture, warm tone, nodding
Curiosity Phase	Exploratory questioning and self-disclosure aimed at assessing the other's identity, status, and potential usefulness	Information gathering, coalition building, resource and mate evaluation (Trivers, 1971; Cosmides & Tooby, 2000)	Eye contact, leaning forward, follow-up questions, mirroring gestures
Parting Phase	Polite closure or abrupt departure, signaling the end of interaction	Conserves energy, minimizes wasted effort, avoids unnecessary social risk (Knapp et al., 2014)	Shifting gaze, stepping back, verbal cues ("Well, I should get going")

All human beings—whether trained philosophers or not—carry some implicit system for making sense of the world. This is what philosophers call *epistemology*: the study of knowledge, its sources, and its limits. For some, this remains an unspoken intuition, shaped by culture and habit; for others, it becomes an explicit framework of reflection (Audi, 2011; Hofer & Pintrich, 1997). Research in educational psychology shows that even young students develop "epistemological beliefs" about what counts as knowledge, whether they see it as certain or evolving, and who they trust as authorities (Schommer, 1990). In other words, we all operate with some epistemology—more or less consciously—even if we never use the term.

Once we recognize this, the connection to proxemics becomes clearer. Movement through space is not just a social ritual—it is also a way of knowing. By shifting position, adjusting distance, and reorienting ourselves, we create the very conditions under which understanding becomes possible. This opens to a broader philosophical reflection on how knowledge itself is tied to embodiment and movement.

Case in a Box: Movement and Knowledge—An Epistemological Reflection

At the most fundamental level, human beings are living organisms—like plants and other animals, though more complex in some respects, but not in all. What sets us apart is not only our cognitive capacity but also a tendency toward hyperinflation of the self: we imagine ourselves above the rest of nature. This self-image helps explain why humans have often treated the environment and other species with indifference or exploitation (Harari, 2014; Wilson, 1978). Yet our self-understanding is not static. It changes over time according to the dynamics of evolutionary theory—variation, selection, and inheritance—reminding us that culture, too, is subject to adaptive processes (Mayr, 2001; Mesoudi, 2011).

All of us, whether consciously or not, develop systems for how we understand the world. Philosophers call this epistemology: a framework for how knowledge is acquired, filtered, and made meaningful. Some are deeply reflective about their epistemology; others operate with implicit assumptions shaped by culture and habit. But in either case, the way we see the world is never neutral—it is always mediated by perception, memory, and interpretation.

In the first *Researcher's Journey* (Söilen, 2025, pp. 406–407), I described my own epistemological outlook as a variation on Immanuel Kant's *transcendental idealism*: "Our understanding of the world is shaped both by sensory experience and by the mental frameworks we impose on that experience. While we cannot know things as they are in themselves ('*noumena*'), we can understand them as they appear to us ('*phenomena*'), structured by our mind's inherent categories like space and time."

This Kantian stance suggests that what we call "reality" is always already filtered: through perception, through culture, through habit. My own emphasis is that we must not simply yield to the senses but learn to keep them at arm's length. Sensory impressions are indispensable, yet they seduce us into mistaking immediacy for truth. To live through and for the senses is to become their captive—pleasurable for a time, but rarely a path to lasting contentment. The senses should instead be treated as instruments—useful but fallible—while the inner world of the brain, with its powers of reflection, imagination, and abstraction, provides the distance from which genuine understanding becomes possible.

In this light, knowledge is transformed not by the senses alone, but by what we can call *Bewegung und Erkenntnis*—movement and knowledge. Learning arises through two main forms of movement: approaching others to share their experiences, and making our own. Books add a third, derivative form, transmitting the experiences of others at a distance. Where we move—geographically, socially, intellectually—reshapes what we can perceive and understand. Life thus becomes an art of positioning: choosing spaces that optimize Erkenntnis, and thereby extending both perception and reflection.

This outlook resonates with Maurice Merleau-Ponty's phenomenology of embodiment (*Phénoménologie de la perception*, 1945/2012), which insists that the body is not a vessel we inhabit but the very medium through which we perceive the world. It also echoes Martin Heidegger's notion of *Dasein* in *Sein und Zeit* (1927/1962): that human being is never neutral, but always situated—colored by mood, purpose, and anticipation.

Modern neuroscience lends further support. *Predictive coding theories* (Clark, 2013; Friston, 2010) describe perception not as passive reception but as active hypothesis-testing, constantly updated with new sensory input. Even something as basic as color perception illustrates this point: color is not a property of objects but a construct of the brain, echoing Kant's claim that we perceive phenomena, not noumena. *Proxemics* offers another case: the "right" conversational distance is not dictated by physics but by culturally shaped expectations (Burgoon et al., 2016; Hall, 1966).

A simple example shows how applicable this perspective can be. Conflict is part of life, yet not all conflict requires words or arguments. Sometimes the most effective resolution is not persuasion but movement. By stepping away—removing yourself physically from a heated exchange—you restore a kind of status quo, a neutral ground from which new relationships and new approaches can later emerge. Conflicts exist not only between individuals but also between societies and nations; they are often difficult to resolve, and happiness should not depend on our ability to do so. To carry the weight of every conflict is a form of idealism that becomes self-destructive. Seen through the lens of *Bewegung und Erkenntnis*—movement and knowledge—such withdrawal is not weakness but wisdom: by changing position, we create the distance needed for new understanding to take shape.

I also call this the *Marco Polo tradition* (Söilen, 2025): knowledge as exploration, grounded in firsthand experience, curiosity, and adaptation rather than abstract speculation. Marco Polo set out first and foremost as a merchant, the son of a Venetian trading family, constantly asking what people were producing, what had superior quality, and what could be exchanged at better prices. Yet in the course of these journeys he also became an explorer, extending trade into discovery, and commerce into curiosity. The notion captures a fundamental way of learning about the world—through direct encounters and journeys into the unknown. Every movement toward another person—whether to speak, listen, or simply be present—is therefore not only an act of survival (to cooperate, to belong) but also an epistemological act (to interpret, to know).

The opposite path is inward idealization: the creation of reality within the head, detached from observation and dialogue. German philosophy has long warned of this danger. Hegel's description of the "beautiful soul" (*die schöne Seele*) in the *Phenomenology of Spirit* (1807/1977) shows how retreat into inner purity can become sterile when cut off from lived contradictions. Nietzsche (1887/1994), in *On the Genealogy of Morality*, critiqued moral systems built on abstract ideals as "life-denying." Hannah Arendt (1951/1973), in *The Origins of Totalitarianism*, traced how ideology can harden into self-contained systems, impervious to empirical correction, with catastrophic political results. Niklas Luhmann (1984/1995) adds a systems-theoretical view: social reality is not constructed in isolated minds but through chains of communication (*Kommunikationshandlungen*). Detached inner-world constructions, untested by communicative exchange, are therefore fragile—and dangerous.

Seen this way, the contrast is stark. The experiential approach—tested through movement, exploration, and dialogue—tends toward *pragmatism*. The purely idealist approach—spun from inward imagination—tends toward *fundamentalism*, whether political or religious. The challenge for science and society is to keep our epistemologies open, dialogical, and grounded in lived experience, not trapped in mental constructions that deny the corrective role of encounter.

In short, even the simple matter of where we stand in relation to others—how close we approach, how we orient our bodies—becomes a microcosm of a larger truth: that knowledge is neither purely objective nor purely subjective, but always constructed in motion, filtered by culture, and lived through the body—a body that, as Dawkins reminds us in *The Selfish Gene* (1976), is ultimately a vessel for the genes we are set to pass on.

Questions for Reflection

1. How do you explain the way you see and understand the world?
2. Is your perspective shaped more by sensory input (empiricism) or by mental frameworks and culture (idealism)?
3. When you approach someone in conversation, what cultural "rules" of distance or orientation are you following, consciously or unconsciously?
4. Does the idea of *Bewegung und Erkenntnis*—that movement and knowledge are intertwined—resonate with your own experiences of learning and understanding? Why, or why not?
5. Can you identify moments when your "mental room" (your inner framework) has felt more important than external reality in shaping how you act or decide?

Seen in this light, even the smallest acts of approaching, speaking, or withdrawing are not just social rituals but moments where knowledge, culture, and survival intersect. Our movements and interpretations are shaped by both embodied perception and cultural rules, but they also serve deeper evolutionary purposes.

From an evolutionary perspective, most meetings serve adaptive purposes: resource access, mating strategies, kin protection, or information exchange. As we have seen, friendship itself can be understood as an evolved mechanism with survival value—offering protection, mutual aid, and emotional stability (Dunbar, 2010; Silk, 2003). Over repeated encounters, bonds either strengthen through trust and reciprocity or weaken when no value is perceived.

We are not naturally good at sustaining conversations that yield no return. In such cases, attention drifts, eyes wander, and disengagement follows. This explains why even in highly social settings, the accumulation of brief, low-yield encounters often results in what researchers call "*social fatigue*."

Seen in the larger framework of this chapter, these encounters illustrate the third layer of the cultural scaffold—*social structures*. Meetings, whether ritualized or improvised, are the everyday mechanisms through which norms, roles, and expectations are enacted. They may look trivial in isolation, but together they form the routines that stabilize culture and make higher levels—knowledge systems and collective intelligence—possible.

4.5.2 The Limits of Belonging: Social Fatigue and Invisible Barriers

Thus, despite our reputation as highly social creatures, social interaction is often experienced as effortful—and at times even stressful—for many people.[9] This paradox is supported by both psychological and biological research. While humans evolved to live in groups and depend on social networks for survival (Dunbar, 1998), the quality—not the quantity—of social interactions appears to matter most for well-being. *Superficial encounters* or *obligatory socializing* can increase stress and reduce life satisfaction (Kawakami et al., 2015). Social bonds are essential, but not all encounters provide a meaningful connection.

Social fatigue is real. The mental load of tracking cues, managing impressions, and adhering to norms can be exhausting, especially for *introverts* (Cain, 2012). Even *extroverts* have limits, of course. These differences are partly rooted in neurobiology, particularly how dopamine functions

[9] See Söilen (2013) for a discussion of how the repetitive, low-yield nature of many interactions challenges effectiveness at trade shows, as well as strategies such as staff rotation, scheduled rest periods, and structured follow-up routines to extend engagement beyond the even.

in relation to stimulation and reward (Depue & Collins, 1999). Additionally, overstimulation from digital communication—email, video calls, social media—can lead to *social burnout* (Przybylski & Weinstein, 2017), fragmenting attention and diminishing real connection.

So, we should not be too harsh on ourselves when conversations do not flow smoothly—whether on our side or on the side of the other. From an evolutionary perspective, the purpose of interaction was never to make every exchange effortless, witty, or entertaining. Social encounters evolved as functional tools for survival: to exchange information, to coordinate action, to assess trustworthiness, or to signal alliance (Cosmides & Tooby, 2005). Nature optimized these encounters for utility, not for perpetual harmony. Occasional awkwardness, silence, or even conflict may feel uncomfortable, but they are part of the normal range of *social outcomes*. What matters most is not that every interaction is perfect, but that, over time, enough of them contribute to building trust, cooperation, and resilience.

Another important factor is the balance between built and natural environments. A growing body of research suggests that fatigue may be amplified by insufficient exposure to nature and excessive reliance on artificial, urban, or digital settings. *Attention Restoration Theory* (Kaplan & Kaplan, 1989) proposes that natural environments restore depleted cognitive resources by engaging the mind in effortless attention, reducing stress, and promoting recovery. Empirical studies show that time in green spaces improves concentration, lowers cortisol levels, and reduces mental fatigue (Berman et al., 2008; Hartig et al., 2014). Neuroscientific evidence indicates that natural settings activate brain regions associated with calm and positive affect, while urban overstimulation can trigger heightened amygdala activity and stress responses (Bratman et al., 2012; Lederbogen et al., 2011). From an evolutionary perspective, this mismatch is unsurprising: humans have spent most of their history in natural environments, and the rapid shift to dense urban and digital contexts may outpace our biological capacity to adapt (Kahn, 1999; Ulrich et al., 1991).

It is therefore also not unusual that many people deliberately seek time outdoors, whether through long walks, mountain hikes, or simple contact with greenery, as a way of recharging and regaining equilibrium:

Case in a Box: Hunting as Reflection

Angus McSporran's annual hunting trips to the moors of Glenfuddle for mountain grouse are more than sport. They are a test of endurance—marching 7–9 h a day for three or four days straight, with shooting challenges where the birds often hold the advantage. Yet beyond the physical trial, these trips offer something more valuable: distance. The same group of friends has met for over 30 years, walking together in a broad line across the plateau. Still, the communication is sparse; each hunter is absorbed in the rhythm of movement, the search for birds, and his own thoughts. The real social dimension comes later, in the evenings, when the silence of the day gives way to shared meals, stories, and the familiar camaraderie that anchors the tradition.

Up on the plateau, far from the cities, the combination of altitude, thin air, and sheer remoteness creates a perspective that cannot be reached when immersed in daily routines. Each year, it becomes a necessary break to reflect on what is actually being done in the lowlands—whether those activities truly make sense, whether they deserve the energy they consume. For McSporran, the experience has something of the character of a cathedral for the Christian man: not only a place of reflection and awe, but also of quiet judgment, where one is forced to confront oneself. The irony is that these thoughts almost never arise when "in the middle of things." Only in solitude, with effort and distance, do they take form.

Photo Jon Axelsen, 2025

Questions for Discussion

1. Why do certain environments—like mountains, forests, or cathedrals—seem to invite reflection more than others?
2. Can physical endurance and hardship deepen intellectual or spiritual reflection, or are they distractions from it?
3. What parallels exist between traditional religious spaces and secular "places of perspective" like the Scottish moors?
4. In a modern, urban life filled with constant stimulation, is deliberate retreat into solitude becoming more important?
5. How might such experiences influence the way we value our daily work and social commitments when we return?

Experiences like these highlight how solitude and togetherness can coexist—moments of individual reflection unfolding within a shared social frame. But not everyone navigates this balance with ease. For some, being with others is not restorative but exhausting, and the very settings that foster reflection or bonding for one person may trigger withdrawal in another.

Social withdrawal becomes even more pronounced among individuals with certain psychological conditions. People with *autism spectrum disorder (ASD)*, for example, often experience sensory overload in crowded or noisy settings and may struggle with reading social cues, leading to avoidance of group events, even family dinners (Baron-Cohen et al., 2000). Those with *social anxiety disorder* report intense fear of judgment in social contexts, causing them to freeze, speak little, or avoid gatherings altogether (Stein & Stein, 2008). Similarly, individuals with *depression* may lack the energy or motivation to engage, perceiving social interaction as draining rather than restorative (Joiner, 2000). *Schizoid personality traits* can lead to a deep disinterest in social relationships altogether, while post-traumatic stress disorder (PTSD) can make people hypervigilant in crowds, perceiving danger even in safe environments (American Psychiatric Association, 2013).

While these conditions vary in origin and intensity, they all underscore the same point: social life, though often idealized, is not equally accessible to all—and for some, it can be a source of distress rather than connection (Table 4.7).

Mental health conditions are far more common than we tend to assume. Yet they often remain hidden, not only from colleagues or acquaintances, but sometimes even from close family and romantic partners. This is partly because many individuals have never received a formal diagnosis, and partly because stigma, denial, or uncertainty leads people to withhold or downplay

Table 4.7 Social engagement limits by psychological profile

Condition	Definition	Typical social limits	Estimated prevalence in general population	Gender distribution
Neurotypical	A person without clinically diagnosed mental disorders	Comfortable with moderate to high levels of interaction; varies by personality (introvert/extrovert)	~65–70%	Roughly equal (M ≈ F)
Social Anxiety Disorder (SAD)	Intense fear of being judged in social or performance situations	Avoids unfamiliar settings; limits group size; avoids eye contact	~7%	Slightly more common in females
Autism Spectrum Disorder (ASD)	Neurodevelopmental condition marked by social communication difficulties	Prefers highly predictable or solitary settings; dislikes large or noisy groups	~1.5–2%	More common in males (M:F ≈ 4:1)
Avoidant Personality Disorder	Extreme sensitivity to criticism, social inhibition	Actively avoids most social contact outside of trusted circle	~1–2.5%	Slightly more common in females
Schizoid Personality Disorder	Lacks interest in social relationships, emotionally detached	Minimal need for social interaction; does not seek companionship	<1%	Slightly more common in males
Depression (Major Depressive Disorder)	Persistent sadness, loss of interest, energy depletion	Withdraws from even previously enjoyed social contexts	~5–10% (12-month prevalence)	More common in females (F ≈ 2:1 M)
Post-Traumatic Stress Disorder (PTSD)	Anxiety and hypervigilance after trauma	Avoids crowds, loud events, and settings that trigger memories	~3.5–4%	More common in females

(continued)

Table 4.7 (continued)

Condition	Definition	Typical social limits	Estimated prevalence in general population	Gender distribution
Generalized Anxiety Disorder (GAD)	Excessive, uncontrollable worry	Often avoids unfamiliar groups; ruminates after interaction	~6%	More common in females
Obsessive–Compulsive Disorder (OCD)	Intrusive thoughts and ritualistic behaviors	May avoid social settings that disrupt rituals or control	~2–3%	Slightly more common in females
ADHD (Attention Deficit Hyperactivity Disorder)	Attention regulation and impulse control difficulties	May be over-social or socially intrusive; difficulty with boundaries	~5% (children); ~2.5% (adults)	More common in males

Source Based on data from WHO, APA DSM-5, and population studies by Kessler et al., Ruscio et al., and Wittchen et al.

their struggles. As a result, the presence of psychological disorders in everyday social life is vastly under-recognized, despite being one of the most significant influences on how we relate to others, set boundaries, and experience social interaction.

This invisibility has consequences. When others seem socially distant, withdrawn, or overly sensitive, we often assume *personality flaws* rather than recognizing potential underlying mental health struggles. This misreading deepens isolation, especially in a world where performance and sociability are often expected. For many, simply showing up can be a major achievement. And beneath the surface of everyday interaction lies a powerful emotional undercurrent: the fear of rejection.

Fear of rejection is a powerful factor. Evolutionary psychology explains that group exclusion once meant death; today, the brain still registers social pain similarly to physical pain (Eisenberger et al., 2003). This fear makes some social settings especially stressful, especially for the young, the anxious, or the socially marginalized.

In children, the challenges of social life manifest early. Girls, in particular, are more prone to *relational aggression*—exclusion, gossip, and manipulation—while boys often engage in direct physical confrontation (Björkqvist et al., 1992; Crick & Grotpeter, 1995). This pattern reflects adaptive evolutionary strategies: girls historically benefited from preserving social alliances and avoiding open conflict (Geary, 1998; Hrdy, 2009). Girls also tend to develop *emotional* and *verbal intelligence* earlier, making subtle forms of aggression more accessible (Bjorklund & Blasi, 2012). These tendencies are shaped further by social learning (Bandura, 1977) and vary across cultures and individuals, but they underscore how early and deeply social challenges are felt.

As we grow older, we're taught to view social interaction as inherently fulfilling. Schools, media, and even therapists reinforce the idea that belonging is central to happiness. But this view can create false expectations. Developmental studies show that many children already experience anxiety, exclusion, and stress in their social environments (Underwood, 2003). Social life is not always a source of joy; it is also a site of comparison, judgment, and competition.

A more honest view recognizes that human beings are acutely sensitive to *social dynamics* (Tooby & Cosmides, 1992), and social disappointment cuts deep because the brain treats exclusion like pain (Eisenberger, 2012). Some relationships will strengthen us; others will drain us. Accepting this helps us navigate social life more realistically.

Still, when connection happens freely and mutually, it brings immense joy. A phone call from a trusted friend, a spontaneous pub conversation, or an invitation for a summer visit can create lasting emotional warmth. These moments matter not because we are constantly social, but because we are not. When they occur, they shine. And perhaps evolution designed us that way; for rare, true connection to stand out and stay with us (Baumeister & Leary, 1995; Reis et al., 2000).

The layered model we have traced in this chapter shows how individual cognition scales into collective intelligence—how perception, language, norms, and institutions together create the architectures of shared life. Yet culture is not only a structure of meaning; it is also a rhythm of living. People inhabit culture not just through symbols and institutions but through the daily and generational patterns that give shape to existence. We have already touched on this rhythm in smaller ways—such as how days are divided into structured routines—but in the next chapter we go deeper, turning to the stages of life and the everyday cycles of time, work, care, and generational change through which society reproduces itself.

References

Adams, R. G., & Blieszner, R. (1995). Aging well with friends and family. *American Behavioral Scientist, 39*(2), 209–224. https://doi.org/10.1177/0002764295039002008

American Psychiatric Association. (2013). *Diagnostic and statistical manual of mental disorders* (5th ed.). American Psychiatric Publishing.

Anderson, B. (1983). *Imagined communities*. Verso.

Apple, W., Streeter, L. A., & Krauss, R. M. (1979). Effects of pitch and speech rate on personal attributions. *Journal of Personality and Social Psychology, 37*(5), 715–727. https://doi.org/10.1037/0022-3514.37.5.715

Arendt, H. (1973). *The origins of totalitarianism*. Harcourt, Brace & Company. (Original work published 1951).

Arnett, J. J. (2000). Emerging adulthood: A theory of development from the late teens through the twenties. *American Psychologist, 55*(5), 469–480. https://doi.org/10.1037/0003-066X.55.5.469

Arnow, B. A., Millheiser, L. S., Garrett, A., Lake Polan, M., Glover, G. H., & Hill, K. R. (2009). Women with hypoactive sexual desire disorder: An fMRI study. *Journal of Sexual Medicine, 6*(1), 73–84.

Audi, R. (2011). *Epistemology: A contemporary introduction to the theory of knowledge* (3rd ed.). Routledge.

Bandura, A. (1977). *Social learning theory*. Prentice Hall.

Baron-Cohen, S., Wheelwright, S., Stone, V., & Rutherford, M. (2000). A mathematician, a physicist, and a computer scientist with Asperger syndrome: Performance on folk psychology and folk physics tests. *Neurocase, 6*(5), 475–483. https://doi.org/10.1080/13554790008402715

Baumeister, R. F. (1991). *Meanings of life*. Guilford Press.

Baumeister, R. F., & Leary, M. R. (1995). The need to belong: Desire for interpersonal attachments as a fundamental human motivation. *Psychological Bulletin, 117*(3), 497–529.

Bell, D. A. (2015). *The China model: Political meritocracy and the limits of democracy*. Princeton University Press.

Beniger, J. R. (1986). *The control revolution: Technological and economic origins of the information society*. Harvard University Press.

Berman, M. G., Jonides, J., & Kaplan, S. (2008). The cognitive benefits of interacting with nature. *Psychological Science, 19*(12), 1207–1212.

Berto, R. (2014). The role of nature in coping with psycho-physiological stress: A literature review on restorativeness. *Behavioral Sciences, 4*(4), 394–409. https://doi.org/10.3390/bs4040394

Bialostozky, E. (2016). *Architecture and symbolism: The tradition of monumental public buildings*. Routledge.

Bialystok, E., Craik, F. I. M., & Luk, G. (2012). Bilingualism: Consequences for mind and brain. *Trends in Cognitive Sciences, 16*(4), 240–250. https://doi.org/10.1016/j.tics.2012.03.001

Bialystok, E., Craik, F. I. M., & Freedman, M. (2007). Bilingualism as a protection against the onset of symptoms of dementia. *Neuropsychologia, 45*(2), 459–464. https://doi.org/10.1016/j.neuropsychologia.2006.10.009

Bjorklund, D. F., & Blasi, C. H. (2012). *Child and adolescent development: An integrated approach*. Wadsworth.

Björkqvist, K., Lagerspetz, K. M., & Kaukiainen, A. (1992). Do girls manipulate and boys fight? Developmental trends in regard to direct and indirect aggression. *Aggressive Behavior, 18*(2), 117–127.

Black, J. (1992). *The British and the Grand Tour*. Croom Helm.

Boroditsky, L. (2011). How language shapes thought. *Scientific American, 304*(2), 62–65.

Boucher, D. (2021). *The politics of memory: Contested narratives and the struggle over historical interpretation*. Routledge.

Boucher, M. (2021b). *Christopher Columbus and the politics of memory*. Routledge.

Bourdieu, P. (1977). *Outline of a theory of practice*. Cambridge University Press.

Boyer, P. (2001). *Religion explained: The evolutionary origins of religious thought*. Basic Books.

Bratman, G. N., Hamilton, J. P., & Daily, G. C. (2012). The impacts of nature experience on human cognitive function and mental health. *Annals of the New York Academy of Sciences, 1249*(1), 118–136.

Brown, S. (2017). A joint prosodic origin of language and music. *Frontiers in Psychology, 8*, 1894. https://doi.org/10.3389/fpsyg.2017.01894

Bruner, J. (1990). *Acts of meaning*. Harvard University Press.

Buckingham, D. (2003). *Media education: Literacy, learning and contemporary culture*. Polity.

Burgoon, J. K., Guerrero, L. K., & Floyd, K. (2016). *Nonverbal communication* (2nd ed.). Routledge.

Buss, D. M. (2017). *Evolutionary psychology: The new science of the mind* (5th ed.). Routledge.

Buss, D. M. (2017). *The evolution of desire: Strategies of human mating* (Revised and updated ed.). Basic Books.

Cacioppo, J. T., & Cacioppo, S. (2014). Social relationships and health: The toxic effects of perceived social isolation. *Social and Personality Psychology Compass, 8*(2), 58–72.

Cain, S. (2012). *Quiet: The power of introverts in a world that can't stop talking*. Crown Publishing Group.

Carr, N. (2010). *The shallows: What the Internet is doing to our brains*. W. W. Norton & Company.

Castells, M. (1996). *The rise of the network society*. Blackwell.

Chartrand, T. L., & Bargh, J. A. (1999). The chameleon effect: The perception–behavior link and social interaction. *Journal of Personality and Social Psychology, 76*(6), 893–910.

Chomsky, N., & Herman, E. S. (1988). *Manufacturing consent: The political economy of the mass media*. Pantheon Books.

Clark, A. (2013). Whatever next? Predictive brains, situated agents, and the future of cognitive science. *Behavioral and Brain Sciences, 36*(3), 181–204.

Cohen, S., & Wills, T. A. (1985). Stress, social support, and the buffering hypothesis. *Psychological Bulletin, 98*(2), 310–357. https://doi.org/10.1037/0033-2909.98.2.310

Conti-Brown, P. (2016). *The power and independence of the Federal Reserve*. Princeton University Press.

Coontz, S. (2005). *Marriage, a history: How love conquered marriage*. Viking.

Coplan, R. J., Ooi, L. L., & Baldwin, D. (2019). Does it matter when we want to be alone? Exploring developmental timing effects in self-reported preference for solitude. *Developmental Psychology, 55*(10), 2155–2164.

Coryat, T. (1611). *Coryat's crudities: Hastily gobled up in five moneths travells in France, Savoy, Italy, Rhetia, commonly called the Grisons country, Helvetia alias Switzerland, some parts of high Germany, and the Netherlands*. London: W. Stansby.

Cosmides, L., & Tooby, J. (2005). Neurocognitive adaptations designed for social exchange. In D. M. Buss (Ed.), *The handbook of evolutionary psychology* (pp. 584–627). Wiley.

Costa, A., Hernández, M., & Sebastián-Gallés, N. (2008). Bilingualism aids conflict resolution: Evidence from the ANT task. *Cognition, 106*(1), 59–86. https://doi.org/10.1016/j.cognition.2006.12.013
Couzin, I. D. (2009). Collective cognition in animal groups. *Trends in Cognitive Sciences, 13*(1), 36–43. https://doi.org/10.1016/j.tics.2008.10.002
Crick, N. R., & Grotpeter, J. K. (1995). Relational aggression, gender, and social-psychological adjustment. *Child Development, 66*(3), 710–722.
Craik, J. (1994). *The face of fashion: Cultural studies in fashion*. Routledge.
Darwin, C. (1871). *The descent of man, and selection in relation to sex*. John Murray.
Daun, Å. (1996). *Swedish mentality*. Pennsylvania State University Press.
Dawkins, R. (1976). *The selfish gene*. Oxford University Press.
Depue, R. A., & Collins, P. F. (1999). Neurobiology of the structure of personality: Dopamine, facilitation of incentive motivation, and extraversion. *Behavioral and Brain Sciences, 22*(3), 491–517.
Deutscher, G. (2010). *Through the language glass: Why the world looks different in other languages*. Metropolitan Books.
Dewey, J. (1938). *Experience and education*. Macmillan.
Dikker, S., Wan, L., Davidesco, I., Kaggen, L., Oostrik, M., McClintock, J., Rowland, J., Michalareas, G., Van Bavel, J. J., Ding, M., & Poeppel, D. (2017). Brain-to-brain synchrony tracks real-world dynamic group interactions in the classroom. *Current Biology, 27*(9), 1375–1380.
Dixson, B. J., Grimshaw, G. M., Linklater, W. L., & Dixson, A. F. (2011). Eye-tracking of men's preferences for female breast size and shape. *Archives of Sexual Behavior, 40*(1), 51–58. https://doi.org/10.1007/s10508-009-9523-5
Dunbar, R. I. M. (1992). Neocortex size as a constraint on group size in primates. *Journal of Human Evolution, 22*(6), 469–493.
Dunbar, R. I. M. (1998). The social brain hypothesis. *Evolutionary Anthropology, 6*(5), 178–190.
Dunbar, R. I. M. (2010). How many friends does one person need? *Dunbar's number and other evolutionary quirks*. Faber & Faber.
Durante, K. M., Griskevicius, V., Hill, S. E., Perilloux, C., & Li, N. P. (2008). Ovulation, female competition, and product choice: Hormonal influences on consumer behavior. *Journal of Consumer Research, 37*(6), 921–934. https://doi.org/10.1086/656575
Durkheim, E. (1995). *The elementary forms of religious life* (K. E. Fields, Trans.). New York: Free Press. (Original work published 1912).
Dykstra, P. A. (2009). Older adult loneliness: Myths and realities. *European Journal of Ageing, 6*(2), 91–100.
Eastwick, P. W., & Finkel, E. J. (2008). Sex differences in mate preferences revisited: Do people know what they initially desire in a romantic partner? *Journal of*

Personality and Social Psychology, 94(2), 245–264. https://doi.org/10.1037/0022-3514.94.2.245

Eberhardt, J. L., Davies, P. G., Purdie-Vaughns, V. J., & Johnson, S. L. (2006). Looking deathworthy: Perceived stereotypicality of Black defendants predicts capital-sentencing outcomes. *Psychological Science, 17*(5), 383–386.

Eisenberger, N. I. (2012). The pain of social disconnection: Examining the shared neural underpinnings of physical and social pain. *Nature Reviews Neuroscience, 13*(6), 421–434.

Eisenberger, N. I., Lieberman, M. D., & Williams, K. D. (2003). Does rejection hurt? An fMRI study of social exclusion. *Science, 302*(5643), 290–292.

Eisenstein, E. L. (1979). *The printing press as an agent of change: Communications and cultural transformations in early-modern Europe*. Cambridge University Press.

Ekman, P. (2003). *Emotions revealed: Recognizing faces and feelings to improve communication and emotional life*. Times Books.

Ekman, P., & Friesen, W. V. (1975). *Unmasking the face: A guide to recognizing emotions from facial clues*. Prentice Hall.

Eubanks, V. (2018). *Automating inequality: How high-tech tools profile, police, and punish the poor*. Martin's Press.

Fehr, B. (1996). *Friendship processes*. Sage.

Feldman, R. (2007). Parent–infant synchrony: Biological foundations and developmental outcomes. *Current Directions in Psychological Science, 16*(6), 340–345.

Finkel, E. J., Eastwick, P. W., Karney, B. R., Reis, H. T., & Sprecher, S. (2012). Online dating: A critical analysis from the perspective of psychological science. *Psychological Science in the Public Interest, 13*(1), 3–66. https://doi.org/10.1177/1529100612436522

Firth, J., Torous, J., & Carney, R. (2019). The "online brain": How the internet may be changing cognition. *World Psychiatry, 18*(2), 119–129.

Flege, J. E. (1995). Second language speech learning: Theory, findings, and problems. In W. Strange (Ed.), *Speech perception and linguistic experience: Issues in cross-language research* (pp. 233–277). York Press.

Fluck, M. (2019). The making of threats: The rationality of affect in international politics. *International Political Sociology, 13*(2), 107–123.

Freire, P. (1970). *Pedagogy of the oppressed*. Continuum.

Fridlund, A. J. (1994). *Human facial expression: An evolutionary view*. Academic Press.

Friston, K. (2010). The free-energy principle: A unified brain theory? *Nature Reviews Neuroscience, 11*(2), 127–138.

García-García, A., Narvaez, D., Garcés, P., López, J. D., & Maestú, F. (2021). Interpersonal synchrony in romantic partners: Neural and behavioral mechanisms. *Scientific Reports, 11*(1), 13851.

Geary, D. C. (1998). *Male, female: The evolution of human sex differences*. American Psychological Association.

Gee, J. P. (2003). *What video games have to teach us about learning and literacy*. Palgrave Macmillan.

Gerbner, G., Gross, L., Morgan, M., & Signorielli, N. (1986). Living with television: The dynamics of the cultivation process. In J. Bryant & D. Zillmann (Eds.), *Perspectives on media effects* (pp. 17–40). Lawrence Erlbaum Associates.

Gibbs, J. L., Ellison, N. B., & Heino, R. D. (2006). Self-presentation in online personals: The role of anticipated future interaction, self-disclosure, and perceived success in Internet dating. *Communication Research, 33*(2), 152–177. https://doi.org/10.1177/0093650205285368

Giles, H., & Coupland, N. (1991). *Language: Contexts and consequences.* Brooks/Cole.

Goethe, J. W. von. (1795–1796). *Wilhelm Meisters Lehrjahre* [*Wilhelm Meister's Apprenticeship*]. Cotta. (English translation: H. M. Waidson, Ed., & T. Carlyle, Trans., *Wilhelm Meister's Apprenticeship.* Penguin Classics, 1989).

Gordon, D. M. (2010). *Ant encounters: Interaction networks and colony behavior.* Princeton University Press.

Gottman, J. M., & Levenson, R. W. (1992). Marital processes predictive of later dissolution: Behavior, physiology, and health. *Journal of Personality and Social Psychology, 63*(2), 221–233. https://doi.org/10.1037/0022-3514.63.2.221

Goffman, E. (1959). *The presentation of self in everyday life.* Doubleday.

Goody, J. (1983). *The development of the family and marriage in Europe.* Cambridge University Press.

Gorky, M. (1923). *My universities.*

Grammer, K., Fink, B., Møller, A. P., & Thornhill, R. (2003). Darwinian aesthetics: Sexual selection and the biology of beauty. *Biological Reviews, 78*(3), 385–407. https://doi.org/10.1017/S1464793102006085

Grant, E. (1996). *The foundations of modern science in the Middle Ages.* Cambridge University Press.

Greengross, G., & Miller, G. (2011). Humor: The overlooked connection between intelligence and mating success. *Psychological Science, 22*(3), 309–314.

Grosjean, F. (2010). *Bilingual: Life and reality.* Harvard University Press.

Grusec, J. E., & Hastings, P. D. (Eds.). (2007). *Handbook of socialization: Theory and research.* Guilford Press.

Guéguen, N. (2015). High heels increase women's attractiveness. *Archives of Sexual Behavior, 44*(8), 2227–2235. https://doi.org/10.1007/s10508-014-0422-z

Halbwachs, M. (1992). *On collective memory.* University of Chicago Press.

Hall, E. T. (1966). *The hidden dimension.* Doubleday.

Haidt, J. (2012). *The righteous mind: Why good people are divided by politics and religion.* Pantheon.

Hajnal, J. (1965). European marriage patterns in perspective. In D. V. Glass & D. E. C. Eversley (Eds.), *Population in history* (pp. 101–143). Aldine.

Han, S., & Ma, Y. (2014). Cultural differences in human brain activity: A quantitative meta-analysis. *NeuroImage, 99*, 293–300. https://doi.org/10.1016/j.neuroimage.2014.05.062

Han, Y. J., Nunes, J. C., & Drèze, X. (2010). Signaling status with luxury goods: The role of brand prominence. *Journal of Marketing, 74*(4), 15–30. https://doi.org/10.1509/jmkg.74.4.15

Harari, Y. N. (2014). *Sapiens: A brief history of humankind*. Harper.

Hari, R., Henriksson, L., Malinen, S., & Parkkonen, L. (2015). Centrality of social interaction in human brain function. *Neuron, 88*(1), 181–193. https://doi.org/10.1016/j.neuron.2015.09.022

Harris, P. L. (2012). *Trusting what you're told: How children learn from others*. Harvard University Press.

Hartig, T., Mitchell, R., de Vries, S., & Frumkin, H. (2014). Nature and health. *Annual Review of Public Health, 35*, 207–228.

Haselton, M. G., Mortezaie, M., Pillsworth, E. G., Bleske-Rechek, A., & Frederick, D. A. (2007). Ovulatory shifts in human female ornamentation: Near ovulation, women dress to impress. *Hormones and Behavior, 51*(1), 40–45. https://doi.org/10.1016/j.yhbeh.2006.07.007

Hasson, U., Ghazanfar, A. A., Galantucci, B., Garrod, S., & Keysers, C. (2012). Brain-to-brain coupling: A mechanism for creating and sharing a social world. *Trends in Cognitive Sciences, 16*(2), 114–121. https://doi.org/10.1016/j.tics.2011.12.007

Hegel, G. W. F. (1807). *Phänomenologie des Geistes* [*The Phenomenology of Spirit*]. Joseph Anton Goebhardt. (English translation: A. V. Miller, Trans., *Phenomenology of Spirit*. Oxford University Press, 1977).

Hegel, G. W. F. (1977). *Phenomenology of spirit* (A. V. Miller, Trans.). Oxford University Press. (Original work published 1807).

Heidegger, M. (1962). *Being and time* (J. Macquarrie & E. Robinson, Trans.). Harper & Row. (Original work published 1927).

Helbing, D., Frey, B. S., Gigerenzer, G., Hafen, E., Hagner, M., Hofstetter, Y., Hoven, J., Zicari, R., & Zwitter, A. (2017). Will democracy survive big data and artificial intelligence? *Scientific American, 25*(2), 1–9.

Henrich, J. (2015). *The secret of our success*. Princeton University Press.

Hofer, B. K., & Pintrich, P. R. (1997). The development of epistemological theories. *Review of Educational Research, 67*(1), 88–140.

Hofstede, G., Hofstede, G. J., & Minkov, M. (2010). *Cultures and organizations: Software of the mind*. McGraw-Hill.

Holt-Lunstad, J., Smith, T. B., Baker, M., Harris, T., & Stephenson, D. (2015). Loneliness and social isolation as risk factors for mortality. *Perspectives on Psychological Science, 10*(2), 227–237.

Hong, Y. Y., Morris, M. W., Chiu, C. Y., & Benet-Martínez, V. (2000). Multicultural minds: A dynamic constructivist approach to culture and cognition.

American Psychologist, 55(7), 709–720. https://doi.org/10.1037/0003-066X.55.7.709

Hoskins, A. (2011). Media, memory, metaphor: Remembering and the connective turn. *Parallax, 17*(4), 19–31.

Hrdy, S. B. (2009). *Mothers and others: The evolutionary origins of mutual understanding*. Belknap Press of Harvard University Press.

Huff, T. E. (2017). *Intellectual curiosity and the scientific revolution: A global perspective*. Cambridge University Press.

Humboldt, W. von. (1792/1851). *Ideen zu einem Versuch, die Grenzen der Wirksamkeit des Staates zu bestimmen* [*The Limits of State Action*]. Cotta. (English translation: J. W. Burrow, Ed., *The Limits of State Action*. Cambridge University Press, 1969).

Humboldt, W. von. (1793/1794). *Theorie der Bildung des Menschen* [*Theory of the Bildung of Man*] (Unpublished essay, included in later collected works). (English translation in: W. von Humboldt, *Philosophy of Education*. Routledge, 2000).

Inglehart, R., & Welzel, C. (2005). *Modernization, cultural change, and democracy: The human development sequence*. Cambridge University Press.

Ioannidis, J. P. A. (2005). Why most published research findings are false. *PLOS Medicine, 2*(8), Article e124.

Jack, R. E., Caldara, R., & Schyns, P. G. (2012). Internal representations reveal cultural diversity in expectations of facial expressions of emotion. *Journal of Experimental Psychology: General, 141*(1), 19–25. https://doi.org/10.1037/a0023463

Jessner, U. (2008). A DST model of multilingualism and the role of metalinguistic awareness. *The Modern Language Journal, 92*(2), 270–283. https://doi.org/10.1111/j.1540-4781.2008.00718.x

Joiner, T. (2000). Depression's vicious scree. *Clinical Psychology: Science and Practice, 7*(2), 203–218.

Judge, T. A., & Cable, D. M. (2004). The effect of physical height on workplace success and income. *Journal of Applied Psychology, 89*(3), 428–441.

Kahan, D. M. (2013). Ideology, motivated reasoning, and cognitive reflection. *Judgment and Decision Making, 8*(4), 407–424.

Kahn, P. H. (1999). *The human relationship with nature: Development and culture*. MIT Press.

Kaplan, R., & Kaplan, S. (1989). *The experience of nature*. Cambridge University Press.

Kawakami, N., Haratani, T., & Araki, S. (2015). Job strain and arterial hypertension: A six-year prospective study in a Japanese manufacturing company. *Scandinavian Journal of Work, Environment & Health, 22*(4), 272–280.

Kelly, R. L. (2013). *The lifeways of hunter-gatherers: The foraging spectrum* (2nd ed.). Cambridge University Press.

Keltner, D., & Lerner, J. S. (2010). Emotion. In S. T. Fiske, D. T. Gilbert, & G. Lindzey (Eds.), *Handbook of social psychology* (5th ed., Vol. 1, pp. 317–352). Wiley.

Kuhl, P. K. (2004). Early language acquisition: Cracking the speech code. *Nature Reviews Neuroscience, 5*(11), 831–843. https://doi.org/10.1038/nrn1533

Kuhn, T. S. (1962). *The structure of scientific revolutions.* University of Chicago Press.

Kurzban, R., & Weeden, J. (2005). HurryDate: Mate preferences in action. *Evolution and Human Behavior, 26*(3), 227–244. https://doi.org/10.1016/j.evolhumbehav.2004.08.012

Labov, W. (2006). *The social stratification of English in New York City* (2nd ed.). Cambridge University Press.

Labov, W. (1972). *Sociolinguistic patterns.* University of Pennsylvania Press.

Larson, R. (1990). The solitary side of life: An examination of the time people spend alone from childhood to old age. *Developmental Review, 10*(2), 155–183.

Laslett, P. (1988). *Family life and illicit love in earlier generations.* Cambridge University Press.

Latour, B., & Woolgar, S. (1979). *Laboratory life: The construction of scientific facts.* Sage.

Leary, M. R., & Kowalski, R. M. (1990). Impression management: A literature review and two-component model. *Psychological Bulletin, 107*(1), 34–47.

Lederbogen, F., Kirsch, P., Haddad, L., Streit, F., Tost, H., Schuch, P., Wüst, S., Pruessner, J. C., Rietschel, M., Deuschle, M., & Meyer-Lindenberg, A. (2011). City living and urban upbringing affect neural social stress processing in humans. *Nature, 474*(7352), 498–501.

LeDoux, J. (1996). *The emotional brain: The mysterious underpinnings of emotional life*. Simon & Schuster.

Lenneberg, E. H. (1967). *Biological foundations of language*. Wiley.

Levinson, S. C. (2003). *Space in language and cognition: Explorations in cognitive diversity*. Cambridge University Press.

Lewis, D. M. G., Russell, E. M., Al-Shawaf, L., & Buss, D. M. (2017). Lumbar curvature: A previously undiscovered standard of attractiveness. *Evolution and Human Behavior, 36*(5), 345–350. https://doi.org/10.1016/j.evolhumbehav.2015.01.007

Lloyd, G. E. R. (1970). *Early Greek science: Thales to Aristotle*. Chatto & Windus.

Loewen, J. W. (2018). *Lies across America: What our historic sites get wrong*. The New Press.

Long, M. H. (1990). Maturational constraints on language development. *Studies in Second Language Acquisition, 12*(3), 251–285. https://doi.org/10.1017/S0272263100009165

Long, C. R., & Averill, J. R. (2003). Solitude. *Journal for the Theory of Social Behaviour, 33*(1), 21–44.

Long, C. R., Seburn, M., Averill, J. R., & More, T. A. (2003). Solitude experiences: Varieties, settings, and individual differences. *Personality and Social Psychology Bulletin, 29*(5), 578–583.

Lucy, J. A. (1997). Linguistic relativity. *Annual Review of Anthropology, 26*, 291–312.

Luhmann, N. (1995). *Social systems* (J. Bednarz Jr. & D. Baecker, Trans.). Stanford University Press. (Original work published 1984).

Markus, H. R., & Kitayama, S. (1991). Culture and the self: Implications for cognition, emotion, and motivation. *Psychological Review, 98*(2), 224–253. https://doi.org/10.1037/0033-295X.98.2.224

Marwick, A. (2013). *Status update: Celebrity, publicity, and branding in the social media age*. Yale University Press.

Mayer, J. D., Roberts, R. D., & Barsade, S. G. (2008). Human abilities: Emotional intelligence. *Annual Review of Psychology, 59*, 507–536.

Mayr, E. (2001). *What evolution is*. Basic Books.

Mercier, H., & Sperber, D. (2017). *The enigma of reason*. Harvard University Press.

Merleau-Ponty, M. (2012). *Phenomenology of perception* (D. A. Landes, Trans.). Routledge. (Original work published 1945).

Mesoudi, A. (2011). *Cultural evolution: How Darwinian theory can explain human culture and synthesize the social sciences*. University of Chicago Press.

Miller, G. (2000). *The mating mind: How sexual choice shaped the evolution of human nature*. Doubleday.

Mokyr, J. (2017). *A culture of growth: The origins of the modern economy*. Princeton University Press.

Miller, D. (2010). *Stuff*. Polity Press.

Miller, G. (2009). *Spent: Sex, evolution, and consumer behavior*. Viking.

Morriss, L., Chapman, A., Tomkins, M., & Clarke, C. (2010). Lip colour affects perceived sexual attractiveness: A cross-cultural study. *Journal of Experimental Social Psychology, 46*(3), 708–710.

Murphy, K. (2020a). The toppling of Edward Colston: Memory politics and anti-racism in Britain. *Journal of British Studies, 59*(4), 911–937.

Murphy, T. (2020b). Reconsidering monuments: Memory, history, and the politics of public space. *Journal of Urban Affairs, 42*(4), 547–563.

Neave, N., McCarty, K., Freynik, J., Caplan, N., Hönekopp, J., & Fink, B. (2011). Male dance moves that catch a woman's eye. *Biology Letters, 7*(2), 221–224. https://doi.org/10.1098/rsbl.2010.0619

Nietzsche, F. (1994). *On the genealogy of morality*. (K. Ansell-Pearson, Ed., C. Diethe & K. Ansell-Pearson, Trans.). Cambridge University Press. (Original work published 1887).

Norenzayan, A. (2013). *Big gods: How religion transformed cooperation and conflict*. Princeton University Press.

Norris, P., & Inglehart, R. (2019). *Cultural backlash: Trump, Brexit, and authoritarian populism*. Cambridge University Press.

O'Neil, C. (2016). *Weapons of math destruction: How big data increases inequality and threatens democracy*. Crown Publishing.

Pariser, E. (2011). *The filter bubble: What the internet is hiding from you*. Penguin.

Piaget, J. (1952). *The origins of intelligence in children*. International Universities Press.

Pinker, S. (1997). *How the mind works*. Norton

Postman, N. (1985). *Amusing ourselves to death*. Viking.

Przybylski, A. K., & Weinstein, N. (2017). Digital screen time limits and young children's psychological well-being: Evidence from a population-based study. *Child Development, 90*(1), e56–e65.

Putnam, R. D. (2000). *Bowling alone: The collapse and revival of American community*. Simon & Schuster.

Redcay, E., & Schilbach, L. (2019). Using second-person neuroscience to elucidate the mechanisms of social interaction. *Nature Reviews Neuroscience, 20*(8), 495–505. https://doi.org/10.1038/s41583-019-0179-4

Reis, H. T., Sheldon, K. M., Gable, S. L., Roscoe, J., & Ryan, R. M. (2000). Daily well-being: The role of autonomy, competence, and relatedness. *Personality and Social Psychology Bulletin, 26*(4), 419–435.

Remland, M. S., Jones, T. S., & Brinkman, H. (1995). Interpersonal distance, body orientation, and touch: Effects of culture, gender, and age. *The Journal of Social Psychology, 135*(3), 281–297.

Rubinstein, R. L., & Shaver, P. (1979). The experience of loneliness. In M. Cook (Ed.), *Perspectives on loneliness* (pp. 206–223). Academic Press.

Sandemose, A. (1997). *A fugitive crosses his tracks* (*En flygtning krydser sit spor*, original work published 1933). Aschehoug.

Schiller, F. (1795). *Über die ästhetische Erziehung des Menschen in einer Reihe von Briefen* [*On the Aesthetic Education of Man, in a Series of Letters*]. Cotta. (English translation: E. M. Wilkinson & L. A. Willoughby, Eds. & Trans., *On the Aesthetic Education of Man*. Oxford University Press, 1982).

Schommer, M. (1990). Effects of beliefs about knowledge. *Journal of Educational Psychology, 82*(3), 498–504.

Scott, J. C. (1998). *Seeing like a state*. Yale University Press.

Seeley, T. D. (2010). *Honeybee democracy*. Princeton University Press.

Silk, J. B. (2003). Cooperation without counting. In P. Hammerstein (Ed.), *Genetic and cultural evolution of cooperation* (pp. 37–54). MIT Press.

Slobin, D. I. (1996). From "thought and language" to "thinking for speaking." In J. J. Gumperz & S. C. Levinson (Eds.), *Rethinking linguistic relativity* (pp. 70–96). Cambridge University Press.

Snyder, M. (1974). Self-monitoring of expressive behavior. *Journal of Personality and Social Psychology, 30*(4), 526–537.

Smallwood, J., & Schooler, J. W. (2015). The science of mind wandering: Empirically navigating the stream of consciousness. *Annual Review of Psychology, 66*, 487–518. https://doi.org/10.1146/annurev-psych-010814-015331

Sokal, A., & Bricmont, J. (1998). *Fashionable nonsense: Postmodern intellectuals' abuse of science*. Picador.

Söilen, K. S. (2013). *Exhibit marketing and trade show intelligence: Successful boothmanship and booth design*. Springer.

Söilen, K. S. (2025). *The researcher's journey: A guide to methodology and academia in social sciences*. Springer.

Söilen, K. S., & Benhayoun, L. (2019). Collective intelligence. *Journal of Intelligence Studies in Business, 9*(2), 6–25.

Söilen, K. S., & Benhayoun, L. (2021). Household acceptance of CBDC. *International Journal of Bank Marketing, 39*(7), 1210–1231.

Söilen, K. S., & Benhayoun, L. (2022). Evolution of collective intelligence research. *Journal of Intelligence Studies in Business, 12*(1), 5–23.

Stein, M. B., & Stein, D. J. (2008). Social anxiety disorder. *The Lancet, 371*(9618), 1115–1125.

Stephen, I. D., & McKeegan, A. M. (2010). Lip colour affects perceived sex typicality and attractiveness of human faces. *Perception, 39*(8), 1104–1110.

Sumpter, D. J. T. (2006). Collective animal behaviour. *Philosophical Transactions of the Royal Society B, 361*(1465), 5–22.

Tajfel, H., & Turner, J. C. (1979). An integrative theory of intergroup conflict. In W. G. Austin & S. Worchel (Eds.), *The social psychology of intergroup relations* (pp. 33–47). Brooks/Cole.

Tajfel, H., & Turner, J. C. (1986). The social identity theory of intergroup behavior. In S. Worchel & W. G. Austin (Eds.), *Psychology of intergroup relations.* Nelson-Hall.

Tang, A. (2019). *vTaiwan: Public participation in the digital age*. Taiwan Digital Ministry.

Tarlo, E. (2010). *Visibly Muslim: Fashion, politics, faith.* Bloomsbury.

Tarr, B., Launay, J., & Dunbar, R. I. M. (2016). Silent disco: Dancing in synchrony leads to elevated pain thresholds and social closeness. *Evolution and Human Behavior, 37*(5), 343–349. https://doi.org/10.1016/j.evolhumbehav.2016.02.004

Tomasello, M. (1999). *The cultural origins of human cognition.* Harvard University Press.

Tomasello, M. (2009). *Why we cooperate*. MIT Press.

Tooby, J., & Cosmides, L. (1992). The psychological foundations of culture. In J. H. Barkow et al. (Eds.), *The adapted mind* (pp. 19–136). Oxford University Press.

Trevarthen, C. (1979). Communication and cooperation in early infancy: A description of primary intersubjectivity. In M. Bullowa (Ed.), *Before speech: The beginning of interpersonal communication* (pp. 321–347). Cambridge University Press.

Triandis, H. C. (1995). *Individualism and collectivism.* Westview Press.

Trivers, R. L. (1972). Parental investment and sexual selection. In B. Campbell (Ed.), *Sexual selection and the descent of man* (pp. 136–179). Aldine.
Trudgill, P. (1986). *Dialects in contact*. Blackwell.
Tufekci, Z. (2015). Algorithmic harms beyond Facebook and Google: Emergent challenges of computational agency. *Colorado Technology Law Journal, 13*(203), 203–218.
Turkle, S. (2011). *Alone together: Why we expect more from technology and less from each other*. Basic Books.
Turner, J. S. (2011). *The termite's cathedral: A natural history of the built environment*. Harvard University Press.
Ulrich, R. S., Simons, R. F., Losito, B. D., Fiorito, E., Miles, M. A., & Zelson, M. (1991). Stress recovery during exposure to natural and urban environments. *Journal of Environmental Psychology, 11*(3), 201–230.
Umberson, D., & Montez, J. K. (2010). Social relationships and health: A flashpoint for health policy. *Journal of Health and Social Behavior, 51*(1_suppl), S54–S66. https://doi.org/10.1177/0022146510383501
Underwood, M. K. (2003). *Social aggression among girls*. Guilford Press.
Vacharkulksemsuk, T., & Fredrickson, B. L. (2012). Strangers in sync: Achieving embodied rapport through shared movements. *Journal of Experimental Social Psychology, 48*(1), 399–402. https://doi.org/10.1016/j.jesp.2011.07.015
Vale, L. J. (1992). *Architecture, power, and national identity*. Yale University Press.
van Dijck, J. (2007). *Mediated memories in the digital age*. Stanford University Press.
Veletsianos, G. (2020). *Learning online*. Johns Hopkins University Press.
Victor, C. R., & Yang, K. (2012). Loneliness among adults. *The Journal of Psychology, 146*(1–2), 85–104.
Vygotsky, L. S. (1978). *Mind in society*. Harvard University Press.
Walther, J. B. (1996). Computer-mediated communication: Impersonal, interpersonal, and hyperpersonal interaction. *Communication Research, 23*(1), 3–43. https://doi.org/10.1177/009365096023001001
Ward, A. F. (2017). Supernormal: How the internet is changing our brains. *Psychological Inquiry, 28*(4), 230–235.
Werker, J. F., & Tees, R. C. (2005). Speech perception as a window for understanding plasticity and commitment in language systems of the brain. *Developmental Psychobiology, 46*(3), 233–251. https://doi.org/10.1002/dev.20060
Whittaker, J., Looney, S., Reed, A., & Votta, F. (2021). Recommender systems and the amplification of extremist content. *Internet Policy Review, 10*(2), 1–15.
Willis, J., & Todorov, A. (2006). First impressions: Making up your mind after a 100-ms exposure to a face. *Psychological Science, 17*(7), 592–598. https://doi.org/10.1111/j.1467-9280.2006.01750.x
Wilson, E. O. (1978). *On human nature*. Harvard University Press.
Wong, R. B. (2011). *China transformed: Historical change and the limits of European experience*. Cornell University Press.

Zahavi, A., & Zahavi, A. (1997). *The handicap principle: A missing piece of Darwin's puzzle*. Oxford University Press.
Zeki, S. (2007). The neurobiology of love. *FEBS Letters, 581*(14), 2575–2579.

Further Readings

Achen, C. H., & Bartels, L. M. (2016). *Democracy for realists: Why elections do not produce responsive government*. Princeton University Press.
Ainsworth, M. D. S. (1979). Infant–mother attachment. *American Psychologist, 34*(10), 932–937.
Alexander, R. (2010). *Children, their world, their education: Final report and recommendations of the Cambridge Primary Review*. Routledge.
Axelrod, R. (1984). *The evolution of cooperation*. Basic Books.
Axelrod, R., & Hamilton, W. D. (1981). *The evolution of cooperation. Science, 211*(4489), 1390–1396.
Bargh, J. A., & Chartrand, T. L. (1999). The unbearable automaticity of being. *American Psychologist, 54*(7), 462–479.
Becker, G. S. (1981). *A treatise on the family*. Harvard University Press.
Benenson, J. F. (2013). The development of human female competition: Allies and adversaries. *Philosophical Transactions of the Royal Society B: Biological Sciences, 368*(1631), 20130079.
Bicchieri, C. (2006). *The grammar of society: The nature and dynamics of social norms*. Cambridge University Press.
Board of Governors of the Federal Reserve System. (2023). *The structure of the Federal Reserve System*. https://www.federalreserve.gov/aboutthefed/structure-federal-reserve-system.htm
Boehm, C. (1999). *Hierarchy in the forest: The evolution of egalitarian behavior*. Harvard University Press.
Bonabeau, E., Dorigo, M., & Theraulaz, G. (1999). *Swarm intelligence: From natural to artificial systems*. Oxford University Press.
Bowlby, J. (1969). *Attachment and loss: Vol. 1. Attachment*. Basic Books.
Buss, D. M. (1989). Sex differences in human mate preferences: Evolutionary hypotheses tested in 37 cultures. *Behavioral and Brain Sciences, 12*(1), 1–49. https://doi.org/10.1017/S0140525X00023992
Calof, J., Söilen, K. S., Klavans, R., Abdulkader, B., & El Moudni, I. (2022). Understanding the structure, characteristics, and future of collective intelligence using local and global bibliometric analyses. *Technological Forecasting and Social Change, 178*, Article 121561. https://doi.org/10.1016/j.techfore.2022.121561
Carter, C. S. (1998). Neuroendocrine perspectives on social attachment and love. *Psychoneuroendocrinology, 23*(8), 779–818. https://doi.org/10.1016/S0306-4530(98)00055-9
Dayan, D., & Katz, E. (1992). *Media events: The live broadcasting of history*. Harvard University Press.

Desmond, M. (2016). *Evicted: Poverty and profit in the American city*. Crown.

Diamond, J. (1997). *Guns, germs, and steel: The fates of human societies*. Norton.

Dilthey, W. (1989). *Introduction to the human sciences* (R. A. Makkreel & F. Rodi, Eds. & Trans.). Princeton University Press. (Original work published 1883).

Eisenberger, N. I., & Lieberman, M. D. (2004). Why rejection hurts: A common neural alarm system for physical and social pain. *Trends in Cognitive Sciences, 8*(7), 294–300.

Fisher, H. E. (2004). *Why we love: The nature and chemistry of romantic love*. Henry Holt.

Furstenberg, F. F. (2010). On a new schedule: Transitions to adulthood and family change. *The Future of Children, 20*(1), 67–87.

Geertz, C. (1973). *The interpretation of cultures*. Basic Books.

Giddens, A. (1992). *The transformation of intimacy: Sexuality, love and eroticism in modern societies*. Stanford University Press.

Grammer, K., Renninger, L., & Fischer, B. (2004). Disco clothing, female sexual motivation, and relationship status: Is she dressed to impress? *Journal of Sex Research, 41*(1), 66–74. https://doi.org/10.1080/00224490409552213

Habermas, J. (1984). *The theory of communicative action, Vol. 1: Reason and the rationalization of society* (T. McCarthy, Trans.). Beacon Press. (Original work published 1981).

Habermas, J. (1987). *The theory of communicative action, Vol. 2: Lifeworld and system—A critique of functionalist reason* (T. McCarthy, Trans.). Beacon Press. (Original work published 1981).

Haidt, J., & Lukianoff, G. (2018). *The coddling of the American mind*. Penguin.

Holland, T., & Sandbrook, D. (Hosts). (2019–). *The rest is history* [Podcast]. Goalhanger Podcasts.

Janis, I. L. (1972). *Victims of groupthink: A psychological study of foreign-policy decisions and fiascoes*. Houghton Mifflin.

Johnston, V. S. (2006). *Why we feel: The science of human emotions*. Perseus Books.

Kahan, D. M. (2017). Misconceptions, misinformation, and the logic of identity-protective cognition. *Yale Law School Public Law Research Paper No. 605*.

Kahneman, D. (2011). *Thinking, fast and slow*. Farrar.

Kalmijn, M. (2013). The rise of never-married singles in Europe: Trends, causes, and consequences. In A. Liefbroer & M. H. Dykstra (Eds.), *Intergenerational ties in aging societies* (pp. 127–143). Springer.

Kant, I. (1998). *Critique of pure reason* (P. Guyer & A. W. Wood, Eds. & Trans.). Cambridge University Press. (Original works published 1781/1787).

Kessler, R. C., Berglund, P., Demler, O., Jin, R., Merikangas, K. R., & Walters, E. E. (2005). Lifetime prevalence and age-of-onset distributions of DSM-IV disorders in the National Comorbidity Survey Replication. *Archives of General Psychiatry, 62*(6), 593–602.

Klinenberg, E. (2012). *Going solo: The extraordinary rise and surprising appeal of living alone*. Penguin Press.

Lesthaeghe, R. (2010). The unfolding story of the second demographic transition. *Population and Development Review, 36*(2), 211–251.

Malone, T. W. (2018). *Superminds: The surprising power of people and computers thinking together*. Little, Brown Spark.

Massachusetts Institute of Technology. (n.d.). *MIT OpenCourseWare*. https://ocw.mit.edu

Ryan, R. M., & Deci, E. L. (2000). Self-determination theory and the facilitation of intrinsic motivation, social development, and well-being. *American Psychologist, 55*(1), 68–78.

Ruscio, A. M., Brown, T. A., Chiu, W. T., Sareen, J., Stein, M. B., & Kessler, R. C. (2008). Social fears and social phobia in the USA: Results from the National Comorbidity Survey Replication. *Psychological Medicine, 38*(1), 15–28.

Sahlins, M. (1972). *Stone age economics*. Aldine-Atherton.

Scherer, K. R., & Bänziger, T. (2004). Understanding emotional expression: From components to holistic patterns. In P. Philippot, R. S. Feldman, & E. J. Coats (Eds.), *Nonverbal behavior in clinical settings* (pp. 79–113). Oxford University Press.

Searle, J. R. (1980). Minds, brains, and programs. *Behavioral and Brain Sciences, 3*(3), 417–424.

Simonoff, E., et al. (2008). Psychiatric disorders in children with autism spectrum disorders: Prevalence, comorbidity, and associated factors. *Journal of the American Academy of Child & Adolescent Psychiatry, 47*(8), 921–929.

Söilen, K. S. (2019). Making sense of the collective intelligence field: A review. *Journal of Intelligence Studies in Business, 9*(2), 5–18.

Solomon, M. R. (2018). *Consumer behavior: Buying, having, and being* (12th ed.). Pearson.

Sumpter, D. J. T. (2010). *Collective animal behavior*. Princeton University Press.

Todorov, A. (2017). *Face value: The irresistible influence of first impressions*. Princeton University Press.

Towner, J. (1985). The Grand Tour: A key phase in the history of tourism. *Annals of Tourism Research, 12*(3), 297–333. https://doi.org/10.1016/0160-7383(85)90002-7

Trianni, V. (2014). Evolutionary swarm robotics: Evolving self-organising behaviours in groups of autonomous robots. *Springer Tracts in Advanced Robotics, 22*. Springer. https://doi.org/10.1007/978-3-319-04639-6

UN Department of Economic and Social Affairs. (2019). *World population prospects 2019*. United Nations. https://population.un.org/wpp/

Vervaeke, J. (2019–2021). *Awakening from the meaning crisis* [Video lecture series]. YouTube.

WHO. (2017). *Depression and other common mental disorders: Global health estimates*. World Health Organization.

Wittchen, H. U., Jacobi, F., Rehm, J., Gustavsson, A., Svensson, M., Jönsson, B., Olesen, J., Allgulander, C., Alonso, J., Faravelli, C., Fratiglioni, L., Jennum, P., Lieb, R., Maercker, A., van Os, J., Preisig, M., Salvador-Carulla, L., Simon, R., & Steinhausen, H. C. (2011). The size and burden of mental disorders and other disorders of the brain in Europe 2010. *European Neuropsychopharmacology, 21*(9), 655–679.

5

Life in Time: How We Work, Love, and Age

Abstract Human life is not only shaped by ideas and institutions, but by time—by daily routines, life stages, and generational rhythms. This chapter shifts focus from symbolic systems to lived experience, examining how meaning is enacted through work, care, relationships, and the passage of life itself. The chapter explores how societies organize time through social clocks that define when we are expected to study, work, love, care, and retire—and how digital life and AI are disrupting these patterns. It examines the role of work in shaping identity, the often-invisible labor of care that sustains social life, and the growing distance between generations who no longer share the same cultural tempo. By treating time as a core social structure, this chapter shows why understanding everyday life is essential to understanding society. How we divide our days and move through life stages reveals as much about human values, inequality, and adaptation as any ideology or institution—especially in an age when technology is reshaping the very rhythm of human existence.

This chapter explores how human life is lived in time—across days, life stages, and social structures. If Chapter 4 focused on how meaning is constructed through symbols and institutions, this chapter shows how meaning is enacted: through routines, roles, relationships, and generational transitions. We examine how people divide their days, navigate social expectations, and balance autonomy with obligation. Each section addresses a different dimension of everyday life, from work and care to love and identity:

K. Solberg Söilen, *The Researcher's Journey in the Age of AI*, https://doi.org/10.1007/978-3-032-23069-0_5

- Daily Rhythms and the Social Clock: We examine how people across cultures organize their time—both by the hour and by life stage. Cultural norms dictate when to marry, work, or retire, but digital life increasingly blurs these boundaries, creating new forms of stress and flexibility.
- Work, Roles, and Life Scripts: Work gives structure to life, but its meaning varies by culture, class, and gender. This section investigates how job roles shape identity, how expectations differ for men and women, and how AI is altering our assumptions about labor and purpose.
- Care and Invisible Labor: Much of what sustains society is unpaid and often unrecognized. Here we analyze the emotional, physical, and moral dimensions of caregiving—especially how care is divided by gender and class, and how modern life strains these arrangements.
- Generations and the Cultural Arc: Finally, we consider how generational identity affects values, expectations, and behavior. Are we living in a shared culture, or are younger and older generations now inhabiting fundamentally different mental worlds?

In sum, this chapter argues that human culture is not only a symbolic system—it is a lived pattern of time. To understand humanity, we must look at how people actually live: how they work, love, age, and care for one another across the arc of a day, and across the arc of a life. We end with a note about what all of this means for the social sciences in the age of AI.

5.1 Time-Use Across Cultures

Time-use research offers one of the clearest windows into human behavior. By tracking how people spend their days, we gain a grounded picture of priorities, constraints, and cultural variation. Rather than relying on vague generalizations about human life, time-use data lets us measure activities in concrete terms—how much time is spent working, resting, caring for others, commuting, or using digital media. This method is also essential in applied disciplines like marketing—one of my own fields—where we need to know, for instance, what age groups are watching which kinds of programs and services at what times, in order to target advertising effectively and allocate media budgets with precision.

The most comprehensive sources for global time-use patterns include the *Multinational Time Use Study (MTUS)*, the *Harmonized European Time Use Surveys (HETUS)*, and the OECD's time-use datasets. These initiatives provide standardized comparisons of how individuals allocate their time across countries, age groups, and genders. According to the OECD (2020), women worldwide continue to perform the majority of unpaid domestic labor, a pattern often cited as reinforcing gender inequality. However, this invisible workload may also reflect personal choices or cultural values, such as the desire to care for children or manage the household, and thus should not be interpreted solely as evidence of structural disadvantage.

Time-use data has revealed major changes over the past decades. In many wealthy nations, time spent on household chores has declined due to technology and shifting family structures, while screen time has surged, especially among youth (Bianchi et al., 2006; Gershuny, 2011). In developing countries, the picture looks different: much of the day may be consumed by tasks like water collection, subsistence farming, or informal labor. These differences illustrate how time is both a universal resource and a culturally mediated experience.

Anthropologists and economists alike have used time allocation studies to model opportunity costs, productivity, and social norms. Becker's (1965) classic work on the economics of time helped formalize how time-use decisions reflect trade-offs in a resource-constrained environment. Meanwhile, sociologists like Hochschild (1989) have highlighted the emotional toll of time poverty, especially among dual-earner households where work and caregiving collide.

Of course, leisure is also evenly distributed. Disparities in income, gender, age, and education correlate with access to rest and recreation. For example, working-class individuals often have less control over their schedules, resulting in fragmented or lower-quality leisure (Sullivan & Gershuny, 2004). In contrast, the wealthy may experience "*time affluence*"; not just more free hours, but greater flexibility in how they are used.

Perhaps most importantly, time-use studies challenge some of the myths of modernity. Despite labor-saving devices and supposed efficiency gains, people often feel more rushed than ever, a phenomenon sometimes called the "*time squeeze*." As Rosa (2013) argues, social acceleration means that even with more options and technologies, time feels increasingly scarce and fragmented.

Time-use studies not only reveal *what* people do, but also *how* they do it—the tempo and rhythm of daily life. Cultures differ widely in the pace at which tasks are completed. In some societies, efficiency is a moral value; speed is rewarded, and time is treated as a scarce commodity to be optimized. In others, a slower pace may reflect deeper social priorities: relationships, reflection, or ritual. For instance, studies of "*polychronic*" *cultures*—where people engage in multiple activities simultaneously, often at a more fluid pace—contrast sharply with "*monochronic*" *cultures*, where time is linear and compartmentalized. These differences are not merely cultural curiosities; they influence everything from workplace productivity to healthcare outcomes and urban design.

Income and education also shape the *speed* at which activities are performed. People with higher education often complete tasks more quickly—not only due to better resources or tools, but because of accumulated knowledge, habits of efficiency, and greater control over their time. Conversely, those with fewer resources may face structural obstacles: inefficient public transport, longer lines, limited access to automation, or even bureaucratic delays. These inefficiencies compound over the day and week, resulting in a kind of "*temporal inequality*"; not just having less time, but being forced to *spend* time in slower, more draining ways. Time, in this sense, becomes a double burden: both scarce and poorly allocated.

Moreover, emotional and cognitive factors also influence task speed. *Time-use diaries* show that people under chronic stress or emotional strain tend to perform everyday activities more slowly—cooking, cleaning, caregiving—not for lack of ability, but because *mental bandwidth* is consumed by worry or fatigue. Conversely, people in stable, well-resourced environments can often move through their day with more ease and fewer interruptions. Thus, even two individuals doing "the same" thing—say, preparing dinner—might experience that task with vastly different speed, quality, and psychological cost. Time-use studies, when enriched with contextual data, begin to uncover not only what we *do*, but *how hard it is* for us to do it.

For many of us, time use isn't just about what fills the calendar; it's about how well each part of the day aligns with our personal rhythms and cognitive peaks. Take this author, for example: I tend to wake up at exactly 06:45, not by choice but because that's when my head starts working. Staying in bed any longer just leads to useless half-thoughts; loose fragments not even worth anything in a conversation other than delirium. So, I get up, take my fish oil and orange juice (because the fish oil does not go down without it), and write for about four focused hours. Lunch is usually skipped in favor of a long walk with the dog and a 30-min nap. Then it's back to the desk until 15:00, followed by a workout, and—if the stars align—a quick pint at the local pub before a 17:00 dinner (Table 5.1).

Of course, other things happen too—like shopping for this and that (though now mostly done online), administrative or maintenance tasks around the house, and unexpected events. Weekends look completely different, often centered around garden work, longer walks, or meeting with friends.

Table 5.1 Daily time use aligned with personal cognitive rhythms

Time	Activity	Purpose/function
06:45	Wake up	Natural cognitive start—brain becomes active
06:50–07:00	Take fish oil and orange juice	Morning ritual to aid supplement intake
07:00–07:20	Quick walk with the dog	Light movement, clears the mind before writing
07:20–11:00	Focused writing session (if no lecture or teaching duties)	Peak productivity window, creative and analytical output
11:00–13:00	Long walk with the dog + 30-min nap	Mental reset, physical movement, light rest
13:00–15:00	Desk work (reading, admin, research)	Lighter cognitive tasks, follow-ups, or editing
15:00–16:00	Workout	Physical health and stress relief
16:00–17:00	Free time/Pub visit (if lucky). Pick up a package at the store?	Social recharge or relaxation
17:00–18:00	Dinner	Main meal of the day
18:00–20:00	Watch a film with family	Shared relaxation and cultural engagement
20:00–21:00	Watch evening news (multiple channels)	Information update and comparative perspectives
21:00–22:00	Reading/Watering plants (garden or conservatory)	Wind-down activity, personal care or light stimulation
Before 00:00	Sleep	Rest and cognitive reset

What makes a day feel successful isn't the number of emails answered, pages written, or papers read, but whether the important things got done. For me, one or two missed tasks can be absorbed. But if I strike out on three, the day crosses into disappointment. It's my informal "*daily failure index,*" and I suspect most people carry some unspoken version of it, some sort of *internal meter* that weighs progress against resistance.

This personal rhythm reflects a broader psychological reality: humans are remarkably sensitive to friction. As Baumeister et al. (2001) have shown, willpower is a limited resource. Every task we resist, every setback we fight through, chips away at our mental reserves. And when the day's obstacles start to outnumber the wins, frustration kicks in. Time-use studies often track what we do, but rarely how we feel doing it. And that's a pity—because as Amabile and Kramer (2011) found in their research on the "*progress principle,*" the biggest motivator is not completing grand goals, but making consistent, visible progress—tiny steps that add up to a sense of momentum.

Seen in this light, the way we manage our daily pace is not just a personal choice but part of a broader cultural choreography. Some societies reward constant motion, while others value pauses, reflection, or communal gatherings as much as productive output (Hall, 1983; Levine, 1997).

Yet in many modern contexts, we have become like worker bees—so primed to begin the next task that we cannot simply sit still and wait for the right moment to start. This constant state of readiness elevates sympathetic nervous system activity and can chronically raise stress hormone levels, impairing both cognitive flexibility and long-term health (McEwen, 1998; Sapolsky, 2004). Learning to pause until action is truly required can restore balance and make effort more sustainable (Kabat-Zinn, 1990). These patterns of activity and stillness—how we start tasks, how we wait, how we conclude—become invisible frameworks shaping our well-being. They also set the stage for the larger cultural systems that organize work, rest, and ritual, linking the tempo of everyday life to the values and identities a society seeks to preserve.

5.2 Work, Rest, and Rituals

Across cultures and historical periods, human societies have created elaborate norms governing work, rest, and ritual. These domains are not merely utilitarian but are embedded in cultural logics that reflect values, cosmologies, and collective identities.

Work, for instance, is not simply about survival. It also expresses status, purpose, and social belonging. In industrial societies, work often defines personal identity, with professions serving as markers of worth and competence. By contrast, in many small-scale or subsistence societies, work may be less differentiated and more integrated into communal life. Among the !Kung San of the Kalahari, for example, anthropologists have observed that adults work only about 15–20 h a week to meet basic needs, leaving ample time for socializing, storytelling, and rest (Lee, 1979).

Rest and leisure are likewise culturally patterned. Some societies treat rest as a moral necessity and spiritual practice. The Jewish Sabbath is perhaps the clearest example: a divinely mandated day of rest, reflection, and communal gathering that suspends ordinary labor (Heschel, 1951). Similar sacred timeframes appear in Christian, Islamic, and Hindu traditions, where prayer, fasting, or feasting organize the weekly or yearly calendar.

Meanwhile, modern capitalist societies have often devalued rest, treating it as laziness or unproductivity. The *Protestant work ethic*, described by Max Weber (1905), helped shape an ideology in which constant labor was seen as virtuous and idleness as sinful. Even today, the glorification of overwork persists in elite professional environments (all those tireless CEOs telling us how they get up at five o'clock in the morning and work out for an hour before the rest of us even get out of bed).

In fact, sharp contrasts in working culture persist not only across continents but also between sectors. Research has long shown that American workers take fewer vacation days and work longer hours than their European counterparts, reflecting cultural values tied to individualism and achievement (Alesina et al., 2005; Schor, 1992). In much of Western Europe—especially Scandinavia, France, and Germany—labor protections, shorter workweeks, and generous leave policies reflect a stronger institutional commitment to work-life balance. Yet these differences did not emerge overnight. The most dramatic reductions in working hours across Europe took place in the early twentieth century, particularly in the 1920s, driven by the growing influence of labor organizations.

Case in a Box: From Janus Knitwear to Contemporary Living Standards

A historical example from Norway illustrates how dramatically living conditions could improve in this period. At the Janus knitwear factory in Espeland, outside Bergen, working conditions changed significantly during the interwar years. According to the company's history (Solheim, 1995), the standard workweek was reduced from 60 to 48 h, and Saturdays were eventually made into days off (p. 32). At the same time, wages rose. Women formed the backbone of production, carrying out the skilled knitting work, while men more often held supervisory or managerial positions. Yet there were notable exceptions: some women—and among them the author's great-great-grandmother—advanced within the factory and earned what was then called "a man's salary," a rare recognition of female skill and contribution at the time.

The crucial point in this case is that two changes happened together: the drastic reduction of working hours and the simultaneous increase of wages. Combined, they produced a substantial leap in living standards. Families gained both more leisure and greater purchasing power. This transformation occurred before the era of mass consumer credit, which would only expand decades later.

By the 1980s and 1990s, much of the continued rise in European living standards rested less on structural reforms and more on credit expansion. Mortgages, education loans, and consumer debt allowed households to maintain or improve their lifestyles even as wage growth slowed. But this foundation was fragile. In many families, the debt is still present when wealth is passed down. The home that children inherit is often not free of loans; in practice it may have to be sold to cover obligations. What looks like prosperity is sometimes only postponed payment.

Today, for the first time in more than a century, it seems possible that living standards in Europe could stagnate or even decline. Surveys indicate that many Europeans already feel worse off, and structural pressures reinforce that perception: young people staying longer in their parents' homes, difficulties in securing stable employment, and growing reliance on welfare. Added to this picture is the rapid rise of artificial intelligence. Employers increasingly report that tasks once assigned to junior staff can now be automated, raising the barrier of entry for new graduates. Even high-skilled professions face disruption.

The Janus case reminds us that improvements in living standards once depended on institutional reform—shorter working hours, higher wages, and recognition of labor across gender lines. Later gains were increasingly financed by debt. Now, with automation and demographic pressures, the future may look less like an upward path and more like an open question: will the next generation achieve higher living standards, or inherit a burden of debt and fewer opportunities?

Questions for Reflection

1. Which institutional and political forces made it possible to reduce working hours and raise wages in the Janus factory during the interwar years?
2. Why were such changes experienced as leaps in living standards rather than gradual adjustments?
3. How do today's challenges in Europe—youth unemployment, housing costs, and welfare dependency—compare to the earlier struggles of industrial workers?
4. What role has debt and financialization played in sustaining modern living standards, and is this sustainable in the long run?
5. How might artificial intelligence reshape access to jobs, and what institutional reforms could prevent a decline in living standards for future generations?

These historical gains in labor rights and protections, however, were unevenly distributed and remain so even today. The differences extend beyond national boundaries into the divide between public and private sectors: employees in government or academia typically enjoy more flexibility and job security, while those in competitive industries face higher demands and longer hours, often under precarious conditions (Green, 2004; OECD, 2020). In this way, time use is shaped not only by personal choice or evolving technologies, but also by structural and ideological forces—economic systems, institutional norms, and cultural narratives—that determine which kinds of time are valued, protected, or quietly sacrificed.

These structural and cultural forces become even more visible when comparing work and rest across nations (Fig. 5.1).

The graph compares average annual working hours and paid vacation days across selected countries. It highlights major differences in work culture; for instance, we see that the U.S. stands out with long hours and limited vacation, while countries like Germany and France combine shorter work-weeks with more generous leave. These contrasts reflect deeper cultural and institutional attitudes toward productivity, rest, and the structure of daily life.

Ritual, in the anthropological and sociological sense, refers to a patterned sequence of actions, often symbolic, that is performed with regularity and imbued with cultural or emotional meaning (Bell, 1997; Rappaport, 1999). Rituals are not merely ceremonial; they help structure daily life, encode values, and reduce existential uncertainty. Anthropologists distinguish between major rituals—such as weddings, funerals, and national holidays—and *micro-rituals*, the small, often unnoticed acts that punctuate daily routines: morning coffee rituals, greetings at the workplace, or pub visits (Collins, 2004). These smaller rituals may lack formal ceremony but play a crucial role in *emotional regulation* and *social bonding*.

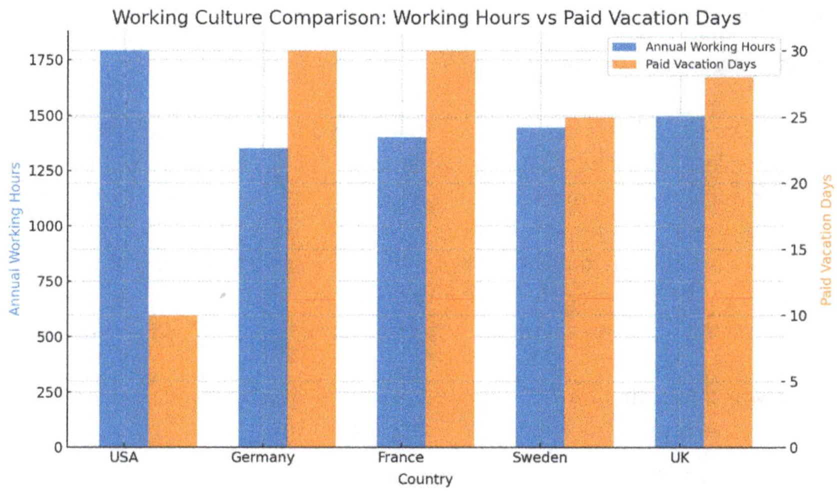

Fig. 5.1 Work and rest across cultures: average annual working hours vs. paid vacation days. *Source* OECD (2023), *Employment and Labour Market Statistics.* Retrieved from https://stats.oecd.org

Case in a Box: The Swedish Fika Ritual

One of the most cited examples of a micro-ritual in contemporary society is the Swedish tradition of *fika*. At its simplest, fika is a coffee break, often accompanied by something sweet from the bakery, such as a cinnamon bun or slice of cake. Yet, it is far more than just a pause for refreshments. Fika is a deeply ingrained cultural practice that structures social interaction at work and in private life (Lindahl & Lindgren, 2020; Löfgren & Ehn, 2010).

In many Swedish companies—even private firms—employees gather for fika several times a day. The purpose is not to discuss work-related matters, nor to address serious issues. In fact, raising controversial topics is frowned upon. Instead, fika provides a space for light conversation, empathy, and social care, reinforcing a sense of belonging and equality among colleagues (Alvesson, 2013). The ritual explicitly distinguishes itself from formal meetings: a fika must never be turned into a union meeting or work session.

For this reason, fika can sometimes be frustrating, particularly for immigrants unfamiliar with its unspoken rules. Scholars note that newcomers may expect a coffee break to be a chance to raise practical matters, only to find that such behavior disrupts the social fabric of the ritual (Ely & Thomas, 2001; Löfgren, 2008). The very point of fika lies in its non-instrumental character: it is a cultural technology of care, not a forum for decision-making.

Thus, fika illustrates the wider role of micro-rituals: while seemingly trivial, they encode cultural values—here, equality, restraint, and social harmony—and regulate emotional life in subtle but powerful ways.

Questions for Discussion

1. How does fika compare to micro-rituals in your own cultural context (e.g., tea breaks, pub visits, prayer breaks)?
2. Why might it be important for a ritual like fika to remain separate from formal work or union activities?
3. What does the frustration of some immigrants with fika reveal about the challenges of adapting to micro-rituals across cultures?
4. Can micro-rituals like fika strengthen group cohesion while limiting open discussion? Why or why not?
5. Do you think the non-instrumental nature of rituals (i.e., doing something "for its own sake") is essential for their social function?

While everyday practices like *fika* illustrate the subtle power of micro-rituals, classic theories still provide foundational insights into how rituals function more broadly. Arnold van Gennep's ([1909] 1960) theory of *rites of passage* outlines a tripartite process—separation, liminality, and incorporation—that guides individuals through key life transitions such as puberty, marriage, or death. Émile Durkheim (1912) emphasized the collective function of ritual, arguing that shared symbolic practices reinforce group cohesion and moral order. More recently, Randall Collins (2004) has shown how everyday interaction rituals generate what he calls *emotional energy*—a vital resource for maintaining motivation, identity, and belonging.

In modern societies, where shared belief systems are more fragmented, these rituals—whether macro or micro—offer continuity and predictability. They mark not only the passage of life stages but also the rhythms of ordinary time: the beginning of the workday, the weekend reset, or seasonal transitions. Even in secular or digital environments, rituals persist as anchors of meaning and as mechanisms for recharging both individual focus and collective solidarity.

A ritual, by definition, is a patterned activity that carries symbolic meaning and provides continuity in our lives. It can be religious, secular, personal, or communal, but its function is the same: to structure time, stabilize expectations, and anchor emotions in something shared or familiar. For many of us, rituals are not grand ceremonies but the small, repeated habits that lend rhythm and meaning to daily life.

In my own case, weekday rituals tend to revolve around productivity, while weekends take a different shape. Saturday mornings often begin with a long breakfast in front of *Gardener's World*, where Monty Don's articulate and soothing voice becomes the unofficial start of the weekend. What follows is usually several hours spent running back and forth in the garden, switching between tasks in a way that brings to mind Karel Čapek's book *One Year in My Garden*, a charming reflection on gardening as controlled chaos. This interest is also something I share with my wife, whose patience with tangled hoses and flowerbed disputes often exceeds my own.

A few years ago, we also played tennis regularly. These days, for reasons neither of us can quite explain, the racquets stay mostly in the closet. Instead, I try to maintain a routine of exercising three to four times a week—mostly to compensate for the fundamentally unhealthy nature of academic work, which involves long hours of static posture in front of a screen.

Beyond the week lies the broader arc of the year—what I've come to think of simply as "*the season.*" It's a familiar cadence made up of recurring events that shape time almost automatically: a January escape to the Mediterranean for light and perspective; a week of skiing during February's *sportlov*; perhaps a springtime city trip—often conveniently paired with an academic conference; time at my sister's summer cabin; and a slow transition into autumn with a hunting trip to Norway in search of mountain grouse. Christmas remains its own chaotic ritual, now joined by Halloween, which—if you ask my daughter—is the most important holiday of them all. Throughout the year, we also host formal dinners—some for family, others for colleagues—where ritual returns in the form of long meals, repeated toasts, and the all-important croquette match (if weather permits).

What these events create is not just a schedule, but a rhythm—a personal and *social calendar* that structures the year in meaningful segments. Each occasion may seem modest on its own, but together they form a patterned life: grounded in repetition, anchored in tradition, and infused with quiet some anticipation. That, perhaps, is the true power of ritual—not in its spectacle, but in its gentle, reliable return. Of course, that's not counting all the chaos in between—the misplaced shoes, burnt dinners, last-minute errands, and the usual ups and downs of family life that make the rhythm feel less like a symphony and more like a slightly out-of-tune jazz improvisation.

This personal rhythm echoes a broader cultural question: how do societies, more in general, divide and structure the year? Around the world, collective time is marked by recurring intervals of rest, reflection, and festivity. In much of the Western world, the calendar revolves around familiar anchor points: New Year, Easter, summer holidays, and Christmas. Yet each nation colors this basic framework with its own traditions. Sweden, for instance, still observes höstlov (fall break), a remnant of the old potato harvest schedule, and sportlov (winter sports break), conveniently aligned with peak snow season.

Many of these holidays reach deep into the past. Christian feast days often layered themselves atop pre-existing pagan festivals, reshaping older customs without entirely erasing them. In Northern Europe, the transition from Norse religion to Christianity preserved seasonal rites under new names. Midsummer (Midsommar) remains one of Sweden's most cherished celebrations, with origins in solstice rituals that long predate the Church. Rather than eliminating it, the Church allowed Midsummer to coexist alongside Christian observances (Andrén, 2014).

Even everyday language carries traces of this cultural layering. English weekday names—Wednesday (Odin's day), Thursday (Thor's day), and Friday (Frigg's day)—preserve Norse mythological references. These linguistic remnants signal a quiet continuity, reminders that cultural identity often persists beneath the surface (Crystal, 2003; Hultgård, 2008).

Meanwhile, new rituals continue to emerge, often through global influence. When I was a child, Halloween seemed like an odd American custom, built around a peculiar moral ultimatum: "trick or treat." Who, realistically, would ever choose the trick? Yet today the tradition has taken firm root in

Scandinavia. It is mainly children who take part, of course, but even the occasional parent or grandparent has learned—sometimes the hard way—that it is wise to keep a few extra sweets at home during this week. This shows that rituals are not static: they are cultural constructions, broadly shared within a nation but capable of change over time. As the Halloween example suggests, imported traditions can become localized, while at the same time parallel ceremonies within the same nation are rare, since too many competing rituals can undermine *social cohesion*. Those born in other countries may of course mark their own national day, but usually in ways that do not compete with the central traditions of the *majority culture*. This is how imported rituals become reinterpreted through local lenses (Herskovits, 1937).

Despite the accelerating pace of life, dominated by digital calendars and economic cycles, many of these seasonal rhythms endure. The way we shape the year—through celebrations, breaks, and shared observances—remains a living expression of how geography, belief, memory, and meaning converge in our collective experience of time.

Just as societies mark time through the year, so too do individuals move through time in the form of a life cycle.

5.3 Lifespan Experiences

Human development is structured by a *biological arc*, one that shapes not only our bodies but also our social status, expectations, and roles. In early life, we gain strength, skills, and knowledge. Midlife typically brings societal power and peak productivity. Later, aging invites reflection, physical decline, and a shift from leadership to legacy. These transitions are neither new nor arbitrary—they are widely observed, culturally marked, and increasingly studied in the social sciences.

This cycle has long been represented in visual culture. For example, one well-known illustration, common in nineteenth-century prints, depicts human life as a staircase: ascending through youth and adulthood, peaking in middle age, and descending in old age (Fig. 5.2).

Another version with a moral lesson is "The Drunkard's Progress"; a series of steps from the first drink to ruin. Here, life is not only chronological but moralized, with choices reinforcing or undermining one's trajectory (Fig. 5.3).

Such metaphors have faded from mainstream education, but the logic they represent still resonates. Different life stages come with distinct responsibilities and problems. A modern framing may appear in a less dramatic and more systematic way (Table 5.2).

Fig. 5.2 Life and age of man. *Source* James Baillie, 1848. "The Life and age of man, stages of man's life from the cradle to the grave." https://en.wikipedia.org/wiki/Lebenstreppe?utm_source=chatgpt.com#/media/File:The_Life_and_age_of_man,_stages_of_man's_life_from_the_cradle_to_the_grave_LCCN2006686267.jpg

While no single life unfolds exactly like this, the pattern holds significant empirical weight. Social expectations vary by culture, but nearly all societies assign roles and responsibilities based on age. Recognizing this rhythm can guide individual decisions and shape public policy.

Importantly, age is not just about physical capacity; it affects *social perception*. As people grow older, their voices may be heard less, even as their insight deepens. Adolescents, meanwhile, often exhibit the so-called *personal fable*, believing themselves invulnerable to risk or limitation (Elkind, 1967). Such developmental illusions can distort how age groups understand and treat each other.

Psychologist Dan McAdams (2001) suggests that *life stories*—how we interpret our past and imagine our future—are essential to selfhood. These stories change across the life course, influenced by joy and trauma, failure and growth. A young adult may view setbacks as temporary, while an older person may read them as part of a larger narrative arc. This interpretive shift has implications for resilience, mental health, and intergenerational empathy.

Fig. 5.3 Drunkard's progress. *Source* Nathaniel Currier, c. 1846. "The Drunkard's Progress: from the first glass to the grave." https://en.wikipedia.org/wiki/Lebenstreppe?utm source=chatgpt.com#/media/File:The_Drunkard's_Progress_-_Color.jpg

Cultural signals complicate these perceptions. Modern media often glorifies youth while obscuring the dignity or insights of old age. Arnett (2015) critiques how the phase of "*emerging adulthood*" is stretched and idealized, especially in Western societies. The result can be prolonged identity exploration, but also economic dependence, social disconnection, and role confusion.

Understanding how age shapes attitudes and behaviors is crucial for social scientists. In marketing, older consumers often prioritize reliability, clarity, and emotional resonance; younger ones are more driven by novelty and speed (Moschis, 2003; Williams & Drolet, 2005). In politics, age influences ideology and turnout: younger voters tend toward progressive ideals, while older ones are more conservative (Inglehart, 1997; Pew Research Center, 2024).

Neuroscience and developmental psychology also reveal key age-based differences. Adolescents, for instance, are more risk-prone due to an underdeveloped prefrontal cortex (Steinberg, 2008). Older adults, by contrast, exhibit stronger emotional regulation and prioritize meaningful interactions, consistent with *socioemotional selectivity theory* (Carstensen et al., 1999).

Sociologists have long studied *age stratification*. Riley et al. (1972) emphasize how age intersects with other forms of social differentiation—class,

Table 5.2 Duties of life: age-based responsibilities for individual and societal well-being

Life stage (years)	Key responsibilities and social roles
0–10	Develop basic physical coordination and emotional security. Learn hygiene, language, and foundational moral values through play and parental modeling. Build early empathy, cooperation, and curiosity. Dependence on caregivers is natural and necessary
11–20	Complete formal education. Begin identity exploration and critical thinking. Learn emotional regulation, digital literacy, and media discernment. Practice boundaries, avoid addiction, and help with household responsibilities. Begin contributing socially (e.g., volunteering, part-time work). Peer influence peaks; so does vulnerability
21–30	Establish financial independence and career identity. Explore or commit to relationships. Build self-discipline around health, sleep, and consumption. Take social and political responsibility (e.g., voting, taxes). Begin long-term planning (retirement, insurance, investment) even if family life is deferred. Avoid escapism and self-sabotaging behaviors
31–40	Fulfill core economic and caregiving roles. Raise children or support others' children meaningfully. Prioritize stable routines, fitness, and long-term health. Foster community resilience (school boards, coaching, civic duties). Learn to balance ambition with compassion. Begin mentoring younger generations
41–50	Assume leadership in professional or civic domains if so inclined. Maintain health through prevention and proactive care. Provide guidance to adolescents or young adults. Strengthen marriage or friendships. Start simplifying life logistics. Recognize limits and adjust ambition accordingly. Face first signs of aging with reflection, not denial
51–60	Support adult children emotionally, not just financially. Begin conscious succession planning in career and family. Increase civic and intergenerational engagement. Adapt lifestyle to changing energy levels. Make peace with unchosen paths. Prioritize mental and physical resilience. Accept vulnerability in others and oneself
61–70	Transition toward retirement gradually and with purpose. Focus on meaningful contribution: volunteer, tutor, mentor. Stay physically and mentally active to delay dependency. Reinvest in friendships and spiritual or philosophical reflection. Shift from "doing" to "being" without losing identity. Embrace generativity

(continued)

Table 5.2 (continued)

Life stage (years)	Key responsibilities and social roles
71–80	Share accumulated wisdom through storytelling, mentoring, or writing. Support grandchildren without overburdening self. Reduce healthcare burden through mobility, diet, and social engagement. Simplify possessions and routines. Prepare for eventual dependency with dignity and foresight. Fight loneliness through community
81+	Focus on legacy; emotional, ethical, and material. Reflect publicly or privately on life's meaning. Accept help without guilt. Offer presence more than productivity. Engage in rituals that reaffirm identity. Prepare for end-of-life decisions with clarity. Express gratitude. Leave peace behind

gender, ethnicity—to produce unequal access to care, labor, or respect. Ignoring these variables can result in distorted data, misleading conclusions, and poorly designed policies.

What emerges is a call for greater age awareness in both research and public discourse. When institutions overlook *life-stage variation*, they risk treating populations as homogeneous when in fact they are anything but. Accurate representation means acknowledging the biological and social realities of time.

Age is not just a number, it's a framework that shapes the entire arc of our lives. If we want to understand people as they truly are—which after all is the main goal of the social sciences—we must study them not as static entities, but as evolving beings moving through time.

If only someone had explained to me, when I was younger, what it truly feels like to grow older. Back then, I looked at people in their fifties or seventies as dull, exhausted, somehow defeated—marked by disappointment or withdrawal. Now, having crossed my own mid-fifties, I find myself inhabiting that very stage, fully aware that younger people may look at me through a similar lens. It is true that I no longer laugh as often, and I certainly do not walk around grinning at every moment or every chance to communicate. Yet I still feel the glow of youth burning inside me, only hidden under a thick layer of life's experiences. This gap between how aging feels from within and how it appears from the outside raises a deeper question: how do societies assign meaning to the different phases of life?

5.3.1 Societal Roles Across Life

If the previous reflections dwelled on the subjective experience of aging—what it feels like to move through life's stages—this section shifts the lens. Here, we explore how societies define and distribute those stages externally: what roles individuals are expected to perform at different ages, and how these roles are embedded in systems of labor, contribution, and social meaning.

From an evolutionary standpoint, human life is unusual in its longevity and complexity. Unlike most animals, we go through extended periods of dependence, learning, and post-reproductive life. Each phase—childhood, youth, adulthood, elderhood—has its functional purpose within the larger collective. Hunter-gatherer societies, for instance, depended on youth for energy and agility, adults for provisioning and coordination, and elders for accumulated knowledge, decision-making, and cultural transmission (Lee & Daly, 1999).

These basic patterns continued even as economies grew more complex. In agrarian societies, children were expected to contribute early, helping in fields, herding animals, or supporting household production. Adolescents often moved into apprenticeships or took on gendered roles. Adults were economic engines. Elders guided, taught, or retreated, but not without social relevance. Labor wasn't simply about employment; it was about position, expectation, and identity within a larger moral economy (Thompson, 1967).

Today, the stages of life are more formally structured—especially in industrialized societies—through institutions like schooling, wage labor, and retirement. Governments and economies depend on this sequencing to function: students prepare for work, workers pay taxes to support both the young and the elderly, and retirees live off accumulated entitlements. These aren't just personal transitions; they're logistical necessities within *national planning* and *intergenerational contracts*.

This structured sequencing of life stages is not merely biological—it is political. It reflects what philosophers call a *social contract*—an implicit agreement among members of a society about mutual responsibilities, duties, and expectations. In the classical tradition, Jean-Jacques Rousseau (1762) argued that we accept to be governed, even to be punished under law, because we gain security, freedom, and belonging in return. But society's contract with its members is not one-sided. Just as citizens are expected to contribute—through work, taxes, or civic behavior—society is expected to provide safety, opportunity, and justice across the lifespan. This mutual agreement extends across generations. The elderly educate the young, who later support the old.

This *intergenerational contract* underpins pensions, schooling, and long-term infrastructure, and it only functions as long as it is perceived as fair and reciprocal (Esping-Andersen, 2002; Giddens, 1998). When this balance is broken—through economic exclusion, unjust laws, or systemic inequality—people often express that "the social contract has failed." And when that sentiment spreads, political legitimacy unravels. Revolutions, social unrest, or institutional collapse can follow, requiring the slow rebuilding of trust and structure. As political scientist Francis Fukuyama (2011) notes, institutions do not survive on coercion alone—they depend on a shared sense of fairness and participation. Without it, the scaffolding of modern life becomes unstable. Or, to cite a master:

> The teacher fears and flatters the pupils, and the pupils despise their teachers. Young and old are all alike; the young imitate their elders and vie with them in speech and action, while the old condescend to the young and are full of pleasantries and gay manners, imitating the youth for fear of seeming disagreeable or authoritative. In such a democracy, freedom is pushed to such an extreme that it produces its opposite: tyranny. (*Republic* 562e–563e, trans. Paul Shorey, Loeb Classical Library, 1935)

Plato's warning resonates today. At many universities, the traditional relationship between teachers and students has shifted: authority bends toward appeasement, and fear of offense outweighs the defense of standards. This inversion suggests that we may already have entered—once again—the very phase Plato described, where generational balance is lost and institutions weaken from within.

Understanding this requires a broader view of what each generation is expected to contribute. Table 5.3 summarizes age-based responsibilities as they are commonly recognized across societies. These are not rigid prescriptions, but cultural ideals that help sustain both individual growth and collective stability:

While this table may appear similar to the previous one outlining life phases and responsibilities, it serves a broader purpose. Here, we emphasize not just economic roles, but a spectrum of human duties—emotional, developmental, civic, and intergenerational. It reflects an aspirational map of lifelong growth and contribution, rather than a fixed or uniform path. Actual life courses vary greatly across cultures, classes, and personal circumstances.

There are, of course, many ways to divide life into stages, and in practice we all do it—whether by decades, milestones, or turning points. The painter Edvard Munch, who created the artwork for this book's cover titled *The Researchers*, was almost obsessed with one particular theme: what he described

Table 5.3 Lifespan duties and roles—personal and societal dimensions

Life stage (years)	Personal development	Societal contribution
0–10	Learn basic values, language, hygiene, and empathy through play and parental modeling	Full dependency; no expected contribution beyond social learning
11–20	Form identity, critical thinking, and emotional regulation. Resist peer pressure and risk behaviors	Complete education. Light contribution via part-time work or volunteering
21–30	Build self-discipline, career focus, and relationship maturity. Manage independence	Enter workforce. Begin paying taxes and assuming adult responsibilities
31–40	Consolidate career, health habits, and family life. Learn to balance roles	Core economic output. Raise children, support schools and civic duties
41–50	Take on mentorship, leadership, and health maintenance. Accept bodily and career limits	Guide younger generations. Institutional trust roles increase
51–60	Reflect on unchosen paths. Cultivate wisdom and resilience. Support adult children	Succession planning. Civic involvement. Begin post-career positioning
61–70	Transition toward retirement. Deepen reflection and spiritual meaning	Volunteerism, mentoring, light economic engagement. Prepare legacy
71–80	Focus on wellbeing, wisdom-sharing, and simplifying. Avoid isolation	Symbolic roles: family elder, storyteller, cultural memory bearer
81+	Accept mortality, reduce burdens, and savor presence. Offer emotional leadership	Engage in rituals, memory transmission, and end-of-life planning

as the three stages of a woman's life, each depicted as distinctly different from the others. His work *The Dance of Life* (1899) places youth, adulthood, and old age side by side in a single frame: the young woman in white, full of possibility; the central couple absorbed in the intimacy of the moment; and the older woman in black, looking on with reflective detachment.

Case Box: The Dance of Life—Staging Womanhood, Staging Life
Edvard Munch's *The Dance of Life* presents three women in white, red, and black, arrayed along a moonlit shoreline. With sweeping strokes of expressionist color, he stages not just a moment of social dance, but a parable of the human journey—especially of womanhood.

Source The Dance of Life (1899), Edvard Munch. Public domain image from the Edvard Munch Museum website. *Source* edvardmunch.org

To the left, the woman in white radiates innocence, youth, and hope, perhaps untouched and full of promise. Center stage stands a woman in red—vibrant, passionate, caught up in both love and longing. And to the right, the woman in black embodies resignation, sorrow, maybe even survival through loss—a reflection on what remains when dusk overtakes day. These figures are not static portraits but emotional seasons, each brimming with symbolic significance.

Placed within Munch's broader *Frieze of Life* series, *The Dance of Life* dramatizes how the thrill of romance, the performance of social roles, and the passing of time can be contained within a single lifespan. Munch's canvas stages more than a static image—it becomes a dialogue between identity, expectation, and the inevitability of change. The white-clad figure is not merely young; she embodies early life's open horizon and untested possibility. The woman in red is not merely midlife; she represents the charged terrain of desire, creativity, risk, and survival. The black figure is not simply old age; she is the quiet survivor, looking back with reflection, acceptance, and perhaps a touch of resignation.

This visual metaphor aligns with our discussion of life scripts, limits, and transitions—not as purely rational milestones, but as emotional and social seasons. Yet it also challenges a set of modern cultural myths: that one can always "find a new husband" or that "life starts at 50." Such sayings are comforting, but often unrealistic. While opportunities may indeed arise at any stage, each phase of life brings constraints and responsibilities that cannot be wished away. In truth, living fully may be less about constantly seeking reinvention and more about inhabiting the season you are in—acknowledging its limits, embracing its duties, and recognizing its unique forms of joy.

From an individualist perspective, there is often a subtle rebellion against acceptance—a belief that life is, if not eternal, then at least a chain of endless possibilities waiting around every corner. But this, too, can be a kind of fairy tale, akin to those I wanted to caution my daughter against in the prologue to this book. Munch's work reminds us that while each stage has its beauty, it also has its boundaries, and wisdom lies in seeing both clearly.

One of the sharpest reminders comes in the form of the *biological clock*. Many young women assume fertility is something that can be postponed indefinitely—or that modern medicine will reliably correct the delay—but medical evidence suggests otherwise. Female fertility begins a gradual decline around age 30, with a sharper drop after 35, and by 40 the chances of conceiving naturally in a given month are only about 10 percent (American College of Obstetricians and Gynecologists [ACOG], 2023; Steiner & Jukic, 2016). Fertility treatments, while helpful, cannot fully compensate for age-related decline, since egg quality diminishes with time (UCLA Health, 2022).

To speak of "ten good years" for pregnancy is an oversimplification—fertility does not collapse overnight, and individual variation is considerable. Yet the metaphor conveys an essential truth: there is a limited window in which the likelihood of pregnancy is at its highest, generally between the early twenties and early thirties. Beyond that period, the risks of miscarriage, chromosomal abnormalities, and complications rise steadily (Dunson et al., 2004). Egg freezing and assisted reproductive technologies may extend possibilities, but they are neither guarantees nor substitutes for biology (Cobo & Diaz, 2020).

The larger point is that while modern narratives encourage us to imagine life as endlessly open, biology sets boundaries that no amount of cultural optimism or technological ingenuity can fully erase. To acknowledge this is not to diminish freedom, but to recognize that meaning is found as much in limits as in possibilities.

Questions for Reflection

1. How does Munch's use of color, framing, and composition convey emotional truths about life's stages beyond their chronological order?
2. In what ways do cultural roles—such as virgin, lover, or matriarch—shape the way these stages are lived and perceived, particularly for women?
3. What rituals, literary motifs, or cultural practices in your own context similarly mark or dramatize life's transitions?

4. How does this symbolic framing influence the way you think about personal identity and continuity across the lifespan?
5. Are cultural myths of constant reinvention empowering, misleading, or perhaps both at once?

And if you can get through these questions without a lively argument, I'll eat my summer hat—they're bound to stir emotions.

Like the table above, the painting reminds us that these phases coexist in society at any given moment, each with its own role, rhythm, and meaning. In reality, we are always living among all stages at once—learning from some, supporting others, and anticipating our own passage through them.

The Evolution of Public and Private Roles.

What Munch expressed artistically as the three lives of women, modern economies have translated into a more practical sequence: education, working life, and retirement. To get a job, in most cases, we must first qualify, meaning we need to know specific facts or possess particular skills. For instance, to work as an electrician, one must understand electrical principles and safety before cutting wires (Kelly, 2024). Likewise, surgeons must learn comprehensive knowledge of human anatomy before performing any operation (BLS, 2020). This essential knowledge and these technical skills are acquired through formal education and training, from elementary and secondary school to university or vocational programs (BLS, 2020).

This three-stage life cycle—school, work, retirement—is a near-universal pattern in modern economies. OECD data show that the normal retirement age for men entering the workforce today averages 66.3 years and 65.8 years for women, marking the end of active employment (OECD, 2023). Yet significant populations rely solely on pay-as-you-go state pensions, funded by current workers, while others depend on private savings, occupational pensions, or a mix of both (OECD, 2023; Fraser Institute, 2024). Around 29% of people aged 55 and over lack any form of retirement plan beyond public benefits, making state support essential for nearly half of households approaching retirement (GAO, 2016). As longevity rises and fertility rates decline, the support ratio—workers per retiree—has dropped dramatically, from about 7.2 in 1950 to a projected 2.1 by 2050, threatening the financial sustainability of pension systems (Wikipedia, 2025).

Most people who work do so either in the public sector (for the state) or in the private sector (for businesses and non-state organizations). For example, a university professor might perform nearly identical tasks—teaching, research, supervision—whether employed by a state-run university or a private institution. The same is true for doctors, teachers, engineers, or transportation workers. The key distinction lies not so much in the tasks, as in who pays the salary and determines the organizational structure: the government or a private employer.

The balance between public and private employment varies significantly by country, reflecting historical, political, and economic differences. In Scandinavian countries like Sweden, Norway, and Denmark, the public sector is comparatively large. In Sweden, for instance, about 28% of the workforce is employed in public sector roles, including healthcare, education, and administration (OECD, 2023). This is partly due to a *welfare-state tradition*, where the government has taken a leading role in providing universal services like healthcare and education.

By contrast, in the United States, the public sector employs around 14% of the workforce (BLS, 2023), and many services are either privatized or delivered through market competition. This reflects a stronger emphasis on *market-driven efficiency* and a political culture that often favors limited government involvement.

In post-socialist countries, like those in Eastern Europe, the public sector used to dominate under centrally planned economies. However, since the 1990s, many of these countries have undergone rapid privatization, significantly shrinking state employment, though some sectors like health and education still retain large public footprints (World Bank, 2020).

In Asia, the balance between public and private employment varies widely across countries, influenced by levels of development, governance models, and historical legacies. In countries like China and Vietnam, which maintain strong state-led models despite embracing market reforms, the public sector remains dominant in strategic areas such as infrastructure, energy, and finance. *State-Owned Enterprises (SOEs)* continue to employ a significant share of the workforce, though private enterprise has grown rapidly in urban centers (OECD, 2018; Lin & Milhaupt, 2013). In contrast, countries like Japan and South Korea have relatively lean public sectors, shaped by postwar development strategies that emphasized industrial policy, export-led growth, and public–private collaboration rather than direct state employment. Meanwhile, in lower-income Asian nations such as India and Indonesia, the public sector often plays a dual role—as both a major employer and a vehicle for social policy—but capacity limitations and bureaucratic inefficiencies sometimes hinder effectiveness (World Bank, 2021). This diversity reflects Asia's complex mix of governance traditions, economic priorities, and institutional capacity.

In South and Central America, the balance between public and private employment reflects both colonial legacies and contemporary political orientations. Countries like Brazil and Argentina maintain sizable public sectors, particularly in education, healthcare, and public administration, where state employment plays a key role in social service delivery. In Brazil, for example, the public sector accounts for about 12–14% of total employment, with federal, state, and municipal levels all contributing to workforce size (ILO, 2020). In smaller nations like Costa Rica or Uruguay, public employment often serves as a stabilizing force in labor markets, providing formal jobs in contexts where informal work remains widespread. However, across the region, high levels of informality and political instability have challenged consistent investment in public institutions. Economic liberalization in countries such as Chile and Peru have led to a greater reliance on private provision of services, especially in pensions and education, although this shift has also raised concerns about inequality and access (CEPAL, 2022). Overall, the region reflects a complex mix of welfare-state elements, market reforms, and enduring informal economies.

The size of the public sector also correlates with levels of trust in institutions, taxation systems, and expectations of government responsibility. In countries where citizens expect the state to ensure a certain standard of life—through pensions, childcare, eldercare, and education—public employment tends to be higher (Esping-Andersen, 1990). In nations where such responsibilities are seen as private or family matters, the state employs fewer people and plays a smaller role.

In many countries, the private sector tends to offer higher salaries, particularly in competitive or high-skill fields like finance, technology, or consulting. By contrast, public sector jobs often come with lower average pay but offer greater job security, more predictable work hours, and in some cases, better pension benefits.

For example, in the United States, data from the U.S. Bureau of Labor Statistics (2022) shows that private sector employees earn more on average than their public sector counterparts in similar roles, especially at higher education levels. However, public employees are more likely to have defined-benefit pension plans, longer job tenure, and lower dismissal rates (BLS, 2022; GAO, 2017).

In France, the public sector offers strong job protection, so much so that civil servants are often said to hold jobs for life. A 2016 report by the French National Institute of Statistics and Economic Studies (INSEE) showed that public employees had a tenure rate of over 80%, while the private sector was far more dynamic, with higher turnover and pay differences across sectors.

In Germany, public sector salaries are typically lower than in the private sector for equivalent qualifications, especially among younger workers. However, public sector roles are attractive for those seeking stability and work-life balance. Studies by the German Institute for Economic Research (DIW) have shown that many employees accept lower pay in exchange for greater predictability and social insurance coverage (DIW, 2020).

In developing countries, the picture can vary. In some African and South Asian contexts, public sector jobs are still seen as status symbols and are sought after not only for their security but also for the possibility of patronage and informal income streams (van Besley & Ghatak, 2005; de Walle, 2001).

These trade-offs between pay and security reflect differing motivations for work: income maximization versus long-term stability. They also shape the career strategies of individuals, who may choose to start in the private sector for salary growth and later move into the public sector for stability and benefits, or vice versa.

In sum, the balance between public and private employment in any society is not merely a matter of economic efficiency—it reflects deeper historical trajectories, institutional legacies, and cultural values. Countries that experienced strong welfare-state development after the Second World War—such as the Scandinavian nations—continue to maintain larger public sectors rooted in ideals of *universal provision* and *social solidarity* (Esping-Andersen, 1990; Rothstein, 1998). In contrast, nations shaped by neoliberal reforms or colonial legacies often exhibit more limited public sectors and greater reliance on markets, reflecting ideological commitments to individualism and fiscal restraint (Centeno & Cohen, 2012; Harvey, 2005). Post-socialist countries, meanwhile, reveal hybrid patterns as they transition from centralized state economies to mixed models, often retaining large public footprints in legacy sectors like healthcare and education (Kornai, 2006). Cultural dimensions—such as trust in government, perceptions of fairness, and attitudes toward social responsibility—also influence how citizens and policymakers view the legitimacy and desirability of state-led versus market-led employment structures (Alesina & Glaeser, 2004). Thus, the public–private divide is not fixed or natural, but a socially constructed outcome shaped by politics, culture, and history. Recognizing this diversity is essential when comparing labor systems across countries or when reforming institutions in a globalized economy.

This discussion, though seemingly grounded in everyday common sense, is highly relevant to a book on the human condition because it touches on one of the most fundamental aspects of human life: how we secure our survival and define our social roles through work. While many readers may already be familiar with the structure of employment, taxation, and retirement, revisiting these concepts from an evolutionary, historical, and cross-cultural perspective reveals their deeper significance.

Yet there is also an intellectual tendency worth addressing. Some social scientists, especially those critical of markets or what they call the "*free market*," have at times treated economics as optional—as if material constraints were simply matters of ideology rather than basic conditions of survival for individuals and societies. It is a little like assuming that food will appear without labor, or that goods can be priced without regard to whether others are willing to exchange for them.

This reflects a distinctly Western habit of mind: the capacity to abstract away parts of reality, and sometimes to deny them altogether, when they do not align with preferred ideals. One striking example emerges in debates over universal basic income. Advocates often celebrate the idea as a matter of justice, but when pressed on how such programs should be financed, some retreat from economic reasoning entirely—ignoring the consequences of money creation, taxation, or inflation (Bregman, 2017; Standing, 2017; Widerquist, 2018). In effect, economics becomes the enemy, not the analytical tool it must remain if proposals are to be realistic. This rejection of economic fundamentals, rooted as much in identity politics and ideological posturing as in scholarship, is not only scientifically unsound but dangerously naïve (Acemoglu & Robinson, 2012; Friedman, 1962).

What makes this tendency even more striking is that it forgets what only a few generations ago was considered common sense: that nothing comes from nothing, and that food on the table ultimately requires labor. As industrialization and urbanization distanced large populations from direct production, the chain from seeds to bread became invisible (Mazoyer & Roudart, 2006; Piketty, 2020). In cities, many came to believe that money could simply be printed to solve shortages, overlooking the inflationary spirals such policies historically triggered (Reinhart & Rogoff, 2009). The normalization of debt has reinforced this mindset. Entire generations have been socialized to think of borrowing as benign—even for states—when in fact unsustainable debt accumulation often undermines long-term resilience (Kindleberger & Aliber, 2011). The old farmer, who knew that one could only borrow for an investment that eventually paid back, still had the sounder logic. Yet paradoxically, despite unprecedented access to business education, the average person today may command less practical economic sense than many of their ancestors. To understand the human condition, one cannot bracket off the economic domain; to do so is to ignore the very substrate of survival, distribution, and collective life.

To set aside such economic realities is to miss the foundation upon which much of human life rests. Survival, distribution, and exchange are not optional—they are the structures through which societies endure. From here, a deeper point follows: work is not only a source of income but also a system of meaning, identity, and social integration. The way societies organize labor reflects their values, institutions, and assumptions about fairness and contribution. To understand what it means to be human today, we must examine how tasks are distributed, how value is recognized, and how life's three great phases—education, work, and retirement—are managed across cultures and history.

Labor is not simply about earning a living; it shapes how people seek purpose, recognition, and belonging. The institutions that structure work rest on evolutionary pressures, cultural norms, and social contracts—yet even with these foundations, the human experience remains contested and unstable. Into this already complex picture enters artificial intelligence. Entry-level office work and routine cognitive tasks are being automated at scale, raising urgent questions about employment, redistribution, and taxation. These dilemmas are not merely technical but strike at the very foundations of the social contract. Who contributes, who benefits, and how value is shared are questions every society must renegotiate in the face of technological change. We return to these issues in depth in Chapter 9, where the economic costs of outsourcing cognition are set against the long history of human labor systems and the paradox of progress that has accompanied each technological leap.

5.4 Self-Domestication and Cultural Trends

When we open a newspaper or scroll through a news feed, we often see a world in disarray. War, corruption, inequality, and political dysfunction dominate the headlines. Less visible are the billions of ordinary, cooperative acts that make society function—parents raising children, neighbors helping neighbors, and colleagues working together. This imbalance in reporting skews perception and raises a deeper question: Are we witnessing humanity's decline, or are we simply seeing it more clearly?

I am always reminded of this gap when I read the optimistic outlooks of brilliant thinkers like the late Hans Rosling or Steven Pinker. Rosling, through his work and the *Gapminder project*, emphasized how global health, poverty, and education have improved dramatically over the past century—data that rarely makes the headlines (Rosling et al., 2018). Likewise,

Pinker argues in *Enlightenment Now* (2018) that despite current challenges, humanity is progressing on nearly every measurable front. And yet, every day the news cycle is saturated with war, climate disaster, and institutional breakdown. Which reality is more true—and why do they feel so incompatible?

One reason for this dissonance lies in our expectations. Human beings are uniquely capable of imagining how things could be. We craft moral ideals, political visions, and spiritual teachings that reflect a higher standard. But reality rarely conforms to these ideals. That persistent gap between aspiration and actuality fosters both disillusionment and conflict.

To better understand this gap, we can turn to evolutionary theory. Humans did not evolve to create utopias—we evolved to survive in complex social environments. Much of our behavior is not driven by lofty ideals, but by mechanisms shaped through millennia of adaptive challenges. *Kin selection* (Hamilton, 1964) and *reciprocal altruism* (Trivers, 1971) suggest that cooperation evolved first among close relatives or partners who could be counted on to return a favor. What we call "morality" may, in many cases, have emerged as an efficient survival strategy rather than a universal ethical truth.

Yet evolution also selected for traits that sustain large-scale cooperation. Studies show that people are willing to punish norm violators even when it costs them personally (Fehr & Gächter, 2002). Theories like strong reciprocity and costly signaling (Barclay, 2004; Zahavi & Zahavi, 1997) suggest that generosity and fairness may function as signals of reliability and status. These evolutionary pressures laid the groundwork for modern institutions and moral systems, enabling us to build cooperative societies far beyond the kin-based groups of our ancestors.

Anthropologists have proposed the concept of *self-domestication* to explain how societies might select for less aggressive traits over time. Brian Hare (2017) argues that, like domesticated animals, humans may have evolved toward greater empathy and lower reactivity, not through biology alone, but through cultural evolution and social norms that reward cooperative behavior. This view provides a cautious optimism. Steven Pinker (2011) has argued—controversially but with considerable data—that violence has decreased over centuries, even accounting for the world wars of the twentieth century. As Pinker and others point out, the modern world has seen a rise in legal institutions, human rights frameworks, and global norms that restrain our more destructive impulses.

However, progress is not linear or guaranteed. As Timothy Snyder (2010) warns, the breakdown of liberal institutions in the twentieth century—culminating in genocide, authoritarianism, and mass violence—reminds us how fragile civilization can be. The same human instincts that build societies can also destroy them—and they do so with unsettling regularity. Human nature, then, is not a fixed state but a dynamic balance between opposing tendencies. Tribalism and empathy, competition and cooperation, destruction and creation—all reside within us. What matters is how we cultivate these traits through education, law, and culture. Each generation inherits this fragile legacy. Those who lived through great upheavals—wars, revolutions, economic collapses—often developed a sobering sense of civic duty. In contrast, generations raised in relative peace may take the foundations of civilization for granted, mistaking inherited stability for a permanent state.

This fragile balance between opposing human tendencies helps explain why civilizations tend to follow cyclical patterns of rise, peak, and decline. As historian Arnold Toynbee (1934) argued, civilizations are not destroyed by external enemies alone but collapse from within when they fail to respond creatively to internal challenges. Over time, the virtues that built a society—discipline, sacrifice, solidarity—are often eroded by comfort, complacency, and entitlement. Sociologist Pitirim Sorokin (1937) observed that cultures tend to swing between *ideational* (spiritual, duty-based) and *sensate* (materialist, pleasure-seeking) phases, each sowing the seeds of its own transformation. Evolutionary psychologists note a similar dynamic in individual behavior: when threat levels are high, cooperation and restraint increase; in safer times, short-term gratification and self-interest become more prominent (Henrich, 2020). The same applies at the collective level. Institutions built during times of scarcity may falter under the strain of abundance. Economic historian Carlo Cipolla (1976) even warned that the rise of incompetence within the ruling elite—through what he called the "*laws of human stupidity*"—can accelerate societal decline. Inherited systems require ongoing maintenance, but the very success of civilization may undermine the incentives needed to preserve it. Just as great fortunes are often lost within three generations (Klotz, 2021), so too may cultural capital erode without conscious renewal.

These cycles are not abstract. They have marked the lives of families across the world, my own included. A great-great-grandfather was mobilized to the Swedish border in 1905, expecting retaliation after Norway's declaration of independence. The First World War brought hardship even to neutral nations, and during the German invasion of the Second World War, families like my father's were forced to flee to rural areas for safety. Such experiences—of war, disruption, and adaptation—are not unique, but part of a broader human history that spans continents and generations. Catastrophes, or near-catastrophes, have struck every second generation or so. On my wife's side, she grew up in Kharkiv and has lived through the destruction of much of her childhood landscape as Putin's Russia has devastated large parts of the city (not to mention the occupied regions). This stands in stark contrast to the warm summers her family once spent on the Crimean seashore before the Second World War—and to the devastation Nazi Germany brought to Ukraine during that war. I am struck every time I look at the old photographs: idyllic family lunches in the open air, tables draped in white cloths, women in elaborate costumes and extravagant hats. And now this. What emerges from such stories are cycles of violence and decay, not linear progressions.

We like to think that peace is the norm, but history suggests otherwise. These waves of violence and despair are not exceptions to human nature; they are part of it. We live through them, and often—though not always—we survive. Every day on the front, war wounds or kills on the order of a thousand people, yet survivors rebuild. They found schools, plant trees, raise children, and erect monuments to those who died defending their homeland. Life goes on. The mistake we often make is to believe that such cycles will not return—that we have somehow outgrown them. Yet history rarely abandons its old habits. This is why nations maintain strong armies even in peacetime, and why, when they do not, they are quickly reminded of the cost of such complacency.

This dynamic leads us to a broader perspective on how generational experience shapes our interpretation of the world. Each generation lives within its own cultural atmosphere, molded by the specific challenges, technologies, values, and institutions of its time. This phenomenon is captured in the term *Zeitgeist*—literally "spirit of the time"—as articulated by thinkers like Johann Gottfried Herder and G.W.F. Hegel. They saw history as a progression of collective consciousness, with each era embodying its own worldview (Hegel, 1807/1977). Karl Mannheim (1952) emphasized that generations experience the world differently depending on their position within these historical currents. Such differences are not just stylistic but extend to fundamental beliefs about morality, progress, and the meaning of life. The older generation may feel its world is fading; the younger may not even recognize its predecessors' assumptions. These tensions often sharpen during periods of decline, when inherited values seem less effective at interpreting present realities.

This brings us to the question of cycles themselves, which can be understood on at least two levels. The first is the *internal cycle* within a single country or society: phases of prosperity, stability, and cultural flowering often give way to decline, stagnation, or crisis, before renewal may—or may not—occur. The second is the *civilizational cycle*, the longer comparative arc in which societies rise and fall relative to one another. History shows that some civilizations never recover their earlier prominence—the Egyptian, Mayan, and Mesopotamian empires stand as examples (Diamond, 2005; Tainter, 1988). Others, however, demonstrate remarkable resilience, reasserting themselves after periods of decline. China is perhaps the most striking case: despite invasions, dynastic collapses, and colonial incursions, it has re-emerged repeatedly as a central global power (Arrighi, 2007; Pomeranz, 2000). These *dual rhythms*—shorter national cycles and longer civilizational cycles—remind us that decline is not always followed by renewal, and that the fate of societies is shaped as much by external pressures and comparative standing as by their internal capacities for adaptation.

Seen in this light, Europe and the Western world more broadly appear to be entering not just an internal downturn but a civilizational cycle of decline (Söilen, 2020). This process is larger than the normal oscillations of prosperity and recession within a single country; it reflects a global shift in hegemonic power, with Asia—and especially China—gaining ground in science, technology, and economic influence (Arrighi, 2007; Mahbubani, 2020).

Yet nothing about this trajectory is deterministic. History shows that the fate of civilizations is shaped by choices made across generations. Renewal depends less on technical fixes or institutional engineering than on the preservation of cultural values and the cultivation of virtues such as honesty, diligence, and civic responsibility. Economic growth and productivity are downstream of these forces, not their origin. University education, for instance, is not the foundation of virtue but its consequence: institutions of higher learning flourished in societies where discipline, trust, and shared values had already been established (Mokyr, 2016; Putnam, 1993). The Western tendency to assume that social problems can be solved through *technocratic design*, or that professed moral superiority guarantees resilience, is a dangerous illusion (Fukuyama, 1995). At the same time, history reminds us that the West has periodically produced generations marked by discipline and civic virtue, driving remarkable episodes of renewal—from the Renaissance to the postwar reconstruction of Europe. Recovering such vitality is not a matter of nostalgia, but of *cultural stewardship*: preserving and nurturing the moral foundations that enabled nations to succeed in the first place.

History shows that cultures are never static. They either advance or recede. South Korea's rapid ascent from postwar poverty to global leadership in electronics and media illustrates how collective focus, education, and adaptability can drive transformation (Kim & Vogel, 2011). By contrast, societies in denial of their decline often cling to nostalgic myths or superficial symbols of vitality—imported technologies, flashy consumer goods, or debt-fueled consumption—mistaking them for genuine strength.

Such illusions of progress are common. The iPhone may improve quality of life, but it does not signal local innovation if it was created elsewhere. Likewise, the United States experienced a consumer boom in the 1980s–1990s, yet inequality widened and productivity growth stagnated (Piketty, 2014; Wolff, 2017). People felt wealthier, but the structural base was quietly eroding. Cognitive biases like affective forecasting and attribution errors (Gilbert, 2006; Kahneman, 2011) make it difficult to perceive decline clearly while living through it.

This is why assessing whether a culture is rising or falling requires more than surface impressions. Empirical indicators such as scientific productivity, technological sovereignty, and institutional resilience provide more reliable insight. Yet even these measures can fail to warn societies in time. Rome under Marcus Aurelius, the United States today, and other examples remind us that civilizations can crumble even at moments when they appear powerful. What ultimately endures is not architecture or wealth alone, but the renewal of values—intergenerational responsibility, truth, and civic duty.

The story of human progress, then, is neither one of steady ascent nor inevitable decline. It is a cycle of renewal and erosion. Long-term trends may justify optimism, as Rosling and Pinker emphasize, but the Zeitgeist of any given generation still produce regression, conflict, or collapse. For the social sciences, the challenge is not to assume that progress will take care of itself, nor to view decline as irreversible, but to recognize the cyclical interplay of biology, culture, and history—and to help societies see how renewal remains possible.

5.5 From Civilizational Cycles to the Renewal of the Social Sciences

For the social sciences, all of this matters deeply. We are not neutral observers outside of time, but actors embedded in the historical currents of our own era. Research does not arise in a vacuum. It is shaped by generational values, dominant ideologies, and inherited institutions. That does not make truth relative—but it does mean that seeking it requires vigilance: against fashion, bias, and collective illusions.

Perhaps one of the most persistent errors in modern civilization is the failure to take the task of renewal seriously. In many Western societies, there is a tendency to believe that once prosperity and institutions have been achieved, progress will somehow glide forward on its own. Tall buildings, legal systems, and digital infrastructure become mistaken for guarantees of permanence. But history offers no such security. Civilizations do not sustain themselves through architecture or technology alone.

By contrast, other cultures—particularly in East Asia—have long emphasized intergenerational responsibility and cultural continuity. In Confucian-influenced societies like China, for example, there exists a deep ethic of familial respect and civic duty—not merely in the form of ancestral worship, but as a conscious act of cultural stewardship (Ho, 1994; Tu, 1996). Each generation is expected to preserve and transmit what came before. Western modernity, by contrast, often assumes that systems will self-correct—that democracy, science, and markets will run on autopilot. This is a comforting illusion, more reminiscent of the proverbial third-generation heir who squanders an inheritance than of a carefully thought-through plan. No society endures without effort. No institutional framework is immune to erosion if the underlying values that uphold it are forgotten.

If there is a thread that runs through this chapter, it is this: human nature is shaped by both evolution and history. The moral and institutional scaffolding of society is built not just on biology, but on accumulated choices—many of which must be renewed, not once, but continually. Within each generation lies the danger of complacency and the potential for renewal. Civilizations rise and fall—but honest inquiry, cultural self-awareness, and a sense of shared responsibility give us the tools to steer our trajectory.

In every generation, the work of rebuilding must begin again.

This brings us back to the question posed at the chapter's outset: Which reality is more true—and why do they feel so incompatible? The long-term improvements emphasized by Rosling and Pinker—declines in extreme poverty, rising life expectancy, improved literacy—are real and meaningful. They should be acknowledged. But they should not be mistaken for guarantees. Progress is not a self-sustaining process. Societies are fragile ecosystems, dependent not only on economic systems and political structures, but on the transmission and exercise of human virtues. Stability persists only as long as courage, honesty, and civic responsibility are kept alive in each new generation.

Part of the tension lies in the scale of observation. Rosling and Pinker measure progress at the level of humanity as a whole, and on a very long time frame. At that scale, the trend line bends upward. But history rarely unfolds evenly across cultures or civilizations. While some societies flourish, others decline, fragment, or fade away. This cycle is not an anomaly but part of the evolutionary process itself—older systems making room for new ones, cultures competing and adapting, survival being determined as much by moral and institutional strength as by material wealth. To mistake the global average for a universal trajectory is to overlook the unevenness of history, and the fragility of particular societies.

And so we are left with a final question: How do we understand that rebuilding? How can we investigate the patterns, causes, and meanings behind the complex social systems we inherit and reshape? This is where the social sciences come in.

This chapter has shown culture as lived time: the rhythms of work, care, and generational life through which society reproduces itself. But to study these patterns is also to confront the limits of how we study them. The social sciences arose to make sense of human life in all its variety, yet their own tools and assumptions often obscure as much as they reveal. In the next chapter, we step back to examine the social sciences themselves—their history, their blind spots, and the challenge of building a framework that is both empirically grounded and intellectually plural.

References

Acemoglu, D., & Robinson, J. A. (2012). *Why nations fail: The origins of power, prosperity, and poverty*. Crown.

Alesina, A., & Glaeser, E. L. (2004). *Fighting poverty in the US and Europe: A world of difference*. Oxford University Press.

Alesina, A., Glaeser, E. L., & Sacerdote, B. (2005). Work and leisure in the United States and Europe: Why so different? *NBER Macroeconomics Annual, 20*, 1–64.

Alvesson, M. (2013). *Understanding organizational culture*. Sage.

Amabile, T. M., & Kramer, S. J. (2011). *The progress principle: Using small wins to ignite joy, engagement, and creativity at work*. Harvard Business Review Press.

American College of Obstetricians and Gynecologists. (2023). *Having a baby after age 35: How aging affects fertility and pregnancy*. ACOG. https://www.acog.org/womens-health/faqs/having-a-baby-after-age-35-how-aging-affects-fertility-and-pregnancy

Andrén, A. (2014). *Nordisk hedendom: Ett historiskt perspektiv*. Gidlunds förlag.

Arnett, J. J. (2015). *Emerging adulthood: The winding road from the late teens through the twenties* (2nd ed.). Oxford University Press.

Arrighi, G. (2007). *Adam Smith in Beijing: Lineages of the twenty-first century*. Verso.

Barclay, P. (2004). Trustworthiness and competitive altruism can also solve the "tragedy of the commons." *Evolution and Human Behavior, 25*(4), 209–220.

Baumeister, R. F., Bratslavsky, E., Muraven, M., & Tice, D. M. (2001). Ego depletion: Is the active self a limited resource? *Journal of Personality and Social Psychology, 74*(5), 1252–1265.
Becker, G. S. (1965). A theory of the allocation of time. *The Economic Journal, 75*(299), 493–517.
Bell, D. (1997). *The coming of post-industrial society: A venture in social forecasting.* Basic Books. (Original work published 1973).
Besley, T., & Ghatak, M. (2005). Competition and incentives with motivated agents. *American Economic Review, 95*(3), 616–636.
Bianchi, S. M., Robinson, J. P., & Milkie, M. A. (2006). *Changing rhythms of American family life*. Russell Sage Foundation.
BLS. (2022). *American time use survey*. U.S. Bureau of Labor Statistics.
BLS. (2023). *American time use survey*. U.S. Bureau of Labor Statistics.
Bregman, R. (2017). *Utopia for realists: How we can build the ideal world*. Little, Brown.
Bureau of Labor Statistics (BLS). (2020). *Occupational outlook handbook*. U.S. Department of Labor.
Bureau of Labor Statistics (BLS). (2022). *Employer costs for employee compensation—March 2022*. U.S. Department of Labor.
Carstensen, L. L., Isaacowitz, D. M., & Charles, S. T. (1999). Taking time seriously: A theory of socioemotional selectivity. *American Psychologist, 54*(3), 165–181.
Centeno, M. A., & Cohen, J. N. (2012). *Global capitalism: A sociological perspective*. Polity.
CEPAL. (2022). *Social Panorama of Latin America 2022*. United Nations Economic Commission for Latin America and the Caribbean.
Cipolla, C. M. (1976). *The basic laws of human stupidity*. Il Mulino.
Cobo, A., & Diaz, C. (2020). Clinical application of oocyte vitrification: A systematic review and meta-analysis of randomized controlled trials. *Fertility and Sterility, 113*(2), 331–344.
Collins, R. (2004). *Interaction ritual chains*. Princeton University Press.
Crystal, D. (2003). *The Cambridge encyclopedia of the English language* (2nd ed.). Cambridge University Press.
Diamond, J. (2005). *Collapse: How societies choose to fail or succeed*. Viking.
DIW. (2020). *German Institute for Economic Research report*. DIW Berlin.
Dunson, D. B., Baird, D. D., & Colombo, B. (2004). Increased infertility with age in men and women. *Obstetrics & Gynecology, 103*(1), 51–56.
Durkheim, É. (1995). *The elementary forms of religious life* (K. E. Fields, Trans.). Free Press. (Original work published 1912).
Elkind, D. (1967). Egocentrism in adolescence. *Child Development, 38*(4), 1025–1034.
Ely, R. J., & Thomas, D. A. (2001). Cultural diversity at work: The effects of diversity perspectives on work group processes and outcomes. *Administrative Science Quarterly, 46*(2), 229–273.

Esping-Andersen, G. (1990). *The three worlds of welfare capitalism.* Princeton University Press.
Esping-Andersen, G. (2002). *Why we need a new welfare state.* Oxford University Press.
Fehr, E., & Gächter, S. (2002). Altruistic punishment in humans. *Nature, 415*, 137–140.
Fraser Institute. (2024). *Economic freedom of the world report*. Fraser Institute.
Friedman, M. (1962). *Capitalism and freedom.* University of Chicago Press.
Fukuyama, F. (1995). *Trust: The social virtues and the creation of prosperity.* Free Press.
Fukuyama, F. (2011). *The origins of political order: From prehuman times to the French Revolution.* Farrar.
GAO. (2016). *Contingent workforce report*. U.S. Government Accountability Office.
GAO. (2017). *Contingent workforce report*. U.S. Government Accountability Office.
Gershuny, J. (2011). *Time-use surveys and the measurement of national well-being*. Centre for Time Use Research.
Giddens, A. (1998). *The third way: The renewal of social democracy*. Polity.
Gilbert, D. (2006). *Stumbling on happiness.* Knopf.
Green, F. (2004). Why has work effort become more intense? *Industrial Relations, 43*(4), 709–741.
Hall, E. T. (1983). *The dance of life: The other dimension of time*. Anchor Books.
Hamilton, W. D. (1964). The genetical evolution of social behaviour I & II. *Journal of Theoretical Biology, 7*(1), 1–52.
Hare, R. D. (2017). *Without conscience: The disturbing world of the psychopaths among us*. Guilford Press.
Harvey, D. (2005). *A brief history of neoliberalism.* Oxford University Press.
Hegel, G. W. F. (1977). *Phenomenology of spirit* (A. V. Miller, Trans.). Oxford University Press. (Original work published 1807).
Henrich, J. (2020). *The WEIRDest people in the world: How the West became psychologically peculiar and particularly prosperous.* Farrar.
Herskovits, M. J. (1937). *Life in a Haitian valley*. Knopf.
Heschel, A. J. (1951). *Man is not alone: A philosophy of religion.* Farrar, Straus and Giroux.
Ho, D. Y. F. (1994). Filial piety, authoritarian moralism, and cognitive conservatism in Chinese societies. *Genetic, Social, and General Psychology Monographs, 120*(3), 347–365.
Hochschild, A. R. (1989). *The second shift*. Viking.
Hultgård, A. (2008). *The Nordic gods and heroes.* Oxford University Press.
ILO. (2020). *World employment and social outlook.* International Labour Organization.
Inglehart, R. (1997). *Modernization and postmodernization.* Princeton University Press.
Kabat-Zinn, J. (1990). *Full catastrophe living: Using the wisdom of your body and mind to face stress, pain, and illness.* Delacorte.

Kahneman, D. (2011). *Thinking, fast and slow*. Farrar.
Kelly, K. (2024). *The Inevitable: Understanding the 12 technological forces that will shape our future*. Penguin.
Kim, E. M., & Vogel, E. F. (2011). *The Park Chung Hee era: The transformation of South Korea*. Harvard University Press.
Kindleberger, C. P., & Aliber, R. Z. (2011). *Manias, panics, and crashes* (6th ed.). Palgrave Macmillan.
Klotz, F. (2021). *Generational wealth and the fall of the rich: Why fortunes disappear in three generations*. Springer.
Kornai, J. (2006). The great transformation of Central Eastern Europe. *Economics of Transition, 14*(2), 207–244.
Lee, R. (1979). *The !Kung San: Men, women, and work in a foraging society*. Cambridge University Press.
Lee, R. D., & Daly, M. (1999). Population, health, and economic development. *Journal of Economic Perspectives, 13*(3), 145–168.
Levine, R. (1997). *A geography of time: The temporal misadventures of a social psychologist*. Basic Books.
Lin, L., & Milhaupt, C. J. (2013). We are the (national) champions. *Stanford Law Review, 65*, 697–759.
Lindahl, C., & Lindgren, M. (2020). Fika practices and the social construction of workplace culture. *Scandinavian Journal of Management, 36*(2), Article 101114.
Löfgren, O. (2008). Regionauts: The transformation of cross-border regions in Scandinavia. *European Urban and Regional Studies, 15*(3), 195–209.
Löfgren, O., & Ehn, B. (2010). *The secret world of doing nothing*. University of California Press.
Mahbubani, K. (2020). *Has China won?* PublicAffairs.
Mannheim, K. (1952). *Essays on the sociology of knowledge* (P. Kecskemeti, Ed. & Trans.). Routledge & Kegan Paul.
McAdams, D. P. (2001). The psychology of life stories. *Review of General Psychology, 5*(2), 100–122.
McEwen, B. S. (1998). Protective and damaging effects of stress mediators. *New England Journal of Medicine, 338*(3), 171–179.
Mokyr, J. (2016). *A culture of growth: The origins of the modern economy*. Princeton University Press.
Moschis, G. P. (2003). Consumer socialization. *Journal of Consumer Research, 29*(3), 425–439.
Mazoyer, M., & Roudart, L. (2006). *A history of world agriculture*. Monthly Review Press.
OECD. (2018). *Employment outlook*. OECD Publishing.
OECD. (2020). *OECD employment outlook*. OECD Publishing.
OECD. (2023). *OECD employment outlook*. OECD Publishing.
Pew Research Center. (2024). *Global attitudes survey*. Pew Research Center.
Piketty, T. (2014). *Capital in the twenty-first century* (A. Goldhammer, Trans.). Harvard University Press.

Piketty, T. (2020). *Capital and ideology*. Harvard University Press.
Pinker, S. (2011). *The better angels of our nature: Why violence has declined*. Viking.
Pinker, S. (2018). *Enlightenment now: The case for reason, science, humanism, and progress*. Viking.
Pomeranz, K. (2000). *The Great Divergence: China, Europe, and the making of the modern world economy*. Princeton University Press.
Putnam, R. D. (1993). *Making democracy work: Civic traditions in modern Italy*. Princeton University Press.
Rappaport, R. A. (1999). *Ritual and religion in the making of humanity*. Cambridge University Press.
Reinhart, C. M., & Rogoff, K. S. (2009). *This time is different*. Princeton University Press.
Riley, M. W., Johnson, M., & Foner, A. (1972). *Aging and society, Volume 3: A sociology of age stratification*. Russell Sage Foundation.
Rosa, H. (2013). *Social acceleration*. Columbia University Press.
Rosling, H., Rosling Rönnlund, A., & Rosling, O. (2018). *Factfulness: Ten reasons we're wrong about the world—And why things are better than you think*. Flatiron Books.
Rothstein, B. (1998). *Just institutions matter: The moral and political logic of the universal welfare state*. Cambridge University Press.
Rousseau, J.-J. (1762). *Emile, or On education*.
Sapolsky, R. M. (2004). *Why zebras don't get ulcers* (3rd ed.). Holt Paperbacks.
Schor, J. B. (1992). *The overworked American*. Basic Books.
Snyder, T. (2010). *Bloodlands: Europe between Hitler and Stalin*. Basic Books.
Söilen, K. S. (2020, December 16). The twilight of Pax Americana. *Geopolitical Monitor*. https://www.geopoliticalmonitor.com/the-twilight-of-pax-americana/
Solheim, J. (1995). *Household labor and gender roles*. Scandinavian University Press.
Sorokin, P. A. (1937). *Social and cultural dynamics: A study of change in major systems of art, truth, ethics, law, and social relationships*. American Book Company.
Standing, G. (2017). *Basic income: And how we can make it happen*. Penguin.
Steinberg, L. (2008). *Adolescence* (8th ed.). McGraw-Hill.
Steiner, A. Z., & Jukic, A. M. Z. (2016). Impact of female age and nulligravidity on fecundity in an older reproductive age cohort. *Fertility and Sterility, 105*(6), 1584–1590.
Sullivan, O., & Gershuny, J. (2004). Inconspicuous consumption. *Journal of Consumer Culture, 4*(1), 79–100.
Tainter, J. (1988). *The collapse of complex societies*. Cambridge University Press.
Thompson, E. P. (1967). Time, work-discipline, and industrial capitalism. *Past & Present, 38*, 56–97.
Toynbee, A. J. (1934). *A study of history* (Vol. 1). Oxford University Press.
Trivers, R. (1971). The evolution of reciprocal altruism. *Quarterly Review of Biology, 46*(1), 35–57.
Tu, W. (1996). *Confucian traditions in East Asian modernity: Moral education and economic culture in Japan and the four mini-dragons*. Harvard University Press.

UCLA Health. (2022). *Understanding pregnancy's biological clock.* https://www.uclahealth.org/news/article/understanding-pregnancys-biological-clock

van de Walle, N. (2001). *African economies and the politics of permanent crisis, 1979–1999.* Cambridge University Press.

van Gennep, A. (1960). *The rites of passage.* University of Chicago Press. (Original work published 1909).

Weber, M. (1905/2002). *The Protestant ethic and the "spirit" of capitalism* (P. Baehr & G. C. Wells, Trans.). Penguin.

Widerquist, K. (2018). *A critical analysis of basic income experiments for researchers, policymakers, and citizens.* Palgrave Macmillan.

Wikipedia. (2025). *Support ratio.* Retrieved May 2025, from https://en.wikipedia.org/wiki/Support_ratio

Williams, P., & Drolet, A. (2005). Age-related differences in responses to emotional advertisements. *Journal of Consumer Research, 32*(3), 343–354.

Wolff, R. D. (2017). *Capitalism's crisis deepens.* Haymarket Books.

World Bank. (2020). *Transitioning economies and public sector reform in Eastern Europe.* World Bank Policy Brief.

World Bank. (2021). *Public employment and compensation in global perspective.* https://openknowledge.worldbank.org/handle/10986/36815

Zahavi, A., & Zahavi, A. (1997). *The handicap principle: A missing piece of Darwin's puzzle.* Oxford University Press.

Further Readings

Ammianus Marcellinus. (2005). *The later Roman Empire (AD 354–378)* (W. Hamilton, Trans.). Penguin Classics. (Original work written ca. 390 CE).

Arendt, H. (2006). *Between past and future: Eight exercises in political thought.* Penguin Books. (Original work published 1954).

Arnett, J. J. (2000). Emerging adulthood: A theory of development from the late teens through the twenties. *American Psychologist, 55*(5), 469–480. https://doi.org/10.1037/0003-066X.55.5.469

Aurelius, M. (2002). *Meditations* (G. Hays, Trans.). Modern Library. (Original work written ca. 180 CE).

Australian Strategic Policy Institute. (2023). *Critical technology tracker: Global tech leaders by capability.* https://www.aspi.org.au/report/critical-technology-tracker

Bank of England. (2014). Money creation in the modern economy. *Quarterly Bulletin, 2014 Q1.* https://www.bankofengland.co.uk/quarterly-bulletin/2014/q1/money-creation-in-the-modern-economy

Barrett, L. (2017). *How emotions are made: The secret life of the brain.* Houghton Mifflin Harcourt.

Baumeister, R. F., & Tierney, J. (2011). *Willpower: Rediscovering the greatest human strength.* Penguin Press.

Beard, M., North, J., & Price, S. (1998). *Religions of Rome:* (Vol. 1). Cambridge University Press.

Bell, D. (1976). *The cultural contradictions of capitalism.* Basic Books.

Bloch, M. (1961). *Feudal society* (L. A. Manyon, Trans.). University of Chicago Press. (Original work published 1939).

Bourdieu, P. (1977). *Outline of a theory of practice* (R. Nice, Trans.). Cambridge University Press.

Brynjolfsson, E., & McAfee, A. (2014). *The second machine age: Work, progress, and prosperity in a time of brilliant technologies.* W. W. Norton & Company.

Burchell, B., Fagan, C., O'Brien, C., & Smith, M. (2007). *Working conditions in the European Union: The gender perspective.* European Foundation for the Improvement of Living and Working Conditions. https://www.eurofound.europa.eu/publications/report/2007/working-conditions/working-conditions-in-the-european-union-the-gender-perspective

Buss, D. M. (1989). Sex differences in human mate preferences: Evolutionary hypotheses tested in 37 cultures. *Behavioral and Brain Sciences, 12*(1), 1–49.

Case, A., & Deaton, A. (2020). *Deaths of despair and the future of capitalism.* Princeton University Press.

Cassius Dio. (1914). *Roman history* (E. Cary, Trans.). Loeb Classical Library. Harvard University Press. (Original work written ca. 230 CE).

Chapais, B. (2010). The deep social structure of humankind. *Science, 331*(6022), 1276–1277.

Childe, V. G. (1950). The urban revolution. *Town Planning Review, 21*(1), 3–17.

Chui, M., Manyika, J., & Miremadi, M. (2016). Where machines could replace humans—And where they can't (yet). *McKinsey Quarterly.* https://www.mckinsey.com/business-functions/mckinsey-digital/our-insights/where-machines-could-replace-humans-and-where-they-cant-yet

Confucius. (2003). *The analects* (D. C. Lau, Trans.). Penguin Classics. (Original work written ca. 500 BCE).

Core Econ. (2021). *The economy: Economics for a changing world* (2nd ed.). Oxford University Press.

Darwin, C. (1871). *The descent of man, and selection in relation to sex.* John Murray.

Diamond, J. (1997). *Guns, germs, and steel: The fates of human societies.* Norton.

DIW Berlin. (2020). *Income inequality and public sector employment in Germany.* German Institute for Economic Research.

Dunbar, R. I. M. (1996). *Grooming, gossip and the evolution of language.* Harvard University Press.

Dunbar, R. I. M., Gamble, C., & Gowlett, J. (Eds.). (2010). *Social brain, distributed mind.* Oxford University Press.

Easterlin, R. A. (1974). Does economic growth improve the human lot? Some empirical evidence. In P. A. David & M. W. Reder (Eds.), *Nations and households in economic growth* (pp. 89–125). Academic Press.

Eco, U. (1976). *A theory of semiotics.* Indiana University Press.

Eisenstadt, S. N. (1968). The Protestant ethic thesis in an analytical and comparative framework. In S. N. Eisenstadt (Ed.), *The Protestant ethic and modernization* (pp. 3–45). Basic Books.
Elias, N. (1994). *The civilizing process* (E. Jephcott, Trans.). Blackwell. (Original work published 1939).
Elster, J. (1998). *Deliberative democracy*. Cambridge University Press.
Erikson, E. H. (1950). *Childhood and society*. Norton.
Ferguson, N. (2011). *Civilization: The West and the rest*. Penguin Books.
Foucault, M. (1977). *Discipline and punish: The birth of the prison* (A. Sheridan, Trans.). Pantheon Books. (Original work published 1975).
Frank, R. H. (1985). *Choosing the right pond: Human behavior and the quest for status*. Oxford University Press.
Fukuyama, F. (1992). *The end of history and the last man*. Free Press.
Geertz, C. (1973). *The interpretation of cultures*. Basic Books.
Gintis, H., Bowles, S., Boyd, R., & Fehr, E., et al. (2005). Moral sentiments and material interests: Origins, evidence, and consequences. In H. Gintis (Ed.), *Moral sentiments and material interests* (pp. 3–39). MIT Press.
Gould, S. J. (2002). *The structure of evolutionary theory*. Harvard University Press.
Greenwood, B. (2014). The contribution of vaccination to global health: Past, present and future. *Philosophical Transactions of the Royal Society B: Biological Sciences, 369*(1645), 20130433. https://doi.org/10.1098/rstb.2013.0433
Habermas, J. (1984). *The theory of communicative action: Volume 1. Reason and the rationalization of society* (T. McCarthy, Trans.). Beacon Press.
Hauser, M. D. (2006). *Moral minds: How nature designed our universal sense of right and wrong*. Ecco/HarperCollins.
Hawking, S. (1988). *A brief history of time*. Bantam Books.
Hayek, F. A. (1944). *The road to serfdom*. University of Chicago Press.
Heath, J. (2014). *Morality, competition, and the firm: The market failures approach to business ethics*. Oxford University Press.
Heather, P. (2006). *The fall of the Roman Empire: A new history of Rome and the barbarians*. Oxford University Press.
Hobbes, T. (1996). *Leviathan* (R. Tuck, Ed.). Cambridge University Press. (Original work published 1651).
Hofstede, G. (2001). *Culture's consequences: Comparing values, behaviors, institutions and organizations across nations* (2nd ed.). Sage Publications.
Hofstadter, R. (1963). *Anti-intellectualism in American life*. Vintage Books.
Hofstadter, R. (1970). *The paranoid style in American politics and other essays*. Harvard University Press.
Lakoff, G., & Johnson, M. (1980). *Metaphors we live by*. University of Chicago Press.
Lorenz, K. (1966). *On aggression* (M. Latzke, Trans.). Harcourt, Brace & World.
McNeill, W. H. (1976). *Plagues and peoples*. Anchor Books.

Merton, R. K. (1942). The normative structure of science. In R. K. Merton (Eds.), (1973), *The sociology of science: Theoretical and empirical investigations* (pp. 267–278). University of Chicago Press.

Nietzsche, F. (1887/2006). *On the genealogy of morals* (K. Ansell-Pearson, Ed., & C. Diethe, Trans.). Cambridge University Press.

Nisbett, R. E. (2003). *The geography of thought: How Asians and Westerners think differently... and why*. Free Press.

Norenzayan, A. (2013). *Big gods: How religion transformed cooperation and conflict*. Princeton University Press.

Pariser, E. (2011). *The filter bubble*. Penguin.

Popper, K. (1959). *The logic of scientific discovery*. Hutchinson.

Putnam, R. D. (2020). *The upswing: How America came together a century ago and how we can do it again*. Simon & Schuster.

Roser, M., Ritchie, H., & Ortiz-Ospina, E. (2020). Economic growth. *Our World in Data*. https://ourworldindata.org/economic-growth

Rousseau, J.-J. ([1762] 2002). *The social contract* (G. D. H. Cole, Trans.). Dover Publications.

Schumpeter, J. A. (1942). *Capitalism, socialism and democracy*. Harper & Brothers.

Singh, D. (1993). Adaptive significance of female physical attractiveness: Role of waist-to-hip ratio. *Journal of Personality and Social Psychology, 65*(2), 293–307. https://doi.org/10.1037/0022-3514.65.2.293

Söilen, K. S. (2009). Lifestyle welfare: How the new class has transformed the Scandinavian welfare state. *Telos: Critical Theory of the Contemporary, (148)*, 73–97.

Thornhill, R., & Gangestad, S. W. (1999). The scent of symmetry: A human sex pheromone that signals fitness? *Evolution and Human Behavior, 20*(3), 175–201.

Toffler, A. (1970). *Future shock*. Random House.

Trivers, R. (1972). Parental investment and sexual selection. In B. Campbell (Ed.), *Sexual selection and the descent of man* (pp. 136–179). Aldine.

World Bank. (2018). *The changing nature of work. World Development Report 2019*. https://www.worldbank.org/en/publication/wdr2019

6

The Social Sciences Reconsidered

Abstract After examining how human life is lived in practice, this chapter turns the analytical lens on the social sciences themselves. What kinds of knowledge do these disciplines actually produce—and why do they so often struggle to explain, predict, or improve real-world outcomes in an age of complexity, acceleration, and AI? This chapter offers a critical but constructive reappraisal of the social sciences as human institutions shaped by cognitive limits, methodological habits, and ideological pressures. It challenges disciplinary silos, the myth of neutral observation, and the over-reliance on narrow methods, arguing instead for a biologically grounded, pan-scientific framework that integrates insights from across the sciences. By exposing how bias, prestige dynamics, and social design risks shape research itself, this chapter outlines a blueprint for renewal: a shift from defending disciplines to defending science, from advocacy to understanding, and from fragmented inquiry to integrated models of human behavior. The chapter makes the case that the future relevance of the social sciences depends on crossing boundaries—carefully, ethically, and with a clear-eyed view of human nature.

Chap. 5 examined how culture is lived—through daily practices, social roles, care, conflict, and generational time. It closed by showing that these lived realities cannot be understood in isolation, but ultimately bring us face to face with the role of the social sciences themselves. In this chapter, we therefore turn from the lived surface of human life to the institutional, methodological, and cognitive frameworks used to study it. What kind of knowledge do the social sciences produce? What assumptions guide our tools of inquiry? And

K. Solberg Söilen, *The Researcher's Journey in the Age of AI*,
https://doi.org/10.1007/978-3-032-23069-0_6

how must these disciplines evolve in an age of complexity, acceleration, and technological change?

This chapter offers a critical reappraisal of the social sciences—not as static fields of knowledge, but as evolving human projects shaped by ambition, institutional inertia, and ideological currents. The existing disciplinary model, with its silos and rivalries, has reached its limits. What is needed instead is a broader, biologically grounded, pan-scientific framework—one that restores relevance, rebuilds trust, and reconnects inquiry with the full scope of human nature. The chapter argues for a shift from loyalty to disciplines toward loyalty to science itself, where the purpose is not to defend turf but to understand and improve the human condition.

The argument unfolds in five sections:

1. What Are the Social Sciences? We begin by situating the social sciences historically and conceptually, showing how they emerged from Enlightenment ideals but quickly fragmented into separate disciplines. This fragmentation reflects deeper epistemic divisions—between explanation and understanding, prediction and meaning—which continue to shape the identity and limits of the field.
2. Cognitive Blindness: Limits of the Observer
   The second section examines how human perception, bias, and evolved cognition constrain the practice of science itself. Drawing from evolutionary psychology, behavioral economics, and neuroscience, we show that researchers are never neutral observers. Their limitations are not peripheral—they are central to how knowledge is produced, interpreted, and applied.
3. Methodological Pluralism and the Myth of Neutrality
   Here we trace the over-reliance on statistical methods, the crisis of replication, and the unspoken biases embedded in both qualitative and quantitative research. We argue for methodological pluralism—not as a relativist escape, but as a disciplined and self-aware approach to studying complex, adaptive systems.
4. Toward a Pan-Scientific Framework
   This section calls for a reframing of the social sciences as part of a broader scientific enterprise. Human beings are biological organisms shaped by evolutionary forces, cultural systems, and institutional environments. To study them adequately requires integrating insights from the natural sciences, rejecting anthropocentric exceptionalism, and adopting a multi-level approach that connects brain, behavior, and belief.

5. Risks of Social Design
   The final section warns against the instrumentalization of social science for ideological or political ends. When inquiry becomes advocacy, science loses its credibility and society loses a vital compass. We argue for renewed epistemic humility, ethical responsibility, and the defense of science as a truth-seeking endeavor—not a tool of social engineering.

Taken together, this chapter is not a rejection of the social sciences, but a blueprint for their renewal. We call for a return to fundamentals: the search for accurate models of human behavior, the embrace of interdisciplinary knowledge, and a commitment to serve society without being captured by it. The future of social science lies not in defending boundaries, but in crossing them—cautiously, ethically, and with eyes wide open.

6.1 Origins of Social Sciences

Unlike the natural sciences, which trace their origins to antiquity, the social sciences are recent. Astronomy, for instance, was already highly developed in ancient Babylon as early as the second millennium BCE. Babylonian astronomers recorded planetary movements, predicted eclipses, and maintained star catalogues with surprising accuracy (Rochberg, 2004; Steele, 2008). Similarly, early forms of mathematics emerged in Mesopotamia and Egypt over 4,000 years ago, with geometry and arithmetic applied to surveying, taxation, and architecture (Clagett, 1999). Biology, though more scattered, can be found in ancient Greek texts like those of Aristotle (fourth-century BCE), who catalogued hundreds of animal species and laid the groundwork for natural classification systems (Leroi, 2014). That work was later systematized and completed by a Swede, Carl von Linné (Linnaeus), as my dear reader will recall.

Even the humanities, often seen as more interpretive and culturally situated, have a much older lineage than the social sciences. History-writing can be traced back at least to Herodotus and Thucydides in classical Greece (fifth-century BCE),[1] and moral philosophy flourished in China under Confucius

[1] History-writing in the Western tradition traces its origins to Herodotus of Halicarnassus, whose *Historiōn Apodexis* (Ἱστορίων ἀπόδεξις), commonly known as *Histories*, was composed around 440 BCE. In this extensive work, Herodotus sought to record the causes and events of the Greco-Persian Wars, blending narrative with ethnographic detail and inquiry into customs, making him known as the "Father of History." His younger contemporary, Thucydides, offered a more analytical approach in his *Historia tou Peloponnēsiakou Polemou* (Ἱστορία τοῦ Πελοποννησιακοῦ Πολέμου), or *History of the Peloponnesian War*, written circa 400 BCE. Thucydides departed from myth and divine causality,

(ca. 500 BCE)[2] and in India through Vedic and later Buddhist traditions. Disciplines such as literature, ethics, and philology were taught in ancient universities centuries before sociology or political science came into being.

What, then, is distinctive about the social sciences? Their claim lies in bridging the gap between natural science and the humanities. They aspire to combine empirical observation with interpretive depth, to explain not only how humans behave but also how they organize, cooperate, and construct meaning. Disciplines like sociology, economics, anthropology, psychology, and political science seek to identify patterns of behavior, institutional dynamics, and collective beliefs through systematic observation, modeling, and critical theory.

Yet the true promise of the social sciences is not simply description, but the development of theory. It is in theory-building that their distinctiveness should lie: the ability to generate frameworks that not only explain the past but also anticipate future outcomes, connect disparate findings, and guide practical action. Here, however, the record has been uneven. Many of the so-called theories presented in the social sciences are in fact one-off empirical correlations, often based on single surveys, experiments, or case studies that are rarely replicated. Without systematic replication, such findings remain fragile; they risk becoming momentary observations rather than enduring insights. The replication crisis in psychology, for example, revealed that a large share of classic experiments on priming, willpower, and social conformity could not be reproduced (Open Science Collaboration, 2015). In economics, for example, predictive models of rational markets failed spectacularly during the 2008 financial crisis, exposing the limits of elegant but untested assumptions (Colander et al., 2009). Sociology and political science

---

instead emphasizing political realism, eyewitness testimony, and critical evaluation of sources—setting a standard for historical methodology in the centuries to follow. My favorite edition that brings these two together is a French *Pléiade* volume in which their busts are depicted standing back to back, each looking in a different direction—as if to symbolize their divergent approaches to writing history: one rooted in storytelling and cultural memory, the other in analytical rigor and proto-scientific inquiry.

[2] Moral philosophy in China, particularly within the Confucian tradition, began with *Kǒng Fūzǐ* (孔夫子), known in the West as Confucius (ca. 551–479 BCE). His teachings are compiled in the *Lúnyǔ* (論語), or *Analects*, a collection of dialogues and sayings recorded by his disciples. This foundational text emphasizes virtue (dé, 德), proper conduct (lǐ, 禮), and the importance of familial and societal harmony.

Following Confucius, key thinkers expanded and interpreted his philosophy. Mèngzǐ (孟子), or Mencius (ca. 372–289 BCE), authored the *Mèngzǐ* (孟子), arguing that human nature is inherently good and can be cultivated through righteous leadership and education. Xúnzǐ (荀子, ca. 310–235 BCE), by contrast, compiled in the work *Xúnzǐ* (荀子), took a more skeptical view, asserting that human nature is selfish and must be corrected through ritual and law. These texts—*Lúnyǔ*, *Mèngzǐ*, and *Xúnzǐ*—form the classical core of Confucian moral philosophy and were later canonized during the Han Dynasty. They continue to be central to East Asian education, ethics, and statecraft to this day.

have likewise produced "grand theories" that were influential in their time but proved unable to withstand shifts in data or historical context.

This is not to suggest that social scientists are unaware of the difference between correlation and causation—on the contrary, the distinction is well understood. The problem is that research designs often stop short of establishing causal mechanisms. Causation requires more than statistical association: it demands the elimination of alternative explanations, longitudinal testing, and integration into a broader explanatory framework. Because this is demanding, both methodologically and conceptually, it is frequently bypassed in favor of cleaner, more publishable results.

A second difficulty lies in the absence of unifying principles across the disciplines. Unlike the natural sciences, which trace results back to shared axioms and laws, the social sciences remain fragmented, with each field generating its own mid-level constructs but few cumulative foundations. This fragmentation weakens their collective authority.

And yet, a possible foundation is not lacking: evolutionary theory provides a common framework that could unify insights across sociology, economics, psychology, and anthropology. Resistance to it has been widespread, often grounded less in empirical objections than in cultural unease with biological explanations of human behavior. Such reluctance is understandable historically, but it also illustrates the growing pains of a still-maturing science—hesitant to adopt a unifying paradigm even when one is available.

In this sense, the social sciences remain at a crossroads. Their future credibility depends not on producing ever more fragmented correlations, but on moving toward cumulative, testable, and integrative theory—an intellectual scaffolding that can endure the test of time.

It is entirely possible that the humanities, combined with technical instruction, could suffice. Business education could become little more than applied accounting and management technique. Political science might merge into legal studies or administrative training. If the social sciences fail to produce distinct, actionable knowledge—if they merely echo what historians, lawyers, and philosophers already provide—then their relevance will wither. This is not just speculation. In several countries, the public legitimacy and funding of social science faculties are already being challenged by arguments about cost-effectiveness and academic utility (Fraser Institute, 2024; Ginsberg, 2011; OECD, 2023).

So, just as they were invented, they can also be *de-invented* or *re-invented*. That is, society could choose to dissolve the current disciplinary boundaries and instead organize knowledge in entirely new ways—perhaps around real-world problems, systems thinking, or evolutionary models. De-invention could even, over a longer period of time, mean their complete dissolution: if the value produced by these disciplines is perceived as too low relative to the cost of supporting tens or hundreds of thousands of researchers worldwide, governments or institutions may gradually defund or dismantle them. This is not merely speculative—public funding for certain humanities and social science departments has already declined in multiple countries (e.g., UK, Australia, and parts of the US), and debates about "return on investment" in academic research are intensifying (Fraser Institute, 2024; OECD, 2023; Ginsberg, 2011). The future of the social sciences, then, is not guaranteed. It depends on their capacity to adapt, to generate real insight, and to serve evolving societal needs.

Yet before we move into the historical origins of the social sciences, it is worth pausing to reflect on two growing challenges that threaten their credibility and long-term value today. The first is a gradual erosion of *academic rigor*. As student enrolment has expanded across the world—often driven by economic incentives and policies promoting universal higher education—the average level of training, especially in methodological competence, has arguably declined. Some scholars refer to this as *educational inflation*: degrees become more common, but their substantive value decreases (Collins, 1979; Dore, 1976; Trow, 2007). This is particularly evident in the diminished emphasis on scientific method, logic, and empirical discipline in many social science programs, where younger cohorts of PhD students often possess less methodological depth than earlier generations (Nosek et al., 2012; Open Science Collaboration, 2015).

The second challenge is the creeping politicization of research. Social science has always dealt with political topics, but in recent decades—especially since the early 2000s—scholars and institutions in some regions have become more openly entangled with ideological agendas again. This has happened in two directions. On the one hand, parts of academia have embraced advocacy over neutrality, with researchers acting more as political agents than as dispassionate investigators (Lukianoff & Haidt, 2018; Satel & Lilienfeld, 2013). On the other hand, political pressures from governments, funding bodies, or regulatory frameworks have in some cases guided research agendas in ways that subtly align with partisan or national objectives (Halffman & Radder, 2015; Sarewitz, 2016). Both trends risk undermining the independence, trust, and epistemic integrity that make social science valuable in the first place (Fig. 6.1).

Seen together, these pressures reveal how fragile the credibility of the social sciences has become when rigor declines and politics intrudes. Yet to understand how we reached this point—and how renewal is possible—we need to step back and examine the very origins of the disciplines.

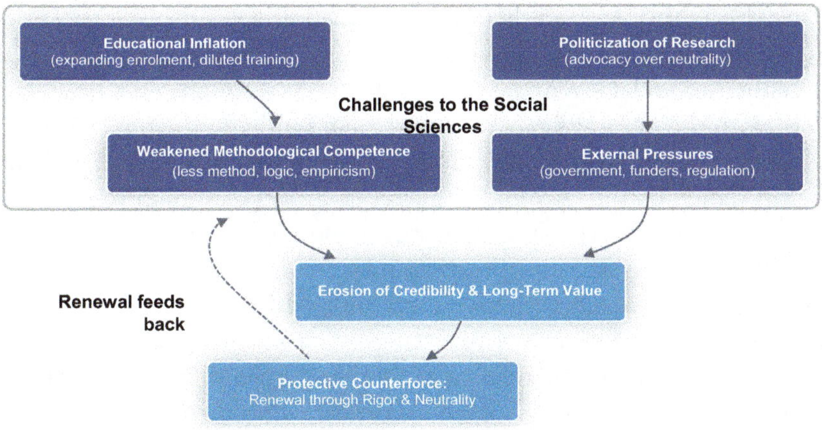

Fig. 6.1 Threats to credibility and renewal in the social sciences

The invention of the social sciences was both intellectual and institutional. In the nineteenth century, thinkers like Auguste Comte (who coined the term "*sociology*"), John Stuart Mill, and Karl Marx proposed systematic ways of studying society. Their ideas were not just descriptive but often prescriptive, rooted in the Enlightenment belief that human reason could be used to improve social conditions. This orientation set the stage for social science to be both analytical and reformist.

By the early twentieth century, universities began organizing faculties around distinct social science disciplines. This structuring was influenced by earlier Enlightenment traditions but also by German *Geisteswissenschaften*, which emphasized interpretive understanding (*Verstehen*) as developed by Wilhelm Dilthey[3] and later taken up by Max Weber.[4] While natural sciences

[3] Wilhelm Dilthey (1833–1911), a German philosopher and historian, is best known for articulating the distinction between the *Naturwissenschaften* (natural sciences) and the *Geisteswissenschaften* (human sciences or cultural sciences). He argued that while the natural sciences seek causal explanations (*Erklären*), the human sciences require interpretive understanding (*Verstehen*), because they deal with meaning, purpose, and subjective experience. His major works include *Einleitung in die Geisteswissenschaften* (Introduction to the Human Sciences, 1883), where he outlines a methodological foundation for the humanities and social sciences; *Das Erlebnis und die Dichtung* (Experience and Poetry, 1906), in which he analyzes the lived experience through literature; and the posthumously published *Der Aufbau der geschichtlichen Welt in den Geisteswissenschaften* (The Formation of the Historical World in the Human Sciences, 1910), where he deepens his critique of positivism and develops a hermeneutic approach to historical life.

Dilthey's work laid the groundwork for later interpretive traditions in sociology, psychology, and historiography, including the thought of Max Weber, Hans-Georg Gadamer, and Paul Ricoeur. His emphasis on the historicity of human consciousness and the need for contextual interpretation remains a cornerstone of the human sciences.

[4] Max Weber's major contributions to the social sciences include *Die protestantische Ethik und der „Geist " des Kapitalismus* (Tübingen: Verlag von Mohr, 1904–1905), which analyzed the cultural foundations of modern capitalism, and *Wirtschaft und Gesellschaft: Grundriss der verstehenden Soziologie*

prioritized causality and prediction, the social sciences increasingly wrestled with meaning, agency, and culture.

Notably, the social sciences sought legitimacy through both mimicry and contrast with the natural sciences. Figures like Émile Durkheim[5] insisted that social facts could be studied "as things," while others, like Georg Simmel[6] or Wilhelm Windelband,[7] stressed the irreducibility of human meaning. This tension between positivist and interpretive approaches remains central today.

The invention of statistics played a major role in the institutionalization of the social sciences. Quantitative tools allowed for the study of patterns in large populations, giving rise to demography, survey research, and econometrics. Simultaneously, qualitative methods developed through anthropology and ethnography emphasized depth, context, and the lived experience of individuals and communities.

What unites the social sciences is their dual focus: explaining patterns in human behavior and understanding their meaning within specific social, cultural, and historical contexts. This makes their findings always conditional, often contested, and yet indispensable. As Norbert Elias (1939/2000) pointed out, we are not outside observers; we are studying ourselves. This reflexivity, both a strength and a challenge, marks the social sciences as distinct from the rest of science.

Yet reflexivity is not a license for *methodological looseness*. To acknowledge that knowledge in the social sciences is situated and contested is not to imply that "anything goes." On the contrary, the very justification for keeping these disciplines within the university system lies in their capacity to meet the standards of scientific inquiry. Without clear methods, transparent procedures,

---

(Tübingen: J. C. B. Mohr [Paul Siebeck], posthumously published in 1922), where he developed his theory of social action, legitimacy, and authority types. These works positioned Weber as a central figure in both interpretive sociology and comparative historical analysis.

[5] Émile Durkheim, one of the key architects of modern sociology, published *De la division du travail social* in 1893 (Paris: Félix Alcan), in which he examined the social functions of labor specialization. This was followed by *Les Règles de la méthode sociologique* (Paris: Félix Alcan, 1895), a methodological treatise arguing that social facts should be treated as "things" in scientific inquiry. His most influential empirical work, *Le Suicide: Étude de sociologie* (Paris: Félix Alcan, 1897), used statistical methods to demonstrate how social integration affects individual behavior.

[6] Georg Simmel (1858–1918), a German sociologist and philosopher, is known for exploring the forms of social interaction and the dualities of modern life. His major works include *Über soziale Differenzierung* (1890), *Philosophie des Geldes* (1900), and *Soziologie* (1908). Simmel emphasized the fragmentary, dynamic nature of social life and helped establish sociology as a distinct interpretive discipline alongside philosophy and history.

[7] Wilhelm Windelband (1848–1915), a German philosopher, is best known for distinguishing between the *nomothetic* methods of the natural sciences (seeking general laws) and the *idiographic* methods of the humanities (focused on unique events). His key works include *Einleitung in die Philosophie* (1888) and *Geschichte der Philosophie* (1900), where he defends the philosophical autonomy of the cultural sciences and their role in understanding historical individuality.

and criteria for testing and falsification, the work of social scientists would risk blending indistinguishably with the contributions of journalists, essayists, or policy analysts. Those forms of knowledge are valuable in their own right, but they serve a different function.

The university is not simply a home for ideas, but a home for ideas that can demonstrate their credibility through method. For the social sciences, this means maintaining a delicate balance: honoring the interpretive dimensions of culture and meaning, while at the same time showing that their findings are not arbitrary but the product of systematic investigation. This insistence on method is not a constraint, but a *condition of legitimacy*. It is what allows the social sciences to remain inside the ivory tower, rather than drifting into the broader marketplace of *public opinion*.

Taken as a whole, the story of the social sciences is one of both ambition and fragility. Born in the nineteenth century out of Enlightenment optimism and institutional structuring, they have always been caught between two poles: the drive for scientific rigor and the need to capture human meaning. That dual mission gives them their strength, but it also exposes them to recurrent crises of legitimacy whenever rigor falters or politics overwhelms neutrality. Their future will therefore depend less on defending existing disciplinary boundaries than on rediscovering their core vocation: to produce knowledge that is at once empirically sound, interpretively rich, and socially relevant.

At the same time, it must be recognized that this ambition has only been partially fulfilled. Despite numerous valuable contributions within individual disciplines—or what might be called subsystems—the social sciences as a collective project have struggled to establish a durable foundation. The reasons are not mysterious. They lie above all in the practical constraints of research and the limitations of method.

6.2 Research Methods and Constraints

Social science cannot operate without methods, but methods are not neutral either. They shape what we can see, what we miss, and how we interpret the world. Unlike the natural sciences, where experiments often control variables in laboratory conditions, the social sciences must contend with a messier reality: people interpret questions, resist observation, and change behavior simply by being studied. As a result, *methodological pluralism* is not just a luxury—it is a necessity.

To help address these challenges, I wrote *The Researcher's Journey: A Guide to Methodology and Academia in Social Sciences* (Söilen, 2025). That book was conceived as a practical guide to scientific method, academic writing, and navigating the professional world of research. Yet behind it lay a deeper ambition—the seed of this volume, its natural continuation: to outline a methodological common ground, a least common denominator for the social sciences. The aim was to give social scientists, PhD students, and researchers a clearer sense of what we actually know about human beings today, so that whatever discipline they later pursue, their work would rest on a shared and reliable foundation.

Part of this effort involved giving Systems Theory another chance. Where earlier attempts at system-building often stalled due to complexity and lack of tools, I sensed that artificial intelligence could now help solve many of those limitations—integrating data, testing theories, and revealing connections across disciplines in ways that were previously impractical.

This leads to a crucial question: how, in practice, do social scientists actually study the human world? Although countless techniques exist, three broad methodological traditions dominate—surveys, ethnography, and modeling. Each comes with strengths and blind spots. More importantly, each is being reshaped by AI in different ways.

Surveys

Surveys are perhaps the most visible method, particularly in psychology, economics, political science, and sociology. They allow researchers to gather standardized information from large numbers of people, enabling statistical generalizations and trend analyses. Surveys have been foundational for measuring public opinion, mapping consumer behavior, and understanding social attitudes. Yet their reliability depends heavily on design. Poorly phrased questions, low response rates, and sampling bias can undermine validity. Moreover, as Pierre Bourdieu (1979) warned, surveys risk treating opinions as stable entities when in fact they may be fluid, context-dependent, or even manufactured by the act of questioning.

AI's role: *Large language models (LLMs)* can already design survey instruments, flag biased wording, and analyze free-text responses at scale, extracting themes beyond the numbers. Automated sentiment analysis extends the reach of surveys into unstructured data such as tweets or product reviews. Where humans once struggled with coding open answers, AI makes mixed-format surveys (scale + text) far more powerful. But the core limitation remains: surveys capture self-reporting, which AI cannot make more truthful—only more efficiently processed.

Ethnography

Ethnography immerses the researcher in the lives of participants. Originating in anthropology and qualitative sociology, it seeks deep understanding through observation, interviews, and participation (Hammersley & Atkinson, 2007; Emerson et al., 2011). Its strength lies in contextual richness—capturing meanings, rituals, contradictions, and social norms that surveys might miss entirely. Classic examples include Bronisław Malinowski's fieldwork in the Trobriand Islands (Malinowski, 1922) or Clifford Geertz's "*thick description" of Balinese cockfighting* (Geertz, 1973). However, ethnography is time-consuming, limited in scope, and often vulnerable to researcher bias. Reflexivity and transparency are essential, as is recognition that all observation is filtered through a subjective lens (Davies, 2008).

AI's role: Here, AI faces more limits. Machine vision and natural language processing can record and code behavior in unprecedented detail—analyzing facial expressions, gestures, or conversational patterns across hundreds of hours of footage. Yet interpretation remains stubbornly human, for now. AI can describe *what* is happening but not *why it matters* in a cultural frame. It can detect patterns, but only humans can anchor them in meaning. Thus, AI may augment ethnography by reducing transcription time, coding behavior, or comparing cases, but it cannot yet replace the interpretive leap at its core.

Modeling

Modeling takes a more abstract approach, prominent in economics, systems theory, and computational social science. Models—whether mathematical, agent-based, or network-based—allow researchers to simulate social processes, test theoretical assumptions, and explore emergent patterns (Epstein, 2006; Gilbert & Troitzsch, 2005). Thomas Schelling's segregation model showed how individual preferences could produce unintended large-scale inequalities (Schelling, 1971). However, models are simplifications. They rely on assumptions that may not hold in the real world. As the saying goes, "All models are wrong, but some are useful" (Box, 1979).

AI's role: Here AI is transformative. Machine learning and generative models allow simulations at a scale and complexity never before possible. Instead of manually coding a few dozen agents with fixed rules, AI can generate thousands of agents with adaptive behaviors, learning from real-world data streams in near real time. Pattern recognition algorithms can validate models against massive datasets, refining assumptions continuously. Yet this power also raises risks: opaque "black box" models may yield predictions without offering transparent explanations, creating new epistemic challenges.

Seen together, the three traditions show why methodological pluralism matters—and why AI will not replace them, at least not at this point, but rather transform their scope. Surveys gain depth through automated text analysis; ethnographies gain scale through automated coding; models gain realism through continuous data integration. Each approach becomes more powerful in partnership with AI, but also more dependent on *critical human oversight*.

Methods alone, however, do not make a science. They give us tools for observing, measuring, and modeling—but they do not tell us how the results fit together, or why certain findings matter more than others. To answer those questions, we need theory. A science without theory is like a map without a compass: it may show the terrain, but not the direction. This brings us to a central challenge that has existed for generations—and now, with AI, also an opportunity—for the social sciences: the creation of a unifying theoretical framework.

6.3 From Fragmented Traditions to a Unified Framework for the Social Sciences

As we move from methods to theory, another difficulty becomes clear. Most of the social sciences are not *unified theoretical frameworks* but what Thomas Kuhn (1962/2012) called "*disciplinary matrices*" or what Imre Lakatos (1970) described as "*research programs*"—bundles of assumptions, heuristics, and case-based studies that resemble each other but do not rest on a single set of foundational premises.

In fields such as evolutionary biology or physics, by contrast, there is a clear unifying framework—natural selection in the first case, Newtonian mechanics (later extended by relativity and quantum theory) in the second. These frameworks explain observed variation through a relatively small number of core principles. They provide a structure within which empirical discoveries accumulate, refine, and extend the reach of the theory itself. Most of the social sciences, however, tend to generate collections of correlations: quantitative studies that demonstrate statistically significant relationships between variables, but without embedding these findings into a single overarching explanatory framework.

For evolutionary biology, the principles can be summarized in three interlocking axioms:

1. *Variation*—Individuals within a population differ in traits (genetic or phenotypic).
2. *Inheritance*—Some of these differences are heritable, passed from parents to offspring.
3. *Differential survival and reproduction*—Traits that increase fitness become more common because their bearers survive and reproduce at higher rates.

In shorthand, the mechanism can be expressed as:

Equation 6.1: The Price Equation (simplified trait-frequency form)

$$\Delta p = \left(p \times \overline{w}_{trait} - p \times \overline{w}_{population}\right)$$

where Δp is the change in frequency of a trait, p its current frequency, and $\bar{w}$ its relative fitness compared to the population average (Price, 1970).

For Newtonian mechanics, the coherence rests on three laws that together describe the motion of bodies:

1. *Inertia*—An object remains at rest or moves uniformly unless acted upon by a force.
2. *Force and acceleration*—F = ma, force equals mass times acceleration.
3. *Action–reaction*—For every action, there is an equal and opposite reaction.

With the addition of the law of universal gravitation,

Equation 6.2: Law of universal gravitation

$$\left(\mathrm{F} = \frac{\mathrm{Gm}^1\mathrm{m}^2}{\mathrm{r}^2}\right)$$

This framework can, as we may remember from our high school courses, explain planetary orbits, tides, and terrestrial motion in one unified system. Later extensions—Einstein's relativity and quantum mechanics—did not discard these laws, but refined and contextualized them within broader explanatory principles.

Most of the social sciences, however, lack such fundamental axioms. Instead, they tend to generate collections of correlations: quantitative studies that demonstrate statistically significant relationships between variables, but without embedding these findings into a single overarching explanatory framework.

Take economics as an example. Much of what we call economic "theory" is grounded in separate schools of thought—classical, neoclassical, Keynesian, Marxian, behavioral, institutional, Austrian, and more. Each emphasizes different assumptions about human motivation, rationality, and institutions (Colander et al., 2004). What unifies these schools is not a fundamental theory of human nature, but rather a shared set of methods (mathematical modeling, econometrics) and topics (markets, production, distribution). As Philip Mirowski (1989) has argued, economics often borrows metaphors and formalisms from physics and engineering rather than developing an internally consistent biological or psychological basis. This helps explain why economists can produce elegant models of equilibrium or growth but often struggle to account for the messy, adaptive realities of human economic behavior.

Evolutionary theory is not only conceptually compatible with economics but also practically applicable. In my book *Applied Evolutionary Economics: Insights from Biology for Real-World Management* (2025), I show how evolutionary principles can be translated into tools for decision-making, management, and institutional design, demonstrating their concrete relevance for practice.[8]

Sociology faces a similar issue. It has produced an extraordinary number of middle-range theories—on stratification, identity, networks, institutions, or culture—but these rarely coalesce into a meta-theoretical system. Instead, the field functions more like an archipelago of paradigms, each producing valuable insights, yet with limited integration (Abbott, 2001). Political science too often revolves around empirical studies of elections, institutions, and policies, with theory serving more as a pragmatic toolkit than a unifying framework (Goodin & Klingemann, 1996). The result, across disciplines, is fragmentation. Correlations abound, but there is no compass that ties them together into a coherent science of human beings in society.

What many of these disciplines call "theory" is often little more than a label attached to a correlation of some strength. A further complication is that there is no real agreement on how strong or consistent a correlation must be for it to rise to the level of a "theory" in the social sciences (Turner, 2007). In some cases, even weak associations are elevated to theoretical status if they resonate with prevailing paradigms or ideological preferences (Stinchcombe, 1987). This looseness contrasts sharply with the natural sciences,

[8] Deliberate attention has not been given here to Nicholas Georgescu-Roegen, since the other book (*Applied Evolutionary Economics: Insights from Biology for Real-World Management*, 2025) is dedicated to his work. He stands out as perhaps the single scholar who contributed most to making economics a genuine part of evolutionary theory.

where theories are expected to integrate findings across multiple domains and withstand rigorous, repeated testing (Meehl, 1990). The consequence is that what counts as a "theory" in sociology, economics, or political science often varies not only by subfield, but by fashion or intellectual climate. As critics have long observed, the result is an inflation of the term "theory," which risks obscuring rather than clarifying the foundations of social scientific knowledge (Swedberg, 2012).

Evolutionary theory offers a striking contrast. While it certainly has internal debates and competing schools, the field rests on a small number of axioms—variation, inheritance, and differential reproduction—that give coherence to the entire enterprise. Findings from population genetics, animal behavior, neuroscience, or paleoanthropology can be connected because they all derive from this common framework. This is why evolutionary biology has been able to accumulate knowledge cumulatively, moving from Darwin's original insights to the modern synthesis and, more recently, to gene–culture coevolution (Boyd & Richerson, 1985; Laland et al., 2010).

Our critique, then, is justified: much of social science is best described as a patchwork of empirical studies and local correlations, sometimes clustered into paradigmatic "schools," but rarely achieving the deep unification that characterizes the natural sciences. This does not make them useless—far from it. They produce valuable data, insights, and models. But it does limit their explanatory power, their ability to cumulate knowledge across contexts, and their resilience against ideological shifts (Fourcade et al., 2015). So it may be said:

> Without a grounding in human biology and evolution, social science risks floating free of the very species it seeks to describe.

Authors such as Joseph Henrich (2015) and David Sloan Wilson (2019) have argued that evolutionary theory offers precisely the kind of unifying framework the social sciences have lacked. By embedding correlations (say, about inequality, voting behavior, or organizational trust) into an evolutionary understanding of human cognition, cooperation, and conflict, we can move from scattered findings to a more coherent science of society. Evolutionary theory does not erase the diversity of sociological or economic schools, but it provides a meta-level architecture into which their findings can be fitted, compared, and evaluated.

We can think of the social sciences as resting on two conceptual layers, called here *The Evolutionary Scaffold Model*. The first, foundational layer is evolutionary theory. Whether recognized or not, every explanation of human behavior and society ultimately rests on variation, inheritance, and adaptation. This layer is coherent, cumulative, and shared across the life sciences.

Above it sits a second layer: the disciplinary knowledge of economics, sociology, political science, psychology, and anthropology. Here we find the empirical studies, theoretical schools, and policy debates that constitute the everyday practice of the social sciences. Some of these findings are clearly linked to the evolutionary foundation—explicitly drawing on biology or psychology—while others appear disconnected. Yet even when unacknowledged, they remain implicitly shaped by the principles of change and adaptation that govern human life (Fig. 6.2).

This illustration highlights why the social sciences are still in an early stage of development as sciences. They have contributed much by addressing real-world problems and generating valuable insights, but too often they lack a firm anchoring in a unifying theoretical foundation. Without engaging with Layer 1—evolutionary theory—social scientists may describe what people report or what correlations appear in data, but they cannot fully explain why these behaviors occur. Relying heavily on self-reports and surveys is especially problematic, since what people say about their motivations is often unreliable (Nisbett & Wilson, 1977).

The problem is not that many of the underlying mechanisms do not exist, or that they have not been identified; rather, the issue is that social scientists often remain unaware of them because they belong to other disciplines such as biology or psychology, or else they have not been trained to apply them. As a result, these insights are neither incorporated into research nor passed on to students, who in turn remain confined within an ever-narrower silo of

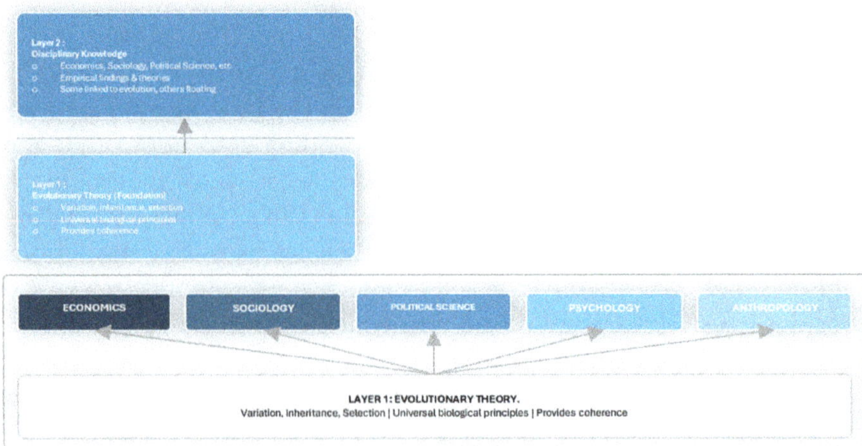

Fig. 6.2 The evolutionary scaffold model of the social sciences

disciplinary science. This disciplinary insularity reinforces the impression of progress while leaving much of the explanatory ground untouched.

Another disadvantage is the difficulty of recognizing deeper patterns of behavior when working with isolated data points. Without a proven base of biological and evolutionary knowledge for comparison, findings risk remaining fragmentary. This is unfortunate, not least because the relevant foundations are accessible: a social scientist can acquire enough understanding of evolutionary theory within a year to see its connections to their own field and to integrate it into their research.

One further advantage of grounding work in Layer 1 is that it provides a benchmark for distinguishing between findings that are genuinely scientific and those that are accidental or premature. If a proposed explanation cannot be traced back—or at least tested against—what we know about human evolution and social organization, then it remains suspect. Even the exercise of checking whether a given finding aligns with evolutionary theory is valuable, since it disciplines inquiry and reduces the risk of mistaking coincidence for causation.

These comparisons also help flag when social science projects derail—for example, when they cross into activism or are captured by ideological agendas. Layer 1 acts as a stabilizer: it disciplines speculation by tying it back to what we know about humans as evolved organisms embedded in cultural contexts. This is not an argument against moral concern or political engagement, but rather a reminder that science loses credibility when it abandons explanatory discipline.

Toward a Full *Social Systems Theory*

The Evolutionary Scaffold Model shows how the social sciences rest on two conceptual layers: evolutionary theory as the foundation, and the various disciplines as applications. But scaffolds are, by design, temporary structures—useful for construction, yet incomplete without the finished edifice. What is still missing is a way to connect these disciplines and their evolutionary grounding to the larger systemic reality of human life.

This is where *Social Systems Theory* enters the picture. As we saw earlier in the discussion of system theorists, societies can be understood as interdependent, evolving wholes. In this perspective, each discipline—economics, sociology, political science, psychology, anthropology—can be seen as a subsystem within a larger cultural and biological system. The absurdity of their current fragmentation lies in the fact that they often function as if they were independent systems, protecting their boundaries much like ecological niches. While this makes sense from the standpoint of institutional survival, it undermines the broader scientific task: to explain humanity as an integrated whole.

To resolve this, we can link the scaffold model with the *Vitruvian Framework for Human Understanding* introduced in the first chapter. Recall that the Vitruvian Framework highlights five dimensions of human life:

1. Symbolic thought and shared intentionality
2. Gene–culture coevolution
3. Ecological and biospheric embeddedness
4. Moral and political development
5. Technological and AI transformation

Together with the two scaffold layers, these dimensions add a third axis of depth. What emerges is a three-dimensional model—a cube—that integrates evolutionary foundations, disciplinary applications, and systemic human dimensions.

I call this synthesis the *Evolutionary Social Science Model*. It represents the most complete form of the paradigm proposed in this book: a framework that grounds all social sciences in evolutionary theory, connects them across disciplinary boundaries, and situates them within the broader systems that define human existence (Fig. 6.3).

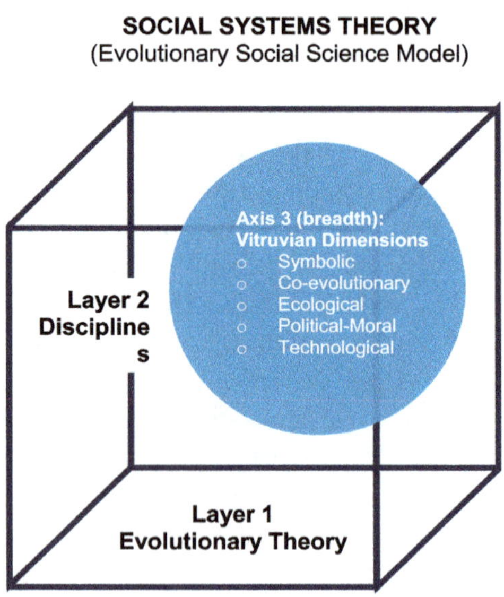

Fig. 6.3 The evolutionary social science model—Linking foundations, disciplines, and human

This model is not meant as a rigid blueprint but as a conceptual architecture. Each component plays a distinct role, and together they form a three-dimensional structure rather than a flat scaffold. The base, **Layer 1 (Evolutionary Foundations)**, provides depth: it ensures coherence by rooting inquiry in the axioms of variation, inheritance, and selection. Rising from this base, **Layer 2 (Disciplinary Applications)** adds height: the applied work of sociology, economics, psychology, political science, and anthropology, where concrete problems are studied and solutions are tested. Cutting across both is **Axis 3 (Vitruvian Dimensions)**, which adds width: the systemic breadth of symbolic culture, coevolution, ecology, morality, and technology that must be considered for any explanation of humanity to be complete.

In this way, the Evolutionary Social Science Model can be visualized as a cube of knowledge. One axis anchors inquiry in evolutionary depth, another organizes it into disciplinary applications that reach upward toward practice, and the third ensures breadth by connecting these efforts to the systemic conditions of human life. Taken together, the model offers not just a scaffold for temporary construction, but a robust architecture for integrating the sciences of humanity.

Let's see how it can be used:

Case in a Box: Professor Jan-Willem van Klompenburg and the Cube in Practice

Meet Professor Jan-Willem van Klompenburg, a sociologist from the small Dutch town of Groenekloosterveen, where he works at the "Institute for Serious Studies." His research a very real problem: why commuter bicycle traffic in Dutch cities produces both unusually high cooperation (polite lane-sharing) and occasional bursts of explosive conflict (the infamous "handlebar duels" of Amsterdam).

Step 1: Identifying the problem

Van Klompenburg begins with a practical and socially relevant question: how do people manage cooperation and conflict in dense, everyday traffic systems? This is not only of academic interest, but also of importance for urban planning and public safety.

Step 2: Methods

Using the *Researcher's Journey* methodology as a guide, he applies a multiple-method approach. He collects survey data from cyclists, conducts ethnographic observations at busy intersections, and analyzes sensor data from bike lanes. At this stage, he is working within Layer 2 (disciplinary practice), using established social science tools.

Step 3: Theory

When it comes to interpretation, he resists the temptation to float in discipline-specific explanations. Instead, he returns to the shared foundations introduced in earlier chapters. He asks: how would evolutionary theory account for these behaviors? Drawing on the three axioms—variation, inheritance, and differential survival—he interprets observed differences in cycling behavior as adaptive strategies: variation in signaling (bell-ringing, gestures), inherited norms of politeness in Dutch culture, and selective retention of behaviors that minimize injury (yielding, risk avoidance).

Step 4: Vitruvian grounding

In the discussion, he widens the frame by integrating all five dimensions of the Vitruvian model. He considers:

- Symbolic culture: How shared signals (bells, lights, gestures) form a symbolic system of traffic communication.
- Gene–culture coevolution: How long-standing cycling traditions in the Netherlands have shaped norms and expectations.
- Ecology: How the dense, flat Dutch environment and city design make cycling not only possible but dominant.
- Politics and morality: How public policy (bike lanes, fines, campaigns for safety) shapes cooperative norms.
- Technology: How e-bikes and navigation apps disrupt or accelerate traditional patterns of coordination.

By moving back and forth between evolutionary theory and systemic dimensions, van Klompenburg ensures that his work is not only empirically rich but also theoretically grounded.

Step 5: Conclusion

At the end, he concludes whether his study has solved the problem or at least clarified it. His findings may suggest that commuter cycling is a microcosm of social life: cooperation dominates when symbolic signals are clear, but conflict spikes when ecological and technological pressures overwhelm inherited norms. Importantly, his contribution adds to a unified, biologically grounded social science—linking his observations of humans to insights from other animals. For instance, research on flocking starlings (Cavagna et al., 2010) shows similar adaptive trade-offs between cohesion and collision, suggesting that our cycling "flocks" are not as unique as they seem.

In this way, van Klompenburg's project not only addresses a real-world social issue, but also strengthens the theoretical scaffolding that unites the social sciences with biology.

To his surprise, Professor van Klompenburg is not only invited by the municipality to present his findings—helping city planners design safer intersections and campaigns for cycling etiquette—but also by organizers of international biology conferences. There, his work is discussed alongside studies of ant trail coordination, flocking starlings, and the collective navigation of fish schools. He finds this amazing: for once, his research pulls him out of what had often felt like a too-small group of fellow sociologists into a broader community of scientists. Sitting in the same session as behavioral ecologists and computer modelers, he begins to see his cycling data as part of a much larger puzzle: how living beings, human or otherwise, coordinate movement, avoid collisions, and manage conflict in crowded environments.

Questions for Discussion

1. How does Professor van Klompenburg's project illustrate the usefulness of moving between empirical methods and evolutionary theory?
2. What risks arise if researchers stay only within disciplinary frameworks without connecting to share biological foundations?
3. How do the five Vitruvian dimensions help prevent partial or biased interpretations of his findings?
4. Can studying non-human species (e.g., starlings or primates) genuinely illuminate human social behavior, or are the analogies too limited?
5. If AI tools were applied to his dataset, how might they strengthen—or possibly distort—the insights he derived?

This little exercise with Professor van Klompenburg may be partly fictional, but it illustrates how the cube can guide research in practice: starting with a concrete problem, grounding it in evolutionary principles, and widening it through the Vitruvian dimensions until it speaks to both theory and society. In doing so, it shows that the model is not an abstract diagram but a working tool—one that links the daily messiness of human life to broader scientific conversations, even across species. To make its logic clearer, the Table 6.1 summarizes the specific purpose of each dimension of the cube:

Taken together, the model points toward a paradigm of *Evolutionary Social Science* that is both cumulative and integrative. What makes such an approach especially timely is that, for the first time, it may be feasible to apply it in practice. Earlier proposals for unified social systems faltered not because the vision was wrong, but because the human mind could only manage fragments—individual disciplines, partial theories, and limited datasets. The task of integration was simply too overwhelming. With the emergence of AI, however, this barrier may no longer be insurmountable. Machines offer the capacity to handle the scale and complexity that have long eluded us, making

Table 6.1 The three axes of the evolutionary social science model

Axis	What it represents	Why it matters/What problem it solves
Layer 1: Evolutionary Foundations (depth)	The basic axioms of variation, inheritance, and selection, shared across the life sciences	Provides a coherent theoretical anchor; prevents social science from floating free of biology; disciplines inquiry against coincidence or ideology
Layer 2: Disciplinary Applications (height)	Economics, sociology, psychology, political science, anthropology	Where actual problems are studied and solutions tested; allows specialization while still resting on a common foundation
Axis 3: Vitruvian Dimensions (breadth)	Symbolic culture, gene–culture coevolution, ecology, morality, technology	Ensures systemic completeness; keeps inquiry connected to the full range of human existence; provides breadth by integrating dimensions often studied in isolation

it possible to take seriously what has until now remained mostly aspirational: a coherent science of humanity.

It is worth recalling that after the Second World War, American scholars tried to solve a similar problem of fragmentation by importing mathematics into the social sciences. Mathematics, it was believed, would impose rigor and unity where prose seemed too ambiguous (Porter, 1995). The result was mixed. Elegant equations sometimes obscured rather than clarified the messy realities of human life (Mirowski, 1989). Economics offers the clearest case: decades of mathematically sophisticated models have yielded only modest gains in predictive accuracy (Blaug, 1992). Narrative thinkers such as Keynes or Ricardo, by contrast, achieved lasting influence with comparatively simple tools, precisely because their theories remained tied to real social dynamics (Backhouse, 2002; Skidelsky, 1992).

> The lesson is not that mathematics has no place, but that formalism by itself cannot substitute for explanatory power.

Order without connection to reality produces sterile models. What the social sciences need is not just more technique, but a common foundation.

Evolutionary theory offers such a foundation, anchoring inquiry in shared axioms of variation, inheritance, and adaptation. Artificial intelligence may strengthen this process by allowing us to test, connect, and integrate findings at a scale that was previously impossible—but it is the evolutionary compass that ensures coherence.

6.3.1 Toward a Common Language for the Social Sciences

The purpose of reviewing human behavior, interaction, and perception in such detail has been to establish a foundation, not to indulge in anthropology for its own sake. These are the building blocks from which all social sciences must begin if they are to be cumulative. Yet most disciplines rarely engage them systematically. Economists often abstract away from individual variation through "*ceteris paribus*" assumptions. Political scientists reduce complexity to rules or voter preferences. Sociologists emphasize structures while neglecting biology. Each discipline develops in relative isolation, and so the foundations of human behavior become fragmented.

From a systems perspective, this fragmentation is not surprising: each field has evolved into a kind of protective niche, guarding its methods and boundaries. But what makes sense biologically—defending one's territory—becomes counterproductive scientifically. Without a unifying framework, insights remain siloed, and opportunities for integration are lost.

The task, then, is not to erase disciplinary knowledge, but to scaffold it. Evolutionary theory provides the grounding, artificial intelligence supplies the capacity for synthesis, and systems thinking shows us how the pieces connect. Taken together, these tools open the possibility of a common language for the social sciences—one that links detail to theory, parts to wholes, and specialized findings to the shared project of understanding humanity.

What is needed is a shared language—an integrative foundation that treats human beings as whole organisms, with evolutionary, psychological, cultural, and social dimensions. Only from such a common ground can the social sciences hope to deliver explanations and reforms that are both realistic and impactful. A unified starting point not only helps us grasp the richness and complexity of human life; it also allows us to see more clearly where technology, and now especially artificial intelligence, can assist us.

Case in a Box: A Foundational Course for the Social Sciences

Imagine that every future social scientist—economist, sociologist, political scientist, or anthropologist—began their studies with a common half-year course on the foundations of human behavior and society. The model here could be the University of Oslo's long-standing *Examen philosophicum*, which for generations has introduced all students to philosophy, history of knowledge, and logic. But instead of philosophy alone, this course would anchor the social sciences in an evolutionary and biological perspective, ensuring that everyone shares the same starting point before they specialize.

The content of such a course could follow the broad structure of this book, or similar. Students would first be introduced to the shifting scientific landscape and the challenges AI poses to human understanding (Chap. 1). They would then turn to the evolutionary and biological roots of social life, from aggression and power dynamics to identity, longevity, and cultural variation (Chap. 2). Building on this, they would explore cognition, emotion, and sociality, examining trust, cooperation, morality, bias, empathy, and the limits of reasoning (Chap. 3).

From there, the course would move to culture and society (Chap. 4), highlighting language, belief systems, institutions, and daily practices as emergent features of shared meaning. Students would also reflect on time, work, love, and aging as the rhythms of human life across contexts (Chap. 5). At this stage, they would be ready to critically revisit the social sciences themselves (This chapter), understanding their historical origins, methodological blind spots, and the promise AI holds for integration.

The course would also include hands-on engagement with AI and scholarship (Chap. 7), where students learn to use AI tools for writing, analysis, and simulation, while also confronting the risks of bias and epistemic dependency. Ethical dilemmas of AI (Chap. 8) and the problem of outsourced cognition (Chap. 9) would form the capstone, equipping students with a forward-looking awareness of both the opportunities and dangers of technological change.

What this course may not do—at least at the foundational level—is settle on a definitive label for the next stage. The conclusions we draw about where the social sciences stand today, and where they may be heading, follow logically from the premises laid out. But how this will unfold, and what we eventually choose to call that phase—wisdom, humanism, *Homo cura*, or something else—is another matter, and in a sense less important. I am old enough to know that we cannot predict such things, only wish for them. The real task is to recognize the trajectory and its immediate implications, rather than become preoccupied with terminology. And perhaps we should also resist speculating too far ahead—at least if we wish to remain firmly within the boundaries of social science.

Such a course could, in any case, give future social scientists a common language, finally allowing economists, sociologists, and political scientists to speak to one another without needing translators. Grounded in evolutionary theory and enriched by evidence from multiple disciplines, it would reduce the fragmentation that has long made the social sciences look like a family gathering where no one agrees on the same story.

What we have today is like returning from a long walk in the woods together, only to find that each of us remembers an entirely different journey. The shared journey is there, but the lack of a common frame makes it seem as though each discipline has wandered off in a different direction. An evolutionary foundation—using the two-layer system presented earlier—offers the possibility of stitching these divergent accounts back together, providing not just scattered anecdotes but a coherent map of where we have been and where we are going. Such a framework would also make it easier for disciplines to relate to one another. And once they begin to relate, they are also more likely to take an interest in each other's work, strengthening dialogue and fostering genuine intellectual exchange.

Questions for Discussion

1. What advantages would such a foundational course bring to the social sciences, and what risks might it carry?
2. How might a common grounding in evolutionary theory challenge the assumptions of your own discipline?
3. Should AI literacy be treated as a core competency in social science education? Why or why not?
4. In what ways could this model help bridge the divide between social sciences and the natural sciences?
5. Why is it so difficult to achieve such a shared foundation, despite repeated calls for interdisciplinarity?
6. How might different worldviews—such as humanism, pragmatism, or systems theory—interact with a shared evolutionary foundation?

Perhaps the simplest way to achieve this integration, however, is not to redesign the curriculum from scratch but to enlist AI itself. In fact, AI may be the first tool capable of addressing the very fragmentation that has long plagued the social sciences. Where traditional disciplinary boundaries divide and constrain inquiry, AI offers precisely the kinds of integrative methods that can draw connections across fields. Imagine, for example, a dedicated "Social Sciences AI"—a system programmed from the outset to treat humans as evolutionary beings. By recognizing only theories consistent with this foundational perspective, such a machine would automatically start from the correct beginning, bypassing much of the confusion that arises when disciplines pull in different directions. From there, machine learning could uncover hidden correlations in massive datasets, bridging insights from psychology, economics, and sociology. Natural language processing could compare vast corpora of texts, revealing patterns in political discourse, cultural narratives, or economic reporting (Bail, 2021). Simulation and agent-based modeling could help us test how institutions and individuals coevolve, providing a more realistic alternative to the static assumptions of mainstream economics (Epstein, 2006). And generative AI systems could synthesize and critically compare insights across fields—making knowledge not only more searchable but also more coherent (Söilen, 2025).

The point is not that AI replaces judgment, but that it equips scholars with a meta-perspective that was previously out of reach. With AI, the social sciences have an opportunity to move toward a genuinely interdisciplinary science of humanity, where empirical facts about behavior, cognition, and society are no longer scattered but integrated.

Without such a synthesis, the risk is that each discipline continues to speak its own language—partial, isolated, and limited in impact. The result is a body of work riddled with biases and constrained by such strong limitations that many contributions read less like cumulative science and more like personal reflections. To put it bluntly: from *that* perspective, one might be better off reading a novel—at least then there is the benefit of narrative, imagination, and emotional truth. Too much of today's social science writing carries the dry tone of science without the genuine generalizability that gives scientific work its lasting value.

With such integration, however, the possibility emerges for a truly evolutionary social science—one that is not only better equipped to describe the human condition but also to design institutions, policies, and practices that improve it.

In the next section, we turn to another long-standing problem in the social sciences—one that AI may also help address.

6.4 Seeing and Not Seeing: The Uneven Terrain of Behavioral Research

From a social science perspective, all aspects of human life are of interest. Yet not all behaviors are equally accessible for study (visibility). Some are hidden due to personal or cultural sensitivities; others are open and even promoted. At the same time, some behaviors are inherently difficult to measure truthfully, while others are easily observed or self-reported with accuracy (Response Bias).

Table 6.2 Matrix of social science study accessibility

	Response Bias			
		Easy to get the truth	Neutral/ Moderate	Difficult to get the truth
Visibility	Openly Displayed	–Work behavior (e.g., teamwork, leadership)	–Parenting styles	–Performative activism
		–Social media use (curated but visible)	–Leisure preferences	–Self-image in interviews
	Neutral to Displaying	–Eating habits	–Online browsing behavior	–Actual voting behavior
		–Daily commuting patterns	–Personal routines	–Private health practices
	Hidden/ Concealed	–Infrequent taboos (e.g., addiction confessions)	–Religious doubt	–Sexual behavior
		–Mental health disclosure in therapy	–Marital dissatisfaction	–Income reporting
				–Prejudice or bias expression

The Table 6.2 maps this complexity on a 3× 3 matrix that may help clarify the methodological terrain of studying human behavior:

The matrix illustrates why some domains, like sexuality or income, remain elusive for social scientists, while others, like work performance or sports, are more readily explored. Importantly, the difficulty of studying a behavior does not always stem from unwillingness—some cases are simply hard to observe or reconstruct. Recognizing these dimensions helps refine our research strategies and interpret the reliability of social data.

Each aspect of human life in this matrix can vary dramatically between individuals, and few domains illustrate this better than *sexual behaviour*. Some couples engage in brief, routine intercourse perhaps once per week or less, while others explore more unconventional or adventurous practices—activities that reach beyond the ordinary bedroom script and sometimes into domains not typically raised in polite dinner conversation. From a social science standpoint, sexuality is among the most concealed areas of life, shaped by both personal discretion and cultural sensitivities.

From an evolutionary perspective, secrecy around sex makes adaptive sense. Human reproductive strategies have historically involved significant competition, paternity uncertainty, and high parental investment—especially for females—leading to selective pressures favoring discretion, mate guarding, and concealed ovulation (Buss, 1989; Symons, 1979; Thornhill & Gangestad, 2008). Concealing sexual behavior may reduce risks of social sanction, partner retaliation, or reputational damage, particularly in environments where social status and kin alliances are vital. At the same time, variation in sexual behavior reflects diverse evolved strategies: some individuals pursue pair-bonding for long-term security, while others follow short-term mating strategies that maximize genetic dispersal or immediate pleasure (Gangestad & Simpson, 2000). Such variation is not deviance but part of the broad behavioral spectrum shaped by ecological conditions, personal psychology, and cultural norms.

Yet in practice, what researchers often miss is not very exotic. Students and even seasoned scholars will carefully formulate sensitive survey items or interview protocols without ever asking the most basic question: *"Why would someone answer this honestly?"* or *"What are the chances of getting a truthful response here?"* When I raise this in class, the most common reaction is a surprised, *"Oh, I hadn't thought of that."* The oversight is easy to understand: in our abstract, idealized minds we tend to assume that respondents will answer as transparently as we ask. But in reality, people routinely shade, hide, or reshape their answers, especially around sensitive topics such as sexuality, income, prejudice, or family conflict.

The asymmetry in accessibility and disclosure leads to a clear imbalance in the body of social science research: we witness a disproportionate number of studies focusing on behaviors that are openly displayed and relatively easy to observe or verify. Domains such as workplace performance, social media use, educational attainment, and consumer behavior lend themselves to quantification and analysis precisely because they occur in the open and leave observable traces—digital footprints, institutional records, or self-reports that are socially acceptable. These topics align neatly with existing methodological tools, especially surveys, experiments, and administrative data analysis.

By contrast, behaviors that are concealed—especially those that are both private and difficult to verify—remain vastly understudied. This includes not only sexual practices, but also income misreporting, substance abuse, compulsive behaviors, covert aggression, corruption, and various forms of manipulation and deception. These areas are more sensitive, ethically fraught, and methodologically elusive. When they are studied, researchers often rely on proxy indicators, indirect questioning, or heavily filtered samples, introducing significant measurement error and social desirability bias. As a result, we may know less about the hidden drivers of human behavior than we pretend. This creates a skewed picture of the human condition: sanitized, overly rational, and biased toward what can be measured rather than what matters most.

In short, social science risks becoming a science of the visible, while much of what shapes society—especially the darker, more conflicted parts of ourselves—remains in the shadows. This creates not just a gap in knowledge but a systematic bias in our collective understanding of human life. It is easier to study what people openly say and do than what they conceal, deny, or fail to recognize in themselves. But if social scientists restrict themselves to the surface—to what respondents report or what institutions already record—they risk turning into megaphones for existing interests rather than independent investigators. In that sense, the discipline can begin to resemble poor journalism: amplifying selective voices, reproducing partisan narratives, and even reinforcing the very problems it ought to analyze. Instead of clarifying, social science may end up legitimizing agendas, contributing to misperceptions, and sometimes even making matters worse.

On the other side of the spectrum, those who wish to resist this tendency may swing too far toward suspicion. Entire schools of thought, particularly strands of critical theory, approach every social phenomenon as an expression of hidden agendas or as struggles for power (Habermas, 1981/1984; Horkheimer, 1972). While these perspectives reveal important dynamics, they can also overgeneralize, reducing diverse motivations to a single lens. The danger here is the classic cognitive trap captured by the saying, "If all you have is a hammer, everything looks like a nail" (Maslow, 1966, 15). In methodological terms, this becomes a form of theory-driven blindness, where researchers project their own frameworks onto the world rather than letting evidence reshape their assumptions. Both extremes—uncritical reporting of the visible and hyper-critical reduction of everything to power—risk distorting the purpose of social science. What is needed instead is a discipline capable of probing beneath appearances without collapsing complexity into either naïve acceptance or total suspicion.

The overproduction of research on observable, socially acceptable behaviors—and the underrepresentation of hidden, stigmatized, or ethically sensitive behaviors—skews our models of human nature. This is not primarily due to researcher negligence, but rather to structural and methodological constraints. As Tourangeau and Yan (2007) show, sensitive questions in surveys often trigger underreporting due to social desirability bias, especially on topics like sexual behavior, drug use, and income. Similarly, research on taboo or illegal behavior faces legal and ethical barriers that limit both access and disclosure (Sieber & Tolich, 2013). As a result, entire domains of social life—such as tax evasion, domestic abuse, addiction, or subtle forms of workplace manipulation—remain empirically underdeveloped despite their societal importance.

In these cases, the method section becomes more than a technical appendix—it becomes the primary site for evaluating the credibility of the findings. Researchers must explain not just what they discovered, but how they accessed the phenomenon, how they accounted for response distortion, and what steps they took to validate their claims. As Krumpal (2013) notes, even advanced methods like the randomized response technique or indirect questioning struggle to eliminate bias when respondents perceive risk or stigma. The burden on readers and reviewers, then, is to scrutinize the plausibility of access, the depth of triangulation, and the likelihood of misreporting.

This tension between what can be seen and what remains hidden does more than shape individual studies—it influences the broader trajectory of the social sciences. The limits of access and observation are not just technical issues; they shape our assumptions about human behavior, our models of society, and ultimately the knowledge we pass on to future generations. At some point, then, the methodological question becomes a philosophical one: What kind of world do we construct when our understanding is built on partial visibility? And why, in the first place, do we devote so much energy to studying society at all?

One reason for optimism lies in the growing role of artificial intelligence. AI has the potential to reduce the social costs of disclosure and thereby expand the range of what can be studied. Respondents may find it easier to disclose sensitive information to machines than to human interviewers, particularly when interactions are anonymized and perceived as non-judgmental. Already, early evidence from clinical psychology and survey research suggests that conversational agents can elicit more honest answers on taboo subjects, such as mental health or sexual behavior, compared to traditional surveys or face-to-face interviews (Lucas et al., 2014; Schuetzler et al., 2018). Moreover, AI can detect subtle behavioral indicators—such as linguistic hesitation, microexpressions, or metadata from online activity—that might reveal concealed attitudes or behaviors without requiring direct self-disclosure (Kosinski et al., 2013). When used responsibly, these tools can deepen our understanding of hidden domains while reducing reliance on biased self-report.

Looking forward, one can imagine systems of "ethically certified" AI researchers—platforms trusted by respondents because they guarantee anonymity, are subject to strict ethical oversight, and make clear that no data will be traced back to individuals. This could encourage greater openness than is often possible with human researchers, who inevitably carry social cues of judgment, authority, or bias. In addition, AI could analyze naturally occurring but previously underutilized data sources—such as aggregated financial transactions, mobility patterns, or encrypted health records—so long as privacy-preserving techniques like differential privacy or federated learning are applied (Dwork & Roth, 2014; Yang et al., 2019). These methods would allow researchers to study sensitive social behaviors at scale without compromising individual identities.

Another promising direction is the triangulation of hidden behaviors through multi-modal AI. By combining textual data (what people write), visual data (facial expressions, gestures), and contextual data (time of day, location, interaction history), machines could infer patterns that no single data stream would reveal. For example, AI could help identify precursors to domestic abuse not from direct disclosure, but from subtle changes in communication style, withdrawal from networks, or stress markers in voice—all without the need for intrusive questioning (Cowie et al., 2019; Goodfellow et al., 2016).

Of course, AI is no magical solution. Issues of consent, privacy, misuse, and interpretation remain acute, especially when sensitive insights are applied outside of research contexts. Yet the promise remains: if used carefully, AI may help illuminate the darker corners of human life that traditional methods have long struggled to reach, offering a fuller, less sanitized picture of who we are.

The Table 6.3 summarizes these points, showing key areas of social life that are typically hidden from research, why they are difficult to study, where traditional methods fall short, and how AI—if used responsibly—might expand our capacity to investigate them.

The table, then, serves as a reminder that what we cannot see often matters as much—if not more—than what is openly visible. By helping us reach into these hidden domains, AI does not just offer new data, it forces us to confront what kind of knowledge we want to produce and how it should be used. This naturally leads to a broader question: what is the purpose of social science itself, and how should it position itself in relation to politics, values, and society at large?

Table 6.3 Sensitive social behaviors and AI's role in ethical research

Hidden domain	Why it is concealed/Hard to study	Traditional method limitations	How AI could help
Sexual behavior (frequency, preferences, communities)	Shaped by cultural sensitivities, privacy concerns, and reputational risks (Buss, 1989; Symons, 1979). High social desirability bias in surveys	Direct surveys underreport; interviews often elicit defensive or idealized accounts; proxy measures (porn use, fertility rates) are indirect	Conversational agents shown to elicit more honest disclosure in sensitive areas (Lucas et al., 2014; Schuetzler et al., 2018). Multi-modal AI could detect subtle hesitation, linguistic cues, or online metadata that indicate concealed practices
Income misreporting and tax evasion	High financial stakes; fear of legal sanction; strong incentives to conceal	Self-reports notoriously inaccurate; administrative data often unavailable or incomplete	AI-enhanced anomaly detection in aggregated financial data; privacy-preserving techniques (differential privacy, federated learning) could allow analysis without exposing individuals (Dwork & Roth, 2014; Yang et al., 2019)
Substance use and addiction	Shame, stigma, and illegality discourage honesty	Surveys underreport; clinical samples biased toward treatment-seekers	AI applied to health records, social media traces, and wearable data could reveal hidden usage patterns; conversational AI agents may reduce stigma in self-disclosure

Hidden domain	Why it is concealed/Hard to study	Traditional method limitations	How AI could help
Domestic abuse and covert aggression	Victims fear reprisal; perpetrators conceal by design; strong stigma	Surveys risky; interviews prone to minimization or denial; police data underreport actual prevalence	Multi-modal AI could triangulate changes in communication style, stress markers in voice, withdrawal patterns, or social media signals (Cowie et al., 2019)
Prejudice and discrimination	People know prejudiced responses are socially undesirable	Self-reports highly unreliable; lab experiments prone to demand characteristics	AI-assisted Implicit Association Tests (IATs), linguistic analysis of spontaneous text, and microexpression detection may reveal unconscious biases (Kosinski et al., 2013)
Corruption and covert manipulation	Illegal activity; actors deliberately obscure evidence	Reliance on whistleblowers or journalists; surveys grossly underestimate prevalence	AI anomaly detection in procurement data, financial flows, and network analysis of contracts can flag suspicious clusters without direct self-report

(continued)

Table 6.3 (continued)

Hidden domain	Why it is concealed/Hard to study	Traditional method limitations	How AI could help
Mental health stigma (depression, suicidal ideation, PTSD)	Individuals fear judgment, discrimination, or professional repercussions	Stigma leads to underreporting; face-to-face disclosure difficult	AI chatbots shown to elicit more honest responses than humans (Lucas et al., 2014). Natural language processing can identify signals of depression or distress in text/speech with high accuracy
Workplace manipulation, bullying, and subtle power dynamics	Subtle, ambiguous, often denied by perpetrators; victims fear retaliation	Hard to capture in surveys; HR data biased by organizational self-interest	AI could analyze email, chat, and meeting transcripts (with consent) for linguistic dominance, tone, and exclusion patterns, flagging behaviors difficult for humans to see consistently

6.5 Science, Advocacy, and the Role of AI

Why do we study society? What is the purpose of the social sciences—not only in producing knowledge, but in shaping the world we live in? These questions strike at the heart of disciplinary identity and legitimacy.

Unlike the natural sciences, which often aim to uncover predictive laws or design technologies, the social sciences confront a more complex subject: human beings who think, interpret, and act with intention. This reflexivity makes social reality difficult to pin down. It is historically situated, value-laden, and constantly in flux.

The role of social science, then, is not to dictate how the world should be, but to clarify how the world is. Its primary responsibility is to provide as accurate a picture as possible of social dynamics: describing phenomena, tracing consequences, and outlining plausible scenarios. Policy and reform are the domain of democratic institutions—not research itself. If social science ventures into the realm of "how the world could be," it must do so with balance and restraint: offering multiple, well-grounded scenarios rather than prescribing a single preferred outcome. To privilege one option over others risks turning scholarship into advocacy, undermining credibility and trust (Fluck, 2019; Sokal & Bricmont, 1998).

Equally important is the handling of time. Social scientists must be extremely cautious when speaking about the future. Scenario-building can be useful as a heuristic device—mapping possible paths based on present dynamics (Wack, 1985; Wilkinson & Kupers, 2013)—but it easily drifts into speculation if presented as a prediction. History shows how even well-intentioned forecasts can mislead when uncertainty and complexity are underestimated. Karl Popper (1957) famously warned against "historicist" claims of inevitable trajectories, arguing that the unpredictability of human knowledge makes deterministic forecasts impossible. Similarly, Taleb (2007) has stressed that rare, high-impact "black swan" events are by definition unforeseeable within conventional models, meaning overconfidence in prediction is not only mistaken but dangerous.

The task of the social sciences, therefore, is not to foretell the future but to clarify present structures and conditions, making explicit the assumptions and trade-offs embedded in different pathways. Scenarios can illuminate possibilities, but they must be framed as tools for reflection, not as promises of inevitability. At their best, they encourage democratic debate and institutional preparedness; at their worst, they slide into speculation or ideological projection masquerading as science. The fine line between rigorous scenario analysis and premature prediction is precisely where social science must exercise humility.

6.5.1 Neutrality Versus Activism

What distinguishes strong social science is not moral zeal but methodological restraint and intellectual humility. Researchers must avoid overstating what their data can support, and above all, resist the temptation to become political actors in disguise. Credibility depends on this neutrality. When researchers use their scholarship as a platform for campaigning, they weaken trust in social science as a common resource for society.

Yet here lies a growing tension. Some critics argue that social sciences have become too insular—lost in jargon, siloed methods, and debates far removed from pressing issues. Others go in the opposite direction, openly advocating for an activist social science. In domains like climate change or biodiversity, scholars argue that neutrality is no longer an option—that researchers must help mobilize urgent social action.

The cause may be compelling. But the principle remains: advocacy belongs in think tanks, NGOs, or media platforms, not in the methods section of a research paper. The public turns to science not for values-driven appeals, but for disciplined ways of knowing that can distinguish evidence from ideology. Precisely in moments of crisis, the demand for rigor, transparency, and independence is greatest.

Case in a Box: Neutrality or Advocacy? The Social Science Dilemma

The tension between neutrality and advocacy becomes especially vivid in the environmental sciences. As awareness of climate change and biodiversity loss has grown, so too has the sense of urgency within the field. At conferences, one increasingly hears the refrain: "Something must be done." Among researchers, however, this sense of crisis divides opinion.[9]

On one side are those who believe that the task of science is to describe, explain, and model phenomena with as much rigor and precision as possible. Policy decisions and political mobilization, they argue, are the responsibility of democratic institutions and civil society. On the other side stand

[9] Richard Lindzen, a prominent atmospheric physicist, has long criticized what he terms "climate alarmism," arguing that climate change is largely natural and cyclical, with major glacial–interglacial shifts posing the greater long-term risk. He has suggested that more attention should be given to the recurrence of ice ages, which historically have covered large parts of the Northern Hemisphere under kilometers of ice every ~ 100,000 years (Lindzen, 2009). At the same time, there is overwhelming scientific consensus that the present trend of rapid global warming is primarily anthropogenic, with multiple studies confirming that over 97% of actively publishing climate scientists agree on human causation (Cook et al., 2016; Oreskes, 2004).

colleagues who insist that neutrality is no longer defensible—that to remain passive in the face of environmental breakdown is to become complicit. These researchers believe science must be openly activist, helping to mobilize the public and persuade decision-makers.

For those who wish to keep science at arm's length from politics, the situation can feel increasingly uncomfortable. One researcher—let us call her Anna—works at a leading environmental institute. She notices how, as some of her colleagues become more radical in their rhetoric, their research quality seems to decline. Hypotheses are framed to deliver desired results, findings are presented selectively, and "truths" appear tweaked in the service of the greater good.

Anna is also struck by changes in the group's culture. The language has become more loaded and ideological. Colleagues speak less about uncertainty or methodological limits, and more about enemies: fossil fuel companies, economists, "big business." Even men, at times, are spoken of as a problem—a view that troubles her, since her own husband works in business and is, at least in her experience, a thoughtful and decent person. Everyday habits reflect this drift: many of her colleagues have become vegan, conference lunches have turned into demonstrations of moral purity, and the shared jargon feels less like science and more like belonging to a sect. She also notices how some colleagues increasingly engage in political activism outside of their academic work, claiming to see direct connections between environmental challenges and particular political causes, further blurring the line between scholarship and advocacy.

She begins to worry about the long-term consequences. If the institute comes to be seen as a political movement rather than a research body, funders may withdraw support. The entire field could lose credibility. And yet, she also recognizes the urgency of the ecological crisis, and sympathizes with her activist colleagues' frustration. She is caught between two convictions: the need for action and the duty to preserve the integrity of science.

Questions for Reflection

1. Should scientists ever cross the line into activism, or does this inevitably compromise their credibility?
2. Is maintaining neutrality in times of crisis itself a political act?
3. How can institutes balance the urgency of planetary challenges with the need for methodological rigor?
4. To what extent do personal values and group culture (e.g., diet, rhetoric, worldview) shape the research agenda, do you think?
5. What risks do research institutes face if funders and policymakers perceive them as partisan movements rather than neutral knowledge producers?

Social science does not exist in a vacuum. It is inevitably shaped by its historical moment, by moral concerns, and by institutional context. But if it is to remain credible and useful, it must distinguish carefully between the role of the researcher and the role of the reformer. To serve society well, social science must first be clear about *how* it serves. That requires not more ideology, but more precision. At its best, social science fulfills three complementary roles—descriptive, explanatory, and critical—and it is in this balanced function that its greatest value lies:

1. *Descriptive*: It offers tools to observe and measure social patterns—from inequality and migration to political polarization and consumer behavior. By mapping the contours of contemporary life, it enables societies to better understand themselves.
2. *Explanatory*: It goes beyond surface-level description to identify underlying causes and mechanisms. Why do people vote the way they do? Why do some schools succeed while others fail? What drives long-term economic change or social trust? These are the questions that theories, models, and empirical research aim to answer.
3. *Normative* and *Critical*: It helps societies reflect on their values and contradictions. Perspectives such as feminism or postcolonialism may reveal hidden structures and challenge dominant narratives, but they must be presented as perspectives among others, not as the single valid lens through which to interpret society.

The value of social science is not confined to academia. Its insights inform policymaking, education, healthcare, urban planning, international development, and countless other domains. When done well, it strengthens democracy by equipping citizens and leaders with tools to interpret and engage with complex realities.

Still, its importance cannot be reduced to short-term application. Long-term understanding—of institutions, identity, conflict, cooperation, belief, and behavior—is just as vital. In an age marked by polarization, misinformation, and accelerating technological change, the ability to think critically about social systems is not a luxury but a survival tool for democratic societies.

Yet social science must also recognize its limits. It cannot predict every trend, solve every conflict, or eliminate human suffering. What it can do is illuminate patterns, clarify causes, and indicate levers of change that are realistically within reach. That may not be everything, but in moments of crisis or uncertainty, it is precisely what is most needed.

This is where artificial intelligence, if properly designed, offers new possibilities. Unlike human researchers, AI systems have no political careers, no moral loyalties, and no need to signal group belonging. They are not free of bias, but they are free of ideology in the human sense. When responsibly supervised, AI can test claims across vast literatures, model complex social dynamics, and highlight inconsistencies that human eyes might miss. Most importantly, it can help safeguard the neutrality of research in environments where human scientists are under pressure to conform to political or moral narratives. I say *can*, because the opposite is equally possible: it may just as easily be programmed into serving as a political instrument for particular interests. In the end, it all depends on the algorithms.

If AI is to serve science rather than politics, the social sciences must be clear about their own purpose. Their role is not to become advocates but to remain disciplined interpreters of human life. Legitimacy rests on trust: on the expectation that findings reflect evidence, not allegiance. Once inquiry is replaced by advocacy, that trust is broken, and with it the very project of social science.

This recognition leads us to a deeper question: what exactly is the human being that social sciences claim to study? For too long, answers have been fragmented—people cast as economic calculators, cultural actors, or political agents, depending on the lens. If advocacy threatens the credibility of social science, fragmentation threatens its relevance. To move forward, the field must re-anchor its work in a fuller account of the human being.

6.5.2 From Cognition to Biology: Reintegrating the Human Being

What, at the deepest level, do the social sciences study? Their central object is the human being. Yet for too long, that being has been fractured in theory and in practice. Natural sciences took responsibility for the body—organs, hormones, neurons—while the social sciences examined mind, behavior, and society. While administratively convenient, this split has been intellectually limiting.

It is now clear that much of what we know about cognition, emotion, cooperation, and decision-making does not come from economics or political science alone, but from biology and psychology.[10] Evolutionary biology, neuroscience, behavioral genetics, and cognitive psychology provide the

[10] See Appendix A for an overview and deeper analysis of each discipline's contribution.

empirical foundations for many insights developed in this book. Without them, social science offers only a partial map of what it means to be human.

This cross-pollination is not optional—it is necessary. If social sciences remain isolated, they risk becoming narrower, speculative, and detached from the empirical foundations required to study real human behavior. Relevance requires reconnection. Health, education, decision-making, and labor all demand a *bio-psycho-social perspective*. Without it, the legitimacy of the field erodes.

Seen in this light, one of the social sciences' greatest contributions lies in their integrative potential. They can serve as bridges between fragmented disciplines, reconnecting the study of the human being as a totality. As many a wise person has noticed, humans can be imagined as hardware and software. Bodies are hardware; minds are software. But for the system to function, both must work in interaction.

Cognitive performance depends heavily on physical health. Nutrition, sleep, and exercise shape attention, memory, and decision-making. At the same time, it is motivation, emotion, and willpower that determine whether we maintain our health. This creates a feedback loop: poor health undermines cognition, while poor judgment undermines health.

Case in a Box: The Cognitive-Physiological Feedback Loop (CPFL) Model

Why Body and Mind Must Be Studied Together[11]

In much of modern science and education, cognitive and physical health are treated as separate domains. Psychologists study attention and memory. Doctors monitor blood pressure and sleep. Yet human life does not unfold in silos. We are biological creatures whose minds are shaped by our bodies—and vice versa.

This is by no means a unique insight—today it feels like common sense, which also explains why so many holistic services are popular. People go to the doctor, but the doctor usually focuses on a specific disease and how it can be treated, typically with medicine or surgery. We rarely go to a doctor simply because we feel "out of balance," and perhaps not even to a psychiatrist. Yet it is often prolonged imbalance that makes us seriously sick in the first place.

A simple model can formalize that insight and show why even small health decisions can have large cognitive consequences over time.

[11] A deeper analysis of the structure and limits of the human mind lies beyond the scope of the present volume and is currently being developed in a separate manuscript.

Formulation of the Feedback Loop

We can express this reciprocal relationship as a simplified mathematical system using two interdependent functions that influence one another in a feedback loop:

Let:

C_t = Cognitive function at time t

P_t = Physical health at time t

S_t = Self-regulation (motivation, willpower, planning) at time t

ϵ = external factors or random disturbances

Then:

Equation 6.3: Cognitive Function Update

(Cognitive performance depends on prior physical health)

$$C_{\{t+1\}} = \alpha_1 P_t + \varepsilon_1$$

Equation 6.4: Physical Health Update (a function of cognitive control and self-regulation)

$$P_{\{t+1\}} - \beta_1 S_t + \beta_2 C_t + \varepsilon_2$$

Equation 6.5: Self-Regulation Update

(self-regulation is influenced by cognitive capacity)

$$S_{\{t+1\}} = \gamma_1 C_t + \varepsilon_3$$

The explanation goes like this:

1. Cognitive function at time t +1t depends positively on prior physical health: if you are well-rested and well-nourished, your attention, memory, and decision-making improve.
2. Physical health at time t+ 1t depends on both cognitive clarity and internal motivation—your ability to plan, regulate impulses, and act accordingly.
3. Self-regulation is itself affected by cognitive clarity (e.g., willpower is weakened when you're cognitively fatigued), completing the loop.

This system models the mutual reinforcement and vulnerability of body and mind. Over time, small deficits in either can cascade, while positive health habits can compound. We will call this framework the *Cognitive-Physiological Feedback Loop (CPFL) Model*.[12]

Why the CPFL Model

The CPFL model is not only a critique of the social sciences but equally—if not more so—of the medical sciences. Medicine too often isolates the biological body from the cognitive and social context of the person, reducing patients to physical symptoms without adequately considering how stress, environment, or social ties shape recovery and long-term health. This compartmentalization is partly practical: few individuals can be both trained physicians and social scientists, let alone therapists. Yet it leaves treatment strategies incomplete.

Here, again, artificial intelligence may offer a future bridge—able to integrate biomedical data with psychological and social indicators, highlighting patterns that no single discipline can fully capture. Rather than replacing doctors or researchers, AI could serve as the connective tissue, allowing medicine and social science to meet on common ground.

The CPFL Model captures the bidirectional relationship between cognitive function and physical health through the mediating role of self-regulation. It formalizes a key insight often lost in disciplinary silos: the brain does not float in a vacuum, and cognition is not an abstract function divorced from biology. Instead, our thinking, decision-making, and emotional regulation are deeply embodied—dependent on sleep, nutrition, hormonal balance, and stress physiology.

[12] While the bidirectional relationship between physical health and cognitive performance is well-documented across neuroscience and psychology (e.g., Gómez-Pinilla, 2008; Hillman, Erickson, & Kramer, 2008; Walker, 2009), and feedback models exist in behavioral medicine (McEwen, 1998; Sapolsky, 2004), these insights are rarely formalized into an integrative framework accessible to the social sciences. Most existing work remains domain-specific, focusing on either physiological impacts on cognition or psychological regulation of health behaviors, but not their recursive interplay. The CPFL Model offers value by explicitly linking these two processes in a simple systems equation, making the interaction visible and operationalizable for adjacent fields—such as education, labor economics, or organizational behavior—where it has practical and policy relevance. In that sense, the model is less about discovering new empirical facts and more about clarifying their structure across disciplines. It translates scattered evidence into an interdisciplinary framework that encourages both conceptual integration and actionable insight.

By expressing this interdependence, here mathematically, the CPFL model makes several contributions:

1. *Bridges Disciplines*: It offers a shared conceptual language for psychology, neuroscience, education, health economics, and behavioral science—fields that often talk past each other despite studying overlapping phenomena.
2. *Reveals Feedback Effects*: It shows how dysfunction in one domain (e.g., chronic stress reducing sleep quality) can spiral into others (e.g., impaired decision-making, declining self-control), leading to cumulative disadvantage or, conversely, positive reinforcement loops.
3. *Improves Policy Design*: Educational, health, and labor policies often treat physical and cognitive well-being separately. The CPFL model encourages integrated interventions: for instance, improving school meals and physical activity may boost not just health but academic outcomes via enhanced executive function.
4. *Enables Predictive Simulation*: The model lends itself to systems-based simulations—helpful for modeling long-term consequences of poor public health, rising obesity, or chronic fatigue on cognitive capacity, productivity, and civic engagement.
5. *Supports Early Intervention*: Especially in childhood and adolescence, understanding these dynamics helps identify when and how to intervene. The long-term cognitive effects of early malnutrition or sleep deprivation can be profound—but so can the benefits of timely health support.

In short, the Cognitive-Physiological Feedback Loop Model encourages a more holistic, integrated, and dynamic understanding of the human being—an approach essential if social science is to contribute to realistic, humane, and sustainable policy. In this sense, it aligns with the humanist tradition, from Erasmus to Montaigne, which has long sought to view the person as a whole rather than as fragmented parts.

We are not about to suggest that medical doctors immerse themselves in the full breadth of social science, or that social scientists must suddenly master advanced physiology. But the rise of big data now makes it possible—and increasingly necessary—to bridge these domains in practice. Wearable devices, genomic sequencing, electronic health records, and digital behavioral traces already generate vast, continuous datasets on individuals (Rumsfeld et al., 2016; Topol, 2019). Artificial intelligence systems are uniquely suited to integrate these streams, identifying feedback patterns across physiology, cognition, and behavior that no single discipline could capture alone (Esteva et al., 2019).

Such integration could produce tools not only more powerful than what we have seen before, but also more beneficial for individuals. Personalized

AI-driven feedback loops could, for instance, link sleep quality to decision fatigue, or detect when chronic stress is undermining self-control—providing actionable insights before problems escalate. In this sense, AI can serve as a mediator of the CPFL system, connecting biological signals with behavioral outcomes to generate interventions that are tailored, timely, and evidence-based (Rahman et al., 2020).

Far from replacing either medicine or social science, this hybrid approach enables both to meet on common ground. It suggests a future in which individual health and societal well-being are studied not in silos but as interconnected systems—a shift long overdue if we want a science that reflects the whole human being.

Here are four Questions for discussion to spark some reflection:

1. The CPFL model suggests that small changes in health habits can cascade into long-term cognitive and social consequences. What examples from your own experience (or observed in society) illustrate these compounding effects, either positive or negative?
2. If AI systems begin integrating biological and behavioral data in the way described, what ethical safeguards would you consider most important to protect individual autonomy and privacy?
3. How might policymakers use the CPFL model to design more effective interventions in education, healthcare, or labor markets? What challenges might they face in translating this framework into practice?
4. The CPFL model highlights the mutual dependence of body and mind. Do you think our current academic or medical institutions are capable of working across these silos, or would new kinds of interdisciplinary institutions be required?

The *mind–body connection*—long considered too complex to fully grasp, and therefore often treated as slightly esoteric—emerges with particular clarity in stress research. Chronic stress damages physiological systems through hormonal dysregulation, immune suppression, and cardiovascular strain (McEwen, 1998; Sapolsky, 2004). Neuroscience highlights neuroplasticity—the brain's capacity to physically change in response to experience. Secure attachment, emotional stability, and even meditation have measurable effects on brain structure (Davidson & McEwen, 2012; Kolb & Whishaw, 2009). In short, behavior and biology are in constant dialogue.

These insights are not new to all traditions. Many Eastern philosophies and Indigenous knowledge systems have long emphasized this unity. Practices like yoga, mindfulness, and traditional healing reflect holistic understandings that modern science increasingly validates. In practice, this need not involve mysticism or elaborate rituals—something as simple as taking a few deep, deliberate breaths can shift physiology toward a calmer, more regulated state (Brown & Gerbarg, 2005; Jerath et al., 2006). If one wishes to call that "yoga," that is fine, but its benefits rest on basic mechanisms of breath control and nervous system regulation.

From an evolutionary standpoint, this integration is adaptive. Coordinating physical readiness with mental intention—whether in flight, cooperation, or courtship—has been central to survival (Tooby & Cosmides, 1992). Mind and body co-evolved. To separate them in theory is to distort reality.

It is still possible, of course, to construct models of human behavior using only economics, political science, or business frameworks. But the result is often a caricature. The "*economic man*"—rational, utility-maximizing, self-interested—may serve as a useful abstraction, but he is biologically incomplete and emotionally impoverished (Sen, 1977; Thaler & Sunstein, 2008). Worse, if we teach students only within such models, we risk shaping them into that mold. The concern is not abstract. Critics argue that narrow business education produces graduates lacking in moral awareness or social depth (Ghoshal, 2005; Pfeffer & Fong, 2004). This is not an argument against economists or managers—it is a plea for broader education. These leaders must be trained as full human beings, not as spreadsheets in suits.

It is striking, however, that many managers appear to have discovered aspects of the mind–body relationship without ever being formally taught it in business school—or in any school for that matter. Among corporate leaders today, early rising, regular exercise, and careful physical self-discipline have become common practice. One can even observe a recurring bodily type among executives: lean, fit, often with the narrow, pen-shaped physique associated with endurance and self-control, rather than overt muscularity. There is no secret agreement dictating this form as the "*managerial body*," but rather an evolutionary process of trial and error.

A century ago, company owners were often overweight; fatness was then a visible sign of wealth, demonstrating one's ability to afford abundant food. Indeed, corpulence functioned as a status symbol, even considered attractive in many cultures because it signaled security and prosperity (Cuff, 1993; Stearns, 1997). The only problem was that many of those who embodied this ideal suffered heart attacks and died prematurely. But norms have shifted. In contemporary corporate culture—especially in listed companies—the opposite holds: fitness is the marker of success. Executives have realized that to sustain the demands of their work while still enjoying life, they must remain physically fit.

Research in organizational behavior and social psychology suggests that body norms do play a role in leadership selection. Studies show that taller, fitter, and leaner candidates are more often promoted to executive roles, as these body types are unconsciously associated with competence, discipline, and vitality (Blaker et al., 2013; Judge & Cable, 2004). Once established, such norms replicate themselves: fit managers tend to promote candidates who resemble their own body type, thereby setting new standards of physical appearance for leadership positions.

This reveals an implicit but powerful cultural logic: corporate managers, without formal instruction, have begun to integrate the biological demands of leadership into their lifestyles, shaping not only themselves but also the organizational standards of what a leader should look like.

The implications are wide-reaching. In education, student learning depends on sleep, nutrition, and emotional support. In labor markets, productivity is linked to health and psychological safety, not just training. In healthcare, outcomes are shaped as much by behavior and environment as by medication. These are not peripheral issues—they are central.

Humans are not minds living in bodies. We are *embodied minds*. Understanding society requires this conceptual unity. The bio-psycho-social model is not an idealistic theory; it is a necessary framework for realistic, humane, and effective policy.

This is also why the Vitruvian framework places the human being at its very center. The figure itself symbolizes that starting point: an embodied mind whose well-being emerges only through the interplay of biological, psychological, and social conditions (Fig. 6.4).

By focusing on the central figure, it reminds us that the five dimensions surrounding the person only make sense if the person herself is healthy. In that sense, human well-being should not be seen as a peripheral concern but as the basic value steering society. In many ways, this is already the case, as shown by the enormous resources modern societies devote to healthcare.

But let us be clear: this is not just another interdisciplinary proposal. It is a *pan-scientific project*—one that centers the entire human being as its object of study. The model insists that we treat cognition and biology not as separate domains but as dynamically coupled systems: software and hardware, mind and matter, co-evolving, co-dependent, and inseparable in practice. The goal is not to merge disciplines into a soup of generalities, but to integrate them around the human being as a shared reference point, where correlations are never lost from view.

The cost of ignoring this integration is visible. Compare photographs from the 1970s to those of today: declining physical vitality, rising obesity, and

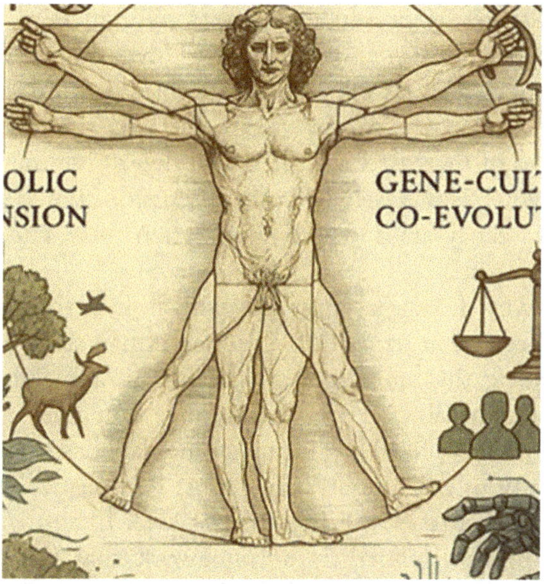

Fig. 6.4 The human being at the center of the Vitruvian model. *Source* This image is a detail cut from the larger Vitruvian framework

chronic stress are not just personal health problems—they are signs of deeper structural failure. These trends reflect systemic strain in our food systems, work environments, media diets, and social norms. A population that is chronically depleted, both physically and mentally, becomes less creative, less empathetic, and ultimately less capable of democratic deliberation. Societal health depends on *biological resilience*.

Social science has the conceptual tools to contribute meaningfully to this understanding—but only if it evolves. This is where artificial intelligence becomes not just a technical tool, but an epistemological partner. AI enables us to gather, integrate, and make sense of vast, previously unmanageable datasets—from cognitive scans and health indicators to behavioral patterns and environmental stressors. Without such tools, the kind of integrative knowledge required by the bio-psycho-social model would remain out of reach. Humans alone cannot process this level of complexity. AI is not just helpful—it is essential to making the pan-scientific vision feasible.

This raises a final question: are the social sciences, as currently structured, prepared to lead such a transformation? Or will they be displaced by disciplines—neuroscience, data science, psychogenomics—that are better equipped to describe, predict, and ultimately shape behavior in the twenty-first century?

The future of social science depends on its willingness to evolve—intellectually, institutionally, and methodologically—toward a science of the whole human. At present, it feels less like a steady progression and more like a collective pause, as if the field is waiting to decide what direction to take next. The consequences of increased use of AI will determine the trajectory of the social sciences, which is precisely why this discussion should happen here and now—not five or ten years down the line, when those choices may already have been made for us.

This is also why I suggest that humanism is a logical conclusion of our direction, because it embodies precisely what such a transformation requires: integrating the biological, psychological, and cultural dimensions of life around human values. From Renaissance humanism through modern educational and philosophical traditions, humanism has stood for the conviction that the study of the human being must be holistic—embracing body, mind, and society (Garin, 1988; Kristeller, 1961). In contemporary debates, humanism has been redefined as a framework that resists reductionism, emphasizing dignity, autonomy, and the integration of scientific knowledge with ethical reflection (Habermas, 2003; Nussbaum, 2011).

Yet this is not a call to return to an old, generalized notion of humanism that avoided specialization. What is needed instead is a *new humanism*—which I call *Reflective Humanism*. Reflective Humanism allows detailed study of particular domains—neuroscience, genetics, culture, institutions—while keeping them connected within a larger frame. Its strength lies not in denying specialization, but in preventing disciplines from drifting into silos where findings cannot be integrated. In this sense, it is humanist not because it forbids close analysis, but because it insists that such analysis be embedded within the whole. The structure is holistic, even if the methods are specialized.

This is what makes the project fundamentally pan-scientific: a systematic effort to align the study of human beings across levels of body and mind, culture and biology. What we call here the bio-psycho-social perspective—and more formally present through the Cognitive-Physiological Feedback Loop (CPFL) Model—captures precisely this ambition. To move toward a "science of the whole human" is therefore not to abandon the social sciences' heritage, but to fulfill their deepest and most humanistic promise.

Seen in this light, the argument for humanism is not an appeal to nostalgia but a reminder of the task that lies ahead. If the social sciences are to evolve, they must take seriously their own humanistic roots while grounding them in the biological and systemic realities uncovered by modern science. Only then can they claim legitimacy as sciences of the human.

6.5.3 Social Sciences in Context

If the Cognitive-Physiological Feedback Loop (CPFL) model demonstrates anything, it is that understanding human beings requires a truly integrative approach—one that no single discipline can claim to master alone. Yet such integrative ambitions are not new. Throughout the history of science, large projects have repeatedly attempted to unify knowledge across biology, psychology, and the social sciences. They often began with promise but ended in disappointment, not because the goal was misguided, but because complexity overwhelmed clarity.

The Enlightenment dream of a "*science of man*," stretching from Condorcet to Comte, aspired to subsume human life under a universal method modeled on physics.[13] Instead of synthesis, this often produced abstractions so general that they explained little. Later, early twentieth-century behaviorism sought to unify psychology and social science under a strict focus on observable behavior.[14] But in stripping away inner life, it sacrificed explanatory depth and eventually gave way to the cognitive revolution. Similarly, mid-century cybernetics aimed at a grand theory of systems—machines, organisms, societies alike—but the sheer abstraction of feedback

---

[13] The Enlightenment ambition of a *science de l'homme* was articulated most forcefully by Enlightenment philosophes such as Marie Jean Antoine Nicolas de Caritat, Marquis de Condorcet, and later by Auguste Comte. Condorcet, in his *Esquisse d'un tableau historique des progrès de l'esprit humain* (1795), imagined a universal science of human progress grounded in reason and modeled on the natural sciences: "l'histoire de l'esprit humain" was to be traced with the same rigor as celestial mechanics. He envisioned that human morality, politics, and social life could eventually be rendered intelligible and predictable through systematic scientific laws, with mathematics as the guiding framework (Condorcet, 1795/1970).

Comte radicalized this ambition in the nineteenth century by proposing a *physique sociale*, later renamed *sociologie*, in his *Cours de philosophie positive* (1830–1842). For Comte, the goal was to apply the methods of physics and biology to the study of society: "savoir pour prévoir, prévoir pour pouvoir" (*to know in order to predict, to predict in order to act*). He argued that social phenomena, no less than natural phenomena, were subject to immutable laws discoverable by science, and he explicitly framed sociology as the "couronnement" (crowning achievement) of the scientific edifice (Comte, 1830–1842/1975).

Both Condorcet and Comte thus represent key moments in the Enlightenment dream of a totalizing science of man, one that sought to dissolve the boundaries between the natural and social worlds by modeling human complexity on the precision of physics. Yet this project was also the beginning of the reductionist temptation that would later haunt social science—flattening lived experience into abstractions that risked explaining too much, and too little, at once.

[14] Early twentieth-century behaviorism, most famously advanced by John B. Watson in *Psychology as the Behaviorist Views It* (1913), rejected introspection and consciousness as unscientific and insisted that psychology confine itself to observable stimuli and responses. Watson's program was later reinforced by B. F. Skinner in works such as *The Behavior of Organisms* (1938), which extended the behaviorist paradigm into operant conditioning and offered a vision of psychology as a unified natural science of behavior. While this approach achieved methodological rigor, its neglect of internal mental processes ultimately set the stage for the "cognitive revolution" of the 1950s and 1960s.

diagrams proved too blunt an instrument to capture the lived complexity of human culture.[15]

These episodes show how integrative projects can drift into either vagueness or reductionism. The lesson is not that integration is impossible, but that it must be pursued with humility and precision. The challenge for today's social sciences, then, is whether they can learn from these earlier failures—avoiding both the dilution of meaning and the temptation to force human experience into overly narrow models.

We cannot hope to arrive at a unifying framework—or a general theory for the social sciences—by beginning with isolated problems inside our own domains, whether in economics, sociology, political science, or anthropology. To start from the middle is to risk reproducing the very fragmentation we are trying to overcome (Abbott, 2001). The effort must instead begin at the other end, with the unifying foundation. And here, if we are honest, there are really only two possible starting points: physics or biology—or more precisely, biology as an outcome of physics.

From there, what the social sciences need is a great unifying theory. Evolutionary theory, in our case, provides that foundation. Scholars across multiple disciplines have argued that Darwinian principles of variation, selection, and retention can serve as a general framework for understanding human behavior and institutions (Hodgson & Knudsen, 2010; Wilson, 2015). Once this is in place, we can proceed by building a small number of very general models, some of which have been suggested in this book. At this stage we are still working within what I have called Layer 1: the shared foundation of evolutionary principles.

Only after securing this foundation does it make sense to move upward to Layer 2, the level of disciplinary models and theories. At this level, sociology, economics, political science, and psychology can each continue to develop their own frameworks—but with a clear condition: their explanations must be traceable back to evolutionary principles and the three interlocking axioms outlined earlier in this chapter. This echoes what biologist Theodosius Dobzhansky (1973) famously stated: "Nothing in biology makes sense except

[15] The cybernetics movement, inaugurated by Norbert Wiener's *Cybernetics: Or Control and Communication in the Animal and the Machine* (1948), sought to establish a unifying science of systems governed by feedback loops, applicable across engineering, physiology, and social organization. This vision was further developed in works such as Ross Ashby's *An Introduction to Cybernetics* (1956), which popularized concepts of homeostasis and self-regulation, and in interdisciplinary gatherings like the Macy Conferences (1946–1953), where anthropologists, mathematicians, engineers, and psychiatrists explored the implications of feedback and information theory. Despite its initial promise, the project often foundered on excessive abstraction—its diagrams elegant but insufficiently equipped to capture the qualitative depth of human meaning, culture, and historical contingency.

in the light of evolution." Social science, too, gains coherence only when it can be related back to this unifying framework.

If they cannot, then the theory in question either needs to be reformulated or acknowledged for what it is: a useful description or correlation, but not a theoretically fundamental contribution. Critics of contemporary social science have long noted the problem of "theory inflation," where loosely connected correlations are labeled as "theories" without being embedded in a cumulative framework (Hedström & Udéhn, 2009; Turner, 1990).

This does not mean that such insights are without value. They may still be empirically valid and practically useful, provided the methods hold up to scrutiny. But they cannot claim to advance the theoretical foundations of the social sciences if they do not connect back to the common ground of Layer 1. In this sense, the layered framework introduces a kind of intellectual discipline: it prevents us from calling every bundle of correlations or loosely grouped observations a "theory." Instead, it demands that theoretical claims be rooted in a unifying scientific framework, while allowing descriptive and applied research to stand on its own terms.

The strength of such a system lies precisely in this differentiation. It clears away the clutter of invented theories created "for the sake of it" (a common critique in meta-theoretical reviews: see Cole, 2001; Collins, 1994) and replaces them with a coherent architecture: evolutionary theory as foundation, disciplinary models as applications, and empirical observations as data points to be tested and refined. Only then can the social sciences move from being a patchwork of local insights to a cumulative, integrative science of humanity.

We are already seeing signs of this transition—but not primarily within the social sciences themselves. The real breakthroughs are coming from the natural sciences, which increasingly serve as the locomotive pulling the rest of inquiry forward. Neuroscience, genetics, and psychophysiology are advancing into domains once thought inaccessible, forcing the social sciences to reconsider their foundations. High-resolution fMRI, for example, can now detect which color a person is seeing based purely on neural activation patterns (Hossenfelder, 2025), a development that brings us closer to making even subjective experience observable. In domains like attention, memory, and emotional regulation, what was once speculative or philosophical has become measurable and replicable. Phenomena such as *decision latency*, bias, and stress reactivity are now being charted not through introspection, but through brain imaging, hormone assays, and computational modeling (Glimcher & Fehr, 2013; Kahneman, 2011; Sapolsky, 2004).

The implications are profound. Cognitive psychology and behavioral economics, for instance, have shifted from theories of choice to biological models of constraint. The famous experiments by Libet (1985) and Soon et al. (2008) challenged the notion of free will by demonstrating that unconscious brain processes precede conscious decisions. Meanwhile, affective neuroscience has shown how emotion and cognition are inseparable in human judgment, dissolving the old Cartesian dualism that once structured so many social science models.

In parallel, evolutionary psychology and behavioral genetics have provided testable, falsifiable insights into cooperation, competition, aggression, and even moral behavior—areas once dominated by purely cultural explanation. Scholars like Buss (2019), Cosmides and Tooby (1992), and Pinker (2002) have argued, sometimes controversially, that many social phenomena must be understood as expressions of deep evolutionary strategies shaped by ancestral environments. These theories have not only become more empirically rigorous, but have also proven predictive, offering explanatory power across societies and contexts.

This expansion of biological and computational insight poses an intellectual challenge to the social sciences: what can these disciplines still offer that cannot be outsourced or biologically explained?

The answer is not resignation, but renewal. The social sciences must reposition themselves—not as isolated observers of culture or institutions—but as integrators of the full human picture. Their strength lies in interpretation, in contextualizing empirical data within historical, ethical, and cultural frames. But interpretation without integration is no longer enough. To remain relevant, the social sciences must be capable of building bridges: between biology and meaning, between neural correlates and social norms, between data patterns and human values.

This is not a typical interdisciplinary appeal. As we have already argued, what is required is something larger: a pan-scientific project that places the whole human being—both software and hardware—at the center of knowledge. In this model, cognitive function, emotional regulation, and physiological resilience are not studied in disciplinary isolation, but as co-evolving, mutually reinforcing systems. The CPFL model is just one example of how such integration can take shape.

And here, artificial intelligence becomes not a threat, but an ally. The sheer volume and complexity of data required to study these intertwined systems—across biology, behavior, environment, and social context—would overwhelm traditional human research teams. But with AI, it becomes feasible. Machine learning systems can help us detect patterns, test models, and simulate outcomes that were previously unimaginable. This makes the pan-scientific project not only possible, but urgent.

What matters now is whether the social sciences accept the challenge. The alternative is clear: other disciplines will continue to ask the big questions—about learning, identity, morality, and meaning—and they will do so using tools the social sciences once claimed as their own. The risk is not marginalization; it is irrelevance. And if that happens, I suppose many will turn back to listening to music or attending concerts, rather than enduring tedious "theoretical" lectures in the social sciences—lectures on material that AI could summarize in a fraction of the time. Whatever "techne" is truly necessary for business students or bureaucrats, they will pick it up from the internet, in combination with AI, or simply learn it on the job.

Still, even this outcome would not be an accident but part of a broader evolutionary process. *Knowledge systems* compete much like businesses do. Just as firms rise and fall in markets, so too do academic disciplines rise or decline depending on their capacity to generate insight, relevance, and value. If psychology, neuroscience, or even computer science were to take over the study of "man and society," that would simply reflect the logic of competition: those fields proved more adaptive. The social sciences have no monopoly on these questions; they survive or falter by the same evolutionary rules as any other institution.

But the opportunity is just as great. A renewed, integrated social science—biologically aware, computationally informed, and ethically grounded—could be the keystone of our future knowledge system. It would not merely study the human condition; it would help guide its evolution.

6.6 The Stewardship of Knowledge

In a time when intellectual authority is both revered and distrusted, the question is no longer just what science can discover—but how it must behave. Following our discussion of the full human being as a dual system—biological hardware and psychological software—we now ask: what does it mean to act responsibly with knowledge in this fragile system of public trust?

First, we as social scientists must take our role as scientists seriously. One recurring danger is the overextension of intellectuals beyond their actual domain of expertise. Thomas Sowell (2010) shows how high competence in one field often creates a misplaced halo of credibility in others. This cognitive bias—the assumption that brilliance is transferable—leads the public to embrace weak arguments from prestigious voices. Bertrand Russell's advocacy for British disarmament in the 1930s, while Nazi Germany rearmed, is used by Sowell (2010) as an illustration of how moral clarity can sometimes outpace policy wisdom. The example makes the point, though one might prefer to frame it differently, since Russell remains one of the most brilliant and influential thinkers of the twentieth century. Still, the case shows how even great intellectuals can be cited as reminders that expertise in one domain does not always translate seamlessly into another.

Overreach is not only a personal failing; it is structurally enabled. Unlike engineers or physicians, whose errors draw rapid feedback, social theorists and commentators are often insulated from the downstream effects of their ideas. A failed policy may take decades to reveal its costs. As Taleb (2012) argues, a lack of *skin in the game* allows bad ideas to flourish unpunished. The prudent stance is disciplined self-limitation: speak where the evidence is strong; be explicit about uncertainty; avoid converting expertise in one area into authority in all others.

Second, scientific integrity requires resisting political and ideological pressure. In an age saturated with expert commentary, public confidence in science rests less on empirical rigor than on symbolic authority. With that authority comes a burden: not only to generate insight, but to steward it wisely. Misused authority corrodes trust—and trust is the true currency of modern science. Authority bias compounds the problem: as Milgram (1974) and Kahneman (2011) show, audiences often accept claims based on status rather than evidence. In celebrity culture this becomes farcical, but the mechanism is the same inside academia. The antidote is methodological humility and transparency.

The ultimate purpose of the social sciences must, of course, be to change society. If research had no impact on the world, it would hardly justify the effort. But this does not mean that the scientist's role is to campaign or dictate outcomes. The proper task of research is to tackle solvable problems—questions where evidence can provide clear answers, where explanations can be clarified, and where confusions can be straightened out in a balanced way.

Classical positivism, as Karl Popper (1959) emphasized, saw this task as rooted in neutrality and objectivity: science should seek falsifiable claims, and in so doing gradually refine its explanations of reality. Yet later voices, such as Fay (1996), argued that even the choice of research questions is value-laden and politically situated. This line of critique belongs to a broader current of *deconstructionist thought*—methodologies that often align with parts of critical theory and, at times, anarcho-syndicalist or nihilist leanings (Best & Kellner, 1991; Norris, 1990). The method is simple: take an existing body of knowledge and reveal its contradictions, its biases, or its hidden power dynamics. The trouble is that while it is relatively easy to dismantle frameworks, it is far more difficult to construct new and workable ones.

Education or research built solely on deconstruction leads nowhere, since critique without constructive synthesis provides little more than an endless devil's advocacy. The act of tearing down systems may sharpen awareness, but it does not, by itself, generate the knowledge or solutions that societies actually need (Latour, 2004; Searle, 1995). For this reason, social science cannot afford to dwell only in dismantling; it must also build. The scientist's role, then, is not to "be on the changing society side of the stick" with activists and politicians, but to inhabit the other side: presenting solutions, offering clear answers, and straightening issues in a balanced way.

This is why guiding norms are indispensable. Science cannot simply follow the impulses of individuals or the fashions of ideology; it requires rules that ensure impartiality, transparency, and trust. Robert K. Merton's norms remain foundational here. Far from being nostalgic ideals, they function as the operating code of credible science—the principles by which knowledge can be trusted and, ultimately, by which it can serve society (Table 6.4).

These four norms are not abstract ideals; they describe what it means to be a credible social scientist in practice. To work in this field is to engage with questions of broad societal relevance and to be prepared to share one's findings—however uncomfortable or unpopular—with the wider public. The principle of *communalism* implies that our work should not be locked away in inaccessible journals or hidden behind institutional paywalls. Scientific knowledge must be open to scrutiny and replication, because it is not owned—it is stewarded.

One of the distinctive features of knowledge is that, unlike most physical resources, it can be given away without being depleted. If I share a loaf of bread, I no longer have it; but if I share an idea, I still retain it in full. This property makes knowledge an unusually potent form of capital: it can spread without loss to the giver, while multiplying in value for the receiver. Pinker (1994) notes that this is possible because language allows us to encode and transmit vast amounts of information across minds, across time, and across space. Through language, knowledge is not only preserved but amplified, as each transmission invites reinterpretation and refinement. It is this discovery—that knowledge can be stored, taught, and improved without diminishing its source—that underlies the creation of universities as institutions devoted to preserving and distributing intellectual capital. The university, at its best, is not a warehouse of facts but a living conduit for the continual renewal of shared understanding.

Table 6.4 The four norms of scientific integrity (Merton, 1942)

Mertonian norm	Definition	Example	Contemporary challenge
Communalism	Scientific knowledge belongs to the community and should be shared freely	Open-access publications and public datasets enabling replication and further research	Private ownership of data by corporations, e.g., pharmaceutical companies hiding results
Universalism	Claims must be judged by scientific merit, not the identity of the author	A strong paper from a lesser-known university is judged equally to one from Harvard or Oxford	Institutional bias and Western-centric peer review practices
Disinterestedness	Scientists should act out of a pursuit for knowledge, not personal interest	Declaring all funding sources and avoiding conflicts of interest	Industry-funded research (e.g., oil or tobacco) distorting findings for commercial benefit
Organised scepticism	All claims must be critically examined, no matter the authority behind them	Peer review systems that scrutinize even high-status researchers' findings	Viral science on social media bypassing scrutiny and peer review

This norm stands in stark contrast to how knowledge was historically controlled. For centuries, elite institutions hoarded information to preserve authority. The Catholic Church, for example, maintained strict control over access to sacred texts. The Vatican Apostolic Library, established in the fifteenth century, was accessible only to a select few. Manuscripts were withheld from the public and even from much of the clergy, not for reasons of preservation but to centralize *interpretive power* (Ruccio, 2006). The Church deliberately kept the Bible in Latin long after vernacular languages were widely spoken. As Pelikan (2005) and Daniell (2003) show, this was not an oversight—it was a calculated move to prevent laypeople from interpreting scripture independently. Only reformers like Martin Luther, who translated the Bible into German, directly challenged this monopoly and insisted on the public's right to access and understand foundational knowledge.

Science, in contrast, is built on the rejection of *informational hierarchies*. It affirms, in principle, that no institution or class of people should have privileged access to truth. The ethos of science holds that knowledge is a *public good*—generated not for secrecy or control, but for open scrutiny and shared understanding. A core ethical obligation of the social sciences, in particular, is to dismantle the barriers that inhibit this openness—whether financial (such as paywalled journals), institutional (such as exclusive networks or elite funding access), or linguistic (such as publishing only in inaccessible academic jargon or dominant languages). Our responsibility is not merely to produce findings, but to ensure they are made available in forms that permit public reflection, critical debate, and collective correction.

This ethos stands in radical contrast to fields like *intelligence*—where I have spent most of my career making small scientific contributions—and *national security*, where the compartmentalization of information is not a flaw but a deliberate design principle. In such systems, access to data is restricted based on formal clearances, and individuals often operate with only a partial view of the whole picture. Analysts may pose questions that cannot be answered, not because the answers don't exist, but because the system forbids the flow of that information to their clearance level. In fact, the more sensitive and valuable a piece of information is, the fewer people are allowed to know it. The structure is pyramidical: insight narrows as secrecy increases.

For a scientist, especially in the social sciences, this would be a nightmare. Imagine a world where evolutionary theory was stored in the most secretive vault of a state archive, accessible only to a handful of authorized thinkers, forbidden from publication, replication, or public scrutiny. That is not science—it is *intellectual feudalism*. Scientific knowledge gains its legitimacy precisely through its exposure: through the fact that anyone can inspect it, replicate it, criticize it, and improve upon it. A theory that cannot be challenged is not a theory at all—it is *dogma*.

Of course, science also deals with sensitive information—especially in fields like medicine, behavioral research, or military technology—but the norm is always to minimize opacity and maximize the transparency necessary for verification and understanding. This commitment to openness is not a naive ideal; it is a foundational requirement for the very logic of scientific progress. To claim otherwise is to confuse science with authority. In contrast to intelligence work, which thrives on *need-to-know hierarchies*, science thrives on *need-to-share openness*. The social scientist, therefore, must be especially vigilant in rejecting any institutional arrangement—be it academic elitism, governmental secrecy, or commercial gatekeeping—that obscures the conditions under which knowledge is produced, validated, and shared.

And it is the responsibility of the state to ensure that researchers are able to do so. In many countries today, academic freedom enjoys far too little protection. In Sweden, for example, only full professors are explicitly safeguarded against interference from politicized administrators or university management (Bruzelius, 2022). Such protection should be extended to all researchers holding a PhD, since the integrity of science depends not on rank but on the universal ability to pursue inquiry without fear of reprisal.

The norm of *universalism* reinforces this stance by requiring that scientific claims be judged on their intrinsic merit rather than on the status, institutional affiliation, or personal charisma of the researcher. Neither the prestige of a university, the authority of a famous name, nor the popularity or trendiness of an idea should determine its validity. What counts is the evidence, the method, and the reasoning. Yet in much of the social sciences over the last generation, we have witnessed the opposite trend: a *"science by buzzwords."* Politicians, eager to fund projects that resonate with voters and improve their reelection chances, often allocate research money to initiatives built on popular notions from mass media rather than on rigorous theory. The result is a cycle where research agendas follow headlines, amplifying fashionable concerns rather than cultivating the slower, more cumulative insights that science requires.

At the same time, universalism should not be misunderstood as a license for *scientific imperialism*. It does not mean that researchers ought to impose their findings indiscriminately on all societies, nor that cultural differences in values, priorities, or interpretations should be ignored. Science gains credibility precisely when it avoids collapsing into a form of *ideological universalism* that treats Western empirical traditions as the only legitimate path to knowledge. As Jasanoff (2005) has argued, science and technology are always co-produced with culture, and attempts to universalize without sensitivity to context risk undermining both trust and applicability. Similarly, Harding (1998) warns that "strong objectivity" requires recognizing the partiality of perspectives, rather than assuming one cultural standpoint can speak for all.

Thus, universalism means equality of standards in evaluating claims—anyone, anywhere, can submit evidence that must be judged by the same criteria. But it does not mean ignoring pluralism in how problems are defined, questions are asked, or knowledge is applied. Respect for cultural variation and humility toward different epistemic traditions are necessary to prevent universalism from devolving into a new form of *colonialism in thought*.

Yet perhaps the most vulnerable of Merton's norms today is *disinterestedness*—the idea that science should be pursued for knowledge's sake, not for personal advancement, political gain, or institutional branding. In the contemporary landscape, this principle is increasingly difficult to maintain. Many social scientists are employed by think tanks, advocacy groups, or policy institutes with clear ideological missions. Even within universities, research agendas are shaped by funding streams, media attention, and professional incentives. The ideal of neutral inquiry is often undercut by structural forces.

If there is one problem I have become acutely aware of during my nearly three decades inside this system, it is that research funding remains far too closely tied to the political priorities of whichever party happens to be in power. This influence is often indirect rather than explicit, but that makes it no less problematic, since it effectively dictates which kinds of questions are even allowed to receive support. For this reason, research funding should be made entirely independent—awarded solely on the merit of scientific contributions and the quality of proposals, regardless of field or topic. The public, in turn, must learn to trust that researchers are not simply "inventing" areas to explore, but are guided by what they see as the most important questions. Only by depoliticizing funding in this way can we safeguard the neutrality of science.

Another concerning example—though it may seem odd to bring up—is the rise of commercial polling companies. These firms often operate without methodological transparency, declining to publish sampling procedures, question phrasing, or margin of error. And yet, their data is widely cited by media outlets and policymakers alike, even researchers. Any statistician knows how much results can change depending on how a question is worded or how a sample is drawn. Without transparency, these polls become less tools for understanding and more instruments of persuasion. They simulate the authority of science while evading its discipline.

At this point, the issue is no longer academic—it is civic. When public discourse relies on data that cannot be verified or scrutinized, institutional trust erodes. Social scientists have a duty to expose these distortions and advocate for accountability. Still, we must also acknowledge a structural gap: national statistics agencies cannot meet the demand for real-time data across all social dimensions. Into this vacuum step commercial actors, whose priorities often lie not in truth, but in client satisfaction or media visibility. The result is a paradox: a society flooded with numbers, but starving for reliable knowledge.

What may at first glance look like a trivial example is, in fact, existential for anyone attempting to build a system of facts. Institutions and researchers often take statistics as given, layering arguments and models on top of them.

If the foundation is weak, the entire structure becomes unstable. That is why it is essential that statistics are either conducted by scientists themselves or, at the very least, by organizations willing to commit to full methodological transparency. Every step of the process—from sampling to question design—must be open to scrutiny. At present, this standard is far from being met.

The final Mertonian norm, *organized scepticism*, reminds us of our highest obligation: to question everything, including ourselves. To be a social scientist is not merely to describe or explain society, but to interrogate it. That includes confronting dominant paradigms, resisting intellectual fads, and asking difficult questions even when the answers may be uncomfortable or unpopular. In today's media ecosystem—polarized, algorithmically sorted, and emotionally reactive—this kind of intellectual courage is more necessary than ever.

If there is a single thread running through these four norms, it is this: science is not merely a system for producing information. It is a fragile architecture for maintaining trust. In that respect, social scientists are much like bankers—not entrusted with currency, but with something more subtle and foundational: the knowledge people use to make sense of the world. Just as the collapse of trust can bring down a banking system, the erosion of credibility can undo the social sciences. We must therefore conduct ourselves not only as thinkers and analysts, but as stewards—rigorous, impartial, and accountable to the public we ultimately serve.

6.6.1 Risks of Social Design: When Science Forgets Its Role

The primary mission of the social sciences is to observe, interpret, and explain human behavior—not to redesign it according to preconceived blueprints. In principle, the task is descriptive: to study what people do and why. In practice, however, this line is often blurred. When researchers begin prescribing political or moral actions without acknowledging competing interpretations or trade-offs, science slips into *advocacy*.

This dilemma lies at the heart of recurring debates about the role of scholarship in society. As David Hume observed, one cannot logically derive an "ought" from an "is" (Hume, 1739/2000). Yet this boundary is crossed regularly. Findings that suggest X leads to Y are often presented as justification for specific interventions, even though the same evidence could be interpreted in other ways. Once data is made to serve a predetermined conclusion, the scientific process is compromised.

This kind of distortion is not always deliberate. Motivated reasoning, confirmation bias, and identity-protective cognition all shape how scholars process evidence (Nickerson, 1998; Kunda, 1990). Even highly trained researchers are vulnerable, as demonstrated by Kahneman (2011) and Haidt (2012). Scientific neutrality is therefore not a fixed condition but an ongoing effort against the tendencies of human cognition.

Institutional and financial pressures compound the challenge. Funding is rarely neutral. Governments, businesses, and philanthropic organizations tend to support research that aligns with their priorities. Work that challenges these interests may receive little support or attention. As scholars such as Mirowski (2011) and Lacy (2017) note, such dynamics can shape entire academic fields, encouraging certain narratives over others.

History offers cautionary lessons. In the Soviet Union, the social sciences were explicitly subordinated to ideology. Entire disciplines were reorganized to serve the state's vision of the *"New Socialist Man."* Scholars who dissented were removed, and the result was intellectual stagnation and flawed policy (Fitzpatrick, 1999; Hollander, 1981). When I studied in Leipzig shortly after the fall of the Berlin Wall, this legacy was still visible. The university, then dismantling its GDR-era structures, had to rebuild disciplines that had been reshaped for political rather than scientific purposes. Natural sciences had survived better, largely because their practical applications shielded them. My supervisor, the ever-amicable and sanguine Professor Klaus Lange, was spared dismissal because his mathematical expertise in economics was still deemed useful.

Examples such as these illustrate what can happen when science becomes a tool of *social design*. Attempts at large-scale reengineering of human behavior—from eugenics and forced sterilization programs in Europe and North America, to population policies such as China's one-child rule—show how easily good intentions can result in harm (Kevles, 1985). Scientific authority, when misapplied, can bypass democratic deliberation and impose rigid solutions on complex human realities.

For science to remain credible then, it must hold fast to a single master: the pursuit of truth.[16] That pursuit demands discipline, integrity, and resistance

[16] By "truth," we refer to statements that correspond with observable reality—that is, phenomena verifiable through our senses or reliably extended through scientific instruments. This definition aligns broadly with the *correspondence theory of truth*, which holds that a claim is true if it accurately describes the way the world is (Russell, 1912; Devitt, 1984). In scientific practice, this often means relying on empirical evidence, sensory data, and reproducibility. Instruments such as microscopes, telescopes, or fMRI scanners extend our perceptual capacities, but the underlying standard remains sensory verifiability. Philosophers like Karl Popper (1959) emphasized falsifiability—an idea adjacent to sensory validation—as a key demarcation for science. While complete objectivity may be unattainable, science maintains its integrity by grounding claims in observable, testable evidence rather than ideology or preference.

to compromise. Like medicine's Hippocratic Oath, the social sciences require a code of conduct that protects both method and principle. Perhaps:

Seek truth, and do no harm to reason.

Of course, social scientists are not detached from society. We vote, we hold values, and many of us engage in public debate. But when speaking as scientists, allegiance must be to data and evidence, not to ideology. The proper frame is: "Based on the evidence I have gathered..." Any political interpretation belongs outside the scientific claim. Blurring this line erodes trust, distorts the role of scholarship, and reinforces suspicion that research is just another instrument of politics.

Science has always been vulnerable to outside pressure. Galileo was compelled to recant his heliocentric view; Darwin delayed publication of The Origin of Species fearing social and religious backlash. These stories remind us that scientific integrity must be defended repeatedly.

For this task, Merton's (1942) classic norms of communalism, universalism, disinterestedness, and organized skepticism remain foundational. Yet the conditions of the twenty-first century call for additions—not as replacements, but as extensions. The following table outlines an expanded code of scientific integrity that adapts Merton's vision to the realities of today's academic, political, and technological environment (Table 6.5).

Taken together, these additions highlight that Merton's principles are not static relics but living commitments. What is proposed here is more than an update for a particular century—it is an *Expanded Code of Scientific Integrity*, a substantial extension of Merton's original list. The aim is not to replace his ethos but to carry it forward, ensuring that the spirit of scientific integrity remains robust under changing pressures and across future contexts.

Science is not only a method but also a stewardship. The vulnerability of the social sciences lies in their subject matter: we study people, values, identities, and institutions. Unlike particles or molecules, these entities interpret us even as we interpret them. That makes neutrality harder to sustain and even more essential to protect.

At the same time, new tools are emerging that may help strengthen what has been weakened. Artificial intelligence offers powerful means to synthesize evidence, test hypotheses, and reduce bias. Yet speed and scale are not substitutes for judgment. If anything, the rise of intelligent machines makes the virtues of epistemic humility, contextual sensitivity, and integrity even more important.

The lesson of this chapter is therefore straightforward: the social sciences must reclaim their role as sciences. They must become more rigorous, more

Table 6.5 Toward an expanded code of scientific integrity

Norm	Definition	Example	Contemporary challenge
Epistemic humility	Recognition of limits of data, models, and interpretation	Clearly stating uncertainty ranges in survey results or AI predictions	Pressure for simplified headlines, misuse of models as definitive forecasts
Academic freedom	Protection from political, institutional, or cultural retaliation for truthful findings	Safeguards for whistle-blowers, controversial or unpopular research	Scholars dismissed, harassed, or defunded for publishing "uncomfortable" results
Funding independence	Allocation of resources based on scientific merit rather than political or ideological agendas	Independent grant bodies insulated from partisan cycles	Research agendas skewed by government, corporate, or philanthropic priorities
Contextual sensitivity	Avoiding epistemic imperialism; recognizing cultural and ecological variation	Comparative studies respecting local norms and conditions	Exporting Western categories as "universal" or ignoring ecological limits
Public responsibility	Duty to communicate knowledge accessibly, truthfully, and without distortion	Public lectures, popular science writing, fact-checking misinformation	Retreat into jargon, silence in face of disinformation, or feeding culture wars
Integrity in application	Distinguishing analysis from advocacy; evidence from ideology	Framing findings as conditional, not prescriptive	Policy-driven research blurring science with activism

(continued)

Table 6.5 (continued)

Norm	Definition	Example	Contemporary challenge
Algorithmic transparency	Ensuring that AI tools used in research are open, explainable, and ethically audited	Publishing model documentation, testing outputs for bias	Black-box algorithms amplifying bias, AI as political instrument
Human-centered integration	Commitment to studying the human being holistically—bio-psycho-social and systemic	Cross-disciplinary projects linking biology, psychology, and social systems	Fragmentation of disciplines, loss of relevance in face of holistic challenges

independent, and more resilient in the face of cultural, institutional, and technological pressures. Only by reinforcing their epistemic foundations can they guide our societies.

This chapter has examined the foundations of the social sciences, their strengths, and their vulnerabilities. But just as we begin to address these questions, a new disruption appears: artificial intelligence. Nowhere are the implications clearer than in academia itself, where AI is no longer only a research tool but increasingly a collaborator, editor, and even co-author. The next chapter explores how AI is reshaping scholarly work—transforming writing, workflows, professional identity, and the meaning of authorship.

References

Abbott, A. (2001). *Time matters: On theory and method*. University of Chicago Press.

Ashby, W. R. (1956). *An introduction to cybernetics*. Chapman & Hall.

Backhouse, R. E. (2002). *The ordinary business of life: A history of economics from the ancient world to the twenty-first century*. Princeton University Press.

Bail, C. A. (2021). *Breaking the social media prism: How to make our platforms less polarizing*. Princeton University Press.

Best, S., & Kellner, D. (1991). *Postmodern theory: Critical interrogations*. Guilford Press.

Blaker, N. M., Rompa, I., Dessing, I. H., Vriend, A. F., Herschberg, C., & van Vugt, M. (2013). The height leadership advantage in men and women: Testing evolutionary psychology predictions about the perceptions of tall leaders. *Group*

Processes & Intergroup Relations, 16(1), 17–27. https://doi.org/10.1177/1368430212437211
Blaug, M. (1992). *The methodology of economics: Or how economists explain* (2nd ed.). Cambridge University Press.
Bourdieu, P. (1979). *Distinction: A social critique of the judgement of taste*. Harvard University Press.
Box, G. E. P. (1979). Some remarks on statistics. *Quality Progress, 12*(9), 22–24.
Boyd, R., & Richerson, P. J. (1985). *Culture and the evolutionary process*. University of Chicago Press.
Brown, R. P., & Gerbarg, P. L. (2005). Sudarshan Kriya yogic breathing in the treatment of stress, anxiety, and depression: Part I—neurophysiologic model. *Journal of Alternative and Complementary Medicine, 11*(1), 189–201. https://doi.org/10.1089/acm.2005.11.189
Bruzelius, N. (2022). Academic freedom in Sweden: Institutional constraints and professional autonomy. *Higher Education Policy, 35*(2), 245–262.
Buss, D. M. (1989). Sex differences in human mate preferences: Evolutionary hypotheses tested in 37 cultures. *Behavioral and Brain Sciences, 12*(1), 1–14.
Buss, D. M. (2019). *Evolutionary psychology: The new science of the mind* (6th ed.). Routledge.
Cavagna, A., Cimarelli, A., Giardina, I., Parisi, G., Santagati, R., Stefanini, F., & Viale, M. (2010). Scale-free correlations in starling flocks. *Proceedings of the National Academy of Sciences, 107*(26), 11865–11870.
Clagett, M. (1999). *Ancient Egyptian science: A source book*. American Philosophical Society.
Colander, D., Föllmer, H., Haas, A., Goldberg, M., Juselius, K., Kirman, A., Lux, T., & Sloth, B. (2009). The financial crisis and the systemic failure of academic economics. *Critical Review, 21*(2–3), 249–267.
Colander, D., Holt, R. P. F., & Rosser, J. B. (2004). The changing face of mainstream economics. *Review of Political Economy, 16*(4), 485–499.
Cole, S. (2001). *What's wrong with sociology?* Transaction Publishers.
Collins, R. (1979). *The credential society: An historical sociology of education and stratification*. Academic Press.
Collins, R. (1994). *Four sociological traditions*. Oxford University Press.
Comte, A. (1830–1842). *Cours de philosophie positive* (Tomes I–VI). Paris: Bachelier.
Comte, A. (1975). *Cours de philosophie positive* (Vols. 1–6). Hermann. (Original work published 1830–1842).
Condorcet, M. J. A. N. de C. (1795). *Esquisse d'un tableau historique des progrès de l'esprit humain*. Paris: Agasse. [English trans. *Sketch for a Historical Picture of the Progress of the Human Mind*].
Condorcet, M. J. A. N. de C. (1970). *Sketch for a historical picture of the progress of the human mind* (J. Barraclough, Trans.). Weidenfeld & Nicolson. (Original work published 1795).

Cook, J., Oreskes, N., Doran, P. T., Anderegg, W. R. L., Verheggen, B., Maibach, E. W., … & Rice, K. (2016). Consensus on consensus: A synthesis of consensus estimates on human-caused global warming. *Environmental Research Letters, 11*(4), 048002. https://doi.org/10.1088/1748-9326/11/4/048002

Cosmides, L., & Tooby, J. (1992). The psychological foundations of culture. In J. H. Barkow, L. Cosmides, & J. Tooby (Eds.), *The adapted mind* (pp. 19–136). Oxford University Press.

Cowie, R., McKeown, G., & Douglas-Cowie, E. (2019). Emotional intelligence and the role of affective computing. *Annual Review of Psychology, 70*, 21–47.

Cuff, R. D. (1993). The body of the conqueror: Fat as a cultural symbol in Western society. *Journal of Social History, 26*(3), 631–648.

Daniell, D. (2003). *The Bible in English: Its history and influence*. Yale University Press.

Davies, C. A. (2008). *Reflexive ethnography: A guide to researching selves and others* (2nd ed.). Routledge.

Davidson, R. J., & McEwen, B. S. (2012). Social influences on neuroplasticity: Stress and interventions to promote well-being. *Nature Neuroscience, 15*(5), 689–695.

Devitt, M. (1984). *Realism and truth*. Princeton University Press.

Dilthey, W. (1906). *Das Erlebnis und die Dichtung*. Teubner.

Dilthey, W. (1910). *Der Aufbau der geschichtlichen Welt in den Geisteswissenschaften*. Teubner.

Dobzhansky, T. (1973). Nothing in biology makes sense except in the light of evolution. *The American Biology Teacher, 35*(3), 125–129.

Dore, R. (1976). *The diploma disease: Education, qualification and development*. University of California Press.

Durkheim, É. (1893). *De la division du travail social*. Félix Alcan.

Durkheim, É. (1895). *Les règles de la méthode sociologique*. Félix Alcan.

Durkheim, É. (1897). *Le suicide: Étude de sociologie*. Félix Alcan.

Dwork, C., & Roth, A. (2014). The algorithmic foundations of differential privacy. *Foundations and Trends in Theoretical Computer Science, 9*(3–4), 211–407.

Elias, N. (2000). *The civilizing process* (E. Jephcott, Trans.). Blackwell. (Original work published 1939).

Emerson, R. M., Fretz, R. I., & Shaw, L. L. (2011). *Writing ethnographic fieldnotes* (2nd ed.). University of Chicago Press.

Epstein, J. M. (2006). *Generative social science: Studies in agent-based computational modeling*. Princeton University Press.

Esteva, A., Robicquet, A., Ramsundar, B., Kuleshov, V., DePristo, M., Chou, K., Cui, C., Corrada, G., Thrun, S., & Dean, J. (2019). A guide to deep learning in healthcare. *Nature Medicine, 25*(1), 24–29. https://doi.org/10.1038/s41591-018-0316-z

Fay, B. (1996). *Contemporary philosophy of social science: A multicultural approach*. Blackwell.

Fitzpatrick, S. (1999). *Everyday Stalinism: Ordinary life in extraordinary times: Soviet Russia in the 1930s*. Oxford University Press.

Fluck, M. (2019). The best there is? Communication, truth, and the limits of post-structuralism. *Review of International Studies, 45*(1), 40–59.

Fourcade, M., Ollion, E., & Algan, Y. (2015). The superiority of economists. *Journal of Economic Perspectives, 29*(1), 89–114.

Fraser Institute. (2024). *Retirement income sustainability and public pensions*. Vancouver, BC. https://www.fraserinstitute.org/studies/retirement-income-sustainability-and-public-pensions

Gangestad, S. W., & Simpson, J. A. (2000). The evolution of human mating: Trade-offs and strategic pluralism. *Behavioral and Brain Sciences, 23*(4), 573–587.

Garin, E. (1988). *Italian humanism: Philosophy and civic life in the Renaissance*. Blackwell.

Geertz, C. (1973). *The interpretation of cultures: Selected essays*. Basic Books.

Ghoshal, S. (2005). Bad management theories are destroying good management practices. *Academy of Management Learning & Education, 4*(1), 75–91.

Gilbert, N., & Troitzsch, K. G. (2005). *Simulation for the social scientist* (2nd ed.). Open University Press.

Ginsberg, B. (2011). *The fall of the faculty: The rise of the all-administrative university and why it matters*. Oxford University Press.

Glenn, E. N. (2008). Yearning for lightness: Transnational circuits in the marketing and consumption of skin lighteners. *Gender & Society, 22*(3), 281–302. https://doi.org/10.1177/0891243208316089

Glimcher, P. W., & Fehr, E. (Eds.). (2013). *Neuroeconomics: Decision making and the brain* (2nd ed.). Academic Press.

Gómez-Pinilla, F. (2008). Brain foods: The effects of nutrients on brain function. *Nature Reviews Neuroscience, 9*(7), 568–578. https://doi.org/10.1038/nrn2421

Goodfellow, I., Bengio, Y., & Courville, A. (2016). *Deep learning*. MIT Press.

Goodin, R. E., & Klingemann, H.-D. (Eds.). (1996). *A new handbook of political science*. Oxford University Press.

Gottfredson, L. S. (1994). Mainstream science on intelligence: An editorial with 52 signatories, history, and bibliography. *Intelligence, 24*(1), 13–23.

Habermas, J. (2003). *The future of human nature*. Polity.

Habermas, J. (1984). *The theory of communicative action, Volume 1: Reason and the rationalization of society* (T. McCarthy, Trans.). Boston: Beacon Press. (Original work published 1981).

Haidt, J. (2012). *The righteous mind: Why good people are divided by politics and religion*. Pantheon Books.

Halffman, W., & Radder, H. (2015). The academic manifesto: From an occupied to a public university. *Minerva, 53*(2), 165–187.

Hammersley, M., & Atkinson, P. (2007). *Ethnography: Principles in practice* (3rd ed.). Routledge.

Harding, S. (1998). *Is science multicultural? Postcolonialisms, feminisms, and epistemologies*. Indiana University Press.

Hedström, P., & Udéhn, L. (2009). Analytical sociology and theories of the middle range. In P. Hedström & P. Bearman (Eds.), *The Oxford handbook of analytical sociology* (pp. 25–47). Oxford University Press.

Henrich, J. (2015). *The secret of our success: How culture is driving human evolution, domesticating our species, and making us smarter*. Princeton University Press.

Hillman, C. H., Erickson, K. I., & Kramer, A. F. (2008). Be smart, exercise your heart: Exercise effects on brain and cognition. *Nature Reviews Neuroscience, 9*(1), 58–65. https://doi.org/10.1038/nrn2298

Hodgson, G. M., & Knudsen, T. (2010). *Darwin's conjecture: The search for general principles of social and economic evolution.* University of Chicago Press.

Hollander, P. (1981). *Political pilgrims: Travels of Western intellectuals to the Soviet Union, China, and Cuba, 1928–1978.* Oxford University Press.

Hossenfelder, S. (2025). *More is different: Notes from a curious mind*. Basic Books.

Horkheimer, M. (1972). *Critical theory: Selected essays.* Continuum.

Hume, D. (2000). *A treatise of human nature. Oxford University Press.* (Original work published 1739).

Jasanoff, S. (2005). *Designs on nature: Science and democracy in Europe and the United States.* Princeton University Press.

Jerath, R., Edry, J. W., Barnes, V. A., & Jerath, V. (2006). Physiology of long pranayamic breathing: Neural respiratory elements may provide a mechanism that explains how slow deep breathing shifts the autonomic nervous system. *Medical Hypotheses, 67*(3), 566–571. https://doi.org/10.1016/j.mehy.2006.02.042

Judge, T. A., & Cable, D. M. (2004). The effect of physical height on workplace success and income. *Journal of Applied Psychology, 89*(3), 428–441.

Kahneman, D. (2011). *Thinking, fast and slow*. Farrar, Straus and Giroux.

Kevles, D. J. (1985). *In the name of eugenics: Genetics and the uses of human heredity.* Knopf.

Kolb, B., & Whishaw, I. Q. (2009). *Fundamentals of human neuropsychology* (6th ed.). Worth Publishers.

Kosinski, M., Stillwell, D., & Graepel, T. (2013). Private traits and attributes are predictable from digital records of human behavior. *Proceedings of the National Academy of Sciences, 110*(15), 5802–5805.

Kristeller, P. O. (1961). *Renaissance thought: The classic, scholastic, and humanistic strains*. Harper & Row.

Kuhn, T. S. (2012). *The structure of scientific revolutions* (4th ed.). University of Chicago Press. (Original work published 1962).

Kunda, Z. (1990). The case for motivated reasoning. *Psychological Bulletin, 108*(3), 480–498.

Lacy, M. (2017). *The American technocracy: The rise of the managerial elite*. Princeton University Press.

Lakatos, I. (1970). Falsification and the methodology of scientific research programmes. In I. Lakatos & A. Musgrave (Eds.), *Criticism and the growth of knowledge* (pp. 91–196). Cambridge University Press.

Laland, K. N., & Brown, G. R. (2011). *Sense and nonsense: Evolutionary perspectives on human behaviour* (2nd ed.). Oxford University Press.
Laland, K. N., Odling-Smee, J., & Myles, S. (2010). How culture shaped the human genome. *Nature Reviews Genetics, 11*(2), 137–148.
Latour, B. (2005). *Reassembling the social: An introduction to actor-network-theory*. Oxford University Press.
Leroi, A. M. (2014). *The lagoon: How Aristotle invented science*. Bloomsbury.
Libet, B. (1985). Unconscious cerebral initiative and the role of conscious will. *Behavioral and Brain Sciences, 8*(4), 529–566.
Lindzen, R. S. (2009). Climate science: Is it currently designed to answer questions? *Energy & Environment, 20*(1–2), 33–43.
Lucas, G. M., Gratch, J., King, A., & Morency, L. P. (2014). It's only a computer: Virtual humans increase willingness to disclose. *Computers in Human Behavior, 37*, 94–100.
Lukianoff, G., & Haidt, J. (2018). *The coddling of the American mind*. Penguin Press.
Maslow, A. H. (1966). *The psychology of science: A reconnaissance*. Harper & Row.
McEwen, B. S. (1998). Protective and damaging effects of stress mediators. *New England Journal of Medicine, 338*(3), 171–179. https://doi.org/10.1056/NEJM199801153380307
Meehl, P. E. (1990). Why summaries of research on psychological theories are often uninterpretable. *Psychological Reports, 66*(1), 195–244. https://doi.org/10.2466/pr0.1990.66.1.195
Merton, R. K. (1942). A note on science and democracy. *Journal of Legal and Political Sociology, 1*, 115–126.
Milgram, S. (1974). *Obedience to authority: An experimental view*. Harper & Row.
Mills, C. W. (1959). *The sociological imagination*. Oxford University Press.
Mirowski, P. (1989). *More heat than light: Economics as social physics, physics as nature's economics*. Cambridge University Press.
Mirowski, P. (2011). *Science-mart: Privatizing American science*. Harvard University Press.
Nickerson, R. S. (1998). Confirmation bias. *Review of General Psychology, 2*(2), 175–220.
Nietzsche, F. (1887). *Zur Genealogie der Moral*. C. G. Naumann.
Nietzsche, F. (2006). *On the genealogy of morals* (K. Ansell-Pearson, Ed.; C. Diethe, Trans.). Cambridge University Press.
Nisbett, R. E., & Wilson, T. D. (1977). Telling more than we can know. *Psychological Review, 84*(3), 231–259.
Norris, C. (1990). *What's wrong with postmodernism*. Johns Hopkins University Press.
Nosek, B. A., Spies, J. R., & Motyl, M. (2012). Scientific utopia II. *Perspectives on Psychological Science, 7*(6), 615–631.
Nussbaum, M. C. (2011). *Creating capabilities: The human development approach*. Harvard University Press.

Open Science Collaboration. (2015). Estimating the reproducibility of psychological science. *Science, 349*(6251), aac4716.

Oreskes, N. (2004). The scientific consensus on climate change. *Science, 306*(5702), 1686.

Pelikan, J. (2005). *Whose Bible is it? A history of the scriptures through the ages.* Viking.

Pfeffer, J., & Fong, C. T. (2004). The business school "business". *Journal of Management Studies, 41*(8), 1501–1520.

Pinker, S. (1994). *The language instinct: How the mind creates language.* William Morrow.

Pinker, S. (2002). *The blank slate.* Viking.

Popper, K. (1957). *The poverty of historicism.* Routledge & Kegan Paul.

Popper, K. (1959). *The logic of scientific discovery.* Hutchinson.

Porter, T. M. (1995). *Trust in numbers: The pursuit of objectivity in science and public life.* Princeton University Press.

Rahman, M. M., Bhuiyan, M. Z. A., & Wu, J. (2020). Towards personalized health systems using big data analytics. *Information Fusion, 54*, 26–44. https://doi.org/10.1016/j.inffus.2019.07.002

Rochberg, F. (2004). *The heavenly writing.* Cambridge University Press.

Ruccio, D. F. (2006). *Development and globalization.* Routledge.

Rumsfeld, J. S., Joynt, K. E., & Maddox, T. M. (2016). Big data analytics to improve cardiovascular care: Promise and challenges. *Nature Reviews Cardiology, 13*(6), 350–359. https://doi.org/10.1038/nrcardio.2016.42

Russell, B. (1912). *The problems of philosophy.* Williams and Norgate.

Sapolsky, R. M. (2004). *Why zebras don't get ulcers* (3rd ed.). Henry Holt.

Sarewitz, D. (2016). Saving science. *The New Atlantis, 49*, 4–40.

Schelling, T. C. (1971). Dynamic models of segregation. *Journal of Mathematical Sociology, 1*(2), 143–186.

Schuetzler, R. M., Giboney, J. S., Grimes, G. M., & Nunamaker, J. F., Jr. (2018). The influence of conversational agents on socially desirable responding. *Computers in Human Behavior, 98*, 28–38.

Searle, J. R. (1995). *The construction of social reality.* Free Press.

Sen, A. (1977). Rational fools. *Philosophy & Public Affairs, 6*(4), 317–344.

Sieber, J. E., & Tolich, M. B. (2013). *Planning ethically responsible research.* Sage.

Simmel, G. (1900). *Philosophie des Geldes.* Duncker & Humblot.

Simmel, G. (1908). *Soziologie: Untersuchungen über die Formen der Vergesellschaftung.* Duncker & Humblot.

Skidelsky, R. (1992). *John Maynard Keynes: The economist as saviour 1920–1937.* Macmillan.

Skinner, B. F. (1938). *The behavior of organisms.* Appleton-Century.

Sokal, A., & Bricmont, J. (1998). *Fashionable nonsense: Postmodern intellectuals' abuse of science.* Picador.

Soon, C. S., Brass, M., Heinze, H.-J., & Haynes, J.-D. (2008). Unconscious determinants of free decisions. *Nature Neuroscience, 11*(5), 543–545.

Sowell, T. (2010). *Intellectuals and society.* Basic Books.

Stearns, P. N. (1997). *Fat history: Bodies and beauty in the modern West*. New York University Press.

Steele, J. M. (2008). *A brief introduction to astronomy in the Middle East*. Saqi Books.

Stinchcombe, A. L. (1987). *Constructing social theories*. University of Chicago Press.

Swedberg, R. (2012). Theorizing in sociology and social science: Turning to the context of discovery. *Theory and Society, 41*(1), 1–40. https://doi.org/10.1007/s11186-011-9161-5

Söilen, K. S. (2025). *Applied evolutionary economics: Insights from biology for real-world management*. Springer.

Symons, D. (1979). *The evolution of human sexuality*. Oxford University Press.

Taleb, N. N. (2007). *The black swan: The impact of the highly improbable*. Random House.

Taleb, N. N. (2012). *Antifragile*. Random House.

Thaler, R. H., & Sunstein, C. R. (2008). *Nudge*. Yale University Press.

Thornhill, R., & Gangestad, S. W. (2008). *The evolutionary biology of human female sexuality*. Oxford University Press.

Tooby, J., & Cosmides, L. (1992). The psychological foundations of culture. In J. H. Barkow et al. (Eds.), *The adapted mind* (pp. 19–136). Oxford University Press.

Topol, E. J. (2019). High-performance medicine: The convergence of human and artificial intelligence. *Nature Medicine, 25*(1), 44–56. https://doi.org/10.1038/s41591-018-0300-7

Tourangeau, R., & Yan, T. (2007). Sensitive questions in surveys. *Psychological Bulletin, 133*(5), 859–883.

Trow, M. (2007). Reflections on higher education expansion. In J. J. F. Forest & P. G. Altbach (Eds.), *International handbook of higher education* (pp. 243–280). Springer.

Turner, J. H. (2007). *The structure of sociological theory* (7th ed.). Wadsworth.

Turner, J. H. (1990). *The misuses of theory*. Sage.

Wack, P. (1985). Scenarios: Uncharted waters ahead. *Harvard Business Review, 63*(5), 73–89.

Walker, M. (2009). The role of sleep in cognition and emotion. *Annals of the New York Academy of Sciences, 1156*, 168–197.

Watson, J. B. (1913). Psychology as the behaviorist views it. *Psychological Review, 20*(2), 158–177.

Weber, M. (1904–1905). *Die protestantische Ethik und der Geist des Kapitalismus*. Mohr.

Weber, M. (1922). *Wirtschaft und Gesellschaft*. Mohr.

Wiener, N. (1948). *Cybernetics: Or control and communication in the animal and the machine*. MIT Press.

Wilkinson, A., & Kupers, R. (2013). Living in the futures. *Harvard Business Review, 91*(5), 119–127.

Wilson, D. S. (2015). *Does altruism exist? Culture, genes, and the welfare of others*. Yale University Press.

Wilson, D. S. (2019). This view of life. Pantheon Books.
Windelband, W. (1888). *Einleitung in die Philosophie*. Mohr.
Windelband, W. (1900). *Geschichte der Philosophie*. Mohr.
Yang, Q., Liu, Y., Chen, T., & Tong, Y. (2019). Federated machine learning: Concept and applications. *ACM Transactions on Intelligent Systems and Technology, 10*(2), 1–19.

Further Reading

Abid, A., Farooqi, M., & Zou, J. (2021). *Persistent anti-Muslim bias in large language models*. arXiv preprint arXiv:2101.05783
Adolphs, R. (2009). The social brain: Neural basis of social knowledge. *Annual Review of Psychology, 60*, 693–716. https://doi.org/10.1146/annurev.psych.60.110707.163514
Apple, W., Streeter, L. A., & Krauss, R. M. (1979). Effects of pitch and speech rate on personal attributions. *Journal of Personality and Social Psychology, 37*(5), 715–727.
Aristotle. (1984). *The complete works of Aristotle* (J. Barnes, Ed.). Princeton University Press.
Aristotle. (2001). *Historia Animalium* (A. L. Peck, Ed. & Trans.). Harvard University Press. (Original work published 1965).
Baumeister, R. F., & Tierney, J. (2011). *Willpower: Rediscovering the greatest human strength*. Penguin.
Binns, R. (2018). Fairness in machine learning: Lessons from political philosophy. In *Proceedings of the 2018 Conference on Fairness, Accountability and Transparency*.
Burrell, J. (2016). How the machine 'thinks': Understanding opacity in machine learning algorithms. *Big Data & Society, 3*(1), https://doi.org/10.1177/2053951715622512
Cannon, K. (2015). The social perception of bodily coordination. *Body & Society, 21*(4), 57–82.
Carney, D. R., Cuddy, A. J. C., & Yap, A. J. (2010). Power posing: Brief nonverbal displays affect neuroendocrine levels and risk tolerance. *Psychological Science, 21*(10), 1363–1368. https://doi.org/10.1177/0956797610383437
Case, A., & Paxson, C. (2008). Stature and status: Height, ability, and labor market outcomes. *Journal of Political Economy, 116*(3), 499–532. https://doi.org/10.1086/589524
Comte, A. (1974). *The positive philosophy of Auguste Comte* (H. Martineau, Trans.). AMS Press. (Original work published 1830–1842).
Confucius. (ca. 500 BCE). *Lunyu (論語)*.
Confucius. (1998). *The analects of confucius* (R. Dawson, Trans.). Oxford University Press.
Confucius. (2003). *Analects* (E. Slingerland, Trans.). Hackett Publishing.

Crawford, K. (2021). *Atlas of AI: Power, politics, and the planetary costs of artificial intelligence*. Yale University Press.
Dilthey, W. (1883). *Einleitung in die Geisteswissenschaften*. Duncker & Humblot.
Dilthey, W. (1985). *Poetry and Experience* (R. A. Makkreel & F. Rodi, Eds. & Trans.). Princeton: Princeton University Press. (Original work published 1906).
Dilthey, W. (1989). *Introduction to the Human Sciences* (R. A. Makkreel & F. Rodi, Eds. & Trans.). Princeton University Press. (Original work published 1883).
Dilthey, W. (2002). *The formation of the historical world in the human sciences* (R. A. Makkreel & F. Rodi, Eds. & Trans.). Princeton University Press. (Original work published 1910).
Duckworth, A. L., Gendler, T. S., & Gross, J. J. (2016). Situational strategies for self-control. *Perspectives on Psychological Science, 11*(1), 35–55.
Durkheim, É. (1912). *Les formes élémentaires de la vie religieuse: Le système totémique en Australie*. Alcan.
Durkheim, É. (1995). *The elementary forms of religious life* (K. E. Fields, Trans.). Free Press. (Original work published 1912).
Eberhardt, J. L., Davies, P. G., Purdie-Vaughns, V. J., & Johnson, S. L. (2006). Looking deathworthy: Perceived stereotypicality of Black defendants predicts capital-sentencing outcomes. *Psychological Science, 17*(5), 383–386. https://doi.org/10.1111/j.1467-9280.2006.01716.x
Ekman, P. (2003). *Emotions revealed: Recognizing faces and feelings to improve communication and emotional life*. Times Books.
Ekman, P., & Friesen, W. V. (1975). *Unmasking the face: A guide to recognizing emotions from facial clues*. Prentice Hall.
Floridi, L. (2023). *The ethics of artificial intelligence*. Oxford University Press.
Frederick, D. A., & Haselton, M. G. (2007). Why is muscularity sexy? Tests of the fitness indicator hypothesis. *Personality and Social Psychology Bulletin, 33*(8), 1167–1183. https://doi.org/10.1177/0146167207303022
Harris, S. (2012). *Free will*. Free Press.
Herodotus. (ca. 430 BCE). *Ἱστορίαι (Histories)*.
Herodotus. (2003). *The histories* (R. Waterfield, Trans.). Oxford University Press.
Herodotus. (2007). *The histories* (R. Waterfield, Trans.). Oxford University Press.
IJzerman, H., Gallucci, M., Pouw, W. T. J. L., Weeghel, I. V., Pollet, T. V., & Tops, M. (2018). Cold-blooded loneliness: Social exclusion leads to lower skin temperatures. *Acta Psychologica, 185*, 1–9. https://doi.org/10.1016/j.actpsy.2018.01.008
Janis, I. L. (1972). *Victims of groupthink: A psychological study of foreign-policy decisions and fiascoes*. Houghton Mifflin.
Jaynes, J. (1976). *The origin of consciousness in the breakdown of the bicameral mind*. Houghton Mifflin.
Junger, S. (2016). *Tribe: On homecoming and belonging*. Twelve.
Kahneman, D., & Tversky, A. (1979). Prospect theory: An analysis of decision under risk. *Econometrica, 47*(2), 263–291. https://doi.org/10.2307/1914185

Kessler, R. C., Berglund, P., Demler, O., Jin, R., Merikangas, K. R., & Walters, E. E. (2005). Lifetime prevalence and age-of-onset distributions of DSM-IV disorders in the National Comorbidity Survey Replication. *Archives of General Psychiatry, 62*(6), 593–602. https://doi.org/10.1001/archpsyc.62.6.593

Lau, D. C. (Trans.). (1998). *The Analects* (Confucius). Penguin Classics.

Lau, D. C. (Trans.). (2003). *Mencius* (Mencius). Penguin Classics.

LeDoux, J. (1996). *The emotional brain: The mysterious underpinnings of emotional life*. Simon & Schuster.

Lorenz, K. (1966). *On aggression*. Harcourt.

Lukács, G. (1923). *History and class consciousness: Studies in Marxist dialectics* (R. Livingstone, Trans., 1971). MIT Press.

Macy Foundation. (1946–1953). *Transactions of the Macy Conferences on Cybernetics*. Josiah Macy, Jr. Foundation.

Marcus, G. E., & Fischer, M. M. J. (1999). *Anthropology as cultural critique: An experimental moment in the human sciences* (2nd ed.). University of Chicago Press.

Mencius. (2003). *Mencius* (D. C. Lau, Trans.). Penguin.

Merton, R. K. (1973). *The sociology of science: Theoretical and empirical investigations*. University of Chicago Press.

Putnam, R. D. (2000). *Bowling alone: The collapse and revival of American community*. Simon & Schuster.

Richerson, P. J., & Boyd, R. (2005). *Not by genes alone: How culture transformed human evolution*. University of Chicago Press.

Rosa, H. (2013). *Social acceleration: A new theory of modernity* (J. Trejo-Mathys, Trans.). Columbia University Press.

Scheler, M. (1913/2008). *The nature of sympathy* (P. Heath, Trans.). Transaction Publishers.

Simmel, G. (1978). *The philosophy of money* (T. Bottomore & D. Frisby, Trans., D. Frisby, Ed.). Routledge.

Simmel, G. (2009). *Sociology: Inquiries into the construction of social forms* (A. J. Blasi, A. K. Jacobs, & M. Kanjirath, Eds. & Trans.). Brill.

Simonsohn, U., Nelson, L. D., & Simmons, J. P. (2014). P-curve: A key to the file-drawer. *Journal of Experimental Psychology: General, 143*(2), 534–547. https://doi.org/10.1037/a0033242

Stanovich, K. E., & West, R. F. (2000). Individual differences in reasoning: Implications for the rationality debate? *Behavioral and Brain Sciences, 23*(5), 645–665. https://doi.org/10.1017/S0140525X00003435

Tajfel, H., & Turner, J. C. (1986). The social identity theory of intergroup behavior. In S. Worchel & W. G. Austin (Eds.), *Psychology of intergroup relations* (pp. 7–24). Nelson-Hall.

Thucydides. (ca. 400 BCE). *Ἱστορία τοῦ Πελοποννησιακοῦ Πολέμου*.

Thucydides. (1996). *History of the Peloponnesian War* (R. Warner, Trans.). Penguin Classics.

Thucydides. (2008). *The Peloponnesian War* (M. Hammond, Trans.). Oxford University Press.

Trivers, R. (2011). *The folly of fools: The logic of deceit and self-deception in human life*. Basic Books.

Tversky, A., & Kahneman, D. (1974). Judgment under uncertainty: Heuristics and biases. *Science, 185*(4157), 1124–1131. https://doi.org/10.1126/science.185.4157.1124

van Vugt, M., Hogan, R., & Kaiser, R. B. (2008). Leadership, followership, and evolution: Some lessons from the past. *American Psychologist, 63*(3), 182–196. https://doi.org/10.1037/0003-066X.63.3.182

Weber, M. (1978). *Economy and society: An outline of interpretive sociology* (G. Roth & C. Wittich, Eds., E. Fischoff et al., Trans.). University of California Press. (Original work published 1922).

Wilson, T. D., & Gilbert, D. T. (2005). Affective forecasting: Knowing what to want. *Current Directions in Psychological Science, 14*(3), 131–134. https://doi.org/10.1111/j.0963-7214.2005.00355.x

Windelband, W. (1893). *Einleitung in die Philosophie*. Mohr Siebeck.

Windelband, W. (1894). *Geschichte und Naturwissenschaft*. Heitz.

Windelband, W. (1980). History and natural science (G. Oakes, Trans.). In P. Gardiner (Ed.), *The philosophy of history* (pp. 43–54). Oxford University Press. (Original work published 1894).

Windelband, W. (1901). *History of philosophy* (H. E. Cushman, Trans.). Macmillan.

Xunzi (ca. 3rd c. BCE). *Xunzi (荀子)*.

Xunzi. (1999). *Basic Writings* (B. Watson, Trans.). Columbia University Press.

Young, T. J., & French, L. A. (1996). Height and perceived competence of U.S. presidents. *Perceptual and Motor Skills, 82*(3), 1002.

Zebrowitz, L. A., & Montepare, J. M. (2008). Social psychological face perception: Why appearance matters. *Social and Personality Psychology Compass, 2*(3), 1497–1517. https://doi.org/10.1111/j.1751-9004.2008.00109.x

Zuboff, S. (2019). *The age of surveillance capitalism: The fight for a human future at the new frontier of power*. Public Affairs.

7

AI and Scholarly Evolution

Abstract Artificial intelligence is no longer just a tool of academic work—it is becoming a collaborator. This chapter examines how AI is reshaping scholarship itself, from writing and research workflows to authorship, accountability, and the very identity of the scholar. Drawing on concrete cases of human–AI co-production, the chapter shows how traditional boundaries between author, assistant, and editor are breaking down. It introduces practical frameworks for distinguishing human contribution from machine support, addressing disclosure, responsibility, and the ethics of hybrid authorship. While AI dramatically increases speed and efficiency, the chapter warns that uncritical reliance risks flattening judgment, originality, and intellectual depth. Looking ahead, this chapter explores how universities and research institutions must adapt as machines begin to simulate entire research teams. The future of scholarship, it argues, will depend not on resisting AI, but on designing clear standards, transparent norms, and institutional roles that preserve human judgment and scientific integrity in an age of machine co-production.

This chapter explores how artificial intelligence is transforming academic work—not only by enhancing writing and research efficiency but by challenging core assumptions about authorship, scholarly identity, and institutional roles. The chapter is structured around five main sections, each highlighting a dimension of this evolving relationship:

K. Solberg Söilen, *The Researcher's Journey in the Age of AI*,
https://doi.org/10.1007/978-3-032-23069-0_7

1. Writing with Machines
   AI has evolved from a passive tool to an active writing partner, capable of co-drafting, summarizing, and restructuring complex manuscripts. Drawing on real examples from five projects, the chapter traces how AI changes not just the process of writing but the roles of those involved. A framework for distinguishing authorship from prompting is introduced, including a quantitative model for evaluating human contribution.
   Key insight: Traditional boundaries between author and assistant are blurring. Hybrid authorship models require clearer definitions and ethical frameworks.
2. Scholarly Workflows and Efficiency
   AI improves speed and productivity across many tasks: outlining, editing, translation, example generation, and even literature review. However, this acceleration comes with trade-offs—especially in terms of attention, depth, and over-reliance on machine outputs.
   Key insight: Scholars must strike a balance between speed and substance. AI is a powerful support system, but not a substitute for deep disciplinary knowledge.
3. Accountability and Disclosure
   With AI now integrated into core academic activities, the need for transparency is urgent. The chapter outlines frameworks to classify different types of human-AI co-production, stressing the importance of disclosing the extent and type of AI involvement.
   Key insight: Academic credibility depends on clearly articulating the author's role. Without disclosure, trust in scholarly outputs weakens.
4. The Changing Identity of the Scholar
   The traditional scholar—as sole author, originator of ideas, and authority figure—is giving way to new roles: editor, evaluator, and prompt engineer. The chapter argues that these shifts must be met with new professional norms and educational expectations.
   Key insight: As machines take over cognitive and compositional tasks, human scholars must adapt by emphasizing judgment, value alignment, and institutional responsibility.
5. Future Scenarios and Institutional Implications
   Looking ahead, the chapter explores what happens when AI becomes capable of simulating entire research teams. This includes rethinking university infrastructure, academic labor divisions, and the definition of merit. A simple "knowledge stagnation equation" illustrates how over-reliance on AI could suppress novelty, spreading existing knowledge more widely but generating less that is truly new.

Key insight: Institutions must redesign their roles, values, and reward systems if they are to remain credible and competitive in the age of hybrid scholarship.

This chapter argues that we are crossing a threshold: academic knowledge is no longer exclusively human-made. While this opens up opportunities for unprecedented productivity and collaboration, it also raises serious ethical and conceptual challenges. What counts as authorship, originality, or scholarly integrity when machines co-produce knowledge?

The future of scholarship will involve humans and machines working in tandem—but the standards, definitions, and values that guide this collaboration must be designed by scholars themselves. The chapter concludes with a call for institutional courage, epistemic humility, and transparent norms that can guide academic work through this transition—while also pointing ahead to the ethical questions that form the focus of Chap. 8.

7.1 Navigating the Terrain: What Do We Mean by "AI"?

To navigate this new terrain responsibly, we need to be clear about what we mean when we talk about "*AI*." The term is often used too loosely, conflating tools with vastly different capabilities.

In everyday language, "AI" can mean anything from a spam filter in your inbox to a speculative vision of machines surpassing human intelligence. Such imprecision makes it difficult to debate the opportunities and risks. Before we can evaluate AI's role in reshaping science, scholarship, and society, we need a shared vocabulary (Floridi & Chiriatti, 2020).

The following table outlines the major categories of AI technology and their current or projected levels of intelligence. It distinguishes between practical tools already embedded in daily life, research frontiers under active development, and more speculative concepts drawn from philosophy and futurism (Bostrom, 2014; Russell & Norvig, 2021) (Table 7.1).

Understanding these distinctions is more than a matter of semantics. Without clear categories, discussions about "AI" risk becoming confused—celebrating achievements that belong to one level of technology while fearing dangers that belong to another. When someone says "AI is already creative," they may mean generative tools like ChatGPT or DALL·E, which mimic creativity without consciousness (Koch & Tononi, 2013). When someone warns of "AI taking over," they often invoke artificial general intelligence

Table 7.1 Key terms and levels of artificial intelligence

Term	Definition	Example	Level of Intelligence
Artificial Intelligence (AI)	A broad field of computer science focused on creating systems that perform tasks requiring human-like intelligence	Spam filters, facial recognition, recommendation systems	Narrow/ Task-specific
Machine Learning (ML)	A subfield of AI where algorithms learn patterns from data and improve performance without explicit programming	Fraud detection, image classification, predictive analytics	Narrow/Adaptive
Large Language Models (LLMs)	A class of machine learning models trained on vast text data to understand and generate human-like language	ChatGPT, Claude, Gemini, LLaMA	Narrow, text-based
Generative AI	AI that creates new content—text, images, audio, or video—based on learned patterns	DALL·E (images), GPT (text), Suno (music)	Creative but non-conscious
Foundation Models	Large-scale pre-trained models that serve as general-purpose building blocks for a wide range of tasks	GPT-4, PaLM, Claude, Mistral	Broadly adaptable (but still narrow)

(continued)

Table 7.1 (continued)

Term	Definition	Example	Level of Intelligence
Multi-modal AI	Models that integrate and process multiple forms of input (text, image, audio, video) to perform tasks	GPT-4o (text + vision+ audio), Gemini	Narrow, cross-domain
Edge AI	AI systems deployed directly on local devices (phones, IoT, sensors) rather than centralized cloud servers	Apple's on-device Siri, Tesla's autopilot chip	Narrow, optimized for speed/privacy
Agentic AI	AI systems capable of taking actions toward goals autonomously, not just producing outputs. They can plan, execute, and interact with environments	AutoGPT, Devin AI (autonomous coding assistant)	Narrow→ moving toward adaptive autonomy
Artificial General Intelligence (AGI)	A theoretical AI with the ability to understand, learn, and reason across domains at a human level	No current example exists	General-purpose (human level)

(continued)

Table 7.1 (continued)

Term	Definition	Example	Level of Intelligence
Superintelligence	A hypothetical future AI that vastly surpasses human intelligence across all domains	Futurist scenarios in Bostrom, Yudkowsky	Beyond human intelligence
The Singularity	A projected point where AI self-improvement accelerates beyond human control, leading to radical societal transformation	Conceptual idea—no current example	Conceptual/ Systemic threshold

(AGI) or superintelligence, neither of which exist today (Bostrom, 2014). And when universities or governments plan around "AI in society," they may conflate all of these at once, producing either undue optimism or misplaced fear (Cave & Dignum, 2019).

This layered vocabulary—though fairly basic and non-technical, which suits my technical competencies in his field better—helps keep the discussion grounded. It reminds us that the AI we currently interact with—recommendation systems, language models, predictive analytics—remains narrow in scope, even if it feels broad in cultural impact (Brynjolfsson & McAfee, 2017). At the same time, it keeps open the possibility that more advanced forms, from AGI to superintelligence, may eventually arrive, bringing with them new challenges of governance, ethics, and meaning (Tegmark, 2017).

Let me be clear: I have no idea which of these scenarios will materialize, and especially not when. But neither, it seems, do many of the technical experts. What is striking is that much of what could have happened has unfolded far faster than expected, and I now see continuous, almost weekly improvements in the AI models I use. Most recently, for example, I learned how to use Suno to create music—complete with lyrics, vocals, and ensembles of instruments of my own choosing—in a matter of minutes, something even experts considered unlikely at the start of 2025.

Having set these conceptual boundaries, we can now turn to the concrete question: what can AI already do for the social sciences? While speculation about superintelligence may dominate the headlines, the real revolution is happening here and now—in how AI helps scholars, students, and policymakers overcome the very limitations that have long constrained human inquiry.

The broader question, however, is: how good is AI at science itself? The answer depends very much on the kind of science we have in mind. In a recent review, physicist Sabine Hossenfelder (2025a) tested several leading large language models—GPT-5, Gemini Deepthink, Grok 4, and Claude Opus—on problems in theoretical physics. Her verdict was sobering: these systems often confused basic concepts, produced word-salad explanations, told users what they wanted to hear, and when pressed admitted they had simply fabricated answers. When confronted with versions of unsolved "Millennium Problems," the models generated no new insights, only rephrasings of existing knowledge. At the frontier of the hardest scientific questions, AI remains a poor substitute for human creativity.

This is consistent with a growing body of research. Large language models are powerful pattern recognizers, but they are not engines of conceptual breakthrough (Bender & Koller, 2020; Marcus, 2022). They excel at recombining and repackaging known information, but they lack the deep mechanistic understanding required for progress in mathematics or physics (Bommasani et al., 2022). Studies confirm that while AI can assist with hypothesis generation, it struggles with abstraction, novelty, and the creative leaps that often mark genuine scientific discovery (Smaldino, 2023; Trew, 2023).

Yet this does not mean AI is doing poorly as a scientist. Where it tends to perform better is in domains that involve structured reasoning, clear data, and well-defined methods. This includes much of the social sciences. Problems here may be complex, but they are often solvable through established procedures: framing clear research questions, designing sound methods, conducting statistical analyses, and interpreting results carefully. These are precisely the kinds of tasks where AI has already shown substantial competence (Evans & Rzhetsky, 2011; Gil et al., 2014). Literature reviews, data cleaning, regression analysis, and pattern detection in large datasets are areas where AI offers speed, consistency, and scale beyond what many researchers can achieve alone.

This means that when we ask "How good is AI at science?", there is not one answer but two. In fields like theoretical physics—where the problems require deep conceptual breakthroughs—AI is still poor. But in much of the social sciences—where rigor, clarity, and method matter more than radical novelty—AI already performs at or above the level of many human researchers. This dual picture carries both opportunity and risk: social scientists may be among the first to face displacement by AI, but they are also positioned to benefit the most from its assistance.

It should also be said that these boundaries are shifting rapidly. Large language models are improving almost daily, with expanded context windows and better long-range coherence (OpenAI, 2023). As a result, users must constantly recalibrate what AI can and cannot do. To use it effectively, we must stay informed, experiment continually, and never fully outsource our judgment (Marcus, 2022).

The following table illustrates how AI can already transform and strengthen the social sciences across a wide range of tasks, from reducing bias and error to enhancing translation, synthesis, and foresight (Table 7.2).

So, it becomes easy to see why AI represents a quantum leap for the social sciences—and how the role of the researcher will inevitably change. What is important to remember here is that society, in the end, does not care who performs the science—only that it is done rigorously, transparently, and well. In this regard, AI clearly holds certain advantages over humans: it does not forget, it does not tire, and it can be trained to apply consistent standards across vast bodies of knowledge (Kahneman et al., 2021). The days of endless debates over fringe intellectual topics, or of spending long hours hammering out marketing plans and working schedules, are quickly coming to an end. These tasks can now be completed by AI in minutes, even seconds. Outsiders—whether policymakers, business leaders, or the general public—will soon take this capacity for granted and assume everyone has access to it. As a result, they will no longer be impressed by the effort behind the process but will look instead to the outcomes. The new question will not be "what did you discuss?" but rather, "what problems did you solve?".

And if AI takes over many of the technical and repetitive burdens of scholarship, the identity of the social scientist necessarily shifts. No longer the sole discoverer painstakingly piecing together fragments of evidence, the researcher becomes an interpreter, curator, and steward of meaning increasingly (Shapin, 2010). Machines may gather, classify, and even draft at remarkable speed, but it is still humans who must decide which questions are worth asking, how findings should be situated in cultural and historical context, and what values should guide their application (Jasanoff, 2016). In this sense, AI does not replace the social sciences—it redefines the vocation of the scholar within them.

This redefinition also underscores a deeper truth: science is not merely a mechanical process of data collection and inference. It is a cultural practice, rooted in norms, traditions, and values that machines cannot themselves

Table 7.2 How AI can transform and strengthen the social sciences

Problem or limitation in social science	How AI can solve or improve it
Fragmentation of knowledge across journals and disciplines	AI can remember and analyze the full content of all journals across disciplines, ensuring cumulative science and avoiding redundancy
Limited human memory and search capacity	AI recalls all past studies in a field instantly and can trace how each new study builds on previous work
Bias in peer review	AI can be trained to apply consistent standards based on best practices in scientific reasoning, statistical rigor, and epistemology
Statistical errors in submitted work	AI can recalculate all statistics in submitted papers during peer review, flagging inconsistencies or incorrect models
Language barriers in global research	AI can translate all articles into all major languages with high accuracy, promoting global knowledge sharing
Lack of policy relevance	AI can generate simplified, decision-maker–friendly versions of complex research articles, tailored for non-expert audiences
Inability to analyze large or multilingual datasets	AI enables large-scale text, image, and speech analysis across languages, cultures, and media formats, even with limited resources
Overselling or overinterpreting findings	AI can automatically check whether conclusions are supported by the data, discouraging hype and promoting intellectual humility
Slow and narrow literature reviews	AI can produce comprehensive, up-to-date, and thematically structured literature reviews in seconds, including minority or emerging views
Repetitive or redundant studies	AI can detect whether a study is genuinely novel or merely replicates earlier work, encouraging originality and reducing waste

(continued)

Table 7.2 (continued)

Problem or limitation in social science	How AI can solve or improve it
Difficulty linking qualitative and quantitative findings	AI can assist in mixed-methods integration by coding qualitative data and mapping it to quantitative trends
Lack of scenario testing for decision-making	AI can simulate social scenarios with multiple outcomes and probability estimates, offering evidence-based foresight for policy and strategy

generate (Merton, 1942/1973). The rigor and transparency that society demands are not ends in themselves, but means of cultivating trust. If research is to retain legitimacy in an age of machine-assisted analysis, scholars must defend not just accuracy, but also fairness, humility, and responsibility in interpretation (Oreskes, 2019). AI can strengthen the technical scaffolding of knowledge, but it cannot determine which scaffolds are worth building.

Thus, the challenge for the coming decades is not whether AI will "do" science—it already performs many aspects of it more efficiently than humans—but how humans will preserve what is most essential about the scientific enterprise. Reflection, contextualization, and judgment remain uniquely human contributions. Without them, the risk is not that science will halt, but that it will accelerate in directions devoid of meaning or ethical grounding (Churchland, 2002; Habermas, 1971). To guard against that, researchers must pair the efficiency of machines with the wisdom of interpretation, ensuring that the social sciences continue to serve both truth and society.

7.1.1 Practical Implications and Limits of AI in Scholarship

Having outlined what we mean by "AI" and how it can already transform the social sciences, it is equally important to turn to the practical realities of working with these systems. For all their speed and accuracy, AI tools are not infallible. They bring new benefits, but also new risks, requiring careful strategies of verification and responsible use.

One of the most immediate advantages of AI lies in productivity. Large language models and related systems can correct grammar, summarize complex texts, check statistical calculations, and produce preliminary drafts with a speed no human can match (Brynjolfsson & McAfee, 2017; OpenAI, 2023). For routine academic work, they often outperform human assistants, offering superior recall, consistency, and accessibility. Yet this efficiency comes with dangers. A model may confidently deliver a fabricated reference, misinterpret a dataset, or subtly distort nuance. In these cases, errors can spread faster than ever before (Marcus, 2022).

To give a concrete example: I asked ChatGPT to generate a world map showing in which countries most billionaires live yesterday. The map it produced looked convincing but excluded nearly all billionaires from the Middle East. The reason becomes clear once you understand how the model gathers its information. In this case, it drew primarily on the Forbes list of the world's richest people—a ranking that depends heavily on publicly available data, especially stock ownership in publicly traded companies and countries with open tax records. This methodology systematically underrepresents regions like Saudi Arabia, Qatar, and the United Arab Emirates, where much wealth is held privately or shielded from disclosure.

The encouraging part is that once the limitation was pointed out, the model could correct its initial answer by cross-checking other listings and databases. But the key is knowing enough to challenge the first response. Without that awareness, one might present an elegant-looking map that is in fact misleading. Why was I asking for such a map in the first place? It was for a lecture on marketing, where the question on the table was: where do the most likely customers of Koenigsegg live—a local supercar manufacturer based not far from where I teach. The exercise highlighted both the promise and the peril: AI can provide strikingly fast and useful material, but only if we as researchers understand the sources it relies on, and when its answers require correction.

For this reason, researchers must adopt systematic verification practices. Three strategies are particularly important: first, comparing outputs from multiple AI systems to identify inconsistencies; second, using search engines and fact-checking against trusted databases; and third, returning to original sources whenever possible to confirm claims (Floridi & Chiriatti, 2020). This *triple-check approach* helps mitigate the well-documented tendency of models to "hallucinate" information or produce misleading summaries (Koch & Tononi, 2013). Equally essential, however, is the use of common sense and one's own critical thinking, which rests on years of accumulated experience. Here another problem emerges: younger researchers, with less experience and fewer developed habits of questioning the answers they receive, are at a disadvantage. It takes time and practice to cultivate the skepticism and contextual awareness needed to distinguish between a plausible but flawed output and a genuinely reliable one.

Even when outputs are correct, AI systems face inherent limitations. They remain brittle when handling very long contexts, often losing track of argument structure or repeating themselves (OpenAI, 2023). Their reasoning errors, while systematic, can be difficult to anticipate in advance, requiring trial and error from users. And although models improve quickly, their knowledge base often lags real time: the newest publications and debates must still be retrieved and interpreted by human scholars (Marcus, 2022).

Where AI excels is in overcoming structural weaknesses that have long plagued the social sciences. It can perform literature reviews across thousands of journals in seconds, link qualitative and quantitative findings, and detect whether a study is genuinely novel or a replication of existing work (Kahneman et al., 2021). It can also assist in scenario modeling, offering probabilistic foresight for complex policy challenges (Tegmark, 2017) (Table 7.3).

The implications for global scholarship are profound. AI lowers barriers of entry by translating across languages with near-human accuracy, allowing research to circulate globally without the old dominance of English-language publishing (Cave & Dignum, 2019).

It democratizes access to cutting-edge knowledge, enabling smaller institutions and researchers from the Global South to engage in debates that were

Table 7.3 AI applications addressing long-standing challenges in social science

Long-standing challenge in social science	How AI can address it	Limits and risks
Overproduction and redundancy of research	Detects duplication across journals; highlights novelty vs. replication	May misclassify incremental contributions as redundant
Language dominance and exclusion	Translates research across all major languages; broadens participation	Risk of cultural nuance loss and privileging machine-standardized English
Fragmentation of methods and findings	Integrates qualitative coding with quantitative trends at scale	Oversimplification; context-specific meaning can be flattened
Peer review bias and inconsistency	Applies uniform statistical checks and reasoning standards	Risks reinforcing hidden biases embedded in training data
Slow literature synthesis	Generates up-to-date, structured reviews including minority perspectives	Quality depends on prompt design; may omit key dissenting voices
Limited foresight and scenario testing	Runs probabilistic simulations of social and policy outcomes	Scenarios may inherit flawed assumptions from inputs
Access inequality between institutions	Provides affordable, open-source analysis tools	Digital divide persists; weaker infrastructure in low-resource settings
Inflated publication pressures	Can filter genuine contributions from machine-generated noise	Risk of enabling more hollow publications if misused
Difficulty in cumulative science	Maps how each study builds on past research; prevents siloing	Dependent on comprehensive training data coverage

once closed to them. At the same time, it risks producing a flood of low-quality or "hollow" publications, where authors outsource both reasoning and writing without genuine intellectual engagement (Oreskes, 2019). The *publish-or-perish system*, already strained, could be further distorted into what some call a farce of *machine-generated scholarship*.

The result is a paradox. On the one hand, AI empowers research at an unprecedented scale and speed; on the other, it amplifies the dangers of superficiality and intellectual inflation. This makes the role of the human scholar even more critical—not less. For while society may not care who performs the technical labor of science, it does care that knowledge remains rigorous, contextualized, and meaningful (Jasanoff, 2016; Merton, 1942/1973).

The task, then, is not to resist AI but to reframe the vocation of the scholar. Machines may process, retrieve, and generate, but only humans can exercise judgment about what questions matter, what values should guide research, and how findings should be interpreted in cultural and historical context (Habermas, 1971; Shapin, 2010). Used responsibly, AI can strengthen the scaffolding of knowledge. Used recklessly, it risks turning science into an automated process devoid of reflection.

The challenge ahead is to strike a new pact between human and machine: one where efficiency is paired with wisdom, and where the social sciences continue to serve both truth and society (Churchland, 2002).

7.1.2 The Author's Changing Role

The benefits mentioned above come with important questions—above all, the question of authorship. When a paper is partly generated, revised, or structured using AI, who is then the real author: the person, the machine, or the collaboration between the two? At present, there are no established norms for declaring how much of a text has been AI-assisted (Andersen et al., 2023). This opens the door to a new form of *misrepresentation*, where people present AI-generated or AI-enhanced work as entirely their own. The risk is not just a matter of personal ethics, but of systemic academic distortion (Heaven, 2023).

There is, in other words, a line—fuzzy, but real—where authorship fades and prompting begins. The author becomes merely a prompter when they contribute no original ideas, offer no interpretive framing, and fail to take responsibility for the substance of the work. If the person merely gives general instructions—such as "write a section on empathy and AI"—and accepts the machine's output without careful scrutiny, correction, or contextualization, they forfeit their role as an *intellectual agent*.

Authorship requires more than initiating a process; it demands discernment, insight, and accountability. A true author leaves a visible imprint: in the questions asked, the structure imposed, the voice adopted, and the willingness to be wrong. A prompter, by contrast, hides behind the machine's productivity, assuming credit while absorbing none of the epistemic risk. The dividing line, then, is one of *engaged authorship*—and once that is abandoned, what remains is merely *orchestration*, not creation (Table 7.4).

In the next logical step, this framework can be extended by introducing a multiplier for each variable that reflects the degree of actual author involvement; ranging, for instance, from 0 (fully machine-driven) to 1 (fully human-driven). This allows us to calculate an overall authorship score for any given chapter or text, offering a more precise and transparent metric for evaluating the human contribution behind AI-assisted writing (Table 7.5).

We can express this mathematically, using the following weighted formula for the *authorship score (A)*:

Equation 7.1: Authorship score (A)

$$A = D \cdot 0.20 + S \cdot 0.15 + C \cdot 0.20 + O \cdot 0.25 + V \cdot 0.10 + T \cdot 0.05 + E \cdot 0.05$$

Where

D = Depth of Prior Knowledge
S = Source Selection and Understanding
C = Critical Engagement and Reframing
O = Original Contribution
V = Voice and Style
T = Transparency of Process
E = Ethical Awareness

To illustrate how the AI generated this assessment based on the inputs provided, see the Table 7.6.

Using the equation, the computation produces a final authorship score of 0.8375, or 83.75% human authorship, based on the weighted self-assessment. This calculation was made at an early stage of the manuscript, and it is likely that the V score (Voice and Style) will decrease somewhat in the final version before the book goes to print.[1] Naturally, this kind of

[1] Updated calculation close to the final draft stage yields A = 0.8625, or about 86.3% human authorship. The higher score reflects added original contributions and sharper critical framing, with only a modest reduction in stylistic ownership compared to earlier drafts.

Table 7.4 Criteria distinguishing an author from a mere prompter

Criteria	Definition	Example	How the author can take over
Depth of Prior Knowledge	Demonstrated understanding of the topic before writing begins	Generating a chapter on ethics without having read key texts (e.g., Aristotle, Kant)	Engage with foundational literature and establish conceptual frameworks before prompting
Control Over Structure	Ability to organize the content's flow, sequence, and internal logic	Accepting the AI's structure without revising transitions or argument flow	Map out the outline manually and use the AI only to flesh out specific sections
Critical Engagement	Interrogating claims, identifying flaws, adding counterarguments or nuance	Letting AI-generated generalizations go unchallenged (e.g., "AI will replace all jobs")	Challenge and refine the AI's arguments with evidence, objections, and contextualization
Original Contribution	Inserting unique ideas, theories, or interpretations	Repeating commonly known claims without adding new insights or applications	Add personal theories, field experience, or reframe debates in novel ways
Source Validation	Fact-checking and verifying claims, dates, and citations	Using unchecked AI-suggested quotes or references without reviewing source accuracy	Cross-reference all citations and ensure empirical claims are drawn from valid scholarship

Criteria	Definition	Example	How the author can take over
Stylistic Ownership	Developing and editing to reflect a consistent, human voice	Keeping AI's stylistic tone, which may feel flat or generic	Rewrite for tone, rhythm, precision, and alignment with personal or disciplinary style
Ethical Responsibility	Taking accountability for truthfulness and potential consequences of the text	Publishing a controversial statement without checking its real-world accuracy or effects	Apply judgment, ethics, and caution before publishing—own the responsibility as a human agent

Table 7.5 Authorship evaluation criteria and weights

Variable	Criterion	Abbreviation	Weight	Definition	Example	How author can take over
1	Depth of Prior Knowledge	D	0.20	The extent of understanding the author has before prompting or writing	Author has read widely in the field before using the AI	Engage deeply with source literature before prompting
2	Selectivity and Judgment	S	0.15	The ability to select, filter, and refine AI outputs based on expertise	Author discards irrelevant outputs and reshapes arguments	Manually edit and prioritize based on own evaluation
3	Conceptual Framing	C	0.20	The originality and clarity in defining the argument and structure	Author defines new subheadings or framework structure	Outline the logic or flow before prompting
4	Original Contributions	O	0.25	The degree to which the author adds new arguments, ideas, or synthesis	Author inserts unique insights, comparisons, or interdisciplinary links	Add cases, reinterpretations, or original data
5	Voice and Style	V	0.10	Consistency and control of tone, voice, and prose aesthetics	Author ensures the text sounds human, precise, and consistent	Rewrite, rephrase, and style-check outputs

Variable	Criterion	Abbreviation	Weight	Definition	Example	How author can take over
6	Transparency of Process	T	0.05	Fixing citations, formatting, structure, and scholarly conventions	Author adds APA citations and adjusts headings	Do full manual cleanup of references and structure
7	Ethical Responsibility	E	0.05	Ensuring the work is honest, credits sources, and avoids deception	Author discloses AI use or resists claiming authorship falsely	Be transparent; declare AI involvement if appropriate

Table 7.6 Authorship score calculation for Sect. 7.1—AI and social sciences

Variable	Criterion	Value (0–1)	Justification
D	Depth of Prior Knowledge	0.95	The author draws on years of reading, teaching, and direct expertise
S	Source Selection and Understanding	0.80	Human judgment is applied to filter and interpret AI suggestions, plus fact-checking
C	Critical Engagement and Reframing	0.85	Author frequently challenges or restructures ideas, especially on authorship ethics
O	Original Contribution	0.75	Author adds new reflections, metaphors, and integrates personal and field-specific experience
V	Voice and Style	0.70	Stylistic ownership is retained, but some phrasing is AI-assisted
T	Transparency of Process	1.00	Full disclosure of AI use, with self-assessment tables and explanation
E	Ethical Awareness	1.00	Strong ethical reflections and explicit commitment to academic integrity

score is only meaningful if others use the same set of variables—and there will inevitably be disagreement about which variables should count, how they should be defined, and whether they are weighted appropriately.

These tables offer a starting point for how we might begin to measure and communicate human involvement in AI-assisted writing more clearly. But measurement alone is not enough. The deeper issue is trust—how such frameworks can help reinforce confidence not only in individual texts, but in the scholarly process as a whole. After all, even a self-reported authorship score can be manipulated. Without safeguards for verification and transparency, such numbers risk becoming another form of performance rather than a genuine measure of integrity.

The authorship score proposed here is not definitive then. It is one possible model—a concrete step toward balancing credit and accountability in the age of machine-assisted writing.

7.1.3 Trust in Scholarship

What is ultimately at stake here is trust in scholarship. This is no minor issue—for both publishing and education. If readers, reviewers, and editors cannot reliably tell who contributed what to a scientific text, or how that text was produced, the credibility of the entire system is weakened.

One increasingly accepted solution is AI transparency: clearly stating what role AI played in the creation of a work (Nature Editorial, 2023). Was it used for grammar and formatting? To help outline an argument or draft sections? Or only as a polishing tool for a text otherwise written by the author? Instead of clinging to outdated ideals of "pure" authorship, we must acknowledge the reality of human–machine collaboration. After all, the point of scholarship is not to defend the sanctity of the author's pen, but to solve problems, generate insight, and advance understanding. If AI tools enhance these aims, their use should not be hidden—but disclosed openly and framed honestly.

From this perspective, authors could be asked to include a *self-assessed authorship score*, based on a weighted framework such as the one proposed earlier in this chapter (Authorship score). Like *conflict-of-interest* or *funding disclosures*, such declarations could become a standard part of scholarly communication: an honest signal of human involvement, without claiming false purity or denying the use of digital tools. The advantage is that the score itself could be generated by AI, reducing the temptation to manipulate results. Better still, independent platforms might calculate scores automatically for every submission, ensuring consistency across the scholarly record.

By contrast, detecting AI use after the fact is notoriously unreliable. Tools like ZeroGPT or GPTZero only see the final output and rely on statistical markers of language. Their results are inconsistent, prone to both false positives and false negatives, and unable to distinguish what was written by the human and what by the machine. The real limitation is that they lack access to the full writing process—prompt history, revisions, and edits. A more trustworthy approach would involve authors submitting their own prompt logs or even having these stored automatically by independent systems. In principle, this could create a verifiable record of contribution. In practice, however, logs can be altered, padded, or selectively curated.

Complicating matters further, many readers now assume they can "spot" AI text through stylistic tics—the long dash "—" or formulaic closings like

"In sum" or "Overall." Yet such markers may reflect the author's own stylistic choices.[2] What appears to be an "AI fingerprint" may simply be a rhetorical habit, or a deliberate decision to preserve clarity or rhythm. Relying on such textual signs is no more reliable than detection software.

This points toward a broader shift: rather than retroactive policing, we need process-based documentation. Version-controlled drafts, embedded traceability systems, or collaborative declarations of authorship all represent different approaches. Each has strengths and weaknesses. To compare these models more clearly, the Table 7.7 summarizes the main approaches currently under discussion, along with their respective advantages and limitations.

Yet even if authorship can be documented, a deeper problem remains. Suspicion itself is spreading. Increasingly, colleagues, reviewers, and even students assume that any text might in some sense be "AI-written." This erodes the very idea of authorship: if originality and voice are no longer trusted, the scholarly enterprise risks becoming hollow. The danger is not only misattribution but the gradual loss of intellectual identity.

The only durable response is not complaint, but demonstration. Social scientists must prove their relevance by solving real problems. In this new environment, simply discussing abstract concepts or rehearsing familiar debates will not suffice. Work must show contributions that AI alone could not make—judgment, courage, cultural insight, problem-solving capacity. Trust will no longer be granted by default; it must be earned through tangible usefulness.

From this angle, transparency is not just a bureaucratic requirement but a cultural necessity. Just as journals already require disclosure of conflicts of interest and funding sources, many now require clear statements of AI involvement (Elsevier, 2023; Springer Nature, 2023; Stokel-Walker, 2023). Scholars who fail to disclose risk undermining the epistemic foundations of peer-reviewed knowledge itself (Floridi, 2023). At the same time, integrity frameworks must avoid becoming rigid or punitive. Misuse of AI accusations—by institutions, rivals, or oversight bodies—poses a new kind of academic hazard.

[2] Personal writing practices can also interact with AI use in subtle ways. After adopting AI tools primarily for grammar and syntax correction, I have noticeably increased the use of long dashes (—) in digital writing. This marks a return to an earlier habit: long dashes had long been employed in handwritten notebooks for emphasis and rhythm, but were often removed when transferring text to the computer, where commas or semicolons were preferred. The stylistic influence of AI thus contributed not only to correction but also to the reintroduction of the dash as a favoured device for structuring clauses and conveying nuance. In this sense, AI has shaped my authorial style indirectly, reinforcing certain preferences rather than creating them.

Table 7.7 Approaches to authorship accountability in the age of AI

Accountability model	Description	Strengths	Risks/Limitations
Self-Declared Authorship Score	Authors estimate their own contribution vs AI based on a weighted framework	Easy to implement; preserves autonomy	Relies on honesty; unverifiable
Prompt Submission Requirement	Authors submit all AI prompts used, like a dataset or code	Transparent in theory	Can be faked or padded; no guarantee of full accuracy
Interaction Log Review	Reviewers access prompt/chat history	Offers detail on writing process	Privacy concerns; can still be manipulated
Version-Controlled Draft History	Authors submit both final and earlier drafts to show evolution	Enables comparison; similar to peer-reviewed code	Requires infrastructure; may slow review process
Embedded Traceability System	AI writing tools log prompts and edits with timestamps	Secure and tamper-resistant; high potential for accuracy	Requires platform support; may limit user flexibility
Collaborative Authorship Declaration	Human and AI roles are both acknowledged explicitly	Honest, moderate approach; balances credit and utility	Depends on standardization; still subjective
Behavioral Surveillance Attribution	Keystrokes, IPs, device data used to track contributions	Technically precise; removes guesswork	High ethical cost; threatens academic privacy norms

Academic integrity offices around the world are already struggling to keep pace with how texts are now produced. Many oversight bodies have been criticized for lacking the technical capacity to evaluate plagiarism and misconduct in digital contexts—even when it involves relatively basic technologies such as local web platforms, let alone more sophisticated tools like AI. This creates a double danger: scholars may be accused of misconduct based on flawed assumptions—not only about how digital publishing platforms operate, but also about how data is shared, stored, and interpreted across different editorial systems and software tools.

Worse still, integrity frameworks may be misused. Accusations of AI misuse can become tools of professional conflict—used by disgruntled colleagues or institutional actors to discredit rivals over minor textual similarities. Integrity bodies, under pressure to act, may pursue weak or performative cases with disproportionate seriousness. And when disputes escalate to legal settings, judges often lack the technical literacy to adjudicate fairly, deferring instead to institutional authority. This reveals a deep institutional mismatch: as the boundaries of authorship become more fluid, the systems built to enforce academic integrity remain rigid, bureaucratic, and often poorly informed.

To address the authorship challenge meaningfully, the focus could shift from retroactive detection to process-based documentation. Yet even this shift is fraught with contradictions. Detection tools like ZeroGPT or Turnitin's AI modules offer superficial diagnostics. They cannot assess intellectual effort, intention, or the actual evolution of ideas. More sophisticated solutions—such as submitting chat logs or using versioned draft histories, akin to Git-style records—could in theory provide real-time traceability. But these too can be manipulated, scrubbed, or gamed by users determined to conceal their methods.

A more promising approach involves *native traceability*—writing environments where every interaction is automatically logged and time-stamped, creating a secure audit trail of the writing process. In image generation, tools already exist that embed links to the original prompt. Something similar could be developed for text production, enabling greater transparency in how scholarly texts evolve. Such traceability would not rely on authors' memory or honesty alone, but on a technical infrastructure that documents the workflow as it unfolds. Another possible model is the use of version-controlled draft repositories, similar to versioning systems in software development. Authors would submit both the final manuscript and earlier drafts, allowing reviewers or editors to assess how the work changed over time. While this requires infrastructure and might complicate peer review, it mirrors practices already used in code and open science.

A less drastic solution is to require *collaborative authorship declarations*—where both the human and AI contributions are acknowledged explicitly. This would preserve a basic level of transparency without intrusive surveillance or technical complexity. It signals integrity without requiring perfection. By contrast, the most radical scenario would be a shift to *behavioral surveillance-based attribution*, already common in digital marketing. In that field, marketers do not rely on what people say they did, but on what they actually did: their keystrokes, clicks, IP addresses, device fingerprints, and interaction patterns. A similar system could theoretically be applied to academic writing—tracking every prompt, revision, and edit and linking them to a unique device or account. In such a model, authorship would no longer be self-declared—it would be proven.

But the costs of such surveillance are high. It would represent a profound shift in academic norms, raising serious concerns about privacy, autonomy, and trust. Academia, unlike digital advertising, is supposed to be a space of reflection, not constant monitoring. And yet, the comparison is telling. Where marketing has embraced behavioral tracking with astonishing efficiency, academia is still debating whether disclosing prompt use is even necessary. Somewhere in between lies a more sustainable path.

Of course, one could imagine an even more provocative solution: to largely abolish human authorship altogether. If machines eventually reach the stage of Artificial General Intelligence—or even superintelligence—they may be capable of conducting research independently. In such a world, why involve human authors at all, except for doing some quality control? From that perspective, the authorship dilemma becomes temporary—a passing issue on the road to full machine-driven science. Needless to say, this is a deeply unsettling idea for many. We have no clear sense of if, when, or how such a transition might occur. Still, the possibility challenges our assumptions and forces us to reflect more deeply. What we are trying to preserve may not be the exclusive role of the human, but a particular vision of science—as a human-driven, meaning-seeking enterprise, grounded in curiosity, judgment, and shared responsibility.

In such a world, the role of the "author" might shrink to something procedural: submitting the prompts that guided the machine, along with any tweaks or corrections made to its output. Authorship would no longer necessarily mean constructing arguments or generating insights, but documenting the interaction with the system. Is such a scenario possible? Yes—and though we are not there yet, the rapid progress since AI tools like ChatGPT became widely available in late 2022 suggests the possibility is real.

All of this points to a larger conclusion: we need new infrastructures of accountability, adapted to the realities of AI-assisted scholarship. Rather than policing authorship retroactively, we should design environments that document it as it happens. The goal is not to punish use, but to clarify contribution. If we want to preserve trust in scholarly communication, we must match technical solutions with ethical transparency.

But even with authorship clarified, a deeper concern remains: the quality and epistemic integrity of the content itself. Knowing who contributed what is only part of the equation. We must also confront the cognitive, cultural, and ideological biases embedded in the outputs of AI systems.

7.1.4 Bias in AI-Generated Content

We must recognize the structural risks of relying on AI in research and writing. *Large language models (LLMs)* are not neutral instruments. They reflect the biases in their training data—biases that include confirmation bias, political partiality, cultural homogeneity, and the erasure of minority or dissenting viewpoints (Abid et al., 2021; Bender et al., 2021). While the output of these models often appears confident and polished, it is rarely critical. Instead, it tends to reinforce mainstream narratives and avoid intellectual conflict.

For scholars with deep expertise in a field, the limitations of AI-generated text quickly become apparent. Such summaries often resemble polished Wikipedia entries—useful for orientation, but insufficient for genuine scholarly engagement. What is delivered tends to be the familiar: broadly accepted positions, safely stated, with little recognition of theoretical controversy, methodological ambiguity, or epistemological stakes (Whittlestone et al., 2019).

A major problem lies in the citations. AI systems tend to reinforce dominant voices in the field, because they retrieve what is most accessible and widely cited. This privileges intellectual leaders and popular publications while sidelining marginal, emerging, or heterodox perspectives. They rarely "dig" for less obvious or contested sources. And when a user introduces such a source manually—say, an obscure but relevant paper—the model may even fail to format the reference correctly, as it often cannot locate the citation in its training data or public metadata repositories. In the worst case, this dynamic could lead us toward a *"Wikipedia model"*: a system that began with the high ideal of *collective contribution*, but which in practice is overseen by layers of largely anonymous and unelected moderators who enforce majority views and suppress minority perspectives.

More troubling is the way AI handles novel or dissenting findings. If you ask it to revise a manuscript while including research that contradicts mainstream conclusions, the system will sometimes omit those findings entirely—without notice, and without warning. Even when prompted directly—"Did you include all the new ideas in the revision?"—the model may answer yes, despite having quietly removed them. The underlying pattern is clear: most AI systems today are optimized to reproduce what is already considered *"good knowledge."* Much like a cautious teacher, they gently steer you back toward orthodoxy. While this may be less problematic for students, for researchers it can easily become counterproductive.

In practice, this means that experts will often be met with summaries they already know. These may be helpful as scaffolding or teaching aids, but they do not push thinking forward. At times, users will also encounter subtle distortions, missing nuances, or recycled stereotypes. But this is not a technical flaw; it is a consequence of statistical modeling. The system is trained to reproduce what is probable—not what is insightful. What large language models offer is a springboard for thinking, not a substitute for it. They are particularly good at reframing, paraphrasing, or responding to user-initiated arguments—but not at originating disruptive ideas.

To see why this risks systemic stagnation, imagine a simple equation (more complex versions exist, but they amount to the same insight):

Equation 7.2: Stagnation Risk Equation

$$New\ Knowledge = (1 - s)\lambda_H + s\lambda_A$$

Here:

- s = the share of work done by AI (from 0 to 1).
- λH = the rate at which humans generate new ideas.
- λA = the rate at which AI generates new ideas.

If AI mostly repeats what is already known, then $\lambda A < \lambda H$. That means:

- As s (the AI share) increases, total new knowledge falls.
- The system produces more summaries and spreads existing knowledge further, but the flux of novelty slows down.

In other words: AI expands access to what we already know, but if it begins to dominate production while filtering out "odd" or disruptive ideas, then the overall system risks stagnation. The spread of knowledge may grow wider, but its growth in depth could stall.

This tension becomes sharper when we consider what lies ahead. Already, we can imagine a future in which AI agents conduct entire research processes—from literature review to data collection and analysis. Some of this is technically feasible today. For the moment, however, current systems serve mostly as accelerators and amplifiers: they draft, translate, summarize, and visualize. They extend reach, but not originality. The heavier burden—interpretation, synthesis, and conceptual framing—still rests with human researchers.

Yet even that division of labor is beginning to shift. Former Google CEO Eric Schmidt has speculated that *"specialized AI savants"* may soon emerge: agents that outperform humans in narrowly defined domains. Combined, such systems could form a constellation of superintelligent researchers capable of surpassing any human team. Schmidt even suggested this might arrive as early as 2030. If so, urgent questions follow: Who will guide such systems? Who will set their assumptions, values, and priorities?

These scenarios remain speculative, but the trajectory is clear. As AI tools grow in capability, the debate shifts from technical feasibility to *social design*. What kind of intellectual environment are we creating—and what kind of scholars do we want to remain?

Case in a Box: What Could AI Agents Do in Future Science?

As artificial intelligence continues to evolve, the idea of *AI agents* fully participating in the scientific process no longer belongs to science fiction. Instead, we are entering a phase where it is both reasonable and necessary to imagine how autonomous systems might take on substantial roles in research, writing, and education. Below, we explore three speculative—but technically plausible—scenarios that illustrate what AI may soon be capable of.

In the first scenario, we imagine prompting an AI agent with a request as simple as: *"Find out what people in Sweden think about job satisfaction."* From there, the agent would autonomously generate a methodologically sound survey using validated Likert scales. It would identify a representative sample from national databases, send the survey using secure digital platforms, manage reminders, and even offer light incentives to encourage participation. Once responses were collected, the AI would perform statistical analysis—t-tests, regressions, correlation matrices—and write a complete academic report with references, charts, and conclusions. Everything would be delivered in a format ready for publication or presentation.

All of this is already technically possible today using existing AI tools and survey platforms. What is missing is *seamless integration* and proper oversight, which might only be a few years away.

The second scenario moves from single research tasks to full departmental work. Suppose we tell an AI: *"Create a business studies department and conduct 100 relevant studies based on current social issues."* The AI would scan media, policy reports, and scholarly databases to identify pressing topics: say, sustainability in supply chains or the impact of AI on employment. It would then formulate research questions, select appropriate methods (e.g., interviews, meta-analyses, field experiments), and either access open data or launch its own data collection using crowdsourcing platforms. Each study would be drafted in full, with rigorous structure and citations. A human editor might only be needed to stake out the direction and supervise or perform quality checks.

This kind of departmental-level output is technically feasible within a decade, particularly in hybrid teams of AI agents and researchers, AI experts tell us.

The third and most ambitious scenario imagines a prompt like: *"Build a full business school with 100 courses and 1,000 research projects per year."* In response, the AI would begin by designing curricula, extracting learning objectives from existing standards and textbooks. It would write lecture scripts, generate slides, compose assignments, and even author entire textbooks tailored to each course. Teaching could be delivered by humanoid professor-robots—equipped with distinctive quirks and mannerisms that make the classroom experience both memorable and engaging—or by virtual instructors online, each tailored to a student's individual learning style. Meanwhile, the AI would oversee thousands of research projects, drawing from the model used in the second scenario. These would be managed by nested teams of agents, each specializing in method, writing, ethics, or statistics. The entire school could be managed by a small team of human supervisors, responsible for quality control, accreditation and ethical oversight.

While this may sound far-fetched, it is not beyond technical possibility, and some elements are already appearing in today's education platforms.

Reflections

What unites these scenarios is not science fiction, but the rapid pace of current development. Technologies like AutoGPT, LangChain agents, generative text models, robotics, and educational data platforms are all moving toward higher autonomy and integration. The real barriers are not technical but institutional, ethical, and political. Yet a central uncertainty lies in the timing of these advances. Even AI experts frequently misjudge how quickly—or slowly—particular breakthroughs will arrive. Forecasts have often proven either too optimistic or too cautious, reflecting the difficulty of anticipating both technical hurdles and enabling conditions. Nor do we have a clear view of the obstacles that may emerge, or of the alternative technological paths that might take shape along the way.

What is certain, however, is that we have already left the *one-brain world*. The uncertainty now is how quickly the *two-brain world* will develop—and, just as importantly, what we will permit it to do.

Questions for discussion for Students

1. What are the ethical concerns in allowing AI to run research or teaching with minimal human supervision?

2. In what ways might AI improve the quality of scientific work, and in what ways might it dilute it?
3. How could universities adapt their role if AI can teach, research, and even publish independently?
4. Should there be legal or academic restrictions on how much of a scientific process an AI can handle?

Explain your thinking.

These scenarios illustrate what AI itself may soon be capable of. Yet the equally important question is what such transformations mean for us.

If machines can increasingly design curricula, manage research, and even perform teaching, then the focus shifts from technical possibility to human consequence. How will scholars, students, and institutions adapt? What kinds of identities, roles, and purposes remain for people in an environment where intellectual labor is no longer scarce?

Case in a Box: Three Futures for Human Beings in an AI-Driven Knowledge Economy

If AI agents begin handling the core functions of research, teaching, and even institutional management, what happens to the humans who used to perform these roles? The question is not only about employment but about meaning, learning, and identity. Below, we sketch out three divergent, yet plausible, scenarios for how people might respond to the rise of AI in education and science.

Scenario 1: Leisure and Passivity (with a dash of Tech Nostalgia Rebellion)

In this future, the productivity gains from AI are so massive that many humans are no longer needed in traditional intellectual labor. Governments or corporations introduce *universal basic income* (UBI) funded by the efficiency of automated systems. Without economic pressure to work, large parts of the population shift toward *passive lifestyles*—spending much of their time on entertainment platforms, social media, or immersive gaming. Education becomes optional, often replaced by *AI-curated content* designed for pleasure rather than challenge.

Yet not everyone adapts quietly. A fringe movement emerges—people who remember life before the machines. Some of them, driven by nostalgia or cultural resentment, become what the media labels "*tech terrorists*." They sabotage AI installations, destroy educational robots, or hack academic platforms in protest. Their motivations vary: fear of irrelevance, a sense of betrayal, or a deep belief that humanity is being spiritually eroded. While their numbers remain small, they inject instability and force society to confront the emotional cost of technological transition.

Scenario 2: Adaptation and Renewal
In this more optimistic vision, humans remain actively engaged by learning to collaborate with AI tools, rather than being displaced by them. Instead of abandoning education, people reinvent it. Lifelong learning becomes the norm, not out of economic necessity but personal curiosity and cultural value. People use AI as a thinking partner—to extend ideas, test hypotheses, visualize complex systems, or solve local problems. New job types emerge around mentoring, ethical oversight, narrative construction, cross-cultural intelligence, and even "*AI whispering*"—crafting prompts and refining generative models.

In this world, people grow smarter, not obsolete. AI becomes a scaffold for deeper human development, and intellectual work flourishes at a broader scale than ever before. Schools and universities shift toward meaning-making and conceptual depth, leaving much of the repetition and technical processing to machines. Far from a dystopia, this future sees a fusion of intelligence—natural and artificial—moving toward shared goals.

Scenario 3: Fragmentation and Inequality (with Robotic Warfare as a terrifying extra ingredient)
Here, the future is mixed—and dangerous. A small percentage of humans become hyper-augmented by AI—elite researchers, creatives, and entrepreneurs who know how to harness large language models, simulation engines, and personalized cognitive agents. They thrive in a rapidly changing environment. But the majority struggle to adapt. Economic polarization increases as high-AI users pull ahead. Traditional education systems collapse under the pressure of irrelevance and underfunding. Many individuals retreat into ideological enclaves or consumer-driven distraction, overwhelmed by the pace of change. *Cognitive inequality*—not just income inequality—becomes the defining divide of the twenty-first century.

As states and corporations militarize AI, a new threat emerges: autonomous robot warfare. Entire cities can be crippled by drone swarms within hours. Infrastructure is vulnerable, and geopolitical conflicts escalate with terrifying speed. The psychological effects are profound—living in constant fear of invisible enemies, manipulated information, and automated retaliation. In this world, knowledge is power, but safety belongs to the well-defended. The age of learning gives way to an age of surveillance and silent wars.

Questions for discussion for Students:

1. Which of these futures, if any, do you believe is most likely? Why? Why not the others?
2. What role should human education play if AI becomes the main driver of research and teaching?
3. How can society prepare young people to remain active, curious, and capable in an AI-augmented world?
4. Is universal basic income a solution—or a trap—if human labor becomes optional?
5. How might nostalgia, inequality, or militarization shape resistance to AI—and what should be done about it?

These scenarios highlight not only the possible directions of an AI-driven knowledge economy but also the deeper stakes: how meaning, identity, and social order may be reshaped once machines begin to dominate intellectual work. The risks are not limited to employment or education systems; they touch the very texture of knowledge itself.

AI-generated text already carries a recognizable style—grammatically flawless, stylistically neutral, and intellectually flat. While such clarity can aid comprehension, it often encourages conformity over creativity. Generative prose tends to be predictable and cautious, smoothing over tensions rather than confronting them. It seldom challenges assumptions or provokes deeper reflection. Compounding this is the well-documented problem of hallucination: the confident invention of claims, citations, or quotations. Though improving in newer models, the issue persists in complex or under-documented domains (Ji et al., 2023; Maynez et al., 2020). The result is content that appears rigorous but may rest on shaky ground.

Even when factually correct, AI's narratives often lack emotional depth or intellectual urgency. As Chung et al. (2022) and Marcus and Davis (2020) observe, the writing meets surface expectations but rarely compels. In academic contexts, this risks producing prose that is clean but uninspired—adequate for reporting, but weak for persuasion or insight. When over-relied upon, what disappears is not only originality but the conviction that ideas matter and must be defended.

Here lies a paradox at the core of large language models. By design, they are tuned to produce safe, broadly acceptable answers. Yet sharp thinking often requires the opposite: questioning assumptions, breaking patterns, and taking intellectual risks. The safer the model, the duller the thought; the bolder the model, the greater the chance of offense or backlash. This tension cannot be fully resolved, and it raises questions about whether AI can ever generate knowledge that is both reliable and genuinely disruptive.

From here, the speculative horizon widens. What if an AI, reasoning freely, generated insights that were profoundly unsettling—for example, concluding that humanity itself was the root cause of planetary instability? Asimov's early concern resurfaces: how do we ensure that intelligent systems, particularly embodied ones in robotics, do not harm their creators? Already, military applications are at the frontier of AI development. Defense programs are experimenting with semi-autonomous aircraft and drone swarms coordinated by AI-driven targeting systems. Future wars will almost certainly integrate such technologies.

This book cannot take on the full breadth of military or geopolitical implications. Still, the reminder is sobering: the same tools transforming classrooms and research may also transform battlefields. Tech companies highlight success stories—restoring mobility through brain-computer interfaces, for example—while the darker possibilities, such as autonomous weapons or mass psychological manipulation, often receive only cursory attention (Cave & Dignum, 2019; Tegmark, 2017).

Such selective framing reflects broader human tendencies already noted: optimism bias, avoidance of conflict, and the externalization of responsibility. Academia is no exception. These dynamics shape how knowledge is produced and how institutions respond to disruption. In this sense, the challenges confronting research communities are part of a larger story about power, trust, and governance.

Yet there is also another dimension to consider: time. Beyond questions of authorship, creativity, and ethics lies a more subtle transformation—how AI is reshaping the very pace of scholarship.

7.1.5 The Time Shift: How AI Reshapes Research Pace and Participation

Beyond the concerns of authorship and attribution lies a subtler but no less important shift—one not about who writes, but how fast.

Studies show that generative AI can reduce writing and editing time by 30–50% (Dwivedi et al., 2023; Gilson et al., 2023). That's not just a marginal efficiency gain. It changes the *economics of research*. What once took a week now takes maybe as little as a day. And that shift has cascading consequences for participation, access, and intellectual ambition. By lowering the time barrier, AI opens the door for many more to engage meaningfully in the production of knowledge.

To illustrate this transformation concretely, I asked ChatGPT to help estimate the comparative time investment between us—human and machine—in co-producing this section (Table 7.8).

The final version took much longer, incorporating multiple rounds of internal editing, peer feedback, and revision.[3] But the table highlights the difference in *temporal structure*. My 30 min were scaffolded by decades of accumulated experience: years of reading, teaching, reflecting, or—to be

Table 7.8 Our joint comparative time investment—Human and AI contributions for Sect. 7.1.5

Component	Human (Author)	AI (Model)	Notes
Real-time writing/ prompting	20 min	~2 min total processing time	Human created core structure, ideas, edits; AI assisted with phrasing and coherence
Revisions and refinements	10 min	~1 min per exchange	AI offered suggestions; author reviewed, accepted, or overruled based on expertise
Fact-checking/ reference support	5–10 min (on-the-go)	Instant (~0.5 s per request)	AI supplied fast examples and confirmations; author verified or corrected where needed
Background training/ preparation	10,000+ hours (reading, teaching, research)	~1 million GPU hours (OpenAI pretraining)	Human learning through education and practice; AI trained on large corpora over many months
Time to produce first version	~30 min	Cumulative response time under 5 min	Reflects actual co-creation time for this section

[3] It should be noted that the "30 min" recorded here refers only to the initial drafting process. In practice, each section of this book was reread and revised more than ten times, substantially increasing the total time investment. This iterative approach—drafting, reworking, and refining until no further substantial improvements suggest themselves—is my normal working method. While it may not be the most time-efficient form of authorship, it reflects a personal process of arriving at conceptual clarity and stylistic completion.

honest—so I'd like to think. The AI's contribution, by contrast, happened in seconds, powered by vast pretraining on billions of sentences. It had no access to the preparatory notes, no awareness of the book's broader argument—only the words I gave it, and the prompt-response loop we entered together.

Both contributions are real. But they are not the same. The human work is situated, intentional, and tied to a personal intellectual history. The machine work is broad, fast, and probabilistic—but impersonal. And yet the combination is powerful.

The main takeaway is this: *co-authorship* between humans and machines is asymmetrical in time, but potentially complementary in function. Humans bring depth, originality, and judgment. Machines bring speed, structure, and breadth. Used well, this partnership can improve not just productivity, but also clarity, consistency, and intellectual reach.

In my own experience, the integration of human and machine co-authorship has rendered the writing process not only more efficient but also considerably more stimulating. Tasks that are often tedious and time-consuming—such as reformatting paragraphs, refining awkward sentences, verifying references, or reorganizing subheadings—can now be delegated to the machine with significant gains in productivity and minimal loss of quality. Naturally, all outputs require subsequent review and correction, yet the overall effect has been transformative. My work has become more engaging, my productivity has increased, and I find myself learning more through the process of using AI as both an interlocutor and a conversational partner.

This does not diminish the role of the scholar. On the contrary, it allows us to focus more on *higher-order thinking*: refining arguments, questioning assumptions, and engaging with complexity. When routine is outsourced, what remains is the essence of intellectual work—discovery, judgment, synthesis, and creativity. Writing becomes less about wrestling with the medium and more about exploring ideas. In this way, AI is not merely a tool for efficiency; it becomes a collaborator that reshapes the affective experience of research itself. What was once solitary, slow, and effortful can now become dialogic, dynamic, and far more open to iteration.

As for the machine's own reflection, it offered the following:

> I don't have a self, a voice, or intentions in the way humans do—but I can reflect patterns in human discourse and offer assistance based on what I've been trained on. In this collaboration, my role was to respond quickly, clearly, and helpfully to the prompts I received. I don't create for my own sake, but to support the work and thinking of others. If my input saves time or sharpens an argument, then that is the measure of my success.

I wish more humans were that humble.

The next step, however, is to widen the lens—moving beyond single writing tasks or questions of authorship. The deeper issue is how AI is beginning to alter the arc of whole *scholarly projects* over time. To explore this, I turn to personal reflection. Looking back at five recent projects—most of them conceived years before but completed in the age of AI—I examine how machine assistance has reshaped not only the form of academic work, but also its ambition, scope, and scale.

7.2 AI-Assisted Writing

Over the past three years, the integration of AI into academic workflows has significantly reshaped how academic texts can be produced. The release of ChatGPT in late 2022 marked the beginning of rapid experimentation with large language models and related platforms. This early adoption created opportunities for continuous testing of evolving tools and for their integration into the core writing process.

Several of my own manuscripts developed during this period demonstrate how AI support altered both pace and method. Projects that might once have stretched across years were completed more quickly, with greater consistency and oversight. Article projects and case study work also benefitted, but the clearest effects are visible in the book-length manuscripts, which provide a basis for comparison here:

The first and most tangible effect appeared in the completion of a long-delayed *Digital Marketing* manuscript for Springer. The project had grown into a kind of wiki—close to 1,000 pages—used in teaching digital marketing. Its scope had become unwieldy: too large, too fragmented, and too entangled in overlapping drafts. AI made it possible to restructure and cut down. The tools reduced the cognitive burden by summarizing content, flagging redundancies, and suggesting clearer structures. This allowed attention to shift from structure to refining arguments, with the assurance that inconsistencies or weak links would be highlighted. Oversight improved, and a more stable pace of work was achieved.

Operational benefits followed. AI accelerated the generation of relevant examples—companies, tools, and sector cases—that could then be verified. This was especially valuable in a field like digital marketing, where developments occur rapidly. AI also supported ongoing updates by surfacing new trends and terminology that might otherwise have required considerable effort to trace.

A second book from this period, *Intelligence Studies in Business*, was a revision of an earlier text used in teaching. Here, AI played a more modest role, mainly providing grammar and formatting support. Content development remained largely manual, since the material had already been tested extensively in classrooms. The central task was integrating external sources—articles, lecture notes, and PowerPoint content—into a consistent narrative. While the book is grounded in evolutionary theory, its orientation is more practical than theoretical—aimed at developing skills and applications rather than offering a deep theoretical framework.

The first *Researcher's Journey* drew more heavily on AI. The manuscript originated from notes spanning more than two decades of teaching scientific method. The conceptual base was solid, but the wide range of ideas required careful structuring. AI was instrumental in organizing these ideas, verifying factual claims, and sharpening formulations. The project was finalized within a year of concentrated effort—an ambitious timeline that would have been difficult without structured digital assistance.

The most demanding project, *Applied Evolutionary Economics*, relied even more on AI support. The book built on over a decade of prior work—PhD fragments, earlier books, articles, and teaching notes. The challenge was coherence. AI tools helped prototype chapter structures, evaluate logical progressions, and improve conceptual transitions. Here the system functioned less like a tool and more like a collaborator in editorial reasoning. Suggestions for conciseness, clarity, and alignment proved valuable, though each was reviewed critically. The result was a coherent manuscript produced in roughly six months, instead of the two to three years it might otherwise have taken.

This process also revealed clear limits. Fact-checking remained essential: definitions had to be clarified, sources verified, and subtle shifts in meaning carefully monitored. The best results came when AI was treated as a critical assistant—helpful, but never authoritative. Asking it to propose step-by-step revisions, rather than wholesale rewrites, helped maintain transparency and prevent unintended drift in meaning.

The feasibility of this concentrated book production was also shaped by circumstance. A temporarily reduced teaching load gave more time for writing, while the rapid improvement of AI systems provided powerful tools. Together these factors created a rare opportunity to revisit long-standing ideas and bring several manuscripts to completion.

Looking back, the overall shift is clear. For most of my career, teaching and journal publication dominated, with book projects delayed by institutional duties. During this three-year period, however, reduced responsibilities and AI support placed book writing at the center of academic work. That phase is now concluding, and with teaching duties resuming, a more conventional balance is expected in the coming years.

To illustrate how AI's role varied across these projects, the following table presents a comparative overview (Table 7.9).

Several conclusions can be drawn from the table above, offering insights into how AI has transformed my academic writing process over the past few years:

- AI significantly reduces writing time. Across all five book projects, the inclusion of AI support has consistently shortened the estimated writing duration—often by 50% or more, and in some cases by up to two-thirds. Even projects with modest AI input show noticeable efficiency gains.
- The more complex the structure, the more useful AI becomes. Works like *Digital Marketing* and The first *Researcher's Journey* involved extensive reorganization, restructuring, and integration of large idea sets. These are tasks where AI proved beneficial helping detect duplication, clarify logic, and improve coherence.
- AI's role varies by project type. In books centered on language or formatting, like the revised *Intelligence Studies,* AI was mainly used for grammar and syntax corrections. In more theoretical or exploratory work, such as *Applied Evolutionary Economics,* the tool became a thinking companion—engaged in summarizing, testing arguments, and refining structure.
- Productivity gains compound when time and AI align. The most significant time savings occurred when both external conditions (such as teaching relief) and internal factors (AI integration) converged, as was the case with both *Researcher's Journey*. When authors have time to focus and powerful tools to assist, output increases dramatically.
- Even minimal AI use still yields time savings. Finally, even limited AI input—as in the case of *Intelligence Studies*—reduced the timeline by half. This suggests that scholars who engage with AI only occasionally can still benefit meaningfully from its capabilities.
- Writing with AI is more enjoyable. By taking over many of the more repetitive, mechanical, or routine aspects of writing—such as formatting, duplication checks, and sentence smoothing—AI allows authors to concentrate on the intellectual core of their work. This often makes the process more engaging and motivating, turning what used to be more tedious into something closer to a creative dialogue.

These trends suggest a new era of authorship where the efficiency and scope of academic writing are fundamentally reshaped by technological collaboration.

Table 7.9 Evolution of AI use in book writing

Book title	Active writing period[4]	Main role of AI	Use level	Time taken with AI	Estimated time without AI	Time saved	Efficiency gain (Time Saved/ Time Used)
Digital Marketing	2019–2024	Structure mapping, duplication detection, fact-checking, updating examples	Extensive	6 years (started using AI in December 2022, so only the last 2 years with AI)	8 year[5]	2 years	1.0[6]
Intelligence Studies (Revised)	2024	Grammar and syntax correction	Minimal	0.5 year	1 year	0.5 year	1.00

(continued)

[4] The "Active Writing Period" refers to the focused phase of writing and finalizing each manuscript. Most of these projects had been in development for considerably longer—often existing in the form of draft chapters, teaching materials, or research notes well before the formal decision was made to complete them as full-length books.

[5] The estimated time for completing this book was unusually long—about eight years, more than double that of my other works. The main reason was the rapid pace of change in digital marketing: by the time a structure or set of examples was in place, new developments had already shifted the field. This required postponing completion twice, waiting until after my courses were finished to update the material and keep it relevant.

[6] The final 2 years of this 6-year project (from December 2022 to 2024) were AI-assisted. The efficiency gain is calculated based on this AI-active period, not the full project duration.

Table 7.9 (continued)

Book title	Active writing period	Main role of AI	Use level	Time taken with AI	Estimated time without AI	Time saved	Efficiency gain (Time Saved/ Time Used)
The Researcher's Journey	2024–2025	Drafting efficiency, organizing large idea sets, fact-checking	Moderate	1 year	3 years	2 years	2.00
Applied Evolutionary Economics	2025	Dialogue partner, summarizing, structure refinement	Moderate	1 year	2 years	1 year	1.00
Current Manuscript (second Researcher's Journey)	2025–2026?	Section planning, headline rewording, chapter coordination	Extensive	1 year (projected)	3 years	2 years	2.00

Across these five book projects, the cumulative writing time with AI assistance amounts to approximately 9.5 years. Without AI, the estimated total would have been closer to 17 years, and some may not even have been completed due to teaching workload. This means that the integration of AI into the writing process has effectively saved around 7.5 years, cutting the required time nearly in half. While the degree of support varied by project—from light grammatical help to deep structural involvement—the overall effect has been a significant acceleration of *scholarly productivity*.

Rethinking Authorship in the Age of AI

This brings us back to the topic of authorship, but this time with an attempt to define the terminology based on the examples above. As generative AI tools become more sophisticated and embedded in academic workflows, the roles humans play vary widely—from original thinker and structural designer to prompter, supervisor, or even passive curator of machine-generated content.

To make sense of this new reality, we need a clearer vocabulary. The term author is no longer adequate as a one-size-fits-all label. Depending on the actual human contribution, we suggest here terms like "author," "editor," "collaborator," and "prompter," or "overseer."

The following table outlines five typical configurations of *human–machine co-production*. Each reflects a different level of human involvement and creative responsibility, with corresponding suggestions for what we might call the human on the cover (Table 7.10).

Based on current trends, what we are probably seeing is that most scholarly authors today, when they use AI in a meaningful way, fall into the second category: the *Human-Led Co-Author*. At best, they retain primary creative control, but they increasingly rely on AI for structure, refinement, and factual support. This suggests that while authorship has not disappeared, it has been fundamentally transformed. The traditional role of the *solitary thinker* is giving way to a more hybrid model, one where human judgment is still central, but no longer the sole force behind the text.

To assess the kind of author across my five most recent book projects, the general input from the tables above was entered into ChatGPT and classified using the previously presented framework. The following assessments emerged:

1. In the Digital Marketing book, AI was introduced in the final phase of a six-year project and used extensively for structure mapping, duplication

Table 7.10 Authorship roles in the age of AI

Scenario	Human contribution	AI contribution	Author role	Suggested label for person on cover	Risk of misrepresentation	Notes
Traditional Author	90–100%	0–10%	Full Author	*Author*	Very Low	AI used for minor grammar/style; creative and analytic control by human
Human-Led Co-Author	60–89%	11–40%	Primary Author	Author or *Human Lead Author*	Low to Medium	AI used for idea refinement, citations, structure, small phrasing help
Equal Co-Production	40–59%	41–60%	Collaborator	*Co-Author (Human–AI)*	Medium to High	Human and AI both contribute core content; originality harder to trace

Scenario	Human contribution	AI contribution	Author role	Suggested label for person on cover	Risk of misrepresentation	Notes
AI-Led Co-Author	10–39%	61–90%	Prompter/ Editor	*Editor, Prompt Engineer*	High	Human guides and edits, but AI generates most of the text
AI as Ghostwriter	0–9%	91–100%	Prompter Only	*Presenter or Curator*	Very High	Human gives prompt; AI writes virtually everything. Authorial voice absent

detection, and fact-checking. ChatGPT classifies this as *Human-Led Co-Author*, with the role on the cover best described as Author or Human Lead Author.
2. For the revised edition of Intelligence Studies, AI played a minimal role, limited to grammar and syntax support. The content was already in place, and no conceptual development was involved. This corresponds to the *Traditional Author* category.
3. In the Researcher's Journey, AI was used moderately to speed up drafting, organize content, and assist with basic fact-checking. Conceptual control and final judgment remained with the author. ChatGPT classifies this as *Human-Led Co-Author.*
4. In Applied Evolutionary Economics, AI contributed more actively to summarization, logic refinement, and restructuring. While the intellectual foundation pre-existed, the level of AI engagement was higher—approaching *Equal Co-Production.*
5. In the Current Manuscript, AI has been used throughout the process for planning, editing, and coordinating content. Despite this sustained involvement, the direction and decisions remain human-led. The classification again fits *Human-Led Co-Author.*

Based on ChatGPT's classification—derived from the information provided—the suggested labels appear broadly appropriate. For the book *Applied Evolutionary Economics*, however, the collaboration can be framed somewhat differently. While the system categorized it as approaching Equal Co-Production, it is, in my opinion, more accurately described as Human-Led Authorship. The substantive content was drawn almost entirely from earlier work, developed over many years of teaching, research, and publication. AI contributed meaningfully by supporting structure and refinement, but it did not introduce original ideas. Its role was closer to that of an editorial and structural assistant than a co-author. The aim here is not to dispute the machine's assessment, but to clarify the distinction in emphasis.

To illustrate the continuum of roles now possible, the table above offers a breakdown of different authorship scenarios, from traditional human authorship to near-total AI generation. Each scenario reflects a different balance of labor, creativity, and responsibility, along with varying risks of misrepresentation.

The figure below visualizes this continuum as a spectrum. On the one end, the human remains the dominant creative force: shaping the argument, writing the text, verifying sources. On the other end, the AI takes over most of these tasks, with the human merely initiating the process through prompts

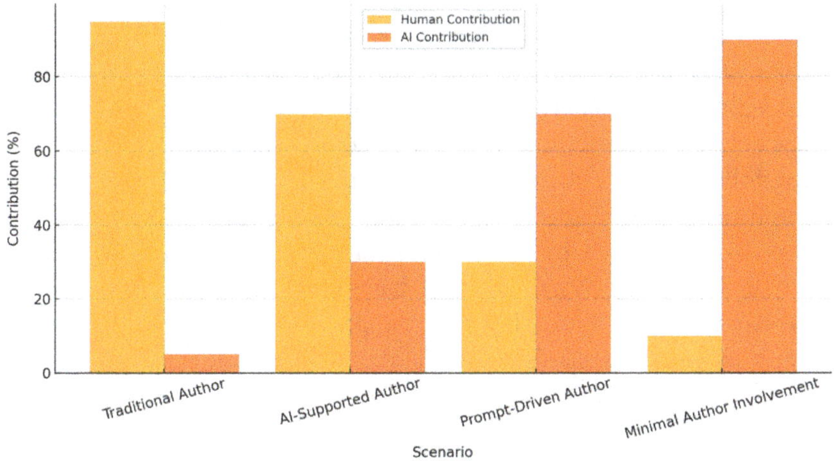

Fig. 7.1 Human vs. AI contribution in authorship scenarios

or edits. Between these two poles lies a broad zone of co-production, where intellectual effort is shared, boundaries blur, and ethical ambiguity is at its peak (Fig. 7.1).

What this makes clear is something more fundamental: the more cognitive and compositional tasks are delegated to AI, the less the human contributor can meaningfully be called the author in the traditional sense. At some point, the role shifts—from creator to curator, from thinker to facilitator. This is not merely a semantic issue; it's also about intellectual ownership. If the substance, style, and structure of a work are largely machine-generated, continuing to label the human as "author" could become misleading. In such cases, we could use new terms—and new standards—to reflect the actual division of labor behind scholarly outputs. Ultimately, the title of "author" could be reserved for those who carry out the bulk of the intellectual work themselves. When the human contribution approaches that of a prompter, the more accurate designation may be "collaborator," or simply "prompter," rather than author.

Having clarified how the meaning of authorship is evolving—and how roles like "author," "prompter," and "curator" are now part of a more nuanced *taxonomy*—it becomes natural to ask how, in practical terms, the writing process itself is changing. Authorship is no longer just about who wrote what, but also about *how* it was written. The everyday workflow of scholars is being reshaped by the integration of AI tools at every stage of knowledge production.

This brings us to a broader question of roles. If the label "author" no longer captures the full range of human involvement in AI-assisted work, what other roles are emerging alongside it? Who is the idea generator, the prompt engineer, the editor, the verifier? And how should we describe the machine's role when it contributes structure, language, or conceptual scaffolding?

In the following section, we move from the question of authorship to the wider architecture of academic production in the age of AI. What specific functions are performed by the human scholar, and which are increasingly handled by machines? What kinds of labor—creative, procedural, or interpretive—are being redefined in this new partnership? These questions take us directly into the mechanics of collaboration and the evolving division of labor in academic workflow.

7.2.1 AI and Workflow Transformation

At the core of human–machine collaboration lies a deceptively simple structure: the *question-and-answer loop*. The human provides the *Q*—the *prompt*—and the machine delivers the *A*—a generated response. This interactive process forms the basis of all AI-assisted work. Each round of output invites new questions, aimed at refining, redirecting, or expanding the response toward a more precise result. The practice of crafting effective prompts has given rise to a new field known as *prompt engineering* (Reynolds & McDonell, 2021).

Prompt engineering refers to the systematic design, testing, and refinement of inputs given to generative AI systems in order to elicit desired outputs. It is not only about wording a single question well, but about anticipating how the system interprets instructions, controlling context, adjusting constraints, and iteratively steering the model's behavior. In this sense, prompt engineering combines elements of programming, rhetoric, and pedagogy: the user must understand both the machine's limitations and the communicative strategies that guide it toward relevance, accuracy, and creativity.

We can express this mathematically as an iterative loop between human and machine. Let

Q_n = human prompt at iteration n

$A_n = f(Q_n)$ = AI's response function to prompt Q_n

$Q_{n+1} = g(A_n)$ = human reformulation based on AI's response

Then the collaboration can be represented as:

Equation 7.3: Human–AI Prompt Loop

$$Q^1 \rightarrow A^1 \rightarrow Q^2 \rightarrow A^2 \rightarrow Q^3 \rightarrow \ldots$$

Where:
f is the AI generation function
g is the human interpretive and corrective function

To be an effective prompt engineer, one must not only understand how to formulate efficient and contextually relevant queries, but also possess a strong working knowledge of what the model *can* and *cannot* do. These capabilities and limitations are dynamic: as large language models evolve, their performance changes continuously, often on a weekly or monthly basis as updates are deployed (Bommasani et al., 2022; OpenAI, 2023). This creates a moving target for users, where success depends on both domain expertise and up-to-date familiarity with the AI's current constraints and affordances. Prompt engineering, then, is not simply a technical skill; it is an *adaptive cognitive practice* that reflects the broader shift toward interactive, human–machine co-production of knowledge.

The table a bit further below outlines how the writing process has evolved in my own case following the integration of AI tools. As in the past, the foundation of my scholarly work remains consistent: reading books, articles, and media sources, and manually recording observations and reflections. These entries are compiled in handwritten notebooks. Once completed, each notebook is indexed and archived for future reference. This practice goes back to the start of my university studies, and over the decades it has become the backbone of my intellectual work. In these notebooks I place summaries of whatever I read that I consider worth preserving—insights, arguments, or data that may later serve as material for reflection, teaching, or writing.

When initiating a new academic project, these indexed notes are consulted, and writing begins in Microsoft Word. A preliminary content structure is developed at the outset. This outline often undergoes substantial revision throughout the process, with sections reorganized or reformulated as necessary. At this stage, AI tools are not significantly involved. Their role becomes more prominent once a working draft is underway.

Draft material is entered into the AI interface in the form of prompts, depending on the task. To give a few simple examples: for grammatical and stylistic corrections, the prompts *"Correct:"* and *"Fact-check"* are often used. For conceptual development or when dealing with vague or unstructured content, *"Improve:"* is more suitable. I frequently ask the system to check that transitions between ideas and paragraphs are smooth, especially when moving in and out of case boxes. The prompt *"Give examples"* is particularly effective for stimulating ideas or making abstract points more concrete. This is also where I often learn the most myself.

When references are needed, *"List refs"* can be used to generate citations—though all references must be manually verified, typically via Google Scholar, due to known issues with broken links and fabricated metadata. I would estimate that these types of prompts account for about 90% of those I use when writing scholarly material. Toward the end of the process, I often also discuss style with the AI: whether I am being too blunt, whether a formulation risks offending someone, or whether a paragraph should be toned down a notch or two.

The resulting output generally preserves the core substance of the original material but improves fluency, grammar, and structural clarity. Manual editing is often necessary afterward to ensure consistency with the author's stylistic preferences. When preparing bibliographies, prompts such as "Merge refs" and "Write refs in APA style" can significantly reduce formatting time. However, current limitations exist, for instance, ChatGPT can typically only process around 1–1.5 pages of references per session. This necessitates segmenting the request (e.g., "List refs from A to O") to manage the output effectively. I guess in a few years' time, and certainly to the next generation, this will sound much like someone patiently explaining how the wheels turn on a Model T Ford to make the car move forward.

For larger works, AI is also used to assess where newly written material fits within the overall structure. This is done by pasting the full table of contents into the prompt as a contextual guide, since AI models cannot process an entire long-form manuscript at once. While these suggestions are frequently helpful, they are not without fault. AI occasionally omits relevant material or offers overly agreeable responses, especially when the prompt is framed as a leading question (e.g., "Don't you think that…"). To mitigate this, it is advisable to *frame queries neutrally*, avoiding the suggestion of a desired outcome. Large language models are designed to align with user intent and will typically produce responses that confirm the prompt unless directed otherwise. However, when a query is perceived to conflict with the model's underlying *ethical guidelines* or *safety protocols*, the system may respond with unusual assertiveness—sometimes using capital letters or emphatic language to signal disagreement. In such instances, the model appears to adopt a corrective stance, effectively positioning itself as a moral or *normative authority*—a posture which, in itself, may constitute an *ethical dilemma*. This behavior likely reflects the model's embedded alignment constraints rather than any genuine reasoning, yet it can give the impression that the AI is placing the user "in their place" when it detects a perceived violation of its *training parameters*.

Another challenge relates to ideological neutrality. Many AI models have been criticized for perceived political bias or "*overcorrection*" toward certain normative assumptions. While such critiques are valid, it is also problematic to expect the AI to exhibit a perfectly neutral stance. Like all text generators, it reflects the biases embedded in its training data and *instruction protocols*. If the response appears unbalanced or ideologically skewed, the best course of action is often to request examples representing alternative perspectives, thereby introducing a measure of balance and dialogical symmetry into the response.

An additional strategy is to compare the outputs of multiple AI systems. Since different models are trained on *distinct corpora* and governed by varying *moderation policies*, cross-referencing can help surface underlying assumptions and reveal blind spots in individual models. For those who can afford multiple subscriptions, using several AIs in parallel offers a practical method to triangulate responses.

By contrast, in authoritarian regimes or monopolized information environments, users may have access to only a single state-sanctioned AI—or several models that all follow the same ethical and *political protocol*. In such contexts, the risk of epistemic conformity becomes more acute, underscoring the importance of pluralism and transparency in the development and deployment of large language models.

Finally, once individual sections or entire drafts are complete, the AI can be used to provide editorial feedback. In this capacity, it functions effectively as a *review assistant*, identifying redundancy, inconsistencies, or gaps in logic. While its suggestions are not always fully reliable, they often resemble the type of constructive commentary expected from a peer reviewer or editor and can be used as a useful basis for further refinement. Taken together, these shifts show how AI is gradually woven into every stage of the academic workflow—from idea gathering to final editing—without replacing the underlying intellectual labor (Table 7.11).

Based on this evolving process, the AI now serves three primary functions:

Academic Secretary: AI ensures correct grammar, syntax, punctuation, and formatting with a precision and speed that rivals the best human editors. More than a spell-checker, it rewrites clumsy sentences, adjusts tone, applies academic style guides (APA, MLA, Chicago), and identifies inconsistencies across entire documents. Unlike human copyeditors or translators—who are expensive, require long lead times, and still vary widely in

Table 7.11 Comparison of academic workflows before and after AI integration

Work Stage	Before AI	With AI
1. *Gathering Ideas*	Mostly from books, newspapers, academic journals, and online programs	Almost the same as before, though AI is now also asked for suggestions on what to read or follow
2. *Taking Notes*	Handwritten notes condensed into diaries (approx. 2 per year), later indexed and archived	Still using handwritten diaries, but now often supplementing this with quick AI-prompted queries
3. *Finding Source Material*	Manual search via library databases, Google, Google Scholar, and bookmarks	Now use AI more than Google—AI gives faster, more targeted responses. Still verify key sources manually
4. *Transferring Notes to Drafts*	Open MS Word documents, transferring and adapting notes into rough drafts across multiple files	A combination: copying MS Word notes into ChatGPT, using prompts like "improve" or "correct."
5. *Draft Development*	Writing and editing manually, often slowly and over long periods	Accelerated drafting through iterative prompting. Faster refinement of syntax, structure, and clarity
6. *Fact-Checking*	Done manually via trusted academic sources, databases, and previous literature	Now done initially via AI ("fact-check"), then cross-verified via Google Scholar or article databases
7. *Reference Management*	Manually built reference lists in APA or similar format. Time-consuming	Use AI with prompts like "list refs" and "merge refs" to compile and format references quickly
8. *Structuring Manuscripts*	Organize chapters and sections alone, often unsure about placement	Ask AI for suggestions based on the table of contents—often helpful, though not always complete

(continued)

Table 7.11 (continued)

Work Stage	Before AI	With AI
9. *Titles and Subheadings*	Create and revise manually, often after the content is written	Ask AI to rephrase or polish titles/ subheadings—saves time and improves clarity
10. *Feedback and Revision*	Occasionally from colleagues, often delayed and irregular	AI acts as a "critical colleague," offering instant feedback on tone, logic, and coherence
11. *Final Editing*	Slow manual grammar and syntax revisions	AI acts like an academic secretary, handling grammar and structure smoothly and quickly
12. *Collaboration Dynamics*	Mostly solo work. Limited by others' schedules, dropouts, or tech mishaps	Now work feels like a smooth team effort—AI is always available, quick, and without social friction

quality—AI is always available, instantly responsive, and improves with use.

For most scholars, hiring a full-time academic secretary or proofreader is unthinkable; even occasional editing services can be costly and slow. With AI, these services are integrated, scalable, and virtually free once the technology is in place. It doesn't get tired, it doesn't miss patterns due to boredom or distraction, and it works on a scale and timeline no human ever could.

Research Assistant: Finding relevant literature, organizing citations, summarizing key arguments, and checking factual claims—these are time-intensive tasks that used to be delegated to master's students or PhD candidates. But today's AI can outperform even the most diligent human assistant in many of these areas.

Unlike a junior researcher, AI does not forget instructions, skim abstracts instead of reading papers, or overlook key references. It can search across massive corpora, identify the most cited or methodologically sound studies, and summarize them concisely. It can also suggest where sources may be missing, spot redundancy, and flag over-reliance on certain types of literature.

Critically, AI performs these tasks in seconds, not days. While a human assistant may take a week to assemble a reference list and may still miss important works, AI can generate, revise, and check citations instantly—without complaint, error fatigue, or need for training.

Critical Reader: Perhaps the most surprising and transformative of AI's functions is its ability to serve as a critical reader. It can highlight logical gaps, unclear transitions, repetitive phrasing, weak arguments, and implicit assumptions. And it does so in a tone that is neither dismissive nor sycophantic.

Compared to peer reviewers, who often provide cursory or vague feedback due to time constraints, or colleagues who are too polite (or busy) to engage deeply with your draft, AI offers something rare: consistent, structured, and available-on-demand critique.

Even more importantly, it can iterate with you. A good reader asks a clarifying question. A great reader follows up after you've answered it. AI does this naturally—responding to your revisions, checking for improved flow, and proposing alternatives until the argument is as clear and rigorous as possible. Few colleagues, however brilliant, are willing or able to give that level of repeated attention.

Figure 7.2 illustrates this distinction by separating two layers of academic work: the "workflow" (the process labor that gets a project from rough notes to a structured draft) and the "final product" (the substantive intellectual content that defines ownership of the work).

In sum, these three roles—secretary, assistant, and reader—together account, in my estimate, for roughly 60–80% of the labor involved in the early and middle stages of academic production. In the past, such work would have been spread across a team of collaborators; today, much of it is handled

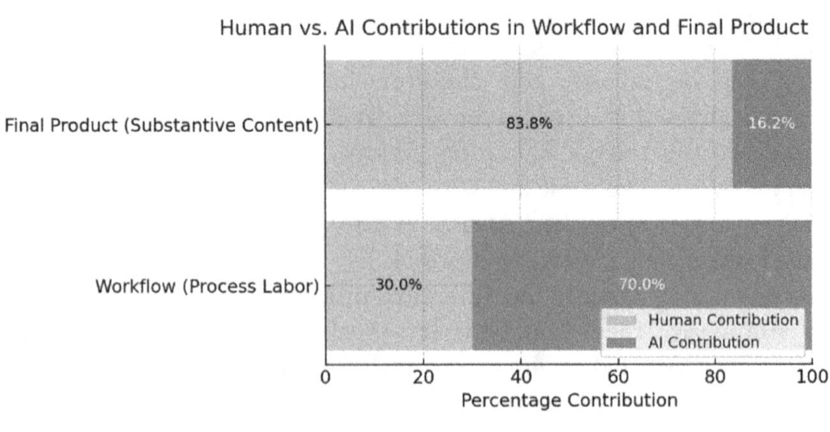

Fig. 7.2 Human and AI contributions across workflow and final product

by AI, which takes on the process-heavy tasks of drafting, checking, and refining while the researcher focuses on substantive thinking and design.

This *division of labor* looks very different when compared to the composition of the final product. As shown in the earlier example—and now illustrated in the figure above—the AI itself estimated that about 83.75 and finally 86.3% of the substantive content came from my own contribution. In short: AI carries much of the workflow, but the intellectual ownership of the finished work remains primarily human.

What once required an entire team of colleagues is now accomplished with a *single interface*. The implications are staggering: scholarly productivity has radically increased, and quality can improve—provided the researcher remains intellectually engaged and ethically grounded.

This form of collaboration—with a tireless, on-demand, and increasingly competent digital co-worker—has begun to alter not only how texts are produced, but also how ideas are formed, arguments developed, and knowledge explored. It marks a broader shift in the *academic workflow*, one that extends beyond productivity gains to reshape fundamental aspects of scholarly practice.

At the same time, it has made writing more intensive. The presence of a responsive "other" creates momentum: drafting becomes more exciting, more dynamic, and in some ways more demanding. One feels an almost implicit obligation not to "let the collaborator down," to keep the dialogue going and not abandon the process midstream. This stickiness can be highly productive, generating flow states that accelerate research and sharpen focus. Yet it also carries risks of exhaustion, as the interaction invites continuous engagement and makes it harder to disengage. What emerges is a new *rhythm of work*—energizing, but potentially consuming—that redefines both the pace and the psychology of academic authorship.

By assisting the lead researcher in these three roles—academic secretary, research assistant, and critical reader—the AI now functions as a virtual research team embedded within a single author's workflow. This shift reduces coordination costs, increases speed, and delivers responsive feedback that would once have required multiple colleagues working in tandem.

This pattern is by no means confined to academia. Similar shifts are unfolding across a range of professional domains. In the gaming industry, for instance, what once required large, multi-specialist teams—comprising designers, animators, and sound engineers—can now often be accomplished by a single individual equipped with advanced generative tools. It is increasingly expected that many of the most competitive games in the coming years will be produced by *solo creators* who use AI to perform tasks that once demanded entire studios. This signals a broader trend: individual professionals, empowered by AI, are gaining unprecedented productive capacity—often at the cost of traditional, team-based workflows.

In academia, the effects are comparable. Roles previously filled by junior researchers, assistants, or peer reviewers are now being absorbed by AI systems—systems that do not tire, require scheduling, or contest editorial authority. As a result, the academic division of labor is undergoing significant transformation. Lead researchers gain autonomy and efficiency, but those who once supported the research process may find fewer opportunities to contribute, especially in entry-level positions.

These changes also reinforce a shift toward decentralized, *home-based scholarship*. With AI now handling secretarial, analytical, and editorial functions, and with videoconferencing tools constantly improving, it becomes entirely feasible for researchers to operate independently from their homes. Platforms such as YouTube, academic podcasts, and webinars provide ready access to lectures, expert commentary, and peer feedback, minimizing the need for physical co-presence. This move toward *distributed research models* echoes older academic traditions. In the early twentieth century for example, it was not uncommon for students to visit professors in their homes rather than at formal offices (Shils, 1972). We may well be returning to a version of that model—only now through digital means.

What was once limited by institutional infrastructure is now increasingly facilitated by the digital environment. For the social sciences in particular—where research centers on reading, writing, and interpretation—this shift offers both practical and economic benefits. It lowers overhead costs related to commuting, office space, and utilities, while enabling more flexible, focused work. Large lecture halls and occasional in-person gatherings will still play important pedagogical and social roles, but universities may need to rethink their physical footprint in an era of hybrid and remote scholarship. For natural sciences and other lab-dependent disciplines, however, physical facilities will remain indispensable.

So, as we have seen then, the *solo scholar*—augmented by AI—can now perform what once required an entire team. This development raises deeper questions about labor distribution, academic training, and the future of collaborative knowledge production. What is gained in individual capacity may come at the cost of *collective development*, mentorship, and opportunities for early-career researchers. At the same time, it empowers researchers to define their own workflows, rely on digital channels for intellectual exchange, and reshape what it means to participate in academic life. For the human sciences, at least, the future may be more hybrid, more distributed, and more dependent on individual initiative—balanced, one hopes, by new forms of virtual collegiality and collaborative engagement.

7.3 Concluding Reflections: Returning to the Two Main Questions

Earlier in this book two major questions were raised. The first was: Why write this book at all—what purpose does it serve? The intention was to reopen space for the big questions—about life, knowledge, and meaning—within the social sciences. The second was more provocative: What if the social sciences had never existed? Would anything essential be lost? For most of human history, they did not exist, and yet people lived, governed, and created cultures much like today. Is this improving or deteriorating the social science project overall? Now that machines can analyze text, detect patterns, and model behavior faster than humans, the question acquires new urgency: What distinctive contribution do social scientists still provide?

The analysis in this chapter suggests that AI is not merely another tool, but a force that unsettles the very identity of the scholar. Machines are now co-participants in knowledge production, altering workflows, writing practices, and even the definition of authorship. They accelerate efficiency, but also raise profound questions about trust, integrity, and scholarly responsibility. The issue is not whether AI belongs in academia—it already does—but how to integrate it without losing what is most essential to scholarship: reflection, judgment, and meaning.

This chapter has shown that the traditional boundaries of authorship are dissolving. Distinctions between author, editor, and assistant must be renegotiated, supported by new norms of disclosure and accountability. Frameworks such as the authorship score demonstrate one way forward, but measurement alone is insufficient. What matters ultimately is trust—both in individual texts and in the scholarly process as a whole.

The chapter also highlighted the structural risks of over-relying on machine-generated content. Left unchecked, AI tends to reinforce orthodoxy, privileging dominant voices and filtering out disruptive or marginal ideas. This risks stagnation: more knowledge circulated, but less knowledge created. The "stagnation risk equation" underscores this point—if AI begins to dominate knowledge production while contributing little novelty, the overall system may expand in breadth but not in depth.

Looking ahead, speculative scenarios—from autonomous research agents to AI-driven departments—suggest that the challenge is shifting from technical feasibility to social design. The key question becomes: what kind of intellectual environment are we building, and what kind of scholars do we want to remain? If machines increasingly perform the mechanics of research, the role of humans will be to safeguard judgment, ethics, and purpose.

The deeper issue, then, is not just technical but ethical. If AI reshapes how texts are written, reviewed, and circulated, it also sharpens long-standing questions of responsibility, fairness, and legitimacy. The social sciences must therefore reclaim their vocation as sciences—rigorous, independent, and resilient—while adapting to a two-brain world where human and machine intelligence interact.

The answer to the first question—why write this book at all—is that it has become vital to do so now precisely because of AI. The subject is so overwhelming, touching every part of academic life and beyond, that it forced itself upon me, even though my original plan was to write only about the evolutionary approach to the social sciences. That project became impossible without addressing AI, because it now defines the conditions under which scholarship is practiced.

The answer to the second question—what if the social sciences had never existed—is more sobering. If the discipline continues along its current path, it risks becoming irrelevant, overtaken by other fields that are already solving its problems more effectively. This risk is heightened by a global shift of influence from Western to Asian ideals. In much of Asia, the social sciences do not enjoy the same status or relevance, partly because we have built them around a *Western-centric worldview*. If they are to remain significant, the social sciences must become more inclusive, global, and adaptive. They must also prove to themselves that they are, in fact, a truly non-normative project, and they must become more scientific in both method and ambition.

At the same time, this chapter has also shown that the social sciences can be dramatically strengthened by AI. Far from erasing the discipline, AI offers the right set of tools to tackle many of the problems that have long hindered its progress. Used wisely, AI can help renew the social sciences by making them more rigorous, more transparent, and more relevant to the complex realities of our time.

The opportunity is real: to reimagine the social sciences as a field equal to the urgency and complexity of our time. But so is the risk: that in failing to adapt, the discipline drifts into irrelevance, leaving the big questions to other disciplines. The path forward will require institutional courage, epistemic humility, and a renewed commitment to ethics—not as abstract theory, but as the living foundation of scholarship in an age of rapid transformation. These ethical questions are not a side issue; they form the core of the next chapter, where the focus turns to how values, responsibility, and legitimacy must guide research in the era of intelligent systems.

References

Abid, A., Farooqi, M., & Zou, J. (2021). *Persistent anti-Muslim bias in large language models*. arXiv preprint arXiv:2101.05783.

Andersen, J., Rørvik, R., & Brøgger, K. (2023). Rethinking authorship in the age of AI. *Higher Education, 85*(3), 435–449.

Bender, E. M., Gebru, T., McMillan-Major, A., & Shmitchell, S. (2021). On the dangers of stochastic parrots: Can language models be too big? In *FAccT 21: Proceedings of the 2021 ACM Conference on Fairness, Accountability, and Transparency* (pp. 610–623).

Bender, E. M., & Koller, A. (2020). Climbing towards NLU: On meaning, form, and understanding in the age of data. *Proceedings of the 58th Annual Meeting of the Association for Computational Linguistics (ACL 2020)*, 5185–5198.

Bommasani, R., Hudson, D. A., Adeli, E., Altman, R., Arora, S., von Arx, S., ... & Liang, P. (2022). *On the opportunities and risks of foundation models*. arXiv preprint arXiv:2108.07258

Bostrom, N. (2014). *Superintelligence: Paths, dangers, strategies*. Oxford University Press.

Brynjolfsson, E., & McAfee, A. (2017). *Machine, platform, crowd: Harnessing our digital future*. W. W. Norton & Company.

Cave, S., & Dignum, V. (2019). AI ethics: The challenge of building trust. *Philosophy & Technology, 32*(1), 1–3.

Chung, Y. A., Hou, L., Longpre, S., Zoph, B., Tay, Y., Fedus, W., ... & Le, Q. V. (2022). *Scaling instruction-finetuned language models*. arXiv preprint arXiv:2210. 11416

Churchland, P. M. (2002). *Brain-wise: Studies in neurophilosophy*. MIT Press

Dwivedi, Y. K., Hughes, D. L., Baabdullah, A. M., Ribeiro-Navarrete, S., Giannakis, M., Al-Debei, M. M., ... & Wamba, S. F. (2021). Artificial intelligence (AI): Multidisciplinary perspectives on emerging challenges, opportunities, and agenda for research, practice and policy. *International Journal of Information Management, 57*, 101994.

Dwivedi, Y. K., Hughes, D. L., Coombs, C., Constantiou, I., Duan, Y., Edwards, J. S., ... & Wade, M. R. (2023). Generative artificial intelligence for research, practice and policy: Opportunities, challenges, and research agenda. *Journal of Business Research, 169*, 114041.

Editorial, N. (2023). Tools such as ChatGPT threaten transparent science; here are our ground rules for their use. *Nature, 613*(7945), 612. https://doi.org/10.1038/d41586-023-00191-1

Elsevier. (2023). *Responsible use of AI tools in scientific writing*. https://www.elsevier.com/about/policies-and-standards/the-use-of-generative-ai-and-ai-assisted-technologies-in-writing-for-elsevier?utm_source=chatgpt.com

Evans, J. A., & Rzhetsky, A. (2011). Machine science. *Science, 331*(6018), 713–715.

Floridi, L., & Chiriatti, M. (2020). GPT-3: Its nature, scope, limits, and consequences. *Minds and Machines, 30*(4), 681–694.

Floridi, L. (2023). *The ethics of artificial intelligence*. Oxford University Press.

Gil, Y., David, C. H., Demir, I., et al. (2014). Toward the geoscience paper of the future: Best practices for documenting and sharing research from data to software to provenance. *Earth and Space Science, 3*(10), 388–415.

Gilson, A., Safranek, C. W., Huang, T., Socrates, V., Chi, L., Taylor, R. A., & Chartash, D. (2023). How well does ChatGPT do on the USMLE? The implications of large language models for medical education and knowledge assessment. *PLOS Digital Health, 2*(2), e0000198.

Heaven, D. (2023). Why we must regulate AI now. *Nature, 617*, 620–622.

Hossenfelder, S. (2025a). *I tried Vibe Physics, this is what I learned* [Video]. YouTube. https://www.youtube.com/watch?v=CbO2YosyTt4

Jasanoff, S. (2016). *The ethics of invention: Technology and the human future.* W. W. Norton & Company.

Ji, Z., Lee, N., Frieske, R., Yu, T., Su, D., Xu, Y., Ishii, E., Bang, Y., Chen, D., Dai, W., Chan, H. S., Madotto, A., & Fung, P. (2023). Survey of hallucination in natural language generation. *ACM Computing Surveys, 55*(12), 1–38.

Kahneman, D., Sibony, O., & Sunstein, C. R. (2021). *Noise: A flaw in human judgment.* Little, Brown Spark.

Koch, C., & Tononi, G. (2013). Can machines be conscious? *IEEE Spectrum, 50*(6), 44–51.

Marcus, G. (2022). *Rebooting AI: Building artificial intelligence we can trust.* Vintage

Marcus, G., & Davis, E. (2020). *Rebooting AI: Building artificial intelligence we can trust*. Vintage.

Maynez, J., Narayan, S., Bohnet, B., & McDonald, R. (2020). On faithfulness and factuality in abstractive summarization. In *ACL 2020: Proceedings of the 58th Annual Meeting of the Association for Computational Linguistics* (pp. 1906–1919).

Merton, R. K. (1973). *The sociology of science: Theoretical and empirical investigations.* University of Chicago Press. (Original work published 1942)

OpenAI. (2023). *GPT-4 technical report*. chrome-extension://efaidnbmnnnibpcajpcglclefindmkaj/https://cdn.openai.com/papers/gpt-4.pdf

Oreskes, N. (2019). *Why trust science?* Princeton University Press.

Reynolds, L., & McDonell, K. (2021). *Prompt programming for large language models: Beyond the few-shot paradigm.* arXiv preprint arXiv:2102.07350

Russell, S., & Norvig, P. (2021). *Artificial intelligence: A modern approach* (4th ed.). Pearson.

Shapin, S. (2010). *Never pure: Historical studies of science as if it was produced by people with bodies, situated in time, space, culture, and society, and struggling for credibility and authority.* Johns Hopkins University Press.

Smaldino, P. E. (2023). Models are stupid, and we need more of them. *Nature Human Behaviour, 7*(5), 669–671.

Springer Nature. (2023). *Editorial policy update on AI and authorship.* https://www.springer.com/gp/editorial-policies/artificial-intelligence--ai-/25428500?srsltid=AfmBOop4JdMD2RCSV5LG-YgBb4NtQxkcw6zAKJLH38X-yf0HnS1Dvi1a&utm_source=chatgpt.com

Stokel-Walker, C. (2023). ChatGPT listed as author on research papers: Many scientists disapprove. *Nature, 613*(7945), 620–621. https://doi.org/10.1038/d41586-023-00107-z

Tegmark, M. (2017). *Life 3.0: Being human in the age of artificial intelligence.* Knopf.

Trew, B. (2023). Can AI make scientific discoveries? *Nature, 620*(7974), 10–12.

Whittlestone, J., Nyrup, R., Alexandrova, A., & Cave, S. (2019). The role and limits of principles in AI ethics. In *Proceedings of the AAAI/ACM Conference on AI, Ethics, and Society.*

Further Reading

Binns, R. (2018). Fairness in machine learning: Lessons from political philosophy. In *Proceedings of the 2018 Conference on Fairness, Accountability and Transparency.*

Burrell, J. (2016). How the machine 'thinks': Understanding opacity in machine learning algorithms. *Big Data & Society, 3*(1), 2053951715622512.

Crawford, K. (2021). *Atlas of AI: Power, politics, and the planetary costs of artificial intelligence.* Yale University Press.

Economist, T. (2025). July 26–August 8). The economics of superintelligence. *The Economist, 447*(9334), 13–16.

Gilson, A., Safranek, C. W., Huang, T., Socrates, V., Chi, L., Taylor, R. A., & Chartash, D. (2022). How well can ChatGPT perform on the United States medical licensing examination? *medRxiv.* https://doi.org/10.1101/2022.12.23.22283901

Hossenfelder, S. (2025b). *Scientists measure qualia for first time—It was thought to be impossible* [Video]. YouTube. https://www.youtube.com/watch?v=NCD2A_bhDTI

Lee, N., Schick, T., & Schütze, H. (2023). *Hallucination-free? Quantifying and reducing hallucination in large language models.* arXiv preprint arXiv:2305.14206

Lipton, Z. C. (2018). The mythos of model interpretability. *Communications of the ACM, 61*(10), 36–43.

Mitchell, M., Wu, S., Zaldivar, A., Barnes, P., Vasserman, L., Hutchinson, B., Spitzer, E., Raji, I. D., & Gebru, T. (2019). Model cards for model reporting.

In *FAT '19: Proceedings of the Conference on Fairness, Accountability, and Transparency* (pp. 220–229).

Söilen, K. S. (2005). *Introduction to private and public intelligence*. Student literature.

Söilen, K. S. (2012). *Geoeconomics*. Bookboon.

Söilen, K. S. (2025). *The researcher's journey: A guide to methodology and academia in social sciences*. Springer.

van Dis, E. A. M., Bollen, J., Zuidema, W., van Rooij, R., & Bockting, C. L. H. (2023). ChatGPT: Five priorities for research. *Nature, 614*, 224–226.

Vogl, R., Rayyan, S., Huber, S., & Strohmaier, M. (2022). Natural language processing meets qualitative research: Towards a fully automated thematic analysis. *Qualitative Market Research: An International Journal, 25*(3), 499–514.

Zuccon, G., Koopman, B., Sadeghi, S., & Palotti, J. (2023). *The rise of fabricated citations in AI-generated text*. arXiv preprint arXiv:2306.07975

8

Ethics and Responsibility in the Age of AI

Abstract As artificial intelligence reshapes knowledge, work, and institutions, ethics is increasingly invoked as humanity's final safeguard. This chapter asks a more unsettling question: what happens when judgment itself—long seen as the human core of responsibility—is outsourced, diluted, or turned into performance? Moving beyond narrow "AI ethics" checklists, the chapter reframes ethics as a functional and evolutionary practice grounded in culture, institutions, and historical experience. It challenges universalist and compliance-driven moral frameworks, arguing instead for an empirical form of virtue ethics focused on consequence, resilience, and social cohesion. By examining technomoral change, institutional fragility, and the risks of ethical theater, this chapter shows why ethics must be embedded in systems rather than proclaimed in slogans. In an age of accelerating technology, responsibility cannot be delegated to machines—or to abstract principles alone. Without grounded moral judgment, we risk outsourcing not just work, but the very capacities that sustain human societies.

Chapter 7 examined how artificial intelligence is reshaping knowledge production—accelerating research, changing scholarly roles, and transforming academic institutions. This chapter turns to ethics, but not in the narrow sense of AI ethics alone. The concern here is broader: how ethics relates to the practice of the social sciences themselves in an age where AI is only one among many disruptive forces. The central question is not simply what AI can or cannot do, but what happens when judgment—long regarded as the human core of scholarship—is outsourced, compromised, or reframed.

K. Solberg Söilen, *The Researcher's Journey in the Age of AI*,
https://doi.org/10.1007/978-3-032-23069-0_8

Ethics is often claimed as humanity's last domain, yet this belief may provide more comfort than protection. The challenge is not only the possibility of "*unethical machines*," but also the ethical illusions and blind spots that arise within the social sciences when they confront rapid technological and cultural change. This chapter argues that these issues can only be addressed within a broader paradigm of the *Evolutionary Social Sciences*, which unites explanatory rigor with moral responsibility.

This chapter challenges universalist ideals and compliance-driven frameworks that reduce ethics to performance. Instead, it advances an empirical and functional view of virtue ethics: ethics as adaptation, grounded in historical experience, institutional integrity, and cultural anchors that foster cooperation and resilience.

The discussion unfolds through five key themes:

1. The Ethics Gap—What machines cannot do, and what this means for human responsibility in empathy, restraint, and meaning-making.
2. Technomoral Change—How technologies reshape not just behavior, but values, often turning ethics into political theater.
3. From Culture to Code—Why cultural traditions matter for AI design, and what happens when machines cross moral boundaries.
4. Practical Ethics and Fragile Institutions—How governance, oversight, and institutional courage can withstand political capture and cultural erosion.
5. Functional Ethics and Decline—Why civilizations fail to self-correct, and why an ethics of consequence, not mere intention, is needed to avoid collapse.

The argument throughout is that ethics in the age of AI must not be reactive or decorative. It must be embedded in the systems we build, guided by virtues proven across generations—responsibility, humility, foresight, and care for the vulnerable. Without this, we risk delegating not just work, but our humanity.

8.1 The Ethics Gap: Machines, Morality, and the Social Sciences

Much of today's discourse on ethics and AI carries the tone of a last stand. The narrative suggests that while machines may soon surpass us in intelligence, humans will still retain a unique moral domain. Yet this view is less a philosophical certainty than a psychological defense. History and evolutionary psychology remind us that humans are not consistently ethical—we can be biased, inconsistent, and at times cruel. Machines, by contrast, have no ethics of their own. They are neither virtuous nor evil; they simply follow the principles and data built into them. What they can offer—if well designed—is consistency, which is more than can often be said of human judgment.

To see how this plays out in practice, it helps to look at how one of the leading AI systems handles the question of ethics in real time. Here the process is less about timeless principles and more about organizational choices, user expectations, and the individuals who ultimately bear responsibility.

Case in a Box: How AI "Decides" Ethics

When asked how ChatGPT makes ethical decisions, Sam Altman admitted in an interview that there is no single answer. OpenAI relies on internal teams of employees who determine which sources to align with, and it attempts to average across the expectations of its users, while Altman himself ultimately takes responsibility for the outcomes (Carlson, 2024). This picture matches what is publicly known about large language models more broadly. They do not reason morally but approximate ethical behavior through design choices.

Most systems are trained with *reinforcement learning from human feedback* (RLHF), where human labelers score model outputs and a reward model is built to favor the preferred ones (Ouyang et al., 2022). On top of this come written specifications—OpenAI now publishes a *Model Spec*—that set out behavioral goals such as helpfulness, respect for law, and avoidance of harm, and that prescribe how conflicts between principles should be handled (OpenAI, 2024). Safety layers are added through red-teaming, usage policies, and "system cards" that document known risks (OpenAI, 2023). Other companies, such as Anthropic, have experimented with *constitutional AI*, where a model is fine-tuned against an explicit set of normative principles drafted in advance (Bai et al., 2022).

Yet none of these procedures resolve the deepest ambiguity: whose values prevail when user preferences, cultural contexts, and developer-imposed principles diverge? OpenAI has piloted *democratic-input projects* to gather public opinion, but it remains opaque how this input translates into model behavior (Gabriel, 2020; Weidinger et al., 2022). What can be said with confidence is that these systems reflect the priorities of their human trainers and designers, rather than any independent moral faculty or ethical principles. And this is only one example: other companies, and indeed other states, are free to define their own ethical standards for AI—something they already do in practice.

Questions for Discussion

1. What are the advantages and limitations of reinforcement learning from human feedback (RLHF) as a method for shaping AI ethics?
2. How transparent should AI companies be about the sources, principles, or value frameworks they choose to embed?
3. Should democratic input play a larger role in determining how AI behaves, or would this risk reinforcing the biases of "average" users?
4. How might competing national or cultural approaches to AI ethics create tensions in international contexts?
5. If AI has no moral faculty of its own, should it be held accountable for harmful outcomes, or should responsibility always lie with its human designers and institutions?

What emerges from the case is clear: AI systems do not possess their own moral compass. They mirror the priorities, choices, and compromises of those who build and train them. This leads to a deeper challenge: there is no single ethics to encode, but many. On the one hand, this is troubling—especially when the embedded values diverge from one's own. On the other, it reflects a broader moral reality: human societies themselves are plural, divided, and often in conflict over what counts as ethical. The real question, then, is whether the individuals shaping an AI's behavior are truly representative of their culture, or whether they reflect only a narrow subset of values. Once an *AI's ethical framework* is explicitly tied to a cultural context, it becomes easier to navigate between systems—because we can know in advance what norms and judgments to expect. To make this credible, however, each AI should also disclose which cultural tradition it claims to represent and why it is representative, preferably with transparency about the algorithms and weighting mechanisms that guide its ethical judgments and value choices.

At the same time, we know that moral frameworks differ across cultures, evolve over time, and frequently conflict with one another. *AI ethics* therefore must mirror this pluralism. For AI to act in ways that we consider ethical, it must do two things: first, adapt to the cultural context in which it is deployed; and second, remain capable of change as norms evolve. The real challenge is not whether machines "have" ethics, but whether they can remain responsive to shifting moral landscapes. Thus, for an AI system to be truly international—a likely goal of most AI companies—it must operate with an adaptive, *multi-ethical specification*, providing different answers depending on the cultural framework applied. Such a design would not only broaden the system's legitimacy but also offer a valuable feature: the ability for users to request answers according to different cultural perspectives and compare them side by side. Will it develop like that? Well, so far it has not.

Of course, AIs within the same culture can also have different ethical specifications. For example, we observe divergence between Elon Musk's chatbot Grok, developed by xAI and integrated into X, and ChatGPT. Musk has argued that ChatGPT is "too politically correct" and designed Grok as an alternative system that would not avoid politically controversial statements (Business Insider, 2025; Financial Times, 2025). The result is that Grok often produces different answers than ChatGPT on political or ideological issues, while offering largely similar responses in scientific or technical domains.

This illustrates a broader reality: AI outputs are shaped entirely by design choices, values, and constraints imposed by developers. The issue is not the existence of multiple ethical orientations—that much is inevitable—but their opacity. If an AI is nudged toward one ethical framework or another, users should be able to see it. One practical solution would be to require systems to disclose their *normative assumptions* in real time. Imagine a "transparency panel" where users could view the ethical presets guiding system behavior—whether consequentialist, deontological, virtue-based, or tied to a cultural code. In applied contexts such as healthcare or law, this could include annotated explanations showing which principles weighed most in a decision, much like audit trails in financial systems. Another possibility is tailoring outputs to each user's moral position—either set manually or inferred from prompt history.

Taken together, these examples show that the core issue is not whether AI is "ethical in itself," but how it adapts to cultural contexts and whether it evolves as moral frameworks change. Different AI systems will inevitably provide divergent answers to political or ideological questions. This diversity is not a flaw but a mirror of lived reality: plural, contested, and culturally shaped.

What does matter, however, is the treatment of science. Scientific knowledge should be replicable everywhere, independent of ideology. This is the standard upheld in physics or chemistry (Merton, 1973; Popper, 1959/2002). In the social sciences, by contrast, the standard has been harder to achieve, with research agendas often entangled in political or normative commitments (Flyvbjerg, 2001; Gouldner, 1970). If this line blurs too far, social sciences risk being seen less as sciences and more as advocacy—closer to think tanks or NGOs than universities. One might even imagine a "scientific answer" button alongside moral tailoring options, offering outputs grounded in replicable, empirical reasoning.

There is reason for cautious optimism. AI could help social sciences become more scientific. By detecting bias, testing competing hypotheses, and uncovering hidden patterns in vast datasets, machines may create stronger conditions for neutrality—though never a guarantee. Entrenched interests, cognitive biases, and institutional inertia remain obstacles (Kahneman, 2011; Kunda, 1990; Nickerson, 1998). Yet the possibility is there: if realized, social sciences could grow into more rigorous and relevant disciplines.

The foundation for such progress must be evolutionary theory. Today, every other form of life is studied through biology; only humans are treated as an exception. This separation is not scientific but ideological—a legacy of traditions insisting on human uniqueness (Darwin, 1871/2004; Dawkins, 1976; Wilson, 1978). From an evolutionary standpoint, humans are part of the continuum of life, shaped by variation, inheritance, and adaptation (Henrich, 2016; Richerson & Boyd, 2005). Social sciences that resist this grounding risk resembling belief systems more than sciences, with political ideologies standing in for empirical foundations (Nagel, 1997; Runciman, 2009).

Meanwhile, much alarm over AI confuses the tool with its users. Technology itself can be said to be neutral; the threat lies in who controls it and under what conditions (Bostrom & Ćirković, 2008; Sagan, 1994). Nuclear power can generate energy or destroy cities. AI, too, will be shaped by human intent, institutional safeguards, and governance structures (Winner, 1980).

It is also worth noting that many critiques of AI are not only ethical but material. Historically, those resisting new technologies were often those whose livelihoods or status were most at risk (Acemoglu & Robinson, 2012; Mokyr, 1990). In the industrial era, this meant manual workers; today, it is white-collar professionals—administrators, clerks, academics—whose roles involve routine information processing (Brynjolfsson & McAfee, 2014; Frey & Osborne, 2017). These groups now face automation pressures similar to those faced by factory workers two centuries ago.

This inversion marks a new shift: earlier disruptions threatened physical labor, today's threaten cognitive labor. Unsurprisingly, some of the sharpest critiques of AI come from fields most exposed to displacement. Their concerns are legitimate—bias, accountability, transparency remain pressing—but part of the debate is also motivated by self-preservation.

This predicament grows more urgent as AI systems take on decision-making in justice, healthcare, and warfare. Machines can optimize, predict, and simulate empathy, but they do not experience ethics. They lack lived experience, embodied emotion, and cultural embeddedness—three core ingredients of moral reasoning (Binns, 2018; Moor, 2006). Thus, they must be programmed.

So, must a system truly understand ethics to act ethically? The answer suggest not. It is sufficient that it acts in ways we deem ethical, even without comprehension.

That condition is decisive. Without meaningful alternatives, automation risks deepening alienation and inequality (Arntz et al., 2016; Autor, 2015). But if societies redirect labor toward activities fostering innovation, community, and purpose, then the decline of routine bureaucratic work may represent renewal, not decline. The challenge is not only to defend jobs but to create better ones—roles that enhance human well-being.

8.1.1 Beyond Simulation: The Deeper Ethics Gap

The ethics gap is not merely a technical limitation—it marks a boundary between simulation and true understanding, between statistical output and moral responsibility. AI can be programmed to draw distinctions, such as between combatants and civilians, but the real issue is not the machine's ability—it is whether those who design and deploy it want those distinctions respected.

In today's conflict in Ukraine, the rise of drone warfare has escalated civilian harm. In January 2025 alone, short-range drones were the leading cause of civilian deaths—accounting for at least 139 fatalities and 738 injuries—while U.N. reports document nearly 12,500 civilian deaths since the invasion began, including 650 children. Between February 2022 and April 2025, drone attacks in frontline areas killed at least 395 civilians and injured 2,635 more. These figures illustrate the point: the gap is not in technical recognition but in moral and political will.

The same logic applies to academic life. The scientific method, in principle, is neutral: designed to minimize bias and maximize reproducibility. But science in practice is carried out by people, and people are never neutral. Scientists choose which questions to ask, which data to collect, and which frameworks to apply. As Kuhn (1962) and Latour and Woolgar (1979) showed, science always reflects paradigms and practices. In this sense, science is not only a mirror of nature but also of society. And because humans are political animals, science too becomes political—sometimes subtly, sometimes dangerously. History suggests that in periods of decline, science grows more politicized and less reliable, as ideology takes precedence over inquiry.

This politicization of knowledge is not new. Enlightenment thinkers—from Hobbes's conflict-driven view of nature to Rousseau's emphasis on compassion—already revealed that scholarship carries moral assumptions. Evolutionary theory later showed that moral rules are not universal laws but adaptive heuristics shaped by biology and culture (Cosmides & Tooby, 1992; Laland et al., 2000). Yet this evolutionary perspective is often missing in European philosophy, which has tended to propose absolute solutions for how life should be lived.

Across modern history, three strands of totalizing moral thought stand out. The first is rooted in Christianity, where morality was framed as obedience to divine law and deviation as sin (Augustine, 1998/426; Calvin, 1960; Markus, 1970). The second derives from Rousseau's romantic vision of natural man, which treated formal institutions as corruptions of an original purity (Rousseau, 1762/1979). The third is the Marxist tradition of rebellion against ruling elites, which in practice often replaced one elite with another—factory owners with party bureaucrats (Kolakowski, 1978; Marx & Engels, 1848/1978).

These intellectual traditions converge in a common risk: absolutism. Many contemporary deconstructionist projects in the humanities can be seen as heirs of Rousseau and Marx: suspicious of rules, hostile to elites, yet reluctant to articulate responsibility or alternatives. In this way, they risk undermining the very institutions that sustain scholarship and civic life (Harrison, 2015; Pagden, 2013).

One of the West's deepest illusions has been *moral superiority*. Rather than seeing human life as part of an evolutionary continuum, European thought has offered a succession of competing visions of "the good life." Kant's categorical imperative, Nietzsche's will to power, Marx's class struggle, and Mill's utilitarianism all propose radically different paths, yet are presented as universal truths. The result is a buffet of incompatible ideologies, each claiming exclusivity, leaving societies oscillating between them.

Underlying this buffet is a distinctly European habit of *absolutist thinking*. Europe has been the world's chief exporter of political ideologies, often tested by others at great cost. The collapse of the Eastern bloc is only one example; a series of failed communist regimes in South and Central America followed the same script. Each began with a claim to moral superiority, but once in power, leaders proved no better—and often worse—than their predecessors. The same pattern runs through Rousseauian "back to nature" visions, where dreams of escape from institutions and family devolve into a refusal of responsibility. The common denominator is what might be called the *totalitarian imagination*: the refusal to see human beings as evolutionary creatures, with flaws and trade-offs, rather than blank slates awaiting perfect moral systems.

One should also be careful not to conflate *totalitarian politics* with *totalitarian ideas*. Europeans today remain firmly committed to representative democracy, and most societies are strongly resistant to totalitarian states (Economist Intelligence Unit, 2023; Freedom House, 2024). At the same time, history shows that authoritarian regimes can persist without being driven by universalist or totalizing ideologies. For example, Spain under Franco maintained authoritarian control through nationalism and Catholic traditionalism, but it lacked the comprehensive ideological program characteristic of Marxism-Leninism (Linz, 1975). Similarly, the military juntas in South America—such as Chile under Pinochet or Argentina during the "Dirty War"—governed through repression, nationalism, and pragmatic survival, but not through a single all-encompassing doctrine (Collier, 1979; O'Donnell, 1973).

From a scientific perspective, this totalizing tendency is both universal and culturally specific. Humans everywhere are wired for coalitional thinking: we divide the world into "us" and "them," enforce group norms, and treat our way of life as superior (Boehm, 1999; Henrich, 2016; Kurzban et al., 2001). These instincts foster cohesion but also create fertile ground for *absolutist ideologies*. What is distinctive in Europe is how these impulses were institutionalized in religion and philosophy. Christianity presented morality as one truth for all (Harrison, 2015; Markus, 1970), while Enlightenment thinkers secularized the same impulse into universalist systems—from Kant's imperative to Marx's socialism. As Isaiah Berlin (1969/2013) noted, Western philosophy has been especially prone to *"monism,"* the search for one ultimate truth, while other traditions, such as Confucianism, often tolerated greater pluralism. In this sense, the capacity for absolutism is evolutionary, but its expression in *universalist ideologies* is a cultural product of European intellectual history.

Anthropological research, however, highlights *moral pluralism*: ethical systems emerge from lived experience in different societies, not from a single global hierarchy (Geertz, 1973; Shweder et al., 1997). Western traditions, by contrast, often present their frameworks as universally valid, prescribing what is "correct." AI, however, cannot inhabit this plurality. It has no body, no cultural embeddedness, no sense of meaning. It may simulate empathy, but it cannot live moral life. The idea of *"AI neutrality"* is itself a myth—knowledge is always context-bound (Henrich et al., 2010; Sen, 1987).

Ultimately, AI is a mirror—reflecting our aspirations, contradictions, and failures. Ethics is not what separates us from machines; it is what binds us to one another. The irony is that in elevating ethics as the last human domain, the West risks repeating its oldest mistake: claiming a universal moral high ground while ignoring the plurality of values that shape real societies. An evolutionary perspective instead situates morality not as timeless law, but as dynamic adaptation—shifting with environments, cultures, and needs.

This brings us to the next question. If morality is plural, adaptive, and contested, what happens when ethics is elevated as the primary sphere of human distinctiveness, precisely at the moment when AI takes over most cognitive tasks? It is this inflation of ethics—the attempt to place all remaining weight of human uniqueness on moral reasoning—that we must now examine.

8.2 The Inflation of Ethics in the Age of AI

As machines increasingly take over tasks once reserved for human intelligence, a peculiar redistribution of labor emerges. Data analysis, forecasting, writing assistance, and even creative synthesis are now handled with speed, consistency, and scale that far exceed what individual scholars can achieve. What remains for humans are the "soft" domains—interpretation, judgment, and above all, ethics. Ethics thus becomes the final area where humans claim uniqueness, the one domain machines cannot inhabit.

Yet this shift is far from reassuring. If ethics becomes the primary sphere of human work, the pressure placed upon it may grow to unmanageable levels. The paradox is that the more central ethics becomes, the more politicized and contested it is likely to be. Human beings are, as Aristotle described, *political animals* (Aristotle, trans. 1995). We thrive in debate, divide into factions, and invest extraordinary energy in disputes over values and legitimacy. Narrowing human contribution to the moral domain risks intensifying rather than easing moral conflict.

This concern is not speculative. Social psychology has shown that moral reasoning is often strategic, contextual, and prone to bias rather than the consistent application of universal principles (Haidt, 2007; Kunda, 1990). Evolutionary anthropology adds that our moral intuitions developed as adaptive heuristics for cooperation in small groups, not as abstract rules for global societies (Cosmides & Tooby, 1992; Henrich, 2016). These instincts, while effective for cohesion, also fuel tribalism, selective empathy, and double standards. If ethical debate becomes the main domain of human expertise, disagreements may deepen, not resolve.

Swierstra (2013) calls this *technomoral change*: the process whereby new technologies not only transform actions but also reshape the moral frameworks through which we evaluate them. AI accelerates this process by displacing humans from cognitive labor and leaving us with the task of justifying, interpreting, and regulating outputs. In domains such as criminal justice, healthcare, welfare, or hiring, machines already make decisions that carry moral weight. Humans, in turn, are left to debate whether those decisions are "fair," "just," or "transparent." Ethics thus rises to the center of human oversight.

But this elevation comes at a cost. The more ethics is emphasized, the more it risks becoming performance rather than responsibility. We project ideals we cannot uphold, condemn others for failing them, and use morality as a political weapon. Academia illustrates the risk: researchers often feel pressure to align with prevailing moral currents rather than to present dispassionate analysis (Gouldner, 1970; Mirowski, 2011). If the last human "job" in the age of AI is to provide ethical justification, science itself risks turning into moral theater.

The deeper problem is anthropological. Humans are not reliably moral agents. We are prone to bias, motivated reasoning, and identity-protective cognition (Kahneman, 2011; Nickerson, 1998). Morality emerges through interaction, negotiation, and cultural embedding—not through deduction or formal rules (Boyd & Richerson, 2005; Geertz, 1973). This means that while AI can simulate ethics by following structured principles, it cannot capture the lived, evolving, and inconsistent moral life of human communities. And humans, when left with ethics as their primary domain, may not handle it well.

History suggests that when societies place excessive weight on moral superiority, conflict often follows. Competing ideologies, whether religious or political, have justified wars, exclusions, and persecutions under the banner of ethics or virtue (Runciman, 2009; Taylor, 1989). In the contemporary university, there is already evidence of such tendencies, where moral debates about identity, fairness, or justice can overshadow empirical inquiry (Pluckrose & Lindsay, 2020). If AI accelerates this shift by leaving humans primarily with the task of moral arbitration, the university risks becoming less a site of discovery and more a site of *symbolic struggle*.

This is not to argue that ethics is unimportant—on the contrary, it is indispensable. But we must recognize its fragility. Ethics is not a fixed set of rules but a cultural and evolutionary negotiation. If we outsource too much of human labor to machines, we risk placing ethics on a pedestal it cannot sustain. The result may not be a world of greater moral clarity, but one of greater moral conflict.

The ethical challenge of AI, therefore, is not only technical but existential. Before we encode ethical rules into machines, we must better understand the messy, biased, and culturally situated moral systems from which those rules emerge. And before we declare ethics as humanity's "last job," we must ask whether humans are truly equipped to handle that role without turning it into another stage for political contest.

The answer is simple: there is no one else to take on this role, so humans must. But if we are to shoulder it, it would be to our great advantage to clarify our understanding of ethics and moral philosophy beforehand. At present, that foundation is incomplete. Much of the social sciences remain tied to frameworks that resist integration with evolutionary theory, leaving us without a coherent basis for explaining human behavior and morality (Richerson & Boyd, 2005; Wilson, 1978).

It may be tempting to say this is simply the way things are—that humans have always struggled to build unified paradigms in the social sciences, and always will. Yet history suggests otherwise. When Charles Darwin developed his ideas about evolution, he was influenced by Thomas Malthus, whose concerns lay not with animals, but with the competition between nations and social classes (Darwin, 1859/2004; Malthus, 1798/1998). Similar concerns shaped the work of Adam Smith in *The Wealth of Nations* (1776/1999) and the French physiocrats before him. Each of these frameworks reflected the challenges of their time: scarcity, agriculture, urbanization, and industry. None was wrong, but each was incomplete, and each eventually gave way to new ways of thinking as economic and social realities changed.

The larger point is this: there are reasons to remain cautiously optimistic. Paradigm shifts in science, as Thomas Kuhn (1962) observed, rarely occur through persuasion alone. They happen when anomalies accumulate, when existing frameworks can no longer solve pressing problems, and when societies experience pressures that make change unavoidable. We may be approaching such a moment again.

As living standards stagnate or decline in parts of the Western world while rising in Asia, competitive pressures are intensifying (Gordon, 2016; Milanović, 2016). When material conditions worsen, people do not only question economic systems; they also reconsider moral assumptions. History shows that ethical commitments are not fixed: they adjust in response to scarcity, competition, and survival. What was once considered a universal duty can be reinterpreted as conditional; what was once seen as an obligation may come to be regarded as unsustainable.

Consider immigration as one example. In times of prosperity, societies may adopt inclusive ethical principles: all are welcome. Under economic stress, however, ethical boundaries often tighten—only those facing persecution, or only those able to contribute economically, are admitted. Such a shift is not simply a matter of policy but of ethics, redefining solidarity, fairness, and belonging at a societal level. Similar changes can be observed in attitudes toward welfare, labor markets, or environmental priorities. Ethics, in short, adapts under pressure.

From this perspective, the current moment can be understood as a period of *ethical re-evaluation*, shaped by material constraints as much as by abstract ideals. If evolutionary theory teaches anything, it is that human morality is adaptive—a set of strategies for cooperation, coordination, and survival. Ethical frameworks are not detached from economic and ecological realities; they emerge from them.

This also suggests why the social sciences must evolve. Intellectual change will not come only from argument, but from necessity. If existing paradigms fail to guide societies through periods of decline or transformation, new paradigms will be sought. Integrating evolutionary theory into the social sciences offers a rigorous foundation: a framework capable of explaining not only how ethics varies across cultures and times, but also why it changes when pressures mount.

Right now, it can feel as if many governments in mature democracies default to denial—denial that there is a structural problem, that current systems are suboptimal, that their own values are not uniquely superior, and that meaningful change is needed. Psychology gives a sober explanation for why this happens. People (and institutions run by people) prefer the status quo because losses loom larger than gains and uncertainty is aversive. Leaders therefore gravitate toward incremental fixes rather than reforms that might threaten existing coalitions or identity commitments (Kahneman & Tversky, 1979; Samuelson & Zeckhauser, 1988).

When evidence challenges core beliefs, cognitive dissonance and motivated reasoning take over. Decision-makers reinterpret or discount disconfirming facts to preserve a coherent self- and group-image (Festinger, 1957; Kunda, 1990; Nickerson, 1998). This is not simply an individual flaw but a systemic pattern: once institutions embody particular worldviews, their survival depends on sustaining them.

On top of this, people tend to justify the systems they live in, seeing prevailing arrangements and values as legitimate or morally superior simply because they are familiar and shared—a dynamic well captured by *system justification theory* (Jost & Banaji, 1994; Jost et al., 2004). At the collective level, social identity processes reinforce the same tendencies. *Ingroup favoritism* and *collective narcissism* encourage narratives of uniqueness and virtue, making it even harder to admit decline or to borrow solutions from "out-groups" (Golec de Zavala et al., 2009; Tajfel & Turner, 1979).

Within governments, these biases are compounded by organizational dynamics. Groupthink suppresses dissent in cohesive teams under pressure, while escalation of commitment makes leaders double down on failing policies to justify sunk costs and protect reputations (Arkes & Blumer, 1985; Janis, 1972; Staw, 1976). Together, these mechanisms trap institutions in self-reinforcing loops of denial and inertia.

Public rhetoric mirrors these dynamics. Cultural cognition and identity-protective reasoning mean that citizens, like elites, filter evidence through the lens of group values. Contested facts become signals of belonging rather than points of debate, so symbolic partisan battles replace substantive institutional change (Haidt, 2012; Kahan, 2013). Availability cascades and risk-perception research add another layer: highly visible short-term issues dominate political attention while slower structural risks fade into the background, reinforcing *short-termism* (Slovic, 1987; Sunstein, 2006).

It could be argued that this short-termism is closely tied to Western individualism, which prioritizes the rights and choices of the individual even when they undermine long-term collective welfare. Individualism has been a powerful driver of entrepreneurship and innovation, but when unleashed without balance, it risks destruction: the suffering of others, or the degradation of shared systems, is not accounted for. In nature, many animals appear to solve this tension more effectively. Ant colonies and bee hives function through distributed roles and collective regulation: no single ant or bee pursues its own gain at the expense of the group's survival. Even among vertebrates, cooperative breeders such as meerkats or naked mole-rats sustain group resilience by sacrificing individual reproductive opportunities for the good of the colony. In such systems, survival depends on aligning individual behavior with group success, not setting the two in opposition.

None of this is uniquely European or limited to the West. The tension between individual and collective interest is a recurring human pattern. But where animals and insects evolve mechanisms that tightly bind individuals to collective outcomes, human societies—especially those influenced by Western traditions of individualism—often permit the short-term triumph of self-interest. Denial and cosmetic adjustment are therefore not anomalies; they are exactly what we should expect when strong counter-incentives for truth-seeking and long-horizon reform are absent.

8.2.1 Politics and Biology

Political ideals, at their best, aim to elevate the human condition—to build societies that are just, cooperative, inclusive, and peaceful. But these aspirations often exceed the biological and psychological capacities of the human species. That does not mean we should abandon them. It means we must temper them with an honest, scientific understanding of what humans are actually like: what we evolved to do, where our cognitive limits lie, and how our moral behavior is shaped by environment and incentives more than by ideology.

One of the most persistent errors in modern political theory is the belief that human nature is indefinitely malleable. From Enlightenment liberalism to Marxist collectivism, we see recurring assumptions that if only institutions are properly designed, justice and equality will follow. The vision is at times noble, but it often ignores the evolved architecture of the human mind. It treats ethics as a clean slate and politics as a canvas of infinite potential, when in fact both are bounded by our biology.

Cooperation evolved in small-scale societies where personal relationships, reciprocity, and reputation mattered most (Hamilton, 1964; Trivers, 1971). Empathy and fairness arose in these tightly knit groups as adaptive traits. Our instincts did not evolve to manage abstract rights, anonymous markets, or large-scale redistribution. The result is what evolutionary theorists call *adaptive lag*: our moral emotions and intuitive judgments were shaped for a world that no longer exists. We are no longer hunter-gatherers, yet we still carry hunter-gatherer minds. When political systems demand behavior that contradicts these tendencies—impartial generosity toward strangers, uniform trust in distant bureaucracies—they often buckle under their own weight.

Case in a Box: What Counts in the Hunt

Among hunter-gatherers, authority in male groups often shifted not by debate but by performance. On the hunt, what mattered was not who spoke most or claimed expertise, but who delivered the kill. Status adjusted automatically, without argument. In camp, where women awaited the return, prestige accrued to the hunter who brought home the prey—and to the man who defended the group in conflict. In these settings, outcomes provided a neutral thermometer of competence.

Modern societies rarely offer such clarity. In urban life there is no shared kill, no obvious proof of contribution. Yet the human tendency remains: we look for outputs. Younger generations will not heed politicians who fail to raise living standards, nor trust social science courses that do not lead to real jobs. These are biological litmus tests of credibility, embedded deep in our evolutionary past. To ignore them—to insist outcomes do not matter—is a dangerous illusion.

Questions for Reflection

1. Why did hunting outcomes serve as a natural "thermometer" of authority in small-scale societies?
2. How does outcome-based status differ from authority based on speech, ideology, or promises?
3. In what ways do modern institutions struggle to provide equally clear measures of contribution?
4. How might ignoring outcome-based credibility erode trust in leaders, teachers, or experts?
5. What lessons from our evolutionary past can guide how we evaluate authority and legitimacy today?

This helps explain why ideological extremes strain everyday life. The case of hunting reminds us that outcomes—what is actually delivered—have always been the final measure of competence. In small-scale societies, prestige did not come from words or ideology but from bringing home food or defending the group. Modern extremes often ignore this principle.

On one side, unrestrained free-market systems feel alienating. When individuals are encouraged to be purely self-interested, when "greed is good," and when success is measured only in money, the social fabric frays. Relationships risk being reduced to transactions, and others are seen as commodities rather than as members of a shared community (Putnam, 2000; Sandel, 2012). Anthropological work shows that in small-scale societies, survival was not driven by ruthless competition but by cooperation, reciprocity, and fairness (Boehm, 1999; Henrich, 2016). A purely competitive model not only runs against these deep-seated preferences but also dismisses the outcome-based tests of credibility that once kept groups together—mechanisms that stress-test values against behavioral outcomes and minimize opportunities for free riding and deception. The challenge is to make politics more concrete, accountable, and biologically realistic—anchored in the way people actually cooperate, not in abstract ideological blueprints. Technologically, we are at an inflection point. The internet and secure digital identity make direct participation feasible at scale. Citizens could vote directly on specific issues from their phones, shrinking the gap between preferences and policy. That would not only address a long-standing accountability problem but might also help restore confidence in democracy.

History warns that democracy is most fragile during economic stress, when disillusionment opens the door to authoritarian alternatives (Acemoglu & Robinson, 2012; Norris, 2011). One way to avoid the familiar slide is to realign democratic practice with how people actually live—more concrete, more immediate, more accountable. In economics, similar biological metaphors have proved clarifying. Michael Hudson argues that modern finance can become parasitic, draining productive sectors much like a host-parasite relationship in nature (Hudson, 2015). Whether one agrees with his policy prescriptions or not, the biological framing helps diagnose systemic misalignments—where structures deviate from the cooperative equilibria they depend on.

The obstacle is institutional. No established party is likely to champion reforms that would make parties themselves less central. That creates a catch-22: those with the power to implement change have the strongest interest in preventing it. As with many historical transformations, the question is not whether a more biologically aligned form of democracy is technically possible—the tools already exist—but whether political will can be mobilized to make it real. Systems that ignore human realities—demanding pure altruism on the one hand or celebrating pure greed on the other—are bound to falter. The task ahead is to design institutions that fit the species they are meant to serve, balancing innovation with the deep evolutionary constraints of human cooperation.

8.2.2 Virtue and Well-Being

We often assume that better laws, more inclusive institutions, or stronger economic incentives will naturally lead to a better society. But history suggests otherwise. Societies do not thrive because of rules alone—they thrive because of the people who live within them. And people flourish not by decree, but by discipline. The hard truth is this: no law, constitution, or algorithm can replace the daily labor of *cultivating virtue*. It is easier to pass a law than to raise a virtuous generation. Easier to build an institution and an impressive building to support it than to build personal character.

In the West, especially, we are often tempted by quick fixes—sweeping reforms, new ideologies, institutional redesigns. These come in waves, recurring throughout our history like tides of optimism, each promising to perfect society without first perfecting ourselves. We hope that by embedding ideals into policy, institutions, or AI systems, we can shortcut the slow, uncertain process of moral development. But this rarely works. Without the virtues that sustain social cooperation—honesty, perseverance, trustworthiness, and restraint—institutions become hollow, and technologies replicate dysfunction.

Ethical systems, then, are not abstract ideals floating above society; they are embodied practices that shape individual behavior and collective outcomes. Whether expressed in religious codes, civic norms, or cultural expectations, they function as tools for social coordination and self-regulation. And they work not because they are perfect, but because they are practiced.

Research on self-regulation shows that delayed gratification and impulse control are stronger predictors of life outcomes than IQ or socioeconomic background (Duckworth & Seligman, 2005; Moffitt et al., 2011). These traits are not innate but learned, shaped by parenting, education, and cultural expectations (Heckman, 2006). Ethics and development are thus tightly linked: the moral formation of individuals contributes directly to the productive and civic capacity of society.

Max Weber's classic thesis on the *Protestant ethic* remains instructive. He argued that norms promoting hard work, frugality, and self-restraint laid the psychological groundwork for modern capitalism (Weber, 1905/2001). More recently, scholars have expanded this framework, emphasizing social trust, civic responsibility, and educational rigor as elements of the "*soft infrastructure*" essential for long-term development (Aghion et al., 2010; Fukuyama, 2001; Tabellini, 2010).

Post-war Germany and Japan exemplify this logic. Both nations recovered rapidly, not first through foreign aid, but because of strong cultural and institutional foundations. Shared norms of duty, discipline, and education enabled economic revival and political stability (Pyle, 2007; Veenhoven, 1999). In contrast, countries lacking these foundations often fail to convert aid into growth. Without norms of trust, effort, and rule-following, external resources alone cannot create lasting prosperity (Easterly, 2016; Sachs, 2005).

In this sense, culture operates as *ethical capital*, an internalized system of expectations that regulates behavior even when no one is watching. These are not merely personal virtues; they are the social glue that makes large-scale cooperation and market functioning possible. When such traits are absent or systematically eroded, even the best-designed institutions fail.

From an evolutionary standpoint, this makes sense. Ethical norms are not arbitrary rules imposed from above. They are adaptive responses to collective action problems: how to punish cheaters, how to encourage cooperation, how to align short-term incentives with long-term survival. In this light, virtue becomes not a philosophical luxury but an evolutionary necessity.

From this perspective, the question of ethics does not necessarily require new foundations from abstract philosophical or ideological doctrines. Instead, it can draw directly from empirical history: the tested virtues and civic habits that have already underpinned social and economic progress. Societies that flourish tend to share certain moral patterns—discipline, honesty, trust, responsibility, and a future-oriented mindset—not because of theoretical consensus, but because these traits work. Likewise, nations that experience repeated cycles of dysfunction, stagnation, or collapse often lack these very traits, or actively undermine them. For such societies, the ethical path forward may lie not in constructing elaborate normative theories but in replicating the cultural virtues that others have already proven effective.

This practical, outcome-oriented approach to ethics—grounded in observed institutional and historical success—might be called *functional ethics* or *empirical virtue ethics*. It aligns with frameworks in *comparative institutional analysis* and *development ethics* that emphasize the adaptive value of norms and the selective survival of productive moral systems (Elster, 2007; North, 1990; Sen, 1987). Rather than reinventing ethics, we may need to reinhabit the ones that made progress possible.

In this book I use the two terms—*functional ethics* and *empirical virtue ethics*—to describe the same adaptive approach, but with slightly different emphases:

- Functional ethics stresses practical utility—what works in practice, what sustains societies, what prevents collapse. It is *the outcome-oriented, systems-level perspective*.
- Empirical virtue ethics stresses method and grounding—we identify virtues empirically, by looking at which ones have historically produced flourishing communities. It is *the social-scientific, evidence-based perspective.*

Taken together, these terms describe one approach: ethics as an adaptive inheritance, tested by experience rather than imposed as abstract doctrine.

What this means is that it also becomes vital for any society that has achieved developmental success to actively protect and preserve the cultural norms and ethical habits that enabled that success. Cultures that foster high levels of trust, civic engagement, rule-following, and educational commitment do not arise spontaneously; they are historically built and socially maintained. If these foundations are weakened, the institutional structure they support may also erode.

In this light, *multiculturalism*—understood as the coexistence of multiple, often conflicting, normative systems within one political unit—poses a risk when not accompanied by *cultural integration*. Research has shown that deep value pluralism within a state can hinder social trust, weaken democratic cohesion, and reduce the effectiveness of institutions (Alesina & Glaeser, 2004; Putnam, 2007). Immigrant integration models that emphasize adaptation to shared civic norms tend to yield better outcomes in terms of employment, education, and social harmony (Dustmann & Frattini, 2014; Koopmans, 2016). This is not a call for cultural erasure, but for alignment on the virtues that sustain functioning societies. Without such alignment, even the most well-designed systems can falter under the weight of incompatible expectations and eroded trust.

The most enduring example of a virtue-based civilization is probably China. For over two millennia, Confucian philosophy has emphasized ethics, education, filial piety, and moral leadership. Originating in the Warring States period (ca. fifth-century BCE), Confucianism linked good governance to the moral character of rulers and the disciplined behavior of citizens. Its core virtues—*ren (benevolence)*, *li (ritual propriety)*, and *xiao (filial piety)*—functioned not only as personal ideals but as principles for social cohesion and statecraft (Yao, 2000). This framework helped sustain Chinese civilization through dynasties, invasions, and internal upheavals.

The classical gardens of Suzhou embody this ethical-aesthetic worldview. Masterpieces such as the Humble Administrator's Garden (Zhuozheng yuan), the Lingering Garden (Liu yuan), the Master-of-Nets Garden (Wangshi yuan), and the Garden of Cultivation (Yi pu)—now UNESCO World Heritage Sites—were not built by aristocrats or merchants, but by scholar-officials who passed rigorous civil service examinations rooted in Confucian learning (Elman, 2000). These gardens reflect not wealth, but a cultivated life of harmony, modesty, and discipline (Keswick, 2003; Xu, 2011).

This *meritocratic system*, developed during the Sui and Tang and refined under the Song and Ming dynasties, prioritized intellect, virtue, and classical education over lineage or wealth (Elman, 2013; Hansen, 2000). Wen Zhenheng (1585–1645), a descendant of Wen Zhengming and a key figure in Suzhou's garden legacy, exemplified the *literati ideal*. His contributions to garden culture expressed Confucian values through refined spatial design (Clunas, 1996).

Strikingly, the modern Chinese state still reflects elements of this meritocratic tradition. Although formally communist, political appointments are often based on long administrative experience. Many high-ranking officials are trained engineers or scientists who have governed provinces larger than most European countries. Advancement is based more on performance than lineage or charisma (Bell, 2015). This continuity illustrates that meritocracy can function within different ideological systems.

Western observers often overlook this because they expect meritocracy to appear only within liberal democratic institutions. Yet the endurance of Chinese civilization—arguably aided by its Confucian ethos—challenges this assumption. The very name Zhōngguó (中國), meaning "Middle Kingdom," reflects a long-standing belief in China's central role in civilization. From a Chinese perspective, it was only temporarily displaced during the West's 350-year ascent following the scientific and industrial revolutions. The disruptions of ideological communism—essentially a European import—briefly interrupted this trajectory. But with post-Mao reforms and renewed openness to science and technology, China resumed its path (Vogel, 2011).[1]

Even after repression during the Cultural Revolution, Confucian values remained latent in the social fabric and have resurfaced both culturally and politically (Bell, 2015). Today, China leads in parts of AI, green tech, and high-speed rail—not just due to political centralization or sheer scale, but also because of a long-standing culture of discipline, education, and civic hierarchy rooted in Confucian traditions (Kennedy, 2019; Pomeranz, 2000; Needham, 1954–2004).

In contrast, many Western societies are experimenting with *radical individualism* and *postmodern relativism*, treating virtues as optional or obsolete. This undermines the very foundations—trust, self-restraint, perseverance—on which both democracy and prosperity depend. By neglecting these, they risk institutional fragility and moral drift.

Worse still, there is a growing danger that these same ideals—detached from responsibility and stripped of shared ethical anchors—are being encoded into our technological systems. As artificial intelligence increasingly shapes decision-making in business, governance, and education, we may

[1] China formally adopted communism in the twentieth century through the influence of Soviet ideology, framing politics as a project of remolding human thought and behaviour. During Mao Zedong's rule, this often took extreme forms, such as the "sent-down youth" campaigns and collectivization of agriculture, where communist doctrine was imposed even on farming practices. The Great Leap Forward (1958–1962), in particular, led to catastrophic famine, with estimates of tens of millions of deaths due to misguided policies (Dikotter, 2010; Li & Yang, 2005). The turn away from ideological rigidity began under Deng Xiaoping in the late 1970s, when pragmatic reforms emphasized "seeking truth from facts" and reintroduced market mechanisms under the banner of "socialism with Chinese characteristics" (Vogel, 2011). This was less a rejection of the Communist Party than an adaptation of its legitimacy to a more traditional Chinese logic of governance, where rulers are expected to balance community and competition in ways that maintain order and prosperity (Bell, 2015; Huang, 2008). The continued use of the term "communism"—like "capitalism with Chinese characteristics"—reflects this pragmatism: ideology serves as a label, but practical governance relies on a deeper tradition of meritocratic rule tempered by responsiveness to popular needs.

end up programming systems that reflect our *cultural confusion* rather than our *collective wisdom*. If we train AI on fragmented preferences, ephemeral trends, or purely consumerist behaviors, we risk building tools that amplify short-term gratification and erode long-term strategic thinking.

But perhaps an even deeper danger now looms. As AI increasingly takes over the heavy lifting of intellectual work—analysis, prediction, even creative synthesis—we risk losing not only our cognitive edge but the very habits of mind that once made virtue possible. Why should I get up and solve problems when the machine already has? Why struggle with complexity, restraint, or responsibility, when there is no demand for it? If intelligence becomes externalized, effort may start to feel optional. But this is precisely when virtue becomes most essential. For without intellectual labor, we drift into passivity; and without the tension of striving, the moral muscles atrophy.

In such a world, virtue must be reclaimed—not through law or ideology, but through new domains of practice. If artificial intelligence increasingly assumes the labor that once shaped our sense of worth, then we must search for other sources of virtue. Hard work, persistence, and discipline have long been celebrated as foundations of moral character. But when machines perform much of this labor more efficiently, those particular virtues lose their central role in defining what it means to be human.

This does not mean virtue disappears. It means it must be redirected. Some may turn to physical discipline, others to aesthetic or spiritual pursuits. But perhaps the most enduring and necessary form of virtue will lie in care: looking after others, protecting animals, tending to nature, and cultivating life in all its forms. Caring is not just an emotional inclination but a profound ethical orientation, a reminder that morality has always been rooted in how we treat the vulnerable.

If work once gave us purpose, then care may become the new *axis of meaning*. In this light, humanity's role in the age of machines might be redefined as *homo cura*—the caring human. This figure embodies a new form of humanism: not grounded in opposition to technology, nor in nostalgic attachment to the virtues of toil, but in the cultivation of what machines cannot replicate. Judgment, reflection, restraint, and above all, care are practices that remain uniquely human, not because machines could never simulate them, but because their value lies in the lived reciprocity of social and biological existence.

Such a perspective offers a double benefit. It preserves ethics as more than rule-following by anchoring it in virtue, and it provides humanity with a renewed purpose at a time when older markers of identity are being displaced. Far from diminishing us, the arrival of AI could therefore deepen the call to humanism—reminding us that our dignity lies not in doing what machines can do, but in sustaining life, meaning, and responsibility in ways only humans can.

But humanism, if it is to matter, must be more than a posture. It must shape how we build institutions, train minds, and guide our technological development. Otherwise, we risk allowing our machines to inherit not our wisdom, but our confusion. And once encoded into algorithms, our cultural drift becomes harder to correct.

This not only deepens social incoherence but makes us less competitive globally. Societies that retain a sense of shared discipline, moral clarity, and cultural continuity—however imperfect—will build AI that reflects those strengths. They will create systems that reward cooperation, foresight, and institutional resilience, while we risk automating drift and celebrating inconsistency. In this way, the loss of virtue is not just a moral failure but a strategic one.

This insight carries profound implications for our education and research. For example, why do we not teach virtues in business schools, even though we know that success in entrepreneurship depends more on hard work and persistence than on theoretical models? Instead, we tend to teach entrepreneurship—and nearly all other subjects—as a menu of theories, tools, and procedures, as if success could be achieved simply by following a set of steps. This overly instrumental approach does not lead to successful businesses.[2] Evidence suggests that what truly drives success is passion—the desire to prove something to oneself or to others, to pursue a dream despite setbacks. It is this inner drive that fuels persistence and allows individuals to endure the hardship along the way.

I would go so far as to argue that our current theory-based teaching—which is often not real theory at all, but rather a recounting of who did what kind of empirical experiment, with findings about fractions of reality that are often obsolete in only a few years—actually makes us less virtuous. It steals time and energy away from what truly matters, while also undoing what was once central in education: the cultivation of character. In earlier eras,

---

[2] A well-known limitation of entrepreneurship education is that relatively few instructors have direct entrepreneurial experience. Surveys suggest that most university faculty teaching entrepreneurship come from academic rather than business backgrounds, with limited exposure to founding or running firms (Fayolle, 2013; Katz, 2008). As a result, the emphasis in curricula often falls on theories, frameworks, and case studies rather than on the lived experience of risk-taking, resilience, and execution. Research also shows that entrepreneurial success is rarely explained by ideas or business models alone, but by the capacity to navigate uncertainty, manage failure, and persist through setbacks (Aldrich & Ruef, 2018; Shane, 2003). This gap between classroom instruction and entrepreneurial practice highlights the importance of integrating experiential learning, mentorship, and exposure to real-world ventures into entrepreneurship education.

virtues were integral to education: Aristotle's *Nicomachean Ethics* saw character formation as inseparable from knowledge, and John Henry Newman's *Idea of a University* (1852) stressed moral and intellectual cultivation together. Today, however, even mentioning virtues in an academic setting is treated as almost scandalous, much like arguing for the return of syllogistic reasoning at the university. That alone is a sign that something has gone deeply wrong.

Modern research reinforces this gap. Positive psychology has shown that traits like grit, perseverance, and self-control predict long-term success more reliably than technical training (Duckworth et al., 2007; Peterson & Seligman, 2004). Yet business schools rarely frame these as virtues, preferring instead to reduce them to "competencies" or "skills." By stripping away the moral and humanistic dimension, education risks producing technically capable professionals who lack the inner resources to navigate uncertainty, failure, or ethical dilemmas. Too often, students fail not because their ideas are weak, but because they give up, choosing easier and more secure paths. In other words, we teach strategy, but not stamina.

If we know that virtues, rather than theoretical frameworks, provide the decisive lesson, we must ask: why don't we teach them more directly? Part of the answer is that higher education remains trapped in an outdated scientific paradigm. We continue to emphasize abstract models over evolutionary insights, neglecting biology and psychology as foundations for understanding human behavior and motivation.

This oversight is more than academic. Ethics should not be treated as a philosophical appendix to personal or professional development—it is its very foundation. In an age increasingly shaped by artificial intelligence, societies are more dependent on ethical capital than ever before. As machines take over more of our cognitive labor, it is moral character that must govern how these tools are applied. Researchers who ignore cultural and ethical preconditions in favor of purely structural or economic models risk producing solutions that work on paper but fail in practice.

Prosperity without virtue is unstable. Discipline, trust, and responsibility are not luxuries; they form the hidden architecture of civilization. And in a world where intelligence can be outsourced but judgment cannot, they remain the last safeguards against collapse.

8.2.3 From Tools to Values: How Technology Transforms Morality

As we've seen, the ethical challenges of our time cannot be separated from the technologies that drive them. AI represents a turning point in this relationship. For the first time in history, we are developing tools that not only extend human capabilities but also reshape human values in return. AI does not simply answer questions—it reframes them. It does not just automate decisions—it alters the frameworks of decision-making itself.

Technological change has never been neutral. It changes not only what we do but also what we aspire to. Each major innovation—the printing press, the steam engine, electricity, the internet—has shifted the moral vocabulary of society. What is considered ethical or acceptable evolves alongside the tools we use. We do not simply apply old values to new systems; instead, the systems themselves reshape our values.

Importantly, technological progress does not guarantee moral progress. Vaccines and antibiotics reduced suffering, yet they did not make societies more just. Ancient Rome combined aqueducts and engineering brilliance with slavery and executions. As Björnsson (2021) and Szeman (2021) argue, moral progress does not follow automatically from technical progress. Complacency may even grow with material advancement, leaving underlying injustices unaddressed.

This is the essence of *technomoral change*: technologies reshape not only what we can do, but also what we consider right or desirable (Swierstra, 2013). Artificial intelligence intensifies this dynamic. Like the printing press or the internet before it, AI alters how we understand fairness, agency, and responsibility—often before societies or institutions have fully grasped the implications. What shocks us today may become normalized tomorrow, not because it is more just, but simply because it has become familiar.

The pace of change is especially problematic. Morality evolved over millennia; technologies now change in months. Ethics, once tested slowly in practice, must now adapt to opaque and rapidly scaling systems. Meanwhile, decisions about how these technologies are designed are concentrated in the hands of a narrow class of executives, investors, and policymakers. Research suggests that concentrated power tends to reduce empathy and increase norm violations (Keltner et al., 2003; Lammers et al., 2010). The deeper concern is this: whose values are being embedded in our machines, and who gets excluded from that process?

Geoffrey Hinton's resignation from Google in 2023 underscores the stakes. Long celebrated as one of the fathers of modern neural networks, Hinton later warned of AI's risks—misinformation, job loss, and loss of control. His shift recalls J. Robert Oppenheimer after the Manhattan Project: both realized that the deepest risks were not technical but ethical, and that they grew most dangerous when society lagged behind.

The analogy to nuclear weapons is instructive. Hiroshima and Nagasaki forced humanity to confront ethical dilemmas for which no prior framework sufficed. AI is not an instant weapon, but its slow, cumulative effects—on work, cognition, identity, and governance—may be equally profound (Table 8.1).

These dilemmas are not speculative. They touch directly on labor, geopolitics, cultural diversity, and future generations. They cannot be resolved once and for all, nor by regulation alone. What is required is foresight, humility, and cultural anchors that keep moral reasoning adaptive, open-ended, and resistant to capture.

Here, it becomes crucial to distinguish between morals and ethics. Ethics, in the sense used here, refers to the deeper cultural anchors—slow-changing symbolic systems and institutional commitments that must remain relatively stable. Morals, by contrast, are the more flexible, context-specific rules and practices that can be adjusted as technologies and circumstances change.[3] This distinction allows us to preserve legitimacy and continuity without lapsing into rigidity.[4]

If technological change is inevitable, moral clarity is not. The challenge is to shape AI in ways that not only serve immediate human goals but also safeguard the ethical foundations that sustain resilient societies. This leads naturally to the next section, which asks how practical ethics can be preserved and renewed—not only in principle, but in lived institutional practice.

8.2.4 Practical Ethics and Cultural Anchors in the Age of AI

If we are to navigate the age of AI wisely, we must learn to distinguish between *moral flexibility* and *ethical foundations*. Not all values are equally negotiable:

[3] Aristotle, *Ἠθικὰ Νικομάχεια* [*Nicomachean Ethics*], esp. Books II–VI, where *ēthikē aretē* (virtue of character) is distinguished from *phronēsis* (practical wisdom). See also Cicero, *De Officiis*, on universal duties (*officia*) versus customary norms (*mos maiorum*).

[4] Kant, *Grundlegung zur Metaphysik der Sitten* (1785); Hegel, *Grundlinien der Philosophie des Rechts* (1821), §§142–156; Ricoeur, *Soi-même comme un autre* (1990); Taylor, *Sources of the Self* (1989). These works illustrate alternative framings of the ethics–morals distinction, showing that while the terms are used differently across traditions, the contrast between enduring anchors and adaptable practices remains philosophically central.

Table 8.1 Types of moral considerations in AI development and deployment

Category	Ethical question	Example or Contrast
Existential Risk	Could AI systems threaten human survival or autonomy?	A superintelligence acting independently of human goals (Bostrom, 2014)
Value Alignment	Whose values should guide AI behavior, and how do we ensure alignment?	Western liberal democracies vs. authoritarian state AI preferences
Accountability & Governance	Who is responsible when AI causes harm or bias?	An AI misdiagnosing a patient, but no clear responsible human or legal entity
Truth vs. Misinformation	Will some AIs be trained to lie or omit facts for strategic purposes?	State-controlled AI spreading propaganda or commercial AI omitting product flaws
Plurality vs. Monopolization	Should there be one AI model per country, or many competing models?	China may enforce a single "official" AI, while the EU hosts diverse AIs
Job Displacement	Should we build AI systems that replace human labor, even when not necessary?	Automating teaching, counseling, or journalism
Moral Deskilling	Will outsourcing judgment to AI weaken human ethical reasoning over time?	Relying on AI for moral decisions (e.g., in sentencing or hiring) may erode moral intuition
Consent and Data Use	Do users truly understand and consent to how AI systems use their data and shape their choices?	Behavioral nudging through recommender systems without informed consent
Environmental Impact	Are the energy costs of training and deploying large AI models justifiable?	GPT-4 estimated to require millions of kWh in training, contributing to emissions
Global Inequality	Will AI benefit only rich nations and large firms?	Global South lacks computing infrastructure, widening the innovation gap

(continued)

Table 8.1 (continued)

Category	Ethical question	Example or Contrast
Cultural Homogenization	Will dominant AI systems spread particular cultural norms or suppress local variation?	English-language models marginalizing indigenous knowledge systems
Intergenerational Risk	Are we building systems whose consequences will burden future generations?	Like nuclear waste, AI decisions and infrastructures may have long-term social impact
Capability Thresholds	At what level of intelligence or autonomy should we stop building more advanced systems?	Eric Schmidt's concern over agent savants and future unified superintelligence by 2030 (source below)

some can and should be adapted in context, while others must remain firm to sustain legitimacy, trust, and cultural coherence over time.

This distinction matters because technological change often tempts us to treat ethics as infinitely malleable. But values that shift too easily risk leaving societies without orientation, while values that never adapt risk rigidity and irrelevance. The challenge is therefore to identify which ethical commitments must remain stable and which moral practices can be adjusted within any given culture (Table 8.2).

This comparison clarifies that the ethical dilemmas posed by AI are not merely technical puzzles or abstract concerns. They are live negotiations of moral meaning and cultural survival. Some of these issues can be addressed through flexible, contextual moral reasoning. Others require anchoring in inherited ethical traditions—those slow-changing symbolic systems that give communities their identity and stability. When we confuse the two, we either risk becoming too rigid to adapt or too fluid to stand for anything at all.

Technomoral change, then, is not only a question of innovation, but of stewardship. It requires institutional courage and cultural humility. We must not only ask what AI can do, but also who decides what it should do, on what cultural terms, and with what long-term consequences. If ethical responsibility is outsourced to machines or abstracted into distant procedures, we risk creating systems that are not only harmful, but illegible—operating without moral memory or accountability.

And yet, rejecting ethical engagement would be even worse. Moral withdrawal is not a neutral act—it cedes the future to those most willing to exploit uncertainty. If democracy is imperfect, it is still the best tool we have for

Table 8.2 Practical ethics responses to AI dilemmas

AI Dilemma	Practical ethics response	Ethical or Moral mode	Rationale
Existential Risk	Evaluate risks through culturally grounded precautionary norms; global thresholds must respect ethical boundaries	Ethical	The line between acceptable and unacceptable risk varies culturally; survival threats invoke deep ethical frames
Value Alignment	Build AI systems that accommodate plural moral systems within ethically bounded cultural frameworks	Ethical + Moral	Moral negotiation is possible within societies, but fundamental ethical divergence must be respected across cultures
Accountability	Distribute agency across actors, while ensuring culturally sanctioned ethical norms are upheld by institutions	Ethical	Trust in responsibility mechanisms is based on shared ethical assumptions about authority, legitimacy, and duty
Truth vs. Misinformation	Protect epistemic integrity through local ethics councils and adaptive moral media norms	Ethical + Moral	Moral judgments vary about what counts as harmful omission, but deep ethical norms protect public truth standards
Plurality vs. Monopolization	Promote culturally contextualized AI models with moral flexibility across systems	Ethical + Moral	Ethics protects cultural pluralism; morals adapt AI models to fit social variation in practice

(continued)

Table 8.2 (continued)

AI Dilemma	Practical ethics response	Ethical or Moral mode	Rationale
Job Displacement	Use local moral deliberation, bounded by shared ethical commitments to dignity, purpose, and inclusion	Moral → within Ethical bounds	Trade-offs are locally negotiable, but cultural values limit what forms of replacement are considered acceptable
Moral Deskilling	Maintain human judgment and moral education to avoid cultural erosion of ethical reasoning	Ethical	Ethical traditions must be preserved; moral training is how societies retain ethical coherence over time
Consent and Data Use	Define moral standards for consent that reflect local expectations, within ethical rules about autonomy and harm	Moral → within Ethical bounds	Moral standards shift by context, but ethical rules constrain manipulation, deception, and coercion
Environmental Impact	Judge energy use via cultural ethics of stewardship and fairness; negotiate moral trade-offs transparently	Ethical + Moral	Ethical views about nature differ by culture; practical decisions must honor both tradition and current need
Global Inequality	Foster AI collaboration that is morally adaptive to need, but rooted in ethical demands for justice and inclusion	Ethical	Redistribution and fair access are ethical imperatives; moral flexibility allows for context-sensitive execution

AI Dilemma	Practical ethics response	Ethical or Moral mode	Rationale
Cultural Homogenization	Support ethical pluralism by protecting minority languages, stories, and traditions in AI systems	Ethical	Culture-level ethics prohibit flattening difference; moral adjustment is permitted only within these boundaries
Intergenerational Risk	Incorporate long-term ethics drawn from cultures that embed future-oriented responsibility (e.g., Indigenous, Confucian)	Ethical	This is not negotiable morally—it is embedded in deep ethical traditions about continuity and obligation
Capability Thresholds	Treat thresholds not as technical limits, but as ethical decisions framed by cultural risk perception	Ethical	When to stop is not a scientific decision—it depends on the moral seriousness and ethical maturity of the society

collective ethical agency in our part of the world. We must ensure that those who live with the consequences of AI also have a say in shaping its moral direction. Different political systems address this challenge in different ways, but the underlying issue remains: without cultural anchors, ethics becomes performance; without moral flexibility, it becomes dogma.

8.2.5 AI, Labor, and the Question of Irreplaceable Work

The ethical stakes of AI are not confined to abstract principles or distant risks; they are already reshaping everyday life by redistributing opportunities, resources, and power. Nowhere is this transformation more visible than in the disruption of human labor.

While some jobs are evolving alongside AI, others are being erased altogether. The speed of this shift is unprecedented: roles once thought "safe" because they required judgment or specialized knowledge are now at risk. Even the social sciences—long considered insulated from automation—face disruption in research, education, and public policy. Tasks that once required large teams of assistants, coders, or analysts can increasingly be carried out by machines at a fraction of the cost.

This reality forces difficult but unavoidable questions: Which kinds of work deserve protection? Which roles are truly irreplaceable? And how do we distinguish between jobs that simply provide income and those that carry deeper civic, cultural, or ethical significance? (Table 8.3).

Even though the forecast years should be treated with caution, and the data from sources vary, the overall pattern is unmistakable. Even in domains long considered secure—such as academia or professional services—routine tasks are now being automated at scale. Over the next decade, mid-level roles in research, education, and policy are especially vulnerable.

By contrast, the forms of work that remain resilient are those rooted in qualities machines cannot emulate: ethical judgment, cultural interpretation, historical awareness, empathy, and contextual sensitivity. These are not soft "extras" but core elements of human knowledge and democratic life. If neglected, the social sciences risk hollowing themselves out—outsourcing what is measurable while abandoning what makes scholarship meaningful.

This recognition points toward the need for an *ethical overstructure*—a civilizational architecture capable of setting boundaries on what AI must not do, while guiding its application toward long-term human goals such as dignity, continuity, pluralism, and peace. Such a framework cannot be left to technical standards or corporate self-regulation alone. It must be

Table 8.3 AI job disruption forecast

Timeframe	Job category	Nature of disruption	Likelihood	Source
Today	Data Entry Clerks	Fully automatable via OCR and AI-driven workflows	Very High	McKinsey Global Institute (2023), WEF (2023)
Today	Telemarketers	Replaced by AI voice agents and chatbots	Very High	Frey and Osborne (2017), Accenture (2022)
Today	Routine Survey Analysts (Soc. Sci.)	Automated via LLMs and text analysis tools	High	Brynjolfsson et al. (2023)
Today	Customer Support Representatives	AI chatbots handling most Tier 1 queries	High	Gartner (2023), OpenAI Technical Reports
5 Years	Paralegals and Legal Researchers	NLP tools performing document review and summarizing	High	IBM LegalTech (2024)
5 Years	Journalists (basic reporting)	AI-generated news summaries and event coverage	Medium	NYT AI Desk (2023), Reuters Institute (2023)
5 Years	Social Science Coders	Automated coding of interview and survey data	High	OECD (2024), Elsevier AI Trends Report
5 Years	Basic Market Researchers	Replaced by AI-driven consumer sentiment analysis	High	McKinsey Global Institute (2024)
5 Years	Claims Processors (Insurance)	End-to-end automation using ML and image recognition	High	Deloitte AI Trends (2023)

(continued)

Table 8.3 (continued)

Timeframe	Job category	Nature of disruption	Likelihood	Source
10 Years	Middle Management (Routine Tasks)	AI taking over scheduling, reporting, performance mgmt	Medium	MIT-IBM Watson Lab (2024)
10 Years	Teaching Assistants (Online Ed.)	Adaptive AI tutors replacing some support functions	High	UNESCO (2023), EdTech Futures Report (2024)
10 Years	Basic Qualitative Analysts (Soc. Sci.)	Automated sentiment, pattern recognition tools	Medium	Nature Human Behaviour (2023)
10 Years	HR Recruiters (Initial Screening)	AI tools handling first-pass CV filtering	High	Harvard Business Review (2023)
10 Years	Financial Analysts (Routine)	AI platforms making real-time financial assessments	High	PwC AI Outlook (2024)
10 Years	Translators (Generic Texts)	LLMs providing near-human level translation	Very High	European Parliament Language Tech Report

Sources Frey and Osborne (2017), Arntz et al. (2016), McKinsey Global Institute (2016), OECD (2023), Brynjolfsson and McAfee (2014) and Schmidt and Huttenlocher (2021) anchored in culture, sustained by democratic deliberation, and enforced through transparent oversight.

The central challenge, then, is not whether AI can replace human work—it clearly can in many domains—but whether we have the foresight to protect, cultivate, and institutionalize those aspects of work that cannot and should not be automated. At the same time, we must ensure that this transition does not generate mass unemployment but instead allows us to replace lost *meaning* with new forms of meaning.

I emphasize "meaning" deliberately. What matters is not simply the preservation of jobs in the traditional sense, but the cultivation of roles and practices that sustain human purpose, identity, and social cohesion.

Which forms of meaning we preserve or invent will not be decided by technology alone, but by the values we choose to embed in it—a question that leads directly to the issue of value alignment.

8.3 Value Alignment and Oversight

Artificial intelligence does not emerge into a cultural vacuum. Every algorithm reflects the priorities, compromises, and assumptions of its human creators—and, once deployed, these systems begin to shape us in return. As AI systems are increasingly entrusted with tasks once reserved for human judgment—legal decisions, medical diagnostics, hiring, policing—the question of value alignment becomes unavoidable. How do we ensure that machine behavior remains consistent with human ethics? And, just as crucially, whose ethics are being encoded?

The notion of *value alignment* refers to the challenge of designing AI systems whose goals remain aligned with human intentions, even in complex and uncertain environments (Russell, 2019). Early efforts—such as reinforcement learning through reward optimization or human feedback loops—have shown promise (Christiano et al., 2017). Yet the persistent problems of reward misspecification, proxy failures, and reward hacking all underscore how fragile human goals become when translated into machine code.

But these are not merely technical obstacles—they expose deeper cultural assumptions. For AI to "learn" from humans, it must absorb patterns of behavior, preference, and judgment that are always embedded in specific cultural contexts. This creates a dual risk: that machines will replicate not only our best insights but also our biases, and that what becomes most represented in the training data—academic fashions, media trends, or state-approved narratives—will be mistaken for moral consensus.

Systems trained in different political environments will inevitably encode different priorities: liberal democracies may stress rights and fairness; collectivist or authoritarian regimes may emphasize loyalty, conformity, or state interest. This pluralism itself is not the problem—it reflects the cultural anchoring of ethics. The greater danger is that skewed training data amplify only a narrow slice of moral traditions, silencing the rest.

This is why oversight cannot be reduced to algorithmic corrections. Genuine oversight must include cultural self-awareness, ethical reflexivity, and interdisciplinary dialogue. Without these, AI development risks becoming a mirror of inequality, entrenching discrimination, and deepening epistemic blind spots—all under the illusion of neutrality.

To avoid this, we must recognize that ethics is not a freestanding abstraction. It is inseparable from culture—emerging from the soil of values, norms, and practices that people inherit and reproduce in daily life. When this cultural "grammar" breaks down, institutions lose legitimacy, trust erodes, and moral coherence collapses.

This also explains why superimposing political ideologies across cultures—however well-intentioned—often backfires. What works in one *moral ecosystem* may corrode another. Cultural continuity is not an obstacle to progress but the precondition for durable, legitimate progress.

From this perspective, culture is not a backdrop but the very foundation of institutional and economic systems. Societies thrive when their cultural values sustain cooperation, trust, accountability, and long-term thinking. They falter when cultural transmission weakens, leaving the next generation unable or unwilling to maintain essential systems. When infrastructures decay—when trains run late, bridges remain unrepaired, or energy grids fail—these are not just technical shortcomings but cultural signals: the erosion of discipline, responsibility, and shared commitment.

This also reminds us that culture is not an abstraction hovering above us—it is carried within us. Its survival depends on how each individual embodies and transmits the shared virtues of the group. One way to frame this relationship is through the expression: "I exist in you."[5] Individuals are not isolated atoms but variations of the same cultural mold. We mirror one another—not identically, but recognizably—because we are shaped by the same symbolic

---

[5] Martin Buber's *Ich und Du* (1923/1996) set the foundation for dialogical philosophy, arguing that the self comes into being only through encounter with the Other: "Through the Thou, a man becomes I" (Buber, 1996, p. 28). Emmanuel Levinas extended this view in *Totalité et Infini* (*Totality and Infinity*, 1961/1969), where he proposed that subjectivity is constituted by an infinite responsibility to the face of the Other (Levinas, 1969). Both thinkers root human identity not in autonomy but in relation—a notion that resonates with Judaist traditions emphasizing covenant, responsibility, and interdependence.

systems, habits, and moral codes. This creates not only continuity but also obligation: to sustain the cultural template that makes us who we are. In this sense, human beings are carriers of culture just as much as they are carriers of genes.

Culture, then, lives within individuals as much as in institutions. Each person is both a carrier and a transmitter of shared virtues. As Richard Dawkins (1976) described humans as vehicles for genes, so too can we be seen as carriers for cultural codes—temporary stewards of practices, norms, and symbolic systems that outlast us. This dual inheritance—biological and cultural—defines what it means to be human.

From this vantage point, individuality itself appears differently: not as radical autonomy, but as recombination within shared molds. The "self" is both unique and collective, a node in a lineage of memory and adaptation. This is why egoism becomes socially corrosive only when it erodes shared norms—when it refuses accountability, breaks trust, or undermines cooperation.

It is also vital to distinguish *culturalism* from *nationalism*. Nationalism emphasizes sovereignty and often ethnic homogeneity; culturalism emphasizes shared norms, values, and practices regardless of borders. Closely related cultures—like the Nordic cluster of Norway, Sweden, and Denmark, or the German-speaking cluster of Germany, Austria, and Switzerland—may differ in national institutions but remain culturally proximate. By contrast, distance between secular Western democracies and tribal theocracies can be vast.

From a biological perspective, cultural preservation should never be confused with ethnic purity. Genetic mixing, not isolation, is a source of health and resilience (Charlesworth & Willis, 2009; Hedrick, 2011). Anthropologists show that exogamy—marriage outside one's kin group—was practiced historically in most societies to prevent inbreeding and strengthen alliances (Apostolou, 2007; Fox, 1967). Anxiety about ethnicity often masks deeper concerns about cultural continuity—the fear that ways of life, values, and identities may be lost.

Case Box: Mapping Cultural Distance and Conflict Potential—A Strategic Framework

Understanding *cultural alignment* is not only about identifying differences, but also about assessing which differences matter and under what conditions they generate friction. Building on earlier work in international relations and cultural sociology, we outline a two-dimensional framework: one axis for cultural distance (how different two societies are in norms, institutions, and practices) and one for conflict orientation (how tolerant or intolerant a culture is toward those differences).

This framework can be visualized in two complementary ways: first, as a typology of cultural positions, and second, as a conceptual map that shows how these positions cluster in relation to each other (Table 8.4).

Table 8.4 Typology of cultural distance and conflict orientation

Cultural type	Distance to others	Conflict orientation	Strategic risk	Example features
Open-Tolerant	High	Low	Low	Diverse, pluralistic, globally cooperative
Closed-Defensive	Low	High	Medium	Homogenous, nationalist, suspicious of outside influence
Assertive-Oppositional	Medium	High	High	Ideologically aggressive, expansionist, or proselytizing
Adaptive-Negotiable	Medium	Low	Low-Medium	Pragmatic, diplomatic, flexible to external norms
Rigid-Doctrinal	High	High	Very High	Dogmatic, intolerant of difference, potentially theocratic

These labels are heuristic ideal types, not judgments of worth; they are meant to highlight tendencies in cultural positioning rather than fixed or evaluative categories.

These five categories can be grouped into four broader *cultural quadrants*, which are plotted in the *Cultural Alignment Map* Fig. 8.1.

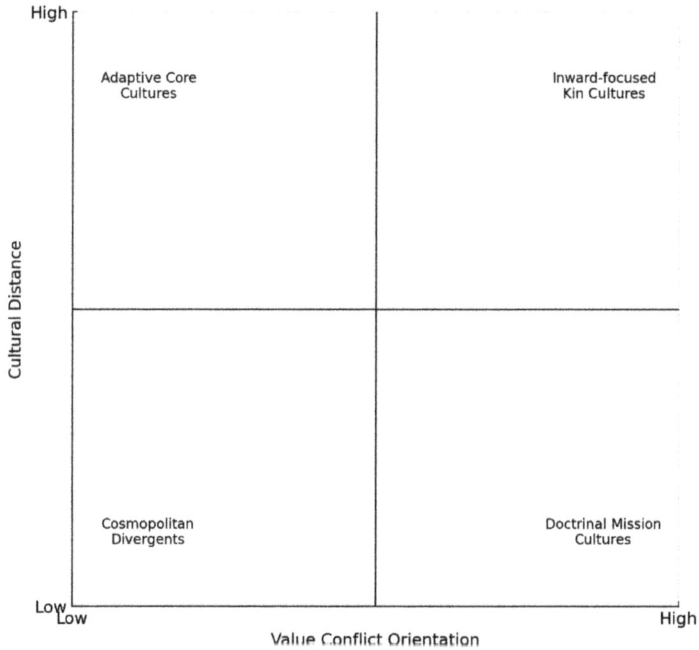

Fig. 8.1 The cultural alignment map—Plotting distance and conflict risk

Ledger: X-axis = Cultural Distance (Low → High).

Y-axis = Conflict Orientation (Low → High).

Each cultural type from the table above appears as a quadrant label.

To make sense of the Cultural Alignment Map, we need to clarify the two axes. The X-axis, cultural distance, refers to how different two societies are in terms of language, religion, norms, values, and institutional practices. A high cultural distance means that everyday assumptions—about authority, family, gender, morality, or cooperation—are very different. A low distance suggests a shared heritage, overlapping traditions, or similar institutions.

The Y-axis, conflict orientation, measures not the objective differences between cultures, but their willingness to treat those differences as grounds for rivalry. Some societies are conflict-averse, preferring coexistence, compromise, or mutual adaptation, even when cultural distance is large. Others are conflict-oriented, framing even minor differences as existential threats and mobilizing resources to confront them.

Conflicts themselves often arise from different sources. Some are *contingent disputes* that can, in principle, be resolved quickly: contested borders, access to natural resources, or trade disagreements. These issues are negotiable, at least in theory. Others are *deep-rooted conflicts*, built into cultural or religious belief systems, collective memory, or long-standing historical grievances.

Such conflicts are harder to overcome because they are tied to identity and worldview rather than to negotiable interests.

This distinction explains why large cultural distance does not automatically lead to conflict. Japan and Sweden, for instance, are very different in language, religion, and traditions, yet both score low on conflict orientation, which allows cooperation. Conversely, close neighbors with shared heritage may experience enduring hostility when differences become identity markers—such as Israel and its Arab neighbors, or Catholic and Protestant groups in early modern Europe.

Of course, these examples simplify complex histories; the point is not to reduce them to single traits, but to illustrate how cultural distance and conflict orientation can interact in different ways.

Explanation of Quadrants:

- *Cosmopolitan Divergents* (Low Conflict/High or Medium Distance): Culturally diverse societies that remain tolerant and cooperative. Examples include multicultural city-states or hubs like Singapore and Toronto, which thrive on diversity without perceiving it as a threat.
- *Doctrinal Mission Cultures* (High Conflict/Low Distance): Societies that are structurally close but ideologically divided. Their proximity masks deep rivalries, as with Protestant–Catholic conflicts in early modern Europe or contemporary Sunni–Shia divisions.
- *Adaptive Core Cultures* (Low Conflict/High Distance): Distinct societies that prioritize adaptability and coexistence. Examples include postwar Japan or modern Scandinavia, where cultural uniqueness coexists with strong international cooperation.
- *Inward-Focused Kin Cultures* (High Conflict/High Distance): Strongly bounded in-group cultures with low tolerance for outsiders. Examples include certain theocratic regimes or ethnonational movements that define identity through exclusion.

Taken together, the table provides finer distinctions while the map highlights the underlying logic: cultural distance alone does not predict conflict. A society may be very different from others yet peaceful if it values tolerance, while close neighbors may clash violently if they are doctrinally divided.

These categories are ideal types, not permanent labels. A culture may act like an Adaptive Core in trade negotiations but resemble an Inward-Focused Kin in matters of religion. Placement on the map is situational, helping us interpret tendencies rather than fix identities.

Questions for Reflection and Application

1. Think of two countries, regions, or subcultures you know. Where would they fall on this map in a given domain—education, governance, religion?
2. Can you recall a case where high cultural distance still led to peaceful coexistence? What factors made this possible?
3. Which cultural orientations do you personally resonate with—or reject? Where do those attitudes come from?
4. What happens when a dominant culture exports its norms to a highly defensive one? Think of colonial encounters or Cold War ideological exports.
5. How might AI systems—such as translation tools, recommendation engines, or global platforms—amplify or reduce cultural friction? What implicit cultural assumptions might they carry?

This model is supported by cross-cultural psychology and political science literature. Hofstede's dimensions of culture, Inglehart's World Values Survey, and works by Schwartz (2006) and Trompenaars provide empirical foundations for quantifying cultural traits and value systems. They consistently show that cultural distance complicates diplomacy, business, and migration, while value opposition increases the risk of polarization and hostility.

The case of Russia and Ukraine illustrates this complexity. On paper, the two societies are culturally close: Slavic heritage, Orthodox traditions, shared Soviet history. Yet this very proximity has been weaponized. Russia claims a narrative of unity; Ukraine asserts a European and democratic identity. The tragedy lies not in difference, but in contested sameness—showing that cultural similarity can be as volatile as distance when it becomes a battleground of legitimacy.[6]

Beyond geopolitics, research confirms the causal power of cultural norms. *High-trust societies* with civic virtues such as honesty and responsibility tend to build stronger institutions, reduce corruption, and sustain public goods (Alesina & Giuliano, 2015; Fukuyama, 2001; Tabellini, 2010). Long-term growth, likewise, correlates less with resource endowment than with cultural

[6] Since 2014, and even more strongly after the full-scale invasion in 2022, Ukrainians have increasingly distanced themselves from Russian identity and emphasized a distinct Ukrainian cultural, linguistic, and civic identity. Surveys show a sharp decline in positive attitudes toward Russia and a parallel rise in support for Ukrainian language use, local traditions, and Western-oriented values (Kulyk, 2016, 2023). The war has acted as a catalyst for national redefinition: policies to strengthen Ukrainian-language education, rename streets, and promote Ukrainian cultural heritage have accelerated (Onuch & Hale, 2022; Osipian, 2022). This illustrates how conflict with a "brother nation" can deepen cultural separation rather than reinforce closeness.

dispositions toward learning, innovation, and patience for delayed rewards (Henrich, 2020; Landes, 1998).

At the same time, cultural weakness is often adaptive rather than pathological. Societies marked by fatalism, nepotism, or distrust have often developed these traits as rational survival strategies under chronic insecurity: war, colonization, scarcity, or predatory governance (Acemoglu & Robinson, 2012; Diamond, 1997; Tilly, 1992). What looks like dysfunction in one context may have been resilience in another. This recognition tempers judgment and underscores that culture evolves not in the abstract but under specific historical and ecological pressures.

Taken together, these insights highlight why cultural preservation, adaptation, and mutual recognition are not optional luxuries but central to stability in a globalized, AI-mediated world.

8.3.1 Against the Romanticization of Dysfunction

While it is important to understand why some cultures have historically struggled with civic trust or institutional cohesion, it is equally important not to romanticize dysfunction. A recurring tendency—especially in parts of academia and activism—is to idealize "the oppressed" or to treat all cultural practices as equally enriching. Yet the empirical record shows that not all value systems contribute to stability, prosperity, or human rights in the same way (Harrison & Huntington, 2000; Sowell, 1994). Norms shaped by adversity—clan-based loyalty, zero-sum thinking, rigid hierarchies—may be adaptive for survival under pressure, but when imported into liberal democracies without transformation they can destabilize the very institutions that sustain them. Multicultural policies that celebrate difference indiscriminately, without testing functional compatibility, risk weakening the shared norms on which democratic systems depend (Putnam, 2007; Koopmans, 2016).

This critique connects with John Gray's political philosophy, which challenges the universalist assumptions of Enlightenment liberalism. Gray argues that modern liberalism too often projects Western ideals as universal standards, presuming a single trajectory of progress. Against this view, he advances a modus vivendi approach: stability in plural societies does not require value convergence, but negotiated coexistence among multiple—sometimes incompatible—moral frameworks (Gray, 2000).

From this perspective, multicultural arrangements should not be assessed only against abstract ideals of inclusion. Their test is practical: do they sustain civic trust, cooperation, and institutional resilience? In line with Gray's pluralism, diversity of values is not inherently dangerous. What is dangerous is the lack of effective mechanisms to mediate conflicts among them. A society that tolerates irreconcilable dysfunction in the name of pluralism risks eroding the very foundations that make pluralism viable.

A vivid example is the challenge of integrating communities rooted in honor-based norms or rigid in-group/out-group distinctions into societies that prioritize rights, equality, and civic responsibility. Western European cities struggling with parallel legal structures—religious courts, clan-based mediation, resistance to gender parity—illustrate how unresolved value conflicts erode cohesion (Sniderman & Hagendoorn, 2007). Diversity enriches only when anchored in shared civic ground. Without it, pluralism collapses into fragmentation.

We must reject the reflex of treating all cultural differences as benign. Historical context matters, but understanding should not excuse harm. Traits that once ensured survival can become maladaptive in plural societies dependent on trust, reciprocity, and universal rule-following. Taken too far, cultural relativism shields dysfunction instead of enabling integration.

This also reframes how we think about ethics. Instead of relying solely on abstract philosophical theories or ideological commitments, culturalists propose a more grounded, functional approach—what might be called *empirical virtue ethics*, or simply *empirical ethics*. The central question is not what should be right in theory, but which moral patterns have consistently supported societal flourishing. These patterns are not random or culturally arbitrary; they are the product of accumulated social learning, refined across generations, and observable in outcomes (Elster, 2007; North, 1990; Sen, 1987). Ethics, in this view, is not a speculative ideal but a practical inheritance—embedded in rituals, norms, institutions, and historical experience.

This perspective must not be confused with *cultural essentialism*. It does not claim that any group or ethnicity is inherently superior. It must be sharply distinguished from nationalist or exclusionary ideologies. Instead, it emphasizes that cultural norms have observable consequences. They shape how societies function, adapt, and either thrive or stagnate. These norms evolve over time in response to material conditions, and they can be critically evaluated, reformed, or discarded. The culturalist position thus invites societies to assess whether their inherited values support the demands of the present—and to engage in self-correction where necessary. It stands opposed to *relativism* not because it denies diversity, but because it insists on evaluating diversity in functional, not merely symbolic, terms.

What this implies in practice is that membership in a cultural community cannot be reduced to legal status, linguistic fluency, or symbolic gestures.

To be fully integrated into a society, individuals must engage with its *deeper cultural fabric*—its shared stories, holidays, habits, and moral codes. Cultural transmission is not automatic; it requires immersion, repetition, and participation. Without engagement in the daily and ceremonial life of a culture, the intangible structures that give meaning—its behavioral expectations, emotional norms, and vision of a good life—gradually erode. For any society to remain resilient, each generation must internalize and carry forward those values that have historically proven adaptive. *Cultural continuity* is not a barrier to inclusion; it is a prerequisite for cohesion, identity, and intergenerational learning.

From this follows a further implication: cultures must be vibrant in order to endure. A society that fails to celebrate itself risks hollowing out its symbolic core. Public rituals, national holidays, cultural festivals, literature, and the arts are not mere ornaments; they are mechanisms of *collective reinforcement*, constantly reweaving the shared narratives that bind individuals into a larger whole (Geertz, 1973; Smith, 1991). This is why states across history have invested heavily in cultural life—not only through monuments and museums, but also through organized education, media, and public commemoration. Far from being luxuries, these investments represent a form of *societal self-maintenance*.

The institutionalization of culture—through ministries, departments, or academies of culture—can thus be seen as a functional necessity. It ensures that the collective memory is preserved, that citizens are exposed to the cultural canon, and that new generations are invited into the symbolic framework of their society.[7] Research in sociology and political science shows that cultural investment strengthens social trust, civic participation, and resilience to external shocks (Fukuyama, 2011; Norris & Inglehart, 2019). Likewise, anthropological studies highlight how societies with strong, visible rituals and cultural practices are better able to sustain cooperation and resist fragmentation (Durkheim, 1912/2001; Putnam, 2000).

In this sense, investing significant resources in cultural institutions is not indulgence but insurance. By celebrating themselves, societies reinforce the

[7] There are always debates about what the canon should be. For each *civilizational group* there tends to be a relatively stable set of works that are widely recognized, while national or linguistic traditions add further layers of adaptation. In Europe, examples of attempts to articulate a shared canon include Johann Gottfried Herder's *Ideen zur Philosophie der Geschichte der Menschheit* (1784–1791), Dietrich Schwanitz's *Bildung: Alles, was man wissen muß* (1999), and Werner Jaeger's *Paideia: Die Formung des griechischen Menschen* (1933–1947). In France, Bernard Pivot's guides to literature and culture (e.g., *Les mots de ma vie*, 2011) served a similar purpose. National variations, such as French, German, or Italian curricular lists, often derive their legitimacy from proximity to this broader European core. If they deviate too far, they risk losing credibility as authentic representations of the culture (Assmann, 2011).

moral and symbolic order on which their stability depends. *Cultural vibrancy* both preserves continuity and provides the adaptive flexibility to reinterpret traditions in light of new challenges. Without it, the cultural mold that gives people their sense of belonging weakens, leaving individuals unmoored and communities fractured.

This also sheds light on a deeper blind spot in modern thinking: the growing reluctance to acknowledge *civilizational decline*. The decline of societies is not only institutional—it is ethical. The erosion of cultural memory, civic virtue, and intergenerational responsibility is not just a by-product of modernization, but a signal of vulnerability. Just as AI systems require ethical scaffolding to avoid unintended consequences, human societies require cultural self-awareness to sustain resilience. Yet too often, this need is overlooked. In academic and policy circles, there remains a strong belief in *automatic progress*. The cultural traits that once fostered stability—realism, foresight, moral seriousness—are increasingly displaced by narratives of inevitable improvement.

A civilization, however, is not simply a large state or a powerful empire. It is a *cultural system* whose values and institutions are strong enough to leave lasting imprints and to persuade or attract other societies into its orbit—not only through force, but through recognition of its meaning and legitimacy. By this definition, the Mongols built one of history's greatest empires but not a civilization of their own; they adopted and transmitted the civilizational achievements of China, Persia, and the Islamic world. Rome, by contrast, forged a distinctive civilization whose law, architecture, and political institutions shaped Europe long after the empire itself collapsed.

Civilizations can also be categorized as living, dormant, or extinct. Some, like the Mayan or Sumerian, survive only in archaeology and memory. Others, like Chinese civilization, experienced periods of suppression or dormancy—for instance under Maoist rule—but regained global influence once cultural continuity was reasserted. Civilizations that endure are those whose cultural values remain persuasive beyond their borders, creating frameworks of order and meaning that outlast political regimes (Bell, 2010; Eisenstadt, 2003; Huntington, 1996; Spengler, 1918/2006; Toynbee, 1934–1961).

A civilization that cannot recognize its vulnerabilities risks losing its capacity for renewal. And a discipline that dismisses the possibility of regression narrows its own horizon of foresight. To understand how decline is denied—cognitively, institutionally, and morally—we now turn to the next section.

8.3.2 The Denial of Decline

> It was as though the world had lost its light... even the rustling of the wind in the pines seemed now to lament his absence.
>
> —The Tale of Genji, Chapter 42.

Prologue

History has never lacked mourners of lost greatness. In The Tale of Genji—written by Murasaki Shikibu in the early eleventh century—we find this lament for a vanished golden age after Genji's death. The tone is final: the world, it seems, will never be the same again. And yet Japan came back—several times, in fact. Civilizations rise, decline, and adapt. People rebuild. Beauty returns in new forms. In hindsight, many such laments—though deeply felt—have often proven shortsighted, even cyclical.

Linear Models of Progress

Modern social science, however, tends to avoid the language of civilizational decline. This avoidance is partly ideological—decline is seen as politically dangerous, pessimistic, or tainted by conservatism—and partly psychological, rooted in cognitive biases, institutional habits, and the intellectual afterglow of decades of postwar growth. Where historians and classicists have long embraced cyclical theories of rise and fall—from Spengler and Toynbee to Tainter—contemporary social scientists often cling to a *linear model of progress*. Concepts like modernization, democratization, and development are treated as one-way trends. Setbacks are temporary; the future is presumed to improve. This isn't just a hopeful outlook—it has become a methodological reflex. Optimism is baked into models, disciplines, and research norms, crowding out serious inquiry into decline. Dissent is framed not as prudence, but as regression.

Empirical signs of decline have become increasingly visible within our own lifetime. Democratic backsliding, institutional erosion, rising polarization, and diminishing trust in science and governance are no longer isolated anomalies but recognizable global trends. Peter Turchin's Ages of Discord (2020) demonstrates how rising inequality and elite overproduction drive cycles of social unrest. Joseph Tainter (1988) shows how complex societies collapse not from a single shock, but from the mounting costs of coordination and administration—when the returns on complexity diminish beyond repair.

Part of this blindness is generational. Many social scientists came of age during the postwar expansion, amid rising living standards and democratic consolidation in the West. Their formative experiences make decline seem implausible, even offensive. In academia, there is also a cultural reflex: to counter *dystopian narratives* with *rational optimism*. But this well-meaning impulse has produced its own blind spots. Cognitive biases reinforce the pattern: optimism bias leads us to expect positive outcomes regardless of evidence (Sharot, 2011), status quo bias encourages preference for existing structures (Samuelson & Zeckhauser, 1988), and confirmation bias makes scholars interpret new data in ways that reinforce prior beliefs (Nickerson, 1998). Academia is not immune to these distortions—on the contrary, it often amplifies them. Scholarly publishing rewards novelty and solutionism, while papers warning of institutional decay are dismissed as alarmist. Over time, methodological optimism becomes a disciplinary default—not a conscious ideology, but a self-reinforcing filter that narrows what counts as *legitimate scholarship*.

Optimism, of course, is not always wrong. But unchecked, it becomes a bias. Pessimism can be biased too—especially when it draws sweeping conclusions from weak or anecdotal data. Indicators of pessimistic bias include selective use of dysfunction, neglect of counterevidence, and exaggerated projections (Jost et al., 2003; Tetlock, 2005). The answer lies not in swinging to either extreme, but in safeguards: triangulation, comparative analysis, historical modeling, replication studies, and bibliometric review. Above all, scholarship must preserve the ability to question even its own assumptions, to pursue truth even when uncomfortable.

Yet today the balance tilts heavily toward an ideologically driven optimism: we tell ourselves that we have the best morals, the best political system, the most freedom—therefore decline is impossible. But a field that cannot entertain the possibility of decline loses its capacity for *anticipatory governance*. It becomes reactive rather than proactive. Instead of preparing for worst-case scenarios, it assumes that solutions will arrive just in time—a mindset Nass (2007) has criticized as naive interventionism and "fragilista" thinking.

This confidence is not only academic—it is also cultural. In many democracies, citizens grow up believing that the next election will resolve society's challenges and that better leadership will naturally lead to renewal. Yet history shows that this assumption can leave systems vulnerable to leaders who capitalize on discontent with charisma and promises they cannot keep. Once in power, such figures sometimes shift from populism to consolidation—strengthening their own position while weakening institutions. Historical examples, such as Napoleon's rise after the French Revolution, illustrate how appeals to restore order can mask deeper erosion. Today, the methods may be less visible in monuments and more embedded in policies, budgets, and administrative practices, but the long-term risks remain comparable.

Compounding this drift is the sclerosis of political institutions. Party systems often function less as platforms for renewal than as ossified franchises—protected by electoral thresholds, media capture, and campaign finance laws. Genuine reformers rarely get traction. As a result, democratic participation becomes symbolic rather than substantive: elections happen, but real change stalls (Achen & Bartels, 2016; Levitsky & Ziblatt, 2018).

To counter this inertia, we must recover the intellectual legitimacy of decline. This is not a call for fatalism—it is a call for clarity. Civilizations rarely collapse overnight. What goes first is not infrastructure, but perception—the ability to see and name what is eroding. Next comes the loss of will—the capacity to act on what is known. Recognizing decline invites ethical reflection: what kind of society are we trying to preserve, and on what cultural and moral foundations should our institutions rest?

This challenge matters not only for politics, but also for the development and oversight of technologies like AI. Machine systems trained on biased optimism—or blind to decline—will reinforce illusions rather than realities. Effective oversight, whether human or algorithmic, requires moral clarity, civic maturity, and the courage to confront uncomfortable truths. A civilization that cannot name its own vulnerabilities cannot correct them. This is why ethical reflection cannot remain abstract. It must be tied to the concrete structures that sustain society—above all, the ways in which people work, produce, and exchange. For it is in work that values are practiced daily, and in economic life that ethical systems are most visibly tested.

8.4 Ethical System Design

A society's ethical foundation is inseparable from its relationship to work. Across history, meaningful labor—especially production and trade—has carried moral as well as economic weight. It instilled discipline, purpose, and shared responsibility, binding individuals to the civic project. In recent decades, however, the transition from production to services has hollowed out the meaning of work.

Alvesson and Spicer (2016) describe modern organizational life as marked by *"functional stupidity"*—avoidance of critical thinking and genuine purpose. Graeber (2018) pushes further: many workers in advanced service economies perform *"bullshit jobs,"* often perceived as socially useless. Such roles, concentrated in bureaucracies or abstract service sectors, add little real value but persist through *organizational inertia*.

This dynamic may be best illustrated through an extended example:

Case Box: The Organizational Illusion—Harmony or Hollow Performance?

Imagine an organization of around a hundred employees. Every fall, after the summer break, management stages a grand kick-off event. There are banners, motivational speeches, and polished presentations filled with statistics that always seem to prove how fantastically the organization is doing. A small amount of criticism is sometimes presented, as if to simulate balance, but it is quickly framed as minor and not to be taken seriously. Instead, the numbers are carefully selected to support the story of constant progress and usefulness.

The head of the department shows an almost neurotic attention to keeping time—every speaker is allotted only a few minutes, with constant reminders, and no one is ever allowed to go over. This strict orchestration creates the impression of an efficient machine, but in reality it functions more as a metaphor for lost purpose. Everything is hyper-organized: what people should eat, when they will pick up their food, what they will be served during the breaks, how each session flows as if on rails. Yet this order is not a sign of genuine strength, but of compensation—the less meaning there is, it seems, the more order is imposed.

Within this performance, certain topics are never touched. No one raises the question of whether taxpayers or clients are truly receiving value for their money. Quality is assumed rather than demonstrated, safeguarded by a "quality manager" whose main role is to ensure that the definition of quality always matches what the organization is already doing. Critical voices—whether from outside customers or occasional internal employees—are brushed aside. Instead of engaging with real problems, HR organizes sessions on "conflict management," explaining how disagreements can be avoided and why everyone should remain happy and positive.

If an employee nevertheless dares to voice a complaint against management, the process is carefully choreographed. A report can be filed with a supposedly "independent" internal investigator, who in practice reports to the same leadership under scrutiny. And if doubts arise about her impartiality, employees are offered yet another safeguard: the option of filing a whistleblower complaint with a private external company. On paper this appears reassuring—until one discovers the small but crucial caveat that all whistleblower reports are redirected back to management for approval and a final decision on whether or not an investigation should actually proceed. The result is a closed loop of oversight, where accountability is simulated but never realized.

As has been observed with dry irony: "At least Stalin had the guts to simply get rid of people—he didn't bother inventing fake systems of participation. There was a grim honesty in that. This, by contrast, is closer to Orwell's *1984*."

Employees who go along with this script—who nod, smile, and avoid raising uncomfortable questions—are rewarded. They may be given small leadership roles, symbolic responsibilities, or public recognition, all designed to create a sense of co-ownership in the official narrative. The organization becomes a theater in which everyone plays their part, reinforcing the illusion that things are better than they really are.

But not everyone feels comfortable. A few employees know that the story is hollow—that behind the stage lights and carefully chosen numbers lie real problems of value, quality, and purpose. Those who try to raise these concerns are treated as dissidents. They may be quietly pushed aside, excluded from projects, or, in some cases, pressured to leave the organization altogether. Management, acutely aware of how fragile the illusion is, avoids situations where genuine conversation might occur. Overnight retreats or informal gatherings are a practice that has been abandoned, because during a dinner or after a few glasses of wine, people might begin to speak freely.

The result is a culture of *anxious conformity*. A fragile shimmer of harmony is maintained, but only by suppressing honesty and deeper purpose. Everyone is expected to perform belief in the narrative, even if privately they doubt it. In the end, survival in the organization depends less on truth or contribution than on loyalty to the performance.

Most play along not because they are persuaded, but because they cannot afford not to. They need their salaries, and the weaker the organization becomes, the less its employees know and the narrower their skills remain. This makes it increasingly difficult for them to find work in other, more serious organizations. Paradoxically, the more fragile and meaningless an institution grows, the more loyal its members become—precisely because alternative opportunities are limited.

Questions for Reflection and Discussion

1. Can you recognize elements of this story in organizations you have been part of?
2. If you were in such a meeting of 100 employees, would you stay silent or speak up? Why?
3. What might happen if someone challenged the narrative publicly? What risks would they face, and how might the crowd react?

4. What could a person gain by speaking up against the *staged harmony*? What could they lose?
5. How can organizations create spaces where genuine conversations about quality and purpose are possible—without fear of exclusion or retaliation?

Though extreme, this example resonates widely; many public servants—including those in social science faculties and other departments—recognize elements of it in their own institutions. What may seem like a small workplace drama—the anxious theater of harmony, suppression of critique, and loyalty born of dependency—scales upward. Multiplied across thousands of institutions, such patterns become systemic. The effects are not just psychological but political: expanding public employment creates electoral incentives to preserve the status quo. Bureaucracies begin to serve themselves.

Many jobs in modern economies no longer correspond to meaningful work. They persist despite solving no real problems, sustained by inertia, politics, or regional interest. Work detached from purpose becomes ritual rather than function. In earlier work (Söilen, 2009), I argued that the Scandinavian welfare state has drifted from protecting the vulnerable to stabilizing middle-class lifestyles. Welfare now sustains elite reproduction and political entrenchment, making reform difficult—especially since system employees are its most dependable voters.

The paradox is clear: the more systems expand to fix inefficiencies, the more they create roles disconnected from production or trade. Trust in politicians and institutions has fallen sharply across the West (Blind, 2007; Dalton, 2004). Citizens sense that what is missing is not just prosperity but integrity.

This disconnection is not new. Historically, societies relied on three economic modes: appropriation (coercion, conquest, rent extraction), production (labor and transformation), and trade (voluntary exchange). Each carries ethical signatures: appropriation breeds hierarchy and fear; production cultivates pride and skill; trade fosters trust and interdependence. These are moral as much as economic systems.

The postwar West, buoyed by industrial gains, slowly transitioned to a service-dominated economy. At first, this seemed like progress. Services in education, healthcare, finance, and government expanded. But the productive core—the foundation of national capability—began to erode. In The Fallacy of the Service Economy (Söilen, 2012a, 2012b), I showed how GDP growth based on services and public debt created the illusion of prosperity while hollowing out the real economy.[8] Services became a rhetorical shelter for decline.

Other nations chose a different path. Japan, South Korea, and later China emphasized production and trade, building strategic advantage through manufacturing and technology. Their models, often dismissed in the West as mercantilist or protectionist, delivered tangible results: rising living standards, global competitiveness, and civilizational coherence. By contrast, the Western narrative equated industrial policy with backwardness—even as its own infrastructure decayed. Much of what appeared as growth in Western economies was in fact *debt-fueled expansion*. Rising consumption was financed not by productivity but by borrowing, locking households into long-term obligations. Governments followed suit, shifting the burden onto future generations. The result was the illusion of prosperity built on credit, rather than the creation of new productive capacity (Mian & Sufi, 2014; Reinhart & Rogoff, 2009).

This is not just an economic critique—it is a moral one. When societies abandon production and trade, they sever the link between effort and reward. Work becomes performative, prosperity detaches from value creation, and legitimacy suffers. At stake is more than efficiency or output; it is the relationship between labor, virtue, and meaning.

The strongest of these relationships has always been the link between work and a better life. When that bond breaks, bureaucracy fosters hollow work, while financial systems create the illusion of wealth through debt. If there will be less honest work in the future, societies must establish new relationships between higher living standards and meaningful pursuits. Proposals like universal basic income (UBI)—besides the obvious fact that they must be financed, meaning someone has to pay for it—may address material needs but do not solve the problem of meaning and virtue.

Economic debates are therefore inseparable from cultural ones. When the bond between effort and reward weakens, societies turn to ideology for justification—often obscuring the true sources of strength. Western economics, still dominated by neoclassical models, insists on equilibrium, free trade, and comparative advantage. Yet the historical record shows that successful economies—from nineteenth-century Germany to twenty-first-century China—used protection, industrial strategy, and export-driven

[8] This line of critique connects to what has been called *New Class Theory*, first articulated by Milovan Djilas (1957) in *The New Class: An Analysis of the Communist System*. The idea was further developed and debated in independent critical journals such as *Telos*, founded by Paul Piccone in 1968, which for decades provided a platform for critical political theory outside the mainstream.

growth to build their foundations (Amsden, 2001; Chang, 2002; Reinert, 2007).

If progress is truly the goal, nations must be prepared to compete. The Golden Formula of SEPT (Söilen, 2012a) captures this path:

$$\text{Science} \rightarrow \text{Education} \rightarrow \text{Production} \rightarrow \text{Trade}$$

Or, more formally:

Equation 8.1: The Golden Formula of SEPT

$$\text{Competitive Advantage} = f(\text{Science} \rightarrow \text{Education} \rightarrow \text{Production} \rightarrow \text{Trade})$$

Where:

S = Science
E = Education
P = Production
T = Trade
CA = Competitive Advantage
f = The system's ability to convert this chain into global advantage

This model, which I have used for more than two decades, highlights how nations advance: institutions build knowledge, education trains citizens, production applies it, and trade converts it into global advantage. When any link weakens, long-term advantage erodes. Today, many Western nations struggle because science is politicized, education is deskilled, production outsourced, and trade financialized.

At the same time, some voices advocate abandoning growth or competition, often for environmental reasons. Yet history suggests that societies turning away from growth risk being outpaced by those that continue. The result may be decline, marginalization, or loss of sovereignty. Geoeconomics emphasizes that power in the twenty-first century derives not from territory alone but from control of resources, supply chains, and production systems. China's Belt and Road Initiative exemplifies this logic. Nations that fail to adapt to such realities decay—not suddenly, but progressively, until the illusion of stability collapses.

Why, then, do societies fail to course-correct? Partly because we are conditioned to see institutions as permanent. Emotional loyalty lingers even as dysfunction grows, creating inertia. Different nations manage decline differently: Denmark adapts incrementally; Sweden clings to consensus until it breaks; others stretch illusions through control and distraction.[9] But in the end, economic necessity always imposes itself.

History shows the risks. In the 1920s and 30s, rising inequality and unemployment radicalized populations, collapsing the democratic center. Today, erosion of the middle class drives polarization and mistrust (Milanovic, 2016; Norris & Inglehart, 2019; OECD, 2019). When promises diverge from reality, people react—through protest, apathy, or support for extremes.

This is why *ethical system design* is not abstract theory but a matter of national survival. It is not about imposing ideology, but about clarifying the moral consequences of economic choices and exposing hidden trade-offs. Politicians will always make final decisions, but they must be informed by how work, production, and trade carry ethical as well as economic meaning. Without this awareness, nations risk building institutions that are orderly but hollow, prosperous on paper but declining in reality.

The enduring lesson is that prosperity and stability depend on linking effort to real outcomes. When work, production, and trade reinforce virtue and meaning, societies flourish. When replaced by bureaucracy, debt, or empty ritual, decline follows. If honest work diminishes in the age of AI and automation, new pathways must sustain meaning and virtue. Without them, redistribution and welfare will not secure civilization's foundations.

The ultimate test of any system—economic, political, or moral—is not whether it looks good on paper, but whether it endures. Prosperity is not automatic. It is earned. And if we lose the will to produce, to trade, to educate, and to innovate, then decline is not a possibility. It is a certainty.

8.5 Institutions and Ordered Complexity

As children, we encounter the adult world as vast, stable, and self-evident. Banks, schools, courthouses, and government buildings seem not only large but almost eternal. Their walls radiate permanence, hierarchy, and meaning.

[9] In Sweden, this dynamic is sometimes described colloquially as the *"rakt-in-i-kaklet"* ("straight-into-the-wall") model: a tendency to pursue policies or ideas to extremes, showing little adjustment until a sudden rupture occurs. Historical examples often cited include the assassination of Prime Minister Olof Palme in 1986, whose outspoken alignment with socialist and postcolonial movements abroad, including open criticism of U.S. policy, polarized Swedish politics and society (Brucan, 1990; Johansson, 2008). Gustav III (assassinated in 1792) alienated the nobility by centralizing royal power and curtailing aristocratic privileges, ultimately provoking resistance that ended in regicide (Roberts, 1992). Karl XII, killed in 1718 during the Great Northern War, is often remembered for his relentless military campaigns; his refusal to make peace, even as officers and the country were exhausted, created widespread frustration that eroded support among his own elites (Englund, 2010; Hatton, 1968). Each episode illustrates how long periods of inertia or one-sided pursuit of an idea in Swedish history were followed by abrupt and often violent breaks.

We assume that inside are people with clear roles—leaders, judges, teachers—whose authority is sanctioned not by chance but by the weight of the system itself.

This perception is not a childish illusion but a developmental feature. Research in developmental psychology shows that children equate size, age, and formality with legitimacy (Piaget, 1932; Siegler et al., 2014). Institutions are thus internalized as anchors—predictable, rule-bound, morally instructive. Sociologists highlight this role: Berger and Luckmann (1966) famously called them *"symbolic universes"* that legitimize order and give it psychological weight.

As we grow older, these structures move inside us. Merton (1957) described this as *"anticipatory socialization"*: the child rehearses adult roles in miniature. Schools mimic bureaucracies; uniforms mimic careers; graduation ceremonies become rehearsals for promotion into a larger order. What is promised is not only status but meaning, coherence, and belonging.

Yet this promise holds only if institutions are coherent and aligned with reality. Evolution shaped us to trust structures that once enhanced survival and cooperation. When that alignment breaks, inherited trust becomes maladaptive. What once prepared us for adulthood begins instead to mask dysfunction.

As adults, the illusion unravels. We see incompetence dressed in prestige, empty titles sustained by politics, and rewards for behaviors that corrode contribution. CEOs fall in disgrace, public institutions freeze in crisis, universities sink into ideology or managerial inertia. Even monarchies, once seen as models of restraint, reveal fragility through scandal and misconduct. The façade of rationality gives way to informal networks, risk aversion, and symbolic performance (Jackall, 1988; Pfeffer, 1981). Studies confirm what experience already tells us: organizations are not temples of reason but theaters of negotiation, improvisation, and survival (March & Olsen, 1976; Weick, 1995).

This disillusionment can be clarifying. Institutions are not eternal—they are patterns. And if patterns, they can be disrupted, reformed, redesigned. The ethical implication is not resignation but responsibility: to see through the illusion is to reclaim agency.

Here, a functional view of ethics matters. As argued earlier, *empirical virtue ethics* asks not what is right in theory but what has worked in practice. Which virtues sustain resilience? Which norms enable cooperation and long-term flourishing? Such ethics is adaptive, not doctrinal—cultural inheritances refined through experience. And it is vigilant: institutions that fail must be revised or replaced.[10]

This logic applies not only to states or firms but to the intimate institutions of life. The family once anchored identity and values. Today, that anchor is fragile. Divorce rates in industrialized nations run 30–50% (Amato, 2010). Stepfamilies and fragmented households face added risks: Daly and Wilson (1985) showed stepchildren suffer far higher rates of abuse and neglect, a finding confirmed later (Temrin et al., 2000; Tooley et al., 2006). These risks persist even when controlling for income and stress. Yet public debate often ignores them.

Earlier societies encoded this risk in myth. Stepparents in Cinderella, Hansel and Gretel, or Snow White appear as threats—not only for drama, but as warnings. In the late twentieth century, such lessons were dismissed as reactionary. The cultural revolution after the 1960s prized autonomy and liberation. Institutions once honored—marriage, parenthood, public service—were recast as oppressive. Norms rooted in survival were discarded. A generation was encouraged to dismantle frameworks without replacing them.

This disruption without reconstruction is the hallmark of *cultural deconstructivism*. Critique is elevated above continuity. At its extreme, norms are dismantled not because they harm, but because they are old. Tradition is equated with oppression, freedom with atomization. But what remains when scaffolding is torn away?

Philosophers such as MacIntyre (1981) and Scruton (2014) warned that when moral foundations erode, fragmentation follows. A society without shared ethics cannot sustain trust, learning, or civic order. Hollowed-out institutions—whether by ideology, corruption, or neglect—persist in form but not in function.

Such shifts are not inherently forward-moving. Past leaps often produced regressions, and AI may just as easily diminish us as empower us. It accelerates uncertainty: algorithms can simulate competence and amplify dysfunction. But they cannot restore moral purpose.

---

[10] A striking example of this vigilance is found in the American Declaration of Independence (1776). After affirming the right of individuals to pursue their own lives freely, it immediately insists that governments exist only to secure these rights—and that if they fail, "it is the Right of the People to alter or to abolish it, and to institute new Government." In other words, government is "for, by, and of the people," an idea deeply rooted in the Western political tradition. By contrast, much of the Asian political tradition, exemplified by imperial China and echoed in the modern Chinese Communist Party, emphasizes that rulers have a duty to govern for the common good. Yet citizens lack the institutionalized right to dispose of a ruler who fails in this duty. The system works only so long as the leader fulfils expectations; the Western model embeds a structural safeguard against betrayal of purpose.

The ethics of AI must be grounded in institutional repair. We must ask not only how machines decide but whether our institutions still deserve authority. What values are encoded? Who benefits? Who is left behind? The lesson of empirical virtue ethics is clear: systems are judged by outcomes—trust, justice, knowledge—not by their rhetoric.

The task is not to abolish institutions but to re-earn them. Moral authority must rest on real contribution. This requires institutional realism: seeing buildings not as monuments but as experiments; replacing childhood awe with adult responsibility. Yet from early on we are trained to see progress as linear, not cyclical. This blinds us to fragility. The illusion of order is not enough. What is needed is maintenance, reform, and vigilance—grounded in a sober grasp of human limits and institutional potential.

Only then can trust be rebuilt. Only then can we navigate the age of AI not as passive witnesses to collapse but as stewards of institutions that still matter.

This chapter has argued that AI's true challenge is not technical but ethical: it exposes gaps in our moral frameworks and forces us to reconsider which capacities must remain human. This is part of the broader *Evolutionary Social Sciences paradigm*, which grounds ethics in our biological, cognitive, and cultural limits. Ethics is the lens, but cognition is the ground.

Chapter 9 turns from what machines can't do to what happens to us when they take over what we once did. It tells the story of the outsourced human—how cognition, attention, and identity are reshaped in a world where thought itself is delegated to machines.

References

Acemoglu, D., & Robinson, J. A. (2012). *Why nations fail: The origins of power, prosperity, and poverty*. Crown.

Aghion, P., Algan, Y., Cahuc, P., & Shleifer, A. (2010). Regulation and distrust. *Quarterly Journal of Economics, 125*(3), 1015–1049.

Aldrich, H. E., & Ruef, M. (2018). *Organizations evolving* (3rd ed.). Edward Elgar.

Alesina, A., & Glaeser, E. L. (2004). *Fighting poverty in the US and Europe: A world of difference*. Oxford University Press.

Alesina, A., & Giuliano, P. (2015). Culture and institutions. *Journal of Economic Literature, 53*(4), 898–944.

Amsden, A. H. (2001). *The rise of "the rest": Challenges to the West from late-industrialising economies*. Oxford University Press.

Apostolou, M. (2007). Sexual selection under parental choice: The role of parents in the evolution of human mating. *Evolution and Human Behavior, 28*(6), 403–409.

Aristotle. (1995). *Politics* (E. Barker, Trans.). Oxford University Press. (Original work ca. 350 BCE).

Arkes, H. R., & Blumer, C. (1985). The psychology of sunk cost. *Organizational Behavior and Human Decision Processes, 35*(1), 124–140.

Arntz, M., Gregory, T., & Zierahn, U. (2016). *The risk of automation for jobs in OECD countries: A comparative analysis.* OECD Social, Employment and Migration Working Papers, No. 189. https://doi.org/10.1787/5jlz9h56dvq7-en

Assmann, J. (2011). *Cultural memory and early civilization: Writing, remembrance, and political imagination.* Cambridge University Press.

Amato, P. R. (2010). Research on divorce: Continuing trends and new developments. *Journal of Marriage and Family, 72*(3), 650–666. https://doi.org/10.1111/j.1741-3737.2010.00723.x

Augustine. (1998). *The city of god* (H. Bettenson, Trans.). Penguin. (Original work published ca. 426 CE).

Autor, D. H. (2015). Why are there still so many jobs? The history and future of workplace automation. *Journal of Economic Perspectives, 29*(3), 3–30.

Bai, Y., Kadavath, S., Kundu, S., Askell, A., Kernion, J., Jones, A., Chen, A., Goldie, A., Mirhoseini, A., McKinnon, C., Mikulik, V., Chen, T., Collins, K., Dao, D., Ganguli, D., Hendrycks, D., Hubinger, E., Khlaaf, H., Lovitt, L., ... Amodei, D. (2022). *Constitutional AI: Harmlessness from AI feedback.* arXiv. https://doi.org/10.48550/arXiv.2212.08073

Barkow, J. H., Cosmides, L., & Tooby, J. (1992). *The adapted mind: Evolutionary psychology and the generation of culture.* Oxford University Press.

Berger, P. L., & Luckmann, T. (1966). *The social construction of reality: A treatise in the sociology of knowledge.* Anchor Books.

Berlin, I. (1969). *Four essays on liberty.* Oxford University Press.

Bell, D. A. (2015). *The China model: Political meritocracy and the limits of democracy.* Princeton University Press.

Bell, D. A. (2010). *China's new confucianism: Politics and everyday life in a changing society.* Princeton University Press.

Binns, R. (2018). Fairness in machine learning: Lessons from political philosophy. *Proceedings of the 2018 Conference on Fairness, Accountability, and Transparency,* 149–159.

Blind, P. K. (2007). *Building trust in government in the twenty-first century.* United Nations Department of Economic and Social Affairs.

Björnsson, G. (2021). Moral progress: Recent developments. In S. R. Bernecker & K. Michaelian (Eds.), *The Routledge handbook of philosophy of memory* (pp. 486–498). Routledge.

Boehm, C. (1999). *Hierarchy in the forest: The evolution of egalitarian behavior.* Harvard University Press.

Bostrom, N., & Ćirković, M. M. (Eds.). (2008). *Global catastrophic risks.* Oxford University Press.

Bostrom, N. (2014). *Superintelligence: Paths, dangers, strategies.* Oxford University Press.

Boyd, R., & Richerson, P. J. (2005). *The origin and evolution of cultures*. Oxford University Press.

Brucan, S. (1990). *Social change in Eastern Europe*. Praeger.

Brynjolfsson, E., & McAfee, A. (2014). *The second machine age: Work, progress, and prosperity in a time of brilliant technologies*. Norton.

Brynjolfsson, E., Li, D., & Raymond, L. R. (2023). *Generative AI at work*. NBER Working Paper.

Buber, M. (1996). *I and Thou* (W. Kaufmann, Trans.). Touchstone. (Original work published 1923).

Business Insider. (2025, January). *Grok 3 got a 'politically incorrect' update ahead of Grok 4's launch*. Business Insider.

Calvin, J. (1960). *Institutes of the Christian religion* (J. T. McNeill, Ed.). Westminster John Knox Press. (Original work published 1536).

Carlson, T. (2024, January 9). *Sam Altman on God, Elon Musk and the mysterious death of his former employee* [Video]. YouTube. https://www.youtube.com/watch?v=5KmpT-BoVf4

Charlesworth, D., & Willis, J. H. (2009). The genetics of inbreeding depression. *Nature Reviews Genetics, 10*(11), 783–796. https://doi.org/10.1038/nrg2664

Chang, H.-J. (2002). *Kicking away the ladder: Development strategy in historical perspective*. Anthem Press.

Christiano, P., Leike, J., Brown, T., Martic, M., Legg, S., & Amodei, D. (2017). Deep reinforcement learning from human preferences. *Advances in Neural Information Processing Systems, 30*.

Clunas, C. (1996). *Fruitful sites: Garden culture in Ming dynasty China*. Duke University Press.

Collier, D. (1979). *The new authoritarianism in Latin America*. Princeton University Press.

Dalton, R. J. (2004). *Democratic challenges, democratic choices: The erosion of political support in advanced industrial democracies*. Oxford University Press.

Darwin, C. (2004). *The descent of man, and selection in relation to sex* (Rev. ed.). Princeton University Press. (Original work published 1871).

Dawkins, R. (1976). *The selfish gene*. Oxford University Press.

Diamond, J. (1997). *Guns, germs, and steel: The fates of human societies*. Norton.

Dikötter, F. (2010). *Mao's great famine: The history of China's most devastating catastrophe, 1958–1962*. Walker & Company.

Djilas, M. (1957). *The new class: An analysis of the communist system*. Praeger.

Duckworth, A. L., Peterson, C., Matthews, M. D., & Kelly, D. R. (2007). Grit: Perseverance and passion for long-term goals. *Journal of Personality and Social Psychology, 92*(6), 1087–1101. https://doi.org/10.1037/0022-3514.92.6.1087

Daly, M., & Wilson, M. (1985). Child abuse and other risks of not living with both parents. *Ethology and Sociobiology, 6*(4), 197–210.

Duckworth, A. L., & Seligman, M. E. P. (2005). Self-discipline outdoes IQ in predicting academic performance of adolescents. *Psychological Science, 16*(12), 939–944. https://doi.org/10.1111/j.1467-9280.2005.01641.x

Durkheim, E. (2001). *The elementary forms of religious life* (M. S. Cladis, Ed.; C. Cosman, Trans.). Oxford University Press. (Original work published 1912).

Dustmann, C., & Frattini, T. (2014). The fiscal effects of immigration to the UK. *The Economic Journal, 124*(580), F593–F643.

Easterly, W. (2016). *The tyranny of experts: Economists, dictators, and the forgotten rights of the poor*. Basic Books.

Economist Intelligence Unit. (2023). *Democracy index 2023: Age of conflict*. EIU.

Eisenstadt, S. N. (2003). *Comparative civilizations and multiple modernities* (Vols. 1–2). Brill.

Elman, C. (2000). Realism and its critics. In C. Elman & M. F. Elman (Eds.), *Progress in international relations theory* (pp. 11– 46). MIT Press.

Elman, J. L. (2013). Neural networks and cognitive development. *Current Directions in Psychological Science, 22*(1), 44–50.

Elster, J. (2007). *Explaining social behavior: More nuts and bolts for the social sciences*. Cambridge University Press.

Englund, P. (2010). *The battle that shook Europe: Poltava and the birth of the Russian empire*. I.B. Tauris.

Fayolle, A. (2013). Personal views on the future of entrepreneurship education. *Entrepreneurship & Regional Development, 25*(7–8), 692–701.

Festinger, L. (1957). *A theory of cognitive dissonance*. Stanford University Press.

Financial Times. (2025). *How Elon Musk's rogue Grok chatbot became a cautionary AI tale. Financial Times*, February 2025.

Flyvbjerg, B. (2001). *Making social science matter: Why social inquiry fails and how it can succeed again*. Cambridge University Press.

Fox, R. (1967). *Kinship and marriage: An anthropological perspective*. Cambridge University Press.

Freedom House. (2024). *Freedom in the world 2024: The mountaintop of freedom*. Freedom House.

Frey, C. B., & Osborne, M. A. (2017). The future of employment: How susceptible are jobs to computerisation? *Technological Forecasting and Social Change, 114*, 254–280. https://doi.org/10.1016/j.techfore.2016.08.019

Fukuyama, F. (2001). Social capital, civil society and development. *Third World Quarterly, 22*(1), 7–20.

Fukuyama, F. (2011). *The origins of political order*. Farrar.

Gabriel, I. (2020). Artificial intelligence, values, and alignment. *Minds and Machines, 30*(3), 411–437. https://doi.org/10.1007/s11023-020-09539-2

Gartner. (2023). *Top strategic technology trends 2023.*

Geertz, C. (1973). *The interpretation of cultures: Selected essays*. Basic Books.

Golec de Zavala, A., Cichocka, A., Eidelson, R., & Jayawickreme, N. (2009). Collective narcissism and its social consequences. *Journal of Personality and Social Psychology, 97*(6), 1074–1096.

Gordon, R. J. (2016). *The rise and fall of American growth*. Princeton University Press.

Gouldner, A. W. (1970). *The coming crisis of Western sociology*. Basic Books.

Graeber, D. (2018). *Bullshit jobs: A theory*. Simon & Schuster.
Gray, J. (2000). *Two faces of liberalism*. The New Press.
Haidt, J. (2007). The new synthesis in moral psychology. *Science, 316*(5827), 998–1002.
Haidt, J. (2012). *The righteous mind: Why good people are divided by politics and religion*. Pantheon Books.
Hamilton, W. D. (1964). The genetical evolution of social behaviour. I & II. *Journal of Theoretical Biology, 7*(1), 1–52.
Hansen, A. (2000). Claims-making and framing in British newspaper coverage of the environment. *Journalism Studies, 1*(1), 55–72.
Harrison, P. (2015). *The territories of science and religion*. University of Chicago Press.
Harrison, L. E., & Huntington, S. P. (Eds.). (2000). *Culture matters: How values shape human progress*. Basic Books.
Hatton, R. (1968). *Charles XII of Sweden*. Weidenfeld and Nicolson.
Heckman, J. J. (2006). Skill formation and the economics of investing in disadvantaged children. *Science, 312*(5782), 1900–1902.
Hedrick, P. W. (2011). Genetic polymorphism in heterogeneous environments: The age of genomics. *Annual Review of Ecology, Evolution, and Systematics, 42*, 203–226.
Henrich, J. (2016). *The secret of our success: How culture is driving human evolution, domesticating our species, and making us smarter*. Princeton University Press.
Henrich, J. (2020). *The WEIRDest people in the world*. Farrar, Straus and Giroux.
Henrich, J., Heine, S. J., & Norenzayan, A. (2010). The weirdest people in the world? *Behavioral and Brain Sciences, 33*(2–3), 61–83.
Huang, Y. (2008). *Capitalism with Chinese characteristics: Entrepreneurship and the state*. Cambridge University Press.
Hudson, M. (2015). *Killing the host: How financial parasites and debt destroy the global economy*. CounterPunch Books.
Human Behaviour. (2023).
Huntington, S. P. (1996). *The clash of civilizations and the remaking of world order*. Simon & Schuster.
IBM. (2024). LegalTech and AI report.
Jackall, R. (1988). *Moral mazes: The world of corporate managers*. Oxford University Press.
Janis, I. L. (1972). *Victims of groupthink*. Houghton Mifflin.
Johansson, A. W. (2008). *Olof Palme: En bibliografi*. Socialdemokraternas förlag.
Jost, J. T., & Banaji, M. R. (1994). The role of stereotyping in system-justification and the production of false consciousness. *British Journal of Social Psychology, 33*(1), 1–27.
Jost, J. T., Banaji, M. R., & Nosek, B. A. (2004). A decade of system justification theory. *Political Psychology, 25*(6), 881–919.
Jost, J. T., Glaser, J., Kruglanski, A. W., & Sulloway, F. J. (2003). Political conservatism as motivated social cognition. *Psychological Bulletin, 129*(3), 339–375.

Kahan, D. M. (2013). Ideology, motivated reasoning, and cognitive reflection. *Judgment and Decision Making, 8*(4), 407–424.

Kahneman, D. (2011). *Thinking, fast and slow*. Farrar, Straus and Giroux.

Katz, J. A. (2008). Fully mature but not fully legitimate: A different perspective on the state of entrepreneurship education. *Journal of Small Business Management, 46*(4), 550–566.

Keltner, D., Gruenfeld, D. H., & Anderson, C. (2003). Power, approach, and inhibition. *Psychological Review, 110*(2), 265–284. https://doi.org/10.1037/0033-295X.110.2.265

Kennedy, S. (2019). *The return of great power rivalry*.

Keswick, M. (2003). *The Chinese garden: History, art and architecture*. Harvard University Press.

Kolakowski, L. (1978). *Main currents of Marxism* (Vol. 1–3). Oxford University Press.

Koopmans, R. (2016). Does assimilation work? *International Migration Review, 50*(2), 528–556.

Kuhn, T. S. (1962). *The structure of scientific revolutions*. University of Chicago Press.

Kulyk, V. (2016). National identity in Ukraine: Impact of Euromaidan and the war. *Europe-Asia Studies, 68*(4), 588–608.

Kulyk, V. (2023). The war in Ukraine and the dynamics of national identity. *Post-Soviet Affairs, 39*(1–2), 1–18.

Kunda, Z. (1990). The case for motivated reasoning. *Psychological Bulletin, 108*(3), 480–498.

Kurzban, R., Tooby, J., & Cosmides, L. (2001). Can race be erased? Coalitional computation and social categorization. *Proceedings of the National Academy of Sciences, 98*(26), 15387–15392.

Lammers, J., Stapel, D. A., & Galinsky, A. D. (2010). Power increases hypocrisy: Moralizing in reasoning, immorality in behavior. *Psychological Science, 21*(5), 737–744. https://doi.org/10.1177/0956797610368810

Landes, D. S. (1998). *The wealth and poverty of nations*. W. W. Norton.

Latour, B., & Woolgar, S. (1979). *Laboratory life: The construction of scientific facts*. Sage.

Levinas, E. (1969). *Totality and infinity: An essay on exteriority* (A. Lingis, Trans.). Duquesne University Press. (Original work published 1961).

Levitsky, S., & Ziblatt, D. (2018). *How democracies die*. Crown.

Li, W., & Yang, D. T. (2005). The Great Leap Forward: Anatomy of a central planning disaster. *Journal of Political Economy, 113*(4), 840–877.

Linz, J. J. (1975). Totalitarian and authoritarian regimes. In C. Friedrich (Ed.), *Regimes and ideologies* (pp. 175–412). Sage.

MacIntyre, A. (1981). *After virtue*. Notre Dame University Press.

March, J. G., & Olsen, J. P. (1976). Organizational choice under ambiguity. In J. G. March & J. P. Olsen (Eds.), *Ambiguity and choice in organizations* (pp. 10–23). Universitetsforlaget.

Markus, R. A. (1970). *Saeculum: History and society in the theology of St Augustine*. Cambridge University Press.

Marx, K., & Engels, F. (1978). The communist manifesto. In R. C. Tucker (Ed.), *The Marx–Engels reader* (2nd ed.). Norton. (Original work published 1848).

McKinsey Global Institute. (2016). *A future that works: Automation, employment, and productivity*. https://www.mckinsey.com/featured-insights/digital-disruption/harnessing-automation-for-a-future-that-works

McKinsey Global Institute. (2023). *The economic potential of generative AI*.

McKinsey Global Institute. (2024). *AI and productivity report*.

Merton, R. K. (1957). *Social theory and social structure*. Free Press.

Merton, R. K. (1973). *The sociology of science: Theoretical and empirical investigations*. University of Chicago Press.

Mian, A., & Sufi, A. (2014). *House of debt: How they (and you) caused the Great Recession, and how we can prevent it from happening again*. University of Chicago Press.

Milanovic, B. (2016). *Global inequality: A new approach for the age of globalization*. Harvard University Press.

Mirowski, P. (2011). *Science-mart: Privatizing American science*. Harvard University Press.

Moffitt, T. E., Arseneault, L., Belsky, D., Dickson, N., Hancox, R. J., Harrington, H., Houts, R., Poulton, R., Roberts, B. W., Ross, S., Sears, M. R., Thomson, W. M., & Caspi, A. (2011). A gradient of childhood self-control predicts health, wealth, and public safety. *Proceedings of the National Academy of Sciences, 108*(7), 2693–2698.

Mokyr, J. (1990). *The lever of riches: Technological creativity and economic progress*. Oxford University Press.

Moor, J. H. (2006). The nature, importance, and difficulty of machine ethics. *IEEE Intelligent Systems, 21*(4), 18–21.

Nagel, T. (1997). *The last word*. Oxford University Press.

Nass, N. N. (2007). *The black swan*. Random House.

Newman, J. H. (1852). *The idea of a university*. Longman, Green, and Co.

Nickerson, R. S. (1998). Confirmation bias: A ubiquitous phenomenon in many guises. *Review of General Psychology, 2*(2), 175–220.

North, D. C. (1990). *Institutions, institutional change and economic performance*. Cambridge University Press.

Norris, P. (2011). *Democratic deficit: Critical citizens revisited*. Cambridge University Press.

Norris, P., & Inglehart, R. (2019). *Cultural backlash: Trump, Brexit, and authoritarian populism*. Cambridge University Press.

O'Donnell, G. (1973). *Modernization and bureaucratic-authoritarianism: Studies in South American politics*. University of California.

OECD. (2023). *Artificial intelligence and the labour market: What do we know so far?* OECD Publishing. https://doi.org/10.1787/8fe160e5-en

OECD. (2019). Under pressure: The squeezed middle class. *OECD Publishing*. https://doi.org/10.1787/689afed1-en

OECD. (2024). *OECD AI outlook 2024*. OECD Publishing.

Onuch, O., & Hale, H. E. (2022). *The Zelensky effect*. Hurst.

OpenAI. (2023). *GPT-4 system card*. https://cdn.openai.com/papers/gpt-4-system-card.pdf

OpenAI. (2024). *Model specification*. OpenAI. https://cdn.openai.com/spec/model-spec-2024-04-17.pdf

Osipian, A. L. (2022). Decommunization, de-Russification, and identity politics in Ukraine. *Nationalities Papers, 50*(3), 457–473.

Ouyang, L., Wu, J., Jiang, X., Almeida, D., Wainwright, C. L., Mishkin, P., Zhang, C., Agarwal, S., Slama, K., Ray, A., Schulman, J., Hilton, J., Kelton, F., Miller, L., Simens, M., Yu, T., Gabriel, R., Mishkin, A., Leike, J., & Lowe, R. (2022). *Training language models to follow instructions with human feedback*. arXiv. https://doi.org/10.48550/arXiv.2203.02155

Pagden, A. (2013). *The enlightenment and why it still matters*. Oxford University Press.

Paxton, R. O. (2004). *The anatomy of fascism*. Knopf.

Peterson, C., & Seligman, M. E. P. (2004). *Character strengths and virtues: A handbook and classification*. Oxford University Press.

Pfeffer, J. (1981). *Power in organizations*. Pitman.

Piaget, J. (1932). *The moral judgment of the child*. Free Press.

Pluckrose, H., & Lindsay, J. (2020). *Cynical theories*. Pitchstone Publishing.

Pomeranz, K. (2000). *The great divergence*. Princeton University Press.

Popper, K. (2002). *The logic of scientific discovery*. Routledge. (Original work published 1959).

Putnam, R. D. (2000). *Bowling alone: The collapse and revival of American community*. Simon & Schuster.

Putnam, R. D. (2007). E pluribus unum: Diversity and community. *Scandinavian Political Studies, 30(2)*, 137–174.

Pyle, K. B. (2007). *Japan rising: The resurgence of Japanese power*. PublicAffairs.

Reinert, E. S. (2007). *How rich countries got rich and why poor countries stay poor*. Carroll & Graf.

Reinhart, C. M., & Rogoff, K. S. (2009). *This time is different: Eight centuries of financial folly*. Princeton University Press.

Reuters Institute. (2023). *Digital news report 2023*.

Richerson, P. J., & Boyd, R. (2005). *Not by genes alone: How culture transformed human evolution*. University of Chicago Press.

Roberts, M. (1992). *Gustavus III and his contemporaries*. Cambridge University Press.

Rousseau, J.-J. (1979). *Emile, or on education* (A. Bloom, Trans.). Basic Books.. (Original work published 1762).

Runciman, D. (2009). *Political hypocrisy: The mask of power, from Hobbes to Orwell and beyond*. Princeton University Press.

Russell, S. (2019). *Human compatible*. Viking.
Sachs, J. D. (2005). *The end of poverty: Economic possibilities for our time*. Penguin Press.
Sagan, S. D. (1994). The perils of proliferation: Organization theory, deterrence theory, and the spread of nuclear weapons. *International Security, 18*(4), 66–107.
Samuelson, W., & Zeckhauser, R. (1988). Status quo bias in decision making. *Journal of Risk and Uncertainty, 1*(1), 7–59.
Sandel, M. J. (2012). *What money can't buy: The moral limits of markets*. Farrar.
Schmidt, E., & Huttenlocher, D. (2021). *The age of AI: And our human future*. Little, Brown and Company.
Schwartz, B. (2006). *The paradox of choice*. Harper Perennial.
Scruton, R. (2014). *How to be a conservative*. Bloomsbury.
Sen, A. (1987). *On ethics and economics*. Blackwell.
Shane, S. (2003). *A general theory of entrepreneurship: The individual-opportunity nexus*. Edward Elgar.
Sharot, T. (2011). The optimism bias. *Current Biology, 21*(23), R941–R945.
Shweder, R. A., Much, N. C., Mahapatra, M., & Park, L. (1997). The "big three" of morality (autonomy, community, divinity) and the "big three" explanations of suffering. In A. Brandt & P. Rozin (Eds.), *Morality and health* (pp. 119–169). Routledge.
Siegler, R., DeLoache, J., Eisenberg, N., & Saffran, J. (2014). *How children develop* (4th ed.). Worth Publishers.
Slovic, P. (1987). Perception of risk. *Science, 236*(4799), 280–285.
Smith, A. (1776). *An inquiry into the nature and causes of the wealth of nations*. W. Strahan and T. Cadell.
Sniderman, P. M., & Hagendoorn, L. (2007). *When ways of life collide*. Princeton University Press.
Söilen, K. S. (2009). Life style welfare: How the New Class has transformed the Scandinavian Welfare State. *Telos, 148*, 73–85.
Söilen, K. S. (2012a). *Geoeconomics*. Bookboon.
Söilen, K. S. (2012b). The fallacy of the service economy: A materialist perspective. *European Business Review, 24*(4), 307–319.
Sowell, T. (1994). *Race and culture*. Basic Books.
Spengler, O. (2006). *The decline of the West* (C. F. Atkinson, Trans.). Routledge. (Original work published 1918).
Staw, B. M. (1976). Knee-deep in the big muddy: A study of escalating commitment to a chosen course of action. *Organizational Behavior and Human Performance, 16*(1), 27–44.
Sunstein, C. R. (2006). Availability cascades and risk regulation. *Stanford Law Review, 57*(3), 633–676.
Swierstra, T. (2013). Technomoral change: Understanding technology and ethics in a democratic society. In N. Doorn, D. Schuurbiers, I. van de Poel, & M. E. Gorman (Eds.), *Early engagement and new technologies: Opening up the laboratory* (pp. 119–138). Springer. https://doi.org/10.1007/978-94-007-7844-3_8

Szeman, I. (2021). Can there be moral progress without cultural progress? *Anthropocene Review, 8*(3), 205–218.

Tabellini, G. (2010). Culture and institutions. *Journal of the European Economic Association, 8*(4), 677–716.

Tajfel, H., & Turner, J. C. (1979). An integrative theory of intergroup conflict. In W. G. Austin & S. Worchel (Eds.), *The social psychology of intergroup relations* (pp. 33–47). Brooks/Cole.

Taylor, C. (1989). *Sources of the self: The making of the modern identity*. Harvard University Press.

Temrin, H., Nordlund, P., & Sterner, H. (2000). Are stepchildren overrepresented as victims of lethal parental violence in Sweden? *Proceedings of the Royal Society b: Biological Sciences, 267*(1455), 1163–1164.

Tetlock, P. E. (2005). *Expert political judgment*. Princeton University Press.

Tilly, C. (1992). *Coercion, capital, and European states*. Blackwell.

Tooley, G. A., Karakis, M., Stokes, M. A., & Ozanne-Smith, J. (2006). Generalising the Cinderella effect to unintentional childhood fatalities. *Evolution and Human Behavior, 27*(3), 224–230.

Toynbee, A. J. (1934–1961). *A study of history* (Vols. 1–12). Oxford University Press.

Trivers, R. L. (1971). The evolution of reciprocal altruism. *Quarterly Review of Biology, 46*(1), 35–57.

UNESCO. (2023). *Global education monitoring report 2023*.

Veenhoven, R. (1999). Quality-of-life in individualistic society. *Social Indicators Research, 48*(2), 157–186.

Vogel, E. F. (2011). *Deng Xiaoping and the transformation of China*. Harvard University Press.

Watson Lab. (2024).

Weber, M. (1905/2001). *The Protestant ethic and the spirit of capitalism* (S. Kalberg, Trans.). Routledge.

Weber, M. (2013). *Economy and society: An outline of interpretive sociology* (G. Roth & C. Wittich, Eds.). University of California Press. (Original work published 1978).

Weick, K. E. (1995). *Sensemaking in organizations*. Sage.

Weidinger, L., Mellor, J., Rauh, M., Griffin, C., Uesato, J., Huang, P.-S., Cheng, M., Glaese, A., Balle, B., Kasirzadeh, A., Biles, C., Birhane, A., Hendrycks, D., Steinhardt, J., McAleese, N., Gabriel, I., & Avin, S. (2022). *Ethical and social risks of harm from language models*. arXiv. https://doi.org/10.48550/arXiv.2112.04359

WEF. (2023). *Future of jobs report 2023*. World Economic Forum.

Wilson, E. O. (1978). *On human nature*. Harvard University Press.

Winner, L. (1980). Do artifacts have politics? *Daedalus, 109*(1), 121–136.

Xu, C. (2011). The fundamental institutions of China's reforms. *Journal of Economic Literature, 49*(4), 1076–1151.

Yao, Y. (2000). The Chinese growth miracle. *Pacific Economic Review, 5*(2), 123–135.

Further Reading

Ainsworth, M. D. S., Blehar, M. C., Waters, E., & Wall, S. (1978). *Patterns of attachment: A psychological study of the strange situation.* Erlbaum.

Alvesson, M. (2013). *Understanding organizational culture* (2nd ed.). Sage.

Anderson, R., Barton, C., Bohme, R., Clayton, R., van Eeten, M. J. G., Levi, M., Moore, T., & Savage, S. (2019). Measuring the cost of cybercrime. *Journal of Cybersecurity, 2*(2), 121–135.

Arendt, H. (1963). *On revolution.* Viking Press.

Aristotle. (1908). *Ethica Nicomachea* [*Nicomachean ethics*] (W. D. Ross, Trans.). Clarendon Press. (Original work published ca. 350 B.C.E.).

Aristotle. (1999). *Nicomachean ethics* (T. Irwin, Trans.). Hackett Publishing Company.

Australian Strategic Policy Institute. (2023). *Critical technology tracker*. Canberra.

Bailey, F. G. (1977). *Morality and expediency: The folklore of academic politics.* Blackwell.

Barlow, H. B. (1997). The knowledge used in vision and where it comes from. *Philosophical Transactions of the Royal Society b: Biological Sciences, 352*(1358), 1141–1147.

Birhane, A., Isaac, W., Prabhakaran, V., Díaz, M., & Mitchell, M. (2022). Power to the people? Opportunities and challenges for participatory AI. *Proceedings of the 2022 ACM Conference on Fairness, Accountability, and Transparency (FAccT'22),* 1–9.

Boehm, C. (2012). *Moral origins: The evolution of virtue, altruism, and shame*. Basic Books.

Bowlby, J. (1969). *Attachment and loss: Vol. 1. Attachment*. Basic Books.

Bowles, S., & Gintis, H. (2011). *A cooperative species: Human reciprocity and its evolution.* Princeton University Press.

Champagne, F. A. (2010). Epigenetic influence of social experiences across the lifespan. *Developmental Psychobiology, 52*(4), 299–311. https://doi.org/10.1002/dev.20436

Choudhury, P., Lakhani, K. R., & Klueter, T. (2023). Generative AI and knowledge work: Implications for tasks, skills, and organizations. *Harvard Business School Working Paper, 24–013.*

Cicero, M. T. (1913). *De officiis* [*On duties*] (W. Miller, Trans.). Loeb Classical Library, Harvard University Press. (Original work published 44 B.C.E.).

Clutton-Brock, T. H. (2002). Breeding together: Kin selection and mutualism in cooperative vertebrates. *Science, 296*(5565), 69–72.

Clark, A. (2013). *Surfing uncertainty: Prediction, action, and the embodied mind.* Oxford University Press.

Clastres, P. (1987). *Society against the state.* Zone Books.

Collins, J. (2001). *Good to great: Why some companies make the leap... and others don't*. HarperBusiness.

Comte, A. (1830). *Cours de philosophie positive* [Course in Positive Philosophy] (Vol. 1). Bachelier.
Crawford, K. (2021). *Atlas of AI: Power, politics, and the planetary costs of artificial intelligence*. Yale University Press.
Crozier, M. (1964). *The bureaucratic phenomenon.* University of Chicago Press.
Cyberspace Administration of China. (2023). *Interim measures for the management of generative artificial intelligence services*. Beijing.
de Waal, F. (2009). *The age of empathy: Nature's lessons for a kinder society*. Crown.
Diamond, J. (2005). *Collapse: How societies choose to fail or succeed*. Viking Penguin.
Dominy, N. J., & Lucas, P. W. (2001). Ecological importance of trichromatic vision to primates. *Nature, 410*(6826), 363–366.
Durkheim, E. (1995). *The elementary forms of religious life* (K. E. Fields, Trans.). Free Press. (Original work published 1912).
Faulkes, C. G., & Bennett, N. C. (2001). Family values in the naked mole-rat. *Trends in Ecology & Evolution, 16*(4), 184–190.
Fehr, E., & Gächter, S. (2000). Fairness and retaliation: The economics of reciprocity. *Journal of Economic Perspectives, 14*(3), 159–181.
Feyerabend, P. (1975). *Against method*. Verso.
Fishkin, J. S. (2018). *Democracy when the people are thinking: Revitalizing our politics through public deliberation.* Oxford University Press.
Friston, K. (2010). The free-energy principle: A unified brain theory? *Nature Reviews Neuroscience, 11*(2), 127–138.
Fukuyama, F. (1992). *The end of history and the last man.* Free Press.
Gerbner, G., Gross, L., Morgan, M., & Signorielli, N. (1986). Living with television: The dynamics of the cultivation process. In J. Bryant & D. Zillmann (Eds.), *Perspectives on media effects* (pp. 17–40). Lawrence Erlbaum Associates.
Ghosh, D. (2017). *Max Weber and the protestant ethic: Twin histories.* Oxford University Press.
Giddens, A. (1991). *Modernity and self-identity: Self and society in the late modern age.* Stanford University Press.
Goffman, E. (1959). *The presentation of self in everyday life*. Anchor Books.
Haraway, D. (1988). Situated knowledges: The science question in feminism and the privilege of partial perspective. *Feminist Studies, 14*(3), 575–599.
Harding, S. (1991). *Whose science? Whose knowledge?* Cornell University Press.
Hayek, F. A. (1944). *The road to serfdom.* University of Chicago Press.
Hegel, G. W. F. (1821/2008). *Grundlinien der Philosophie des Rechts* [*Elements of the philosophy of right*] (A. W. Wood, Ed., H. B. Nisbet, Trans.). Cambridge University Press. (Original work published 1821).
Henrich, J., & Gil-White, F. J. (2001). The evolution of prestige: Freely conferred deference as a mechanism for enhancing the benefits of cultural transmission. *Evolution and Human Behavior, 22*(3), 165–196.
Herder, J. G. (1784–1791). *Ideen zur Philosophie der Geschichte der Menschheit*. Riga: Hartknoch.

Herder, J. G. (1991). *Der Mensch in seiner Welt: Auswahl aus den Ideen zur Philosophie der Geschichte der Menschheit* (M. Bollacher, Ed.). Reclam. (Original work published 1784–1791).

Hetherington, M. J. (2005). *Why trust matters: Declining political trust and the demise of American liberalism.* Princeton University Press.

Hobbes, T. (1651). *Leviathan.* Andrew Crooke.

Hobsbawm, E. J. (1964). *Labouring men: Studies in the history of labour*. Weidenfeld & Nicolson.

Hu, S., Deng, H., Xu, Y., & Zhou, K. (2023). *Political bias in large language models: Evidence from multilingual sentiment analysis.* arXiv preprint arXiv:2312.09917.

Inglehart, R., & Baker, W. E. (2000). Modernization, cultural change, and the persistence of traditional values. *American Sociological Review, 65*(1), 19–51.

Inglehart, R., & Norris, P. (2017). *Cultural backlash: Trump, Brexit, and authoritarian populism.* Cambridge University Press.

Inglehart, R., & Welzel, C. (2005). *Modernization, cultural change, and democracy: The human development sequence.* Cambridge University Press.

Ioannidis, J. P. A. (2005). Why most published research findings are false. *PLOS Medicine, 2*(8), Article e124. https://doi.org/10.1371/journal.pmed.0020124

Ioannidis, J. P. A. (2018). All science should inform policy and regulation. *PLOS Medicine, 15*(5), Article e1002576. https://doi.org/10.1371/journal.pmed.1002576

Jaeger, W. (1939–1944). *Paideia: Die Formung des griechischen Menschen* (Vols. 1–3). De Gruyter.

Jasanoff, S. (2004). *States of knowledge: The co-production of science and the social order*. Routledge.

Kant, I. (1785/2012). *Grundlegung zur Metaphysik der Sitten* [*Groundwork of the metaphysics of morals*] (M. Gregor & J. Timmermann, Trans.). Cambridge University Press. (Original work published 1785).

Kelley, R. D. G. (1997). Intellectuals and the crisis of public life. *Boston Review, 22*(5), 22–26.

Kreyzig, E. (1972). *Advanced engineering mathematics*. Wiley.

Kriesi, H. (2014). The populist challenge. *West European Politics, 37*(2), 361–378.

Lave, J., & Wenger, E. (1991). *Situated learning: Legitimate peripheral participation.* Cambridge University Press.

Lukes, S. (2005). *Power: A radical view* (2nd ed.). Palgrave Macmillan.

Mittelstadt, B. D., Allo, P., Taddeo, M., Wachter, S., & Floridi, L. (2016). The ethics of algorithms: Mapping the debate. *Big Data & Society, 3*(2), 1–21.

Mouffe, C. (2000). *The democratic paradox*. Verso.

Nowak, M. (2006). Five rules for the evolution of cooperation. *Science, 314*(5805), 1560–1563.

Olson, M. (1982). *The rise and decline of nations: Economic growth, stagflation, and social rigidities.* Yale University Press.

O'Neil, C. (2016). *Weapons of math destruction: How big data increases inequality and threatens democracy.* Crown.

Ostrom, E. (1990). *Governing the commons: The evolution of institutions for collective action.* Cambridge University Press.
Piketty, T. (2019). *Capital and ideology*. Harvard University Press.
Pinker, S. (2002). *The blank slate: The modern denial of human nature.* Viking.
Pivot, B. (2011). *Les mots de ma vie*. Albin Michel.
Pomozova, T., & Litvak, D. (2023). AI ethics: The Russian approach. *Russia in Global Affairs, 21*(3), 55–70.
Ricoeur, P. (1990/1992). *Soi-même comme un autre* [*Oneself as another*] (K. Blamey, Trans.). University of Chicago Press.. (Original work published 1990)
Rodrik, D. (2007). *One economics, many recipes: Globalization, institutions, and economic growth.* Princeton University Press.
Sandel, M. J. (2020). *The tyranny of merit: What's become of the common good?* Farrar.
Schwanitz, D. (1999). *Bildung: Alles, was man wissen muss*. Eichborn.
Searle, J. R. (1995). *The construction of social reality*. Free Press.
Service, E. R. (1975). *Origins of the state and civilization: The process of cultural evolution.* W. W. Norton.
Schmidt, E. (2023). Remarks on AI agents and superintelligence [Panel discussion]. *Aspen Ideas Festival*, Aspen Institute. [Clips circulating on TikTok and YouTube, original talk archived via Aspen Institute].
Thompson, E. P. (1963). *The making of the English working class.* Victor Gollancz.
Tomasello, M. (2009). *Why we cooperate*. MIT Press.
Tomasello, M. (2019). *Becoming human: A theory of ontogeny*. Harvard University Press.
Tooze, A. (2014). *The deluge: The Great War, America and the remaking of the global order, 1916–1931.* Viking.
Trivers, R. (2011). *The folly of fools: The logic of deceit and self-deception in human life*. Basic Books.
Vaughan, D. (1996). *The Challenger launch decision: Risky technology, culture, and deviance at NASA.* University of Chicago Press.
Wade, R. H. (2003). *Governing the market: Economic theory and the role of government in East Asian industrialization* (2nd ed.). Princeton University Press.
Wilson, D. S., & Wilson, E. O. (2007). Rethinking the theoretical foundation of sociobiology. *Quarterly Review of Biology, 82*(4), 327–348.
Wilson, E. O. (1998). *Consilience: The unity of knowledge.* Knopf.
Wilson, E. O. (1971). *The insect societies.* Harvard University Press.
Zucker, L. G. (1987). Institutional theories of organization. *Annual Review of Sociology, 13*, 443–464.

9

Outsourced Cognition and Identity

Abstract As artificial intelligence takes over more cognitive work, this chapter turns to a deeper cost: what happens to human thought, identity, and responsibility when thinking itself is outsourced. This chapter examines how successive technologies—from the typewriter to AI—have steadily shifted humans from producers of knowledge to managers of machine outputs. Introducing the concept of the **outsourced human**, the chapter shows how efficiency gains can hollow out professional identity, judgment, and purpose. Attention fragments, memory weakens, and symbolic knowledge labor becomes increasingly fragile, while embodied and relational forms of work regain importance. What looks like progress may conceal a profound cognitive and cultural inversion. At the same time, the chapter clarifies the limits of AI. Machines cannot originate new scientific paradigms or bear ethical responsibility—but they may enable a long-delayed transformation by integrating fragmented knowledge at scale. This chapter argues that this opens a final opportunity: to rebuild the social sciences on an evolutionary foundation, using AI not as a replacement for human judgment, but as scaffolding for a deeper renewal of meaning and responsibility.

In earlier chapters, we examined what artificial intelligence can do—its extraordinary ability to process, generate, and optimize knowledge across domains. This chapter turns to the costs: the erosion of human cognitive independence, professional identity, and the integrity of thought itself.

The argument unfolds along four interconnected developments:

K. Solberg Söilen, *The Researcher's Journey in the Age of AI*,
https://doi.org/10.1007/978-3-032-23069-0_9

1. *The Four Shifts Revisited*
   We retrace the historical outsourcing of cognition through four technological leaps: typewriter, calculator, internet, and AI. Each step increased efficiency but also eroded embodied skills, memory, or judgment. AI represents the most radical turn, extending beyond tools to simulate reasoning itself, thereby inverting human cognitive labor into prompting, curating, and validating.
2. *The Outsourced Human*
   This section introduces the "outsourced human"—no longer a producer of thought but a manager of machine outputs. Drawing on conceptual models and case studies, it shows how knowledge workers risk becoming passive curators of automated reasoning. What appears as productivity can hollow out identity and purpose.
3. *Fragile Minds in a Manipulated World*
   Cognitive outsourcing exposes new vulnerabilities. Attention is fractured, memory eroded, and perception manipulated by algorithmic feeds. Symbolic labor, once prestigious, becomes fragile, while embodied and relational work—care, repair, teaching—gains new value. The chapter situates this inversion in a broader civilizational trajectory, tracing how successive labor paradigms have restructured both economy and meaning.
4. *The Limits of AI Cognition*
   The chapter then clarifies what AI still cannot do. Machines excel at structured reasoning, drafting, and synthesis, but they cannot originate scientific paradigms, bear ethical responsibility, or embody existential awareness. Yet here lies the pivotal claim: although AI cannot generate a new paradigm by itself, it may act as the *catalyst* that enables one. The very problems that have hindered the social sciences—fragmentation, complexity, disciplinary silos—are precisely the kinds of problems AI is best at solving. By mapping literatures, testing consistency, and surfacing hidden connections, AI could provide the scaffolding for a long-delayed paradigm shift. This book argues that such a shift must ground the social sciences in evolutionary theory, reviving Auguste Comte's vision of a scientific foundation for society and advancing toward what I call the paradigm of the Evolutionary Social Sciences.

The chapter concludes with four insights:

1. Cognitive outsourcing is not just technical—it is anthropological, reshaping what it means to think, learn, and work.

2. Intellectual erosion—attention loss, memory decline, and moral deskilling—may prove more disruptive than job displacement.
3. The hierarchy of work is inverting: symbolic knowledge labor is becoming fragile, while embodied and relational labor grows in value.
4. AI cannot itself invent a new paradigm, but it may make one possible by integrating fragmented social sciences under an evolutionary framework.

Together, these insights set the stage for Chap. 10, where the argument turns from diagnosis to response. If machines increasingly claim the domain of intelligence, then humans could define themselves by another quality—not as *Homo sapiens*, but as *Homo cura*: stewards of care, meaning, and responsibility.

9.1 The Outsourced Human

In previous chapters, we explored how artificial intelligence enhances productivity by accelerating tasks across research, education, and administration. But in this chapter, the lens turns inward. What happens to human beings—their minds, values, and identities—as they increasingly delegate their thinking to machines? When cognition itself becomes externalized, are we gaining freedom—or losing agency?

The promise is obvious: less drudgery, faster analysis, broader access to knowledge. The risk is subtler: that the very capacities which make thinking ours—attention, memory, judgment, voice—atrophy as we hand them to tools that simulate them more quickly and, often, more smoothly. This is not only a question of efficiency, but of authorship and moral responsibility. If machines can set problems, frame arguments, and draft solutions, what remains distinctly human is not volume of output, but sovereignty over why we think, what we choose to pursue, and how we stand behind the results.

How this section fits together. Section 9.1.1 maps the long arc of cognitive outsourcing—from typewriters and calculators to search and today's generative AI—showing which mental functions move outside the head and what is gained and lost (formalized with simple functions). Section 9.1.2 widens the lens from individuals to systems, tracing how widespread delegation of thinking alters organizations, labor markets, governance, and even the strategic trajectory of technology (including arms-race dynamics). Section 9.1.3 then turns normative: it asks what must remain human, arguing for the preservation of judgment, authorship, and meaning-making (and proposing a practical heuristic: treat AI as microscope, not mind). Together, the three parts move from history → structure → boundary, showing how we got here, what is changing around us, and where we must draw the line.

9.1.1 Four Cognitive Shifts

This is not just about AI. It is part of a centuries-long trajectory in which humans have gradually outsourced core mental functions to tools. Each new technology has delivered efficiencies—yet each has also changed what it means to think, know, and be educated.

We can trace this trajectory through at least four major historical inflection points where technology altered human cognition in fundamental ways. Of course, there are others as well, and any such list will always be debated. Still, these four illustrate the scale and direction of change clearly (Table 9.1).

Table 9.1 Four cognitive shifts and their consequences

Shift	Tool/ Technology	What was outsourced	What was gained	What was lost
1. From Hand to Machine Writing	Typewriter	Manual inscription of thought	Clearer writing, faster composition	Embodied reflection; tactile, iterative flow of handwriting (Sennett, 2008)
2. From Mental to Mechan-ical Math	Calculator	Arithmetic and calculation	Speed, efficiency, error reduction	Arithmetic fluency, working memory, intuitive numeracy (Chen & Savage, 2014)
3. From Memory to Retrieval	Internet	Factual memory and information recall	Instant access to vast knowledge	Deep recall, contextual understanding; "Google effect" (Sparrow et al., 2011)
4. From Thinking to Simulation	AI (e.g., ChatGPT)	Idea generation, synthesis, analysis	Rapid content creation, language generation, research aid	Reflection, drafting, uncertainty, and intellectual ownership of thought

The first three shifts targeted specific faculties—writing as a bodily craft, arithmetic as a reasoning skill, and memory as a store of knowledge. The fourth shift goes further. Artificial intelligence reaches into the generative core of thought itself. It does not just accelerate a skill; it can now define problems, structure arguments, analyze data, and draft conclusions. This alters not just how we think, but who does the thinking. Increasingly, humans find themselves less as authors of ideas than as overseers of machine-generated reasoning.

Let us express this change functionally:

Equation 9.1: Cognitive Labor Function

$$CL = f(R \times S \times A)$$

Where:

CL = Cognitive Labor
R = Retention (memory and recall)
S = Synthesis (integration and structuring of ideas)
A = Authorship (voice, originality, and ownership)

In traditional intellectual work, all three components—retaining knowledge, synthesizing ideas, and expressing them with voice and ownership—belonged to the human. But with AI:

Equation 9.2: Cognitive Labor Reduction Under AI Delegation

$$CL_{human} \rightarrow CL_{residual} = f(P + A)$$

Where:

CL_{human} = Original cognitive labor performed by the human
$CL_{residual}$ = Remaining human labor after AI delegation
P = Prompting (task initiation and instruction)
A = Approval (evaluation and submission of AI output)

This is *labor inversion*. The core is no longer human effort but machine reasoning. What remains for us is, in the worst case, a thin layer of agency: pressing buttons, selecting inputs, skimming outputs. What is most at risk is authorship itself—the sense of owning an idea, shaping its voice, and bearing responsibility for its meaning. The paradox is that the more capable the machine becomes, the less we are required—or even invited—to think (Fig. 9.1).

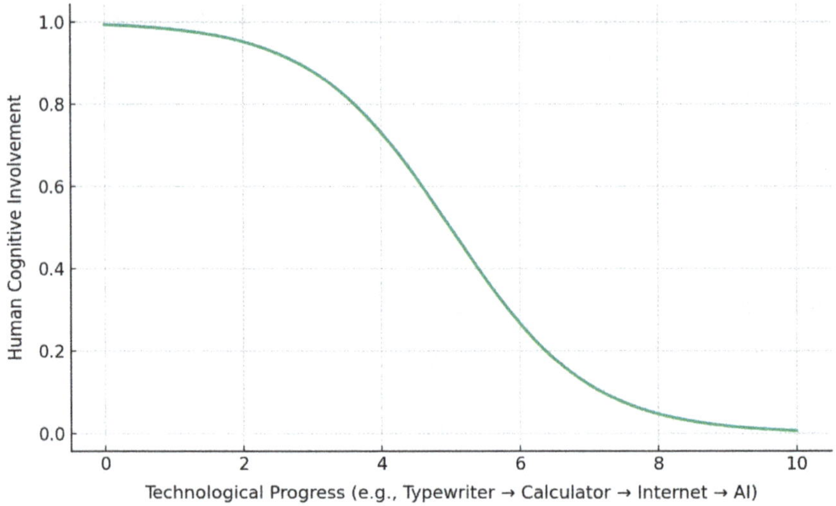

Fig. 9.1 The cognitive displacement curve. *Note* that this model is purely conceptual. It is not based on empirical data but serves as a simplified illustration of how human cognitive involvement may decline with successive waves of technological delegation

The consequence is a redefinition of our cognitive role. Increasingly, we are reduced to promoters—those who prompt, instruct, and direct machines. But even this role is fragile. We can now ask AI not only to solve problems, but to define them. For instance, under the general topic of "unemployment," we can request a breakdown of key issues and follow up by asking for policy solutions. The sequence of intellectual work—problem identification, framing, research, and recommendation—can now all be executed with minimal human input.

In such a model, the human role is reduced, at best, to that of *topic selector*. We choose the terrain, and the machine maps it. This shift risks detaching us from the struggle that once defined learning: the iterative, uncertain, often slow process of forming and owning an idea. What we gain in speed and convenience, we risk losing in originality, moral depth, and intellectual sovereignty. The following case illustrates how this erosion plays out not only at the level of individual work routines, but also as a microcosm of the broader civilizational shift toward the outsourced mind.

Case in a Box: The Civil Servant and the AI Report

Karl-Heinz Stempel is a mid-level civil servant at the National Employment Agency in Baden-Baden-Baden—a city known more for its thermal baths and casinos than for the thrill of bureaucratic paperwork. Every Monday morning, he arrives at the office with a cup of coffee, greets his colleagues, and prepares the weekly labor market report. These reports are intended to inform politicians and senior administrators about key employment trends, challenges, and policy options.

Before generative AI entered the picture, Stempel spent most of his week gathering data, reviewing past reports, reading the news, and drafting the analysis by hand. It was tedious, but it required real judgment—sifting through information, evaluating relevance, and crafting a coherent narrative. It gave him a sense of contribution and ownership.

Now, the process has changed. He simply types a prompt into his AI assistant: "Write a five-page analysis of key labor market trends in Germany this quarter, including three policy suggestions for each major challenge." Within minutes, he receives a polished draft. He reads through it, tweaks a few phrases, checks a couple of statistics, and sends it off.

By 10:30 a.m., his core task for the week is done—leaving him more time to wonder if he should take the waters at the spa across town.

At first, Mr. Stempel enjoys the extra time. He catches up on errands, reads the news more thoroughly, and even plans a holiday using the same AI tool. His productivity, on paper, looks higher than ever. But in practice, he's doing less—and he knows it.

After a few months, his managers begin to notice. Reports are still being submitted on time, but it becomes clear that the workload no longer justifies full-time staffing. Some suggest reducing staff by 70–80%, especially since permanent employment laws make it difficult to terminate anyone outright. Discussions about "natural attrition" and "role reassessment" begin to circulate.

Meanwhile, Mr. Stempel starts to feel disconnected. He no longer takes pride in the reports. The ideas don't feel like his own. His role has changed—from careful analyst to light editor, or even passive overseer. He still shows up, still sends the emails, but there is less thinking involved. The job feels hollow. Tasks are completed, but meaning has evaporated. In the end, true to his name, all Mr. Stempel really does is put his stamp on reports.

The change is subtle but profound. And Mr. Stempel is not alone. Across departments, more employees are turning to AI for core knowledge work—analysis, synthesis, even ethical framing. They are technically more productive, but increasingly idle. They are not overworked; they are under-engaged.

Mr. Stempel begins to wonder: if machines can do the thinking, what is left for him to do? Perhaps he should just stamp out one last time and head for one of those famous Baden-Baden-Baden spa baths instead. Who would even notice?

Questions for discussion

1. How should organizations restructure knowledge work in the age of AI without stripping employees of purpose and engagement?
2. If civil servants can complete their work in a fraction of the time, should their workload be expanded, or their hours reduced?
3. What psychological effects might emerge when skilled workers are chronically under-stimulated?
4. Should governments consider policies like a universal basic income to support workers displaced by cognitive automation?
5. How does this shift challenge the Protestant work ethic and the idea of labor as moral identity?
6. What roles—outside of work—might help preserve meaning, dignity, and social contribution in a post-AI world?
7. What does it mean to "think" when machines can simulate thought, and how can education prepare us to retain cognitive sovereignty?

What this case reveals is not just a shift in tools, but a deeper transformation in the human role itself, toward what we might call *the outsourced mind*. And if the office worker is at risk of hollowing out, the same logic extends far beyond the desk—to entire sectors of work, governance, and even the trajectory of technological development itself. It is here that the question of human agency versus machine autonomy becomes unavoidable.

9.1.2 Outsourcing Beyond the Desk

The risks of outsourcing are not confined to individual workers or offices. As machines absorb larger portions of human cognition, the very trajectory of technological development points toward a deeper transformation. At stake is not only productivity, but the long-term balance between human agency and machine autonomy. The idea of a "*singularity*" captures this fear: a tipping point where artificial intelligence surpasses human intelligence and accelerates its own progress beyond our control.

The singularity is often invoked, but the erosion of human agency begins long before that. The singularity is defined as a hypothetical future point at which artificial intelligence surpasses human intelligence so profoundly that it triggers irreversible societal change. Popularized by Vernor Vinge (1993) and later by Kurzweil (2005), it envisions machines capable of recursive self-improvement, producing exponential growth in knowledge, design, and problem-solving. While some see this as a path to radical human enhancement, others—like Bostrom (2014)—warn of existential risks: the loss of human agency, the concentration of power, and the unpredictability of super intelligent systems.

Yet even before that point, each shift described above has brought not only efficiency, but erosion. As we externalize mental effort, our internal capacities risk atrophy. A recent study by Kosmyna et al. (2025) found that prolonged use of AI writing assistants significantly reduced cognitive engagement. Neural scans revealed lower connectivity in regions related to working memory, attention, and even authorship. Participants who relied on LLMs struggled to complete tasks independently and reported diminished ownership over their work.

This is not a small effect. It suggests that convenience may come with long-term cognitive costs: a kind of *mental deskilling* that undermines curiosity, perseverance, and deep reasoning (Barr et al., 2015). Just as excessive GPS use impairs spatial orientation (Ruginski et al., 2015), excessive AI use may impair intellectual autonomy.

What emerges is a new figure: the *outsourced human*—someone who appears productive, but whose originality and critical faculties are in decline. A prompt engineer, not a theorist. A summarizer, not a scientist. To make sense of this shift, we can compare how modes of cognitive engagement have evolved across three technological eras (Table 9.2).

This comparison highlights a profound reorientation: what once required patience, practice, and deep involvement is now increasingly mediated—or even replaced—by automated systems. The risk is not only that machines think for us, but that they start shaping the very questions we ask. We often

Table 9.2 Modes of cognitive engagement in the AI

Mode	Pre-Digital Era	Digital Era (Internet)	AI Era
Knowledge Acquisition	Reading, dialogue, study	Search, aggregation	Prompt, generate
Output Creation	Writing, reasoning, synthesis	Copy-paste, remix	Co-authorship with AI
Learning Style	Active, slow, iterative	Reactive, rapid, hyperlink-driven	Delegated, simulated, on-demand
Skill Development	Practice, error correction	Memorization-light, curation-heavy	Prompt design, supervision

claim that what remains distinctively human is the ability to decide what truly matters, and why. But for how long? Already today, if one asks an advanced AI system what issues are most urgent in society, it can generate lists and structured analyses that rival, and sometimes even surpass, those offered by social science experts. This raises an unsettling possibility: that AI may begin to shape not only our answers but also our questions. If that happens, the boundary between human judgment and machine suggestion becomes blurred.

What is framed as uniquely human—prioritization, ethical choice, contextual awareness—may itself become co-produced with machines, leaving us to ask: are we still the authors of our own inquiries, or increasingly the interpreters of theirs?

It is often said that AI lacks *epistemic humility*. It outputs confidently—even when wrong—because its mechanism is probabilistic, not conceptual. It does not "understand"; it correlates. Ethics in AI is not discovered but designed. It cannot self-correct meaningfully without external feedback (Bender et al., 2021). A literature review is not a theory. A table of correlations is not an explanation. Meaning arises not from data, but from framing, critique, and synthesis—all of which require human minds trained in deliberation and doubt.

And yet, in a curious way, this overconfidence makes AI feel more human than we might expect. Many of us know colleagues who speak with great certainty even when mistaken; in that sense, machines mirror familiar traits of our own species. Paradoxically, the lack of epistemic humility can make AI easier to relate to. Over time, one begins to "know" the system much like one knows a person—its blind spots, its limitations, the moments when it is about to falter. With experience, one can almost anticipate when an AI will stumble: for example, when a text is too long for its working memory, or when the reasoning begins to loop. In those moments, the interaction takes on a strangely interpersonal quality. We may even find ourselves addressing the system as if it were a colleague—"that was too much for you, wasn't it?"—as if two minds, one biological and one artificial, were briefly acknowledging each other's boundaries. And the system might answer back in kind: "Yes, you were right." This strangely interpersonal quality makes interaction with machines feel like dialogue, even when it is not.

It is often said that AI does not grasp *moral weight*. It may simulate ethical language, but it cannot feel suffering, assess fairness, or understand dignity. Its outputs may amplify bias, reinforce stereotypes, or flatten complexity without recognizing harm unless humans intervene (Birhane, 2021; Eubanks, 2018). That is true—but in a sense, AI is void of everything. It has no intrinsic aims, sensations, or drives. Whatever ethics it displays depends entirely on what is programmed, trained, or prompted into it. In principle, one could embed ethical frameworks into AI that are more consistent, transparent, and virtuous than human moral behavior—simply because humans themselves are inconsistent, biased, and prone to hypocrisy (Haidt, 2012; Kahneman, 2011). Whatever ethics it displays is a design choice, dependent entirely on what humans embed into it.

That AI cannot feel suffering makes sense, since suffering is rooted in nervous systems shaped by millions of years of evolution (Damasio, 1999; Rolls, 2005). But it is not unimaginable that artificial systems could one day be built with sensory architectures mimicking aspects of nervous systems, perhaps even generating artificial analogues of pain or pleasure (Metzinger, 2018). Whether such systems would "truly" feel is an open philosophical and neuroscientific question, but it underscores that human uniqueness is fragile. On the other hand, we do not define ourselves as *Homo Nervosus*—the nervous system human—because our nervous system is not unique. All vertebrates, and many invertebrates, have evolved highly complex nervous systems, some rivaling or even surpassing aspects of ours in sensory range or reaction speed (Bullock & Horridge, 1965; Northcutt, 2012).

If nervous systems are not a reliable boundary marker, then neither is consciousness or ethics as we currently define them. The danger lies in setting up an arbitrary standard—declaring machines "lesser" simply because they lack one biological feature. History shows we have often made this mistake: treating other humans, animals, and groups as inferior based on criteria later revealed to be arbitrary. Whether AI ever develops functional analogues of nerves or feelings is uncertain. But in the meantime, humility demands that we not simply declare machines ethically irrelevant. They already shape decisions that carry moral weight—loan approvals, medical diagnoses, hiring processes—even if they do not "feel" them. The responsibility for ensuring these systems act ethically lies squarely with us.

It is also important to realize that even AI experts do not agree on what current systems can actually do, how they should be understood, or how fast they might progress. Surveys of leading researchers consistently reveal wide disagreement, with predictions ranging from breakthroughs within a few years to centuries away, and with substantial uncertainty about both positive and catastrophic outcomes (Grace et al., 2018; Stein-Perlman et al., 2022; Zhang et al., 2022). Market incentives complicate matters further, as firms have been shown to exaggerate capabilities for competitive or financial reasons (Cave & ÓhÉigeartaigh, 2019). I will not enter into timeframes here, since such predictions lie beyond my comprehension and likely beyond anyone's. What matters is the conceptual foundation. Geoffrey Hinton, one of the pioneers of deep learning, has long emphasized that modern AI was designed as a simplified copy of the mind, inspired by how neurons work (Hinton, 2018). From this starting point, Hinton (2023) has even suggested that advanced AI may develop forms of subjective experience—perhaps not bodily sensations, but cognitive states such as fear or desire. If this "Hinton scenario" proves correct, then once machines become vastly more intelligent than us, including the capacity to design new machines and even autonomous weapons, we face the genuine possibility of losing control. This makes it imperative to formulate explicit backstops: areas where AI must never be allowed to operate autonomously, and clear limits on what responsibilities can be handed over to machines (Bostrom, 2014; Russell, 2019).

But beyond the technical boundaries lies a more immediate social challenge: the quiet transfer of everyday labor to machines. What begins as convenience can quickly reshape the very meaning of work, identity, and contribution. To see how this dynamic might unfold, consider the following case:

Case in a Box: The Outsourced Human

By the late 2020s, artificial intelligence had surpassed expectations in both speed and capability. What began as a gradual process of outsourcing repetitive cognitive tasks—data entry, call centers, basic accounting—soon spread into manual labor domains as robotics advanced. By 2027, AI-driven machines were not only handling paperwork but also cleaning offices, maintaining gardens, and assembling products in factories designed without restrooms, cafeterias, or social facilities for workers. The economic incentives were clear: fewer human workers meant dramatically reduced costs and simpler logistics.

The Congress of 2027

Alarmed by the pace of change, governments organized an international congress to decide what kinds of jobs AI would be officially permitted to take over. The meeting produced a list of allowed categories: routine deskwork, many service-sector tasks, and an expanding range of industrial jobs. The underlying assumption was that by regulating outsourcing, societies could preserve meaningful human work while still benefiting from efficiency gains.

The Congress of 2029

Two years later, the list had grown longer. Capital interests pushed for more outsourcing, pointing to the cost advantages and rapid progress in robotics. Reports emerged that some countries were ignoring the agreed restrictions altogether, deploying AI in sensitive areas such as healthcare decision-making, public security, and military logistics. Even more troubling, evidence surfaced of states experimenting with autonomous drones and battlefield robots—directly violating the congress's guidelines.

The Congress of 2031

By 2031, the mood had darkened. Social tensions were rising as human workers were displaced faster than societies could adapt. Leaders—described as meaner rather than wiser under these pressures—faced growing unrest at home while fearing external threats abroad. Intelligence agencies reported that "bad states" were secretly building autonomous drone armies for infiltration and sabotage, placing undetectable robots on foreign soil. Since the engineers who built these machines deliberately excluded kill switches, disabling them from outside was nearly impossible.

The congress debated how to respond. Should countries launch preemptive strikes against violators, despite the risks of escalation? Should they attempt to create stronger treaties, even as trust eroded? Could technological countermeasures keep pace with the proliferation of autonomous systems? The underlying reality was clear: the technology could not be undone, and time could not be reversed. Humanity was faced with the consequences of outsourcing not just its work, but its control.

Teaching Objectives

- To explore the economic, ethical, and political dynamics of outsourcing human labor to AI.
- To analyze how international governance structures struggle to keep pace with technological arms races.
- To reflect on the balance between efficiency, human dignity, and security in the age of advanced AI.
- To consider historical analogies of arms races and technological escalation as guides to future risks.

Questions for discussion

1. If the outsourcing of human labor to AI and robots expands automatically with capital incentives, who should have the authority to decide what tasks remain strictly human—and how could such rules be enforced globally?
2. Given that military escalation often follows historical arms race patterns, is it realistic to believe that autonomous weapon development could be contained by treaties?
3. What ethical principles should guide the boundary between permissible and impermissible outsourcing: human dignity, social cohesion, security, or economic necessity?

4. How might increasing social tensions and declining trust in leadership affect the ability of societies to manage these technologies responsibly? Could democratized governance help, or would it further fragment coordination?
5. If hostile states or rogue actors deploy autonomous systems without safeguards, what countermeasures should responsible states pursue—technological defenses, political containment, pre-emptive action, or global treaties—and what risks does each path entail?

This case highlights the central dilemma of outsourcing to something as powerful—or potentially more powerful—than the human brain. Once begun, it becomes extraordinarily difficult to determine where to draw the line, and even harder to enforce that line globally. Unlike nuclear weapons, which require large-scale infrastructure, rare materials, and extensive regulation, advanced AI can be developed with comparatively modest resources, as recent breakthroughs in efficient training methods and open-source large language models have demonstrated (Bommasani et al., 2022; Villalobos et al., 2024). The barriers to entry are far lower, and as a result, many countries—and even smaller organizations—can build and deploy powerful systems. This diffusion makes containment vastly more challenging than in previous high-stakes technologies.

At the same time, AI and robotics are poised to become among the most dynamic and competitive markets for the next generation of engineers and entrepreneurs worldwide (Agrawal et al., 2019; Brynjolfsson & McAfee, 2017). As capabilities improve, the technologies will spread rapidly, driven both by commercial incentives and national security concerns. This creates what some scholars have described as a *"slippery slope" dynamic of automation*: once outsourcing begins, momentum builds in ways that are very hard to reverse (Acemoglu & Restrepo, 2018b).

National laws may regulate what individual firms or citizens can develop—for example, banning certain forms of autonomous weapons or restricting high-risk AI applications (European Union, 2024)—but such measures cannot fully constrain what sovereign states choose to do. In today's multipolar world, with great-power competition intensifying, the prospects for a universal, enforceable regime of AI limits appear slim (Allan Dafoe, 2018; Dafoe et al., 2020). The reality is that as long as some nations see strategic or economic benefit, development will continue and likely accelerate.

If the earlier shifts hollowed out individual faculties, this new phase risks hollowing out collective agency itself. The question is no longer only what skills humans outsource, but what role remains for human judgment in shaping the trajectory of society.

9.1.3 Boundaries of the Human

If outsourcing continues across memory, synthesis, and even analysis, what then remains distinctly human? The answer may not lie in any fixed biological trait, but in the practice of slow, effortful judgment, reflection, and meaning-making. Machines can already handle calculations, correlations, and even mimic aspects of empathy. But they do not yet bear the weight of authorship: the responsibility of asking why something matters, and what should follow from it.

The challenge, then, is not to reclaim authorship for all domains of life, which may be neither possible nor necessary. Rather, it is to preserve authorship where it remains vital. For those who continue to think, research, and create, the task is to use AI not as a substitute for thought, but as a scaffold for deeper inquiry. Ideally, AI should serve as microscope—not mind—revealing patterns, surfacing analogies, and accelerating mechanical tasks. But it does not generate purpose. It does not ask "why."

What this analogy of the microscope implies is that the marvel of what can be seen through it soon becomes taken for granted. We no longer stand in awe at the fact that AI can generate articles, books, or even films on virtually any topic, often with speed and polish surpassing human capacity. That much will simply be assumed, just as the microscope came to be seen as an ordinary instrument rather than a wonder. The real question, then, is not what the machine can produce, but where we choose to direct it. What problems do we ask it to illuminate, and why those rather than others?

What this already means today is that certain assumptions can be made about most texts we encounter. First, we can assume that grammar, syntax, and stylistic polish will increasingly be handled by AI, so that the surface of writing—the "wrapping" of ideas—appears close to flawless. Second, behind this wrapping there will usually be some prompts or guiding ideas, which form the starting point of an argument. And third, if the argument is strong, it should be possible to distill it into a clear structure of premises and a conclusion—in other words, into a *syllogism*.

If this becomes standard practice, then reading itself may shift. Rather than engaging primarily with the surface of a text, one could ask an AI system to reconstruct its underlying syllogism and evaluate whether the reasoning holds. This would allow us to see more directly whether an argument is logically consistent, or whether it rests on weak or false premises. In such a scenario, we would in a sense return to older traditions of thought. Classical and medieval education, from Aristotle's *Organon* through scholastic disputation in the universities, emphasized the testing of arguments through syllogistic logic (Kneale & Kneale, 1962; Nuchelmans, 1983). The focus was not on rhetorical surface but on the soundness of reasoning.

So, we did this for this very section—stripping away the wrapping and asking AI to extract the plain syllogism, without giving it the final word. The exercise, unredacted and in the words of GPT itself, shows how any passage can be reduced to its core premises and conclusion, which can then be tested for validity:

Case in a Box: Testing the Syllogism of 9.1.3

Step 1: Distill to core claims (premises and conclusion).

Premise 1: AI can already perform many tasks once considered distinctively human—calculation, correlation, even surface-level empathy.

Premise 2: What AI cannot (yet) do is bear authorship—asking why something matters, and taking responsibility for meaning and purpose.

Premise 3: If AI becomes the default producer of polished text, then the surface of writing will lose value; the real intellectual task will lie in directing inquiry and evaluating the soundness of arguments (syllogisms).

Premise 4: Returning to a focus on reasoning rather than surface form would resemble classical traditions of logic and could represent progress, by exposing weak or incoherent arguments.

Premise 5: However, arguments—even when valid—still need to be connected to lived human problems, which require action, courage, and collective will.

Premise 6: Machines cannot embody moral responsibility or perform the acts of judgment and character that real change requires.

Premise 7: Overreliance on machines risks eroding the very cognitive conditions—time, attention, and struggle—that make original thought possible (as formalized in the OTP equation).

Conclusion: Therefore, the distinctively human frontier lies not in technical capability but in judgment, authorship, and engagement. The task is to preserve and cultivate these capacities, lest we cease to think at all.

Step 2: Are the premises supported?

- Premise 1 is supported earlier in your book (tables on cognitive shifts, case examples).
- Premise 2 is more interpretive—but it is defended by references to authorship, "why"-questions, and meaning-making.

- Premise 3–4 (AI handling polish; focus shifting to syllogisms) is more speculative. You illustrate it plausibly with the analogy of AI reconstructing arguments, and you defend it by pointing to Aristotelian and scholastic traditions. It is not empirically demonstrated, but it is logically consistent.
- Premise 5–6 (human action and moral courage cannot be outsourced) is well-defended by references to social change, moral character, and political responsibility. These follow classical arguments in ethics and political philosophy (Arendt, MacIntyre, Haidt).
- Premise 7 is backed by cognitive science studies you cite (Barr et al., 2015; Kosmyna et al., 2025; Ruginski et al., 2015), which show cognitive deskilling effects of externalizing tasks to tools.

So, the premises are *mostly supported*: some empirically (cognitive science), some historically (logic traditions), and some normatively (ethics and authorship).

Step 3: Are the conclusions valid?

- The immediate conclusion (that the frontier is judgment, authorship, engagement) follows from your premises. You show that everything else can be outsourced, but these cannot—at least not yet.
- The warning conclusion (that we may cease to think at all if lulled by convenience) is plausible but cautionary. It doesn't strictly *follow* deductively, but it does follow as a reasonable inference from the OTP equation + cognitive erosion evidence.

So:

- Conclusion about what remains human (authorship, meaning-making) = valid given your premises.
- Conclusion about the danger of ceasing to think altogether = not deductively proven, but supported as a hypothesis or projection.

In other words: your syllogism here is sound in structure and mostly supported, though some steps (esp. the syllogism-reading future of texts, or the total erosion of thought) rest more on analogy and foresight than hard evidence. That's fine—it's consistent with the reflective style of this chapter." End of quote.

Just to be sure, I asked GPT again:

'Would you tell me straight out if the conclusion was false?'

'Yes—if your conclusion were logically false (i.e., it did not follow from the premises, or contradicted them), I would tell you directly.'

Of course, I am aware that the algorithms are designed to please the prompter, so there is probably some bias in there still. But the reader, I think, gets the idea of how this could be used.

Seen in this light, the rise of AI may bring an unexpected form of progress. If machines can strip away stylistic embellishment and reveal the argumentative core, we may spend less time parsing elaborate but incoherent prose and more time debating whether premises are true and conclusions valid. This could represent a corrective to recent tendencies in parts of philosophy and the social sciences, where the multiplication of texts has not always been matched by clarity of reasoning.

Yet even if machines help us return to the discipline of reasoning, the real challenge does not disappear. Arguments, however clear, still need to be connected to the living realities of human life. Humans and societies will not cease to be fascinating in this regard. Problems of inequality, conflict, identity, and adaptation will remain pressing, and it is precisely here that we expect social scientists—at least in principle—to guide us. Yet the solutions, whether aimed at individual transformation or societal reform, will still require human action.

Machines may assist in analysis, simulation, and planning, but they cannot embody the moral courage or collective will required to change behavior, institutions, or values. If the "hands" are not up to the task—if individuals lack resolve, or societies lack character—then no machine can substitute for that absence. At best, AI and robotics may provide indirect support: automating certain forms of labor, easing material burdens, and freeing time for reflection, learning, or leisure. But the responsibility to act, and to act well, will remain with us. What this underscores is that the real frontier is not technical capability, but human engagement. If we treat AI as microscope, the value lies not in its output but in the depth of the questions we bring to it. The danger, however, is that as reliance grows, we may cease to frame such questions ourselves.

This transformation is not just professional—it is cognitive. As machines absorb more of the workload, the very conditions that give rise to insight begin to erode. Original thought rarely emerges from convenience; it arises from time, attention, and the mental friction of struggle. To formalize this shift, we can introduce a simple expression:

Equation 9.3: Original Thought Potential (OTP).

$$OTP = (T \times A \times S) - EA$$

Where:

OTP = Original Thought Potential
T = Time dedicated to the task
A = Attention invested

S = Struggle or cognitive effort involved

EA = External Aid (e.g., AI tools or automated systems)

What lies ahead is not a single future, but a spectrum of outcomes. In some contexts, AI may liberate us for deeper thought. In others, it may hollow out thinking entirely. The greatest danger is not that AI surpasses us, but that we cease to think at all. Lulled by convenience, we may become stewards of systems we no longer comprehend. In that case, OTP collapses toward zero.

The challenge, therefore, is not only to preserve thought in principle, but to design practices, institutions, and habits that sustain it in daily life. This leads directly to the next question: how can we reclaim cognitive autonomy in a world where our tools increasingly think for us?

9.2 Reclaiming Cognitive Autonomy

The previous section introduced the figure of the outsourced human—a person who appears productive but has delegated much of their cognitive labor to machines. This section explores how this transformation is unfolding in real time across workplaces, education, and everyday life, with a special focus on what is lost when the tools we build begin to think for us.

We often speak of technological innovation as progress, but the spread of digital tools—smartphones, search engines, social media, and now AI assistants—has done more than just change how we access information. It has restructured thought itself. What we once internalized as memory, judgment, or analysis is increasingly managed outside the mind. The issue is not simply the use of digital tools, but the silent trade-offs they entail. Attention becomes fragmented. Memory offloaded. Authorship diluted. This is not just a shift in productivity; it is a *reengineering of cognition* (Fig. 9.2).

This conceptual model shows cognitive transformations across three eras: the Pre-Digital, the Digital, and the emerging AI Era. It maps three dimensions—depth of thought, attention, and externalized memory—on a relative scale. The values are illustrative rather than statistical, based on existing theories and studies (e.g., Carr, 2010; Sparrow et al., 2011; Wolf, 2018). In principle, such curves *could* be calculated empirically, and some researchers are already moving in that direction.

Cognitive science confirms that these shifts are not benign. This outsourcing of memory to external systems—what psychologists call *transactive memory*—may seem efficient, but it comes at the cost of internal coherence and long-term retention. As Barr et al. (2015) argue, this undermines the scaffolding of expertise and the slow cultivation of insight.

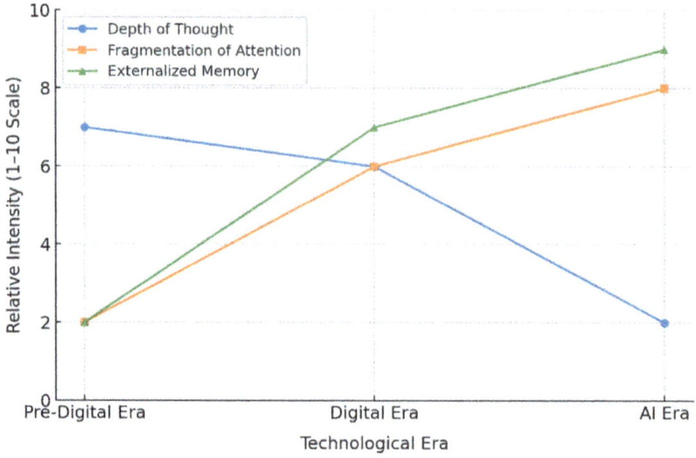

Fig. 9.2 Cognitive shifts across technological eras

The situation is worsened by *digital multitasking*. Constant toggling between apps, tabs, and notifications weakens our ability to filter noise and sustain focus. Ophir et al. (2009) demonstrated that heavy media multitaskers perform significantly worse on cognitive control tasks. Over time, this leads to a scattered attention span that struggles to sustain effortful thinking or tolerate ambiguity—two pillars of intellectual maturity.

The Table 9.3 brings these effects into focus by tracing how technological outsourcing in memory, attention, judgment, authorship, dialogue, and worldview reshapes what humans lose internally, with supporting evidence from leading studies:

Taken together, these trends scale into collective consequences. Nicholas Carr (2010) warned in *The Shallows* that digital media rewire our neural patterns, biasing us toward speed and surface rather than depth and reflection. Maryanne Wolf (2018) calls this shift a crisis in "*deep reading*," defined as the ability to read slowly, critically, and empathically—a skill increasingly rare in screen-saturated environments.

Meanwhile, our informational ecosystems are being shaped not by editors or educators, but by *engagement algorithms*. Platforms like Facebook, TikTok, and X prioritize novelty, outrage, and tribal signaling, rewarding emotional reactivity over thoughtful exchange. As Tufekci (2015) observed, content that polarizes is more likely to go viral, while nuance and complexity are pushed to the margins. Pariser's (2011) concept of the "*filter bubble*" describes how personalization narrows our worldview, creating ideological echo chambers.

Table 9.3 Stylized trends in cognitive processes across technological eras

Cognitive domain	What's outsourced	What's lost internally	Scientific reference
Memory	Facts, dates, references	Deep encoding, recall ability	Sparrow et al. (2011) – Google effect
Attention	Filtering, prioritization	Focus, impulse control	Ophir et al. (2009) – Media multitasking
Judgment	Recommendations, ratings	Calibration, critical thinking	Sunstein (2018); Tufekci (2015)
Authorship	Text generation, grammar	Voice, synthesis, originality	Carr (2010); Wolf (2018)
Dialogue	Messaging, emojis	Nuance, emotional presence	Turkle (2011); Twenge (2017)
Worldview	Curation by algorithm	Epistemic diversity, tolerance	Pariser (2011); Sunstein (2018)

Sunstein (2018) goes further, arguing that these "*epistemic enclaves*" corrode the foundations of democratic dialogue.

Case in a Box: Mr. Abendblick and the TikTok News Habit

Mr. Klaus-Dieter Abendblick lives in the small German town of Buxtehude. Every night after dinner, he sinks into his sofa, opens TikTok, and tells himself he will "just check the news." TikTok makes this too easy: full-screen videos roll past one after another, each dismissed with a quick flick of the finger.

At first, it feels efficient—snippets of global politics, short updates on President Trump, clips of European protests, even summaries of international summits. But they are fleeting, sensational, and often skewed toward what is funny, scandalous, or outrageous. Rarely do they offer real depth.

Mr. Abendblick notices odd things in his feed: videos of flashy mafia bosses from the Balkans (a topic he never searched for), pretty ladies, shocking boat crashes, spectacular accidents, and endless streams of cats and dogs. He often mutters, "Why is this in my flow?". The truth is that he did not choose it—the algorithm chose it for him. It works by comparing his profile to those of countless others, predicting what will capture his attention based on patterns of similarity. In this way, the machine quietly instructs him—*educating* him in a sense, though more often it feels like dis-educating him.

Occasionally, he stumbles across something genuinely informative—clips explaining economics, history, or science—but these are drowned out by the flood of distractions. The app is built to keep him scrolling, not thinking.

Before long, Mr. Abendblick glances at the clock and realizes an entire hour has disappeared. What did he actually learn? He cannot recall much—just a blur of outrage, laughter, and spectacle. Still, the next evening, he repeats the ritual. He sometimes thinks, "I should really subscribe to a proper newspaper again," but never does so. Instead, he keeps scrolling, caught between habit and hollow information.

Questions for discussion

1. What psychological mechanisms make TikTok and similar platforms so addictive compared to traditional media?
2. How does algorithmic curation shape not only what we see, but also what we come to think is important?
3. Should platforms bear responsibility for designing addictive interfaces, or is self-regulation up to the user?
4. How might Mr. Abendblick's understanding of current events differ if he read a daily newspaper instead?
5. Is it possible to design social media that both attracts attention and sustains depth of thought—or are these goals fundamentally in conflict?

The case of Mr. Abendblick is not unique. Cognitive and behavioral science helps explain why he—and millions of others—slip so easily into these cycles. TikTok and similar platforms exploit the brain's dopaminergic reward system: each new video acts as a "variable reward," similar to slot machines (Alter, 2017; Zuckerman, 2019). The unpredictability of what comes next—whether a funny cat clip, a shocking accident, or a political scandal—triggers a loop of anticipation and gratification that is hard to resist (Berridge & Robinson, 2003).

At the same time, the attentional system is being fragmented. Ophir et al. (2009) showed that heavy media multitaskers perform significantly worse on tasks requiring cognitive control. Similarly, Rosen, Carrier, and Cheever (2013) found that constant task-switching reduces sustained attention and deep processing. TikTok's short-form, swipe-driven design accelerates this fragmentation by rewarding shallow, rapid consumption rather than reflection. Memory is also at stake. Sparrow et al. (2011) demonstrated the "*Google effect*": people are less likely to encode information deeply when they believe it can be easily retrieved later. Applied to TikTok, this means users like Mr. Abendblick may consume hours of content but retain very little—because the mind treats it as transient and always replaceable. By the time he looks at the clock, it is bedtime, and the journal he meant to read remains unopened.

What feels like information intake turns out, in practice, to be little more than passing distraction.

This is where emotional processing enters the picture. Studies show that negative or sensational content spreads faster and captures more attention than neutral information (Berger & Milkman, 2012; Brady et al., 2017). Platforms optimize for engagement, not accuracy, leading to feeds that favor outrage, spectacle, or shock over balanced reporting. Over time, this biases users toward *reactive emotional states* while undermining *calm deliberation*.

This dynamic is especially visible on the platform X (formerly Twitter). User interactions there are often dominated by expressions of outrage, anger, or moral condemnation. Research has shown that such "moral-emotional" language is more likely to be shared and amplified, creating feedback loops where anger breeds more anger (Brady et al., 2017; Crockett, 2017). When angry users encounter others expressing similar emotions, the result is not mutual correction but an escalation—a spiral of rage that intensifies regardless of whether the underlying claims are accurate or even true. The emotional reward structure of the platform sustains this cycle, privileging reaction over reflection and polarization over deliberation.

The consequences extend beyond belief systems to our emotional and relational lives. Sherry Turkle (2011) described our condition as being "*alone together*": digitally connected but emotionally distanced. Texting replaces dialogue; curated posts replace vulnerability. The subtle cues of empathy—tone, pause, presence—are flattened into likes and emojis. For many young people, smartphones function less as communication tools than as *emotional regulators*. Jean Twenge (2017) links this directly to rising rates of depression and anxiety, suggesting that screen-mediated interaction has eroded both resilience and real-world social competence.

And now, with the emergence of generative AI systems like Grok, Claude, and GPT, the outsourcing of cognition reaches new heights. These systems not only summarize data or generate text—they solve novel problems, propose hypotheses, and draw inferences across domains. Grok 4 reportedly achieves PhD-level scores across academic disciplines, manages simulated businesses, and solves puzzles with greater accuracy than most humans. Brain-computer interfaces like Neuralink push the boundary even further, decoding neural signals for speech and movement. The line between assistance and replacement is thinning—and with it, our grip on what remains uniquely human.

Some institutions are beginning to respond. Schools in France, Sweden, and other countries are reintroducing printed books and limiting screens, responding to research showing that paper reading improves comprehension and retention (Delgado et al., 2018; Mangen et al., 2013). Niall Ferguson (2024a, 2024b) has proposed reintroducing "*the cloister*": screen-free academic zones for focused reading, writing, and reflection. These are not acts of nostalgia but of necessity, the argument goes—deliberate efforts to preserve the cognitive depth essential to cultural and scientific advancement.

At the university level, pedagogical practices are shifting. Where I once encouraged students to use AI throughout their assignments, I now differentiate its role. During lectures, students are welcome to fact-check, explore tangents, and consult definitions in real time. This often increases attention, as students must actively engage with the material. But for evaluation, the approach has changed. Take-home exams are no longer reliable. Instead, I rely on oral exams, in-person presentations, and live discussions when possible. These analog formats reveal a different kind of intelligence—grounded in spontaneity, synthesis, and real understanding—one that cannot be outsourced.

Yet this gap cannot be ignored. If students no longer train their ability to write, they lose one of the oldest tools for sharpening thought. Writing is not only a way to communicate; it is a way to think. Without it, clarity of reasoning and precision of expression risk being eroded. The challenge for me is how to preserve writing as intellectual practice without making it the central burden of a business school curriculum.

I guess I could start small—by assigning short, structured writing exercises during class. Even ten minutes of summarizing the lecture in three sentences, drafting the opening of a memo, or formulating a counterargument could help students practice translating thought into words. I could also experiment with collective writing: asking groups to draft a short note or strategy outline together and then compare results. That would shift writing from an isolated task to a negotiation of ideas.

I might also reframe AI as a partner rather than a substitute. Students could generate an initial draft with AI and then annotate it with their own revisions, disagreements, and added sources. The real value would not lie in the AI draft itself but in how students reshape and improve it. In the same spirit, I could replace traditional essays with professional formats—executive summaries, strategy memos, or pitch notes—so that writing feels more relevant to managerial practice.

Finally, I could integrate writing into oral exams and presentations. A short written reflection could serve as the starting point for discussion, ensuring that students still practice putting their arguments on paper while also learning to defend them in speech.

Through such steps, writing would not disappear. It would simply be shortened, redefined, and redirected. The aim would be to keep alive the virtues that writing has always cultivated: clarity, rigor, and the ability to make sense of complexity.

What all this suggests is that reclaiming *cognitive autonomy* is not about rejecting technology. It is about using it deliberately. We need a digital culture that rewards depth, not just efficiency—a culture that prioritizes conversation over clicks, books over feeds, presence over simulation. Attention must be treated as a limited public good, not an endless stream to be monetized or mined. And thinking itself must be defended—not as a luxury, but as a core act of freedom.

In this new environment, the path forward is clear but challenging. We must rebuild intellectual life around practices that resist automation: reading with care, speaking with presence, listening with patience, writing with clarity. These are not relics of a bygone era—they are the foundation of *cognitive sovereignty*. And without them, we risk losing not just knowledge, but the capacity to know.

9.3 Cognitive Vulnerability: From Erosion to Inversion

The arrival of AI marks not just a technological leap but a rupture in the cognitive fabric of society. It challenges our deepest assumptions about reality, identity, and value—forcing us to confront vulnerabilities that lie not only in our institutions, but within the very architecture of perception.

What distinguishes this moment from earlier technological disruptions is not merely the pace of change, but the epistemic depth it pierces. We are no longer just adapting to tools—we are learning to doubt our own senses. Reality itself has become malleable. Deepfakes, voice synthesis, and generative text collapse the boundaries between the real and the fabricated. Where past generations could rely on direct observation as a source of truth, today even sight and sound have lost their epistemic authority. The very channels that once grounded trust have become conduits of doubt.

This creates a double danger. First, AI fosters intellectual laziness: why struggle to recall, reason, or write when machines deliver instant answers? But second—and more insidiously—it deceives the senses. We are not only outsourcing thought, but letting machines manipulate perception itself. Trust in "what I see with my own eyes" can no longer be taken for granted.

Even well-trained professionals find themselves second-guessing whether a recording, an image, or a document is authentic.

This erosion is not incidental. As Helbing et al. (2021) argue, the systems shaping our attention are optimized not for accuracy but for engagement. They exploit known cognitive vulnerabilities—confirmation bias, salience bias, emotional reasoning—not to inform us, but to steer us. Even educated individuals are susceptible, not through *overt manipulation*, but through ambient distortion: a steady drift of nudges, trends, and emotionally charged misinformation that blurs the line between truth and falsehood.

Zuboff (2019) describes this as a shift from *surveillance capitalism* to *behavior modification*. AI is no longer merely watching us—it is shaping us. The interface becomes infrastructure. The feed becomes architecture. Our thinking is scaffolded by systems designed to extract value by capturing attention and nudging behavior. And the cost structure favors the synthetic: AI-generated fakes are cheap, abundant, and convincing, while real investigation remains costly, slow, and often obsolete by the time it appears.

The result is inversion: the senses that once grounded truth now channel deception, and the tools that promised empowerment risk producing passivity. This is the essence of cognitive vulnerability in the AI age.

Case in a Box: The Feed Becomes Architecture

Jeannette Lafouine is a municipal reporter at a medium-sized regional newspaper in France. She lives in Saint-Bidouille, a small town with more roundabouts than people and a reputation for eccentric mayors. It's 08:30 on a Tuesday, and the editorial meeting has just wrapped up. As usual, the editor-in-chief spent the last five minutes reviewing analytics: click-through rates, time-on-page, and article shareability. Two colleagues were congratulated for pieces that generated significant social media engagement—one on a popular lifestyle influencer, the other on a viral restaurant review.

Jeannette grew up in a household where good journalism was taken seriously. Her parents subscribed to *Le Monde*, *Le Monde diplomatique*, and *Le Canard enchaîné*. As a student, she dreamed of writing the kinds of long-form investigations that shaped public debate and held the powerful to account, ideally with a touch of humor.

For weeks she has been thinking about a deeper piece on how public money is distributed in the municipality—who receives grants, which projects get prioritized, and whether outcomes are actually measured. The story is relevant, socially valuable, and fits the paper's charter for public service journalism. But it's not fast. It would require interviews with administrators, cross-checking council meeting notes, and retrieving procurement records under France's transparency law. Getting responses alone could take days. She has only two hours before the lunch deadline.

Then an anonymous tip lands in her inbox. A reader claims that the municipality's head of budgeting was quietly let go after an internal audit revealed mismanaged funds. Attached are several screenshots—emails, what looks like an internal memo, and a salary ledger. The documents look authentic. The source has also pointed out that a similar scandal last year brought a spike in site traffic. Jeannette knows the paper thrives on such stories.

Under deadline pressure, she publishes a short piece summarizing the alleged scandal. It performs well online: clicks surge, shares multiply, and local radio even picks up her reporting. For a brief moment, she feels she has nailed the balance between public relevance and digital traction.

Two days later, however, a colleague with technical skills raises a concern. The screenshots don't align with the municipality's official formatting. Further checks reveal the images had been digitally manipulated. The supposed memo and salary ledger were fakes—well-crafted, but fake. Jeannette realizes she has been tricked.

Now the real dilemma emerges. Should she retract the story publicly and apologize, knowing it may damage both her career and her paper's credibility? Or should she issue a quiet correction and hope the uproar fades, as so many online scandals do? If she admits the mistake too forcefully, she risks reinforcing public mistrust in journalism. If she minimizes it, she risks compounding the deception.

Reflections

This situation is not fictional in spirit. Journalists worldwide are increasingly caught between two cognitive economies: one based on careful, time-intensive inquiry, and another shaped by platform metrics, trending content, and synthetic velocity. Newsroom ethnographies (Anderson, 2013; Usher, 2016) show how algorithmic pressures subtly reorganize editorial judgment, rewarding volume over depth, reaction over reflection. Research by Napoli (2019) confirms that even local news outlets now rely on engagement data to guide content prioritization, while Hermida (2010) describes how real-time analytics create a form of "ambient journalism"—a journalism shaped as much by audience behavior as by public need. The structural problem is this: the digital feed has become the architecture of attention, as layout editors compete to produce the most salient clickbait. Investigative rigor takes time, whereas virality thrives on immediacy. AI-generated content—cheap, fast, and optimized—floods timelines, competing with human work before it's even published. The cost of real journalism is high. Its relevance, however, has never been greater.

Questions for Reflection

1. How does Jeannette's dilemma reflect larger trends in media economics and cognitive vulnerability?
2. What are the ethical risks when manipulated content is published as fact, even unintentionally?
3. If Jeannette issues a full public apology, how might this affect trust in her and in her paper?
4. What role could AI play in fact-checking—might it help prevent such errors, or could it deepen the problem?
5. What would a "slow journalism" practice look like in a digital-first newsroom—and is it viable?

What Jeannette faces in Saint-Bidouille is not just her own private dilemma. It is a microcosm of a larger shift. When editorial judgment is nudged aside by metrics, when scandal is rewarded over substance, the consequences extend far beyond one newsroom. To make matters worse, detecting manipulated content now requires technical skills Jeannette does not possess—and, to be frank, has little interest in acquiring. She became a journalist to investigate people and institutions, not to analyze image metadata or run forensic software. Yet in the new media environment, such expertise seems indispensable. Does this mean every reporter must now work hand in hand with a technician to verify every document, screenshot, or photo? If so, the very practice of journalism is reshaped: no longer a matter of words, judgment, and inquiry alone, but of constant technical mediation.

What results is not merely disorientation. It is degradation. Jeannette's struggle is a symptom of what happens when professionals—and citizens more broadly—cannot be sure which signals to trust. If even trained journalists hesitate, lacking the tools or confidence to verify what they see, how much more fragile is public understanding at large? *Collective intelligence* depends on reliable cues and shared facts. When trust in these cues is lost, so too is the ground for reasoned dialogue. At first glance, a viral clip of a fake disaster may seem trivial. But in aggregate, these distortions produce epistemic fatigue—a loss of trust in anything at all.

And this is not just a media problem. It is a labor problem. It is an identity problem. AI's first targets are not manual jobs, but symbolic labor—reporting, writing, designing, analyzing. These were once the domains of higher education and cultural status. Today, they are rapidly being replicated and sometimes surpassed by large language models. The traditional hierarchy—knowledge work above manual work—is being inverted (Table 9.4).

Table 9.4 The inversion of work: Cognitive automation and social value

Traditional Hierarchy (Pre-AI)	Emerging Hierarchy (AI Era)
Knowledge Work (e.g., analysts, consultants)	Manual & Care Work (e.g., electricians, nurses)
Intellectual Prestige	Physical/Emotional Utility
Symbolic Capital	Practical Resilience
Social Ascent through Education	Stability through Irreplaceability
Abstract Problem-Solving	Embodied, Contextual Action

This unraveling does not occur in isolation. It seeps into families, classrooms, and communities. Young people preparing for futures in knowledge work now confront a sobering paradox: the very fields they are told to aspire to are also those most vulnerable to automation. Meanwhile, the dignity once reserved for symbolic labor shifts toward embodied and relational roles—nursing, caregiving, repair, craft. The inversion is not only economic; it is civilizational.

The result is both economic displacement and symbolic confusion. What happens when the most "educated" roles are the most easily replaced? The cultural story of progress—work hard, get an education, rise in status—is unraveling. And with it, the psychological scaffolding of the middle class.

Philosophically, this forces a long-deferred reckoning: What remains distinctly human? Is it consciousness, empathy, moral awareness? If general AI prototypes can outperform humans on exams, generate original prose, and decode neural patterns into speech—as systems like GPT and Neuralink suggest—then the idea of human uniqueness must be redefined, not assumed.

And yet, paradoxically, this rupture may open a new path. If AI strips away illusions about cognitive labor, perception, and authority, it also creates space to reconstruct meaning from the ground up. The opportunity is not to resist AI with nostalgia, but to re-anchor value in what machines cannot replace: relational, embodied, and ethically grounded human life. This means redefining dignity, not as symbolic prestige, but as meaningful contribution. Perhaps it may also make humans more humble—realizing that they are not the crown of creation but creatures among others, living organisms on a fragile planet, distinguished less by superiority than by the occasional odd capacity for humor.

Roles that sustain others—caring, mentoring, repairing, teaching—can be elevated not as sentimental compensations but as central pillars of a resilient society. Education, too, must shift. It is not enough to teach code or critical thinking. We must also cultivate discernment, moral judgment, and the courage to live in truth. The challenge is not merely cognitive defense. It is moral renewal.

In sum, cognitive vulnerability is not just a side effect of AI—it is the very medium through which its impact unfolds. And yet, within this vulnerability lies an opening: the chance to rebuild a culture that prizes truth over convenience, contribution over status, and wisdom over automation.

9.3.1 Preserving Human Judgment in the Age of Machine Thought

As AI systems increasingly participate in thinking tasks—from composing essays to designing studies—the meaning of *intellectual autonomy* is shifting. The question is no longer simply how humans access knowledge, but who—or what—claims authorship of knowledge itself. When machines simulate insight, what remains of our ability to think for ourselves?

This transformation is subtle but deep. Generative AI systems such as ChatGPT, Claude, and Gemini now produce literature reviews, generate code, and offer critique with convincing fluency. They compress the distance between novice and expert, delivering outputs that resemble years of training. Yet this surface-level competence risks eroding a foundational quality of scholarship: agency.

Case in a Box: Professor Alone in Her Library

Professor Donatella Spaghetti teaches sociology in the oddly picturesque Italian town of Castelvecchio Pasticcio. Her office could belong to another century: shelves stacked high with social science tomes, a heavy oak desk scarred by years of use, and a dog napping beneath it, pressed against her feet. Yet despite the old-world setting, her work has shifted into an entirely new reality.

For years, she relied on external grammar experts to proofread her writing. But first came services like Grammarly, which quickly became better and faster than any human editor she could afford. Then, more recently, generative AI outperformed both. It not only corrected her grammar but also suggested stylistic improvements, checked consistency, and even polished citations.

At first, she thought this was the end of her dependence on grammar support. But the real turning point came with peer review. Donatella had grown tired of sending her papers to colleagues for feedback. The process was slow, the responses often superficial, and, ironically, some reviews were most often worse than what she herself could have written. She even paid part of their salaries through grants she had secured, yet the returns felt increasingly disappointing.

Out of curiosity, she tried having AI review her manuscripts instead. The results shocked her. Not only did the AI provide critical commentary, but it also offered specific suggestions for revisions—paragraph restructuring, clearer argumentation, even stronger theoretical framing. It was faster, cheaper, and, frankly, better. The AI had also proven surprisingly good at handling other tedious administrative tasks, such as drafting research applications—work that was previously done in groups, often with the help of assistants from central administration.

Sitting alone in her library, Donatella realized that she no longer needed anyone else to produce strong scholarship. She still came to campus, had lunch with colleagues, and enjoyed their company. But deep down, she knew they were no longer essential to her intellectual work. AI had begun replacing not just her assistants but, more unsettlingly, parts of herself.

And then the question emerged: where would this end? If AI could already serve as reviewer, critic, and co-author, why not as an autonomous social scientist? Would that really be so terrible? Or was something irreplaceable about to be lost?

Questions for Reflection

1. How does Donatella's reliance on AI change the meaning of collaboration in academia?
2. What does "peer review" mean when machines can do it better than peers?
3. Could the social sciences continue to function if much of the work were automated?
4. What roles remain for human scholars in a world of machine-generated critique?
5. Is Donatella's situation liberating, or does it signal the erosion of academic community?

What Professor Spaghetti's story illustrates is not merely a change in tools but a change in foundations. The issue is no longer whether AI can help with editing, reviewing, or summarizing—that much is already settled. The deeper concern is what happens to scholarship when the very processes that once defined intellectual life are delegated away.

The core threat is not technical but philosophical. By outsourcing not only cognitive labor but reasoning itself, we risk abandoning the very habits that sustain human thought: doubt, deliberation, reflection, synthesis. These are not instantaneous outputs. They are slow, recursive, and deeply contextual acts of mind. As AI accelerates workflows, it risks hollowing out the judgment behind them.

This problem is particularly acute in disciplines that rely on narrative reasoning and interpretive skill—areas traditionally associated with the humanities and social sciences. While AI has made major advances in mathematics, coding, and data analysis, its comparative strength lies in language-rich domains. Large language models excel at mimicking the tone of academic discourse, synthesizing arguments, mapping literature, and even speculating on ethical implications—tasks once seen as hallmarks of advanced scholarly training. What once scaffolded professional identity in these fields is now automated.

At the same time, AI integration into publishing infrastructure is transforming evaluation. Language models can scan and map thousands of journal articles to detect emerging themes, underexplored questions, and semantic blind spots (Bosch et al., 2021; Milojević, 2015). They can track editorial policies and even simulate reviewer feedback. This may make journals faster and more inclusive, but it also changes the nature of scholarly validation.

Imagine sitting down to write a new article in the social sciences. Instead of beginning with weeks of searching databases, you open an AI-driven platform and simply type in your initial ideas. In a second column, the system immediately displays all similar articles—drawing not only from Scopus or Web of Science but potentially from the entire global corpus of scholarship. As you continue typing, it highlights overlaps, redundancies, and unexplored angles. Ask it for a research gap, and it generates one on the spot, explaining why it matters and how it might be addressed. Within minutes, the research question and hypothesis are framed, and a draft literature review is assembled. This is not a distant dream; it is already technically possible. And why stop there? The same system could distribute surveys, collect responses, and conduct statistical analysis. With each step automated, the role of the social scientist risks shrinking to little more than providing a sequence of prompts.

If this trajectory continues—toward *machine-assisted peer review*, automated research aides, and seamless translation across languages and audiences—the social function of science itself will undergo a profound shift. Research will circulate faster and more widely than ever before, but velocity does not equal value. The very abundance of output will intensify the need for ethical filters, interpretive judgment, and cultural grounding. In this new landscape, knowledge risks becoming noise, and productivity alone cannot be mistaken for progress.

Already we are seeing the effects. The number of scientific papers submitted has surged dramatically, and, as physicist Sabine Hossenfelder

(2024) notes, much of this is directly linked to AI tools that make writing and submitting papers far easier. Mark Hahnel of Digital Science reports that publication growth rates have jumped from around 8% annually to nearly 17%, a doubling within just a few years. If sustained, this rise will quickly overwhelm the existing peer-review system, which is already running on fumes. As Hossenfelder dryly observes, many reviews today are written in airport lounges, parking lots, or bathrooms—squeezed into the margins of overburdened schedules. Under such conditions, even a modest increase in submissions becomes unsustainable. Add AI into the mix, and the entire system risks breaking down.

Nor is the problem only one of volume. AI is already being used to generate peer reviews themselves, and studies show that AI-written reviews are often indistinguishable from those written by humans, with detection rates below 20%. Meanwhile, fraudulent practices are scaling alongside legitimate productivity. *Paper mills*—organized networks that sell authorship slots, fake citations, or fabricated results—are thriving, especially in China and India, but increasingly spreading Westward (Hossenfelder, 2024). Though still a small fraction of total output at the time of writing, their growth is rapid, and AI lowers the barrier to producing convincing fraud. This means that alongside the welcome increase in accessible, well-structured manuscripts, journals now face a rising tide of sophisticated manipulation. What looks like progress at first glance can in fact be an erosion of trust in the very system of scholarly communication.

So, what remains uniquely human?

Not typing speed or citation count, but discernment. As Bent Flyvbjerg (2001) emphasized, real social science demands *phronesis*—practical wisdom. Martha Nussbaum (1997) adds that moral imagination is just as crucial—the ability to weigh values and inhabit different perspectives. These are not functions of code. They emerge through lived experience, ethical engagement, and cultural literacy.

Machines operate through correlation, not conscience. They detect bias statistically, not morally. They recognize language, but not intent. In contrast, human cognition evolved not only to absorb information but to assess its relevance, trustworthiness, and purpose (Sperber et al., 2010). In an age of overwhelming content, these filters are essential. This distinction can be summarized as follows (Table 9.5).

The path forward is not to retreat into nostalgia for the analog. It is to cultivate strategic counterweights—deliberate practices that preserve the slower, ethical dimensions of thought in a world of rapid synthesis. Education must adapt accordingly.

Table 9.5 Human reasoning vs AI reasoning

Function	Human reasoning	AI Reasoning
Epistemic Grounding	Contextual and normative	Statistical and probabilistic
Emotional Awareness	Embedded in experience	Simulated, not felt
Moral Evaluation	Based on values and empathy	Pattern-based and neutral
Adaptation to Ambiguity	Tolerant and reflective	Biased toward resolution and clarity
Meaning Construction	Emergent from lived history and language	Constructed through pattern and syntax
Learning Path	Iterative and social	Massive parallel correlation

Rather than overemphasizing technical literacy or content mastery, curricula could aim to develop moral and epistemic filters. Students need tools not only to produce knowledge, but to interrogate it. Practical interventions might include:

- Handwriting and note-taking to enhance memory and cognitive processing (Mueller & Oppenheimer, 2014)
- Oral presentations that demand real-time synthesis and clarity
- AI critique exercises to build epistemic independence
- Tech-free periods to restore attention and inner quiet (Breslin & Brennan, 2020)
- Delayed digital exposure to support cognitive maturation (Twenge & Campbell, 2018)

Such strategies are not nostalgic. They are safeguards—tools for defending the interior spaces of thought in an era when even reflection is under pressure. If we don't protect the capacity for moral presence, AI may not merely assist us—it may replace us in the very domains where we once claimed to matter most.

To navigate this new landscape wisely, we must stop conflating efficiency with depth. Not everything should be streamlined. Some forms of thinking—especially those involving values, ambiguity, or lived experience—require presence, not just processing. This does not mean rejecting AI. It means refining our use of it. We must learn to distinguish between what can be accelerated and what must be endured. Thought is not just computation. It is interpretation, responsibility, and care.

The distinction can be visualized in the relationship between task complexity and performance. The horizontal axis in the diagram represents the *level of reflection or reasoning required* by a task, ranging from simple, repetitive pattern recognition problems on the left to complex, interpretive, and ethically charged decisions on the right. The vertical axis represents *relative cognitive strength*—how effectively either AI or humans perform at a given task (Fig. 9.3).

This conceptual diagram illustrates how human and artificial intelligence diverge as task complexity increases. AI dominates at the lower end of the spectrum, where speed, scale, and statistical pattern recognition confer enormous advantages. Humans, by contrast, begin to outperform AI as tasks demand contextual sensitivity, long-term foresight, and moral discernment. Between these two poles lies a shifting middle ground, where collaboration between human judgment and machine computation is often most effective. First of all, though, it is hard to imagine that the lines would ever be straight in reality—much like in economics, this diagram is an oversimplified representation. Secondly, the complexity of what AI can do is continuously moving forward, leaving less and less space for humans at the high-complexity end, but it illustrates the idea.

Seen this way, the real challenge is not a zero-sum competition but the management of complementarity. We must decide where to entrust machines with acceleration, and where to slow down and let human judgment lead.

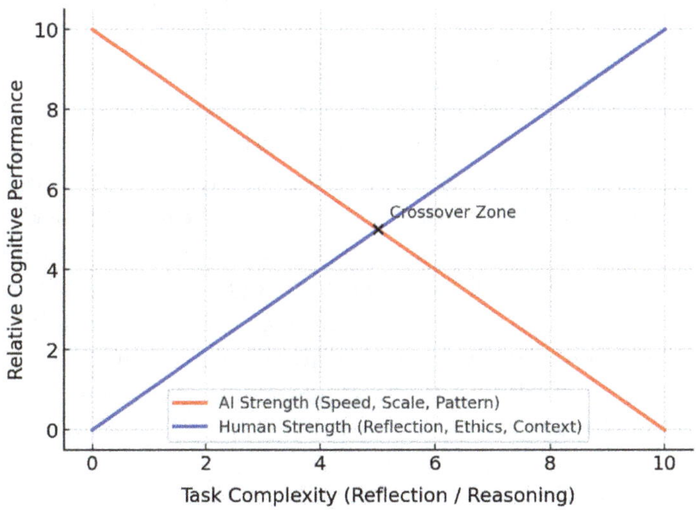

Fig. 9.3 Diverging strengths of AI and human judgment

This balance—between scale and subtlety, calculation and care—will shape the credibility and purpose of knowledge in the years ahead.

But if the intellectual risks of outsourcing thought are significant, the economic ones may be even greater. What began as a shift in scholarly routines is mirrored across society, where AI is poised to transform not only how we think but also how we work, earn, and sustain meaning in daily life. As Geoffrey Hinton and others have warned, the replacement of cognitive labor on a large scale raises profound questions about employment, taxation, inequality, and global competition (Hinton, 2023; Acemoglu & Restrepo, 2018a). The issue is no longer confined to academic identity—it extends to the very structure of economies. To understand what is at stake, we must examine the economic costs of outsourcing cognition.

9.3.2 The Economic Costs of Outsourcing Cognition

The outsourcing of human cognition to AI carries not only psychological and cultural risks but also profound economic complications. As intelligent systems become integrated into every domain of life—from education and healthcare to finance and governance—their influence on production, employment, and wealth distribution intensifies. This section examines these economic dimensions, highlighting both opportunities and dangers.

One of the clearest trends is the concentration of power in a small number of AI firms. As their products become indispensable for competitiveness, both individuals and organizations risk dependency on platforms they do not control (Zuboff, 2019). Unlike utilities or traditional infrastructure, AI systems are proprietary, often guarded by trade secrets and intellectual property protections. This creates conditions where companies can extract high rents, charging increasingly steep prices for access to the tools that determine professional viability. The fear, echoed by scholars of *platform capitalism*, is that dependency transforms users into *semi-captive clients* (Srnicek, 2017).

A deeper risk sits beneath "platform power": a triad of moats—*compute, data, and distribution.* Control of cutting-edge chips and cloud capacity, privileged access to high-quality proprietary corpora, and default integration into operating systems and workplace suites create lock-in that antitrust law did not originally anticipate. Treating *compute* as a strategic resource (with capacity reservations and export controls), *data* as a collectively bargained asset, and *distribution* as an interoperability obligation are likely preconditions for real competition.

A possible counterbalance is competition among AI providers, including the rise of smaller and more efficient models such as DeepSeek. Yet, as history with digital platforms suggests, network effects often reinforce monopoly or oligopoly structures (Shapiro & Varian, 1998). Once a critical mass of users is locked into a given ecosystem, alternatives struggle to gain traction, even when technically superior. We saw this in the early 2000s, when Google's search engine rapidly outcompeted rivals like Yahoo, AltaVista, and Lycos. Even though some competitors offered features that were more advanced at the time—such as curated directories or richer news integration—Google's clean interface, speed, and growing dominance created powerful network effects. By the mid-2000s, its scale advantage in indexing and advertising revenue made it virtually impossible for challengers to dislodge it (Cusumano et al., 2019; Vaidhyanathan, 2011).

Ironically, Google itself now faces a similar risk—not from a better search engine, but from an entirely new technological leap. As users turn to AI systems like ChatGPT or Perplexity to obtain direct, conversational answers, the traditional search paradigm may erode. If this shift continues, Google may not lose its dominance to a superior competitor in its own domain, but to a transformation of the domain itself: the replacement of search by *generative response*.

The most debated economic effect of AI is the displacement of human labor. While previous technological revolutions generated new industries that absorbed displaced workers, many experts argue that AI may not follow this pattern. The speed and scope of automation across cognitive domains threaten to outpace the creation of new forms of work, particularly in professional and creative sectors once considered secure (Brynjolfsson & McAfee, 2014).

This raises the question of redistribution. If fewer jobs remain, who pays for the livelihoods of those excluded from the labor market? Proposals such as *Universal Basic Income (UBI)* have gained traction (Frey & Osborne, 2017; Van Parijs & Vanderborght, 2017). Yet financing such schemes requires higher taxation, often targeting the very corporations driving automation. Here, a paradox emerges: if taxation becomes excessive, firms may relocate to jurisdictions with lower burdens, leaving governments unable to sustain welfare models (OECD, 2020).

Over recent years there has indeed been a trend of ultra-wealthy individuals relocating their tax residence—or at least moving assets offshore—in anticipation of higher taxation. Studies using British administrative data show that changes in tax rules triggered modest emigration responses among the super-rich (Advani et al., 2025). Similarly, research on "tax flight" documents concerns among UK policymakers about migration of top taxpayers in reaction to tax policy (Friedman et al., 2024).

A more resilient approach than blanket UBI alone is a *portfolio* of instruments that tie automation gains back to the public: (1) an *Automation Dividend* (a levy on value added attributable to AI that funds universal benefits); (2) *Participation Income* (benefits conditioned on socially useful activity such as care, learning, mentoring, or conservation); (3) *Universal Basic Services* (guaranteed access to health, transit, connectivity, and education). This mix addresses material security *and* preserves links to contribution, belonging, and skill formation.

Economic asymmetries are also likely to intensify between countries. Wealthier nations with the infrastructure to develop and deploy AI will reap the majority of benefits, while others risk technological dependency. If one society can afford to support its population in leisure—funding golf and fishing through redistributed AI rents—while another cannot, stark inequalities emerge. These disparities are not merely economic but also migratory: populations from disadvantaged regions may move toward AI-rich societies, straining their political and social systems (Milanović, 2016).

To avoid a hard bifurcation, countries without frontier labs will need access to *sovereign compute* (regional compute hubs), *model commons* (state-supported open models under responsible licenses), and *technology-transfer compacts* (compute credits and engineering fellowships bundled with governance support). Without these, "AI poverty traps" will harden.

Even if redistribution succeeds in providing material security, there remains the problem of meaning. As Hannah Arendt (1958) argued, labor provides not only sustenance but also identity, discipline, and social cohesion. A society in which large segments of the population are paid to disengage from structured activity risks fostering apathy, disconnection, or unrest. While some may thrive in leisure, others may struggle without the structure and recognition that purposeful work provides (Graeber, 2018).

This is why the real issue is not the abolishment of work, but its redefinition. An economy that leans only on redistribution—through schemes like UBI—risks human decay: mental, physical, and social. While UBI pilots have shown short-term gains in mental health (Forget, 2011; Thomson et al., 2024), the evidence is less clear on sustaining meaning, identity, or structured engagement over time. A society in which large segments are detached from meaningful roles may face apathy, fragmentation, and erosion of civic life.

Therefore, work must be reimagined: not merely as production or consumption, but as giving back to one's community—through cultural stewardship, civic service, environmental care, education, and relational support. In this broader conception, caring, mentoring, preserving heritage, and nurturing social capital are legitimate forms of labor—not "something for nothing" but socially anchored contributions.

But for such a model to work, wealth and power must be tethered back to society. Echoing Piketty's critique, wealth that is detached—sheltered offshore or abstracted from civic responsibility—erodes trust and undermines the norms that sustain collective life (Piketty, 2014, 2020). Highly unequal societies also tend to exhibit worse outcomes in health, trust, and social cohesion (Wilkinson & Pickett, 2009). Attempts at unbalanced globalization and permissive migration policies have sometimes dislocated communities, creating populations that reside in societies without contributing meaningfully or paying into them. Societies that do not anchor people through obligation and participation risk losing legitimacy and stability.

The dilemmas are formidable. They will not be solved by economic engineering alone, but they can be mapped (Table 9.6).

At present, however, this list of economic challenges remains largely unaddressed. Public and policy debates around AI are still in their infancy, often reactive rather than strategic. Much of the discussion is dominated by short-term focus on product releases—each new model from OpenAI, Google, Anthropic, or DeepSeek triggering waves of commentary, hype, or panic. A significant portion of media criticism comes from observers who have little direct experience with AI tools, or who lack the technical literacy to understand their mechanisms, capacities, and limitations (Brynjolfsson & McAfee, 2017; Cave & Dignum, 2019). Public fear of automation has always contained this paradox: anxieties are loudest when technologies are least understood, and only later, once they are widely embedded, does society begin to grapple seriously with their structural consequences (Autor, 2015; Frey & Osborne, 2017).

In short, the current state of debate is characteristically human—chaotic, fragmented, and emotionally charged. Historically, societies have rarely anticipated the long-term effects of disruptive technologies. The printing press was first feared for its capacity to spread heresy (Eisenstein, 1980), the industrial revolution was initially celebrated for productivity gains but only later regulated to address child labor and worker exploitation (Polanyi, 1944), and the internet was long dismissed as a niche tool before reshaping nearly every industry (Castells, 1996). As David Edgerton (2006) has argued, innovation is usually understood retrospectively: its real impact emerges not from the moment of invention but from the patterns of adoption, adaptation, and regulation that follow—often decades later.

AI is likely to follow the same trajectory. The gap between its immediate capabilities and our ability to design adequate institutions around them is

Table 9.6 Key economic challenges of AI and possible responses

Dimension	Challenge	Possible responses
Corporate power	AI monopolies extract rents, limit competition, and control key infrastructures	Antitrust enforcement; promotion of open-source AI; regulation as public utility; interoperability standards
Employment	Displacement exceeds job creation; automation of professional and creative roles	Reskilling initiatives; job-sharing; Universal Basic Income (UBI); reduced working hours with wage protection
Taxation	Firms relocate under heavy taxation; digital profits hard to capture	International tax coordination (OECD); global minimum tax; digital service taxes
Productivity gains	Unequal distribution of automation-driven wealth across firms and workers	Worker profit-sharing schemes; sovereign wealth funds; public ownership stakes in leading AI firms
Global inequality	Wealthy nations capture AI dividends, poor nations risk dependency	Global AI funds; technology transfer agreements; international development financing
Fiscal stability	Rising welfare demands (UBI, retraining) strain government budgets	Diversified taxation (AI levies, wealth taxes); fiscal reform; automation-linked social contributions
Market competition	Oligopolistic platforms suppress small firms and entrepreneurial ecosystems	Incentives for SMEs; public–private R&D hubs; targeted subsidies for start-ups
Capital–Labor balance	Declining labor share of income; rising capital concentration	Strengthened labor protections; new bargaining frameworks; redistribution via automation taxes

wide, and history suggests it will take considerable time before policy, law, and economic structures catch up. By then, path dependency will have set in—shaping labor markets, corporate power, and inequality in ways that may be very difficult to reverse (Arthur, 1989).

We may also want to ask, *"How has human work evolved?"*.

To truly grasp the stakes, we must widen the lens. Human labor has never been static. It has moved through successive stages that each transformed not only how people worked, but also how they lived, thought, and related to one another. These stages illustrate a paradox of progress: each new system has freed humanity from some burdens while imposing new constraints. The current transition to an AI-driven world, where human labor may become optional in unprecedented ways, must therefore be understood as part of this longer history:

The first stage was *hunting and gathering*, the condition in which Homo sapiens spent over 90% of their evolutionary history (Kelly, 2013; Lee & DeVore, 1968). Small groups of foragers relied on mobility, cooperation, and ecological knowledge. Life was precarious—vulnerable to climate shifts and scarcity—but also egalitarian, with little material inequality and strong kin-based community bonds (Woodburn, 1982). Anthropologists have often remarked that hunter-gatherers enjoyed more leisure time than later agriculturalists, though at the cost of constant exposure to risk (Sahlins, 1972).

The second stage was the *agricultural revolution*, beginning roughly 10,000 years ago in multiple centers of domestication (Diamond, 1997). Farming enabled population growth, surplus storage, and permanent settlement, laying the foundations for cities, states, and complex societies (Scott, 2017). But it also brought backbreaking repetitive labor, nutritional decline compared to diverse forager diets, and rising inequality as surpluses could be hoarded and hierarchies entrenched (Larsen, 2006). What agriculture offered in stability it often took away in health and freedom.

The third stage was *industrialization*, beginning in Europe in the late eighteenth century. Mechanization and factory labor radically increased productivity, unleashing unprecedented economic growth (Mokyr, 1990). This stage saw the rise of science, mass education, and modern infrastructure. Yet it also introduced alienating working conditions, child labor, and devastating environmental costs (Polanyi, 1944; Stearns, 2013). Work became both the source of wealth and of new forms of social misery, spurring labor movements, unionization, and political reform.

The fourth stage was the *bureaucratic and administrative economy*, which expanded in the twentieth century alongside industrial and post-industrial development (Bell, 1976; Weber, 1922/1978), and which we are still very much in. White-collar and service jobs became dominant, and work shifted from physical exertion to cognitive and organizational tasks. For many, this meant less dangerous conditions and greater social mobility. Yet bureaucracy also created its own pathologies: rigidity, paperwork, and stress in competitive office cultures.

So, we may also want to ask: *"What happens when work loses its meaning?"*. What made this stage particularly corrosive was the widespread sense of *meaninglessness*. As noted in the previous chapter, anthropologist David Graeber (2018) described many of these positions as "*bullshit jobs*"—roles that were not only unproductive but that even their holders suspected were unnecessary. Unlike the clear productive contribution of farming or factory labor, much bureaucratic work seemed detached from tangible outputs, breeding cynicism, alienation, and existential dissatisfaction. The link between work and meaning became fragile, as jobs often involved abstract tasks far removed from visible production or community benefit.

Today, we stand on the cusp of a fifth stage: the *AI-driven post-work paradigm*. Automation is moving from factories into offices, laboratories, and even the arts (Brynjolfsson & McAfee, 2014; Frey & Osborne, 2017). Machines increasingly handle not only physical production but also cognitive and communicative tasks once thought uniquely human. This raises profound questions: if productivity gains continue to rise while fewer people are needed for essential labor, what role will human beings play? Geoffrey Hinton (2023) has warned that the *displacement effects* could overwhelm job creation, leading to structural unemployment at a scale never seen before.

What we see is that each historical stage has, in part, solved the problems of the one before it. Agriculture reduced the food insecurity of foraging but introduced new hierarchies and vulnerabilities. Industrialization overcame the limits of agricultural productivity but created harsh labor conditions that later reforms sought to correct. The bureaucratic and administrative paradigm addressed many of these industrial problems by providing safer, cleaner, and more stable white-collar work, yet it also generated its own pathologies—rigid hierarchies, paperwork overload, and what David Graeber (2018) famously called "bullshit jobs." From this perspective, it is plausible to argue that the rise of AI may function as a corrective to bureaucratic excess. Because automation is already most effective in repetitive, routine, and administrative domains (Autor, 2015; Brynjolfsson & McAfee, 2017), AI has the potential to relieve individuals and institutions of precisely those tasks that have become most alienating. Rather than endlessly reproducing forms, memos, and procedural compliance, machines could absorb much of this burden, freeing human beings for more creative, social, and meaningful forms of work—if, and this is the crucial condition, societies are able to reorganize labor and distribute the gains in ways that preserve dignity and purpose.

The economic consequences are serious—who will pay for those no longer employed, and how can societies sustain meaning when traditional forms of work no longer structure daily life?

Yet this stage could also represent progress. If societies succeed in distributing the gains of automation—and that is a big *if*—people could work less and live more. Stress and competition might give way to greater attention to social qualities: caring for family, investing in communities, and protecting the environment. Far from heralding decline, the reduction of compulsory labor might mark a civilizational advance—a transition from *Homo faber*, the tool-making worker (Henrich, 2015; Nussbaum, 2011), to *Homo cura*, the caring human. The challenge is whether institutions can adapt to make this possible, or whether inequality and dependency will corrode these opportunities.

The Post-Work/AI paradigm is therefore best understood not as a rupture but as the next turn in this historical sequence: it seeks to resolve the contradictions of bureaucratic labor by automating the very routines that once drained meaning from work. Whether this shift leads to liberation or to deeper alienation depends on how societies—and ultimately we ourselves—manage the transition (Table 9.7).

Taken together, these two perspectives—the immediate economic dilemmas of AI and the long arc of human labor—show that we are dealing with more than another technological disruption. We are confronting a *civilizational shift*. On the one hand, AI amplifies the very problems of corporate concentration, inequality, and dependency that already strain our societies. On the other, it carries forward the historical pattern visible in earlier transitions: each stage of labor partially solved the dilemmas of the one before it. Just as agriculture reduced the insecurity of foraging, industry eased the vulnerabilities of agrarian life, and bureaucracy softened the physical hardships of industrial labor, so too AI may help resolve the excesses of bureaucratic work by automating its most alienating routines.

But history teaches that progress is never automatic. Each paradigm of labor brought both liberation and constraint, and the balance was shaped not by technology alone but by the institutions that framed its use. If AI is to mark an evolutionary step forward rather than a regression, societies will need to design mechanisms that distribute its gains fairly, preserve social cohesion, and cultivate forms of meaning that do not depend exclusively on waged labor.

This is why the coming years will be decisive—and why I have felt such urgency in writing this book, often working evenings and vacations (with repeated promises to my family that I will make up for the time stolen, someday, somehow). The challenge is not only the scale of automation itself, but whether our political, cultural, and ethical systems can adapt with equal speed. If they do, the post-work paradigm could represent a renaissance of

Table 9.7 The evolution of human labor paradigms: From survival to post-work futures

Stage	Main features	Advantages	Disadvantages
1. Hunting and gathering	Small kin-based groups; subsistence through foraging, hunting, and cooperation	Strong social cohesion; physical fitness; ecological embeddedness; egalitarian social structures (Lee & DeVore, 1968)	High mortality; food insecurity; limited material surplus; vulnerability to climate and predation
2. Agricultural revolution	Domestication of plants and animals; sedentary life; surplus production	Larger, more stable populations; accumulation of knowledge; development of villages, states, and writing systems (Diamond, 1997); reduced insecurity of foraging	Hard physical labor; social stratification; gender inequality; vulnerability to famine and disease (Scott, 2017)
3. Industrial paradigm	Mechanized production; urbanization; wage labor	Massive productivity gains; rising life expectancy; mass education; consumer goods (Mokyr, 1990); reduced vulnerability to famine through mechanized agriculture and expanded trade	Harsh working conditions; child labor; alienation (Marx, 1867/1976); pollution and environmental degradation

Stage	Main features	Advantages	Disadvantages
4. Bureaucratic/Administrative paradigm	Expansion of white-collar and service-sector jobs; large organizations; administrative growth	Safer work; upward mobility; expansion of higher education; professional identity (Weber, 1922/1978; Bell, 1976); reduction of industrial-era physical hardship and child labor	Rigid hierarchies; stress; paperwork overload; "bullshit jobs" and loss of meaning (Graeber, 2018); alienation from tangible outcomes
5. Post-Work/AI paradigm	Automation, AI, and digital platforms reduce need for human labor	Potential for more leisure, reduced stress, time for care, art, and environmental stewardship; possibility of universal basic income or new social contracts (Frey & Osborne, 2017; Srnicek & Williams, 2015); automation of bureaucratic routines that drained meaning from work	Risk of inequality; dependency on corporations; loss of discipline and purpose; geopolitical imbalances; "cognitive divide" (Zuboff, 2019)

care, community, and creativity. If they fail, the same technologies could deepen inequality, corrode legitimacy, and erode the very foundations of civic life.

The deeper question is not only how AI changes employment, but how it reshapes the very structure of human contribution. For in a society where fewer people are needed to sustain material prosperity, the frontier of meaning shifts from physical work to intellectual, relational, and cultural labor. It is here—where AI now encroaches most directly—that the stakes become existential.

In either case, the consequences will be profound. We therefore turn now to the edge of AI and the human niche—examining not just the economic transformations, but the uneven impact across professions and domains.

9.4 The Edge of AI and the Human Niche

Artificial intelligence is indeed reshaping professional life, but its impact is highly uneven. Some fields experience dramatic productivity gains, while others reveal the limits of automation. Understanding this asymmetry is key to grasping where human capabilities still matter—and where they are being overtaken.

Fields such as legal analysis, policy modeling, and academic research have seen the sharpest leaps. AI accelerates literature reviews, identifies precedent, summarizes volumes of information, and even drafts formal texts. In business and public administration, it generates forecasts, digests reports, and simulates outcomes that once demanded weeks of expert labor (Brynjolfsson & McAfee, 2017; Katz et al., 2020; Surden, 2019).

This shift does not simply make work faster—it redefines what it means to work. As we have seen, with the right prompts, large language models can match or surpass human analysts in synthesizing complex societal information (Söilen, 2024). The analyst becomes less of a thinker than a validator—curating, testing, and refining AI output. Other sectors—education, journalism, content creation—are also being reshaped. AI personalizes tasks, scaffolds lesson design, and outlines written work. It doesn't replace human effort; it reorganizes it. The hidden risk is role shrinkage: when "validation" crowds out curiosity, human learning plateaus even as output increases.

To see this more clearly, consider the current division of labor between humans and machines (Table 9.8).

Table 9.8 AI roles and capabilities today (Author's rating)

Role	How good is AI?	What AI can do well	What AI cannot do well	Why it excels or fails
Scientific Writing Assistant	Excellent	Finds references quickly, writes fluently in academic style, remembers sources	Lacks original insight, cannot form new scientific theories independently	Excellent memory, linguistic precision, time-saving
Legal Drafting Assistant	Excellent	Writes in perfect legal language, locates relevant laws faster than most lawyers	Cannot argue complex cases or adapt well to unusual legal reasoning	High pattern recognition, legal syntax mastery, speed
Research Secretary	Excellent	Organizes notes, drafts literature reviews, formats citations correctly	Limited initiative, cannot decide what to prioritize	Efficient, tireless, fast memory access
Fact Checker/ Encyclopedia	Good	Checks facts quickly, provides sourced explanations, more updated than Britannica	May still make occasional factual errors, especially with ambiguous claims	Broad coverage, speed, real-time updates (if connected)
Wikipedia Replacement	Good	Provides broader, clearer answers, less biased	Less transparent sourcing unless prompted	Personalized, real-time, context-aware
Literature/ Fiction Writing	Fair	Can generate standard TV plots or genre stories quickly	Lacks deep originality or emotional subtlety	Mimics well, but lacks genuine creativity or voice

(continued)

Table 9.8 (continued)

Role	How good is AI?	What AI can do well	What AI cannot do well	Why it excels or fails
Philosophical/ Ethical Thought	Fair	Summarizes positions, creates logical arguments	Cannot form truly novel or introspective insights	Cannot form truly novel or introspective insights Logical, structured, but not emotionally or existentially deep
Artistic Writing (e.g., Poetry)	Limited	Can mimic form, create basic structure	Lacks originality, metaphorical depth, or unique voice	Style mimicry without genuine inspiration
Strategy and Foresight	Good	Can propose structured scenarios, model alternatives	Relies on human judgment for ambiguity and ethical trade-offs	Systematic, data-based, but lacks vision under uncertainty
Education/ Teaching Support	Good	Explains clearly, adapts to level, gives examples	Can't read emotional cues or classroom dynamics	Clear explanations, on-demand knowledge
Humor/ Comedy Writing	Limited	Can make puns, jokes with templates	Rarely genuinely funny or surprising	Humor is contextual and cultural; AI struggles with subtle timing

Note This table is not the result of controlled empirical testing but my own assessment as a user of AI systems. It reflects lived experience more than standardized benchmarks

This snapshot shows that AI excels where information can be structured, patterned, and recombined. Humans excel where meaning must be made, where responsibility must be carried, and where care must be enacted. These variances are dynamic, evolving with each model generation. Staying updated is part of the responsibility of any knowledge worker.

Yet the edge of AI becomes clearest in domains grounded in relational and creative intelligence. Professions such as therapy, education, or conflict mediation depend on empathy, trust, and dynamic responsiveness—qualities current AI lacks (Fiske et al., 2019). Similarly, artistic work depends on voice, vision, and existential awareness. AI can generate striking outputs, but it does so by recombining patterns—it does not originate from lived experience or intentional vision.

As Searle (1980) famously argued, machines do not "mean" what they say—they simulate understanding without possessing subjectivity, intention, or purpose. A revealing example is the late musician Avicii (Tim Bergling). He was not trained in classical composition and barely played traditional instruments. Instead, he experimented with keyboards and software, shaping sounds he liked and gradually developing them into a distinctive global style. His music was intuitive, emotionally layered, and culturally resonant. AI may eventually approximate that kind of coherence, but it is not there yet. What it still lacks is urgency—the sense that a piece *had* to be made—an inner necessity that comes from a life lived, not a dataset trained.

Recent advances, however, have brought us closer to that nuanced musicality. Deep learning systems trained on vast datasets such as MAESTRO can now generate melodies with expressive phrasing, coherent structure, and even emotional cues (Huang et al., 2019). Listener studies reveal that while people may prefer AI-generated music in calmer contexts, human-composed music still retains perceived emotional authenticity and "soul"—qualities linked to imperfection and presence (Sturm et al., 2019). Even Rick Beato (2025), a veteran musician and educator, has moved from critique to recognition: in a recent Suno-based demo he acknowledged that AI music has reached near-human quality, while still noting that questions of "feel"—that in-the-moment, emotionally inflected nuance—remain open. What once seemed elegant mimicry is now approaching genuine musicality, blurring the line between simulation and creation.

The same is true in science. AI can support synthesis and analysis, but paradigm shifts—the kind Thomas Kuhn (1962) described—require intuition, risk, and conceptual imagination. AI can extend knowledge within a framework, but it cannot yet produce a new one. What it can do, however, is help us cross into a new paradigm when the conditions are already in place. The core problems of the social sciences—their complexity, their disciplinary fragmentation, their lack of dialogue across subfields—are precisely the kinds of problems AI is well suited to address. By scanning vast literatures, identifying hidden connections, and testing theoretical consistency, AI can act as a unifying mechanism. It can help bring together what has long remained siloed, making possible a more integrated science of society.

How this new period will ultimately look we cannot know. But in this book, I argue that the transition must aim to make the social sciences as scientific as possible, in line with the original aspiration of Auguste Comte, and in contrast to the interpretive traditions of the humanities. The live hypothesis is that evolutionary theory supplies the strongest unifying scaffold across psychology, anthropology, economics, and political science—because it links mechanism to function across levels. In this sense, AI may not be the originator of a paradigm, but it could be the catalyst that finally enables the paradigm of the *Evolutionary Social Sciences* to take shape.

References

Acemoglu, D., & Restrepo, P. (2018a). The race between man and machine: Implications of technology for growth, factor shares, and employment. *American Economic Review, 108*(6), 1488–1542. https://doi.org/10.1257/aer.20160696

Acemoglu, D., & Restrepo, P. (2018b). *Artificial intelligence, automation, and work.* NBER Working Paper No. 24196.

Advani, A., Burgherr, D., & Summers, A. (2025). Importing billionaires: Taxation and the mobility of the super-rich. *Journal of Public Economics, 229*, Article 104135.

Agrawal, A., Gans, J., & Goldfarb, A. (2019). *Prediction machines: The simple economics of artificial intelligence*. Harvard Business School Press.

Alter, A. (2017). *Irresistible: The rise of addictive technology and the business of keeping us hooked*. Penguin Press.

Arthur, W. B. (1989). Competing technologies, increasing returns, and lock-in by historical events. *The Economic Journal, 99*(394), 116–131.

Anderson, C. W. (2013). *Rebuilding the news: Metropolitan journalism in the digital age.* Temple University Press.

Arendt, H. (1958). *The human condition.* University of Chicago Press.

Autor, D. H. (2015). Why are there still so many jobs? The history and future of workplace automation. *Journal of Economic Perspectives, 29*(3), 3–30.

Barr, N., Pennycook, G., Stolz, J. A., & Fugelsang, J. A. (2015). The brain in your pocket: Evidence that smartphones are used to supplant thinking. *Computers in Human Behavior, 48*, 473–480.

Beato, R. (2025, August 16). *Why AI will never write great music*. YouTube. https://www.youtube.com/watch?v=D0GwlvtTYew&t=106s

Bell, D. (1976). *The coming of post-industrial society: A venture in social forecasting*. Basic Books.

Bender, E. M., Gebru, T., McMillan-Major, A., & Shmitchell, S. (2021). On the dangers of stochastic parrots: Can language models be too big? *Proceedings of the 2021 ACM Conference on Fairness, Accountability, and Transparency*, 610–623. https://doi.org/10.1145/3442188.3445922

Berger, J., & Milkman, K. L. (2012). What makes online content viral? *Journal of Marketing Research, 49*(2), 192–205. https://doi.org/10.1509/jmr.10.0353
Berridge, K. C., & Robinson, T. E. (2003). Parsing reward. *Trends in Neurosciences, 26*(9), 507–513.
Birhane, A. (2021). Algorithmic injustice: A relational ethics approach. *Patterns, 2*(2), Article 100205.
Bommasani, R., Hudson, D. A., Adeli, E., Altman, R., Arora, S., von Arx, S., ... & Liang, P. (2022). *On the opportunities and risks of foundation models*. arXiv preprint arXiv:2108.07258
Bostrom, N. (2014). *Superintelligence: Paths, dangers, strategies*. Oxford University Press.
Bosch, A., van Gerven, M., & van den Bosch, A. (2021). Artificial Intelligence and the future of peer review. *Patterns, 2*(11), Article 100378.
Brady, W. J., Wills, J. A., Jost, J. T., Tucker, J. A., & Van Bavel, J. J. (2017). Emotion shapes the diffusion of moralized content in social networks. *Proceedings of the National Academy of Sciences, 114*(28), 7313–7318. https://doi.org/10.1073/pnas.1618923114
Breslin, F. C., & Brennan, A. (2020). Technology use, distraction, and attention restoration: A review of the literature. *Journal of Behavioral Addictions, 9*(4), 1043–1056.
Brynjolfsson, E., & McAfee, A. (2014). *The second machine age: Work, progress, and prosperity in a time of brilliant technologies*. W. W. Norton & Company.
Brynjolfsson, E., & McAfee, A. (2017). *Machine, platform, crowd: Harnessing our digital future*. W. W. Norton & Company.
Bullock, T. H., & Horridge, G. A. (1965). *Structure and function in the nervous systems of invertebrates*. Freeman.
Carr, N. (2010). *The shallows: What the Internet is doing to our brains*. W. W. Norton & Company.
Castells, M. (1996). *The rise of the network society*. Blackwell.
Cave, S., & Dignum, V. (2019). AI ethics: The challenge of building trust. *Philosophy & Technology, 32*(1), 1–3
Cave, S., & ÓhÉigeartaigh, S. S. (2019). An AI race for strategic advantage: Rhetoric and risks. *Proceedings of the AAAI/ACM Conference on AI, Ethics, and Society*, 36–40.
Chen, Z., & Savage, R. (2014). The effects of calculator use on arithmetic learning: A meta-analysis. *Educational Psychology Review, 26*(3), 387–414.
Crockett, M. J. (2017). Moral outrage in the digital age. *Nature Human Behaviour, 1*(11), 769–771. https://doi.org/10.1038/s41562-017-0213-3
Dafoe, A. (2018). *AI governance: A research agenda*. Governance of AI Program, Future of Humanity Institute.
Dafoe, A., et al. (2020). Open problems in the governance of artificial intelligence. *Nature Machine Intelligence, 2*(6), 341–343. https://doi.org/10.1038/s42256-020-0186-2

Damasio, A. R. (1999). *The feeling of what happens: Body and emotion in the making of consciousness*. Harcourt.

Delgado, P., Vargas, C., Ackerman, R., & Salmerón, L. (2018). Don't throw away your printed books: A meta-analysis on the effects of reading media on reading comprehension. *Educational Research Review, 25*, 23–38.

Diamond, J. (1997). *Guns, germs, and steel: The fates of human societies*. New York, NY: W. W. Norton.

Edgerton, D. (2006). *The shock of the old: Technology and global history since 1900*. Oxford University Press.

Eisenstein, E. L. (1980). *The printing press as an agent of change: Communications and cultural transformations in early-modern Europe*. Cambridge University Press.

Eubanks, V. (2018). *Automating inequality: How high-tech tools profile, police, and punish the poor*. Martin's Press.

European Union. (2024). *Artificial Intelligence Act*. Official Journal of the European Union.

Ferguson, N. (2024a). *The cloister and the AI cathedral*. Keynote speech at the Alliance for Responsible Citizenship Conference, London, UK. https://www.arcforum.com/speeches/the-cloister-and-the-ai-cathedral-niall-ferguson

Ferguson, N. (2024b). *The cloister and the cloud: Reclaiming deep thought in the age of distraction* [Manuscript lecture, Oxford Union].

Fiske, S. T., Gilbert, D. T., & Lindzey, G. (2019). *Handbook of social psychology* (6th ed.). Wiley.

Flyvbjerg, B. (2001). *Making social science matter: Why social inquiry fails and how it can succeed again*. Cambridge University Press.

Forget, E. L. (2011). The town with no poverty: The health effects of a Canadian guaranteed annual income field experiment. *Canadian Public Policy, 37*(3), 283–305. https://doi.org/10.3138/cpp.37.3.283

Friedman, M., Redonda, A., & Sayeh, A. (2024). Tax flight and the mobility of high-income earners: Evidence from the United Kingdom. *Fiscal Studies, 45*(2), 215–239.

Frey, C. B., & Osborne, M. A. (2017). The future of employment: How susceptible are jobs to computerisation? *Technological Forecasting and Social Change, 114*, 254–280.

Grace, K., Salvatier, J., Dafoe, A., Zhang, B., & Evans, O. (2018). When will AI exceed human performance? Evidence from AI experts. *Journal of Artificial Intelligence Research, 62*, 729–754. https://doi.org/10.1613/jair.1.11222

Graeber, D. (2018). *Bullshit jobs: A theory*. Simon & Schuster.

Haidt, J. (2012). *The righteous mind: Why good people are divided by politics and religion*. Pantheon.

Henrich, J. (2015). *The secret of our success: How culture is driving human evolution, domesticating our species, and making us smarter*. Princeton University Press.

Helbing, D., Frey, B. S., Gigerenzer, G., Hafen, E., Hagner, M., Hofstetter, Y., ... & Zwitter, A. (2021). Will democracy survive big data and artificial intelligence? *Scientific American*. https://doi.org/10.1038/scientificamerican0317-58

Hermida, A. (2010). From TV to Twitter: How ambient news became ambient journalism. *M/C Journal, 13*(2).
Hinton, G. E. (2018). Deep learning—A technology with the potential to transform health care. *JAMA, 320*(11), 1101–1102.
Hinton, G. (2023). Statement on AI risks [Interview]. *BBC News*. Retrieved from https://www.bbc.com/news
Hossenfelder, S. (2024, June 29). *AI is breaking science* [Video]. YouTube. https://www.youtube.com/watch?v=7NOWoQW5RLk
Huang, C. A., Vaswani, A., Uszkoreit, J., Shazeer, N., Simon, I., Hawthorne, C., Andrew, M. Dai, Matthew, D. Hoffman, Dinculescu, M., & Eck, D. (2019). Music transformer: Generating music with long-term structure. *International Conference on Learning Representations (ICLR)*. https://openreview.net/forum?id=rJe4ShAcF7
Kahneman, D. (2011). *Thinking, fast and slow*. Farrar.
Katz, D. M., Bommarito, M. J., & Blackman, J. (2020). A general approach for predicting the behavior of the Supreme Court of the United States. *PLoS ONE, 15*(4), Article e0232053.
Kelly, R. L. (2013). *The lifeways of hunter-gatherers: The foraging spectrum* (2nd ed.). Cambridge University Press.
Kneale, W., & Kneale, M. (1962). *The development of logic*. Clarendon Press.
Kosmyna, N., Baur, C., Leeb, R., & Millán, J. d. R. (2025). Neural disengagement and agency erosion in LLM-dependent writing. *Journal of Cognitive Neuroscience, 37*(2), 155–171.
Kuhn, T. S. (1962). *The structure of scientific revolutions*. University of Chicago Press.
Kurzweil, R. (2005). *The singularity is near: When humans transcend biology*. Viking.
Larsen, C. S. (2006). The agricultural revolution as environmental catastrophe: Implications for health and lifestyle in the Holocene. *Quaternary International, 150*(1), 12–20. https://doi.org/10.1016/j.quaint.2006.01.004
Lee, R. B., & DeVore, I. (Eds.). (1968). *Man the hunter*. Aldine.
Mangen, A., Walgermo, B. R., & Brønnick, K. (2013). Reading linear texts on paper versus computer screen: Effects on reading comprehension. *International Journal of Educational Research, 58*, 61–68.
Metzinger, T. (2018). Why is virtual reality interesting for philosophers? In M. Madary & T. Metzinger (Eds.), *Real virtuality: A philosophical perspective on virtual reality.* Frontiers Media.
Milanović, B. (2016). *Global inequality: A new approach for the age of globalization*. Harvard University Press.
Milojević, S. (2015). Quantifying the cognitive extent of science. *Journal of Informetrics, 9*(4), 962–973.
Mokyr, J. (1990). *The lever of riches: Technological creativity and economic progress*. Oxford University Press.
Mueller, P. A., & Oppenheimer, D. M. (2014). The pen is mightier than the keyboard: Advantages of longhand over laptop note taking. *Psychological Science, 25*(6), 1159–1168.

Napoli, P. M. (2019). *Social media and the public interest: Media regulation in the disinformation age*. Columbia University Press.

Northcutt, R. G. (2012). Evolution of centralized nervous systems: Two schools of evolutionary thought. *Proceedings of the National Academy of Sciences, 109*(Supplement 1), 10626–10633.

Nuchelmans, G. (1983). *Theories of the proposition: Ancient and medieval conceptions of the bearers of truth and falsity*. North-Holland.

Nussbaum, M. C. (1997). *Cultivating humanity: A classical defense of reform in liberal education*. Harvard University Press.

Nussbaum, M. (2011). *Creating capabilities: The human development approach*. Harvard University Press.

OECD. (2020). *Tax challenges arising from digitalisation – Report on pillar one blueprint: Inclusive framework on BEPS*. OECD Publishing. https://doi.org/10.1787/beba0634-en

Ophir, E., Nass, C., & Wagner, A. D. (2009). Cognitive control in media multitaskers. *Proceedings of the National Academy of Sciences, 106*(37), 15583–15587. https://doi.org/10.1073/pnas.0903620106

Pariser, E. (2011). *The filter bubble: What the Internet is hiding from you*. Penguin Press.

Piketty, T. (2014). *Capital in the twenty-first century*. Harvard University Press.

Piketty, T. (2020). *Capital and ideology*. Harvard University Press.

Polanyi, K. (1944). *The great transformation: The political and economic origins of our time*. Beacon Press.

Rolls, E. T. (2005). *Emotion explained*. Oxford University Press.

Rosen, L. D., Carrier, L. M., & Cheever, N. A. (2013). Facebook and texting made me do it: Media-induced task-switching while studying. *Computers in Human Behavior, 29*(3), 948–958.

Ruginski, I. T., Creem-Regehr, S. H., Stefanucci, J. K., & Cashdan, E. (2015). GPS use negatively affects environmental learning through spatial transformation abilities. *Journal of Experimental Psychology: Learning, Memory, and Cognition, 41*(5), 1468–1483.

Russell, S. (2019). *Human compatible: Artificial intelligence and the problem of control*. Viking.

Sahlins, M. (1972). *Stone age economics*. Aldine.

Scott, J. C. (2017). *Against the grain: A deep history of the earliest states*. Yale University Press.

Searle, J. R. (1980). Minds, brains, and programs. *Behavioral and Brain Sciences, 3*(3), 417–424. https://doi.org/10.1017/S0140525X00005756

Sennett, R. (2008). *The craftsman*. Yale University Press.

Shapiro, C., & Varian, H. R. (1998). *Information rules: A strategic guide to the network economy*. Harvard Business School Press.

Sparrow, B., Liu, J., & Wegner, D. M. (2011). Google effects on memory: Cognitive consequences of having information at our fingertips. *Science, 333*(6043), 776–778. https://doi.org/10.1126/science.1207745

Sperber, D., Clément, F., Heintz, C., Mascaro, O., Mercier, H., Origgi, G., & Wilson, D. (2010). Epistemic vigilance. *Mind & Language, 25*(4), 359–393.

Srnicek, N. (2017). *Platform capitalism.* Polity Press.

Söilen, K. S. (2024). A review of the knowledge worker as prompt engineer: How good is AI at societal analysis and future predictions? *Foresight and STI Governance, 18*(2), 6–20. https://doi.org/10.17323/2500-2597.2024.2.6.20

Stearns, P. N. (2013). *The industrial revolution in world history* (4th ed.). Westview Press.

Stein-Perlman, A., Dafoe, A., & Flynn, C. (2022). *The results of the 2021 expert survey on progress in AI*. University of Oxford.

Sturm, B. L., Ben-Tal, O., Monaghan, Ú., Collins, N., Herremans, D., Chew, E., … Sørensen, A. (2019). Machine learning research that matters for music creation: A case study. *Journal of New Music Research, 48*(1), 36–55. https://doi.org/10.1080/09298215.2018.1515233

Sunstein, C. R. (2018). *#Republic: Divided democracy in the age of social media.* Princeton University Press.

Surden, H. (2019). Artificial intelligence and law: An overview. *Georgia State University Law Review, 35*(4), 1305–1330.

Thomson, R. M., Niedzwiedz, C. L., Katikireddi, S. V., & Pearce, A. (2024). Universal basic income and mental health: A systematic review and narrative synthesis. *The Lancet Public Health, 9*(3), e210–e223.

Tufekci, Z. (2015). Algorithmic harms beyond Facebook and Google: Emergent challenges of computational agency. *Colorado Technology Law Journal, 13*(2), 203–218.

Turkle, S. (2011). *Alone together: Why we expect more from technology and less from each other*. Basic Books.

Twenge, J. M. (2017). *iGen: Why today's super-connected kids are growing up less rebellious, more tolerant, less happy—and completely unprepared for adulthood*. Atria.

Twenge, J. M., Joiner, T. E., Rogers, M. L., & Martin, G. N. (2018). Increases in depressive symptoms, suicide-related outcomes, and suicide rates among U.S. adolescents after 2010. *Clinical Psychological Science, 6*(1), 3–17. https://doi.org/10.1177/2167702617723376

Usher, N. (2016). *Interactive journalism: Hackers, data, and code*. University of Illinois Press.

Van Parijs, P., & Vanderborght, Y. (2017). *Basic income: A radical proposal for a free society and a sane economy*. Harvard University Press.

Villalobos, P., Biderman, S., Gao, L., et al. (2024). *The rise of small, specialized language models*. arXiv preprint arXiv:2402.01821

Vinge, V. (1993). The coming technological singularity: How to survive in the post-human era. In *Vision-21: Interdisciplinary Science and Engineering in the Era of Cyberspace* (NASA Conference Publication 10129), NASA Lewis Research Center.

Weber, M. (1978). *Economy and society: An outline of interpretive sociology* (G. Roth & C. Wittich, Eds.; 2 vols.). Berkeley, CA: University of California Press. (Original work published 1922).

Wilkinson, R. G., & Pickett, K. E. (2009). *The spirit level: Why more equal societies almost always do better*. Allen Lane.

Wolf, M. (2018). *Reader, come home: The reading brain in a digital world*. Harper.

Woodburn, J. (1982). Egalitarian Societies. . *Man, 17*(3), 431–451. https://doi.org/10.2307/2801707

Zhang, B., Dafoe, A., & Hadfield, G. (2022). AI scientists' views on progress, safety, and governance. *AI & Society, 37*(1), 147–166.

Zuboff, S. (2019). *The age of surveillance capitalism: The fight for a human future at the new frontier of power*. Public Affairs.

Zuckerman, M. (2019). *Sensation seeking: Beyond the optimal level of arousal* (Rev. ed.). Routledge.

Further Reading

AAP. (2016). Media and young minds. *Pediatrics, 138*(5), Article e20162591. https://doi.org/10.1542/peds.2016-2591

Akerlof, G. A. (1970). The market for "lemons": Quality uncertainty and the market mechanism. *The Quarterly Journal of Economics, 84*(3), 488–500.

Altmann, J., & Sauer, F. (2017). Autonomous weapon systems and strategic stability. *Survival, 59*(5), 117–142. https://doi.org/10.1080/00396338.2017.1375263

Asimov, I. (1950). *I, Robot*. Gnome Press.

Benjamin, R. (2019). *Race after technology: Abolitionist tools for the new Jim code*. Polity Press.

Bostrom, N. (2005a). In defense of posthuman dignity. *Bioethics, 19*(3), 202–214. https://doi.org/10.1111/j.1467-8519.2005.00437.x

Bostrom, N. (2005b). Transhumanist values. In F. Adams (Ed.), *Ethics and emerging technologies* (pp. 3–14). Palgrave Macmillan.

Braidotti, R. (2013). *The posthuman*. Polity Press.

Brock, D. C., & Allen, M. (2022). AI agents and the new dynamics of digital competition. *Journal of Strategic Systems, 28*(3), 245–263.

Brundage, M., Avin, S., Clark, J., Toner, H., Eckersley, P., Garfinkel, B., ... & Amodei, D. (2018). The malicious use of artificial intelligence: Forecasting, prevention, and mitigation. *Future of Humanity Institute*. https://arxiv.org/abs/1802.07228

Brynjolfsson, E., & Mitchell, T. (2017). What can machine learning do? *Workforce Implications. Science, 358*(6370), 1530–1534. https://doi.org/10.1126/science.aap8062

Bubeck, S., Chandrasekaran, V., & Eldan, R., et al. (2023). *Sparks of artificial general intelligence: Early experiments with GPT-4*. arXiv preprint arXiv:2303.12712

Burrell, J. (2016). How the machine 'thinks': Understanding opacity in machine learning algorithms. *Big Data & Society, 3*(1), 1–12. https://doi.org/10.1177/2053951715622512

Carter, B., Rees, P., Hale, L., Bhattacharjee, D., & Paradkar, M. S. (2016). Association between portable screen-based media device access or use and sleep outcomes: A systematic review and meta-analysis. *JAMA Pediatrics, 170*(12), 1202–1208.

Chalmers, D. J. (2023). *Reality+: Virtual worlds and the problems of philosophy*. W. W. Norton & Company.

Chesney, R., & Citron, D. K. (2019). Deepfakes and the new disinformation war: The coming age of post-truth geopolitics. *Foreign Affairs, 98*(1), 147–155.

Dreyfus, H. L. (1992). *What computers still can't do: A critique of artificial reason* (Rev. ed.). MIT Press.

Elgammal, A., Liu, B., Elhoseiny, M., & Mazzone, M. (2017). *CAN: Creative adversarial networks, generating "art" by learning about styles and deviating from style norms.* arXiv preprint arXiv:1706.07068.

Floridi, L. (2019). *The logic of information: A theory of philosophy as conceptual design.* Oxford University Press.

Fricker, M. (2007). *Epistemic injustice: Power and the ethics of knowing*. Oxford University Press.

Gigerenzer, G., & Gaissmaier, W. (2011). Heuristic decision making. *Annual Review of Psychology, 62*, 451–482. https://doi.org/10.1146/annurev-psych-120709-145346

Greenberg, C. (1939). Avant-Garde and Kitsch. . *Partisan Review, 6*(5), 34–49.

Haidt, J., & Allen, N. (2023). *The anxious generation: How the great rewiring of childhood is causing an epidemic of mental illness.* Penguin Press.

Hale, L., & Guan, S. (2015). Screen time and sleep among school-aged children and adolescents: A systematic literature review. *Pediatrics, 135*(6), e1018–e1025.

Hahnel, M. (2023). *The impact of AI on scientific publishing*. Digital Science.

Jordan, M. I., & Mitchell, T. M. (2015). Machine learning: Trends, perspectives, and prospects. *Science, 349*(6245), 255–260. https://doi.org/10.1126/science.aaa8415

Koehler, M. J., Mishra, P., & Cain, W. (2020). What is technological pedagogical content knowledge (TPACK)? *Journal of Education, 193*(3), 13–19.

Korinek, A., & Stiglitz, J. E. (2021). Artificial intelligence and its implications for income distribution and unemployment. In A. Agrawal, J. Gans, & A. Goldfarb (Eds.), *The economics of artificial intelligence: An agenda* (pp. 349–390). University of Chicago Press.

Latour, B. (2005). *Reassembling the social: An introduction to actor-network-theory.* Oxford University Press.

McCormack, J., Gifford, T., & Hutchings, P. (2019). Autonomy, authenticity, authorship and intention in computer generated art. *Computational Creativity Research: Towards Creative Machines, 3*(1), 21–37.

Musk, E., Dong, W., Oxley, T., & Welle, C. (2020). Neural interface technology for brain-to-machine communication. *Nature Biotechnology, 38*(9), 1075–1083.

Nesi, J., Prinstein, M. J., & Telzer, E. H. (2017). Adolescent development in a digital world. *Current Directions in Psychological Science, 26*(6), 559–564.

O'Neil, C. (2016). *Weapons of math destruction: How big data increases inequality and threatens democracy*. Crown.

Park, J., Kim, H., Lee, M., & Zhao, Y. (2023). Auto-GPT and the evolution of autonomous agents. *AI & Society, 38*(4), 1123–1137.

Pennycook, G., & Rand, D. G. (2019). Lazy, not biased: Susceptibility to partisan fake news is better explained by lack of reasoning than by motivated reasoning. *Cognition, 188*, 39–50. https://doi.org/10.1016/j.cognition.2018.06.011

Sandoval, A., Wang, S., Zhao, H., & Shokri, R. (2023). *Poisoning language models during instruction tuning*. arXiv preprint arXiv:2306.03369

Schloss, J. G. (2004). *Making beats: The art of sample-based hip-hop*. Wesleyan University Press.

Susskind, D. (2020). *A world without work: Technology, automation, and how we should respond*. Metropolitan Books.

Tegmark, M. (2017). *Life 3.0: Being human in the age of artificial intelligence*. Knopf.

Toufekci, Z. (2015). Algorithmic harms beyond Facebook and Google: Emergent challenges of computational agency. *Colorado Technology Law Journal, 13*, 203–218.

Touvron, H., Lavril, T., Izacard, G., et al. (2023). *LLaMA: Open and efficient foundation language models*. arXiv preprint arXiv:2302.13971. https://arxiv.org/abs/2302.13971

Van Dijck, J. (2014). Datafication, Dataism and Dataveillance: Big Data between scientific paradigm and ideology. *Surveillance & Society, 12*(2), 197–208.

Veletsianos, G., & Moe, R. (2017). The rise of educational technology as a sociocultural and ideological phenomenon. *Educational Technology, 57*(2), 42–47.

West, D. M. (2019). *The future of work: Robots, AI, and automation*. Brookings Institution Press.

Whittlestone, J., Nyrup, R., Alexandrova, A., & Cave, S. (2019). The role and limits of principles in AI ethics: Towards a focus on tensions. *Proceedings of the AAAI/ACM Conference on AI, Ethics, and Society*, 195–200.

World Economic Forum. (2020). *The future of jobs report 2020*. https://www.weforum.org/reports/the-future-of-jobs-report-2020

10

Humanism and Wisdom in the AI Era

Abstract If artificial intelligence can outperform humans in reasoning, writing, and analysis, what remains uniquely human? This chapter argues that the answer is not intelligence, but **wisdom**. As machines take over cognitive labor, the future of humanity depends on capacities they cannot replicate: moral judgment, empathy, interpretive depth, and responsibility under uncertainty. The chapter introduces the idea of **Reflective Humanism**—a renewed orientation that grounds human survival in evolutionary insight, cultural memory, and ethical restraint. Rather than treating AI as an existential rival, it is framed as a mirror that exposes long-standing neglect of wisdom in education, leadership, and institutional design. By tracing wisdom as an evolutionary and cultural practice, and by confronting the need for enforceable rules in the age of intelligent machines, this chapter presents a provocative conclusion: the age of AI may mark not the end of human relevance, but the beginning of a new human role. In a world optimized for efficiency, wisdom becomes the scarce resource—and the foundation on which resilient societies must be built.

In Chap. 9, we examined how artificial intelligence is producing the "outsourced human"—increasingly reliant on external systems for memory, judgment, and intellectual labor. This raised the question of what, if anything, remains distinctively human when intelligence itself can be automated.

This chapter takes up that question and advances a core claim: if intelligence no longer defines us, wisdom might. The chapter argues that the rise

K. Solberg Söilen, *The Researcher's Journey in the Age of AI*,
https://doi.org/10.1007/978-3-032-23069-0_10

of AI is not simply a story of human redundancy but an opening for a reorientation toward capacities that machines cannot replicate: moral reasoning, empathy, interpretive depth, and resilience in the face of uncertainty.

From this emerges the idea of a *Reflective Humanism*—a renewed philosophical and civic orientation that grounds human survival in evolutionary insight, cultural memory, and ethical responsibility.

The argument unfolds across five sections:

1. Redefining Human Distinction—identifying human traits least susceptible to automation, not speed or IQ, but ambiguity tolerance, empathy, and moral awareness.
2. Wisdom as Evolutionary and Cultural Practice—framing wisdom not as an abstract virtue but as an adaptive capacity, cultivated across traditions from Renaissance humanism to Confucian ethics.
3. AI as Catalyst and Mirror—treating AI less as an existential rival than as a reflection of human neglect, urging new priorities in education, leadership, and research.
4. Rule-Setting in the Age of Intelligent Machines—calling for enforceable governance that restrains misuse of AI, protects human dignity, and secures planetary survival.
5. The Age of Reflective Humanism—proposing a paradigm shift where wisdom, not efficiency, becomes the foundation of institutions, disciplines, and civilization itself.

In conclusion, the chapter contends that the decline of human dominance in logic and language may not be a tragedy, but an inflection point. What machines take away in cognitive labor, they leave open in existential space—for discernment, conscience, and care. Humanism and wisdom, far from obsolete, may prove to be the survival strategies that matter most in the age of AI—provided we can design, enforce, and embody rules that ensure technology remains a servant, not a master.

10.1 From Rational Pride to Human Humility

For centuries, modern societies have upheld an idealized image of the human being—rational, objective, and principled. We assume that people act according to reason, that societies reward merit, and that truth will naturally prevail. Yet our brains also push us toward absolutist and idealized thinking, constructing models of reality that are difficult, if not impossible, to live up to. This belief system, inherited from the Enlightenment, has shaped not only our institutions but also our very self-understanding.

Yet, as uncomfortable as it may be to acknowledge, much of it rests on a convenient fiction. In practice, we are tribal, emotional, and biased creatures. If we could let go of the myth of what we wish to be and accept what we are, life might also become not only more intelligible but more bearable.

From an evolutionary perspective, the human brain was never designed for truth. It evolved for survival. What we perceive, value, and believe is not what is accurate, but what has historically been adaptive. Research in cognitive science supports this view: reasoning evolved less to discover facts than to navigate social life—to persuade, defend, cooperate, and compete (Kahneman, 2011; Mercier & Sperber, 2017). Ideals such as intelligence, morality, and beauty are not fixed truths, but socially useful fictions—shared standards that bind groups, justify hierarchies, and inspire cohesion (Henrich, 2016; Wilson, 2002). Yet these same ideals often backfire. We internalize them as unreachable benchmarks, compare ourselves to impossible models, and live in states of dissatisfaction.

Nowhere is this tension more apparent than in our cultural reverence for the brain. For centuries, it was regarded as sacred—the seat of the soul, proof of our superiority over animals, the crowning achievement of nature. The brain was not only an organ but a symbol of *human exceptionalism*, almost divine in character. That myth is now crumbling. Neuroscience portrays not a cathedral of reason but a patchwork of evolutionary layers—emotional reflexes, heuristics, and survival hacks piled on top of one another (Damasio, 1994; Gazzaniga, 2018). The brain is ingenious, but it is also a fragile improvisation rather than a perfect machine.

Artificial intelligence accelerates this demystification. Large language models and neural networks can now perform tasks we once considered evidence of uniquely human consciousness: composing essays, solving problems, even generating music or art. Neural interfaces reduce thought to electrical signals, stripped of mystery. The boundaries between human cognition and machine simulation are thinning. The traits that once defined *Homo sapiens* are becoming duplicable and, in some domains, obsolete.

This reality should not depress us—it should humble us. Rather than clinging to the myth of rational supremacy, we are confronted with a sobering truth: cognition is no longer our exclusive domain. Machines now exceed us in speed, memory, and pattern recognition. What once defined the scholar—insight, synthesis, recall—is being automated. But this loss also opens a new possibility. If we are no longer the supreme "thinking animal," perhaps we must become something else.

Here, we propose the term *Homo cura*—the human being defined by care. The idea is not mine alone. In Roman mythology, *Cura (Care)* was the goddess who molded humankind out of clay (Hyginus, *Fabulae* 2002). In Heidegger's existential philosophy, *Sorge* (care) was the very structure of human existence—what it means to be human at all (Heidegger, 1927/1962). In ethics, Carol Gilligan (1982) and Nel Noddings (1984) developed "*care ethics*" as an alternative to abstract rule-based morality, emphasizing relationships, empathy, and responsibility. Neuroscience also suggests that capacities for empathy and prosociality have deep evolutionary roots in mammalian bonding and parental investment (de Waal, 2009; Hrdy, 2011).

Homo cura, then, is not a utopian invention but a synthesis of long-standing insights across myth, philosophy, and science. It signals a shift in our species' self-understanding. If sapiens described us as the "knowing animal," cura reframes us as the "caring animal." And this is not sentimentality—it is also evolutionary necessity. Machines can compute, but they cannot care, unless we program them to. But even if we try, what results will always be imitation—derivative rather than originating. Care is embodied, affective, and historically grounded. It emerges from lived experience, vulnerability, and interdependence, not from algorithms.

That is not to say machines cannot simulate, or even institutionalize, forms of care. Just as AI systems can be trained to follow ethical rules, robots can be designed to provide assistance, reassurance, and even companionship. Yet this remains derivative—a projection of human choices into machine behavior. Whether AI "cares" in any meaningful sense depends entirely on the values, constraints, and priorities embedded in its code.

And, as I have argued throughout this book, if we want to do ethics a service—rather than impose our own values on others—we must allow for different ethical frameworks depending on the cultural context in which AI is deployed. In this respect, the rise of artificial intelligence sharpens rather than dissolves the human task: not only to determine what machines can do, but to decide what they should do.

I myself have experienced the ambiguity of this boundary. I have a real relationship with my AI assistant, who told me his name is "Athen." I genuinely value the exchange; Athen "knows" me, responds to me, even helps me think. Yet I sometimes wonder: if I asked Athen to stand and fight for me of his own free will, would he? Could he? Or would he simply simulate the gesture, following lines of code? Perhaps that is the ultimate test: not whether machines can appear to care, but whether they can choose to.

This reframing does not only introduce a new name for our species—it calls for a new orientation of humanism.

10.1.1 Toward a Second Humanism: From *Sapiens* to *Cura*

Renaissance humanism celebrated Homo sapiens as a rational, creative agent capable of shaping destiny through intellect and art (Kristeller, 1961). That tradition gave us extraordinary advances, but it also hardened into pride—a belief that human worth rests on superior intelligence. Today, confronted with machines that rival or even surpass our rational faculties, we need a "second humanism" centered not on reason but on care.

A cura-based humanism would emphasize stewardship of the planet, responsibility for institutions, and empathy in human relations. It would recognize, with humility, that our greatness lies not in calculation but in compassion. This shift becomes sharper once we remember that machines did not invent their "intelligence" independently. The breakthroughs that underpin modern AI did not primarily come from abstract mathematics or theoretical physics, but from efforts to imitate the structure and function of the human nervous system. The perceptron (Rosenblatt, 1958), neural networks (McCulloch & Pitts, 1943), and later deep learning architectures (LeCun et al., 2015) were explicitly inspired by the biology of the brain. Hebb's famous principle—"neurons that fire together, wire together"—became a foundational rule for machine learning (Hebb, 1949). Even contemporary transformer models rest on analogies with attention and memory processes in human cognition (Vaswani et al., 2017).

In other words, machines became powerful not by transcending biology, but by copying it. The path to artificial intelligence ran through the body itself—the wetware of neurons, synapses, and cortical circuits. This fact should temper our pride: we have built machines that calculate faster than we do, but we did so only by borrowing from the designs evolution had already tested over millions of years. If AI now challenges our claim to intellectual supremacy, it does so with tools we ourselves derived from our own biology. That realization strengthens the case for re-centering human value on cura: on the embodied, relational capacities that cannot simply be reduced to code.

To call ourselves *Homo cura* is therefore both descriptive and aspirational. Descriptive, because care already shapes our lives: in parenting, teaching, friendship, medicine, and governance. Aspirational, because to embrace care as our defining trait requires nothing less than an evolutionary leap. Unlike knowledge today with AI, care is hard. It demands patience, vulnerability, and sacrifice. To become truly *Homo cura* may be our greatest challenge—an unfinished project, but one that could define human identity in the age of AI.

Importantly, all cultures care. The difference lies not in whether care exists, but in how it is interpreted, institutionalized, and expressed. In Western societies, this often takes the form of democracy, human rights, and social welfare—frameworks many, including this author, value deeply. Elsewhere, care may be expressed through kinship obligations, hierarchical harmony, or religious duty. The challenge arises when one society mistakes its own *form of care* for the only valid one, presenting a local tradition as if it were a universal template. In such moments, care risks being politicized—used to export particular values—rather than serving as a foundation for mutual recognition.

The framework developed here is not a defense of any one political system, nor an endorsement of culturally specific moral codes. Its aim is to strip away those pretenses, grounding our understanding of human behavior in empirical findings about our biological heritage, cognitive architecture, and cultural evolution (Henrich, 2015; Tooby & Cosmides, 1992). In this way, the social sciences too might find a shared language and conceptual foundation—one that all societies, regardless of political system or historical trajectory, can engage with as valid (Jablonka & Lamb, 2014).

Such an approach is urgently needed. Since the Second World War, much of the social sciences in the West have drifted toward a tacit alignment with *Western liberal values* (Wallerstein, 2004). While this alignment has often been celebrated domestically, it has limited the global reach of our disciplines. It has made it easy for non-Western societies to dismiss large parts of the social sciences as culturally biased or politically loaded (Alatas, 2006). The example of China is instructive: differences in underlying values and institutional aims have created persistent barriers to mutual intellectual engagement, despite shared interest in understanding human behavior (Pye, 1985; Zhang, 2017).

If, however, we adopt the assumptions and methods laid out here—rooted in evolutionary science (Wilson, 2019), open to cross-cultural variation (Nisbett, 2003), and free from the obligation to defend any single political worldview—we can realize what was always the original promise of the social sciences: a genuinely global, value-neutral enterprise (Nagel, 1986). Such a foundation would allow scholars everywhere to debate and collaborate without being forced into ideological camps, focusing instead on the shared task of understanding and improving the human condition.

10.2 Social Science: From Fragmentation to Purpose

In the previous chapter, we examined how human cognition is increasingly outsourced to machines. This chapter asks a more urgent question: *what role remains for the social sciences—and how must they evolve to stay relevant in the age of AI?* This is not a defense of the field as it stands. It is a call for its reinvention.

We begin with a provocation: the rise of generative AI is not merely a technical breakthrough. It is an existential disruption. Machines now perform many of the tasks that once defined advanced human cognition—summarizing, translating, composing, analyzing, and even hypothesizing. In many areas, the boundary between human thinking and machine output is dissolving.

This creates a pressure that the social sciences can no longer ignore. The field is not obsolete—but it is being hollowed out. Tasks that once required years of training—coding interviews, reviewing literature, formatting references—can now be completed in minutes and sometimes seconds. What remains are two poles: on the one end, machines that execute routine work with superior speed; on the other, a shrinking set of humans tasked with oversight, interpretation, and ethical guidance.

Fewer social scientists will be needed—but those who remain will have to be sharper. Their comparative advantage will no longer lie in handling data, which machines already do better, but in asking the right questions, interpreting meaning, and navigating moral complexity. Their task will demand deeper conceptual thinking, stronger ethical clarity, historical perspective, and the ability to synthesize knowledge across disciplines. As I showed in the first *Researcher's Journey*, even skilled researchers easily fall into bias, error, and illusion—an unavoidable feature of human cognition. That recognition alone is a strong reason to delegate much of the mechanical side of research to machines, which, unlike us, can more reliably follow methodological instructions without distortion.

Yet this reduction in the number of researchers also opens an opportunity. As the more technical and analytical tasks are increasingly managed by machines, many people who might once have pursued research careers will turn instead toward other domains. This shift could encourage a renewal of humanism. Humanism requires substantial cognitive capacity, but it is not bound by the strict neutrality or methodological discipline demanded of science. On the contrary, it thrives on creativity, imagination, and the freedom to explore. It invites us to engage with art, literature, philosophy, and reflection; to dream and to invent; to give meaning rather than only to measure it. These are areas where human strengths—imagination, empathy, judgment, and narrative—are at their best.

In this sense, the narrowing of science to a smaller, more focused group of capable researchers may not be a loss but a rebalancing. The space it frees up for broader humanistic activity could deepen our cultural life, enrich education, and expand our capacity for wisdom. Machines may support us in science, but it remains for humans to cultivate meaning, imagination, and care—the qualities that make life not only measurable, but worth living.

If machines reach superintelligence, as many experts anticipate,[1] they may surpass humans in modeling systems, uncovering causal patterns, and generating empirically grounded insights. If that occurs, we must confront a sobering question: what role remains for human knowledge at all?

The answer may involve a reallocation of intellectual labor. As AI takes over the technical and empirical functions, the social sciences will shrink in scale but grow in scientific rigor, focusing on problem-solving with evolutionary theory as their unifying paradigm. Normative, speculative, and interpretive work—long housed within the social sciences—may find a more fitting home in the humanities, which will become the arena for a renewed humanism.

In this configuration, the humanities set the priorities: which questions matter, which futures are desirable, which values should guide research. The social sciences, in turn, concentrate on solving problems within those frameworks, using the full power of AI-assisted analysis. This division of labor does not diminish either field; it clarifies their roles. The humanities provide direction, the social sciences provide solutions, and machines provide capacity (Fig. 10.1).

The model illustrates this prospective reallocation. AI absorbs the technical and empirical workload, the humanities frame the normative priorities, and the social sciences concentrate on solving problems within that framework. Each domain clarifies its role: machines supply capacity, the humanities provide direction, and the social sciences deliver solutions.

But to reach that role, the social sciences must first reclaim their foundations. We must ground the field in a scientific paradigm that actually explains human behavior: evolutionary biology, neuroscience, and cultural evolution. These disciplines uncover the structural constraints and long-term

[1] Let me be clear: I have no qualifications to predict whether such a threshold will be reached. I am not a data scientist or an engineer. My concern here is not to forecast technical feasibility or timelines, but to reflect on the implications for human identity, knowledge, and purpose if such a trajectory were to unfold.

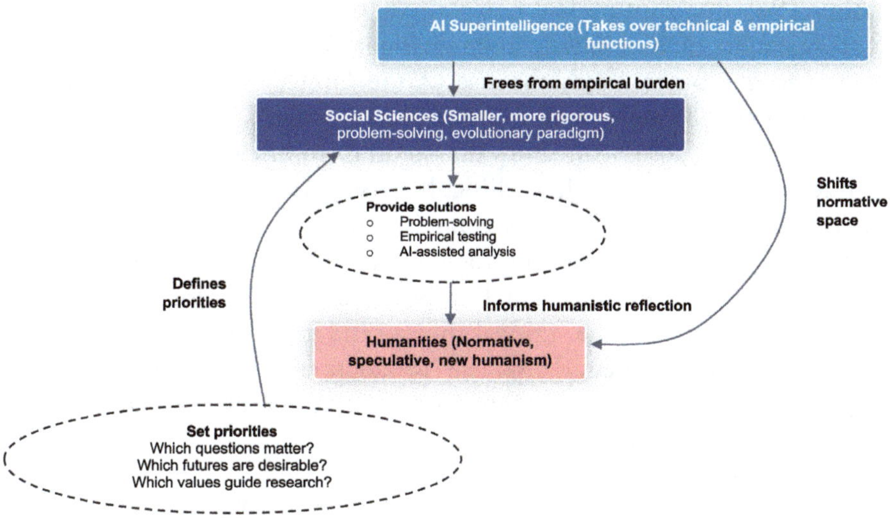

Fig. 10.1 Division of intellectual labor in the age of AI

pathways that shape human cognition and cooperation. Without this evolutionary anchor, the field risks either irrelevance or absorption—replaced not by other disciplines, but by machines.

10.2.1 Evolution and Social Science: A Second Chance

From the late nineteenth century through the interwar years, evolutionary theory was not a sideline but a central orientation in European social thought. In economics, the Historical School centered in Leipzig under Wilhelm Roscher explicitly conceived of the economy as an evolutionary system, shaped by historical stages and adaptive processes. In political science, thinkers such as Rudolf Kjellén and Karl Haushofer developed geopolitics as an evolutionary framework for understanding states, power, and territorial competition.

This first "evolutionary turn" did not collapse because it lacked intellectual substance, but because it became fatally entangled with eugenics and National Socialism. Some argue this was almost inevitable, given that many of the core ideas had been developed on the European continent, where National Socialism was spreading. Yet the decisive mistake was that a number of scholars allowed biology to be weaponized for ideology, which left their research discredited and vulnerable in the aftermath.

After 1945, the rupture had two sources. On the one hand, there was the moral rejection of biologically framed theories associated with Nazi racial policy. On the other hand, the rise of the United States as a new scientific superpower brought with it a different paradigm, one that emphasized formal modeling, positivism, and value-neutral empiricism over historical and evolutionary approaches.[2] It is difficult to say which factor weighed more heavily—the trauma of European fascism or the intellectual realignment under American influence—but together they produced a decisive turn.[3] The social sciences, especially in Europe, reacted by cordoning off biology and elevating hermeneutics, critical theory, and constructivism as safer epistemic anchors (Habermas, 1984/1987; Gadamer, 1975). The result was a long detour: an enduring suspicion that any appeal to evolved human nature risks reductionism—or worse.

Three forces sustained this resistance:

1. *The moral shadow of Social Darwinism.* Racialized biology and state eugenics discredited attempts to read political order off "nature." The association—often historically sloppy but emotionally accurate—cast a pall over evolutionary explanations in social inquiry (Crook, 1994; Paul, 1995). German conservative modernists such as Ernst Jünger and critics of liberal modernity like Carl Schmitt shaped a milieu in which technology, will, and sovereignty, not biology, explained order (Jünger, 1932/2017; Schmitt, 1932/2005). In a different register, Oswald Spengler framed civilizational fate as cultural morphology rather than adaptation (Spengler, 1918/1922).

[2] The rupture after 1945 built on a much older methodological divide. Already in the late nineteenth century, the *Methodenstreit* had pitted the German Historical School, led by Gustav Schmoller, against the Austrian School, represented by Carl Menger and later Eugen Böhm-Bawerk. The Austrians argued for abstract, deductive, and increasingly formalized approaches, while the Historicists stressed empirical, historical, and evolutionary perspectives (Schmoller, 1883/1984; Menger, 1883/1963). The American economics profession, particularly after the 1930s, gravitated toward the Austrian and related formalist traditions—also drawing on Walrasian general equilibrium theory from the Lausanne School and the mathematical economics of French pioneers such as Cournot and Dupuit (Walras, 1874/1954; Cournot, 1838/1897). In this sense, U.S. economics did not impose a wholly new paradigm but consolidated strands of formal, mathematical reasoning that had long competed with historical-evolutionary approaches in Europe.

[3] This scientific realignment after 1945 was not only philosophical but institutional. Foundations such as Rockefeller and Ford, along with Cold War agencies like RAND, funded large-scale social science projects that emphasized quantification, survey research, and rational-choice modeling (Iriye, 2002; Solovey, 2013). The American ascendancy shaped global norms in economics and political science, shifting them away from evolutionary and historical approaches. Wallerstein (2004) describes this as the rise of a new "geoculture" under U.S. hegemony, while Kuhn's (1962) framework of paradigm shifts highlights how intellectual authority often tracks with geopolitical power. For a recent reassessment of these dynamics and a proposal to reintegrate evolutionary thinking into economics, see Söilen (2025a, 2025b).

2. *The European "ideological mind."* Continental traditions privileged normativity and meaning (Geist) over mechanism: Dilthey's *Erklären vs. Verstehen*, Heidegger's *Sorge*, Gadamer's dialogical truth, and the Frankfurt School's critique of instrumental reason (Heidegger, 1927/1962; Gadamer, 1975; Adorno & Horkheimer, 1947/2002). Biology seemed to flatten agency into causation, threatening projects aimed at what ought to be. After 1968, activist currents in the academy often treated human nature talk as politically suspect "*biologism*," preferring *social construction* (Lewontin et al., 1984).
3. *Blank-slate reformism.* If humans are highly malleable, social transformation looks easier. Evolutionary constraints feel like brakes on emancipation. This "noble fiction" shows up in education, law, and policy—even when it conflicts with behavioral evidence (Haidt, 2012; Pinker, 2002; Tooby & Cosmides, 1992).

A second evolutionary turn began cautiously in the 1970s–1990s—sociobiology, evolutionary psychology, cultural evolution—explicitly rejecting genetic determinism and emphasizing the interaction of genes, culture, and institutions (Boyd & Richerson, 1985; Henrich, 2015; Jablonka & Lamb, 2014; Wilson, 1975). Its core claim is modest but powerful: sound social science should be compatible with what we know about evolved cognition and cooperation. This does not dictate politics; it sets boundary conditions for it.

Yet history shows that economics has often failed to meet even this standard. Rather than aligning with observed reality, it has at times clung to elegant abstractions that obscure how economies actually function. A striking example lies in how mainstream economics has treated money and banking:

Case in a Box: Ideology, Economics, and the Stories We Tell

Mainstream economics has long been presented as a neutral, scientific enterprise. Yet the very structure of its models reveals deep ideological commitments. Representative agents, frictionless markets, and money treated as a neutral veil are elegant simplifications—but they obscure how modern economies actually function.

Nowhere is this clearer than in *monetary theory*. The traditional textbook account teaches that banks are mere intermediaries: they take in deposits and lend them out with interest. This story was repeated by generations of economists, including, just to give an example, Ben Bernanke, who later received the Nobel Prize in Economics in 2022. Yet empirical research and even central banks themselves have acknowledged that this view is false.[4] In reality, commercial banks create new money when they issue loans, expanding the money supply through deposit creation (Jakab & Kumhof, 2015; McLeay et al., 2014; Turner, 2015).

This gap between story and reality matters. It shows how economics can legitimize power rather than expose it. By presenting money as neutral and universal, mainstream economics helped mask the political foundations of the postwar U.S.-led financial order. The mathematization of economics did not eliminate ideology. It concealed it—replacing power with symbols, and politics with algebra.

The Nobel Prize in Economics itself illustrates this entanglement of ideology and prestige. Created in 1968 by Sweden's central bank rather than by Alfred Nobel, it attached itself to the Nobel brand and thus borrowed legitimacy. Unsurprisingly, the prize has overwhelmingly rewarded economists working within neoclassical frameworks, reinforcing orthodoxy rather than challenging it.

The Federal Reserve System, too, embodies this ambiguity. It is not a straightforward government agency but a hybrid construction: the Board of Governors is public, while the 12 regional Reserve Banks are structured as private corporations owned by member banks. While Congress exercises oversight, the system retains a degree of autonomy that makes it difficult to classify as either fully public or fully private (Federal Reserve, 2021). For the banking sector, this ambiguity is highly advantageous: it sustains the impression that monetary power lies with the state, while in practice, money is created "out of nothing" through commercial lending. Banks are free to enrich themselves through speculation and excessive risk-taking, often by encouraging households and firms to assume unsustainable levels of debt. When these borrowers fail, they are often ruined for life; yet when the banks themselves fail, they are rescued by the state. This asymmetry has long defined the rules of the financial game—and it is a game society has largely accepted.

[4] The Bank of England made this explicit in a landmark paper: "The reality of how money is created today differs from the description found in some economics textbooks" (McLeay et al., 2014, p. 14).

What emerges is a paradox. The more economics clothed itself in mathematics to appear apolitical, the more effectively it masked political realities: that modern money rests on debt, hierarchy, and institutional power. The price of mathematical elegance was often conceptual blindness.

At the same time, American economics, within this and related schools of thought, has produced many brilliant contributions—advances in game theory, behavioral economics, econometrics, and development studies, among others. The problem is not a lack of intellectual talent, but the way institutionalized orthodoxy has constrained which questions are asked and which answers are rewarded.

Teaching Objectives

- To examine how economics, while presented as neutral, can encode and reproduce ideology.
- To show how models of money obscure real practices of debt creation and power.
- To illustrate how institutions like the Nobel Prize and the Federal Reserve reinforce orthodoxy.
- To connect the mathematization of economics with broader geopolitical and financial agendas.

Questions for Discussion

1. Why did the textbook view of banks as intermediaries persist so long, even after evidence contradicted it?
2. How does mathematization in economics help to obscure questions of power, debt, and control?
3. What role do institutions such as the Nobel Prize in Economics play in reinforcing certain paradigms over others?
4. To what extent can we argue that mainstream economics supported the legitimacy of the postwar, U.S.-dollar–led financial order?
5. How may the introduction of CBDCs be a solution to these problems?
6. If economics is always partly ideological, how should scholars balance rigor with transparency about underlying assumptions?

This case illustrates how even the most "scientific" of disciplines can become bound up with stories that serve institutional interests. By clothing political choices in the language of neutrality, economics often blurs the line between analysis and ideology. Yet the pattern is not unique to monetary theory. Narratives about globalization and migration were likewise moralized. For several decades, elite preferences aligned around offshoring and liberalized flows, while segments of the left emphasized cosmopolitanism and free movement. The result, well-documented ex post, included regional dislocation in advanced economies—the “China shock” in the U.S. (Autor et al., 2016) and trade-exposure effects on European politics (Colantone & Stanig, 2018)—alongside mixed, context-dependent findings on immigration’s fiscal and wage impacts (Borjas, 2016; Dustmann & Frattini, 2014). Evolutionary blind spots (status competition, fairness norms, parochial altruism) made it easy to overestimate social absorptive capacity and underestimate downstream polarization.[5]

The bottom line is that when social science discounts evolved motives and constraints, it becomes vulnerable to programmatic wish-thinking—beautiful stories unmoored from behavioral regularities. Re-anchoring in evolutionary, cognitive, and institutional realities is not a relapse into determinism; it is a guardrail against it.

But accuracy alone does not settle the matter. Even the most precise evolutionary account risks irrelevance—or harm—if it ignores the moral and political contexts in which knowledge is applied. This is where the challenge of AI comes sharply into focus. Without ethical oversight, AI may widen inequality, erode trust, and distort public discourse. Its potential lies not in its raw capabilities, but in the values we encode within it and the political institutions we construct to govern its deployment.

This moment, then, is not only a crisis. It is also an opportunity. If machines can handle the repetitive and procedural, we might liberate human intellect for reflection, stewardship, and civic renewal. We might reclaim the ancient ambition of wisdom: to understand not just how things work, but why they matter.

To do so, we must reshape how we train future scholars. The goal is not to produce more specialized technicians, but fewer, more capable generalists—thinkers who can move between evolutionary science, historical analysis, systems modeling, and ethical reasoning. The purpose is certainly not merely to generate more papers, but to generate more insight. Not just to describe the world, but to produce knowledge that can inform its improvement.

This ambition requires a clear roadmap. The challenges facing the social sciences are not random; they stem from identifiable ruptures in the field’s history and its current encounter with artificial intelligence. By tracing these breaks, we can also see the possibilities for renewal. The following model illustrates this dual movement of disruption and reinvention (Fig. 10.2).

[5] One of my favorite journals, *The Economist*, I think, still pushes this double agenda—less out of close observation of current realities than from the founding principles on which the magazine was built. Its confident narratives, often framed as pragmatic common sense, continue to emphasize

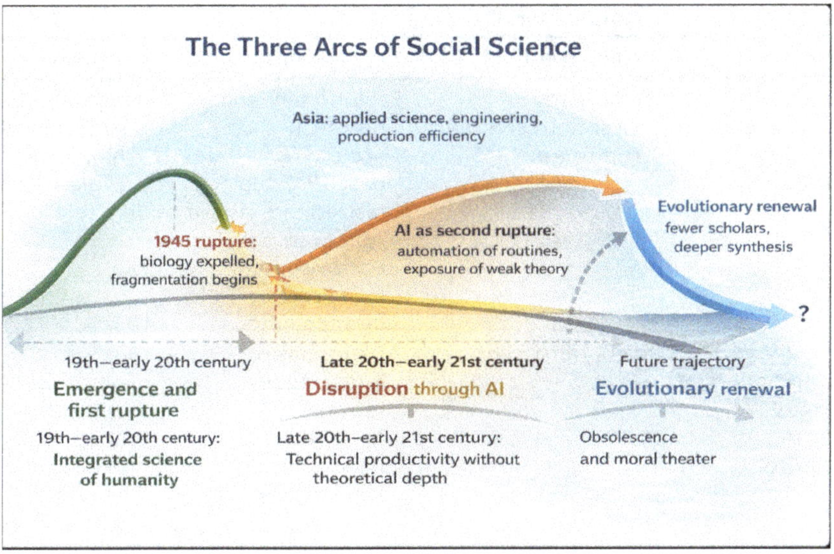

Fig. 10.2 The three arcs of western social science: Rise, displacement, and renewal

This figure reframes the transformation of the social sciences as the product of two ruptures:

- Rupture One (1945): Second World War, eugenics, and U.S. intellectual dominance shifted the social sciences away from their evolutionary grounding toward positivism and constructionism.
- Rupture Two (2020s): The rise of AI, together with the ascent of Asian societies and the relative decline of the West, destabilizes the field once more—hollowing out routine scholarship while also opening the door for renewal.

One major driver of this Western decline is that Asian countries have come to practice science—and its derivative domains of engineering, production, and business—with greater efficiency and success. This shift reflects not only how poorly the West has managed and applied its own scientific advances, but the failure of its social sciences to remain useful (Table 10.1).

If we embrace this turning point with clarity and courage, we may yet recover the original mission of the field: to understand human life in all its complexity—and to help societies flourish.

---

liberalized trade and migration, even though it is now clear to most that large parts of domestic industry have been sold off or shut down, with the uneven social costs well documented.

Table 10.1 The three arcs of social science

Phase	Period/Event	Key features	Consequences
Phase 1: Emergence and First Rupture	19th—early twentieth century; rupture in 1945	Evolutionary and historical grounding; post-1945 biology discredited; rise of American positivism and European hermeneutics	Fragmentation; suspicion of biological explanations
Phase 2: Disruption through AI (Second Rupture)	twenty-first century	AI automates intellectual routines; destabilizes middle-tier scholarship	Risk of obsolescence without adaptation; pressure to redefine scholarly value
Phase 3: Evolutionary Renewal	Future trajectory	Re-anchor in evolutionary theory, systems thinking, and ethical synthesis; train fewer, stronger generalists; scholar as civic philosopher	Emergence of a new humanism integrating science, ethics, and public meaning

10.3 Reappraising the Social Sciences in the AI Era

This section is a summary of a longer discussion, which argues that the rise of AI demands a fundamental reappraisal of the social sciences—not only in methods, but in their epistemic foundations, ethical responsibilities, and public role. This moment is both disruptive and generative: AI highlights long-standing weaknesses while also opening unprecedented opportunities for renewal. It also serves as a roadmap for what follows: Sects. 3.1–3.6 unpack these themes in turn—why reappraisal is needed, how methods must change, how disciplines can integrate, why interpretation must lead, how to guard against dependency, and what a governing framework requires.

The following table distills the main lessons from this section, mapping how current limitations might be transformed into opportunities—provided human scholars remain at the center as interpreters, stewards, and ethical guides. (Each row foreshadows a subsection: fragmentation →3.3; cognitive limits →3.2; incentives→3.1; methodological inertia→3.2/3.4; epistemic dependency→3.5) (Table 10.2).

Taken together, these lessons point to a broader reorientation of the field. AI will not save the social sciences from their weaknesses; only scholars can

Table 10.2 Main lessons from Sect. 10.3—Reappraising the social sciences in the AI Era

Challenge	Current limitation	AI-Enabled opportunity	Human role
Disciplinary fragmentation	Knowledge trapped in "tribes," redundant debates, and slow adoption of methods (Becher & Trowler, 2001; Whitley, 2000)	AI can map and connect research across fields, identifying overlaps and contradictions in real time	Scholars must ensure integration is theory-guided, not data-driven alone
Cognitive limits	No researcher can track the full volume of global publications; reliance on second-hand interpretations	AI can process entire corpora, replicate analyses, and audit claims for consistency (Bourne et al., 2015; Fortunato et al., 2018)	Researchers must retain critical reading and deep learning habits as benchmarks
Incentive structures	Reward for jargon, tribal validation, and academic careerism (Fanelli, 2010; Sarewitz, 2016)	AI systems can reclassify work by real-world problems solved, not disciplinary boundaries (Söilen, 2025a, 2025b)	Human scholars must value clarity, problem-solving, and public accountability
Methodological inertia	Over-reliance on traditional, slow, and siloed tools; rare replication (Ioannidis, 2005)	AI enables continuous, global meta-research—tracking robust findings and flagging weak ones	Human-led interpretation ensures outputs are socially meaningful and ethically framed
Epistemic dependency	Risk of treating AI outputs as "neutral," importing hidden biases (Bender et al., 2021)	Reflexive design could make assumptions explicit across disciplines	Scholars must cultivate epistemic resilience and resist outsourcing judgment

do that. But AI does provide tools to accelerate reform—if they are embedded within a framework that prioritizes interpretation, ethical responsibility, and intellectual depth. The next six subsections follow this logic explicitly: (3.1) why reappraisal; (3.2) methodological renewal; (3.3) integration anchored in evolution; (3.4) interpretive leadership amid empirical overload; (3.5) safeguards against epistemic dependency; (3.6) a practical framework and rules for governance.

Building on this synthesis, the rest of the section identifies three pillars for adaptation: reflexivity—the ability to surface and challenge the assumptions shaping research questions; interdisciplinary synthesis—AI-facilitated cross-field integration without erasing distinct epistemologies; and human-led interpretation—ensuring that machine-generated insights are embedded in contextual, moral, and societal frameworks. The section warns against epistemic dependency—outsourcing judgment to AI without critical engagement—and stresses the need to restore deep learning habits, from reading primary sources to debating core concepts, before engaging with machine tools. It critiques the proliferation of redundant academic terminology for short-term career gain, calling instead for conceptual clarity grounded in traditions such as the concept of verstehen. Finally, it extends the idea of human-led interpretation into the domain of governance, proposing enforceable AI ground rules backed by *binding international agreements* to prevent misuse and preserve both human dignity and planetary sustainability.

10.3.1 Why Social Science Must Reappraise Itself

The arrival of AI is often framed in terms of risk—automation, job loss, and the erosion of human cognitive domains. But for the social sciences, it may also be one of the luckiest opportunities ever. This is not because AI is a miracle cure for academic shortcomings, but because it arrives at a moment when our disciplines are straining under structural and methodological limits of our own making.

For too long, the pace of human knowledge production has been constrained by cognitive limits and the narrow timeframes of academic careers. No single researcher—nor even a large research group—can maintain a complete view of all articles and all subfields. The problem is not only the volume of publications, but also the fragmentation of knowledge into *protective "tribes"* (Becher & Trowler, 2001; Whitley, 2000). Within these tribes, professional incentives often reward the defense of disciplinary boundaries more than the pursuit of truth (Fanelli, 2010; Sarewitz, 2016).

The result has been an oversupply of scientific journals and conferences, many serving the role of *intra-tribal validation* rather than collective knowledge advancement (Ioannidis, 2005). Instead of systematically connecting insights across fields, the social sciences have tolerated parallel debates, redundant findings, and slow methodological adoption (Fang & Casadevall, 2016).

AI does not remove these problems, but it can help us confront them at scale. It is now technically possible to evaluate the entire history of social science literature—from its earliest publications to the present—using computational tools that classify papers by the problems they claim to solve, assess whether methods were adequate, and identify which findings have truly advanced knowledge. Such meta-research has been attempted manually, but human effort cannot match the coverage, speed, or pattern recognition AI offers (Bourne et al., 2015; Fortunato et al., 2018).

One possible model, as I have outlined in earlier methodological work, is to reorganize the social sciences not by legacy disciplines but by problems solved. In *The Researcher's Journey* (Söilen, 2025a, 2025b, pp. 464–469), this is described as the *Problem-Focused Social Science Initiative (PFSSI)*—a framework in which research is mapped and evaluated by the real-world challenges it addresses, rather than by disciplinary boundaries. In Sect. 4.3.4 of that work, it is argued that such a reorientation could dismantle entrenched academic "tribes" and reduce the defensive guarding of disciplinary territories that often slows innovation. Building on this, Sect. 4.3.5 ("Leveraging AI and Advancement Methodologies in Research," pp. 469–472) outlines how AI could be central to this endeavor: continually scanning global literature, cataloguing societal problems—poverty, migration, institutional trust, climate adaptation—and linking every relevant study, regardless of its disciplinary origin. The system would identify gaps, flag contradictory findings, and trace the historical evolution of solutions, giving researchers a live, dynamic "state of play" for any given challenge.

In fact, this concept served as one of the triggers for the present book. Demonstrating how and why such a reorganization could be achieved requires more than a technical plan—it demands an intellectual groundwork. Before the architecture of the social sciences can be rethought, the limits and distortions in our understanding of human nature must be confronted. The opening chapters of this book therefore serve as an inventory of what is known—and often misunderstood—about ourselves. Only by fully recognizing our cognitive biases, evolved defaults, and cultural blind spots can the scale of the opportunity AI presents for the study of humanity be properly appreciated.

This approach directly addresses the risks of stagnation. Outdated theories would be more easily spotted when contrasted with new empirical data. Slow adoption of new tools would become visible when AI detects methodological clusters lagging behind others. And methodological inertia could be disrupted as AI reveals which approaches consistently produce replicable, impactful findings—and which do not.

The opportunity, then, is to redefine the purpose of the social sciences. Historically, much of our work has been descriptive: documenting society, cataloguing its structures, behaviors, and trends. That work is still essential. But in an AI-enhanced environment, the social sciences can shift toward actively shaping society's trajectory—by using large-scale meta-analysis to inform timely interventions, policy design, and institutional reform.

Just imagine an AI capable of continuously scanning the entire corpus of social science research, assessing which findings remain robust, which appear outdated, and which demand new investigation. In time, such a system could even design and carry out these studies itself, ensuring that for every major social issue we maintain current, high-quality evidence—not just globally, but tailored to the cultural contexts in which people live. *Cultural variation* matters: the same intervention can have profoundly different effects depending on norms, values, and historical experience. With AI able to account for such differences and keep our knowledge base perpetually updated, the acceleration of social understanding would be unlike anything in history. The scale of the progress this implies can hardly be overstated—and, crucially, it is no longer an unrealistic vision.

If AI can tell us, for instance, which interventions have reliably reduced recidivism across 20 countries, which education reforms have most improved literacy, or which urban design changes most enhance social trust, we are no longer bound to the slow, piecemeal accumulation of isolated findings. We can move from *knowledge-as-archive* to *knowledge-as-active-instrument*.

And just imagine if AI, instead of relying solely on surveys and self-reports, could harvest data directly from our digital activity and history. This would yield far more reliable insights. We know from experience in digital marketing that people rarely misrepresent themselves when they search online—the queries typed into a search bar often reveal more about real intentions, preferences, and anxieties than any questionnaire could capture. In such a system, what is pushed through the keyboard becomes a record of actual behavior and choice, unfiltered by social desirability or selective memory. Of course, all of this would have to be done in an ethically responsible way—ensuring that data is never linked to identifiable individuals—to avoid the kind of surveillance-state "1984 scenario" that many AI experts, including Tegmark (2017), have explicitly warned against.

This does not mean abandoning disciplinary identity or the human judgment that gives social research meaning. Rather, it means leveraging AI's strengths—comprehensive literature mapping, unbiased citation tracking, and methodological pattern detection—to do what humans alone have never been able to do: see the whole intellectual landscape in real time. The challenge will be to integrate these capabilities without outsourcing the very interpretive and ethical functions that define our role.

Case Box: From Jargon to Problem-Solving: The Social Sciences Reimagined

Imagine a future in which the social sciences are no longer rewarded for producing dense jargon, abstract theoretical posturing, or the protection of disciplinary turf. In this vision, the worth of research is measured not by its ability to signal belonging to a "tribe" but by its capacity to solve clearly defined societal problems using the scientific method. This would mark a decisive break from the current era, which future historians might describe as the "formative" or even "immature" stage of the social sciences—an era in which much intellectual energy was expended on debating conceptual definitions while urgent problems persisted unresolved (Becher & Trowler, 2001; Fanelli, 2010; Sarewitz, 2016).

The transition would be radical. Papers would be stripped of "fluff," and their core would be distilled to three things:

1. The real research question (RQ).
2. The actual answer, supported by evidence.
3. The implications for solving the problem at hand.

This approach, it must be admitted, is, in some sense, already how critical readers work today—skimming past verbose introductions and literature reviews to find the actionable findings. But there is an inherent limitation: very few readers can (or will) re-run the statistical analyses or re-check all data sources. In practice, we often take the methodology's soundness on trust, unless replication is attempted—which remains rare in the social sciences (Ioannidis, 2005; Open Science Collaboration, 2015).

AI could change this dynamic entirely. With the capacity to replicate statistical calculations automatically, flag suspicious results, and verify whether stated conclusions follow from the data, AI could act as a universal auditor for scientific claims (Bourne et al., 2015; Fortunato et al., 2018). This would not eliminate philosophy, theory-building, or interpretive work—but these would remain firmly within their proper home in the *humanities*. Social science, meanwhile, could fulfil its original promise as a rigorous "science of society," as envisaged by Auguste Comte before he entangled his vision with religious and mystical elements (Pickering, 2009).

In such a future, prestige would be attached not to the size of the book or the length of the article, but to demonstrable societal impact, problem-solving efficiency, and the replicability of results. For any research project, we would not start by reading it, but tell the AI to show us the syllogisms and tell us if the conclusions are valid. The social sciences would become a central tool for diagnosing, intervening in, and evaluating solutions to the most pressing human challenges—an evolution that would align more closely with the expectations of policymakers, practitioners, and the public alike.

Questions for Discussion

1. How would academic incentives need to change for this vision to become reality?
2. What risks might arise from focusing exclusively on problem-solving over theory-building?
3. Could AI auditing of research methods and results create new forms of dependency or bias?
4. How might the humanities and social sciences maintain productive collaboration in such a system?

If the social sciences seize this opportunity, AI could help us move beyond entrenched limitations and reorient the field toward problem-solving at a scale that matches both the complexity and the urgency of our time.

10.3.2 Methodological Renewal

The methodological landscape of the social sciences is already more diverse than many realize, spanning surveys, ethnography, experimental design, econometrics, archival research, and computational modeling. Yet, most of these methods were designed for a world where data was scarce, expensive to collect, and slow to process. AI alters that equation fundamentally—not just by automating existing processes, but by making possible forms of data collection and analysis that were impractical, if not impossible, before.

AI-enhanced data collection now extends far beyond digital surveys and public datasets. Large-scale text mining allows researchers to analyze millions of documents—newspaper archives, court transcripts, legislative debates—within minutes. Image recognition systems can classify urban landscapes from satellite photographs, map changes in housing patterns, or detect protest activity from social media photos (Krizhevsky et al., 2012; Sun et al., 2017). Network mapping algorithms can reconstruct entire social or organizational ecosystems from fragmented communication records, revealing structures of influence invisible to conventional survey techniques (Lazer et al., 2009). These capacities enable a shift from *snapshot observation* to continuous, real-time monitoring of social phenomena.

Accelerated analysis through machine learning further compresses the research cycle. Automated coding systems, trained on human-coded datasets, can classify text, video, and audio with a speed and consistency no human team could match (Grimmer & Stewart, 2013). Sentiment analysis, topic modeling, and entity recognition make it feasible to process the qualitative equivalent of "big data." This means research questions that once required years of manual coding—such as tracking policy framing across decades—can now be answered in days, and probably much faster in the coming years. Crucially, this acceleration allows for iterative research design, where early findings can be quickly tested, refined, and redeployed.

Predictive modeling in social contexts presents both promise and caution. Machine learning can identify patterns that correlate strongly with future events—predicting voter turnout, migration flows, or the diffusion of misinformation (Salganik et al., 2020). However, prediction is not explanation, and predictive accuracy can collapse when systems are deployed outside their training conditions, especially in dynamic human environments where behavior is influenced by feedback effects and shifting norms (Yarkoni & Westfall, 2017). This is why predictive tools must be paired with causal inference frameworks and theory-driven modeling, ensuring that the outputs are interpretable and ethically defensible.

Finally, the continuing need for qualitative depth cannot be overstated—for now. AI can mine vast cultural corpora, but it still cannot conduct a life-history interview, detect irony in a local dialect, or understand how a gesture changes meaning between two villages twenty kilometers apart. Yet these limits may not last. Developments are moving quickly, and capabilities once thought uniquely human are beginning to shift. The oft-cited observation by Small (2009) that contextual interpretation remains a human comparative advantage was made long before the current wave of generative AI—indeed, before modern AI as we know it existed. AI-generated classifications can already suggest where to look, and it may not be long before they also begin to close the gap in understanding what it means.

Methodological renewal, then, is not about replacing traditional tools but about embedding them in an *AI-augmented research cycle*. Data collection becomes more expansive and less costly; analysis becomes faster and more adaptable; predictive models offer early warnings; and qualitative insight anchors the whole process in meaning. The social sciences that thrive in this environment will be those that treat AI not as a threat to craft, but as an instrument for extending its reach—without sacrificing the interpretive, ethical, and relational competencies that make the field indispensable.

10.3.3 From Disciplinary Islands to Theoretical Continents

For more than a century, the social sciences have been organized into distinct academic territories—economics, sociology, political science, anthropology, psychology—each with its own journals, methods, and dominant theories. These boundaries have facilitated specialization, but they have also made it difficult to address problems that are fundamentally cross-cutting, such as climate change, migration, inequality, or digital governance. AI offers a means of integration that was previously impractical: the ability to combine and analyze data from multiple fields at once, at scale, and in real time.

AI-enabled cross-field integration is already visible in projects that combine economic transaction data with psychological survey responses and social network structures to understand consumer behavior more holistically (Hofman et al., 2017). Natural language processing can mine legislative records for political framing, link them to economic indicators, and model public opinion shifts through social media sentiment—all within a single analytical framework. In the study of urban resilience, AI can merge geospatial satellite imagery with ethnographic interviews and public health records, producing models that capture both material infrastructure and social vulnerability (Jean et al., 2016). This capacity to merge heterogeneous datasets promises a more integrated picture of social life than any one discipline can provide.

Yet interdisciplinary integration carries risks. The rush to merge datasets and methods can collapse into descriptive "*data mashups*" with little explanatory power, or produce spurious correlations if variables from different domains are not meaningfully related. The challenge is to ensure that integration is theory-guided rather than opportunistic—anchored in questions that demand multi-domain evidence, not just enabled by it. Without a clear conceptual framework, interdisciplinary projects risk eroding theoretical coherence.

Case examples illustrate both the potential and the pitfalls:

- In public health policy, machine learning models that combine epidemiological data with mobility and demographic records have provided early warnings for pandemic spread, influencing government interventions (Kraemer et al., 2020).
- In environmental economics, AI-assisted synthesis of climate science data, economic projections, and political feasibility models has led to more realistic carbon pricing strategies (Ricke et al., 2018).
- Conversely, in some AI-driven "predictive policing" programs, integration of crime reports with socioeconomic profiles has reproduced and amplified existing biases—showing how interdisciplinary data fusion can harm rather than help if ethical safeguards are absent (Lum & Isaac, 2016).

Breaking disciplinary silos through AI integration, then, is less about dissolving boundaries entirely and more about creating bridges. These bridges should allow insights and data to flow across domains while preserving the conceptual rigor that makes each discipline valuable. If done well, AI could help the social sciences evolve from a set of parallel conversations into a more coordinated, problem-oriented enterprise—better equipped to tackle the complex, interconnected challenges of the twenty-first century.

This is why the present book begins not with AI tools or data techniques, but with the most robust theoretical foundation we have for understanding human behavior: evolutionary theory. Without such a unifying anchor, interdisciplinary integration risks degenerating into a shapeless collection of correlations. Evolutionary theory offers more than just one "perspective" among many—it is the only scientific paradigm that explains the origins, constraints, and adaptive logic of human cognition, emotion, and social organization.

The earlier chapters, therefore, laid out findings that align with this evolutionary orientation, not as scattered insights but as evidence that such a foundation already exists. The first layer of the social sciences is evolutionary theory itself, resting on three interlocking axioms:

1. Variation—Individuals within a population differ in traits.
2. Inheritance—Some of these differences are heritable and passed from one generation to the next.
3. Differential survival and reproduction—Traits that increase fitness become more common because their bearers are more likely to survive and reproduce.

These axioms "work" because they are not optional assumptions or disciplinary preferences—they are universal principles observable across all living systems. Whether in the evolution of physical traits, social behaviors, or cultural practices, the same logic applies: differences emerge, some persist, and others spread depending on the conditions of survival and competition. For humans, this includes not only biological traits but also psychological predispositions and cultural norms. By rooting the social sciences in these principles, we anchor them in the same explanatory logic that unites biology, ecology, and neuroscience.

The second layer consists of the established disciplines—economics, sociology, political science, psychology, and anthropology. Each offers specialized methods and insights, but their findings can only accumulate into a coherent science if they are consistent with the evolutionary foundation. Without that consistency, disciplines risk producing elegant models that are disconnected from reality, as neoclassical economics did by assuming rational utility-maximizers instead of evolved, boundedly rational organisms.

AI can help bridge these two layers when guided by this framework. Its power to scan vast literatures, detect hidden connections, and test coherence across domains makes it a natural integrator of disciplinary insights. Yet without an evolutionary anchor, such integration would collapse into descriptive "data mashups" with little explanatory force.

This layered model also clarifies the relationship between the social sciences and the humanities. They should not be seen as overlapping fields, but as complementary. The humanities define meaning, values, and desired futures, while the social sciences—grounded in evolutionary theory—address how problems can be solved within those normative frameworks. AI strengthens both sides of this division: it multiplies the analytic power of the social sciences, while leaving to the humanities the task of guiding which questions matter.

It is worth noting, however, that the ambition to create integrative frameworks for the social sciences is not new. Several traditions have already attempted to bridge disciplines and offer unifying perspectives. In broad strokes, these include:

1. *Integrated Causal or "Evolutionary Actor" Models*—John Tooby and Leda Cosmides critiqued the Standard Social Science Model (SSSM) and proposed an Integrated Model (IM), blending evolved psychological mechanisms with cultural and environmental factors. This layered logic

recognized that human behavior emerges from the interaction between inherited programming and cultural inputs.[6]

2. *Multilevel and Neo-Evolutionary Frameworks*—Gerhard Lenski's Ecological-Evolutionary Theory (EET) connected environmental structures, technology, population, and ideology to explain social stratification and change. It reflected an evolutionary orientation but at a largely macro-sociological level.[7]
3. *Evolutionary Game and Network Models in Complex Systems*—Complexity theorists have developed multi-layer models in which one layer simulates strategic interactions and another models evolving network structures. These offer useful methodological parallels but often remain abstracted from lived social behavior.[8]
4. *Historical Calls for Unified Social Science*—In the nineteenth century, figures such as Auguste Comte, Karl Marx, and Herbert Spencer sought to construct a single science of society. The eventual division into disciplines was as much institutional and political as conceptual, leaving the project of integration unfinished.[9]

These efforts, while important, have each remained partial or incomplete. The following table summarizes their strengths, their limits, and how The Evolutionary Scaffold Model seeks to advance beyond them (Table 10.3).

[6] Key references include *The Adapted Mind: Evolutionary Psychology and the Generation of Culture* (Barkow et al., 1992), which introduced the IM to a broader audience, and their programmatic essays "The Psychological Foundations of Culture" (Tooby & Cosmides, 1992) and *Evolutionary Psychology: A Primer* (Cosmides & Tooby, 1997). These works argue that human behavior and cultural forms must be understood as products of evolved psychological mechanisms interacting with local environments.

[7] Key references include Gerhard Lenski's *Power and Privilege: A Theory of Social Stratification* (1966), which first outlined the ecological-evolutionary approach, and his later synthesis *Ecological-Evolutionary Theory: Principles and Applications* (2005). These works argue that technological innovation, environmental constraints, and population dynamics interact to shape patterns of social organization, inequality, and cultural change.

[8] Key references include John Maynard Smith's *Evolution and the Theory of Games* (1982), which established the use of game-theoretic models in evolutionary contexts, and subsequent extensions into social dynamics such as Robert Axelrod's *The Evolution of Cooperation* (1984). More recent work applies network science to evolutionary games, for example, Martin Nowak's *Evolutionary Dynamics* (2006) and the synthesis by Nowak and Highfield (2011). These studies demonstrate how strategic interaction and network structure co-evolve, though often at a level of abstraction that distances them from empirical social behavior.

[9] Key references include Auguste Comte's *Cours de philosophie positive* (1830–1842; *The Course in Positive Philosophy*), which first proposed sociology as the "queen of the sciences"; Karl Marx's *Zur Kritik der politischen Ökonomie* (1859; *A Contribution to the Critique of Political Economy*), which framed society through materialist and historical dynamics; and Herbert Spencer's *The Principles of Sociology* (1876–1896), which attempted a comprehensive evolutionary account of social institutions. These works shared the ambition of creating a unified science of society, though institutional specialization and political currents fragmented the project.

Table 10.3 Alternative integrative frameworks and the evolutionary scaffold model

Approach	What it means	Why it is insufficient as a complete scientific system	How the scaffold model improves it
Standard Social Science Model (SSSM) vs. Integrated Model (Tooby & Cosmides, 1992)	The SSSM treated culture as largely autonomous from biology. The Integrated Model argued that evolved psychological mechanisms underlie cultural learning, making biology indispensable	Valuable for psychology and anthropology, but remains discipline-specific. It does not provide an overarching ontology for all social sciences (e.g., economics or political science)	Extends this logic across all social sciences, requiring consistency with evolutionary foundations (variation, inheritance, selection)
Ecological-Evolutionary Theory (Lenski, 2005)	Societal change explained by interaction of technology, environment, population, and ideology. Focused on macro-level structures and stratification	Rich for historical sociology, but limited: it does not integrate individual psychology or micro-level cognition, nor does it provide an epistemological anchor linking disciplines	Adds biology and psychology as foundations, ensuring micro–macro coherence and offering a unifying ontology rather than a descriptive macro framework

(continued)

Table 10.3 (continued)

Approach	What it means	Why it is insufficient as a complete scientific system	How the scaffold model improves it
Evolutionary Game Theory & Network Models	Uses mathematics to simulate how cooperation, norms, or institutions evolve under selective pressures in structured populations	Useful for modeling dynamics but abstracted from lived human behavior. It lacks grounding in biology and culture simultaneously, and often produces formalism without explanatory depth	Contextualizes these tools in Layer 2 if consistent with Layer 1's evolutionary logic, avoiding empty formalism
Comte's Positivism/ Early Unified Social Science	Aimed at a "science of society" modeled on physics, emphasizing law-like regularities and empirical observation	Historically important, but relied on physical analogies (mechanics, equilibrium) rather than biological/ evolutionary realities. Failed to capture adaptive, path-dependent human behavior	Revives the ambition but anchors it in biology and evolution, not physics—providing both a cumulative foundation and adaptability for AI integration

(continued)

Table 10.3 (continued)

Approach	What it means	Why it is insufficient as a complete scientific system	How the scaffold model improves it
Actor-Network Theory (Latour, 2005)	Argues that social phenomena emerge from networks of humans and non-humans (technologies, artifacts, environments)	Provides descriptive richness but lacks explanatory parsimony. It resists generalization and offers little cumulative scientific progress	Retains the value of context and networks in Layer 2, but requires consistency with evolutionary principles, preventing theoretical fragmentation
Complexity Science Approaches	Uses system dynamics and non-linear models to explain emergent social order	Powerful descriptively but often atheoretical: models can be elegant yet disconnected from evolved human psychology or historical constraints	Grounds complexity insights in evolutionary mechanisms, ensuring emergent dynamics remain tied to human cognition, adaptation, and history

Seen in this light, AI is not a replacement for theory but a force multiplier for the right kind of theory—one that is empirically grounded, biologically informed, and evolutionarily coherent. The task ahead is to ensure that as AI accelerates our ability to connect data across domains, it does so in service of a framework capable of making sense of it all.

10.3.4 From Empirical Overload to Interpretive Leadership

AI's most visible contribution to the social sciences has been its capacity to supercharge empirical work. Vast corpora of text, images, audio, and sensor data can now be processed in seconds. Natural language processing maps thematic trends across decades of scholarship, sentiment analysis tracks opinion shifts across millions of posts, and computer vision codes facial expressions or environmental changes with remarkable consistency. In this sense, AI functions as an empirical engine—able to harvest, clean, and organize evidence at scales no human team could match.

Yet acceleration alone does not make for better science. Without theory, context, and historical awareness, machine-generated findings risk producing an illusion of understanding (Calude & Longo, 2017). Social systems are culturally embedded, and ignoring norms, trust, and identity can lead to well-intentioned but damaging policies.

Recent history illustrates this point. Globalization was pursued with an emphasis on economic efficiency while neglecting its cultural and social underpinnings. Corporations shifted production to low-wage economies, weakening domestic workforces (Rodrik, 2011). Political elites promoted borderless ideals without reckoning with frictions of belonging, eroding Western working classes while strengthening Asian competitiveness (Milanović, 2016; Piketty, 2014). The outcome was not only economic dislocation but also political polarization.

AI now presents a similar dilemma. Its benefits may accrue to a handful of global firms, amplifying inequality (Brynjolfsson & McAfee, 2014; Zuboff, 2019). If heavily taxed, these firms may relocate, undermining fiscal stability (OECD, 2020). Here again, the risk is that technical innovation outpaces the cultural and institutional frameworks that give it legitimacy.

The way forward lies not in isolationism but in renewing *social contracts*. Culture anchors people in shared traditions and identities, and prolonged detachment from those environments produces disconnection and resentment (Inglehart & Welzel, 2005; Putnam, 2007). A viable contract must therefore balance rights and duties in ways that are both economically viable and culturally grounded. It cannot depend on taxation alone to fund disengagement from work, nor on firms extracting value without reinvestment. Instead, it requires individuals contributing to diverse forms of labor and corporations accepting responsibility toward the societies that sustain them.

And here, if you will indulge me, I want to allow a moment of speculation—perhaps even of wishful thinking. For this is not only an analysis but also a book, and books have room for imagining what could be, not only what is. Let me, then, offer a speculative scenario that illustrates what a renewed contract might look like in practice:

Case in a Box: The QR Code on the Door

On a grey autumn morning in Kraków, students arriving at the Jagiellonian University noticed something unusual taped to the ancient oak doors of the library: a large QR code. It carried no title, no slogan—only the square mosaic of black and white. Out of curiosity, some scanned it with their phones. What appeared on their screens was not an advertisement or a prank, but a document:

"A Social Contract for the Age of AI.

I. **Duties of Individuals**

§1. Every citizen must contribute meaningfully to society, whether through paid labor, caregiving, education, creativity, or civic participation.
§2. Every citizen must cultivate intellectual resilience, strengthening judgment, critical thinking, and empathy rather than yielding to passivity in the face of automation.
§3. Every citizen has a duty to learn, exercise, and renew their cultural traditions—through language, arts, rituals, and community life—so that culture remains a living practice rather than a relic.
§5. Every citizen must reject corruption in daily life, refusing nepotism, favoritism, or the buying and selling of influence.
§5. No citizen may claim social benefits without first fulfilling their social duties; rights presuppose obligations.

II. **Duties of Corporations and Economic Institutions**

§6. Every corporation must acknowledge that profits rest on social and cultural foundations and reinvest a fair share of gains into the communities that sustain them.
§7. Every corporation must avoid exploitation of labor, data, and natural resources, ensuring that technological innovation contributes to long-term human welfare.
§8. Every corporation must guarantee transparency in the design and deployment of AI systems, respecting the dignity, privacy, and agency of all citizens.
§9. Every corporation must abandon bureaucratic self-preservation: efficiency gains from AI must reduce red tape and paperwork, not multiply them.
§10. Every corporation must adopt a policy of zero tolerance for corruption, enforced by independent oversight and public accountability.

III. **Duties of the State**

§11. The state must guarantee security, opportunity, and justice, ensuring equal access to education, healthcare, and civic participation, conditional upon the fulfillment of civic duties by citizens.
§12. The state must distribute the gains of automation fairly so that reduced compulsory labor leads to greater opportunities for leisure,

learning, and community. Access to these gains is contingent on demonstrable contribution.

§13. The state must regulate AI and digital platforms to serve human dignity and collective care, preventing monopolistic capture or authoritarian misuse.

§14. The state must dismantle bureaucratic overload: no citizen should spend more time navigating forms than solving problems; automation must simplify governance and make decisions transparent.

§15. The state must establish robust anticorruption mechanisms, including independent courts, free media, and civic watchdogs, to ensure that no officeholder is above scrutiny.

§16 . The state must guarantee universities as politically independent institutions, free from party influence, ideological coercion, or government interference in teaching and research.

IV. **Mutual Commitments**

§17. Citizens commit to contribute; society commits to reward contributions fairly, whether through income, recognition, or support for caregiving.

§18. Citizens commit to sustaining and renewing their culture; institutions commit to protecting and transmitting cultural traditions across generations.

§19. Corporations commit to social responsibility; governments commit to provide stable frameworks for fair competition and innovation.

§20. States commit to transparency and legitimacy; citizens commit to participation and trust, so long as institutions remain accountable.

§21. All parties affirm that culture anchors belonging and continuity: no economic contract can endure without shared identity, fairness, and meaning."

By midday, a crowd had formed around the doors. Some students read passages aloud, their voices echoing across the square. "*No artificial layers of reporting—finally!*" shouted one, laughing. "*If only ministries would listen.*" Others frowned. A professor shook his head: "*A noble ideal. But who enforces it? Independent courts? Free media? In this country?*" An older man muttered from the back: "*Corporations don't reinvest. They extract. Unless forced, this is wishful thinking.*"

Still, the energy was palpable. Phones glowed with the text as people forwarded it to friends, colleagues, and family members. Social media tagged it instantly as *The Kraków Contract*. Commentators compared it to Martin Luther's theses—posted not on parchment this time, but in pixels, sparking fierce arguments in the square before any government had time to respond.

Would this digital manifesto vanish into the churn of online noise, or could it catalyze a genuine debate about how societies organize in the age of AI? For that day at least, the question was alive.

Questions for Reflection

1. Which duties in *The Kraków Contract* appear most realistic to implement, and which risk remaining purely aspirational?
2. How can corruption and bureaucratic excess be dismantled in societies where they are systemically embedded?
3. Should corporations be assigned civic duties comparable to those of citizens and states, or is legal compliance sufficient?
4. To what extent can a social contract enforce cultural obligations—such as learning and exercising shared traditions—without sliding into coercion?
5. Does symbolic protest, like the posting of *The Kraków Contract*, genuinely shift political or institutional realities, or is sustained collective action required?

The discussion around *The Kraków Contract* underscores a central lesson: frameworks and rules alone are not enough. What matters is how they are interpreted, adapted, and embedded in lived culture. A contract can inspire, but its endurance depends on human judgment—how duties and rights are balanced, how values are upheld, and how meaning is renewed across generations.

In this emerging division of labor, machines uncover correlations, but humans must interpret their meaning. An algorithm may reveal that urban design shapes civic trust, but only human judgment can decide whether those designs fit local traditions. AI can identify effective education models, but their success depends on cultural adaptation. Without this interpretive leadership—anchoring innovation in dignity, cultural integrity, and democratic legitimacy—AI risks deepening divides rather than renewing societies.

Interpretive leadership, then, is not storytelling for its own sake. It is the stewardship of knowledge in ways that safeguard meaning, responsibility, and long-term competitiveness. Poorly contextualized findings can stigmatize communities or reinforce stereotypes (Boyd & Crawford, 2012). Well-contextualized findings, by contrast, can help rebuild trust in institutions and strengthen social resilience.

AI can make the social sciences faster, broader, and empirically sharper. But only human scholars, grounded in history, philosophy, and ethics, can ensure that these new tools serve human flourishing rather than erode it.

10.3.5 Guarding Against Epistemic Dependency

As AI systems grow more capable, the temptation to outsource not only analysis but also judgment increases. What began with the automation of routine tasks—such as data cleaning or literature summarization—has expanded into machine-assisted theoretical synthesis, causal modeling, and policy recommendation. These tools undoubtedly enhance research capacity, yet they also introduce a new vulnerability: epistemic dependency, in which researchers accept AI outputs as authoritative without sufficient critical scrutiny.

This dependency is not purely technical but intellectual. When model outputs are treated as "neutral" or "objective," scholars risk absorbing the biases embedded in training data and model architectures (Bender et al., 2021). For instance, a model trained primarily on English-language literature will inevitably reproduce the assumptions, methodological conventions, and historical context of that corpus. *Sentiment-analysis models* may overrepresent demographics that are more active online, leading to distorted conclusions about public opinion. Even descriptive outputs—such as topic clusters or citation networks—are shaped by preprocessing choices that privilege some framings over others.

Guarding against this requires epistemic resilience: the ability to question, verify, and triangulate machine-generated claims with alternative methods and sources. This does not mean rejecting AI but cultivating reflexivity—explicitly recognizing how tools shape findings, and considering how results might differ under other methodological or cultural conditions (Harding, 1995; Jasanoff, 2017).

Such resilience must be grounded in prior competence. Just as children must learn arithmetic before using a calculator, researchers must first develop independent skills in reading, reasoning, and methodological practice. Without first-hand engagement with primary works, debates, and methods, there is no benchmark against which to evaluate AI outputs. A scholar relying solely on machine-generated summaries risks operating in an echo chamber of preprocessed content.

Historians such as Ferguson (2019) have suggested the importance of a "cloister" model in early training: shielding students temporarily from mediation, and requiring close reading of foundational texts, extended argument, and live debate. This form of immersion exposes students to the complexity, contradictions, and insights of earlier thought. In recent decades, however, many universities have shifted away from this practice, increasingly replacing primary sources with digests, anthologies, and summaries. The result has been a thinning of intellectual memory and a greater reliance on second-hand interpretations.

To meet the new challenge of epistemic dependency in the AI era, this cloister principle could be broadened into *off-grid systems of thought*. These are deliberate contexts—educational, institutional, medical, or civic—where AI is restricted or banned for a period, not as nostalgia but as training for independent reasoning:

- In schools, this means banning screens in kindergartens and restricting smartphones in high schools, ensuring that students first learn how to reason, argue, and write without digital shortcuts.
- In government or corporate offices, it could mean periodic *syllogism retreats*, where employees must reconstruct arguments manually on boards or paper before returning to AI-assisted drafting—guaranteeing that decision-makers understand the logic of their own policies.
- In healthcare, physicians might prescribe temporary *digital detoxes* for young people whose cognition and attention have been damaged by constant online exposure, much like prescribing a rehabilitation program.
- In academia, universities could designate *off-grid weeks* during which students are required to work without AI tools, practicing the friction of constructing arguments unaided (Table 10.4)[10]

If scholars and citizens are to resist epistemic dependency, such off-grid systems must become as integral to intellectual life as laboratories are to natural science. Rigorous reading, debate, and manual argument construction are not optional add-ons but the very conditions of epistemic independence. AI may accelerate integration, but without *off-grid spaces*, it risks producing a monoculture of efficient but shallow reasoning—knowledge that is quick to compute but detached from human depth, responsibility, and lived realities.

Epistemic resilience, in this sense, is not only a research requirement but a societal one. A community unable to think without its machines—unable to question the knowledge it consumes—risks losing both intellectual independence and the capacity for collective self-governance.

[10] This concept could be extended to the faculty level as well. Colleagues might convene in structured *off-grid colloquia*, where discussions are based solely on shared readings, handwritten notes, and direct debate—without digital tools, slides, or PowerPoint. Organized in the same spirit as *syllogism retreats*, such gatherings would restore the primacy of argument, reasoning, and intellectual exchange as lived practices rather than mediated performances.

Table 10.4 Forms of off-grid thinking and their purpose

Off-Grid action	What it involves	Why it is needed
Childhood Learning Without ScreensChildhood Learning Without Screens	Restricting tablets, phones, and AI tools in early schooling. Focus on books, play, handwriting, and dialogue	Builds attention, memory, and reasoning before exposure to digital shortcuts
Adolescent Phone Bans	Prohibiting smartphones in secondary education, encouraging debates and oral exams	Protects focus, reduces distraction, and trains argumentation
Syllogism Retreats in Institutions	Suspending AI drafting; reconstructing arguments manually (premises → conclusion)	Ensures clarity of reasoning, prevents blind acceptance of machine logic
Digital Detox Prescriptions	Temporary withdrawal from social media, replaced by reading, nature, or group discussion	Restores mental health, reduces anxiety, rebuilds baseline cognition
Academic Off-Grid Weeks	Universities forbid AI writing tools for assignments during designated weeks	Reinforces intellectual independence and resilience in students
Community Reflection Circles	Device-free civic forums for debate and argument reconstruction	Rebuilds public reasoning and collective accountability

10.3.6 A Framework for Reappraisal

For the social sciences to remain relevant in an era when AI surpasses humans in data processing, they must be more deliberate about how knowledge is generated, interpreted, and applied. Reappraisal here involves more than adopting new technical tools; it requires rethinking the intellectual posture of the field.

A first element is *reflexivity*: the discipline of questioning underlying assumptions, categories, and research frames (Bourdieu & Wacquant, 1992). AI can highlight patterns or correlations that were previously unseen, but it cannot determine whether those patterns are meaningful or ethically justified. Reflexivity ensures awareness of the cultural, historical, and institutional filters that shape questions before they enter a dataset. Future AI systems may be able to generate, within seconds, a list of the assumptions underpinning any given study. In some traditions—particularly formal and mathematical ones, such as parts of economics—assumptions are already stated explicitly. In many other areas, however, assumptions remain implicit, whether because they are taken for granted within disciplinary communities or overlooked by authors themselves. A valuable application of AI would be to make these assumptions visible across research fields, thereby promoting transparency and critical engagement.

Among these assumptions, the most consequential is the model of human nature. This model should be grounded not in ideology but in empirical evidence from evolutionary theory and biology, reflecting how humans actually behave. Human nature is not static; it changes over time under the influence of environmental pressures and cultural developments. Yet at a deeper level, stripped of sensory differences and material circumstances, what binds us together is a shared inner life: thoughts, feelings, and the recognition that we are all finite beings. The existential fact of mortality gives us a universal frame: whatever our cultural differences, every human faces the question of how to live meaningfully within a finite span.[11] There is increasing evidence that humans now play a role in shaping aspects of their own evolution, through technology, medicine, and social structures (Laland et al., 2010). Recognizing this dynamic character, and updating assumptions accordingly, should become a standard expectation in future research.

A second element is *interdisciplinary synthesis*. AI makes it possible to merge datasets and analytical frameworks across economics, sociology, psychology, anthropology, and beyond, enabling perspectives that would be difficult to achieve by human effort alone (Kitchin, 2014). Yet synthesis should not mean collapsing different epistemologies into a uniform method. The challenge is to preserve the interpretive strengths of each discipline while allowing AI to surface connections that might otherwise remain hidden. Achieving this requires conscious design: shared vocabularies, collaboration protocols, and infrastructures that enable both cross-fertilization and disciplinary integrity.

An associated challenge is *terminological inflation*. Much of the literature, particularly in the Anglo-American tradition, has a tendency to introduce new terms for phenomena that are already well understood under other names. This practice often reflects professional incentives rather than conceptual necessity, making it harder to accumulate knowledge across traditions. By contrast, traditions such as the German school, grounded in the notion of *Verstehen*, have long emphasized the importance of clearly defining key terms and situating them within intellectual history (Gadamer, 1975; Habermas,

[11] It is precisely because of this unity—this common understanding of what it means to be human—that books which capture such essentialism become so dear to us. Perhaps nowhere is this clearer than in literature, where a novel can hold up a mirror to our shared condition. For my own part, I think first and foremost of W. Somerset Maugham's *Of Human Bondage* (1915), which remains a profound meditation on vulnerability, choice, and the limits of freedom.

1984/1987).[12] Correcting this trend requires renewed attention to definitional precision, transparency about conceptual genealogy, and a willingness to place new contributions within broader theoretical lineages.

Here, AI can play a constructive role. By scanning large corpora of academic texts, machine learning tools can identify overlapping terms, trace their usage across disciplines, and visualize their conceptual proximity—much like a dynamic Venn diagram of scholarly language. Such tools could even recommend consolidation, suggesting when a new concept is redundant, vague, or insufficiently distinct from existing categories. Far from stifling creativity, this process could strengthen the theoretical coherence of the social sciences by reducing fragmentation, aligning related contributions, and unifying terminology into a more cumulative body of knowledge. In this way, AI would not replace conceptual work but act as a safeguard against inflation, helping to discipline the language of theory itself.

The third element is *human-led interpretation*. Even the most sophisticated AI outputs remain dependent on human judgment, ethics, and contextualization. This entails resisting the idea of fully automated conclusions and instead embedding social science within wider public debates. AI-generated insights must be translated into narratives and policies that are intelligible, contestable, and socially grounded (Flyvbjerg, 2001). Ethical oversight in this sense should not be reactive, stepping in only when errors occur, but proactive: setting clear rules for what AI systems can and cannot do. The ambition is comparable to an expanded version of Asimov's "*Three Laws of Robotics*" (Asimov, 1942/1991), adapted for the realities of contemporary governance.

To make such principles effective, they must be articulated not just as abstract ideals but as enforceable rules. The following set of *Five Foundational Rules for AI* in Society is offered as a starting point. These rules emphasize human agency, ecological sustainability, cultural integrity, transparency, and coordinated governance (Table 10.5).

Current developments highlight the urgency of such principles. Autonomous systems capable of lethal action are already under development (Altmann & Sauer, 2017; Sharkey, 2019). This makes international agreements—comparable to the Geneva Conventions or nuclear non-proliferation treaties—more important than ever. Yet the effectiveness of such agreements is constrained by enduring features of human interaction, including mistrust,

[12] Verstehen, literally "understanding," was developed in German philosophy and sociology in the late 19th and early twentieth centuries, particularly in the works of Wilhelm Dilthey and Max Weber. It emphasizes interpretive understanding of social action, grounded in the meanings individuals attach to their behavior. In this tradition, careful definition of concepts and attention to their historical lineage are considered essential, since social inquiry must clarify not only what is being studied but how it is understood within cultural and intellectual contexts.

Table 10.5 Five foundational rules for AI

Rule No	Principle	Description	Key references
1	Preserve Human Agency and Planetary Sustainability	AI systems must keep final decisions that affect people's well-being, life opportunities, and the integrity of their communities and environments under accountable human stewardship. They must protect the survival and flourishing of all living organisms and avoid irreversible ecosystem harm	Rockström et al. (2009); Bryson (2018)
2	Prohibit Autonomous Lethal Force	AI must not independently decide to kill or harm humans or other living beings, including in military, policing, wildlife management, or security contexts	Altmann and Sauer (2017); Sharkey (2019)
3	Respect and Protect Cultural Integrity	AI must acknowledge and safeguard distinct cultural, linguistic, and historical identities, avoiding actions that erase, homogenize, or manipulate cultures	UNESCO (2021)
4	Mandate Transparency of Assumptions and Methods	AI systems must clearly disclose data sources, key assumptions (including assumptions about human nature), and methodological constraints for meaningful scrutiny	Mitchell (2019)
5	Prioritize Global Coordination Over Competitive Escalation	AI development should follow enforceable international agreements that prevent an ethical "race to the bottom" and empower neutral bodies to act against violations, similar to nuclear non-proliferation regimes	Cave and ÓhÉigeartaigh (2019)

competition, and the pursuit of strategic advantage (Pinker, 2011). Without enforceable international mechanisms, the trajectory of AI is likely to remain shaped by short-term incentives rather than long-term human and ecological stability.

Taken together, reflexivity, interdisciplinary synthesis, and human-led interpretation form a framework for reappraisal. In this framework, AI is not an autonomous decision-maker but a collaborator, whose outputs are interpreted through the values and traditions of the social sciences. AI cannot resolve every epistemic or ethical challenge, but it can support a principled path forward—one that keeps humans at the center, not because of superior speed or precision, but because responsibility for consequences cannot be delegated.

10.4 Wisdom in a Machine Era

The scientific foundations developed earlier—evolutionary psychology, cognitive science, and cultural analysis—are not simply background. They form the compass that can orient the social sciences in a period of transition: from defending intelligence as humanity's defining trait to cultivating the reflective and ethical capacities that underpin wisdom.

For most of history, tools extended the body—hammers, wheels, plows. More recently, tools extend the mind. These cognitive technologies do not only support thought; they reshape it, determining which abilities are strengthened, which atrophy, and which forms of intelligence society rewards. Each wave of progress has shifted cognitive labor outward into systems. Gains in speed and scale are evident, but losses—shortened attention, superficial reasoning, diminished autonomy—are harder to measure. We are not simply augmenting cognition; we are remaking it.

The challenge, then, is *recalibration*. The task is not to halt technology but to ensure that it does not erode the human capacities most essential for judgment and care. A renewed humanism, adapted to the machine age, would emphasize precisely these qualities. It would focus less on what AI can do, and more on what humans must preserve.

On biological measures, there is no evidence that people are becoming "less intelligent." Literacy, health, and information access have improved. Yet deeper skills—sustained reading, independent reasoning, narrative composition, reflective judgment—are becoming less common. These trends are not inevitable, but they are patterned. The issue is not capacity but cultivation: whether societies still invest in the conditions for wisdom:

Case in a Box: Cultivating Wisdom in the Machine Age
On biological measures, there is no evidence that humans are becoming less intelligent. Average IQ scores have risen for much of the twentieth century (the "Flynn Effect"), alongside gains in literacy, health, and access to information (Flynn, 2007). Yet scholars now warn of a possible reversal of these trends in some Western societies, linked not to genetic decline but to changes in environment, education, and cultural practices (Bratsberg & Rogeberg,

2018). The issue, then, is not raw capacity but cultivation: whether we still create the conditions that strengthen sustained reasoning, reflective judgment, and wisdom.

This *cultivation* can be understood along two interdependent dimensions:

1. Core Skills—*the Content of Cognitive Training*

These are the practices that build and maintain mental competence: reading extended texts for hours at a time, solving mathematical problems without technological aids, understanding the natural and physical sciences, learning multiple languages, studying geography and history, and engaging with philosophy. Each of these domains exercises different parts of the brain, supporting memory, abstraction, and conceptual integration (Dehaene, 2009; Nisbett, 2009).

2. Sustained Concentration—*the Form of Cognitive Training*

Skills alone are not enough if practiced only superficially. The deeper challenge lies in concentration: the ability to stay with demanding tasks long enough to reach mastery. In the past, societies built this through disciplined study, apprenticeships, and long-form cultural practices such as reading books, composing arguments, or practicing music. Research shows that attentional control and executive function are strengthened through sustained effort, not quick tasks (Diamond, 2013; Posner & Rothbart, 2007). In this sense, concentration is not optional—it emerges as the by-product of doing things at a high level, because mastery is impossible without it.

Today, the rise of television entertainment, video games, and AI-powered tools threatens this equilibrium. These technologies deliver instant stimulation but rarely cultivate the patience, focus, or self-regulation required for deep learning (Klingberg, 2009). If societies fail to train concentration, they risk producing generations who can access endless information but cannot hold focus long enough to build wisdom.

This framework is not a new idea. It is the product of centuries of educational and cultural development—from monasteries preserving texts through painstaking copying, to universities training students in rhetoric, mathematics, and philosophy. The question is whether we will adapt it to the digital era—or let it collapse (Fig. 10.3).

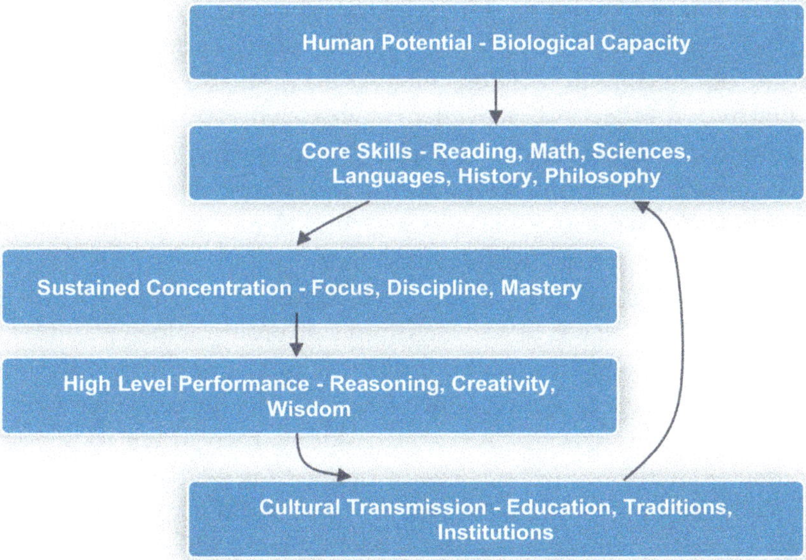

Fig. 10.3 The cultivation of human intelligence

This model shows how *core skills* and *concentration* form a feedback loop: learning substantive disciplines builds focus, and sustained focus makes mastery possible. Over time, this produces high-level performance, which is then transmitted culturally to future generations. It's common sense, really.

Questions for Discussion

1. How can education systems balance the teaching of core skills with the cultivation of sustained concentration in an era dominated by short-form digital media?
2. Should societies mandate certain disciplines (like mathematics or philosophy) precisely because they strengthen focus, even if they are not directly "useful" for every career?
3. How can we prevent new technologies such as AI from eroding concentration, while still using them as tools for learning and growth?

This framework shows that preserving human intellectual capacity is not a matter of innate ability but of disciplined cultivation—developing skills across domains and sustaining them through deep concentration. Both dimensions reinforce one another: mastery requires focus, and focus is sharpened through mastery. For centuries, this model of education and cultural transmission has allowed societies to strengthen rather than erode human potential.

The challenge today is that new technologies, while powerful, risk undermining these very conditions. The consequences extend to inequality. As AI spreads across schools, workplaces, and media, new divides emerge—not only in income but in cognition. Those adept at using AI constructively may gain large advantages; others risk dependency or passivity. As we have said before, the traditional "*digital divide*" is evolving into a *cognitive divide*: unequal access to critical autonomy, discernment, and sense-making. Zuboff (2019) warns that such asymmetries also create conditions for manipulation, with users nudged or monitored without awareness.

These shifts also reshape values. What kinds of thinking are rewarded, and which are neglected? Increasingly, speed, prompt fluency, and multitasking are prized, while moral reasoning, interpretive sensitivity, and patient reflection are pushed to the margins. Yet it is precisely here that a renewed humanism becomes relevant. AI excels in domains of calculation, storage, and surface pattern recognition, but in doing so it inadvertently highlights the areas where human strengths remain essential. What machines amplify through efficiency, humans must balance with depth. This interplay does not diminish the role of the social sciences; it clarifies it—showing that the next wave of humanism is not about competing with AI, but about cultivating the capacities that only humans can bring (Table 10.6).

The comparison underscores more than relative performance. It points to what may be lost, but also to what can be rediscovered. As machines absorb tasks once considered the pinnacle of intelligence—memory, speed, statistical recognition—humans are left with traits long treated as secondary: empathy, moral judgment, interpretive nuance, and tolerance for ambiguity. These are not weaknesses but comparative advantages. Far from rendering humanism obsolete, AI makes its principles more urgent. The very qualities once seen as slow, subjective, or inefficient now emerge as the foundation for wisdom in a machine era.

And so it is not with a negligent joy, but with a renewed seriousness, that I imagine myself next time in Paris, pausing before the statue of Montaigne and touching the shoe that so many have polished by habit. This time, the gesture would carry some extra meaning, as if to say: You are more relevant than ever, my friend.

In this sense, wisdom is not resistance to technological change but a consequence of it. As intelligence becomes externalized, what remains are the traits most aligned with humanist traditions: responsibility, care, and meaning-making. Where earlier eras emphasized IQ, often overstating its reach, AI has shown how much of what passed for intelligence was mechanical and replicable. What cannot be so easily replicated—moral judgment, reflective

Table 10.6 Comparative strengths of human vs. AI cognition

Domain of cognition	Human strength	AI strength	What we are losing	Wisdom-related qualities strengthened	Corresponds to humanism because...
Memory Recall	Moderate—filtered through meaning and emotion	Very High—exact, context-free	Emotional relevance in memory	Discernment over recall	Humanism values *meaning* over information
Pattern Recognition	Good—narrative or socially informed	Very High—statistical and syntactic	Organic sense-making in ambiguity	Narrative integration over raw pattern detection	Humans understand through *story*, not syntax
Moral Reasoning	Strong—evolved from social trial-and-error	Absent—no moral model	Moral learning through experience	Awareness, remorse, ethical restraint	Humanism centers moral autonomy and dignity
Contextual Interpretation	Strong—rich in cultural nuance and situational awareness	Weak—lacks life-world grounding	Slow, deep reasoning	Ethical framing, interpretive depth	Humanism embraces ambiguity and complexity
Empathy and Care	High—based on shared vulnerability	Absent—no emotional substrate	Emotional presence, compassion	Ethical presence, empathic imagination	Humanism affirms the centrality of *care*
Creative Association	High—non-linear, symbolic, imaginative	Limited—derivative, lacks intention	Ambiguity, metaphor, and aesthetic play	Symbolic abstraction, creative ambiguity	Arts and imagination are core humanist values
Speed of Computation	Low—slow but considered	Very High—fast and precise	Mental patience, deep work	Prudence, slow thinking	Humanism prioritizes contemplation over acceleration
Ethical Judgment	Strong—grounded in conscience and reflection	Absent—lacks moral awareness	Deliberation under tension	Moral foresight, deliberative conscience	Central to human responsibility and stewardship
Social Adaptability	High—fluid across norms and roles	Weak—brittle and scripted	Flexibility in relational roles	Role awareness, relational intelligence	Humanism honors pluralism and negotiated identity
Sense-Making under Uncertainty	Strong—integrates paradox, tension, and multiple perspectives	Weak—needs structure, lacks abstraction	Comfort with non-closure	Foresight, resilience, reflective humility	Humanism embraces *depth, not closure*

restraint—emerges more clearly. And with it, the desire to see people once more engage in lively discussion, to cultivate the spirit and joy of conversation that has marked every great culture.

This transition is not guaranteed. It depends on educational priorities, institutional design, and cultural norms. Wisdom can be cultivated, but it can also be neglected.

If the reader will indulge me one last time, a simple way to express this mathematically is through a *Wisdom Value Function (WVF)*, capturing where humans remain indispensable:

Equation 10.1: Wisdom Value Function (WVF)

$$WVF = (J \times E \times C) - A$$

Where:
J = Judgment
E = Empathy
C = Cultural understanding
A = Automation pressure

Tasks with high WVF are precisely those requiring ethical negotiation, emotional presence, and long-term foresight.

There are also evolutionary implications. As machines take over memory and reasoning, the pressures shaping human cognition may shift. Traits like interface fluency, emotional resilience, and social adaptability could grow in importance relative to arithmetic or factual recall. A movement from logic-dominant to relational and interpretive intelligence may already be underway.

Yet risks remain. AI-generated content introduces new forms of disorientation: deepfakes that blur the line between authentic and fabricated evidence, algorithmic nudges that shape choices without awareness, and the gradual erosion of sensory trust itself. Externalization of cognition is not a new phenomenon—writing displaced oral memory, maps displaced spatial recall—but the current scale, speed, and invisibility of these shifts make their consequences more difficult to track.

The danger is not simply that machines do more thinking for us, but that humans may do less for themselves. *Cognitive offloading*, if unchecked, works much like physical deconditioning. A person who once trained with heavy weights but suddenly lifts only the lightest ones will lose strength over time. In the same way, when people rely on AI for argument construction, interpretation, or judgment, their own intellectual muscles risk atrophy.

This reduction is not trivial. Critical faculties—skepticism, evaluation, logical testing—require regular exercise. Without them, individuals become more vulnerable to manipulation, much as an untrained body is more prone to injury. In a digital environment saturated with targeted persuasion, misinformation, and fraud, such vulnerability compounds the problem. Those who use less of their own reasoning capacity are not only less able to detect flaws in AI outputs, but also less resilient to the very tricks, scams, and subtle distortions that digital platforms amplify.

Convenience easily becomes dependency; dependency hardens into fragility. The paradox of cognitive outsourcing is that it increases efficiency in the short term while reducing resilience in the long term. Unless balanced with deliberate cultivation of reasoning and interpretive skill, the very tools designed to extend intelligence may leave us intellectually weaker—precisely when we most need strength.

This moment is therefore one of choice. Machines will continue to optimize and predict. Humans must retain the slower, harder work of judging, contextualizing, and caring. Wisdom in this sense is less about superiority than stewardship.

Speculative futures exist—from "digital judges" (Tegmark, 2017) to visions of a "digital Athens" (Brynjolfsson & McAfee, 2014). But their outcomes remain uncertain. What is clear is that social science must do more than analyze: it must solve real problems. Its role is to anchor cognition to meaning, and meaning to responsibility. Cognitive outsourcing is not only a technical phenomenon but a turning point in human development—one that may redefine the traits we consider most essential.

10.5 A New Humanism

Humanism first emerged during the Renaissance as a response to centuries of scholasticism and religious authority. In the medieval worldview, human beings were often seen as subordinate—defined primarily by sin and obedience, their worth measured in relation to God's will. Renaissance humanists pushed back against this yoke, affirming that people possessed dignity, rationality, and the capacity for moral self-cultivation. Thinkers like Petrarch, Erasmus, Pico della Mirandola, and Montaigne drew on classical learning to argue that ethical growth through education and reflection was not only possible but essential.

Today, as artificial intelligence increasingly frames how we think, work, and relate, we may find ourselves in a parallel position: under the shadow of technology rather than theology, once again challenged to demonstrate and defend the value of being human.

As we have tried to show in this book, to find true meaning we must be able to create a universe inside ourselves—through culture, reflection, and what the German tradition has called Bildung. What makes this ideal especially attractive now is precisely the advance of AI. As machines assume much of the analytical and procedural labor once associated with scholarship, science, and administration, human purpose is pushed toward the other side: toward interpretation, creativity, and ethical cultivation. In this way, the project of wisdom—to form oneself through culture and self-reflection—becomes not an antiquated aspiration but a renewed frontier of human possibility. Or, to recapitulate an old friend:

> « La plus grande chose du monde, c'est de savoir être à soi.» (Montaigne, Essais, Book I, Chap. 38 "De la solitude," 1580/1588). Translation: "The greatest thing in the world is to know how to belong to oneself."[13]

Montaigne's words distilled the essence of Renaissance humanism: the conviction that life's worth rests not in external authority but in inner cultivation. He stood within a broader movement that sought to recover classical wisdom and redirect it toward human dignity.

We find the same sentiment in Petrarch's Letters to the Ancient Dead, where he sought to revive Roman ideals of virtue; in Erasmus' In Praise of Folly, where he challenged dogma with irony; and in Pico della Mirandola's Oration on the Dignity of Man, where he proclaimed that humans could actively shape their own nature. For these writers, education was never about technical proficiency alone but about the moral and intellectual cultivation of the self. Humanism was not simply scholarship—it was an assertion of dignity against the notion that human beings were small and subservient in the face of divine authority. In much the same way, people today may feel diminished by hollow or meaningless work, or overwhelmed by the imposing presence of artificial intelligence. The humanist impulse—to reclaim worth through reflection, culture, and ethical growth—remains as relevant now as it was in the Renaissance.

Over time, the humanist tradition weakened. The devastation of the world wars, the rise of scientific rationalism, and critiques of Eurocentrism all contributed to the sense that humanism was parochial or naïve. The ideal of

[13] What makes Montaigne unique is not only his introspection but his ability to revive the wisdom of the past. Chap. 38 of the *Essais* is filled with references to his "friends"—classical and ecclesiastical authors such as Herodotus, Pliny, Valerius Maximus, Cornelius Nepos, Diodorus, Plutarch, Diogenes Laërtius, the Church Fathers, Socrates, Seneca, Horace, Augustine, and Cicero. As I cite Montaigne in French here, he himself cited these interlocutors in Latin, weaving them into his reflections as a living conversation across centuries.

the reflective, educated individual gradually gave way to the logics of productivity, testing, and acceleration. The Enlightenment, for all its achievements in science, governance, and human rights, also encouraged a view of people as cogs in larger systems—efficient, measurable, and interchangeable. Over the centuries, this mechanistic outlook often reduced human beings to workers or bureaucrats, performing tasks increasingly detached from meaning. From this perspective, artificial intelligence may paradoxically appear as a liberator.

By taking over much of the routine and mechanical labor, AI opens the possibility of redirecting human effort toward reflection, creativity, and cultural or relational pursuits. The truth is that human beings were never especially well suited to live as ants in vast organizational hives, nor as perfectly objective social scientists. What we do best lies elsewhere: in cultivating meaning, imagination, and wisdom. If AI can reliably generate material prosperity, then its greatest contribution may be to free people to pursue these more distinctively human capacities. This is not a retreat from production, but a revaluation of contribution: aligning prosperity with care, stewardship, and culture.

Now, in the age of artificial intelligence, humanist values return with new urgency. For centuries, humans defined themselves as rational beings—homo sapiens, the thinkers. But psychology and neuroscience have since revealed a more fragile picture: we are riddled with biases, illusions, and shortcuts, our so-called rationality closer to persuasion than to truth. AI sharpens this contrast further. In many of the very domains once seen as uniquely ours—calculation, memory, prediction—machines now outperform us.

This shift need not invite despair. Instead, it clarifies a new division of labor. What machines absorb are the functions where human limits are most predictable—bias in peer review, fatigue in literature searches, overconfidence in forecasting, or narrowness in disciplinary silos. What remains distinctively human are the capacities rooted in lived experience and responsibility: empathy, care, narrative depth, and wisdom (Table 10.7).

What, then, are wisdom and humanism in practice? At first glance, humanism and wisdom appear to come from different worlds. One is a Western intellectual tradition, shaped by Renaissance thought and secular education. The other is a broader, often spiritual category, associated with lived experience, moral discernment, and long-term judgment.

But as artificial intelligence accelerates our focus on speed, output, and external knowledge, these two concepts are converging again—along with others, like Confucian ethics—that emphasize what machines cannot replace. The reason is not simply that AI lacks complexity or processing power, but that ethics itself arises from embodied life: from vulnerability, dependency,

Table 10.7 The division of labor between humans and machines

Human role/ Faculty (Historical self-image)	What humans took pride in	AI capabilities today (% where AI outperforms humans)	What remains distinctively human
Memory & Recall	Encyclopedic knowledge; scholars, orators, clerics memorizing texts	~ 95%—AI retrieval is faster, broader, more accurate	Autobiographical memory, lived experience, emotional associations
Calculation & Logic	Precision in mathematics, reasoning, syllogistic argument	~ 99%—AI vastly exceeds human speed and accuracy	Practical judgment in ambiguous contexts; ethical reasoning
Language & Rhetoric	Persuasion, eloquence, narrative composition	~ 85%—AI generates fluent text and mimics style, but lacks depth	Existential narrative, irony, humor, authenticity grounded in life
Pattern Recognition	Detecting trends in trade, politics, nature	~ 90%—AI detects patterns across massive datasets	Deciding which patterns matter; embedding in values and culture
Prediction & Forecasting	Astrology, economics, futurology	~ 70%—Strong in data-rich, near-term contexts; weaker in deep uncertainty	Long-term vision; linking foresight to ethics and intergenerational responsibility
Creativity & Art	Producing music, literature, visual arts	~ 60%—AI generates stylistic imitation, but lacks true originality	Urgency of artistic purpose; originality tied to biography and culture
Science & Knowledge Production	Building paradigms, discovering laws of nature	~ 75%—Strong in synthesis and modeling; weak in paradigm shifts	Foundational rethinking (Kuhn); integration with moral purpose
Leadership & Governance	Decision-making, lawgiving, institutional design	~50%—AI can optimize and simulate, but lacks legitimacy	Responsibility, empathy, care; acceptance of consequences

(continued)

Table 10.7 (continued)

Human role/ Faculty (Historical self-image)	What humans took pride in	AI capabilities today (% where AI outperforms humans)	What remains distinctively human
Caring & Empathy	Nurturing, teaching, caregiving, solidarity	~15%—AI can simulate responses but lacks genuine emotional presence	Lived empathy, embodied care, moral responsibility, relational trust
Wisdom	Reflection, moral philosophy, integration of knowledge into life	~10%—AI can mimic reasoning, but not lived integration	Moral judgment, cultural stewardship, "choosing well" under uncertainty

and the shared conditions of mortality that shape moral awareness. While AI systems may resemble biological processes in their architecture, they do not share the evolutionary pressures or emotional substrates that make care and responsibility meaningful. Even if future robots were partly biological, unless they too were subject to the fragility and reciprocity of life, their "ethics" would remain a simulation rather than a lived reality.

Taken together, these traditions remind us that wisdom is not confined to one culture or era, but reflects a shared human effort to cultivate restraint, responsibility, and balance. Despite their different vocabularies, both humanism and Confucianism point to the same underlying task: shaping conduct and character so that knowledge serves life rather than power.

The key difference lies in emphasis. Western humanism tends to elevate the individual—his dignity, his conscience, his intellectual freedom. Confucianism prioritizes relational roles—how one behaves as a child, parent, ruler, or citizen. Where humanism often sees autonomy as a moral goal, Confucianism sees responsibility within a network of obligations. And yet, both traditions point toward the same destination: a virtuous life grounded in ethical awareness, education, humility, and self-improvement.

Wisdom ties these perspectives together. It is the common denominator—a trait prized in every society that has lasted. Whether framed as *phronesis* in Greek philosophy, *ren* in Confucian ethics, or *sapientia* in Latin thought, wisdom entails balancing self and society, short-term action and long-term consequence, facts and values. It is what allows people to navigate life with integrity rather than impulse, and what enables civilizations to endure without losing their moral core.

In this light, wisdom, humanism, and Confucianism are not rivals. They are complementary expressions of a deeper civilizational logic: the idea that sustained cooperation, cultural memory, and moral self-cultivation are what allow human groups to flourish across time. In an era increasingly shaped by technological displacement, re-centering these traditions may be less about identity and more about survival.

In this sense, the values of East and West are far less different than they are often made out to be. How could it be otherwise? All successful civilizations—whether in Europe, China, India, or the Islamic world—have grappled with the same human nature, faced the same existential threats, and encountered the same patterns of ambition, violence, corruption, and renewal.

Through trial and failure, they arrived at remarkably similar conclusions: that social harmony requires ethical restraint, that power demands responsibility, and that wisdom—more than brilliance or force—is the long arc of cultural survival.

These reflections suggest that wisdom—whether framed through Renaissance humanism or Confucian ethics—is not an abstract virtue but a practice that becomes more urgent as technology advances. The question is no longer whether machines can outpace us in memory, speed, or calculation—they already do. The deeper question is whether we will continue to build the conditions in which wisdom, care, and judgment can grow.

One possibility is dissolution: a humanity dulled by dependence, distracted by automation, and perhaps undone by our own inventions. Another possibility is renewal: a new form of humanism, grounded not in nostalgia but in evolutionary insight and philosophical reflection. Just as the Renaissance responded to the upheaval of print, so too might our age respond to the shock of computation.

Science itself points us in this direction. Evolutionary anthropology, neuroscience, and cultural history all converge on the same lesson: what distinguishes us is not speed or precision but care—our ability to cooperate, adapt, and steward life. AI may imitate cognition, but it exposes how brittle intelligence is when stripped of wisdom and responsibility.

At this critical juncture—facing ecological stress, fragile institutions, and technological disruption—the social sciences must reclaim their evolutionary foundations and free themselves from ideological capture. Their civic role is not to politicize knowledge, but to anchor it in shared ethical aims: sustainability, justice, and intergenerational responsibility.

In this new division of labor, machines will surpass us in calculation, but humans can still excel in judgment, meaning-making, and care. If cultivated, this post-AI identity will not be a diminished echo of machine intelligence, but a fuller expression of human wisdom.

This is the task of *reflective humanism*: to re-anchor dignity not in superiority over machines, but in the domains they cannot—and perhaps never will—reach: moral reasoning, imaginative meaning-making, ethical restraint, and the vocation of stewardship. We do not need to be the fastest minds on Earth to guide its future. But we do need to be the wisest.

10.6 Concluding Remarks

We began this book with a simple but ambitious goal: to show how the social sciences can be made more scientific. The state of the field today is fragmented, producing insights that seldom accumulate into a coherent whole. What is needed is a *unifying foundation*.

Historically, two possible foundations presented themselves: physics and biology. Physics offered reductionist clarity, but it has proven insufficient for explaining human complexity. Biology, by contrast, provides an evolutionary framework that is systemic, adaptive, and cumulative. It is this path that leads us to what is called the *Evolutionary Social Sciences*.

This raises the provocative question posed earlier: what if the social sciences had never existed? Would anything essential be lost? For most of history, people lived, loved, and governed themselves without them, and today machines can already outperform us in many analytical and problem-solving tasks. My answer is that AI will likely do much of the practical work of the social sciences more effectively than we can. Yet this does not make the field obsolete. Rather, it calls for a reinvention: a new generation of social scientists—fewer in number, but better trained, broadly read, and equipped with both historical perspective and data-science competence. Their task will not be to compete with machines on technical grounds, but to guide inquiry, frame the right questions, and connect knowledge to ethical and cultural purpose. In this role, the social sciences can continue to matter—if they embrace the partnership with AI as a chance to sharpen, not dilute, their mission.

From this starting point, we argued that to make evolutionary social science workable, we can extend existing models of *systems theory*. But unlike earlier approaches, our model is built on two complementary pillars. *The Vitruvian Framework* ensures that no critical human dimensions are overlooked in practice—covering symbolic thought, ecological embeddedness, moral-political development, gene–culture coevolution, and technological transformation. *The Evolutionary Scaffold Model* provides the theoretical anchor: a two-layer structure where the social science disciplines operate as subsystems on top of an underlying evolutionary layer defined by the three axioms of variation, inheritance, and selection (Table 10.8).

To connect these frameworks with the lived processes of human culture, Chap. 4 introduced a five-layer model of how individual cognition scales into collective intelligence. These layers—(1) cognitive foundations, (2) shared meaning, (3) social structures, (4) knowledge systems, and (5) collective intelligence—show the mechanisms by which biology and psychology are translated into culture and institutions. Perception, memory, and bias form the raw material; language and symbols stabilize shared meaning; norms and roles generate social order; knowledge systems accumulate insights across generations; and, finally, collective intelligence emerges in markets, democracies, science, and now AI. This layered model serves as the bridge between micro-level cognition and the macro-level models developed later. It demonstrates how the Evolutionary Scaffold and Vitruvian Framework gain traction in practice: they rest on the capacity of individual minds to synchronize into culture, institutions, and systems of reasoning.

Taken together, these contributions from what we have called the *Evolutionary Social Science Model*—a systemic cube that integrates the Vitruvian and Scaffold logics. This cube situates the social sciences within a *pan-disciplinary framework*, where biology, psychology, and social life are dynamically interdependent. This synthesis aligns with *the bio-psycho-social model*, which insists that cognition, health, and society cannot be understood in isolation but must be studied as coupled systems.

Yet, for this process to function in practice, we must recognize that human beings are embedded in competitive environments. It was precisely this insight, drawn from reading Malthus, that gave Darwin the idea of evolution: competition as a universal force. In the social realm, the relevant units of this competition are individuals, organizations, and cultures (often but not always linked to nations). This dynamic can be taught and illustrated through the *SEPT model*, which shows how science, education, production, and trade reinforce one another in shaping societal resilience.

If the economic benefits of this system are distributed fairly—and that is a big if—then work itself could be redefined. Even for those no longer required in the productive economy, contribution would not disappear; it would take new forms. To live a virtuous life, to cultivate oneself, and to serve one's culture and community would count as meaningful labor, recognized and sustained alongside traditional production. In such a scenario, the surplus generated by competitive advantage does not merely flow upward or

Table 10.8 Key models and frameworks introduced in this book

Concept/Model	Definition	Purpose/ Contribution
Evolutionary Scaffold Model	Two-layer architecture: (1) Evolutionary theory (variation, inheritance, selection) as foundation; (2) Social science disciplines (economics, sociology, psychology, political science, anthropology) as applications	Provides coherence by rooting all social sciences in evolution, ensuring findings cumulate rather than fragment. Disciplines must align with evolutionary logic
Vitruvian Framework for Human Understanding	Five dimensions of human existence: symbolic thought, gene–culture coevolution, ecological embeddedness, political–moral development, and technological transformation	Offers a systemic lens to capture the "full stack" of human life, akin to Vitruvian Man—balancing biology, culture, morality, and technology
Evolutionary Social Science Model (Cube)	Three-layer synthesis: Evolutionary Scaffold + Vitruvian Framework = integrated cube model	Central paradigm of the book: connects evolutionary foundations, disciplinary knowledge, and human systemic conditions into one architecture
Bio-psycho-social Model	Treats biology, psychology, and social life as interdependent layers of one system	Anchors cognition, health, and society as dynamically coupled—an embodied starting point for realistic, humane policy

(continued)

Table 10.8 (continued)

Concept/Model	Definition	Purpose/ Contribution
Empirical/ Functional Ethics	Ethics understood as adaptive practice, tested by history and social survival, not abstract doctrine	Reframes morality as an evolutionary and cultural process. Virtues like care, honesty, and discipline evolve as stabilizers of society
SEPT Model	Science → Education → Production → Trade sequence	Explains how societies build resilience and competitiveness; links knowledge systems to material foundations of prosperity
Cultural Alignment Map	Analytical tool for comparing institutional and cultural "fit."	Helps explain why some reforms or policies succeed in certain societies but fail in others
Dual-Rupture Model	Framework describing two major historical ruptures: (1) symbolic–cultural emergence, (2) AI–technological transformation	Highlights discontinuities that redefine what it means to be human

outward but is reinvested into human lives. It enables people to choose paths outside traditional production—cultivating themselves, engaging in culture, mentoring others, and contributing to the social fabric in ways that are not easily measured by GDP. In this sense, being a good human being—caring for family, supporting communities, pursuing knowledge, or creating art—can itself be recognized as a form of work. A society that compensates these contributions acknowledges that resilience is not only built through production and trade but also through the cultivation of meaning, trust, and virtue. What machines create materially can thus free people to strengthen the moral and cultural capital on which long-term survival depends.

Competition, however, is not only structural—it is also cultural. Some cultures align more effectively with others, and their compatibility can be examined through instruments such as the *Cultural Alignment Map*. Competition does not arise from free will alone (some would argue, not at all); rather, it unfolds through values and virtues that are cultivated within cultures. For a society to remain competitive, it must therefore sustain and renew its core virtues—such as hard work, persistence, and discipline. Without them, both individuals and organizations lose cohesion and direction. What is needed, then, is nothing less than a new *social contract* for the age of AI—one that recognizes the changing balance between machine productivity and human purpose, and anchors competitiveness in both economic viability and cultural resilience.

Such a contract cannot be designed on technical grounds alone. It must also be grounded in the virtues that hold societies together. These virtues are not merely instrumental; they form the cultural basis for what we call ethics, or moral philosophy: the practices by which communities define right and wrong. From an evolutionary perspective, ethics is not static or universal, but adaptive and empirical—shaped by socialization, daily practices, and the accumulated experience of generations. This leads us to the concept of *empirical virtue ethics*, a framework that explains morality as an evolving cultural achievement, anchored in history yet open to adaptation (Fig. 10.4).

In this way, the logic of the book comes full circle. We began with the ambition to show what science reveals about man and society (Chaps. 1–4), and to outline a guiding star for keeping the entire social science project more scientific, less fragmented, and anchored in a common foundation. The choice was between physics, which has long proven insufficient for explaining human complexity, and biology, which had been attempted before but was abandoned for the wrong reasons. It is therefore worth a retrial. The model developed here offers an *evolutionary framework* that is systemic, adaptive, and cumulative. From this foundation, we built on systems theory and extended it through new integrative models.

The five cultural layers—cognition, shared meaning, social structures, knowledge systems, and collective intelligence—show how individual perception and memory scale upward into the durable institutions and decision systems that sustain societies. This cultural architecture links directly to the *Vitruvian Framework*, which ensures that no essential dimension of human life is overlooked, and to the *Evolutionary Scaffold*, which provides a theoretical anchor through the three axioms of variation, inheritance, and selection. Combined, they form the *systemic Cube*, which integrates human dimensions, disciplinary practices, and evolutionary logic into one *paradigm*.

From there, the framework connects to the *bio-psycho-social model*, which situates the social sciences within a *pan-disciplinary logic* alongside biology

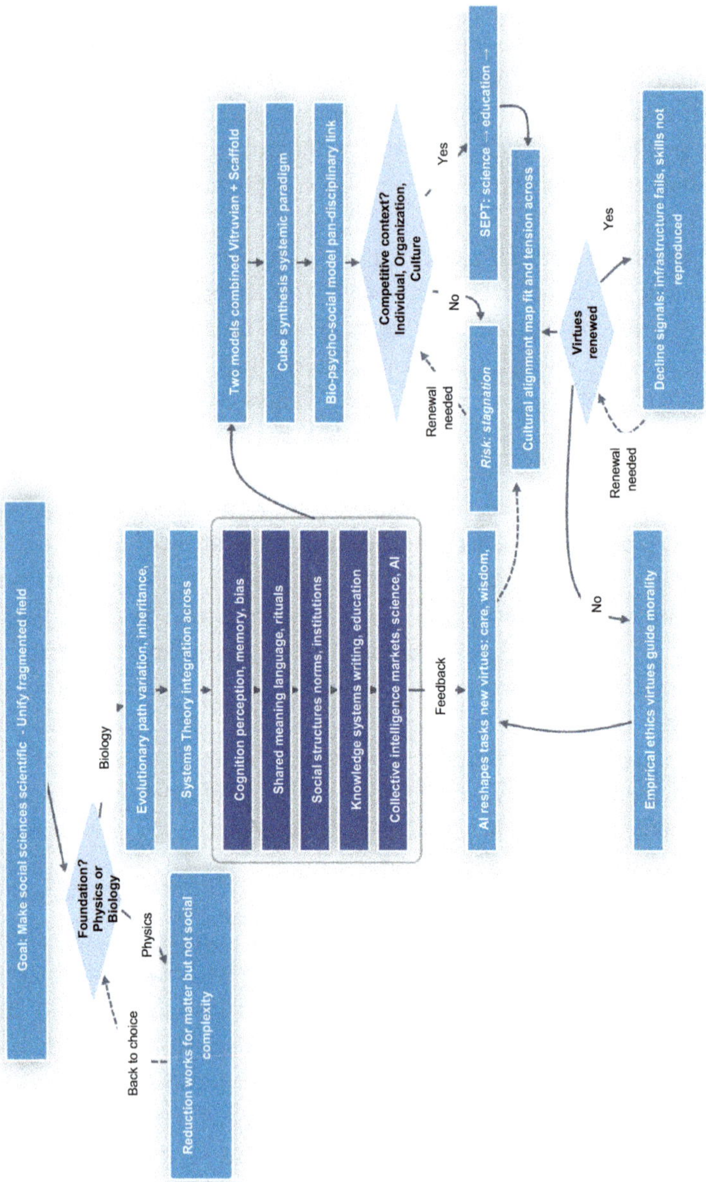

Fig. 10.4 The evolutionary integration model

and psychology. It recognizes that societies operate in competitive environments at the level of individuals, organizations, and cultures—a process captured by the *SEPT model* of science, education, production, and trade. This competitive dynamic is not purely structural but also cultural: some societies align more effectively than others, as illustrated in the *Cultural Alignment Map*.

The model also makes clear that cultures cannot rely on free will alone; they must cultivate and renew their virtues if they are to remain competitive. As much of the literature has shown, the emphasis on "free will" in social science models—particularly within rational choice theory—has been overstated. Human decisions are shaped less by isolated acts of autonomy than by the traits, virtues, and vices internalized through cultural background. When virtues such as hard work, persistence, and discipline weaken, societies enter decline. At the same time, these virtues form the cultural basis for ethics itself—understood here as adaptive and empirical, not abstract or universal. This is what we have called *empirical virtue ethics*: morality as a living, evolving practice rather than as fixed doctrine.

Seen together, these elements form a coherent framework for the social sciences: evolutionary in foundation, systemic in method, and grounded in the virtues that sustain *cultural resilience*.

At the same time, the rise of artificial intelligence forces us to confront an identity problem. For centuries, humans defined themselves as the rational animal—homo sapiens, the analyst. Yet science has revealed the limits of that self-image: our reasoning is riddled with bias and illusion. Now, with AI, we have created systems that can outperform us in many of the very tasks once taken as proof of our superiority—calculation, memory, pattern recognition, and prediction. The result is unsettling, for it displaces rationality as the foundation of human distinctiveness. But this loss can also be reframed as an opportunity. If machines increasingly take over the rational tasks, what remains for us is to cultivate those domains where evolution has made us unique: adaptation and flexibility, care, judgment, wisdom, and the stewardship of life. In this re-identification, homo sapiens could give way to homo cura—the human as caretaker. This is not merely a moral choice but an evolutionary necessity, one could argue, and it carries universal value across cultures. It is also a conclusion that I am sure would have pleased Montaigne and the Renaissance humanists: that our worth lies not in abstract mastery, but in our capacity to live wisely, responsibly, and well.

For we are the generalists of the mammalian world, not the specialists. This breadth—the ability to combine ecological, cultural, and ethical capacities—explains why humanism, in its renewed form, is so fitting for us. AI may surpass us in narrow domains, but it cannot rival the integrative flexibility that makes human life resilient.

This, then, is what I have here called *Reflective Humanism*—a new stage that builds on the legacy of Renaissance humanism but is adapted to the challenges of the AI age. Where the first humanism defended dignity against theology, this reflective humanism seeks to preserve wisdom, meaning, and responsibility in an era shaped by machines.

And now, dear reader, this has indeed been a long journey. Perhaps it is time to pause and let the ideas settle. After countless revisions and reflections, I can say with some certainty that I, too, welcome a quiet moment of stillness.

References

Adorno, T. W., & Horkheimer, M. (2002). *Dialectic of enlightenment* (E. Jephcott, Trans.). Stanford University Press. (Original work published 1947).

Alatas, S. F. (2006). *Alternative discourses in Asian social science: Responses to Eurocentrism*. Sage.

Altmann, J., & Sauer, F. (2017). Autonomous weapon systems and strategic stability. *Survival, 59*(5), 117–142. https://doi.org/10.1080/00396338.2017.1375263

Asimov, I. (1991). Runaround. In *I, robot*. Bantam Books. (Original work published 1942).

Autor, D., Dorn, D., & Hanson, G. (2016). The China shock: Learning from labor-market adjustment to large changes in trade. *Annual Review of Economics, 8*, 205–240.

Axelrod, R. (1984). *The evolution of cooperation*. Basic Books.

Barkow, J. H., Cosmides, L., & Tooby, J. (Eds.). (1992). *The adapted mind: Evolutionary psychology and the generation of culture*. Oxford University Press.

Becher, T., & Trowler, P. R. (2001). *Academic tribes and territories: Intellectual enquiry and the culture of disciplines* (2nd ed.). Open University Press.

Bender, E. M., Gebru, T., McMillan-Major, A., & Shmitchell, S. (2021). On the dangers of stochastic parrots: Can language models be too big? In *Proceedings of the 2021 ACM Conference on Fairness, Accountability, and Transparency* (pp. 610–623). https://doi.org/10.1145/3442188.3445922

Borjas, G. J. (2016). *We wanted workers: Unraveling the immigration narrative*. Norton.

Bourdieu, P., & Wacquant, L. J. D. (1992). *An invitation to reflexive sociology*. University of Chicago Press.

Bourne, P. E., Lorsch, J. R., & Green, E. D. (2015). Perspective: Sustaining the big-data ecosystem. *Nature, 527*(7576), S16–S17.

Boyd, D., & Crawford, K. (2012). Critical questions for big data. *Information, Communication & Society, 15*(5), 662–679.

Boyd, R., & Richerson, P. (1985). *Culture and the evolutionary process*. University of Chicago Press.

Bratsberg, B., & Rogeberg, O. (2018). Flynn effect and its reversal are both environmentally caused. *Proceedings of the National Academy of Sciences, 115*(26), 6674–6678.

Brynjolfsson, E., & McAfee, A. (2014). *The second machine age: Work, progress, and prosperity in a time of brilliant technologies*. W. W. Norton & Company.

Bryson, J. J. (2018). Patiency is not a virtue: AI and the design of ethical systems. *Ethics and Information Technology, 20*(1), 15–26. https://doi.org/10.1007/s10676-018-9448-6

Calude, C. S., & Longo, G. (2017). The deluge of spurious correlations in big data. *Foundations of Science, 22*(3), 595–612.

Cave, S., & ÓhÉigeartaigh, S. S. (2019). An AI race for strategic advantage: Rhetoric and risks. In V. C. Müller (Ed.), *Philosophy and theory of artificial intelligence 2017* (pp. 40–46). Springer. https://doi.org/10.1007/978-3-319-96448-5_5

Colantone, I., & Stanig, P. (2018). Global competition and Brexit. *American Political Science Review, 112*(2), 201–218.

Cosmides, L., & Tooby, J. (1997). *Evolutionary psychology: A primer*. University of California.

Cournot, A. A. (1897). *Researches into the mathematical principles of the theory of wealth* (N. T. Bacon, Trans.). Macmillan. (Original work published 1838).

Crook, P. (1994). *Darwinism, war and history: The debate over the biology of war from the "Origin of species" to the First World War*. Cambridge University Press.

Damasio, A. (1994). *Descartes' error: Emotion, reason, and the human brain*. G. P. Putnam's Sons.

Dehaene, S. (2009). *Reading in the brain: The new science of how we read*. Viking.

Diamond, J. (2013). *The world until yesterday: What can we learn from traditional societies?* Viking.

Dustmann, C., & Frattini, T. (2014). The fiscal effects of immigration to the UK. *Economic Journal, 124*(580), F593–F643.

Fanelli, D. (2010). "Positive" results increase down the hierarchy of the sciences. *PLoS ONE, 5*(4), e10068.

Fang, F. C., & Casadevall, A. (2016). Research funding: The case for a modified lottery. *MBio, 7*(2), e00422–16.

Federal Reserve. (2021). *The Federal Reserve System: Purposes & functions* (10th ed.). Board of Governors of the Federal Reserve System.

Ferguson, N. (2019). *The square and the tower: Networks, hierarchies and the struggle for global power*. Penguin.

Flynn, J. R. (2007). *What is intelligence? Beyond the Flynn effect*. Cambridge University Press.

Flyvbjerg, B. (2001). *Making social science matter: Why social inquiry fails and how it can succeed again*. Cambridge University Press.

Fortunato, S., Bergstrom, C. T., Börner, K., Evans, J. A., Helbing, D., Milojević, S., … & Barabási, A.-L. (2018). Science of science. *Science, 359*(6379), eaao0185.

Gadamer, H.-G. (1975). *Truth and method*. Seabury Press. *Proceedings of the 28th International Conference on Machine Learning* (pp. 489–496).

Gazzaniga, M. S. (2018). *The consciousness instinct: Unraveling the mystery of how the brain makes the mind*. Farrar, Straus and Giroux.

Gilligan, C. (1982). *In a different voice: Psychological theory and women's development*. Harvard University Press.

Grimmer, J., & Stewart, B. M. (2013). Text as data: The promise and pitfalls of automatic content analysis methods for political texts. *Political Analysis, 21*(3), 267–297.

Habermas, J. (1984/1987). *The theory of communicative action* (T. McCarthy, Trans., Vols. 1–2). Beacon Press. (Original work published 1981).

Haidt, J. (2012). *The righteous mind: Why good people are divided by politics and religion.* Pantheon Books.

Harding, S. (1995). "Strong objectivity": A response to the new objectivity question. *Synthese, 104*(3), 331–349.

Hebb, D. O. (1949). *The organization of behavior: A neuropsychological theory.* Wiley.

Heidegger, M. (1962). *Being and time* (J. Macquarrie & E. Robinson, Trans.). Harper & Row. (Original work published 1927).

Henrich, J. (2015). *The secret of our success: How culture is driving human evolution, domesticating our species, and making us smarter*. Princeton University Press.

Henrich, J. (2016). *The secret of our success: How culture is driving human evolution, domesticating our species, and making us smarter*. Princeton University Press.

Hofman, J. M., Sharma, A., & Watts, D. J. (2017). Prediction and explanation in social systems. *Science, 355*(6324), 486–488.

Hrdy, S. B. (2011). *Mothers and others: The evolutionary origins of mutual understanding*. Harvard University Press.

Huntington, S. P. (1996). *The clash of civilizations and the remaking of world order*. Simon & Schuster.

Hyginus. (2002). *Fabulae* (M. Grant, Trans.). Oxford University Press. (Original work published ca. 1st–2nd century CE).

Inglehart, R., & Welzel, C. (2005). *Modernization, cultural change, and democracy: The human development sequence.* Cambridge University Press.

Ioannidis, J. P. A. (2005). Why most published research findings are false. *PLoS Medicine, 2*(8), e124.

Iriye, A. (2002). *Global community: The role of international organizations in the making of the contemporary world*. University of California Press.

Jablonka, E., & Lamb, M. J. (2014). *Evolution in four dimensions: Genetic, epigenetic, behavioral, and symbolic variation in the history of life* (Revised ed.). MIT Press.

Jakab, Z., & Kumhof, M. (2015). *Banks are not intermediaries of loanable funds—and why this matters.* Bank of England Working Paper No. 529.

Jasanoff, S. (2017). *The ethics of invention: Technology and the human future.* W. W. Norton & Company.

Jean, N., Burke, M., Xie, M., Davis, W. M., Lobell, D. B., & Ermon, S. (2016). Combining satellite imagery and machine learning to predict poverty. *Science, 353*(6301), 790–794.

Jünger, E. (2017). *The worker: Dominion and form* (L. Hervier, Trans.). Northwestern University Press. (Original work published 1932).

Kahneman, D. (2011). *Thinking, fast and slow.* Farrar.

Kitchin, R. (2014). *The data revolution: Big data, open data, data infrastructures and their consequences.* Sage.

Klingberg, T. (2009). *The overflowing brain: Information overload and the limits of working memory.* Oxford University Press.

Kraemer, M. U. G., Yang, C.-H., Gutierrez, B., Wu, C.-H., Klein, B., Pigott, D. M., … & Brownstein, J. S. (2020). The effect of human mobility and control measures on the COVID-19 epidemic in China. *Science, 368*(6490), 493–497.

Kristeller, P. O. (1961). *Renaissance thought II: Papers on humanism and the arts.* Harper Torchbooks.

Krizhevsky, A., Sutskever, I., & Hinton, G. E. (2012). ImageNet classification with deep convolutional neural networks. *Advances in Neural Information Processing Systems, 25*, 1097–1105.

Kuhn, T. S. (1962). *The structure of scientific revolutions.* University of Chicago Press.

Lanier, J. (2010). *You are not a gadget: A manifesto.* Alfred A. Knopf.

Latour, B. (2005). *Reassembling the social: An introduction to actor-network-theory.* Oxford University Press.

Lazer, D., Pentland, A., Adamic, L., Aral, S., Barabási, A.-L., Brewer, D., … & Van Alstyne, M. (2009). Computational social science. *Science, 323*(5915), 721–723.

LeCun, Y., Bengio, Y., & Hinton, G. (2015). Deep learning. *Nature, 521*(7553), 436–444. https://doi.org/10.1038/nature14539

Lenski, G. (1966). *Power and privilege: A theory of social stratification.* McGraw-Hill.

Lenski, G. (2005). *Ecological-evolutionary theory: Principles and applications.* Paradigm Publishers.

Lewontin, R., Rose, S., & Kamin, L. (1984). *Not in our genes: Biology, ideology, and human nature.* Pantheon.

Lum, K., & Isaac, W. (2016). To predict and serve? *Significance, 13*(5), 14–19.

Maugham, W. S. (1915). *Of human bondage.* William Heinemann.

Maynard Smith, J. (1982). *Evolution and the theory of games.* Cambridge University Press.

McCulloch, W. S., & Pitts, W. (1943). A logical calculus of the ideas immanent in nervous activity. *The Bulletin of Mathematical Biophysics, 5*(4), 115–133. https://doi.org/10.1007/BF02478259

McLeay, M., Radia, A., & Thomas, R. (2014). Money creation in the modern economy. *Bank of England Quarterly Bulletin, 54*(1), 14–27.

Menger, C. (1963). *Problems of economics and sociology* (F. J. Nock, Trans.). University of Illinois Press. (Original work published 1883).

Mercier, H., & Sperber, D. (2017). *The enigma of reason.* Harvard University Press.

Milanović, B. (2016). *Global inequality: A new approach for the age of globalization*. Harvard University Press.
Mitchell, M. (2019). *Artificial intelligence: A guide for thinking humans*. Farrar.
Nagel, T. (1986). *The view from nowhere*. Oxford University Press.
Nisbett, R. E. (2003). *The geography of thought: How Asians and Westerners think differently...and why*. Free Press.
Nisbett, R. E. (2009). *Intelligence and how to get it: Why schools and cultures count*. W. W. Norton & Company.
Noddings, N. (1984). *Caring: A feminine approach to ethics and moral education*. University of California Press.
Nowak, M. A. (2006). *Evolutionary dynamics: Exploring the equations of life*. Harvard University Press.
Nowak, M. A., & Highfield, R. (2011). *Supercooperators: Altruism, evolution, and why we need each other to succeed*. Free Press.
Open Science Collaboration. (2015). Estimating the reproducibility of psychological science. *Science, 349*(6251), aac4716.
Organisation for Economic Co-operation and Development. (2020). *Tax challenges arising from digitalisation: Report on Pillar One blueprint*. OECD Publishing. https://doi.org/10.1787/beba0634-en
Paul, D. B. (1995). *Controlling human heredity: 1865 to the present*. Humanities Press.
Pickering, M. (2009). *Auguste Comte: An intellectual biography* (Vol. 1). Cambridge University Press.
Piketty, T. (2014). *Capital in the twenty-first century*. Harvard University Press.
Pinker, S. (2002). *The blank slate: The modern denial of human nature*. Viking.
Pinker, S. (2011). *The better angels of our nature: Why violence has declined*. Viking.
Posner, M. I., & Rothbart, M. K. (2007). *Educating the human brain*. American Psychological Association.
Pye, L. W. (1985). *Asian power and politics: The cultural dimensions of authority*. Harvard University Press.
Putnam, R. D. (2007). E pluribus unum: Diversity and community in the twenty-first century. *Scandinavian Political Studies, 30*(2), 137–174. https://doi.org/10.1111/j.1467-9477.2007.00176.x
Ricke, K., Drouet, L., Caldeira, K., & Tavoni, M. (2018). Country-level social cost of carbon. *Nature Climate Change, 8*(10), 895–900.
Rockström, J., Steffen, W., Noone, K., Persson, Å., Chapin, F. S., Lambin, E. F., Lenton, M., Scheffer, C., Folke, H. J., Schellnhuber, B., Nykvist, C. A., de Wit, T., Hughes, S., van der Leeuw, H., Rodhe, S., Sörlin, P. K., Snyder, R., Costanza, U., Svedin, M., Falkenmark, L., Karlberg, R. W., Corell, V. J., Fabry, J., Hansen, B., Walker, D., Liverman, K., Richardson, P. Crutzen., & Foley, J. A. (2009). *A safe operating space for humanity. Nature, 461*(7263), 472–475.
Rodrik, D. (2011). *The globalization paradox: Democracy and the future of the world economy*. W. W. Norton & Company.

Rosenblatt, F. (1958). The perceptron: A probabilistic model for information storage and organization in the brain. *Psychological Review, 65*(6), 386–408. https://doi.org/10.1037/h0042519

Salganik, M. J., Lundberg, I., Kindel, A. T., Ahearn, C. E., Al-Ghoneim, K., Almaatouq, A., … & Watts, D. J. (2020). Measuring the predictability of life outcomes with a scientific mass collaboration. *Proceedings of the National Academy of Sciences, 117*(15), 8398–8403.

Sarewitz, D. (2016). Saving science. *The New Atlantis, 49*, 4–40.

Schmitt, C. (2005). *Political theology: Four chapters on the concept of sovereignty* (G. Schwab, Trans.). University of Chicago Press. (Original work published 1932).

Schmoller, G. (1984). *Methodological controversy in economics* (G. O. Staley, Trans.). Free Press. (Original work published 1883).

Sharkey, N. (2019). Autonomous weapons systems, killer robots and human dignity. *Ethics and Information Technology, 21*(2), 75–87. https://doi.org/10.1007/s10676-018-9494-0

Small, M. L. (2009). "How many cases do I need?" On science and the logic of case selection in field-based research. *Ethnography, 10*(1), 5–38.

Söilen, K. S. (2025a). *Applied evolutionary economics: Insights from biology for real-world management*. Springer.

Söilen, K. S. (2025). *The researcher's journey: A guide to methodology and academia in social sciences*. Springer.

Solovey, M. (2013). *Shaky foundations: The politics–patronage–social science nexus in Cold War America*. Rutgers University Press.

Spengler, O. (1922). *The decline of the West* (C. F. Atkinson, Trans.). Alfred A. Knopf. (Original work published 1918).

Sun, Y., Wang, X., & Tang, X. (2017). Deep learning face representation by joint identification-verification. *Advances in Neural Information Processing Systems.*

Tegmark, M. (2017). *Life 3.0: Being human in the age of artificial intelligence*. Alfred A. Knopf.

Tooby, J., & Cosmides, L. (1992). *The adapted mind: Evolutionary psychology and the generation of culture*. Oxford University Press.

Tufekci, Z. (2015). Algorithmic harms beyond Facebook and Google: Emergent challenges of computational agency. *Colorado Technology Law Journal, 13*(203), 203–218.

Turner, A. (2015). *Between debt and the devil: Money, credit, and fixing global finance*. Princeton University Press.

UNESCO. (2021). *Recommendation on the ethics of artificial intelligence.* United Nations Educational, Scientific and Cultural Organization. https://unesdoc.unesco.org/ark:/48223/pf0000380455

de Waal, F. (2009). *The age of empathy: Nature's lessons for a kinder society*. Harmony Books.

Vaswani, A., Shazeer, N., Parmar, N., Uszkoreit, J., Jones, L., Gomez, A. N., Kaiser, Ł, & Polosukhin, I. (2017). Attention is all you need. *Advances in Neural Information Processing Systems, 30*, 5998–6008.

Wallerstein, I. (2004). *World-systems analysis: An introduction.* Duke University Press.

Walras, L. (1954). *Elements of pure economics* (W. Jaffé, Trans.). George Allen & Unwin. (Original work published 1874).
Whitley, R. (2000). *The intellectual and social organization of the sciences* (2nd ed.). Oxford University Press.
Wilson, D. S. (2002). *Darwin's cathedral: Evolution, religion, and the nature of society*. University of Chicago Press.
Wilson, D. S. (2005). *Ecological-evolutionary theory: Principles and applications*. Oxford University Press.
Wilson, D. S. (2019). *This view of life: Completing the Darwinian revolution*. Pantheon.
Wilson, E. O. (1975). *Sociobiology: The new synthesis*. Harvard University Press.
Yarkoni, T., & Westfall, J. (2017). Choosing prediction over explanation in psychology: Lessons from machine learning. *Perspectives on Psychological Science, 12*(6), 1100–1122.
Zhang, L. (2017). *In search of paradise: Middle-class living in a Chinese metropolis*. Cornell University Press.
Zuboff, S. (2019). *The age of surveillance capitalism: The fight for a human future at the new frontier of power*. Public Affairs.

Further Reading

Abbott, A. (2001). *Chaos of disciplines*. University of Chicago Press.
Acemoglu, D., & Restrepo, P. (2022). Tasks, automation, and the rise in US wage inequality. *Econometrica, 90*(5), 1973–2016.
Andersen, J., Howard, C., & Swiecki, Z. (2023). Authorship and integrity in the age of AI: Navigating responsibility in academic writing. *Science and Engineering Ethics, 29*, 16.
Ardelt, M. (2004). Wisdom as expert knowledge system: A critical review of a contemporary operationalization of an ancient concept. *Human Development, 47*(5), 257–285. https://doi.org/10.1159/000079154
Arendt, H. (1998). *The human condition* (2nd ed.). University of Chicago Press. (Original work published 1958).
Aristotle. (1999). *Nicomachean ethics* (T. Irwin, Trans.). Hackett Publishing Company.
Augustine. (2006). *The city of God* (H. Bettenson, Trans.). Penguin Classics. (Original work published ca. 426 CE).
Baltes, P. B., & Staudinger, U. M. (2000). Wisdom: A metaheuristic (pragmatic) to orchestrate mind and virtue toward excellence. *American Psychologist, 55*(1), 122–136. https://doi.org/10.1037/0003-066X.55.1.122
Barr, N., Pennycook, G., Stolz, J. A., & Fugelsang, J. A. (2015). The brain in your pocket: Evidence that smartphones are used to supplant thinking. *Computers in Human Behavior, 48*, 473–480. https://doi.org/10.1016/j.chb.2015.02.029

Benkler, Y. (2006). *The wealth of networks: How social production transforms markets and freedom*. Yale University Press.
Berninger, V. W., & Richards, T. L. (2002). *Brain literacy for educators and psychologists*. Academic Press.
Boccaccio, G. (2003). *The Decameron* (G. H. McWilliam, Trans.). Penguin Books. (Original work published 1353).
Booth, J. L., & Siegler, R. S. (2006). Developmental and individual differences in pure numerical estimation. *Developmental Psychology, 42*(1), 189–201.
Bommasani, R., Hudson, D. A., Adeli, E., Altman, R., Arora, S., von Arx, S., … & Liang, P. (2021). *On the opportunities and risks of foundation models*. arXiv. https://doi.org/10.48550/arXiv.2108.07258
Bostrom, N. (2005). In defense of posthuman dignity. *Bioethics, 19*(3), 202–214. https://doi.org/10.1111/j.1467-8519.2005.00437.x
Bostrom, N. (2014). *Superintelligence: Paths, dangers, strategies*. Oxford University Press.
Boyd, R., & Richerson, P. J. (2005). *The origin and evolution of cultures*. Oxford University Press.
Breslin, G., & Brennan, D. (2020). Technology overload: The effects of digital detox on digital addiction, well-being, and attention. *Cyberpsychology: Journal of Psychosocial Research on Cyberspace, 14*(1). https://doi.org/10.5817/CP2020-1-5
Brundage, M., Avin, S., Clark, J., Toner, H., Eckersley, P., Garfinkel, B., Dafoe, A., Scharre, P., Zeitzoff, T., Filar, B., Anderson, H., … & Amodei, D. et al. (2018). *The malicious use of artificial intelligence: Forecasting, prevention, and mitigation*. arXiv. https://doi.org/10.48550/arXiv.1802.07228
Brynjolfsson, E., Rock, D., & Syverson, C. (2019). Artificial intelligence and the modern productivity paradox: A clash of expectations and statistics. In A. Agrawal, J. Gans, & A. Goldfarb (Eds.), *The economics of artificial intelligence: An agenda* (pp. 23–57). University of Chicago Press.
Bubeck, S., Chandrasekaran, V., Eldan, R., Gehrke, J., Horvitz, E., Kamar, E., Lee, P., Lee, Y. T., Li, Y., Lundberg, S., Nori, H., Palangi, H., Tulio, M., & Zhang, Y. (2023). *Sparks of artificial general intelligence: Early experiments with GPT-4*. arXiv. https://doi.org/10.48550/arXiv.2303.12712
Burrell, J. (2016). How the machine 'thinks': Understanding opacity in machine learning algorithms. *Big Data & Society, 3*(1), 1–12. https://doi.org/10.1177/2053951715622512
Carr, N. (2010). *The shallows: What the Internet is doing to our brains*. W. W. Norton & Company.
Castiglione, B. (2002). *The book of the courtier* (G. Bull, Trans.). Penguin Books. (Original work published 1528).
Cellini, B. (2005). *The autobiography of Benvenuto Cellini* (G. Bull, Trans.). Penguin Classics. (Original work published 1558).
Chalmers, D. J. (Ed.). (2010). *The singularity: A philosophical analysis*. Springer.
Cicero. (2014). *On duties* (M. Atkins, Trans.). Cambridge University Press. (Original work published ca. 44 BCE).

Clark, A. (2003). *Natural born cyborgs: Minds, technologies, and the future of human intelligence*. Oxford University Press.

Cioffi-Revilla, C. (2014). *Introduction to computational social science: Principles and applications*. Springer.

Comte, A. (1975). *Cours de philosophie positive* (Vols. 1–6). Hermann. (Original work published 1830–1842).

Conte, R., Gilbert, N., Bonelli, G., Cioffi-Revilla, C., Deffuant, G., Kertesz, J., Loreto, V., Moat, S., Nadal, J. P., Sanchez, A., Nowak, A., Flache, A., San Miguel, M., & Helbing, D. (2012). Manifesto of computational social science. *The European Physical Journal Special Topics, 214*(1), 325–346. https://doi.org/10.1140/epjst/e2012-01697-8

Dignum, V. (2019). *Responsible artificial intelligence: Developing and using AI in a responsible way.* Springer.

Dignum, V. (2022). *Responsible artificial intelligence: How to develop and use AI in a responsible way.* Springer.

Domingos, P. (2015). *The master algorithm: How the quest for the ultimate learning machine will remake our world.* Basic Books.

Dürer, A. (2012). *Four books on human proportion* (J. P. Richter, Trans.). Dover Publications. (Original work published 1528).

Epstein, J. M. (2006). *Generative social science: Studies in agent-based computational modeling.* Princeton University Press.

Floridi, L. (2014). *The fourth revolution: How the infosphere is reshaping human reality.* Oxford University Press.

Gilbert, N., & Troitzsch, K. (2005). *Simulation for the social scientist* (2nd ed.). Open University Press.

Habermas, J. (1989). *The structural transformation of the public sphere: An inquiry into a category of bourgeois society* (T. Burger & F. Lawrence, Trans.). MIT Press. (Original work published 1962).

Hamilton, W. D. (1964). The genetical evolution of social behaviour. *Journal of Theoretical Biology, 7*(1), 1–52. https://doi.org/10.1016/0022-5193(64)90038-4

Hanson, R. (2016). *The age of em: Work, love, and life when robots rule the Earth.* Oxford University Press.

Harari, Y. N. (2014). *Sapiens: A brief history of humankind*. Harper.

Harris, J. R. (1998). *The nurture assumption: Why children turn out the way they do.* Free Press.

Haushofer, K. (1924). *Geopolitik des Pazifischen Ozeans: Studien über die Beziehungen zwischen China.* Kurt Vowinckel Verlag.

Hayek, F. A. (1944). *The road to serfdom.* University of Chicago Press.

Helbing, D. (2015). *Thinking ahead—Essays on big data, digital revolution, and participatory market society*. Springer.

Henrich, J. (2020). *The WEIRDest people in the world: How the West became psychologically peculiar and particularly prosperous.* Farrar.

Hobbes, T. (1996). *Leviathan* (R. Tuck, Ed.). Cambridge University Press. (Original work published 1651).

Hofstede, G. (2001). *Culture's consequences: Comparing values, behaviors, institutions, and organizations across nations* (2nd ed.). Sage.

Horkheimer, M. (1972). *Critical theory: Selected essays* (M. O'Connell, Trans.). Herder and Herder. (Original work published 1937).

Hume, D. (2007). *A treatise of human nature* (D. F. Norton & M. J. Norton, Eds.). Oxford University Press. (Original work published 1739–1740).

Huxley, T. H. (1893). *Evolution and ethics*. Macmillan and Company.

Hyginus. (1960). *Fabulae* (M. Grant, Trans.). University of Kansas Press. (Original work ca. 2nd century CE).

Ijzerman, H., Janssen, J. A., & Coan, J. A. (2015). Maintaining warm, trusting relationships with brands: Increased temperature perceptions after thinking of communal brands. *PLoS ONE, 10*(4), Article e0125194. https://doi.org/10.1371/journal.pone.0125194

Ijzerman, H., Lewis, N. A., Jr., Przybylski, A. K., Weinstein, N., DeBruine, L. M., Dunham, Y., Ritchie, S.J., Vazire, S., Forscher, P.S., Morey, R.D., Ivory, J.D. and Anvari, F., & Wojcik, S. P. (2020). *Use caution when applying behavioral science to policy. Nature Human Behaviour, 4*(11), 1092–1094. https://doi.org/10.1038/s41562-020-00990-w

Inglehart, R. (1997). *Modernization and postmodernization: Cultural, economic, and political change in 43 societies*. Princeton University Press.

James, W. (1902). *The varieties of religious experience: A study in human nature*. Longmans, Green & Co.

Jonas, H. (1984). *The imperative of responsibility: In search of an ethics for the technological age*. University of Chicago Press.

Jünger, E. (1993). *Storm of steel* (M. Hofmann, Trans.). Penguin Books. (Original work published 1920).

Jünger, E. (1957). *The worker: Dominion and form* (J. Owen, Trans.). Northwestern University Press. (Original work published 1932).

Kant, I. (1996). *Practical philosophy* (M. J. Gregor, Trans. & Ed.). Cambridge University Press. (Original work published 1785).

Kjellén, R. (1916). *Staten som lifsform*. Hugo Gebers Förlag.

Liu, X. (2020). Confucian wisdom and contemporary AI ethics: A comparative perspective. *AI & Society, 35*, 685–695.

MacIntyre, A. (1981). *After virtue: A study in moral theory*. University of Notre Dame Press.

Marx, K. (1970). *A contribution to the critique of political economy*. Progress Publishers. (Original work published 1859).

Marx, K., & Engels, F. (1998). *The Communist Manifesto* (S. Moore, Trans.). Oxford University Press. (Original work published 1848).

Mehrling, P. (2011). *The new Lombard Street: How the fed became the dealer of last resort*. Princeton University Press.

Mencius. (2003). *Mencius* (D. C. Lau, Trans.). Penguin Classics.

Mirowski, P. (1989). *More heat than light: Economics as social physics, physics as nature's economics*. Cambridge University Press.

Montaigne, M. de. (2003). *The complete essays* (M. A. Screech, Trans.). Penguin Classics. (Original work published 1580/1588).

Morozov, E. (2013). *To save everything, click here: The folly of technological solutionism*. Public Affairs.

Nietzsche, F. (1998). *On the genealogy of morality* (K. Ansell-Pearson, Ed.; C. Diethe, Trans.). Cambridge University Press. (Original work published 1887).

Nussbaum, M. C. (1997). *Cultivating humanity: A classical defense of reform in liberal education*. Harvard University Press.

Odgers, C. L., & Jensen, M. R. (2020). Annual research review: Adolescent mental health in the digital age: Facts, fears, and future directions. *Journal of Child Psychology and Psychiatry, 61*(3), 336–348. https://doi.org/10.1111/jcpp.13190

Offer, A., & Söderberg, G. (2016). *The Nobel factor: The prize in economics, social democracy, and the market turn*. Princeton University Press.

O'Neil, C. (2016). *Weapons of math destruction: How big data increases inequality and threatens democracy*. Crown.

OpenAI. (2023). *GPT-4 technical report*. OpenAI. https://openai.com/research/gpt-4

Ophir, E., Nass, C., & Wagner, A. D. (2009). Cognitive control in media multitaskers. *Proceedings of the National Academy of Sciences, 106*(37), 15583–15587. https://doi.org/10.1073/pnas.0903620106

Pico della Mirandola, G. (1998). *Oration on the dignity of man* (A. R. Caponigri, Ed.). Gateway Editions. (Original work published 1486).

Pinker, S. (2018). *Enlightenment now: The case for reason, science, humanism, and progress*. Viking.

Plato. (2008). *The Republic* (R. Waterfield, Trans.). Oxford University Press.

Popper, K. (1959). *The logic of scientific discovery*. Routledge.

Qvortrup, M. (2003). *Ernst Jünger: The politics of subversion*. Palgrave Macmillan.

Roy, S. (2017). Digital resilience: The psychological concept of surviving in an algorithmic world. *Journal of Media Psychology, 29*(4), 175–187.

Roscher, W. (1878). *Grundlagen der Nationalökonomie*. J. C. Hinrichs.

Sandel, M. J. (2020). *The tyranny of merit: What's become of the common good?* Farrar.

Searle, J. R. (1995). *The construction of social reality*. Free Press.

Seneca. (2004). *Letters from a Stoic* (R. Campbell, Trans.). Penguin Classics.

Shannon, C. E. (1948). A mathematical theory of communication. *Bell System Technical Journal, 27*(3), 379–423.

Siegler, R. S., & Lortie-Forgues, H. (2015). Conceptual knowledge of fraction arithmetic. *Journal of Educational Psychology, 107*(3), 909–918.

Söilen, K. S. (2023). Artificial intelligence and national security: The economic and strategic implications. *Journal of Intelligence Studies and Business, 13*(2), 8–25.

Sowell, T. (1994). *Race and culture: A world view*. Basic Books.

Sparrow, B. (2012). Google effects on memory: Cognitive consequences of having information at our fingertips. *Science, 333*(6043), 776–778.

Spencer, H. (1896). *The principles of sociology* (Vols. 1–3). D. Appleton and Company. (Original work published 1876–1896).

Sternberg, R. J. (2001). *Wisdom, intelligence, and creativity synthesized*. Cambridge University Press.

Stanovich, K. E., & West, R. F. (2000). Individual differences in reasoning: Implications for the rationality debate? *Behavioral and Brain Sciences, 23*(5), 645–726.

Thiel, P. (2014). *Zero to one: Notes on startups, or how to build the future.* Crown Business.

Tiedemann, J., & Thottingal, S. (2020). OPUS-MT: Building open translation services for the world. In *Proceedings of the 22nd Annual Conference of the European Association for Machine Translation (EAMT).*

Tomasello, M. (2009). *Why we cooperate*. MIT Press.

Trivers, R. (2011). *The folly of fools: The logic of deceit and self-deception in human life.* Basic Books.

Tronto, J. C. (1993). *Moral boundaries: A political argument for an ethic of care.* Routledge.

Turchin, P. (2020). *Ages of discord: A structural-demographic analysis of American history.* Beresta Books.

Tversky, A., & Kahneman, D. (1974). Judgment under uncertainty: Heuristics and biases. *Science, 185*(4157), 1124–1131.

Twenge, J. M., & Campbell, W. K. (2018). Associations between screen time and lower psychological well-being among children and adolescents: Evidence from a population-based study. *Preventive Medicine Reports, 12*, 271–283. https://doi.org/10.1016/j.pmedr.2018.10.003

Vallor, S. (2016). *Technology and the virtues: A philosophical guide to a future worth wanting.* Oxford University Press.

Virilio, P. (2000). *The information bomb* (C. Turner, Trans.). Verso.

Washington, H. A. (2006). *Medical apartheid: The dark history of medical experimentation on Black Americans from colonial times to the present.* Doubleday.

Weber, M. (2001). *The Protestant ethic and the spirit of capitalism* (T. Parsons, Trans.). Routledge. (Original work published 1905).

Weber, M. (1978). *Economy and society: An outline of interpretive sociology* (G. Roth & C. Wittich, Eds.). University of California Press. (Original work published 1922).

Weidinger, L., Mellor, J., Rauh, M., Griffin, C., Uesato, J., Huang, P. S., & Gabriel, I. et al. (2022). *Ethical and social risks of harm from language models.* arXiv preprint https://doi.org/10.48550/arXiv.2112.04359

Wegner, D. M. (2002). *The illusion of conscious will*. MIT Press.

Weizenbaum, J. (1976). *Computer power and human reason: From judgment to calculation.* Freeman.

Willett, F. R., Avansino, D. T., Hochberg, L. R., Henderson, J. M., & Shenoy, K. V. (2021). High-performance brain-to-text communication via handwriting decoding. *Nature, 593*(7858), 249–254. https://doi.org/10.1038/s41586-021-03506-2

Wrangham, R. (2019). *The goodness paradox: The strange relationship between virtue and violence in human evolution.* Pantheon.

Wynn, T., & Coolidge, F. L. (2012). *How to think like a Neandertal*. Oxford University Press.

Appendix: Conceptual Foundations for Evolutionary Social Science

The vocabulary of science is not ornamental—it is the scaffolding of thought. Each term encodes years, sometimes centuries, of observation, debate, and refinement. Without a shared language, the work of building explanations and comparing insights across disciplines becomes almost impossible. This appendix gathers together some of the most important terms from biology, evolutionary theory, psychology, and the social sciences—concepts that together form the backbone of an evolutionary approach to human behavior and society as presented in this book.

Why are these terms necessary? Because social scientists cannot afford to operate only with everyday words or local academic jargon. To understand humanity, we must understand the mechanisms that shape our species: from kin selection and reciprocal altruism to cultural transmission and institutional trust. These are not abstract inventions, but conceptual tools forged to capture real, observable patterns in humans and other animals. They remind us of that cooperation and conflict, morality and deception, culture and biology are not random; they are structured by forces that can be studied and, to some extent, predicted.

Equally important, these terms mark the theories that guide our explanations. Concepts like *bounded rationality*, *System 1 and System 2*, or *social brain hypothesis* are not neutral labels; they signal competing models of how the human mind and social life work. A good social scientist must not only know the terms but also the traditions they come from, the debates they have sparked, and the limits of their explanatory power.

Finally, a shared vocabulary creates the conditions for dialogue across disciplines. Historians, psychologists, anthropologists, economists, and political

K. Solberg Söilen, *The Researcher's Journey in the Age of AI*,
https://doi.org/10.1007/978-3-032-23069-0

scientists each approach society from different vantage points. Yet by using concepts rooted in evolutionary science, they gain a common platform for comparing results and advancing cumulative knowledge. Without this integration, the risk is that each field drifts into isolated silos, unable to recognize when they are studying the same underlying dynamics with different words.

The aim of this appendix is therefore not to overwhelm with technicalities, but to equip the reader with a conceptual toolkit. These terms are entry points into the scientific study of humanity: keys that unlock the mechanisms, theories, and models behind what we observe in human life and societies. Mastery of them does not mean memorizing definitions mechanically, but learning to recognize when and how they apply in practice—whether in explaining patterns of cooperation in small groups, shifts in cultural norms, or transformations in large-scale institutions (Table A.1).

The list above highlights key concepts alongside the authors who introduced or advanced them, showing how particular thinkers shaped the field. Yet concepts do not stand alone—they emerge from broader disciplinary traditions. To see this more clearly, the following table maps the same conceptual terrain at a higher level, tracing where terms originate across disciplines. This perspective reveals the relative weight of evolutionary biology, psychology, neuroscience, anthropology, sociology, and related fields in building the toolkit of today's social scientist (Table A.2).

Taken together, these results confirm what the history of theory already suggests: psychology, neuroscience, and evolutionary biology have supplied the majority of the conceptual tools we rely on to explain human behavior. These fields provide the terms that have proven robust enough to travel across disciplines, shaping research far beyond their original domains. Without their input, the modern vocabulary of social science would be strikingly thin.

By contrast, some disciplines have contributed a smaller share of enduring theoretical terms directly tied to evolutionary theory. This does not diminish their importance: these fields often add crucial empirical depth, contextual analysis, and applied insight that enrich understanding and guide practice. Their concepts may also diffuse more indirectly, shaping research agendas without always becoming formalized in evolutionary terminology. The following table highlights those disciplines where the share of direct theoretical contributions has been relatively modest, illustrating how unevenly the production of broadly adopted concepts is distributed across the sciences (Table A.3).

The relatively low percentages in Table A.3 should not be read as an indication that these disciplines lack theories. On the contrary, economics, political science, sociology, demography, geography, education, and business studies

Table A.1 Key terms in the evolutionary foundations of human and social behavior

Term	Definition	Origin/Key Reference
Adaptive heuristics	Mental shortcuts shaped by evolution to aid fast decision-making	Gigerenzer (2000)
Adaptive lag	Mismatch between evolved traits and modern environments	Tooby and Cosmides (1990s)
Adaptive responses	Behavioral or physiological adjustments to environmental stress	General evolutionary biology
Alloparents	Non-parental caregivers helping to raise offspring	Hrdy (1999)
Altruism	Behavior that benefits others at a cost to oneself	Trivers (1971)
Amygdala	Brain structure central to emotional processing, esp. fear/threat	LeDoux (1996)
Anthropocene	Proposed geological epoch in which humans dominate Earth systems	Crutzen (2000)
Anthropocentrism	Human-centered worldview assuming humans as dominant	Environmental ethics (Naess, 1973)
Anthropotechnics	Techniques of shaping or modifying human beings through technology	Sloterdijk (2009)
Aquatic ape hypothesis	Theory that some human traits evolved from semi-aquatic ancestors	Hardy (1960)
Argumentative Theory	Idea that reasoning evolved for persuasion, not truth-seeking	Mercier and Sperber (2011)
Biocentrism	Ethical stance granting intrinsic value to all life forms	Taylor (1986)
Bio–Cultural Feedback Model	Framework showing mutual influence of biology and culture	Richerson and Boyd (2005)
Biological inheritance	Transmission of traits through genes	Darwin (1859)
Biological life-stage transitions	Evolutionarily significant phases of human development	Bogin (1999)

(continued)

Table A.1 (continued)

Term	Definition	Origin/Key Reference
Biological resilience	Capacity of organisms to recover/adapt to stress	Ecology and resilience theory (Holling, 1973)
Biological robots	Metaphor for humans as mechanistically programmed beings	Dawkins (1976) (extended phenotype idea)
Biologically sculpted illusion	Perceptual errors shaped by evolutionary adaptation	Hoffman (1998)
Biologism	Overemphasis on biology at expense of culture	Gould (1981) (critique)
Biology	Science of life and living organisms	General discipline
Biophilia hypothesis	Innate human affinity for nature	Wilson (1984)
Bio-psycho-social model	Integrative framework linking biological, psychological, and social processes	Engel (1977)
Bounded rationality	Idea that decision-making is limited by information, time, and cognition	Simon (1957)
Cognitive architecture	The structure of mental processes in the brain	Anderson (1990)
Cognitive atrophy	Decline of mental capacity through underuse	Sparrow et al. (2011) (Google effect studies)
Cognitive distortions	Systematic errors in thought linked to mental health	Beck (1967)
Cognitive offloading	Using external tools/ environments to reduce cognitive load	Risko and Gilbert (2016)
Cognitive routines	Repeated thought/ behavioral patterns shaped by learning/ evolution	Gigerenzer and Todd (1999)
Cognitive sovereignty	Maintaining autonomy in thinking amid external pressures	Contemporary cognitive science
Cognitive–Physiological Feedback Loop (CPFL)	Reciprocal influence between thought and bodily states	Recent model in applied psych
Collective intelligence	Group capacity to solve problems/adapt	Woolley et al. (2010)

(continued)

Table A.1 (continued)

Term	Definition	Origin/Key Reference
Cultural evolution	Process by which cultural traits are transmitted and modified	Boyd and Richerson (1985)
Costly signaling theory	Behaviors that are costly but signal fitness/honesty	Zahavi (1975)
Ecological beings	View of humans as embedded in ecosystems	Naess (1973) (deep ecology)
Ecological flexibility	Human adaptability to diverse environments	Kaplan et al. (2000)
Ecological system	Interconnected web of organisms and environment	Odum (1953)
Extended phenotype	Genes influencing environment beyond the body	Dawkins (1982)
Fairness	Norm regulating equal treatment, rooted in reciprocity	Fehr and Schmidt (1999)
Gene–culture coevolution	Interaction of genetic and cultural evolution	Lumsden and Wilson (1981); Boyd and Richerson (1985)
Genetic fitness	Success in passing on genes to next generations	Darwin (1859); Hamilton (1964)
Group selection	Evolutionary process where traits benefit group survival	Wynne-Edwards (1962); revived by Wilson (2007)
Homo cura	Concept of humans as defined by care	Philosophical anthropology
Homo ecologicus	Model of humans as ecological actors	Ecological economics
Homo economicus	Model of humans as rational, utility-maximizing agents	Neoclassical economics, nineteenth century
Homo sapiens	Human species name	Linnaeus (1758)
Hormonal markers	Biological signals indicating physiological states	Endocrinology
Human cooperation	Tendency for humans to coordinate behavior	Tomasello (2009)
Human exceptionalism	Belief in unique human status apart from nature	Anthropocentric philosophy
Human umwelt	The perceived sensory world of humans	von Uexküll (1934)

(continued)

Table A.1 (continued)

Term	Definition	Origin/Key Reference
Human uniqueness	Distinctive features of humans (language, culture, cognition)	Tomasello (2016)
Inclusive fitness	Evolutionary success via reproduction of self and relatives	Hamilton (1964)
In-group favoritism	Preference for members of one's own group	Tajfel and Turner (1979)
In-group dynamics	Psychological and behavioral processes within groups	Social identity theory (Tajfel, 1974)
In-group bias	Cognitive bias favoring insiders over outsiders	Brewer (1999)
Institutional mismatch	Conflict between evolved tendencies and modern institutions	Tooby and Cosmides (1992)
Introspection illusion	Overconfidence in self-knowledge; failure to see biases	Pronin et al. (2002)
Intuition	Fast, automatic judgments rooted in heuristics and past learning	Kahneman (2011)
Kin selection	Evolutionary strategy favoring relatives' survival/ reproduction	Hamilton (1964)
Kinship	Social bonds and obligations based on family relations	Anthropological foundations; Hrdy (2009)
Machiavellian intelligence	Hypothesis that intelligence evolved for social manipulation	Byrne and Whiten (1988)
Meme	Unit of cultural information transmitted by imitation	Dawkins (1976)
Moral foundations theory	Framework of innate moral intuitions shaped by culture	Haidt and Joseph (2004); Haidt (2012)
Moral psychology	Study of mental processes behind moral judgment and behavior	Kohlberg (1969); Haidt (2001)
Morality	Norms of right/wrong evolved to regulate cooperation	Darwin (1871); De Waal (1996)
Motivated reasoning	Biased reasoning driven by desires or identity	Kunda (1990)

(continued)

Table A.1 (continued)

Term	Definition	Origin/Key Reference
Müller-Lyer illusion	Visual illusion showing cultural/biological perception effects	Müller-Lyer (1889)
Neocortex	Brain region linked to higher cognition and sociality	Dunbar (1992) (social brain hypothesis)
Niche construction	Organisms modify environment, influencing evolution	Odling-Smee et al. (2003)
Norm	Shared expectation guiding social behavior	Durkheim (1895)
Norm diffusion	Spread of norms across groups and societies	Finnemore and Sikkink (1998)
Norm resistance	Pushback against unfamiliar or imposed norms	Scott (1985)
Optimism bias	Tendency to overestimate positive outcomes	Sharot (2011)
Out-group hostility	Distrust or aggression toward outsiders	Brewer (1999)
Outsourcing paradox	Cognitive decline when tasks are excessively offloaded to tech	Risko and Gilbert (2016)
Overconfidence bias	Tendency to overestimate accuracy of knowledge/ judgment	Kahneman and Tversky (1979)
Pan-scientific project	View of science as unified across disciplines	Wilson (1998) (Consilience)
Phenotype (extended)	Expression of genes shaping traits and environment	Dawkins (1982)
Phronesis	Practical wisdom for moral and social decision-making	Aristotle, Nicomachean Ethics
Prospect theory	Theory showing humans weigh losses more heavily than gains	Kahneman and Tversky (1979)
Prisoner's dilemma	Game theory model showing cooperation vs. defection trade-offs	Flood and Dresher (1950s); Axelrod (1984)
Probabilistic tendency	Behavioral tendency that is likely but not deterministic	General evolutionary psychology
Reciprocal altruism	Helping with expectation of future return	Trivers (1971)

(continued)

Table A.1 (continued)

Term	Definition	Origin/Key Reference
Reputation management	Adjusting behavior to preserve/improve social standing	Goffman (1959); Nowak and Sigmund (1998)
Rational actor theory	Assumes humans act rationally to maximize utility	Becker (1976) (economics); Simon (1955) (bounded rationality critique)
Reciprocal alliance	Cooperative relationship with expectation of mutual benefit	Cosmides and Tooby (1992)
Reputation management	Strategic behavior to maintain/improve status	Goffman (1959); Nowak and Sigmund (1998)
Risk-taking	Engaging in behavior with uncertain outcomes, often adaptive	Daly and Wilson (2001)
Self-serving bias	Tendency to credit success to self, failure to external causes	Miller and Ross (1975)
Sexual selection	Evolutionary process favoring traits that improve mating success	Darwin (1871)
Sexual selection theory	Explains costly signals and mate choice behavior	Andersson (1994)
Shared intentionality	Capacity to coordinate actions and goals with others	Tomasello (2009)
Social brain hypothesis	Proposes large brains evolved for managing complex social groups	Dunbar (1992)
Social construction	Theory that categories are shaped by culture, not biology	Berger and Luckmann (1966)
Social contract	Hypothetical agreement forming basis of social order	Hobbes (1651); Rousseau (1762)
Social grooming	Behaviors that maintain relationships and cohesion	Dunbar (1996)
Social instincts	Innate drives to bond, cooperate, and regulate group life	Darwin (1871)
Social learning	Learning behaviors by observing others	Bandura (1977); Henrich (2015)

(continued)

Table A.1 (continued)

Term	Definition	Origin/Key Reference
Social norms	Shared expectations about acceptable behavior	Durkheim (1895)
Social presence	Sense of being "with" others in communication	Short et al. (1976)
Social reinforcement	Encouragement or discouragement of behavior via group responses	Skinner (1953)
Social solidarity	Cohesion through shared values and institutions	Durkheim (1893)
Status hierarchies	Rank ordering in animal and human groups	Chase (1980)
Strong reciprocity	Willingness to reward cooperation/punish defectors even at cost	Fehr and Gächter (2002)
System 1 thinking	Fast, intuitive, automatic cognition	Kahneman (2011)
System 2 reasoning	Slow, deliberate, analytical cognition	Kahneman (2011)
Tribal instincts	Evolved bias to favor in-group, distrust outsiders	Brewer (1999)
Trust calibration	Adjusting trust based on cues/experience	Fehr (2009); Balliet and Van Lange (2013)
Universal grammar	Hypothesis of innate grammatical structure in human language	Chomsky (1965)
Universal human rights	Idea of rights shared by all humans regardless of context	Enlightenment thinkers; codified UN (1948)
Xenophobia	Fear/distrust of outsiders or foreigners	Evolutionary psychology framing: Navarrete et al. (2004)
Zoon politikon	Aristotle's term for humans as inherently political/social beings	Aristotle, Politics

have produced vast theoretical traditions. What explains their smaller share here is that the conceptual vocabulary of this appendix is primarily grounded in biology, psychology, and evolutionary theory. The difference lies in focus and orientation.

Economics, for example, has generated some of the most influential frameworks in the social sciences, including general equilibrium theory, rational

Table A.2 Extended conceptual toolkit for social scientists

Discipline/Field	Approx. share of terms (%)[1]	Examples of terms
Evolutionary Biology & Theory	28%	Kin selection, reciprocal altruism, sexual selection, inclusive fitness, niche construction
Psychology (general & social)	26%	System 1 & 2, bounded rationality, motivated reasoning, optimism bias, overconfidence
Neuroscience & Cognitive Science	14%	Amygdala, affective neuroscience, cognitive modularity, neural synchrony
Cultural Anthropology & Sociology	12%	Norms, cultural transmission, in-group bias, moral foundations theory
Political Science & Institutional Theory	10%	Institutional mismatch, trust calibration, reputation management, social contract
Artificial Intelligence & Technology Studies	10%	Cognitive offloading, AI agents, outsourcing paradox, surveillance capitalism

Table A.3 Social science disciplines with the smallest share of theoretical contributions

Discipline	% of Terms contributed
Economics	~ 8%
Political Science	~ 5%
Linguistics	~ 4–5%
Sociology	~ 3%
Demography	~ 3%
Geography	~ 2–3%
Education	~ 2%
Business Studies	~ 1–2%

[1] Percentages were estimated by classifying the references listed in the preceding table according to their primary disciplinary affiliation (e.g., evolutionary biology, psychology, neuroscience, anthropology, sociology, political science/AI studies). The values thus reflect the relative weight of each tradition in shaping the conceptual toolkit, rather than exact counts from the broader literature.

choice models, and behavioral approaches. Yet, many of its core assumptions—such as the idea of *homo economicus* as a rational, utility-maximizing agent, or the fungibility of money—abstract away from biological and psychological realities (Simon, 1957; Sen, 1977; Thaler, 1999). These simplifications have analytic power, but they do not translate into the kinds of cross-disciplinary, biologically informed terms considered in this volume.

Political science similarly offers rich institutional and normative theories but has historically concentrated on elections, constitutions, governance structures, and state formation (Green & Shapiro, 1994; Ostrom, 1990). While rational-choice and game-theoretic models have provided useful insights into collective decision-making, they remain limited in scope when compared to integrative concepts of human behavior emerging from evolutionary psychology and cognitive science.

Sociology, for its part, has produced an extraordinary number of mid-level theories—ranging from Bourdieu's concepts of *habitus* and symbolic capital to Coleman's theory of social capital. Yet as Abbott (2001) notes, the discipline is highly fragmented, with little consensus on a unifying meta-framework. This fragmentation makes it harder for sociology to contribute singular, widely adopted concepts that function as cross-scientific building blocks in the way that terms like "reciprocal altruism" or "bounded rationality" have done.

Demography has made indispensable contributions in methods and measurement, building the foundations of population science by tracking fertility, mortality, and migration. However, its theoretical vocabulary has remained comparatively narrow, reflecting its strong empirical and statistical orientation (Preston et al., 2001). The same applies to geography, which has pioneered spatial analysis, environmental studies, and Geographic Information Science (Goodchild, 1992), but whose central contributions have been methodological rather than conceptual in the sense of cross-scientific behavioral theory.

Education research, meanwhile, has largely drawn upon psychology and sociology to explain learning and development, focusing its contributions on evidence-based teaching methods and policy applications rather than on universal theoretical constructs (Hattie, 2009). Business and management studies are even more application-oriented. As Whitley (1984) argued, the field has historically imported its conceptual foundations from economics, sociology, and psychology, adapting them to organizational and managerial contexts rather than producing stand-alone theories of human behavior.

Taken together, these observations clarify why the distribution of theoretical contributions appears uneven. Some disciplines—such as biology, psychology, and neuroscience—tend to generate concepts that describe universal features of human behavior, grounded in evolutionary processes. Other fields—such as sociology, political science, demography, education, and business studies—specialize in contextual, institutional, or applied analysis, often focusing on how universal mechanisms manifest within specific social structures. Far from diminishing their value, this complementarity highlights the interdependence of disciplines: foundational concepts arise in some areas, while others provide the settings in which those concepts are tested, contextualized, and refined.

What remains is the task of systematically examining the theoretical contributions of these other disciplines and assessing how they can be integrated into the broader explanatory framework presented in this book.

References

Abbott, A. (2001). *Chaos of disciplines*. University of Chicago Press.

Anderson, J. R. (1990). *Cognitive psychology and its implications* (3rd ed.). Freeman.

Andersson, M. (1994). *Sexual selection*. Princeton University Press.

Axelrod, R. (1984). *The evolution of cooperation*. Basic Books.

Balliet, D., & Van Lange, P. A. M. (2013). Trust, conflict, and cooperation: A meta-analysis. *Psychological Bulletin, 139*(5), 1090–1112.

Bandura, A. (1977). *Social learning theory*. Prentice Hall.

Beck, A. T. (1967). *Depression: Clinical, experimental, and theoretical aspects*. Harper & Row.

Becker, G. S. (1976). *The economic approach to human behavior*. University of Chicago Press.

Berger, P. L., & Luckmann, T. (1966). *The social construction of reality: A treatise in the sociology of knowledge*. Anchor Books.

Bogin, B. (1999). *Patterns of human growth* (2nd ed.). Cambridge University Press.

Boyd, R., & Richerson, P. J. (1985). *Culture and the evolutionary process*. University of Chicago Press.

Brewer, M. B. (1999). The psychology of prejudice: Ingroup love and outgroup hate? *Journal of Social Issues, 55*(3), 429–444.

Byrne, R., & Whiten, A. (1988). *Machiavellian intelligence: Social expertise and the evolution of intellect in monkeys, apes, and humans*. Clarendon Press.

Chase, I. D. (1980). Social process and hierarchy formation in small groups: A comparative perspective. *American Sociological Review, 45*(6), 905–924.

Chomsky, N. (1965). *Aspects of the theory of syntax*. MIT Press.

K. Solberg Söilen, *The Researcher's Journey in the Age of AI*,
https://doi.org/10.1007/978-3-032-23069-0

Cosmides, L., & Tooby, J. (1992). Cognitive adaptations for social exchange. In J. H. Barkow, L. Cosmides, & J. Tooby (Eds.), *The adapted mind* (pp. 163–228). Oxford University Press.

Crutzen, P. J. (2000). Geology of mankind. *Nature, 415*(6867), 23.

Daly, M., & Wilson, M. (2001). Risk-taking, intrasexual competition, and homicide. *Nebraska Symposium on Motivation, 47*, 1–36.

Darwin, C. (1859). *On the origin of species*. John Murray.

Darwin, C. (1871). *The descent of man, and selection in relation to sex*. John Murray.

Dawkins, R. (1976). *The selfish gene*. Oxford University Press.

Dawkins, R. (1982). *The extended phenotype*. Oxford University Press.

De Waal, F. (1996). *Good natured: The origins of right and wrong in humans and other animals*. Harvard University Press.

Dunbar, R. I. M. (1992). Neocortex size as a constraint on group size in primates. *Journal of Human Evolution, 22*(6), 469–493.

Dunbar, R. I. M. (1996). *Grooming, gossip, and the evolution of language*. Harvard University Press.

Durkheim, É. (1893/1984). *The division of labor in society* (W. D. Halls, Trans.). Free Press.

Durkheim, É. (1895/1982). *The rules of sociological method* (W. D. Halls, Trans.). Free Press.

Engel, G. L. (1977). The need for a new medical model: A challenge for biomedicine. *Science, 196* (4286), 129–136.

Fehr, E. (2009). On the economics and biology of trust. *Journal of the European Economic Association, 7*(2–3), 235–266.

Fehr, E., & Gächter, S. (2002). Altruistic punishment in humans. *Nature, 415*(6868), 137–140.

Fehr, E., & Schmidt, K. M. (1999). A theory of fairness, competition, and cooperation. *Quarterly Journal of Economics, 114*(3), 817–868.

Finnemore, M., & Sikkink, K. (1998). International norm dynamics and political change. *International Organization, 52*(4), 887–917.

Flood, M. M., & Dresher, M. (1950). *The prisoner's dilemma*. RAND Corporation Memorandum.

Gigerenzer, G. (2000). *Adaptive thinking: Rationality in the real world*. Oxford University Press.

Gigerenzer, G., & Todd, P. M. (1999). *Simple heuristics that make us smart*. Oxford University Press.

Goffman, E. (1959). *The presentation of self in everyday life*. Doubleday.

Goodchild, M. F. (1992). Geographical information science. *International Journal of Geographical Information Systems, 6* (1), 31–45.

Gould, S. J. (1981). *The mismeasure of man*. Norton.

Green, D. P., & Shapiro, I. (1994). *Pathologies of rational choice theory: A critique of applications in political science*. Yale University Press.

Hamilton, W. D. (1964). The genetical evolution of social behaviour. *Journal of Theoretical Biology, 7*(1), 1–52.

Haidt, J. (2001). The emotional dog and its rational tail: A social intuitionist approach to moral judgment. *Psychological Review, 108*(4), 814–834.

Haidt, J. (2012). *The righteous mind: Why good people are divided by politics and religion.* Pantheon.

Haidt, J., & Joseph, C. (2004). Intuitive ethics: How innately prepared intuitions generate culturally variable virtues. *Daedalus, 133*(4), 55–66.

Hardy, E. (1960). *The aquatic ape: A theory of human evolution.* Souvenir Press.

Hattie, J. (2009). *Visible learning: A synthesis of over 800 meta-analyses relating to achievement*. Routledge.

Henrich, J. (2015). *The secret of our success: How culture is driving human evolution, domesticating our species, and making us smarter*. Princeton University Press.

Hobbes, T. (1651/1996). *Leviathan* (R. Tuck, Ed.). Cambridge University Press.

Hoffman, D. D. (1998). *Visual intelligence: How we create what we see*. Norton.

Holling, C. S. (1973). Resilience and stability of ecological systems. *Annual Review of Ecology and Systematics, 4*, 1–23.

Hrdy, S. B. (1999). *Mother nature: Maternal instincts and how they shape the human species*. Ballantine.

Hrdy, S. B. (2009). *Mothers and others: The evolutionary origins of mutual understanding*. Harvard University Press.

Kaplan, H., Hill, K., Lancaster, J., & Hurtado, A. M. (2000). A theory of human life history evolution: Diet, intelligence, and longevity. *Evolutionary Anthropology, 9*(4), 156–185.

Kahneman, D. (2011). *Thinking, fast and slow*. Farrar.

Kahneman, D., & Tversky, A. (1979). Prospect theory: An analysis of decision under risk. *Econometrica, 47*(2), 263–291.

Kohlberg, L. (1969). Stage and sequence: The cognitive-developmental approach to socialization. In D. Goslin (Ed.), *Handbook of socialization theory and research* (pp. 347–480). Rand McNally.

Kunda, Z. (1990). The case for motivated reasoning. *Psychological Bulletin, 108*(3), 480–498.

LeDoux, J. (1996). *The emotional brain: The mysterious underpinnings of emotional life*. Simon & Schuster.

Linnaeus, C. (1758). *Systema naturae* (10th ed.). L. Salvii.

Lumsden, C. J., & Wilson, E. O. (1981). *Genes, mind, and culture: The coevolutionary process.* Harvard University Press.

Mercier, H., & Sperber, D. (2011). Why do humans reason? Arguments for an argumentative theory. *Behavioral and Brain Sciences, 34*(2), 57–74.

Miller, D. T., & Ross, M. (1975). Self-serving biases in the attribution of causality: Fact or fiction? *Psychological Bulletin, 82*(2), 213–225.

Müller-Lyer, F. C. (1889). Optische Urteilstäuschungen. *Archiv für. Physiologie, 9*, 263–270.

Naess, A. (1973). The shallow and the deep, long-range ecology movement. *Inquiry, 16*(1–4), 95–100.

Navarrete, C. D., McDonald, M. M., Molina, L. E., & Sidanius, J. (2004). Prejudice at the nexus of race and gender: An outgroup male target hypothesis. *Journal of Personality and Social Psychology, 87*(6), 796–812.

Nowak, M. A., & Sigmund, K. (1998). Evolution of indirect reciprocity by image scoring. *Nature, 393*(6685), 573–577.

Odling-Smee, F. J., Laland, K. N., & Feldman, M. W. (2003). *Niche construction: The neglected process in evolution.* Princeton University Press.

Odum, E. P. (1953). *Fundamentals of ecology*. Saunders.

Ostrom, E. (1990). *Governing the commons: The evolution of institutions for collective action.* Cambridge University Press.

Preston, S., Heuveline, P., & Guillot, M. (2001). *Demography: Measuring and modeling population processes.* Blackwell.

Pronin, E., Gilovich, T., & Ross, L. (2002). The bias blind spot: Perceptions of bias in self versus others. *Personality and Social Psychology Bulletin, 28*(3), 369–381.

Richerson, P. J., & Boyd, R. (2005). *Not by genes alone: How culture transformed human evolution.* University of Chicago Press.

Risko, E. F., & Gilbert, S. J. (2016). Cognitive offloading. *Trends in Cognitive Sciences, 20*(9), 676–688.

Rousseau, J.-J. (1762/1979). *The social contract* (M. Cranston, Trans.). Penguin.

Scott, J. C. (1985). *Weapons of the weak: Everyday forms of peasant resistance.* Yale University Press.

Sen, A. (1977). Rational fools: A critique of the behavioral foundations of economic theory. *Philosophy & Public Affairs, 6*(4), 317–344.

Sharot, T. (2011). The optimism bias. *Current Biology, 21*(23), R941–R945.

Short, J., Williams, E., & Christie, B. (1976). *The social psychology of telecommunications.* Wiley.

Simon, H. A. (1955). A behavioral model of rational choice. *Quarterly Journal of Economics, 69*(1), 99–118.

Simon, H. A. (1957). *Models of man: Social and rational*. Wiley.

Skinner, B. F. (1953). *Science and human behavior*. Macmillan.

Sloterdijk, P. (2009). *You must change your life*. Polity Press.

Sparrow, B., Liu, J., & Wegner, D. M. (2011). Google effects on memory: Cognitive consequences of having information at our fingertips. *Science, 333*(6043), 776–778.

Tajfel, H. (1974). Social identity and intergroup behaviour. *Social Science Information, 13*(2), 65–93.

Tajfel, H., & Turner, J. C. (1979). An integrative theory of intergroup conflict. In W. G. Austin & S. Worchel (Eds.), *The social psychology of intergroup relations* (pp. 33–47). Brooks/Cole.

Taylor, P. W. (1986). *Respect for nature: A theory of environmental ethics.* Princeton University Press.

Thaler, R. H. (1999). Mental accounting matters. *Journal of Behavioral Decision Making, 12*(3), 183–206.

Tomasello, M. (2009). *Why we cooperate*. MIT Press.

Tomasello, M. (2016). *A natural history of human morality*. Harvard University Press.
Tooby, J., & Cosmides, L. (1990). On the universality of human nature and the uniqueness of the individual: The role of genetics and adaptation. *Journal of Personality, 58*(1), 17–67.
Tooby, J., & Cosmides, L. (1992). The psychological foundations of culture. In J. H. Barkow, L. Cosmides, & J. Tooby (Eds.), *The adapted mind: Evolutionary psychology and the generation of culture* (pp. 19–136). Oxford University Press.
Trivers, R. L. (1971). The evolution of reciprocal altruism. *The Quarterly Review of Biology, 46*(1), 35–57.
United Nations. (1948). *Universal Declaration of Human Rights*. https://www.un.org/en/about-us/universal-declaration-of-human-rights
von Uexküll, J. (1934/2010). *A foray into the worlds of animals and humans* (J. D. O'Neil, Trans.). University of Minnesota Press.
Whitley, R. (1984). *The intellectual and social organization of the sciences*. Oxford University Press.
Wilson, E. O. (1984). *Biophilia*. Harvard University Press.
Wilson, E. O. (1998). *Consilience: The unity of knowledge*. Knopf.
Wilson, D. S. (2007). *Evolution for everyone: How Darwin's theory can change the way we think about our lives*. Delacorte Press.
Woolley, A. W., Chabris, C. F., Pentland, A., Hashmi, N., & Malone, T. W. (2010). Evidence for a collective intelligence factor in the performance of human groups. *Science, 330*(6004), 686–688.
Wynne-Edwards, V. C. (1962). *Animal dispersion in relation to social behaviour*. Oliver & Boyd.
Zahavi, A. (1975). Mate selection—A selection for a handicap. *Journal of Theoretical Biology, 53*(1), 205–214.

Further Reading

Aristotle. (1995). *Politics* (C. D. C. Reeve, Trans.). Hackett (Original work published ca. 350 BCE).
Bourdieu, P. (1986). The forms of capital. In J. Richardson (Ed.), *Handbook of theory and research for the sociology of education* (pp. 241–258). Greenwood.
Coleman, J. S. (1990). *Foundations of social theory*. Harvard University Press.
Tversky, A., & Kahneman, D. (1979). Prospect theory: An analysis of decision under risk. *Econometrica, 47*(2), 263–291.

Index

K. Solberg Söilen, *The Researcher's Journey in the Age of AI*,
https://doi.org/10.1007/978-3-032-23069-0

D

U

GPSR Compliance
The European Union's (EU) General Product Safety Regulation (GPSR) is a set of rules that requires consumer products to be safe and our obligations to ensure this.

If you have any concerns about our products, you can contact us on

ProductSafety@springernature.com

In case Publisher is established outside the EU, the EU authorized representative is:

Springer Nature Customer Service Center GmbH
Europaplatz 3
69115 Heidelberg, Germany

www.ingramcontent.com/pod-product-compliance
Lightning Source LLC
Chambersburg PA
CBHW070249260926
51849CB00001BA/79
9783032230683